YEARBOOK OF EUROPEAN LAW

Editorial Statement

The *Yearbook of European Law* seeks to promote the dissemination of ideas and provide a forum for legal discourse in the wider area of European law. It is committed to the highest academic standards and to providing informative and critical analysis of topical issues accessible to all those interested in legal studies. It reflects diverse theoretical approaches towards the study of law. The *Yearbook* publishes contributions in the following broad areas: the law of the European Union, the European Convention for the Protection of Human Rights, related aspects of international law, and comparative laws of Europe.

Contributions for publication in the articles section should be sent to the following address:

Professor Takis Tridimas
Co-editor
Yearbook of European Law
Faculty of Law
University of Southampton
Highfield
Southampton SO17 1BJ
England

Tel. ++44(0) 1703 595761
     ++44(0) 1703 593550
Fax ++44(0) 1703 593024

E-mail: ptt@soton.ac.uk

YEARBOOK OF
EUROPEAN LAW

20

2001

EDITORS

P. EECKHOUT
Professor of European Law
King's College London

T. TRIDIMAS
Professor of European Law
University of Southampton and
College of Europe, Bruges

BOOK REVIEW EDITOR

G. DE BÚRCA

OXFORD
UNIVERSITY PRESS

OXFORD
UNIVERSITY PRESS

Great Clarendon Street, Oxford OX2 6DP

Oxford University Press is a department of the University of Oxford.
It furthers the University's objective of excellence in research, scholarship,
and education by publishing worldwide in

Oxford New York

Auckland Bangkok Buenos Aires Cape Town Chennai
Dar es Salaam Delhi Hong Kong Istanbul Karachi Kolkata
Kuala Lumpur Madrid Melbourne Mexico City Mumbai Nairobi
São Paulo Shanghai Singapore Taipei Tokyo Toronto

with an associated company in Berlin

Oxford is a registered trade mark of Oxford University Press
in the UK and in certain other countries

Published in the United States
by Oxford University Press Inc., New York

Customers wishing to establish a standing order for the Yearbook should write or fax—
Oxford University Press, Saxon Way West, Corby, Northants, NN18 9ES, UK
Fax 01536 746337
Please Quote Series ISBN: 019961 8704

British Library Cataloguing in Publication Data
Data available

Library of Congress Cataloging in Publication Data
Data available
ISBN 0–19–924340–9

1 3 5 7 9 10 8 6 4 2

Typeset by Hope Services (Abingdon) Ltd
Printed in Great Britain
Biddles Ltd, Guildford and King's Lynn

Editorial Committee

Contents

REVIEWS OF BOOKS

Abbreviations

AAL	*Anglo-American Law Review*
AC	Appeal Cases
ACP	Africa-Caribbean-Pacific
A&E	Adolphus & Ellis
AEL	*Academy of European Law*
AETR	Accord européen relatif au travail des équipages des véhicules effectuant des transports, internationaux par route (also ERTA)
AFDI	*Annuaire français de droit international*
AG	Aktiengesellschaft
AJ	Aide Judiciaire – Legal Aid
AJCL	*American Journal of Comparative Law*
AJDA	*l'Actualité juridique droit administratif*
AJIL	*American Journal of International Law*
ALJR	Australian Law Journal Reports
All ER	All England Law Reports
ALR	Australian Law Reports
Ann Eur	*Annuaire européen* (European Yearbook)
Ann Suisse DI	*Annuaire suisse de droit international*
Aör	*Archiv des öffentlichen Rechts*
AOW	*Algemene Ouderomswet*
APEC	Asian-Pacific Economic Co-operation
Art	Article
ASEAN	Association of South-East Asia Nations
ASIL	*Proceedings of American Society of International Law*
Aust YIL	*Australian Yearbook of International Law*
AWD	Aussenwirtschaftsdienst des Betriebs-Beraters
AWW	*Algemene Weduwen-en Wezenwet*
BCLC	Butterworths Company Law Cases
BGB	Burgerliches Gesetzbuch
BGB1	Bundesgesetzblatt
BGE	Entscheidungen des Schweizerischen Bundesgerichtes
BGH	Bundesgerichtshof
BISD	Basic Instruments and Selected Documents (GATT)
BJE	*Bulletin des juristes européens*
BJIBFL	*Butterworths Journal of International Banking and Financial Law*
BJIR	*British Journal of Industrial Relations*
BKA	Bundeskartellamt
BLEU	Belgo-Luxembourg Economic Union

BL Rev	*Business Law Review*
BOCCRF	*Bulletin Officiel de la Concurrence de la Consommation et de la Répression des Fraudes*
BOE	*Boletín Official del Estado*
BPIL	*British Practice in International Law*
Bull civ V	*Bulletin des arrêts de la Cour de cassation Chambre 5e*
B VerfG	Bundesverfassungsgericht
B VerfGE	Entscheidungen des Bundesverfassungs-gerichts
BYIL	*British Yearbook of International Law*
CA	Court of Appeal
CAP	Common Agricultural Policy
CBNS	Common Bench, New Series
CCH	Commerce Clearing House
CCP	Common Commercial Policy
CCT	Common customs tariff
CDE	*Cahiers de droit européen*
CE	Conseil d'Etat
CEN	European Committee for (technical) Standardization
CENELEC	European Committee for Electro-technical Standardization
CEPS	Centre for European Policy Studies
CERIFI	Centre for the Information Discussion and Exchange on the Crossing of Frontiers and Immigration
CES	Comité economique et social
CET	Common external tariff
CFI	Court of First Instance of the European Communities
CFSP	Common Foreign and Security Policy
Ch	Chancery Division of the High Court
Chap	Chapter
Cie	Compagnie
CIM-DH	Conference Informelle Ministerielle-Droits de l'Homme
CIS	Commonwealth of Independent States
CJ	Chief Justice
CJHA	Co-operation in the field of Justice and Home Affairs
CJQ	*Civil Justice Quarterly*
Cl & F	Clark & Finnelly
CLJ	*Cambridge Law Journal*
CLP	*Current Legal Problems*
CLR	Commonwealth Law Reports
CMLR	Common Market Law Reports
CML Rev	*Common Market Law Review*
Cmnd (Cd, CmdCm)	Command Paper
CMR	Common Market Reporter

COCOR	Comité de Coordination
Comm	Commission Documents
Co Rep	Colle's Reports
COREPER	Committee of Permanent Representatives to the European Communities (abbreviation of comité dés représentants permanents)
Crim App R	Criminal Appeal Reports
Crim L Rev	*Criminal Law Review*
CS	Court of Session
CSCE	Conference on Security and Co-operation in Europe
DA	*Deutschland-Archiv*
DET	*Droit européen des transports*
DF	Droit Fiscal
DLR	Dominion Law Reports
DOAR	*Droits des Affaires, Ondernermingsrecht*
DöV	Die öffentliche Verwaltung
D & R	Decisions and Reports
DS	*Dalloz Sirey*
DTI	Department of Trade and Industry
DVBI	*Deutsches Verwaltungsblatt*
EAEC	European Atomic Energy Community
EAGGF	European Agricultural Guarantee and Guidance Fund
EAT	Employment Appeal Tribunal
EBRD	European Bank for Reconstruction and Development
ECA	European Communities Act
ECB	European Central Bank
EC Bull	*Bulletin of the European Communities*
ECE	Economic Commission for Europe
ECHR	European Convention on Human Rights
ECJ	European Court of Justice
ECLR	*European Competition Law Review*
ECMT	European Conference of Ministers of Transport
ECR	European Court Reports
ECSC	European Coal and Steel Community
ECTS	European Credit Transfer System
ECU	European Currency Unit
EDF	European Development Fund
EEA	European Economic Area
EEAA	European Economic Area Agreement
EEC	European Economic Community
EELR	*European Environmental Law Review*
EFA Rev	*European Foreign Affairs Review*
EFTA	European Free Trade Area

EGBGB	Einführungsgesetz zum Bürgerlichen Gesetzbuch
EHRLR	*European Human Rights Law Review*
EHRR	European Human Rights Reports
EIB	European Investment Bank
EIPR	*European Intellectual Property Review*
EIRR	European Industrial Relations Reports
EJIL	*European Journal of International Law*
ELJ	*European Law Journal*
ELQ	*Ecology Law Quarterly*
EL Rev	*European Law Review*
EMF	European Monetary Fund
ENDS Rep	*Environmental News Data Services Report*
EPC	European Political Co-operation
EPCA	Employment Protection Consolidation Act
EP Debate	European Parliament Debate
EP (or PE) doc	European Parliament document
EPL	*European Public Law*
EPOR	European Patent Office Reports
ERASMUS	European Community Action Scheme for the Mobility of University Students
ERDF	European Regional Development Fund
ERM	Exchange Rate Mechanism
ERPL	*European Review of Private Law*
ERTA	European agreement concerning the work of crews of vehicles engaged in international road transport (also AETR)
ESCB	European System of Central Banks
ESF	European Social Fund
ETL	*European Transport Law*
ETS	European Treaty Series
EUA	European unit of account
EuGRZ	*Europäische Grundrechte-Zeitschiest*
EUI	European University Institute
EuR	*Europarecht*
Euratom	European Atomic Energy Community
Eur Ct HR	European Court of Human Rights
Europe Bulletin	Daily Bulletin produced by Agence Europe, Brussels-Luxembourg
EuZW	*Europäische Zeitschrift für Wirtschaftsrecht*
EVst	Einfuhr- und Voratsstelle
Ex	Exchequer Cases
F	Federal (used in American case citations)
FA	Finanzamt
FAO	Food and Agriculture Organisation

FEOGA	Fonds européen d'orientation et de garantie agricole (European agricultural guidance and guarantee fund)
FIDE	Fédération internationale de droit européen
FILJ	*Fordham International Law Journal*
FLR	Federal Law Reports
FL Rev	*Federal Law Review*
FSR	Fleet Street Reports
FTA	Free Trade Agreement
GATS	General Agreement on Trade and Services
GATT	General Agreement on Tariffs and Trade
GG	Grundgesetz
GI	*Giurisprudenza italiane*
GmhH	Gesellschaft mit beschränkter Haftung
GP	*Gazette du Palais*
GSP	Generalized System of Preferences
GVBI	*Berlin Gesetz-un-Verordnungsblatt*
GYBIL	*German Yearbook of International Law*
HA	High Authority of the ECSC
Harv LR	*Harvard Law Review*
HC	House of Commons
HC Deb	House of Commons Debates
HL	House of Lords
HL Deb	House of Lords Debates
HMSO	Her Majesty's Stationery Office
HRLJ	*Human Rights Law Journal*
HRQ	*Human Rights Quarterly*
HR Rev	*Human Rights Review*
HZ	Historicle Zeitung
HZA	Hauptzollamt
ICCLR	*International Commercial Cases Law Review*
ICCPR	International Covenant on Civil and Political Rights
ICJ Rep	International Court of Justice Reports
ICLQ	*International and Comparative Law Quarterly*
ICR	Industrial Court Reports
IEPG	Independent European Programme Group
IFOR	Implementation Force
IGC	Intergovernmental Conference
IIC	*International Review of Industrial Property and Copyright*
ILJ	*Industrial Law Journal*
ILM	International Legal Materials
ILO	International Labour Organisation

ILPr	International Litigation Procedure
ILF	International Law Reports
ILRM	Irish Law Reports Monthly
IMF	International Monetary Fund
ImmAR	Immigration Appeal Reports
IMO	International Maritime Organisation
Ind JIL	*Indian Journal of International Law*
IPD	Intellectual Property Decisions
IR	Irish Reports
IRLR	Industrial Relations Law Reports
JBL	*Journal of Business Law*
JCMS	*Journal of Common Market Studies*
JCP	*Jurisclasseur périodique*
JDI	*Journal du droit international*
JEL	*Journal of Environmental Law*
JEPP	*Journal of European Public Policy*
JESP	*Journal of European Social Policy*
JICL	*Journal of International and Comparative Law*
JLS	*Journal of Legal Studies*
JO	Journal Officiel (des Communautés européennes)
JORF	Journal Officiel de la République française
JSWFL	*Journal of Social Welfare and Family Law*
JT	*Journal des tribunaux* (Belgium)
JWT	*Journal of World Trade*
JZ	Juristenzeitung
KB	King's Bench
KG	Kommanditgesellschaft
KSE	*Kölner Schriften zum Europarecht*
LEd	Lawyers Edition
LGDJ	Librairie Générale de Droit et de Jurisprudence
LIEI	*Legal Issues of European Integration*
LIJ	*Law Institute Journal*
Lloyd's Rep	Lloyd's Law Reports
LMCLQ	*Lloyd's Maritime and Commercial Law Quarterly*
LNTS	League of Nations Treaty Series
LQR	*Law Quarterly Review*
MB	*Moniteur Belge*
Mercosur	Mercado Común del Sur (Southern Common Market)
MEP	Member of the European Parliament
MJ	*Maastricht Journal of European and Comparative Law*
MLR	*Modern Law Review*

MMC	Monopolies and Mergers Commission
MP	Member of Parliament
n	footnote
NATO	North Atlantic Treaty Organisation
Neth ILR	*Netherlands International Law Review*
NILQ	*Northern Ireland Law Quarterly*
NILR	Northern Ireland Law Report
NJ	*Nederlandse Jurisprudentie*
NJW	*Neue Juristische Wochenschrift*
NLJ	*New Law Journal*
NQHR	*Netherlands Quarterly of Human Rights*
NTB	*Nederlands Tÿdschrift voor Bestuwisrecht*
NTER	*Nederlands Tÿdschrift voor Europees Recht*
NV	Naamloze Vennootschap
OAU	Organisation of African Union
OECD	Organisation for Economic Co-operation and Development
OEEC	Organisation for European Economic Co-operation
OHG	Offene Handelsgesellschaft
OJ	Official Journal (of the European Communities)
OJLS	*Oxford Journal of Legal Studies*
OPPO	Opposition
OSCE	Organisation for Security and Co-operation in Europe
P	On appeal to European Court of Justice from the Court of First Instance—after case number
Pas	*Pasicrisie*
PC	Privy Council
PCIJ	Permanent Court of International Justice
PCA	Partnerships and Co-operation Agreements
PE (or EP) doc	European Parliament document
PL	*Public Law*
PLC (or plc)	Public Limited Company
P-R	Pourvoi-Référé
QB	Queen's Bench Division of the High Court
QSR	Queensland State Reports
R	référé, denotes a decision taken on an application for interim measures—after case number ·
Rabels Z	*Rabels Zeitschrift*
RBDI	*Revue belge de droit international*
RCADI	*Recueil des cours de l'académie de droit international de la Haye*

RCDIP	*Revue critique de droit international privé*
RDE	*Rivista di Diritto Europeo*
RDH	*Revue des droits de l'homme*
RDIDC	*Revue de droit international et de droit comparé*
RDIPP	*Rivista di diritto internazionale privato e processuale*
RDP	*Revue du droit public*
Rec	*Recueil de la jurisprudence de la Cour de Justice des Communautés européennes*
RECIEL	*Review of European Community and International Environmental Law*
REICE	*Revista de Estudios y de Investigaciones Europeas*
Res-DH	Resolution-Droits de l'Homme
Rev	Revision
Rev de l'integ europ	*Revue de l'intégration européenne*
Rev Soc	*Revue des Sociétés*
RFAP	*Revue française d'administration publique*
RFDA	*Revue française de droit administratif*
RGDIP	*Revue générale de droit international public*
RIAA	Reports of International Arbitral Awards
RIDC	*Revue internationale de droit comparé*
RIDPC	*Rivista Italiana di Diritto Pubblico Comunitario*
RIIA	Royal Institute of International Affairs
RIW	*Recht Internationale Wirtschaft*
RJD	Reports of Judgments and Decisions
RJF	*Revue de Jurisprudence fiscale*
RJW	*Revue juridique de l'environment*
RMC	*Revue du Marché commun*
RMCUE	*Revue de Marché commun et de l'Union européenne*
RMUE	*Revue du marché unique européen*
RPC	Reports of Patent Cases
RSC	Rules of the Supreme Court
RTDE	*Revue trimestrielle de droit européen*
RW	*Rechtskundig Weekblad*
s	section
SA	Société anonyme
SARL	Société à responsabilité limitée
SCt	Supreme Court
SEA	Single European Act
SEW	*Social-economische Wetgeving*
SI	Statutory Instrument
SLT	*Scots Law Times*
Soc	Société
SpA	Società per Azioni
SPEL	*Scottish Planning and Environmental Law*

SPRL	Société de personnes à responsabilité limitée
Sp.St/Lon	Speeches and Statements issued by the French Embassy in London
Stb	*Statsblad*
STC	Simon's Tax Cases
St GB	Strafgestzbuch
St Tr	State Trials
Syd L Rev	*Sydney Law Review*
TACIS	Technical Assistance for the Commonwealth of Independent States
TC	*Tribunal des Conflicts*
TEU	Treaty on European Union
TREVI	Terrorism, Radicalism, Extremism, Violence, and Immigration
TRIPS	Agreement on Trade-Related Intellectual Property Rights
UCLA	*University of California at Los Angeles (Law Review)*
UKTS	United Kingdom Treaty Series
UN	United Nations Organisation
UNCED	United Nations Conference on Environment and Development
UNCTAD	United Nations Conference on Trade and Development
UNESCO	United Nations Educational, Scientific and Cultural Organisation
Uni Chi L R	*University of Chicago Law Review*
UNRWA	United Nations Relief and Works Agency
UNTS	United Nations Treaty Series
USC	United States Code
UWAL Rev	*University of Western Australia Law Review*
VC	Vice Chancellor
Ves	Vesey Junior
Ves Sen	Vesey Senior
VN	*Vereinte Nationen*
WEU	Western European Union
WGI	Working Group on Immigration—a sub-group of the Council of Ministers
WHO	World Health Organisation
WIPR	World Intellectual Property Reports
WLR	Weekly Law Reports
WTO	World Trade Organisation

WuW	*Wirtschaft und Wettbewerb*
YBILC	*Year Book of the International Law Commission*
YECHR	*Yearbook of the European Convention on Human Rights*
YEL	*Yearbook of European Law*
YLJ	*Yale Law Journal*
ZaiAS	*Zeitschrift für ausländisches und internationales Arbeits- und Sozialrecht*
ZAöRV	*Zeitschrift für ausländisches öffentliches Recht und Völkerrecht*
ZHR	*Zeitschrift für das gesamte Handelsrecht und Wirtschaftsrecht*

The Influence of Free Movement of Persons, Services and Capital on National Direct Taxation: Trends in the Case Law of the Court of Justice

MELCHIOR WATHELET*

I. Direct Taxation Falls Within National Competence

Taxation continues to be a central feature of state sovereignty, both as an instrument of economic and social policy and because of its direct effect on economic operators. From the outset, therefore, the Member States have been willing to transfer sovereign rights to the Community in this sphere only to a very limited extent.

Articles 2 and 3 of the EC Treaty do not expressly mention the abolition of tax barriers, even though it is difficult not to take account of them in so far as Article 3(1)(c) speaks of obstacles to free movement, Article 3(1)(g) refers to a system ensuring that competition in the internal market is not distorted, and Article 3(1)(h) speaks of the need for the approximation of national laws to the extent required for the functioning of the common market.

It is true that Articles 90 and 93 of the EC Treaty (formerly Articles 95 and 99 EC) empower the Community to adopt provisions for the harmonization of tax legislation and prohibit discriminatory taxation of imported products, but those provisions are concerned only with indirect taxation and there is no comparable enabling or prohibiting provision in the sphere of direct taxation.

In fact, in that sphere, having regard to the principle of conferred powers and the principle of subsidiarity, the only specific possibility for action by the Community in relation to direct taxation is the adoption of measures for the approximation of laws which have a direct impact on the establishment or functioning of the common market, and the basis for this must be the general provision applicable to all areas, namely Article 94 of the EC Treaty (formerly

* The author, a Judge at the Court of Justice of the EC and Professor at the Faculty of Law, Université catholique de Louvain, is not presenting the position of his institution, but expressing his personal views. The author would like to thank Sophie Graff-Svenningsen, *Référendaire* at the Court of Justice, Luxembourg, and Rainer Becker, advocate, Freshfields chambers, Brussels, for their assistance in preparing this article. This article presents the updated version of the article 'Les incidences de la libre circulation des personnes, des services et des capitaux sur la fiscalité directe nationale', published in French in the *Journal des Tribunaux* (18 November 2000, nr. 5987).

Article 100 EC). It should also be noted that Article 95 of the EC Treaty (formerly Article 100a EC), introduced by the Single European Act, which allows the approximation of laws by a qualified majority decision, is not applicable to tax provisions.

This sole possible course of action made available by Article 94 of the EC Treaty (formerly Article 100 EC) has moreover been resorted to very little in the field of direct taxation.

There is no example in the field of income tax. In the field of corporation tax, three directives are to be mentioned:

—Directive 90/434/EEC of 23 July 1990,[1] on the common system of taxation applicable to mergers, divisions, transfers of assets and exchanges of shares concerning companies of different Member States;

—Directive 90/435/EEC of 23 July 1990,[2] on the common system of taxation applicable in the case of parent companies and subsidiaries of different Member States;

—and to prevent or fight tax evasion or fraud, Directive 77/799/EEC of 19 December 1977,[3] concerning mutual assistance by the competent authorities of the Member States in the field of direct taxation.

II. Although Direct Taxation is a Matter Reserved to the Member States, They must Observe Community Law in the Exercise of their Powers

Notwithstanding this national legislative sovereignty in matters of direct taxation, the national rules in force in each area, including that of direct taxation, must be consonant with the Community provisions.

'Although direct taxation falls within the competence of the Member States, the latter must nonetheless exercise that competence consistently with Community law'—that is the phrase found in every judgment of the Court of Justice on direct taxation.[4]

---

[1] [1990] OJ L225/1. The only judgments of the Court interpreting or applying this Directive are of 17 July 1997 (preliminary reference in Case C–28/95 *Leur-Bloem* [1997] ECR I–1461) and of 19 February 1998 (C–8/97 *Commission* v. *Greece* [1998] ECR I–823).

[2] [1997] OJ L16/98. Two judgments of the Court are related to the interpretation of provisions of this directive: judgment of 17 Oct. 1996, in Joined Cases C–283/94, C–291/94 and C–292/94, *Denkavit International BV and Voormeer BV* [1996] *Bundesamt Finanzen* ECR I–5063 and judgment of 8 June 2000, in Case C–375/98, *Ministerio Publico et Fazenda Publica* v. *Epson Europe BV*, [2000] ECR I–4243.

[3] [1977] OJ L336/15. This directive is referred to, namely in the judgments of 28 January 1992, Case C–204/90, *Bachmann* [1992] (ECR I–249, para. 18) and Case C–300/90 *Commission* v. *Belgium* [1992] (ECR I–305, para. 11), of 12 April 1994, Case C–1/93, *Halliburton Services BV* [1994] (ECR I–1137, para. 22), of 14 February 1995, Case C–279/93 *Schumacker* [1995] (ECR I–225, para. 45), of 11 August 1995, Case C–80/94 *Wielockx* [1995] (ECR I–2493, para. 26), of 15 May 1997, Case C–250/95 *Futura Participations and Singer* [1997] (ECR I–2471, paras. 30 and 41), and of 28 October 1999, Case C–55/98 *Vestergaard* [1999] (ECR I–7641, para. 26).

[4] For the first time, in the judgment of 14 February 1995, Case C–279/93, *Schumacker* [1995] ECR I–225, para. 21 and frequently reproduced since then (for example, in the judgments of 11 August

It is therefore entirely possible that national legislation on direct taxation might be declared incompatible with Community law and, more particularly, with the provisions on the four fundamental freedoms, and as a result the structure of the relevant national tax law is likely to be affected to a considerable extent.

But what does the 'exercise of fiscal competence' involve?

III. The Exercise of Fiscal Competence and the Allocation of Fiscal Competence

The *Gilly* case,[5] which raised the issue of the compatibility with Article 48 of the EC Treaty (now Article 39 EC on free movement of workers) of a Franco-German convention for the avoidance of double taxation, will first illustrate what the exercise of fiscal competence is not.

Mr and Mrs Gilly lived in France. Mr Gilly, of French nationality, was a teacher in France. His wife had dual nationality, French and German, and taught in a German State school.

The first problem raised involved Article 14 of the Double Taxation Convention. According to that Article, people with income paid out of a public budget are taxable in the state which pays that income. An exception is made, however, where the person concerned is a national of another Member State, in which case his income is taxable in the state of residence.

The Double Taxation Convention thus adopts the nationality of taxpayers as its criterion of differentiation. Did this amount to unlawful discrimination on the ground of nationality? The Court clearly answered No. It said: 'such differentiation . . . flows, in the absence of any unifying or harmonising measures adopted in the Community context under, in particular, the second indent of Article 220 of the EC Treaty [now Article 293 EC], from the contracting parties' competence to define the criteria for allocating their powers of taxation as between themselves, with a view to eliminating double taxation'.[6]

The allocation of fiscal powers or competence thus comes before the exercise of such competence and therefore the application of the criterion of nationality and, *a fortiori*, that of residence in order to allocate that fiscal power or competence thus does not constitute discrimination within the meaning of the Treaty.

The second problem raised involved Article 20 of the Convention. In the system established by that Article, Mrs Gilly's German income was exempt in

---

1995, Case C–80/94 *Wielockx* [1995] ECR I–2493, para. 16, of 27 June 1996, Case C–107/94 *Asscher* [1996] ECR I–3089, para. 36, of 15 May 1997, Case C–250/95 *Futura Participations and Singer* [1997] ECR I–2471, para. 19, of 16 July 1998, Case C–264/96 *ICI* [1998] ECR I–4695, para. 19, and of 14 September 1999, Case C–391/97 *Gschwind* [1997] ECR I–5451, para. 20).

[5] Judgment of 12 May 1998 in Case C–336/96, *Époux Robert Gilly* v. *Directeur des services fiscaux du Bas-Rhin* [1998] ECR I–2793.

[6] *Ibid.*, para. 30.

France but, as a result of the fact that the German tax was more steeply progressive, the tax credit granted to Mrs Gilly in France was lower than the
amount of the tax which she had actually paid in Germany.

The result was that Mrs Gilly paid more tax in respect of her professional
activity in another Member State than she would have paid if she had worked
in France. It is obvious that such a system makes the free movement of workers less attractive.

The Court considered, however, that in that case there was no incompatibility with Community law in so far as that unfavourable consequence was the
result 'in the first place of the differences between the tax scales of the Member
States concerned, and, in the absence of any Community legislation in the
field, the determination of those scales was a matter for the Member States'.[7]

In other words, in order to be compatible with Community law, the exercise
of fiscal competence clearly does not mean that the Member States must apply
the same taxation methods or the same tax scales.

Does it follow, however, that where a double taxation convention is involved
the exercise of fiscal competence is automatically compatible with
Community law? No. The Court clearly so stated in its judgment in *Saint-
Gobain*,[8] involving German legislation which withheld from non-resident
companies which were resident in another Member State certain tax advantages deriving from a convention for the prevention of double taxation concluded with a non-Member country which, in the Federal Republic of
Germany's contention, fell outside the scope of Community competence.

The Court stated very clearly that once the power of taxation is allocated,
which involves in particular the power to determine a connecting factor,
which may be nationality or residence, the Member States must comply with
the Community rules and in particular the national treatment principle in
relation to permanent establishments of non-resident companies.[9]

The Court added that the extension of those tax advantages to non-resident
companies had no impact either on the duties of the Federal Republic of
Germany or on the rights of contracting non-member countries, as provided
for in the treaty for the avoidance of double taxation.

---

[7] Judgment of 12 May 1998 in Case C–336/96, *Époux Robert Gilly* v. *Directeur des services fiscaux
du Bas-Rhin* [1998] ECR I–2793, para. 47.
[8] Judgment of 21 September 1999 in Case C307/97, *Compagnie de Saint-Gobain,
Zweigniederlassung Deutschland* v. *Finanzamt Aachen-Innenstadt* [1999] ECR I–6161.
[9] *Ibid.*, para. 58: 'In the case of a double-taxation treaty concluded between a Member State and
a non-member country, the national treatment principle requires the Member State which is party
to the treaty to grant to permanent establishments of non-resident companies the advantages
provided for by that treaty on the same conditions as those which apply to resident companies'.

IV. Compliance with Community Law Concerning Fundamental Freedoms

In relation to the exercise of national competence to impose direct taxation, what is the exact scope of the obligation to comply with Community law, and more particularly the provisions concerning fundamental freedoms?

It should be emphasized in the first place that those freedoms are essentially the free movement of workers, freedom of establishment, freedom to provide services and free movement of capital, since, almost by definition, direct taxation does not affect goods.

The obligation to comply with the provisions relating to the major fundamental freedoms involves, at the outset, two prohibitions:

(a) prohibition of discrimination, that is to say treating differently people who are in objectively comparable situations or applying the same treatment to different situations.[10] Such discrimination may itself fall into two categories:

—discrimination is direct or evident where the national measures are openly associated with the nationality of the persons concerned. This is in fact extremely rare in the case of natural persons since the national fiscal measures relate much more often to residence than to nationality. On the other hand, it may be much more frequent for legal persons, since national legislation often differentiates between the conditions applicable to legal persons by reference to their registered office, which, in the case law of the Court of Justice,[11] determines attachment to a particular national legal order and therefore corresponds, for legal persons, to the criterion of nationality for natural persons.

—Discrimination may also be covert or indirect where the national measure draws no distinction based on nationality and thus applies, formally, without distinction to all citizens of the European Union but, in reality, even if based on other distinguishing criteria, such as residence or possession of a qualification, the national measure concerned in fact affects above all the nationals of other Member States.

(b) The prohibition of restrictive measures or barriers, that is to say national measures which, although not discriminatory, and thus treating nationals of the state in question and those of other Member States alike, have the effect of impeding the exercise of a fundamental freedom or making it less attractive.

---

[10] See as an example in a constant case law, para. 30 of the *Schumacker* judgment, *supra* n. 3.

[11] Judgments of 18 January 1986 in Case 270/83 *Commission* v. *France* [1986] ECR 273, para. 18; of 13 July 1993 in Case C–330/91 *Commerzbank* [1993] ECR I–4017, para. 13; and *ICI, supra* n. 4, para. 20.

This prohibition of restrictions or barriers, expressly provided for by the text of the Treaty in certain instances, has been extended to all fundamental freedoms by the case law of the Court of Justice.

Such discrimination or barriers may, however, be justified:

—either for reasons expressly mentioned in the Treaty, namely in relation to free movement of persons and capital, the exercise of public authority, and grounds of public policy, security or public health (Articles 39(3) (formerly Article 48(3), 45 (formerly Article 55), 46 (formerly Article 56), 55 (formerly Article 66) and 58(1)(b) of the EC Treaty (formerly Article 73d(1)(b)));

—or by what the Court of Justice has called overriding reasons of public interest, which are thus not provided for in the Treaty but which the Court has taken into account only in order to justify *barriers*—discrimination itself can be justified only on grounds expressly provided for in the Treaty.

Such justification must, however, be proportionate, that is to say apt to ensure attainment of the objective pursued, and not go beyond what is necessary to attain that objective. We shall consider several examples of this in relation to direct taxation.

V.   Application of Those Guidelines to Direct Taxation

Applying those principles, those guidelines, to direct taxation, we must immediately draw a distinction between natural and legal persons.

Let me repeat that, for natural persons, the national tax systems do not refer to their nationality but to their residence or tax domicile, which can therefore give rise only to indirect or disguised discrimination. In contrast, the same national tax systems refer, in the case of legal persons, to their registered office, which, I say again, is the equivalent of the nationality criterion for natural persons, thus being capable of giving rise to direct discrimination.

A.   NATURAL PERSONS

(i)   Discrimination

If national legislation attaches a favourable fiscal effect to residence, it will mainly operate to the disadvantage of nationals of other Member States, since it is above all they who, although working in the taxing state, reside in their own. Indirect discrimination is therefore possible.

(a)　The Schumacker *Case Law*

The leading case of the Court of Justice in this sphere is *Schumacker*, in 1995.[12] Mr Schumacker is Belgian, lives in Belgium with his wife and works in Germany. The couple have no income in Belgium.

Under the Belgo-German convention for the avoidance of double taxation, Mr Schumacker's professional income is taxed in his state of employment, namely Germany, which reserves to residents certain tax advantages linked to the personal and family circumstances of taxpayers, and more particularly a lower tax rate, known as 'splitting'.

The issue was whether that difference of treatment, based on residence, also constituted discrimination. Having regard to the definition of discrimination, the question then arose whether the difference of treatment was counter-balanced by the difference of circumstances.

The Court's response was that 'in relation to direct taxes, the situations of residents and of non-residents are not, as a rule, comparable'.[13] In fact, the Court went on, income received by a non-resident is in most cases only part of his total income. His personal ability to pay tax, his aggregate income and his personal and family circumstances can be better appraised at the place where his personal and financial interests are centred, namely his place of residence. Finally, that approach was consonant with international tax law and with the Model Double Taxation Treaty created by the OECD.[14]

Since the situations are different, the difference of treatment was, in principle, thus admissible. It was therefore not contrary to Article 39 EC (formerly Article 48 of the EC Treaty) to tax a non-resident more heavily.

However, the Court held, the position was different in the *Schumacker* case, in which a non-resident received no significant income in his state of residence, so that the latter was not in a position to grant him the tax advantages which would arise if his personal and family circumstances were taken into account.[15]

In that case, therefore, there was no objective difference of circumstances on which to base a difference of treatment between the resident and the non-resident, since the personal and family circumstances of the non-resident were not taken into account for tax purposes anywhere.[16]

The Court concluded that the fact that the state of employment refused to apply the 'splitting' regime to the non-resident, who received no significant income in the state of his residence, constituted indirect discrimination.

Three other judgments have confirmed that rule.

The 1995 *Wielockx*[17] judgment concerned a Belgian residing in Belgium who worked on a self-employed basis in the Netherlands. Dutch legislation allowed residents to deduct only expenses or contributions to a pension reserve.

---

[12] Judgment of 14 February 1995 in Case C–279/93 *Finanzamt Köln-Altstadt* v. *Roland Schumacker* [1995] ECR I–225.

[13] *Ibid.*, para. 31.　　　　[14] *Ibid.*, para. 32.　　　　[15] *Ibid.*, para. 36.　　　　[16] *Ibid.*, para. 37.

[17] Judgment of 11 August 1995 in Case C–80/94, *G.H.E.J. Wielockx* v. *Inspecteur der directe belastingen* [1995] ECR I–2493.

The Court confirmed that such a non-resident taxpayer, whether employed or self-employed, who received all or almost all his income in the state where he worked was objectively in the same situation, as far as income tax was concerned, as a resident of that state who did the same work there, since both were taxed in that state alone and their taxable income was the same.[18]

The Court concluded that the refusal to allow deduction meant that the personal and family circumstances of a non-resident were not taken into account anywhere and that discrimination therefore arose.

The *Gschwind* judgment,[19] in 1999, concerned a Dutch married couple living in the Netherlands. The husband was employed in Germany and earned 58 per cent of the household income, whilst his wife was employed in the Netherlands and her income accounted for 42 per cent of the household income.

German tax legislation reserved the advantage of 'splitting' to residents, unless the non-residents had only very limited foreign income or earned 90 per cent of their aggregate income in Germany.

Applying the *Schumacker* rule, the first paragraph to note was that a significant part of the couple's world income was received in their state of residence, thus constituting an adequate taxable amount allowing account to be taken of the personal and family circumstances of Mr and Mrs Gschwind. The necessary conclusion was that residents and non-residents were not in a comparable situation and that, therefore, the difference in their situation cancelled out the difference of tax treatment.

The recent *Zurstrassen* judgment[20] confirms this case law.

In this case, contrary to the *Schumacker* and *Gschwind* cases, there was no taxpayer who did not reside in his state of employment but a taxpayer—of Belgian nationality—residing in the State where his professional income—i.e. almost the whole family income (98 per cent)—was taxed, i.e. the Grand Duchy of Luxembourg.

However, as in the *Schumacker* case, Mrs Zurstrassen did not reside in the state of employment of her husband, but in Belgium, with their children, for reasons in particular of schooling. Having no income of her own, she was not liable to tax in Belgium, the state of her residence.

To tax his income, the tax authorities of Luxembourg considered Mr Zurstrassen as a single taxpayer, without any dependants, although he was married and had children, because his wife, unemployed and without income of her own, had kept her residence in Belgium.

Mr Zurstrassen argued that this decision was discriminatory in that he and his wife were placed at a disadvantage compared, in particular, with non-

---

[18] Judgment of 11 August 1995 in Case C–80/94, *G.H.E.J. Wielockx* v. *Inspecteur der directe belastingen* [1995] ECR I–2493, para. 20.

[19] Judgment of 14 September 1999 in Case C–391/97, *Frans Gschwind* v. *Finanzamt Aachen-Außenstadt* [1999] ECR I–5451.

[20] Judgment of 16 May 2000 in Case C–87/99, *P. Zurstrassen* v. *Administration des Contributions directes*, not yet reported.

residents who were married and where more than 50 per cent of the earned income of their household was paid in Luxembourg and they both worked in Luxembourg, inasmuch as they were treated as resident for tax purposes and were eligible for joint assessment to tax.[21]

The Court ruled that the condition of residence for both spouses to be entitled to joint assessment to tax was contrary to the equal treatment required by Articles 48(2) of the EC Treaty (now Article 39(2) EC) and 7(2), of Regulation 1612/68.[22]

Indeed, such a condition is easier for nationals of the Grand Duchy to satisfy than for nationals of other Member States, who have settled in the country in order to pursue an economic activity and members of whose family are more liable to reside outside Luxembourg.[23]

The Court also declined to accept that the difference of treatment imposed on Mr Zurstrassen could be justified by considerations linked to the fact that the situations of residents and non-residents are generally different and thus are not generally comparable as far as direct taxes are concerned. Indeed, as Mr Zurstrassen, having his residence in the state of his employment, i.e. Luxembourg, earned in that country almost the entire professional income of his household, the Grand Duchy was in fact the only state which could take into account his personal and family situation.[24]

It should be noted that, as in the *Schumacker* case, the wife of the taxpayer, Mrs Zurstrassen, earned no income of her own in the state of her residence and was not taxable there. The reply given by the Court did not have as a consequence that the personal and family situation of the spouses had to be taken into account twice.

To justify the decision of its administration, the Government of the Grand Duchy had argued that the joint assessment to tax of spouses simplified tax collection because of the solidarity between them. It was then possible for the tax collector to take action against either of them and demand from either payment of the entire tax debt. Such a possibility would not exist if one of the spouses was non-resident.[25]

Without even answering the question whether the objective of facilitating tax collection could justify unequal treatment based on residence, the Court only noted that the Luxembourg tax legislation itself allowed the joint assessment to tax of non-resident couples, provided that more than 50 per cent of the couple's earned income was taxable in Luxembourg, without any consideration for the practical obstacles to recovery of the tax, although they would be greater than in the *Zurstrassen* case.[26]

(b) Other cases

It should not be concluded from the *Schumacker* case law that there is never discrimination when a non-resident has significant income in his state of residence.

---

[21] *Ibid.*, para. 12.   [22] [1968] JO L257/2, [1968] II OJ Spec. Ed 475.
[23] *Ibid.*, paras. 19 and 20.   [24] *Ibid.*, para. 23.   [25] *Ibid.*, para. 24.
[26] *Ibid.*, para. 25.

Since the issue is whether or not a resident and a non-resident are in an objectively comparable situation from the point of view of the rule concerned, discrimination may occur, even if a non-resident has a significant income in his state of residence. The case law of the Court provides a number of examples.

Thus, in *Schumacker*, the Court stated that the refusal to grant non-residents the benefit of annual adjustment procedures applicable to residents constituted unjustified discrimination.[27] The 1990 *Biehl*[28] judgment had held likewise, because Luxembourg tax legislation gave only permanently resident taxpayers the right to obtain repayment of an over-deduction of tax from wages or salaries, whereas the temporarily resident taxpayers (more liable to be non-nationals) could only commence a non-contentious procedure to have their situation reviewed. As far as tax procedure is concerned, residents and non-residents are thus in comparable situations.

The 1996 *Asscher*[29] judgment is very illuminating on this paragraph. Mr Asscher was self-employed in the Netherlands, where he received less than 90 per cent of his aggregate income, and in Belgium. The Dutch legislation applied a tax rate of 25 per cent to the first band of taxable income for non-residents who received less than 90 per cent of their world income in the Netherlands, whereas the rate was only 13 per cent for residents, even if they earned less than 90 per cent of their world income in the Netherlands.

The purpose of the Dutch legislation was 'to offset the fact that certain non-residents escape the progressive nature of the tax because their tax obligations are confined to income received in the Netherlands'.

However, under the convention between Belgium and the Netherlands for the avoidance of double taxation, which in fact conformed with the OECD model, if income from the state of employment is exempted in the state of residence, the latter, in that instance Belgium, could always take them into account, *inter alia*, in order to apply the rule of progressivity.

The Court concluded that being a non-resident did not enable him to avoid the application of the rule of progressivity, and therefore that both residents and non-residents were in a comparable situation with regard to that rule.

(ii)   Barriers

The borderline between covert or indirect discrimination, on the one hand, and barriers or restrictive measures, on the other, is sometimes difficult to identify. That is particularly true in the case of the freedom to provide services (Article 59 of the EC Treaty, now Article 49 EC).

The 1992 *Bachmann* case,[30] which is especially known for its part devoted to the justifications of discriminations or barriers, involved a German national

---

[27] Judgment in *Schumacker, supra* n. 12, para. 58.

[28] Judgment of 18 May 1990 in Case C–175/88, *Klaus Biehl* v. *Administration des contributions* [1990] ECR I–1779.

[29] Judgment of 27 June 1996 in Case C–107/94, *P.H. Asscher* v. *Staatssecretaris van Financiën* [1996] ECR I–3089.

[30] Judgment of 28 January 1992 in Case C–204/90, *Hanns-Martin Bachmann* v. *Belgium* [1992] ECR I–249.

working in Germany who had paid, in Germany, premiums under a sickness-invalidity and life insurance policy taken out before he entered Belgium in order to work there. The problem arose from the fact that Belgian legislation disallowed deduction of those insurance premiums because they were not paid in Belgium.

This measure manifestly constituted a barrier, since it discouraged approaches to insurers established in other Member States, but the Court held that, even if the measure was not based on nationality or residence, there was a risk 'that the provisions in question may operate to the particular detriment of [migrant] workers who are, as a general rule, nationals of other Member States'.[31] That is in fact the definition of indirect discrimination and not of a barrier!

And yet, in theory at least, this differentiation, constituting indirect or disguised discrimination, on the one hand, and a barrier, on the other, is important, since as far as justification is concerned, only those expressly mentioned in the Treaty are acceptable in the case of discrimination, whereas barriers may be justified in addition by what the Court has called 'overriding reasons of public interest'.[32]

In the *Baars*[33] case, the question was whether a Member State's wealth tax legislation which partially or totally exempted from wealth tax assets invested in shares of a company (called 'undertaking exemption') but only if the company in the shares of which the assets have been invested, was established in this Member State was compatible with Articles 52 (now Article 43), 73b and 73d of the EC Treaty (now Articles 56 and 58 EC).

Mr Baars was a Dutch national, resident in the Netherlands. He owned all the shares in a company incorporated under Irish law and established in Ireland. In the assets declared to assess wealth tax, he included the value of these shares. The Dutch authorities refused to allow Mr Baars the 'undertaking exemption' from the wealth tax on this amount since the condition of establishment in the Netherlands of the company in the shares of which the assets had been invested was not fulfilled. Mr Baars submitted that this condition was a restriction both of the freedom of establishment and of the free movement of capital, incompatible with Community law.

The Court's answer tackled only the freedom of establishment, as Mr Baars was the only shareholder of the Irish company. Ruling that the legislation in question was incompatible with the right of establishment, as provided by Article 52 of the EC Treaty (now Article 43 EC), the Court considered it useless to examine the case in relation to the free movement of capital.

It has ruled that the Dutch legislation, by refusing to grant the tax advantage in question to nationals of Member States residing in the Netherlands who, exercising their right of free establishment, manage a company established in another Member State, while granting that advantage to nationals of Member

---

[31] *Ibid.*, para. 9.   [32] See *infra*, part VI.

[33] Judgment of 13 April 2000 in Case C–251/98, *C. Baars* v. *Inspecteur der Belastingen Particulieren/Ondernemingen Gorinchem*, not yet reported.

States, residing in the Netherlands who hold a substantial holding in a company established in the Netherlands, provided for a difference of tax treatment, in principle contrary to Article 52 of the EC Treaty (now Article 43 EC). It was easy to state that the taxpayers were in comparable objective situations, as the criterion to differentiate them was not their residence but the country of establishment of the company of which they were shareholders.[34]

The Court simply stated that the legislation at issue implied a difference of treatment though it could have found either discrimination between residents according to whether or not they had exercised their right of establishment guaranteed by the Treaty or a barrier, inasmuch as the legislation at issue applied to every resident in the Netherlands and made less attractive for them establishment in another Member State.

Actually, as Advocate General Tesauro noted in paragraphs 21 and 24 of his Opinion in the *ICI* case,[35] the answer to the question of identifying whether a difference of treatment constitutes discrimination or a barrier depends on where the emphasis is placed. In the *ICI* case, the Advocate General found it clear that the legislation at issue discriminated between companies resident in the United Kingdom, according to whether or not they had exercised their right of establishment in another Member State, even through a holding company. The difference of tax treatment affected companies whose registered office was in the same Member State and was linked to their decision whether or not to avail themselves of the possibility, guaranteed by Article 52 of the EC Treaty (now Article 43 EC), of setting up subsidiaries in other Member States.

However Advocate General Tesauro observed that, even if the legislation at issue were to be regarded as applying without any distinction, in view of the fact that the requirement was imposed on companies which were all resident in the United Kingdom, the result would be the same, as it would still be incompatible with the rules regarding freedom of establishment.

B. LEGAL PERSONS

Let us now consider legal persons—companies—focusing essentially on freedom of establishment (Article 43 of the EC Treaty, formerly Article 52 EC).

Most of the cases concern tax provisions which subject legal persons whose registered office is abroad, to rules different from those applicable to companies established in national territory, with the result that direct discrimination arises more frequently.

The *locus classicus* in this area is the 1986 judgment in *Commission* v. *French Republic*, the 'tax credit case'.[36] To avoid double taxation, in economic terms, of company profits, through liability first to corporation tax and then to a tax on dividends, French law had provided for the application to the latter of a tax

---

[34] Judgment of 13 April 2000 in Case C–251/98, *C. Baars* v. *Inspecteur der Belastingen Particulieren/Ondernemingen Gorinchem*, not yet reported, para. 30.

[35] Case 264/96, *Imperial Chemical Industries (ICI)* v. *K.H. Colmer* [1998] ECR I–4695.

[36] Judgment of 18 January 1986 in Case 270/83, *Commission* v. *French Republic* [1986] ECR 273.

credit known as the '*avoir fiscal*', but reserved it to dividends distributed by companies with their registered office in France.

Closely following tradition, the Court took the same approach as in *Schumacker*, finding first that the branches or agencies of foreign companies were not, apart from the advantage at issue, in an objectively different fiscal situation from that of companies whose registered office was in France.

In fact, the taxable amount was the same, only profits earned in France being subject to French tax.

The Court therefore concluded that to treat those companies differently as regards availability of the tax credit constituted discrimination.

It held likewise in the 1993 *Commerzbank* judgment,[37] concerning UK legislation which added a supplement to repayments of tax paid but not due provided that the companies concerned had their tax domicile in the United Kingdom. The Court spoke in that case of—albeit indirect—discrimination, since the criterion of differentiation was not strictly the registered office but the fiscal domicile.

I now turn to the recent judgments in which the Court has often spoken of unequal treatment rather than covert discrimination or barriers.

The only recent case in which the Court still referred to discrimination is the *Royal Bank of Scotland* case, in which judgment was delivered in 1999,[38] involving Greek legislation which imposed corporation tax at the rate of 40 per cent for companies whose registered office was in a Member State other than Greece and at the rate of 35 per cent for companies with their registered offices in Greece.

After finding that there was no objective difference of situation as regards determination of the taxable amount as between the two categories, the Court concluded that there was discrimination.[39] The Court did not say so expressly, but it was clearly a case of direct discrimination.

In its 1998 judgment in *ICI*,[40] the Court referred to 'unequal treatment' in the case of a UK law which allowed deduction of losses suffered by a subsidiary of a holding company only to undertakings whose business consisted wholly or mainly in the holding of shares in subsidiaries whose seat was in UK territory. ICI, a UK company, owned Coopers Animal Health (Holdings) ('Holdings') through a consortium. Holdings controlled twenty-three subsidiaries, of which only four were within the United Kingdom, a situation which prompted the UK tax authorities to refuse to allow ICI to deduct the losses of a subsidiary of Holdings.

The Court stated that the UK legislation applied the test of the subsidiaries' seat to establish differential tax treatment of consortium companies

---

[37] Judgment of 13 July 1993 in Case C–330/91, *The Queen* v. *Ireland Revenue Commissioners, ex p. Commerzbank AG* [1993] ECR I–4017.

[38] Judgment of 29 April 1999 in Case C–311/97, *Royal Bank of Scotland plc* v. *Elliniko Dimosio* [1999] ECR I–2651.

[39] *Ibid.*, para. 30.

[40] Judgment of 16 July 1998 in Case C–264/96, *Imperial Chemical Industries plc (ICI)* v. *K.H. Colmer* [1998] ECR I–4695.

established in the United Kingdom,[41] but did not refer to discrimination or to a barrier or obstacle to the right of free establishment.

The 1999 *Saint-Gobain* judgment[42] concerned a German law which reserved certain tax advantages to companies which were subject in Germany to unlimited tax liability (namely, resident companies) and withheld them from companies whose seat was elsewhere, even though they were also taxed in Germany through a branch there, which was regarded as a permanent establishment under German tax legislation.

Once again, after determining that the tax situations were objectively comparable, since the receipt of dividends and the holding of shares were taxable in the same way for both categories, since the limited tax liability of non-resident companies was extended to foreign income, whilst the unlimited tax liability of German companies was in reality limited, which made the two tax obligations comparable, the Court found that there was unequal treatment.[43] It correctly stated that as a result, it was less attractive[44] (which reminds the obstacle or the barrier to free movement) to set up a branch in Germany, to pay dividends there and to arrange for it to hold shares; it could also have spoken of discrimination, but it did not do so.

Finally, let us mention the *AMID* (*Algemene Maatschappij voor Investeringen en Dienstverlening NV/Belgische Staat*) case decided on 15 December 2000.[45]

According to Belgian income tax legislation, AMID, a limited liability company having its seat and fiscal domicile in Belgium as well as a permanent establishment in the Grand Duchy of Luxembourg, was not allowed to deduct losses incurred in the previous year by its Belgian establishment from the profits made by the same establishment in the following year, because these losses should have been set off against the profits made in the Grand Duchy in the previous year. Since, under the Luxembourg tax system, the Belgian loss could not be set off against the Luxembourg profit, AMID argued that companies with branches abroad were disadvantaged in comparison with companies having branches only in Belgium, in which case the losses could have been deducted.

As no objective difference in the respective positions of the two categories of companies had been established and in the absence of any justification presented by the Belgian government, the Court ruled that the difference in treatment as regards the deduction of losses was contrary to the freedom of establishment. There was again no need to qualify with more details this 'difference in treatment' as no justification had even been invoked.[46]

---

[41] Judgment of 16 July 1998 in Case C–264/96, *Imperial Chemical Industries plc (ICI)* v. *K.H. Colmer* [1998] ECR I–4695, para. 23.

[42] Judgment of 21 September 1999 in Case C–307/97, *Compagnie de Saint-Gobain, Zweigniederlassung Deutschland* v. *Finanzamt Aachen-Innenstadt* [1999] ECR I–6161.

[43] *Ibid.*, para. 44.   [44] *Ibid.*, paras. 42–44.

[45] Judgment of 14 December 2000 in Case C–141/99, *Algemene Maatschappij voor Investering en Dienstverlening NV* and *Belgium*, not yet reported.

[46] *Ibid.*, paras. 30–32.

Where the issue is the freedom to provide services rather than freedom of establishment, the Court sometimes speaks of obstacles and sometimes of unequal treatment.

In the 1998 case of *Safir*,[47] involving Swedish legislation laying down different tax conditions for life assurance depending on whether the policy was effected with companies established in Sweden or abroad, the Court referred to an obstacle to the freedom to provide services and to the freedom to take out life insurance abroad.

In its *X AB and Y AB* judgment, in 1999,[48] concerning Swedish legislation withholding tax advantages on intra-group financial transfers where the Swedish company had exercised its right of establishment in other Member States, the Court referred to unequal treatment between different types of financial transfers based on the criterion of subsidiaries' seat.

In the recent 1999 judgment in *Bent Vestergaard*,[49] concerning Danish legislation under which vocational training expenses incurred at tourist locations in other Member States were deemed not to be expenses incurred in the course of employment and could not be deducted as such, but under which the same presumption did not apply to the same expenses incurred in tourist locations in Denmark, the Court referred to a difference of treatment relating to the place (in fact the Member State) where the services were provided.

The *Eurowings* case, also decided in 1999,[50] involved German legislation concerning a tax on capital and earnings, which required earnings from leases to be added back to the taxable amount where a German company had signed the lease with a lessor who was not subject to that tax, which meant in practice a lessor established in another Member State. After restating the fact that the freedom to provide services precluded any restriction and applied both to recipients and to providers of services, the Court concluded that there was difference of treatment based on the Member State where the provider of services was established.

VI. Justifications

Possible justifications for such discrimination, obstacles or differences of treatment remain to be considered.

The rule bears repeating: in the event of discrimination, only justifications expressly provided for by the Treaty can be relied on, whereas in the case of a

---

[47] Judgment of 28 April 1998 in Case C–118/96, *Jessica Safir* v. *Skattemyndigheten* [1998] ECR I–1897.

[48] Judgment of 18 November 1999 in Case C–200/98, *X AB and Y AB* v. *Riksskatteverket* [1999] ECR I–8261.

[49] Judgment of 28 October 1999 in Case C–55/98, *Skatteministeriet* v. *Bent Vestergaard* [1999] ECR I–7641.

[50] Judgment of 26 October 1999 in Case C–294/97, *Eurowings Luftverkehrs AG* v. *Finanzamt Dortmund-Unna* [1999] ECR I–7447.

mere obstacle or restriction, the Court of Justice has allowed other grounds of justification, referring to the 'overriding general interest'.

Let me say straight away that, particularly in relation to direct taxation, the trend in today's case law, with the exception of rare cases of clear and open discrimination, in which the Court would probably examine only justifications expressly mentioned in the text of the Treaty (the *Royal Bank of Scotland* case should be borne in mind), the Court, after finding a difference of treatment, will first examine all the justifications put forward, those mentioned expressly in the Treaty or matters of overriding general interest, without ruling whether or not the measures considered are discriminatory or not.

In fact, if all the justifications invoked are rejected, this point will not have to be settled. But would the Court accept a matter of overriding general interest as justification for unequal treatment; should it not choose between discrimination and mere obstacle or restriction?

Or, on the contrary, would the Court be ready to admit that the reasons of overriding general interest justify mere restrictions as well as discrimination, with perhaps the exclusion of direct discrimination? Up to now, this dilemma has never been presented to the Court in such clear terms, even though in all the cases which I have cited or cite below, there was never any question of justifications expressly mentioned in the Treaty: Member States never rely on the exercise of public authority, public policy, public health or public security to justify their tax measures.

But it is also true that matters of overriding general interest have only rarely been admitted by the Court.

A.   COHESION OF THE TAX SYSTEM

I could willingly say, '*à tout seigneur, tout honneur*'. In fact, fiscal cohesion is almost always invoked by Member States. Perhaps because it is the only justification ever accepted by the Court of Justice, even though, ultimately, that occurred only once. Moreover, it would be tempting to grant it a special status, quite apart from the fact that it is put forward almost systematically. Even though the judgment is not concerned with direct taxation, it should be noted that, in the 1995 case of *Svensson and Gustavsson*,[51] after finding that there was discrimination[52] and after repeating that discrimination can only be justified by the general interest grounds referred to in Article 56(1) of the EC Treaty (now Article 46(1) EC), the Court nevertheless considered the possibility that such discrimination might be justified by the need to ensure the cohesion of a tax system.[53]

The cohesion of the tax system was what made the *Bachmann* judgment[54] famous. It will be remembered that Belgian tax law did not allow life insurance

[51] Judgment of 14 November 1995 in Case C–484/93, *Peter Svensson and Lena Gustavsson* v. *Ministry of Housing and Urbanism* [1995] ECR I–3955.

[52] *Ibid.*, para. 12.   [53] *Ibid.*, paras. 16–18.

[54] Judgment of 28 January 1992 in Case C–204/90, *Hanns-Martin Bachmann* v. *Belgium* [1992] ECR I–249. The Court said the same thing in its Judgment of 28 January 1992 in Case C–300/90, *Commission of the European Communities* v. *Belgium* [1992] ECR I–305.

premiums to be deducted from taxable income where the premiums had been paid abroad. The Belgian authorities contended that, in fact, Belgian tax law gave the insured a choice of either deducting premiums but taxing future benefits or not deducting premiums and exempting future benefits.

It was therefore consistent for Belgium to refuse to deduct premiums paid in Germany because it could have no certainty of being able to tax at a later stage benefits also paid in Germany. In respect of the same taxpayer and in connection with the same tax, it was therefore justified to maintain the balance sought by the Belgian legislature between one tax rule that was favourable and another that was unfavourable.

In the *Asscher* case,[55] the Dutch Government had pleaded that an increase in the rate of tax for non-residents was designed to offset the non-deductibility of social insurance contributions of residents to which, by definition, non-residents were not subject.

The Court took the view that there was not a sufficiently direct link between the increase in the tax for non-residents and the fact that they did not have to pay social contributions in the Netherlands.

First, the increase in the rate of tax gave them no additional social protection and, secondly, if they paid no social contributions in the Netherlands, that was purely and simply by virtue of Regulation 1408/71,[56] which provided for payments to be made to a single social security regime, in that case that of the state of residence. Therefore there could not be any question of another state, even through taxation measures, offsetting that failure to pay contributions to a second social security scheme.

In the *Wielockx* case,[57] according to the Dutch Government, which also invoked cohesion of the tax system, it was logical that a non-resident should not be able to deduct pension contributions since the convention for the avoidance of double taxation between Belgium and the Netherlands provided that pensions were to be taxed in the state of residence. That reasoning was to some extent similar to that in *Bachmann*: premiums could not be deducted if the benefit was also exempt.

However, the Court did not follow that line of argument. It observed that the Netherlands—under the same convention for the avoidance of double taxation—itself taxed the pensions of its residents even if the contributions were the subject of deduction in another country. The Court stated that fiscal cohesion had been realized by the double taxation convention at the level of the global relationships between the two countries, which meant that in some degree the state had waived the right to ensure fiscal cohesion at individual level.

---

[55] Judgment of 27 June 1996 in Case C–104/97, *P.H. Asscher v. Staatssecretaris van Financiën* [1996] ECR I–3089.

[56] [1971] JO L149/2, [1971] II OJ Spec. Ed. 416.

[57] Judgment of 11 August 1995 in Case C–80/94, *G.H.E.J. Wielockx v. Inspecteur der Directe Belastingen* [1995] ECR I–2493.

It is true that, in certain cases, the Netherlands would have to allow deduction of pension contributions without being able to tax the pension when it was ultimately paid; however, in other cases, they would tax pensions when they had not allowed any premium deduction.

Finally, fiscal cohesion was also invoked in the *ICI* case,[58] in which the Court also considered that there was no sufficiently direct link between tax relief for losses suffered by a subsidiary established in the United Kingdom and the taxation of profits of subsidiaries whose seat was outside UK territory.

In the *Baars* case,[59] whether the Dutch Government invoked cohesion of the tax system, saying that it was justified to refuse to grant the exemption to a resident who holds shares in a non-resident company because the non-resident company does not pay the Netherlands' corporation tax and because this exemption had been established in order to compensate the 'double taxation' of a same income: first, the taxation of the profits made by the company which distributes dividends, secondly, the taxation of the patrimony/participation of the shareholder. The Court rejected this argument. There is no link between corporation tax and wealth tax, which are distinct taxes, applying to distinct taxpayers (respectively companies and natural persons).[60]

One excellent example of unequal treatment which might have been justified by the need to preserve fiscal cohesion is provided by a case which will be examined in greater detail in the chapter relating to the free movement of capital. This is Case C–35/98 *Staatssecretaris van Financiën* v. *Verkooijen*, in which the Advocate General, in his Opinion of 24 June 1999,[61] concluded that income-tax legislation such as that in issue in the main proceedings was lawful for reasons relating to the need to preserve the cohesion of the Netherlands tax system. The interest which the initial reasoning of the Advocate General holds for the purposes of this article is in no way diminished by the fact that his initial Opinion was based on an erroneous premiss which warranted the reopening of the oral procedure and the delivery of a fresh Opinion.

Mr Verkooijen resided in the Netherlands, where he worked for a company controlled by the Belgian undertaking Petrofina NV. He acquired shares in the Belgian company within the context of an employees' savings plan ('*werknemersspaarplan*').

The Dutch legislation on the taxation of dividends provided for the exemption, within certain limits, of dividends and income received from shares and holdings in companies: dividends were exempted, up to a specific amount, from income tax payable by natural persons, on condition that those dividends were paid by companies having their seat in the Netherlands.

The situation in that case bears certain similarities to that in the preliminary-ruling case of *Baars*, cited above, save that *Verkooijen* concerned an exemption from income tax rather than wealth tax and the facts of the latter

---

[58] Judgment of 16 July 1998 in Case C–264/96, *Imperial Chemical Industries plc (ICI)* v. *K.H. Colmer* [1998] ECR I–4695.

[59] *Baars, supra* n. 33.   [60] *Ibid.*, paras. 38–40.   [61] [2000] ECR I–4071.

case prompted the Court to examine the issues by reference to the free movement of capital rather than freedom of establishment.

The Dutch Government again sought to argue that the difference in the treatment afforded to Dutch taxpayers, depending on whether the dividends received by them emanated from companies established in the Netherlands or elsewhere, was justified by the need to ensure fiscal cohesion.

As in *Baars*, it maintained that the exemption in respect of income tax was designed to compensate for the effects of the double taxation which would otherwise result from the levying of corporation tax on profits accruing to companies and of income tax on the dividends paid by those companies to private shareholders.

The Advocate General based his view on the premiss that it was not possible in the Netherlands to take account, at the level of the aggregate income tax payable by natural persons at the end of the tax year, of the tax on dividends levied at source when dividends were paid to shareholders. He further observed that, under the double taxation convention concluded between Belgium and the Netherlands, a taxpayer in Mr Verkooijen's position would be entitled, even if dividends received from a Belgian company were to be included for the purposes of the taxation of his aggregate income in the Netherlands, to a partial tax credit in order to take account of the tax levied at source in Belgium when the dividends were paid. Indeed, the existence of such a tax credit is provided for in the model convention drawn up by the OECD.

The Advocate General therefore considered that it was legitimate to reserve the exemption from income tax to taxpayers receiving dividends from companies established in the Netherlands, so as to compensate for the effects of double taxation, which he defined in terms different from those used by the Dutch Government and which would involve an initial levy, consisting of the deduction of dividend tax at source upon the payment of a dividend by a company established in the Netherlands, followed by a second levy in the context of the aggregate income tax due at the end of the year, without necessarily taking into account, for the purposes of calculating that aggregate income tax, the dividend tax paid in advance.

It was likewise legitimate to refuse the benefit of such exemption in the case of taxpayers receiving dividends from a company established in another Member State, since they were not subject to deduction at source.

That being so, was it necessary, in such circumstances, to seek to provide any justification? After all, the unequal treatment could be regarded as having been cancelled out by the objective difference in the respective situations with regard to the taxation of dividends.

At all events, the premiss on which the Opinion was based was incorrect, since Dutch tax law provided for the dividend tax to be taken into account upon the levying of the tax due on the aggregate income in the Netherlands, so that resident taxpayers receiving dividends from companies established in the Netherlands and taxpayers receiving dividends from companies established in another Member State were in a comparable situation as regards the conferment of fiscal advantages such as the exemption in question. In those circumstances, the need to preserve the cohesion of the Dutch tax system was not a justifiable ground for restricting the conferment of such advantages to the shareholders of companies established in the Netherlands. This is apparent from the Advocate General's second Opinion, dated 14 December 1999, which was confirmed by the judgment delivered in this case on 6 June 2000.

Finally, it appears that, save in *Bachmann*, the argument regarding the need to preserve the cohesion of the tax system has invariably been rejected.

In Joined Cases C–397/98 and C–410/98 *Metallgesellschaft and Hoechst*, the arguments put forward by the United Kingdom to justify the provisions at issue in the main proceedings, based on the need to preserve the cohesion of the national tax system, were not accepted by Advocate General Fennelly in his Opinion dated 12 September 2000 nor by the Court in its judgment of 8 March 2001.[62]

It is appropriate, first of all, to recall the legal and factual context of those cases. Under United Kingdom tax law, certain distributions, including the payment of dividends, involve the payment of advance corporation tax or 'ACT'. As its name indicates, such advance payment is made before the aggregate corporation tax for the relevant accounting period (known as 'mainstream corporation tax') is levied. Each quarter, a company resident in the United Kingdom is required to make a return showing the amount of any distribution made and the amount of ACT payable. The ACT due in respect of a distribution must be paid within 14 days after the end of the quarter in which the distribution is made.

A subsidiary resident in the United Kingdom and paying dividends to its parent company may, by making a group income election, avoid having to pay ACT and may thus enjoy a cash-flow advantage (since mainstream corporation tax is not payable until nine months after the end of the accounting period). However, the ability to do so is reserved to subsidiaries resident in the United Kingdom of parent companies which also have their seat in the United Kingdom.

The plaintiffs in the main proceedings are the UK subsidiaries of parent companies having their seat in Germany and the parent companies in question. They are therefore not entitled to make a group income election, and have had to pay ACT on dividends paid to their parent companies.

The financial prejudice arising from the obligation to pay ACT and the inability to make a group income election is said to be considerable. For example, Hoechst UK Ltd maintains that the amounts which it has paid in respect of ACT are in excess of £250,000,000, and that the time value of those advance payments comes to approximately £8,000,000.

The plaintiffs in the main proceedings claim that the United Kingdom's refusal to extend the group income election scheme to non-resident parent

---

[62] Joined Cases C–397/98 and C–410/98, *Metallgesellschaft Ltd. and Others, Hoechst AG and Hoechst (UK) Ltd.* v. *Commissioners of Inland Revenue and H.M. Attorney General*, not yet reported.

companies is contrary to the Treaty rules concerning both freedom of establishment and the free movement of capital.

The UK Government argues that the difference in treatment with regard to
the group income election scheme is justified by the need to preserve the
cohesion of the UK tax system.

Thus, the fundamental principle underlying the UK tax system is that companies are liable to corporation tax on their profits and that their shareholders
are liable to tax when profits are distributed to them by way of dividend. The
straightforward application of that principle would result, in economic terms,
in double taxation of company profits, once in the hands of the paying company, and again in the hands of the shareholder (being either a legal person or
a natural person). The United Kingdom's partial imputation system mitigates
this double taxation by exempting corporate shareholders resident in the
United Kingdom from corporation tax on the dividends they receive.

In order to ensure the cohesion of the UK tax system, it is essential that the
tax exemption applying to the dividend in the hands of the corporate shareholder should be matched by a charge to tax in the form of the imposition on
the company paying the dividend of a liability to account for the ACT. There is
a clear and direct link between the charge of the paying company to the ACT
corresponding to the payment of dividends and the tax exemption accorded to
the corporate shareholder in respect of dividends received.

The abovementioned rule is not contravened by allowing resident subsidiaries of resident parent companies to make a group income election and
by exempting them from having to pay ACT when paying dividends to their
parent companies, for the following reason. Whilst a subsidiary which has
made a group income election is not liable to ACT on the dividends paid to its
parent company, the ACT which that subsidiary has avoided having to pay will
sooner or later be paid by the parent company when it redistributes those
sums in the form of distributions chargeable to ACT.

The United Kingdom analyses the situation of a group of companies comprising a resident subsidiary and a resident parent company in relation to that
of a group comprising a resident subsidiary and a parent company having its
seat in another Member State, and maintains that they are not comparable.
The first group of companies is not relieved of the obligation to match the
exemption of the corporate shareholder (the parent company) by a charge to
ACT since the payment of ACT is deferred. Thus, the charge to ACT is, so to
speak, transferred from the subsidiary to the parent company at the same time
as the dividend is paid by the former to the latter.

The situation of a group comprising a resident subsidiary and a non-
resident parent company is different, inasmuch as, if the resident subsidiary of
such a parent company were permitted to avoid having to pay ACT when
paying dividends to its parent, there would be no ACT capable of being levied
subsequently on the dividends paid and redistributed, since the parent company, being established in another Member State, would not be subject to the
payment of UK ACT on the distributions made by it.

The United Kingdom maintains that, where the first group of companies makes the group income election, payment of the ACT will be deferred; if, by contrast, the second group were permitted to make such an election, the effect would be to grant an exemption from ACT. And this exemption would not be offset by any subsequent payment of ACT by the non-resident parent company when it made distributions, in that it is not subject to UK corporation tax or, therefore, to ACT. Consequently, the United Kingdom maintains that it is justified in refusing to allow UK subsidiaries of non-resident companies the right to make a group income election.

The Court rejected that line of argument. First, it observed that ACT is not a tax on dividends but simply constitutes an advance on the mainstream corporation tax payable by companies. Thus, it is incorrect to suppose that affording resident subsidiaries of non-resident parent companies the possibility of making a group income election would allow the subsidiary to avoid paying any tax in the United Kingdom on profits distributed by way of dividends (paragraph 52 of the judgment). The situation of UK subsidiaries of resident parent companies is comparable to that of UK subsidiaries of non-resident parent companies, inasmuch as their respective profits are liable to UK corporation tax.

Secondly, the fact that a non-resident company is not liable to ACT is attributable to the fact that it is not liable to corporation tax in the United Kingdom, since it is subject to that tax in its state of establishment. Logic therefore requires that a company should not have to make advance payment of a tax to which it will never be liable (see paragraph 56 of the judgment).

Therefore, the difference in the tax treatment of parent companies depending on whether or not they are resident cannot justify a denial of a tax advantage to subsidiaries, resident in the United Kingdom, of parent companies having their seat in another Member State when that advantage is available to subsidiaries resident in the United Kingdom of parent companies also resident in the United Kingdom. All those subsidiaries are in fact liable to mainstream corporation tax on their profits irrespective of the place of residence of their parent companies. The grant to one category of an advantage which is refused to the other cannot be justified by any difference in the liability to corporation tax of the parent companies to which the dividends are paid.

As regards justification by the need to preserve the cohesion of the UK's tax system, the Court considered that, by contrast with the *Bachmann* and *Commission* v. *Belgium* cases, there was not a sufficiently direct link in the present cases between, on the one hand, the refusal to exempt resident subsidiaries of non-resident parent companies from the payment of ACT under a group income election and, on the other hand, the fact that parent companies having their seat in another Member State and receiving dividends from their subsidiaries in the United Kingdom are not liable to corporation tax in the United Kingdom (see paragraph 69 of the judgment).

Parent companies, whether resident or not, are exempt from corporation tax in the United Kingdom in respect of dividends received from their resident subsidiaries. The Court found it irrelevant for the purpose of granting a tax advantage such as an exemption from ACT that, for resident parent companies, such exemption is intended to prevent double-taxation of the profits of resident subsidiaries and that, for non-resident parent companies, that exemption simply results from the fact that they are not in any event subject to corporation tax in the United Kingdom, being subject to a comparable tax in the Member State in which they are established.

B. LOSS OF TAX REVENUE

Loss of tax revenue can never constitute justification for any discrimination or obstacle, either under Article 46 of the Treaty (formerly Article 56 EC) or as a matter of overriding general interest, as the Court stated very clearly in its judgment in *ICI*.[63]

It was thus to no avail that the UK Government pleaded that it was unable to offset the relief granted to resident subsidiaries since it could not tax the profits of subsidiaries located outside the United Kingdom.

In the judgment delivered in 1999 in *Saint-Gobain*, the Court reiterated that principle: 'a reduction of revenue . . . is not one of the grounds listed in Article 56 of the EC Treaty (now, after amendment, Article 46 EC) and cannot be regarded as a matter of overriding general interest which may be relied upon in order to justify unequal treatment that is in principle incompatible with Article 52 of the Treaty'.[64]

It thus rejected the German Government's argument that the refusal to allow non-resident companies having a permanent establishment in Germany certain tax concessions granted to resident companies was justified by the need to prevent a reduction in tax revenue given the impossibility for the German tax authorities to compensate for the reduction in revenue brought about by the grant of the tax concessions in question by taxing dividends distributed by non-resident companies limited by shares operating permanent establishments in Germany.

C. THE ARGUMENT THAT NON-RESIDENT COMPANIES ENJOY OTHER ADVANTAGES

A purported justification to this effect was rejected in the judgments in *Commission* v. *France*,[65] *Asscher*[66] and *Saint-Gobain*.[67] The Court stated very

---

[63] Judgment, *supra* n. 40 above, para. 28.
[64] Judgment, *supra* n. 9 above, para. 51.   [65] Judgment, *supra* n. 36 above, para. 21.
[66] Judgment, *supra* n. 29 above, para. 53: 'The advantage which such non-residents are presumed to enjoy arises, if at all, from the decision of the Netherlands legislature to abolish the right to deduct social security contributions which, by its nature, affects only such taxpayers as are under an obligation to pay them, thus favouring, in the Netherlands Government's submission, those who do not have to pay such contributions in the Netherlands. Such a circumstance may not be offset by tax differentials affecting the latter category, since that would amount to penalizing them for not paying social security contributions in the Netherlands'.
[67] Judgment, *supra* n. 8 above, para. 54.

clearly that, even if such advantages are presumed to exist, they cannot justify a breach of the obligation laid down by Article 52 of the EC Treaty (now, after amendment, Article 43 EC), requiring Member States to treat non-residents in the same way as their own nationals.[68]

D.   PREVENTING THE RISK OF TAX AVOIDANCE

Having stated very generally—perhaps too generally—in its judgment in *Commission* v. *France* that 'the risk of tax avoidance cannot be relied upon in this context', the Court was somewhat more circumspect in the judgment in *ICI*. Whilst it ultimately rejected the argument, this was perhaps because it was applied in too absolute a manner.

The Court observed that the UK legislation did not have the specific purpose of preventing wholly artificial arrangements set up to circumvent United Kingdom tax legislation, but applied generally to all situations in which the majority of a group's subsidiaries were established outside the United Kingdom. It stated that the establishment of a company outside the United Kingdom did not, of itself, necessarily entail tax avoidance, since that company would in any event be subject to the legislation of the state of establishment.[69]

In point 22 of his Opinion of 12 September 2000 in *Metallgesellschaft and Hoechst*, cited above, the Advocate General rejected the United Kingdom's argument that tax avoidance or evasion would be facilitated if the right to make a group income election were extended to UK subsidiaries of non-resident parent companies.

Inasmuch as ACT is merely an advance payment of corporation tax, permitting UK subsidiaries of non-resident parent companies to make that election would simply enable them to enjoy the same cash-flow advantage as that available to resident subsidiaries of resident parent companies. In each case, the subsidiaries' respective profits are chargeable to mainstream corporation tax in the same way. Thus, there would be no risk of avoidance of corporation tax as regards subsidiaries resident in the United Kingdom, whether or not the parent company was resident in that Member State.

E.   INCREASING THE EFFECTIVENESS OF FISCAL SUPERVISION

The Court has consistently held, since delivering its judgment of 20 February 1979 in *Rewe-Zentral* (the *'Cassis de Dijon'* case),[70] that the effectiveness of fiscal supervision constitutes an overriding requirement of general interest capable of justifying a restriction on the exercise of fundamental freedoms guaranteed by the Treaty.

---

[68] For an example of a decision in which the same case law was applied in relation to Art. 59 EC (now, after amendment, Art. 49 EC), see the judgment in *Eurowings, supra* n. 50, para. 44.

[69] Judgment in *ICI, supra* n. 58, para. 26.

[70] Case 120/78, *Rewe-Zentral AG* v. *Bundesmonopolverwaltung für Branntwein* [1979] ECR 649, para. 8.

In *Schumacker*,[71] Germany argued that administrative difficulties prevented the state of employment from ascertaining the income received by non-residents in their state of residence.

The Court rejected that argument, on the basis that Directive 77/799 concerning mutual assistance in the field of direct taxation[72] provided adequate means of overcoming such difficulties in that regard.

In *Futura Participations*,[73] by contrast, the Court accepted that the Luxembourg legislation could make the deductibility of the losses of a subsidiary conditional on the keeping of accounts in accordance with the Luxembourg rules, with a view to ensuring the effectiveness of fiscal supervision.[74]

This was not, however, sufficient to save the Luxembourg legislation, since the Court ultimately held that one element of the rules in question was unacceptable on the ground that it did not respect the principle of proportionality. The Luxembourg legislation provided not only that such accounts were to be drawn up in accordance with the national rules but also that they were to be kept within the Grand Duchy of Luxembourg; the Court held that this went beyond what was necessary in order to attain the objective pursued, namely to ensure the effectiveness of fiscal supervision.[75]

In *Baxter*,[76] the French Conseil d'Etat asked whether Article 52 of the EC Treaty (now, after amendment, Article 43 EC) precluded domestic tax rules such as those applied in France pursuant to a 1996 order on urgent measures for restoring financial stability in the social security system. The legislation in question imposed on pharmaceutical laboratories, for the year 1996, a special levy the basis of assessment of which was the pre-tax turnover achieved in France in the previous tax year in reimbursable proprietary medicinal products, after deduction of the costs accounted for during the same period corresponding to expenditure on scientific and technical research carried out *in France*.

The pharmaceutical laboratories involved as the plaintiffs in the main proceedings argued that a tax mechanism such as that in issue disadvantaged pharmaceutical companies having their main establishment in another Member State and operating in France through a secondary establishment by comparison with pharmaceutical undertakings having their principal establishment in France, since research units are usually located in the same Member State as the undertaking's principal place of business.

The Court observed that, although there existed French undertakings which incurred research expenditure outside France and foreign undertakings which incurred such expenditure within that Member State, it remained the case that

---

[71] *Supra* n. 12.   [72] [1977] OJ L336/15. Cited *supra* n. 3..

[73] Judgment of 15 May 1997 in Case C–250/95, *Futura Participations SA and Singer* v. *Administration des Contributions* [1997] ECR I–2471.

[74] Paras. 31–35 of the judgment.   [75] Paras. 38–40 of the judgment.

[76] Judgment of 8 July 1999 in Case C–254/97, *Baxter and Others* v. *Premier Ministre and Others* [1999] ECR I–4809.

the mechanism governing the tax allowance in question seemed likely to work more particularly to the detriment of undertakings having their principal place of business in other Member States and operating in France through secondary places of business. It was, typically, those undertakings which, in most cases, had developed their research activity outside the territory of the French Republic.[77]

The French Government sought to justify that unequal treatment by maintaining that the special levy made it possible to tax one of the factors which had contributed to the financial imbalance in the social security system, namely the sale of proprietary medicinal products, whilst at the same time allowing a factor contributing to the reduction of expenditure on health, namely the cost of research relating to proprietary medicinal products, to be deducted. In that context, the restriction of the deductibility of research costs to expenditure relating only to research carried out in France was, it submitted, essential so that the French tax authorities could ascertain the nature and genuineness of the research expenditure incurred.

The Court was unwilling, in that case, to accept that the effectiveness of financial or fiscal supervision constituted sufficient justification. Although the effectiveness of such supervision entitled a Member State to apply measures enabling the amount of costs deductible in that state as research expenditure to be ascertained clearly and precisely, it did not justify national legislation which absolutely prevents the taxpayer from submitting evidence that expenditure relating to research carried out in other Member States has actually been incurred.[78]

The effectiveness of fiscal supervision was also invoked in *Vestergaard* by the Danish Ministry of Fiscal Affairs in its attempt to justify the difference in treatment resulting from national rules making it more difficult to deduct expenditure relating to participation in professional training courses where such courses were organised abroad than where they were organised in Denmark. The Court held that, whilst a Member State may, in the interests of the effectiveness of fiscal supervision, apply measures which permit the amount of costs deductible in that state as operating costs to be ascertained clearly and precisely, and in particular those incurred in taking part in professional training courses, that cannot justify an arrangement whereby that Member State may make the deduction subject to different conditions according to whether the courses take place in that state or in another Member State.[79] As in *Schumacker*, the Court referred to Directive 77/799 concerning mutual assistance in the field of direct taxation. It rejected the Danish authorities' argument that the exchange of information between national tax authorities provided for by Directive 77/799 was not sufficient, and pointed out that that Directive allows the competent authorities of a Member State to request all the

[77] Judgment of 8 July 1999 in Case C–254/97, *Baxter and Others* v. *Premier Ministre and Others* [1999] ECR I–4809, para. 13.

[78] *Ibid.*, paras. 18 and 19.   [79] Para. 25 of the judgment in *Vestergaard, supra* n. 49.

information which appears to them to be necessary in order to ascertain the correct amount of revenue tax payable by a taxpayer.

VII.   Recent Developments Concerning the Free Movement of Capital

It is only recently that the Court has tackled the problems surrounding the relationship between direct taxation and the free movement of capital. It did so initially in its judgment in *Safir*[80] and subsequently in its judgment in *X AB and Y AB*.[81] In both those cases, however, the Court held the national legislation to be contrary to Community law in relation, respectively, to freedom to provide services (*Safir*) and freedom of establishment (*X AB and Y AB*), and therefore considered that there was no need to examine whether or not the legislation in question was compatible with Community law regarding the free movement of capital.[82]

In fact, national courts are tending with ever greater frequency to refer to the Court of Justice questions on the interpretation of provisions of Community law relating simultaneously to the free movement of capital, freedom to provide services and/or freedom of establishment. Since the free movement of capital remains an area to which relatively little attention has hitherto been given in the case law, the Court has more often than not chosen—in response to the request made by the parties submitting written observations—to confine the scope of its answer to the more familiar terrain of freedom of movement for persons and freedom to provide services.

Nor, consequently, has the Court stated its views on the grounds of justification which may be invoked in this sphere[83] or on any specific aspects of those grounds.

In fact, such grounds may conceivably differ from those which may be invoked in relation to freedom to provide services or freedom of establishment, particularly inasmuch as Article 73d(1)(a) of the EC Treaty (now Article 58(1)(a) EC) allows Member States to 'apply the relevant provisions of their tax law which distinguish between taxpayers who are not in the same situation with regard to their place of residence or with regard to the place where their capital is invested'. Such a provision, which could be construed as limiting the

[80] Cited in n. 47 above. It is appropriate to recall at this juncture that the earlier judgment delivered on 14 November 1995 in Case C–484/93, *Svensson and Gustavsson* [1995] ECR I–3955, to which reference is made in the section of this article relating to fiscal cohesion, concerned the compatibility with Art. 67 EEC of a national rule in the field of *indirect* taxation.

[81] Cited in n. 48 above.

[82] See para. 35 of the judgment in *Safir* and para. 30 of the judgment in *X AB and Y AB*, nn. 47 and 48 above.

[83] It should nevertheless be noted that the question of possible justification was touched upon, but not considered in depth, in the judgment of 1 June 1999 in Case C–302/98, *Konle* [1999] ECR I–3099. That case concerned the compatibility with the principle of the free movement of capital not of any legislation in the field of direct taxation but of legislation such as the Austrian rules requiring non-nationals to obtain prior authorization for the purchase of building land within Austria.

scope of the prohibition of restrictions on capital movements between Member States contained in Article 73b, does not exist with regard to freedom to provide services or freedom of establishment, in which fields the Court has held in numerous judgments that legislation applying different rules according to residence constitutes discrimination or an impediment.

The case of *Verkooijen*[84] has provided the answers to certain questions in this connection.

The facts in the main proceedings took place prior to 1 January 1994, when Articles 73b and 73d entered into force; consequently, the provisions of Community law applying to the free movement of capital were those laid down in Council Directive 88/361/EEC of 24 June 1988 for the implementation of Article 67 of the Treaty.[85] However, the Member States submitting observations to the Court had as a whole based their arguments on the premiss that, as regards the free movement of capital, the law applying after 1 January 1994 reproduced the law as it stood before that date,[86] so that anything which might be authorized under Article 73d(1)(a) of the EC Treaty could likewise be authorized under the Community law in force prior to that date. They maintained that Article 73d(1)(a) of the EC Treaty authorized (and thus absolved them from having to justify) certain specific restrictions on the free movement of capital which were not covered, according to them, by Article 73d(3), under which 'the measures and procedures referred to in paragraphs 1 and 2 shall not constitute a means of arbitrary discrimination or a disguised restriction on the free movement of capital and payments as defined in Article 73b'. According to the Member States, the term 'measures and procedures' contained in Article 73d(3) related only to the provisions of Article 73d(1)(b) and (2) of the Treaty, to the exclusion of those of Article 73d(1)(a), in which neither of the words in question appears.[87]

In view of the date when the facts occurred, the Court based its judgment on Directive 88/361[88] and held that the receipt of dividends was to be regarded as a capital movement and that the national legislation at issue constituted a

---

[84] Judgment dated 6 June 2000 in Case C–35/98, *Staatssecretaris van Financiën* v. *Verkooijen* [2000] ECR I–4071. For the facts, see Part A (Cohesion of the tax system) of Section VI (Justification), *supra*.

[85] [1988] OJ L178/5. In its judgment in *Sanz de Lera*, the Court interpreted Art. 73b and Art. 73d(1)(b) and (3) EC even though the facts in the main proceedings had likewise taken place before 1 Jan. 1994, the date of entry into force of Arts. 73b and 73d EC.

[86] They based their submission in that regard on the fact that Declaration No 7 annexed to the final act of the TEU provides, in relation to capital movements, as follows: 'The Conference affirms that the right of Member States to apply the relevant provisions of their tax law as referred to in Article 73d(1)(a) of this Treaty will apply only with respect to the relevant provisions which exist at the end of 1993'.

[87] It should be noted that the interrelation between Art. 73d(1)(b) EC and Art. 73d(3) has not generated the same controversy. In para. 21 of its judgment in *Sanz de Lera*, the Court ruled that, pursuant to Art. 73d(3), the measures authorized under Art. 73d(1)(b) were not to constitute a means of arbitrary discrimination or a disguised restriction on the free movement of capital as defined in Art. 73b.

[88] [1988] OJ L178/5.

restriction on capital movements which was prohibited by Article 1 of the Directive in question.

However, before dealing with the question of possible justification, the Court indirectly (using such terms as 'in addition' (paragraph 43), 'in any event' (paragraph 44) and 'furthermore' (paragraph 45)) but clearly rejected the arguments put forward by the various governments.

First of all, it attached minimal significance to the allegedly specific nature of Article 73d(1)(a), which authorized restrictions which are not permissible in respect of establishment or the provision of services. The Court considered that there was nothing very new in that provision, recalling that 'national tax provisions of the kind to which that article refers, in so far as they establish certain distinctions based, in particular, on the residence of taxpayers, could be compatible with Community law provided that they applied to situations which were not objectively comparable' (with reference to *Schumacker*) 'or could be justified by overriding reasons in the general interest, in particular in relation to the cohesion of the tax system' (citing *Bachmann*).

It went on to state that Article 73d(3) is applicable to Article 73d(1)(a),[89] dismissing as irrelevant the Member States' argument that the measures and procedures referred to in Article 73d(3) do not relate to Article 73d(1)(a), in which only the term 'provisions' is used. First, it is difficult to distinguish between 'measures' and 'provisions', and secondly, the term 'measures and procedures' does not appear at all in paragraph 2 even though Article 73d(3) refers expressly to that paragraph.

The judgment in *Verkooijen* also cast light on the grounds which may be invoked in order to justify an obstacle to the free movement of capital. The contents of that judgment enable very close parallels to be drawn with the spheres of freedom of establishment and freedom to provide services:

(a) Logically, the ground of justification founded on the need to preserve the cohesion of the tax system, frequently invoked in relation to the free movement of persons and services, may also be relied on in the context of the free movement of capital. However, the Court in *Verkooijen* considered that ground to be unfounded in the absence of a direct link between the grant to shareholders residing in the Netherlands of an income tax exemption in respect of dividends received and taxation of the profits of companies with their seat in another Member State.[90]

---

[89] It should be recalled that, in his Opinion of 24 June 1999 (*supra* n. 61), Mr La Pergola maintained that, contrary to the argument advanced by all the Member States submitting observations, the restriction mentioned in Art. 73d(3) relates to all the measures referred to in Art. 73d(1) and (2), and not merely those referred to in Art. 73d(1)(b) and (2). In point 58 of his Opinion of 14 October 1999 in *Baars*, not yet reported, Mr Alber likewise considered that, although Art. 73d(1)(a) enables Member States to treat taxpayers differently according to their place of residence or the place where their capital is invested, the measures taken by them in that connection cannot, under Art. 73d(3), constitute a means of arbitrary discrimination or a disguised restriction on the free movement of capital.

[90] Judgment in *Verkooijen*, *supra* n. 61, paras. 57 and 58.

(b) The loss of tax revenue was also relied upon as justification for the restriction on the free movement of capital. The Dutch Government maintained in that regard that the exemption of dividends received by its residents who are shareholders of companies with their seat in other Member States would result in a loss of revenue for the Dutch tax authorities, inasmuch as such companies distributing dividends are not subject to tax on their profits in the Netherlands, so that the grant of the exemption could not be offset by taxing the profits of those companies.

The Court recalled in that connection the settled case law according to which a reduction in tax revenue cannot constitute an overriding reason in the public interest which may be relied on to justify a measure which is in principle contrary to a fundamental freedom.[91]

(c) The UK Government had sought to rescue the impugned provisions of Dutch tax law by invoking a justification founded on the intention to promote the economy of the country by encouraging investment by individuals in companies with their seats in the Netherlands. That argument was rejected by the Court, on the basis of equally settled case law holding that aims of a purely economic nature cannot constitute an overriding reason in the general interest justifying a restriction of a fundamental freedom.[92]

(d) The same response was given by the Court to the argument based on a possible tax advantage for taxpayers receiving dividends from companies established in another Member State: 'unfavourable tax treatment contrary to a fundamental freedom cannot be justified by the existence of other tax advantages, even supposing that such advantages exist'.[93]

The recent judgment in *Commission* v. *Belgium*[94] was delivered in Treaty-infringement proceedings in which the Court was asked for the first time to find that a state had failed to fulfil its obligations under the Community provisions concerning the free movement of capital. In those proceedings, the Commission claimed that the Court should declare that, by prohibiting by Royal Decree of 1994 the acquisition by certain persons resident in Belgium of bonds issued by the Kingdom of Belgium on the Eurobond market, Belgium had failed to fulfil its obligations under Article 73b of the EC Treaty (now Article 56 EC).

The Court's analysis was based on '*a fortiori*' principles. Having recalled that measures taken by a Member State which are liable to dissuade its residents from obtaining loans or making investments in other Member States, or which make a direct foreign investment subject to prior authorization, constitute restrictions on movements of capital within the meaning of Article 73b(1), it stated that the exclusion of the possibility of Belgian residents subscribing to

---

[91] Judgment in *Verkooijen, supra* n. 61, para. 59.   [92] *Ibid.*, para. 48.
[93] *Ibid.*, para. 61.
[94] Judgment of 26 September 2000 in Case C–478/98, *Commission* v. *Belgium*, not yet reported.

the loan in question went well beyond a measure of the kind described and thus 'all the more' constituted a restriction of the free movement of capital.

The Court again confirmed in that judgment that arguments based on the need to ensure fiscal cohesion may justify an obstacle to the free movement of capital, but once again rejected the validity of any such argument in the particular case before it.

The Belgian Government's arguments in that regard were as follows. A particular characteristic of Eurobond loans is that interest is paid without any deduction. By deciding to issue the loan on the Eurobond market, Belgium had to waive deduction of withholding tax. Since the exemption from withholding tax was an essential condition for the state to be able to raise funds on the Eurobond market, the Belgian Government maintained that it was entitled to prevent that exemption from becoming a source of tax evasion—hence the prohibition of the acquisition of the loan securities in question by Belgian residents. According to the Belgian Government, there was a correlation between the exemption from withholding tax and the almost certain loss of the final tax on the interest payable on the securities, which would never be declared by Belgian residents. Indeed, statistics showed that income from securities, especially that received from a foreign source, from which no withholding tax has been deducted is hardly ever declared. The prohibition on the purchase of the securities constituted in that regard a coherent solution safeguarding the interests of the national exchequer.

The Court determined that issue relatively succinctly, observing that there was no direct link between any fiscal advantage and a corresponding disadvantage which ought to be preserved in order to ensure fiscal coherence.[95] The Advocate General had considered the point at greater length:[96] he pointed out that the issue in the proceedings was not the waiver of withholding tax but the prohibition on the purchase of certain securities. By contrast with those cases in which fiscal cohesion had been pleaded, which concerned specific fiscal advantages or disadvantages, no fiscal disadvantage was being challenged in this case. The context in which the measure had been adopted appeared to him far removed from the direct offsetting of counterbalancing fiscal advantages and disadvantages, which represent the only circumstances in which the Court has accepted the argument concerning the need to ensure fiscal cohesion.

What is particularly interesting about the judgment in *Commission* v. *Belgium* is what it says with regard to the justification of a measure designed to prevent tax evasion and to ensure the effectiveness of fiscal supervision, these being matters which, in the context of the free movement of capital, fall within the ambit of Article 58(1)(b) of the EC Treaty (formerly Article 73d(1)(b) EC).

Under Article 58(1)(b) of the EC Treaty, Article 73b(1) is without prejudice to the right of Member States to 'take all requisite measures to prevent infringements of national law and regulations, in particular in the field of taxation

---

[95] *Ibid.*, para. 35.
[96] Opinion of Mr Jacobs of 15 June 2000, [2000] ECR I–7587. See point 57.

. . . , or to lay down procedures for the declaration of capital movements for purposes of administrative or statistical information, or to take measures which are justified on grounds of public policy or public security'.

It is apparent from the judgment in *Bordessa*[97] (as confirmed by the judgment in *Sanz de Lera*[98]) that the measures which are necessary to prevent the commission of certain infringements of tax law, as covered by Article 73d(1)(b), include, in particular, those designed to ensure effective fiscal supervision and to prevent illegal activities such as tax evasion.[99]

The Court inferred from this that the fight against tax evasion and the effectiveness of fiscal supervision may be invoked under Article 73d(1)(b) to justify a restriction on the free movement of capital between Member States. Such a restriction must none the less respect the principle of proportionality, which means that it must be such as to guarantee the attainment of the objective pursued and must not go beyond what is necessary in order to do so.

The Belgian measure did not pass the proportionality test. The Court held that a general presumption of tax evasion or tax fraud cannot justify a fiscal measure which consists in an outright prohibition on the exercise of a fundamental freedom guaranteed by Article 73b of the Treaty. The Belgian Government's argument that the contested prohibition was the only possible measure for avoiding the creation of a domestic loan market with withholding tax and a Eurobond loan market with no withholding tax, both accessible to Belgian residents, was rejected. The Court observed that there was nothing to prevent Belgian residents wishing to invest from acquiring loan securities issued on the Eurobond market by issuers other than Belgium which are also not subject to Belgian tax.[100]

VIII. Conclusion

The case law discussed above is made up almost exclusively of judgments delivered between 1990 and 2000, two thirds of them dating from 1998, 1999, and 2000. Direct taxation has been slow to feature amongst the matters on which the Court of Justice is called upon to adjudicate, although there has

[97] Judgment of 23 January 1995 in Joined Cases C–358/93 and C–416/93, *Bordessa and Others* [1995] ECR I–361, paras. 21 and 22.

[98] Judgment of 14 December 1995 in, *Sanz de Lera and Others, supra* n. 87, para. 22.

[99] It should be noted that, in *Bordessa, supra* n. 97, the Court was requested to give an interpretation of Directive 88/361/EEC for the implementation of Art. 67 EEC. It observed that the first para. of Art. 4 of Directive 88/361 expressly refers to the requisite measures to prevent infringements of the laws and regulations of Member States, '*inter alia*' in the field of taxation and the prudential supervision of financial institutions, and inferred from this that other measures are also permitted in so far as they are designed to prevent illegal activities of comparable seriousness, such as money laundering (para. 21). It referred to Art. 73d(1)(b) only for the purposes of confirming that interpretation. In that regard, it observed that that provision of the EC Treaty essentially reproduces the first para. of Art. 4 of the Directive but also provides that Member States have the right to take measures which are justified on grounds of public policy or public security (para. 22).

[100] Judgment in *Commission* v. *Belgium, supra* n. 94, para. 46.

been no adoption of new legislation, save perhaps in relation to the free movement of capital, which might provide an explanation for this sudden influx of
cases.

Perhaps a greater degree of interaction between the national economies was
needed before Community citizens and undertakings ventured to call into
question the compatibility of national legislation in the field of direct taxation
with the basic freedoms conferred by Community law.

It may be that, if there is a continuing increase in the number of cases
brought, either before the Court of Justice or before the national courts, that
will force the Member States to accelerate moves towards a harmonization of
national laws. In the meantime, the Court's case law has established a number
of guidelines concerning the action to be taken by national tax authorities in a
field which was thought, until quite recently, to be virtually impervious to
infiltration by Community law.

Public Service Provision in Competitive Markets

Erika Szyszczak*

I. Introduction

The process of European integration has resulted in a restructuring of the relationship between the state and the free market. Part of this process has been the recognition that certain services normally regulated and provided or financed by the state, generically known as 'public services' are now a 'key element in the European model of society'.[1] Article 16 EC confirms the place of 'services of general interest' among the shared values of the European Union and their important role in promoting the competitiveness of the European Union as well as social and territorial cohesion. Commentators have argued that Article 16 EC was introduced in order:

to have a moderating influence on the operation of market forces by securing the provision of certain goods and services by, or under the auspices of, the Member States.[2]

However, the official European Union discourse on public services is different. Rather than looking for the *residual* role the state is to play in providing public services the European approach has been to seek a new institutional design. This new institutional design re-models the relationship between the state and the provision of public services, seeking ways to create structures whereby public services can be delivered through competitive markets.

The purpose of this article is twofold. First of all, it attempts to provide a clearer picture of the European Union concept of what were previously described as 'public services'[3] and, secondly, to examine the way in which the new form of public services, generically labelled 'services of general interest', are to be delivered in competitive markets.

---

* Jean Monnet Professor of European Law and Professor of European Competition and Labour Law at the University of Leicester.

[1] *Communication From the Commission Services of General Interest in Europe* COM(2000)580 final, 3.

[2] Flynn, 'Competition Policy and Public Services in EC Law After the Maastricht and Amsterdam Treaties' in O'Keeffe and Twomey (eds.), *Legal Issues of the Amsterdam Treaty* (Hart, Oxford, 1999) 185–99, 188.

[3] The term 'public services' is used throughout this article as a generic term to describe the delivery of goods and services which are alleged to be in the public interest. The term 'public goods' is not a useful term in this context since it is used by economists specifically to denote non-excludable goods where consumption by one individual does not affect the consumption of the good by others.

II. The Background

The economic, political, and social world has been shaped by a number of processes in recent years: most significantly by rapid technological change, globalization of economic activity, the development of capital markets, the liberalization and restructuring of product and service markets and deregulation of markets. Governments and private companies alike have persuaded their electorates and consumers of the capacity of markets to provide not only private goods and services, but also what have traditionally been viewed as publicly provided services.[4] The belief in free markets is premised on the view not only that private enterprise is more efficient than state provision but that it may also be more responsive to consumer wishes. This change in attitude towards free markets has complemented other goals being pursued by governments, particularly the exercise of stricter fiscal discipline on public spending and the embracing of new forms of public management by neo-liberal governments seeking to provide a climate in which markets can develop and flourish.[5] Such beliefs are particularly acute in the EU; indeed liberalization of the public sector has been viewed by one Commissioner responsible for competition, Van Miert, as an *unavoidable* consequence of the establishment of the Internal Market:

It is obvious that a market based on competition and free circulation of goods, services, people and capital is at odds with systems based on national monopolies. Our liberalisation policy was therefore conceived as an indispensable instrument for the establishment of the internal market.[6]

The Internal Market programme demanded the removal of pervasive non-tariff trade barriers in the form of state aids, protectionism in public procurement practices and the maintenance of state monopolies to market forces. This generated a closer examination of perceived distortions of the Internal Market created by state intervention. This programme was relatively easy to trigger since the *legal* tools were entrenched within the original provisions of the EEC Treaty in 1957.

The result has been a radical restructuring of the relationship between the state and the market. A literal view of Article 295 EC suggests that the Treaty took an agnostic or neutral view of how a Member State should organize the

---

[4] The transfer of state assets to the private sector is the most extraordinary economic development of the latter part of the 20th century. From 1990–9 the OECD estimates that some $850bn of state assets were transferred to the private sector, 40% of these transfers took place in Europe. www.oecd.org.

[5] This has been described as not so much a 'hollowing out' of the state but a recognition of, and distrust in, the nationalization process as the most efficient way to run the national economy: Majone, 'Paradoxes of Privatization and Deregulation' (1994) 1 *Journal of European Public Policy* 54–70.

[6] Van Miert, 'Liberalization of the Economy of the European Union: The Game is not (yet) Over' in Geradin (ed.), *The Liberalization of State Monopolies in the European Union and Beyond* (Kluwer, The Hague, 2000), 1–12, at 1.

provision of goods and services within its territory. Indeed, this position has been maintained by the Commission in official documents.[7] But the practical understanding of Article 295 EC has altered as a result of greater cross-border economic activity and the elevation of an EU economic policy based upon an 'open market economy with free competition' to a constitutional principle.[8]

Liberalization has gone hand in hand with privatization[9] when privatization[10] is taken to mean the various ways in which the relationship is changed between state-provided activity and the private sector.[11] The process of liberalization, already evident in a number of the Member States, was hastened by the precise schedule and success of the Internal Market programme. But other influences were present, particularly the fiscal strictures imposed by EMU, greater cross-border trade and rapid technological change.

Liberalization does not necessarily require a change of ownership. Community law merely requires that public and private undertakings operating on the market should compete on a level playing field. However, the results of liberalization and privatization are dramatic. There has been a significant transfer of competence away from the Member State governments: Community competence has become exclusive. Where there are common rules, Member States may no longer adopt conflicting policies or rules and the residual role for the state in providing public services and goods and intervening in a competitive market must constantly be assessed according to Community law norms. Equally the law of the market must be responsive to the changes liberalization and privatization have ushered in. On the one hand the law of the market must take cognizance of the history of state intervention in the economy and be responsive to the culturally specific public and constitutional values inherent in the delivery of certain goods and services. Somewhat paradoxically, the law of the market must also be dynamic and free itself from some of these values if it is to deliver the efficiency enhancing results expected in the areas liberated from what were perceived to be the chains of archaic, rigid, inefficient government bureaucracy.

---

[7] Most notably in the *Commission Communication on Services of General Interest in Europe* COM(96)443 final, 5: 'The Community has nothing to say on whether companies responsible for providing general interest services should be public or private and is not, therefore requiring privatization'. In the later *Communication, supra* n. 1, at 5, the Commission states '[t]he definition of terms, the views and the objectives laid down in the 1996 Communication on the future role of these services in the context of the Single Market remain valid today. This Communication updates that of 1996'.

[8] Art. 4(2) EC. The Court has also recognized the fundamental nature and centrality of the competition law provisions for the achievement of the Internal Market: see, e.g., Case C–126/97, *Eco Swiss China Time Ltd.* v. *Benetton International NV* [1999] ECR I–3055, para. 36.

[9] See European Commission, *23rd Competition Report from the Commission: 1993* (EC Commission, Brussels, 1994), para. 41; Devroe, 'Privatizations and Community Law: Neutrality Versus Policy' (1997) 34 *Common Market Law Review* 267–306; Verhoeven, 'Privatization and EC Law: Is the European Commission "Neutral" With Respect to Public Versus Private Ownership of Companies?' (1996) 45 *International and Comparative Law Quarterly* 861–887.

[10] European Commission, *supra* n. 9, para. 41.

[11] A definition employed by Kay and Thompson, 'Privatization: A Policy in Search of a Rationale' (1986) 96 *Economic Journal* 18–32.

The move towards liberalization and the consequent reliance upon private markets to provide an increasing number of goods and services has not been smooth. The process has not always gained widespread confidence and is far from complete. In some Member States scepticism about the gains from liberalization has resulted in an incomplete, or partial, transfer of state functions to the private sector. Some failures have also raised political debate on the way liberalization has been implemented, whether the process is irreversible and, indeed, have stifled attempts at further liberalization of what are seen as sensitive sectors.

Liberalization has, therefore, brought with it a significant number of new political, legal, and economic issues for the European Union. How to provide public services through the market, using public or private actors and new 'hybrid' actors; the residual role to be played by the public sector in providing public services; how to control public and private power on the market; and, in particular, how to regulate the relationship between private power and residual public power. Equally, amidst the enthusiasm for free, liberalized markets various countervailing tendencies have emerged. One particular theme has been what is the *purpose* of free markets? Effective economic productivity is usually quoted as the obvious rationale. But there are other complex ideas. Notions of citizenship, liberty, and equality of opportunity generated by free markets have also given rise to linkages between free markets and social rights which in turn are linked to the elusive notion of social justice. Sunstein argues:

Certainly there are connections between free markets and social justice. A system aspiring to social justice aspires to liberty, and a system of free markets seems to promise liberty, because it allows people to trade in goods and services as they wish. In fact, a system of free markets seems to promise not merely liberty but equality of an important sort as well, since everyone in a free market is given an equal right to transact and participate in market arrangements.[12]

The ability of free markets to deliver such ideals is questioned sharply in the area where constituencies have long held the view that certain services *cannot* be effectively or fairly delivered by free markets. Although the European Union constructed free trade and competition as fundamental values in its economic constitution neither were absolute values.[13] Equally public reaction to the almost technocratic nature of European integration envisaged under the Maastricht Treaty, alongside a questioning of the political goals of European integration, led to a reorientation of Treaty goals and priorities: shared values, cohesion, and cultural diversity taking their place alongside efficiency and competitiveness. It is thus in this context that the *Europeanization* of public service provision in competitive markets is taking place.

---

[12] Sunstein, *Free Markets and Social Justice* (OUP, Oxford, 1997) 3.
[13] See Szyszczak, 'Free Trade as a Fundamental Value' in Economides *et al.* (eds.), *Fundamental Values* (Hart, Oxford, 2000).

III. The Reach of the Free Market

One of the fundamental principles of the European Union is the adoption of an economic policy, based, *inter alia*, upon the close co-ordination of Members States' economic policies and conducted in accordance with the principle of an open market economy.[14] This principle is reiterated in Article 98 EC and directs the broad economic guidelines of the economic policies of the Member States and of the Community.[15] For the purposes of Community law, or more accurately Community, as opposed to Member State, competence, a line has been drawn between 'economic activities' and 'non-economic activities'. It is only in the former case that Community law is triggered. In relation to 'non-economic activities' the state still enjoys a wide discretion when organizing such activities and may provide and finance such activities in any way it chooses. In contrast 'economic activities' are subject to the free market philosophy of the EC Treaty and its primary and secondary rules.

The binary divide between 'economic' and 'non-economic' activities of the state is not a satisfactory classification or, indeed, an appropriate methodology to delimit competence between the Community and the Member States.[16] Indeed other devices, such as the impact of trade between the Member States and *de minimis* ideas, have also been employed to assess Community, as opposed to Member State, competence. While nationalization of a number of industries has brought state activity into the economic domain the Member States oscillate between nationalization and privatization of the production and delivery of goods and services. Member States continue to experiment with how far they can push back the frontiers of the state, some going as far as subjecting the traditional tasks of revenue protection and the coercive powers of the state (such as the provision of immigration, security, and prison services) to market testing. The reach of Community law has extended to the *regulatory* activity of the state, particularly under the dynamic interpretation of Articles 28 EC and 86 EC and the residual threat of the use of Articles 81 and 82 EC to state regulatory activity.[17] As a result of liberalization and privatization, as well as the Member States' changing perceptions of their role in competitive markets, a number of activities previously considered to be 'non-economic activities' are now open to scrutiny under the EC Treaty rules and principles of free markets and undistorted competition.[18]

A significant feature of the EC Treaty is that it is characterized by a marked lack of formalism. This has enabled the Court of Justice to employ a functional

---

[14] Art. 4(1) EC.

[15] The most recent draft guidelines are to be found at COM(2001)224 final.

[16] The problem is also mirrored in the debates at the national level between what is usually described as the 'public/private' distinction.

[17] Case T–513/93, *Consiglio Nazionale degli Spedizionieri Doganali* [2000] ECR II–1807.

[18] Similarly, as Member States subject even more of their 'non-economic' activities to market principles, the dividing line between the reach of the market and residual public sphere becomes even more blurred.

approach in interpreting the reach of Community law by focusing upon *effects on the market* rather than legal form.[19] Although there is no clear concept of 'economic' activity within the EC Treaty, as with other fundamental concepts, the Court has recognized that the definition of 'economic' activities cannot be left to each Member State to decide: through necessity it is a Community law concept. When looking at the provision of public services the issue is complicated by the fact that the state may perform both a regulatory function and a participatory (provider or financing) function in relation to the supply of public services. The boundary between activities of the state which are of a non-economic nature and which escape the reach of Community law and those activities which are connected to economic activities but may still be legal if they can be brought within one of the exceptions, justifications, or derogations to the Treaty provisions is thus an important, but also a fine and shifting, dividing line.

One solution has been to continue to argue for a functional approach, distinguishing between 'economic' and 'non-economic' activities of the state. Buendia Sierra[20] proposes a solution where he argues for a division between state activities of 'regulation' which would not be considered economic activities and all services offered by the public sector to the general public which would be considered to be economic activities. If followed, this would in effect lead to any public service being defined as an economic activity. Such an interpretation of the Treaty rules would be consonant with present day political economic thinking which suggests that a wide range of public services can, and indeed should, be provided by the market. Such a view is also consonant with the reach of Community law. The Treaty rules already apply to aspects of the public service in that the definition of the public service is a Community law definition and any resort to it as a *derogation* from Treaty rules is not left to unilateral interpretation for each Member State. The Court stipulates that any derogation from the Treaty must be interpreted restrictively and is subject to the principle of proportionality. Thus the Member States' room for manœuvre in the use of public services in the Internal Market is already curtailed.

A weakness of Buendia Sierra's solution is found in the fact that an even greater number of *regulatory* activities of the state are also subject to Community law. Despite the attempt to re-draw the boundary between regulatory activity and market-distorting activity in *Keck*,[21] a Member State will be accountable under Article 28 EC where its regulatory activity does not affect in the same manner, in law and in fact, the marketing of domestic goods and goods from other Member States.

Equally, although the successful cases are few and far between,[22] the Court has affirmed the general principle that while the competition rules of Articles

---

[19] See, e.g., Case C–41/90, *Höfner* v. *Macrotron* [1991] ECR I–1979, paras. 20–22.
[20] Buendia Sierra, *Exclusive Rights and State Monopolies Under EC Law* (OUP, Oxford, 1999), 55ff.
[21] Cases 267–268/91 [1993] ECR I–6097.
[22] See Case 311/85, *Vlaamse Reisbureaus* [1987] ECR 3801; Case 136/86, *Aubert* [1987] ECR 4789; Case 66/86, *Ahmed Saeed* [1989] ECR 803; Case C–35/96, *Commission* v. *Italy* [1998] ECR I–3851; Case T–513/93, *CNSD* [2000] ECR II–1807.

81 and 82 EC are concerned solely with the conduct of undertakings and not with measures adopted by the Member States:

the fact nevertheless remains that [Article 81 EC] . . . in conjunction with [Article 10 EC], requires the Member States not to introduce or maintain in force measures, even of a legislative nature, which may render ineffective the competition rules applicable to undertakings.[23]

Clearly some services of a 'non-economic' nature continue to exist and Buendia Sierra proposes to create a distinction between 'diffuse' and 'specific' services. Diffuse services are described as:

those which benefit the whole population and where the benefit that each individual receives is difficult to evaluate and therefore difficult to substitute with a privately provided service based on a contract between the supplier and the consumer.[24]

Such diffuse services equate with the economist's idea of a public good and would fall outside the reach of Community law. This idea underpins the Court's case law where the Court has ruled that services such as education,[25] and compulsory basic social security schemes based on the principle of solidarity[26] are excluded from the application of Community law. The rationale for the exclusion is the idea that the state 'is not seeking to engage in gainful activity but is fulfilling its duty towards its own population in the social, cultural and educational fields'.[27]

In contrast a specific service is one where:

the benefit obtained by each individual is easily quantifiable and therefore easy to substitute with privately, contractually based services.[28]

Again there are flaws in Buendia Sierra's proposal. It is not a workable division of the activities of the state because of the Europeanization of public services. Even with diffuse services the reach of Community law seems to know few boundaries. One example is the use of the non-discrimination on the grounds of nationality principle found in Article 12 EC, bringing with it ideas of Citizenship rights which cut across the national, solidaristic boundaries traditional 'diffuse' services seek to create.[29] Secondly, even with diffuse services, or what in European Union law we now call 'universal services' or, generically, services of general interest, the state is no longer free to determine how such

---

[23] Case C–35/96, *Commission* v. *Italy* [1998] ECR I–3851, para. 53.
[24] N. 20 above, 56.   [25] Case 263/86, *Belgium* v. *Humbel* [1988] ECR 5365.
[26] Joined Cases C–159/91 and C–160/91, *Poucet and Pistre* [1993] ECR I–637.
[27] *Commission Communication, supra* n. 1, para. 29.
[28] Buendia Sierra, *supra*, n. 20, 56.
[29] The embryonic beginnings of this are seen in Case C–186/87, *Cowan* [1989] ECR 195, and see more recently in Case C–85/96, *Martínez Sala* [1998] ECR I–2691, and Case C–274/96, *Bickel and Franz* [1998] ECR I–7637. Although Art. 12 EC has been closely linked to the fundamental principle of free movement of persons the independent use of Art. 12 EC makes 'it difficult to conceive of any area which is still *ratione materiae* outside the scope of Community law': Poiares Maduro, 'Europe's Social Self: "The Sickness Unto Death"' in Shaw (ed.), *Social Law and Policy in an Evolving European Union* (Hart, Oxford, 2000) 323–49 at 336. Cf. Case C–430/97, *Johannes* v. *Johannes* [1999] ECR I–3475.

services should be supplied. In some sectors, for example, postal services, telecommunications, transport, and utilities, such services are regulated by European Union legislation

The advantage of allowing the Court to define 'economic' activities caught by the Treaty rules, and thus the reach of the market, allows the concept to be dynamic and evolutionary. The disadvantage of this approach is that the Court may address only the issues placed before it, largely by national courts under the Article 234 EC reference procedure, and thus inconsistencies in its case law emerge. Nevertheless, the case law relating to the free movement of goods and services, as well as the application of Articles 81 and 82 EC and 86 EC to state activity, seeks to create a bright line dividing the competence between the Member States and the Community. The demarcation line between the 'economic' and 'non-economic' activity of the state has been fought over where the line passes through the traditional Member State concept of public service. This battle has been fought most vigorously in the litigation using Article 86 EC.[30]

IV. Article 86 EC

Article 86 EC has provided the legal forum whereby individuals have tested the limits of the state to provide public services on a non-competitive basis and also provided the legal basis for liberalization of certain sectors in the rules generated by the Commission under Article 86(3) EC. For this reason the evolution of the case law under Article 86 EC provides a starting point to explain the European Union approach to providing public services through competitive markets.

A two-step approach should be taken under Article 86 EC. The first step is to decide if the activity is an *economic* activity and falling within the scope of Community competence. The second step can be taken only if the activity is subject to Community competence. This involves deciding *either* whether the activity is capable of being justified and therefore may escape the application of the Treaty rules *or* whether it is caught by Article 86(1) EC but may benefit from the derogation from the Treaty rules found in Article 86(2) EC.

Prior to the judgments in *Eurocontrol*[31] and *Poucet and Pistre*[32] the view was that the Treaty rules should apply to services of a general economic interest unless the restrictions imposed by the state could be justified under Article 86(2) EC. In these cases the Court creates a new possibility: the competition rules could simply not be applied as regards certain activities which were in the general or public interest.

[30] See, e.g., Case C–18/88, *RTT* v. *GB-Inno-BM SA (RTT)* [1991] ECR I–5980, para. 22; Case C–393/92, *Almelo* [1994] ECR I–1520, paras. 47, 49 where the Court uses the term 'public service' as synonymous with the concept of 'services of general economic interest'.

[31] Case C–364/92, *SAT* v. *Eurocontrol* [1994] ECR I–43. At para. 20 the Court states: 'it is in the exercise of . . . sovereignty that the states ensure . . . the supervision of their airspace and the provision of air navigation control services'.

[32] Joined Cases C–159 and 160/91 [1993] ECR I–637.

The explanation for the approach adopted by the Court in *Poucet and Pistre* and *Eurocontrol* lies in the limitations of the earlier ruling in *Höfner* v. *Macrotron*.[33] This was the starting point for the Court in creating a role for Community law to shape the exposure of public services to competitive forces. The Court took a functional approach in *Höfner*: the legal status and financing of a particular activity were *not* conclusive of the status of the activity under scrutiny. But this was not sufficient to handle the opportunistic litigation which would emerge, particularly where the liberalization and privatization processes of the European Union encouraged the view that private provision of a number of activities, previously seen as exclusive to the state, were not only conceivable but desirable alternatives to the traditional models of public provision of such services.

In *Höfner* the decisive criterion in deciding that an activity was 'economic' was the fact that the activities were capable of being provided by private market actors. Applying this criterion in *Poucet*, for example, would have opened up the state provision of social security to competition. Thus the Court was obliged to introduce a wider range of factors to identify the borderline between 'economic' and 'non-economic' activities. In particular in relation to 'social' activities, a new Community law concept of 'social solidarity' was born.

Similarly in *Eurocontrol*,[34] a public body was charged with the maintenance and improvement of air navigation safety and with the collection of route charges levied on users of airspace. The undertaking was considered to be a public authority and was not considered to be an undertaking for the purposes of competition law. The application of the legal status/funding criteria of *Höfner* would not have resolved the question satisfactorily. Thus the Court adopted additional criteria such as the public interest character of the activities. This reasoning is followed in the later case of *Calì*.[35] The fact that the anti-pollution surveillance activities of the Port of Genoa were a service of general interest was used by the Court to reach the conclusion that the activities being challenged were 'non-economic' and outside the scope of the Treaty rules.

Unfortunately the Court's reasoning in these cases does not stand up to close scrutiny. The Court blurs the line between what activity should be *outside the reach of the Treaty* and what sort of activity should be caught by the Treaty rules and thus subject to competitive market principles with the possibility of being justified or exempted from the rigours of the market. What the Court appears to be grappling with is an embryonic idea: how far *should* public services, managed by the state, be immune from scrutiny and the potential susceptibility to market forces? This argument is borne out by giving an alternative reading of the social security rulings. In *Poucet* the Court could have

---

[33] Case C–41/90 [1991] ECR I–1979. [34] *Supra* n. 31.
[35] Case C–343/95, *Diego Calì & Figli Srl* v. *Servizi eclogici porto di Genova SpA (SEPG)(Calì)* [1997] ECR I–1588, para. 22. At para. 23 the Court states that the anti-pollution supervision 'constitutes a mission of general interest which is part of the essential tasks of the state relating to the environment within the public domain'.

applied its earlier ruling in *Duphar*[36] where the Court states, in quite categorical terms, that Community law does not detract from the powers of the Member States to organize their social security systems. This would have created a protective zone for the Member States by arguing that the *ratione materiae* was outside the scope of Community law. Instead it might be argued that the Court in *Poucet* is, in reality, looking for a justification of *why* the Member State's social security system might be shielded from competitive forces. This is found in the way the scheme is organized on the basis of social solidarity. It is for this reason that it has been argued by Winterstein that the Court has, in effect, added a new *exemption* from the reach of the Treaty rules:

The Court . . . has chosen a different solution. Instead of assessing insurance services according to their nature, which is undoubtedly economic, and then reviewing the special monopoly rights granted to the entities providing them under Article 86(2) EC, the Court has departed from the functional approach. It has excluded the provision of social insurance services, to which affiliation is compulsory, altogether from the ambit of Community competition law on the basis of the 'solidarity principle'.[37]

In *FFSA*,[38] a ruling two years after *Poucet*, when the Court was faced with a voluntary, complementary, social security system based upon capitalization, the Court was able to conclude that such a scheme (organized by the *choice* of the Member State) was nevertheless an 'economic' activity. There is no reference to the dicta of *Duphar* in the judgment. Instead the *insufficiency* of the social solidarity principle within the scheme is the determining feature in bringing the social security scheme into the economic domain of the Treaty.[39] The application of Article 86(2) EC was left to the national court where, in a subsequent decision, the French Conseil d'Etat ruled that the monopoly rights granted to the social security fund and the tax concessions granted to it were incompatible with Articles 82 and 86 EC. Thus the lack of social solidarity in the social security scheme was a reason for not exempting the social security scheme from the Treaty rules and also a reason for *not* immunizing it against the thrust of market forces.

In the later case of *Albany*[40] supplementary pension funds were found to be pursuing social objectives since they were non-profit making and restrictions were placed upon their investments. There were some elements of solidarity within the social security funds but not enough to exclude them from Community law competence. The Court agreed with the Advocate General in finding that the activities of the pension funds were 'economic' in character and within the domain of the Treaty rules. The funds used the principle of

[36] Case 238/82 [1984] ECR 523, para. 16.
[37] Winterstein, 'Nailing the Jellyfish: Social Security and Competition Law' [1999] *European Competition Law Review* 324–33, 327.
[38] Case C–244/94 [1995] ECR I–4013.
[39] While affiliation to the scheme was not compulsory and there was a link between contributions and benefits (thus denying social solidarity as understood by the Court) other features of the scheme showed aspects of social solidarity: there was no link between contribution and risk and there were possibilities of temporary exemptions.
[40] Case C–67/96 [1999] ECR I–5751.

capitalization. The level of benefits was contingent on the financial results of the funds. The Court found that the funds operated in much the same way as an insurance company engaged in economic activities. But there were a number of features of social solidarity mirroring contemporary Dutch political ideas of social democracy: compulsory membership of the supplementary pension scheme and equal representation of the social partners on the board of the sectoral pension bodies. Individuals were not risk-rated in the Dutch scheme in the way that a private insurance scheme would operate. The mutual indemnification of risk encouraged collective responsibility.[41] The fact that the funds were obliged to offer pensions based upon a solidarity principle made them less competitive than comparable services offered by insurance services thereby justifying the application of Article 86(2) EC.

The Court may not have bargained on the dramatic change of attitude towards the market provision of goods and services and the willingness of litigants to test the limits of state intervention in the market during the 1990s. Its response to the questioning of state activity in the market has been criticized for adopting different and inconsistent lines of reasoning.[42] Equally, it has been argued that the 'eminently casuistic character' of the Court's case law cannot form the basis for the regulation of the diffuse public service interests existing at the national level.[43] But Article 86 EC may continue to assume a role in the normative construction of the provision of public services in competitive markets for a number of reasons. The development of new technologies and emerging markets may create a need in certain sectors for exclusive rights to promote and protect new forms of services of general economic interest. The concept of universal service provision in the liberalized sectors represents only a baseline in the provision of such services and Member States are free to provide additional services above this baseline. Article 86 EC may come into play in assessing the compatibility of such services with the Treaty rules. Similarly, different concepts of universal service are still evident in the Member States, and new forms of universal service not catered for by regulation may emerge.[44] Liberalization of existing markets in the European Union is far from complete or universal. However, as a result of greater liberalization of the market, perhaps less attention must be placed upon the bright line between Member State competence to regulate and offer public services and Community competence. The issue is how to re-regulate such services where they are provided in competitive markets.

[41] Clark and Bennet, 'Dutch Sector-wide Supplementary Pensions: Fund Governance, European Competition Policy, and the Geography of Finance' (2001) 33 *Environment and Planning* 27–48.

[42] Hancher, 'Community, State and Market' in Craig and De Búrca (eds.), *The Evolution of EU Law* (OUP, Oxford, 1999).

[43] Malaret Garcia, 'Public Service, Public Services, Public Functions, and Guarantees of the Rights of the Citizens: Unchanging Needs in a Changed Context' in Freedland and Sciarra (eds.), *Public Services and Citizenship in European Law* (OUP, Oxford, 1998) 57–82 at 79.

[44] For example, a Member State may decide that existing services, such as telecommunications, should be available to a wide range of public services such as schools, hospitals, or new technologies, such as Internet access, compulsory for schools or remote rural areas.

V. The Europeanization of 'Public Service'

While Article 86 EC is the Treaty lynchpin around which the conceptual reform of public services has taken place an analysis of the Court's case law reveals limitations in the reasoning behind the Court's interpretation of 'economic' and 'non-economic' activities. Equally the lack of a consistent appreciation of the relationship between paragraphs (1) and (2) of Article 86 EC explains why there was the need for further legislative intervention at the Community level to create a European Union notion of public services and to regulate the exposure of such services to the rigours of the market. The result has been the evolution of a new, culturally specific concept derived from a mixture of judicial creativity, soft and hard law definitions: a process which has re-invented the role public services are to assume in European society.

A. ARTICLE 86(2) EC: SERVICES OF GENERAL ECONOMIC INTEREST

The starting point for deriving a *Community* definition of public service can be traced back to the original EEC Treaty, where there is the reference to the *derogation* from the Treaty rules for 'services of general economic interest', now found in Article 86(2) EC. Public service obligations were traditionally entrusted to state monopolies as a counterpoint for their special or exclusive rights.[45] As a derogation from a fundamental Community concept Article 86(2) EC is subject to a narrow or strict interpretation in accordance with the principle of proportionality.[46] The underlying principle is that public and private undertakings must follow the Treaty provisions, especially the competition rules, except where the application of the Treaty principles of free trade and competition are unable to fulfil adequately 'services of general economic interest'.

In order to protect a public service a public service provider with special or exclusive rights must meet three conditions. First, the undertaking concerned must have been entrusted with an 'operation of a service of general economic interest' or 'having the character of a revenue-producing monopoly'. Secondly, the application of the Treaty rules would obstruct the performance in law or in fact of the particular tasks assigned to it. Thirdly, the development of trade must not be affected to the extent which would be contrary to the interests of the Community.

In an early, pre-Internal Market case, the Court states that the aim of the derogation is to:

---

[45] Geradin, 'The Opening of State Monopolies to Competition: Main Issues of the Liberalization Process' in Geradin (ed.), *The Liberalisation of State Monopolies in the European Union and Beyond* (Kluwer, Deventer, 2000) 181–205 at 194.

[46] A point reiterated frequently by the Court and the CFI: Case T–106/95, *La Poste* [1997] ECR II–3547, para. 173; Case T–260/94, *Air Inter* [1997] ECR II–997, para. 135.

reconcile Member States' interest in using certain undertakings, in particular in the public sector, as an instrument of economic or fiscal policy with the Community's interest in ensuring compliance with the rules in competition and the preservation of the unity of the Common Market.[47]

This aim is repeated by the Advocates General and the Court in post-Internal Market case law.[48] While the Commission has also confirmed this aim in its *Reports on Competition Policy*, a more aggressive, pro-competition stance is taken by the then Commissioner Van Miert where he states the role of Article 86(2) EC as:

balancing between flexibility and adaptability that comes from the opening of markets and the imperatives of general interest (social and economic solidarity, security of provisions . . .).[49]

The Court has interpreted Article 86(2) EC in a dynamic way, allowing for the concept of a service of general economic interest to adapt to technological change, societal values, and economic conditions. In *RTT* the Court states:

At the present stage of the Community, [a] monopoly, which is intended to make a public telephone network available to users, constitutes a service of general economic interest within the meaning of Article 90(2) [now Article 86 EC].[50]

In fact very rarely[51] has either the Court or the Commission restricted the Member States' discretion to provide a public service; a wide range of activities have been accepted as 'services of a general economic interest'.[52] The Member States' competence to define 'services of general economic interest' is borne out in the Commission's Communication:

[Services of General Economic Interest] . . . is the term used in Article 86 of the Treaty and refers to market services which the Member States subject to specific public service

---

[47] Case C–202/88, *France* v. *Commission* [1991] ECR I–1223, para. 12.

[48] See, e.g., the Court in Case C–157/94, *Commission* v. *Netherlands* [1997] ECR I–5699, para. 37; Jacobs AG in Case C–67/96, *Albany, supra* n. 40, para. 436. At para. 19 of the Commission's *Communication (supra* n. 1) a similar statement is made: 'Article 86 of the Treaty and in particular Article 86(2) EC, is the central provision for reconciling the Community objectives including those of competition and internal market freedoms on the one hand, with the effective fulfilment of the mission of *general economic interest* entrusted by public authorities on the other hand' (emphasis added).

[49] (1999) 2 *Competition Policy Newsletter* 4.   [50] Emphasis added.

[51] The cases of note concern the management of copyright (Case 127/73, *BRT II* [1974] ECR 318) and a monopoly over port activities in Case C–179/90, *Port of Genoa* [1991] ECR I–5931.

[52] See, *inter alia,* the operation of a river port: Case 10/71, *Port of Pertet* [1971] ECR 730; a public telecommunications network: Case C–18/88 *RTT* [1991] ECR I–5979; operation of television services: Case 155/73, *Sacchi* [1974] ECR 409; employment procurement: Case C–41/91, *Höfner* [1991] ECR I–2017; postal services: Case C–320/91, *Corbeau* [1993] ECR I–2568, Case T–106/95, *La Poste* [1997] ECR II–3547, Case C–147/97 and 148/97 *Deutsche Post* [2000] ECR I–825; distribution of utilities: Case C–393/92, *Almelo* [1994] ECR I–1477 and Commission Decision 91/50, *Ijsselcentrale* [1991] OJ L28/43 (electricity), Commission Decision 82/371, *Navewa-Anseau* [1982] OJ L167/48 (water); sectoral pension schemes: Case C–67/96, *Albany* [1999] ECR I–5751 and Joined Cases C–180/98–C–184/98, *Pavlov* [2000] ECR I–6451.

obligations by virtue of a general interest criterion. This would tend to cover such things as transport networks, energy and communications.[53]

The most intellectually challenging task for delimiting the scope of national concepts of public service has been in deciding how the public service should be provided: whether the application of the Treaty rules would obstruct the performance in law or in fact of the particular tasks assigned to the undertaking with exclusive rights or having the character of a revenue-making monopoly. It is within this arena that Community law relies most heavily upon the principle of proportionality.

The Court and Commission approached this issue by focusing upon *how* the economic viability of the undertaking would be affected by being exposed to the full force of Treaty obligations. Both the Court and the Commission took a stringent view. For example, in *Sacchi*[54] the Court stated that Article 86(2) EC would come into play *only* if the relevant Treaty provisions were *incompatible* with the performance of the undertaking's assigned tasks. A strict approach is evident in *RTT*[55] where the Court states that only restrictions which are *indispensable* in order to achieve the objective of general economic interest will be allowed under Article 86(2) EC. These vigorous tests are adopted by the Commission in its Decisions.[56]

Looser criteria have evolved, both in the Court's case law and Commission practice.[57] In *Ahmed Saeed*[58] the Court suggests that ensuring the economic stability of the public service may be an acceptable justification under Article 86(2) EC. *Corbeau*[59] is a decisive case where the Court accepted that a core monopoly, in the pre-liberalization days of the postal sector, merited shielding from the competition rules. The obligation to perform the relevant services in conditions of economic equilibrium presupposed that it would be possible to offset less profitable sectors against the profitable sectors (internal cross-subsidization).[60] This precluded the private free trader from cream-skimming the profitable sector at the expense of the provision of a service of general economic interest. The Court went further: the financial resources used to compensate the non-profitable sectors did not have to emanate from services of general economic interest activities.

A crucial and central issue of much of this case law is how far the survival of an undertaking entrusted with providing a service of general economic interest relies on its ability to resist competition in the profitable parts of the service by competitors in the private sector. The Court addressed the issue of protect-

---

[53] *Supra* n. 1, Annex II: Definition of Terms, 37.
[54] Case 155/73 [1974] ECR 409.   [55] Case C–18/88 [1991] ECR I–5941.
[56] Commission Decision 82/371, *Navewa-Anseau* [1982] OJ L167/48, para. 66; Commission Decision 82/861, *BT* [1982] OJ L360/42.
[57] See Commission Decision 90/16, *Courier Express Delivery Services* [1990] OJ L10/51; Commission Decision 90/456, *International Courier Services Spain* [1990] OJ L233/22.
[58] Case 66/86 [1989] ECR 803.   [59] Case C–320/91 [1993] ECR I–2533.
[60] See also Case C–174/97P, *FFSA* v. *Commission* [1998] ECR I–1303.

ing public services from cream-skimming in *Almelo*.[61] Advocate General Darmon argued for a flexible application of Article 86(2) EC stating that the competition rules should not apply:

not only where they make it impossible for the undertaking in question to perform its public service task but also where they jeopardise its financial stability.[62]

But the Advocate General is stringent in the application of the proportionality principle by demanding that the undertaking invoking Article 86(2) EC must prove that there are no other less restrictive ways of achieving its objectives. In contrast the Court adopts a soft application of the principle of proportionality. The Court does not question the need to create monopoly rights or ask whether other forms of organization which are less restrictive of competition could meet the task entrusted to the undertaking. Instead the specific context in which the activity takes place is relevant:

it is necessary to take into consideration the economic conditions in which the under-taking operate, in particular the costs which it has to bear and the legislation, particu-larly concerning the environment, to which it is subject.[63]

These ideas are continued in later case law.[64]

B. THE RELATIONSHIP BETWEEN ARTICLE 86(2) EC AND OTHER JUSTIFICATIONS AND DEROGATIONS FROM THE TREATY RULES

The crucial role of Article 86(2) EC in protecting public services is seen in its development of justifications and derogations from the Treaty rules beyond the usual coupling of Article 86(1) EC with Article 82 EC. Article 86(2) EC has been used as a reference rule to justify state activity which might otherwise infringe other provisions and principles of Community law.[65] An obvious example is where a Member State uses subsidies to deliver public services. Article 86(2) was raised as a justification for an allegation of illegal state aid in *Banco Exterior de España SA*.[66] The Court of Justice did not rule on the point, finding that the aid at issue was an 'existing aid' and therefore could continue until the Commission decided otherwise,[67] Advocate General Lenz addressed the issue directly. He was of the opinion that Article 86(2) EC may be raised as

---

[61] Case C–393/92, *Municipality of Almelo and others* v. *NV Energiebedrijf Ijsselmij* [1994] ECR I–1477.

[62] *Ibid.*, para. 146.   [63] *Ibid.*, para 49.

[64] See Cases C–147/97 & 148/97, *Deutsche Post* [2000] ECR I–825.

[65] See, e.g., the Opinion of Cosmo AG in the gas and electricity infringement actions: Cases C–157–160/94, *Commission* v. *Netherlands, Italian Republic, French Republic and Kingdom of Spain* [1997] ECR I–5699, para. 89 and the Court's ruling at paras. 47–49; Case C–158/94, *Italian Electricity Monopoly* [1997] ECR I–5789, paras. 41–43; Case C–157/94, *Dutch Electricity Monopoly* [1997] ECR I–5699, paras. 30–32.

[66] Case C–387/92 [1994] ECR I–877.   [67] *Ibid.*, para. 21.

[68] Note, however, that the AG sees Art. 86(2) EC as a procedure. The justification cannot be raised at the outset but must be subject to an evaluation by the Commission of the compatibility of the aid with the Community interest.

a justification for a state aid which would otherwise fall foul of the Treaty rules.[68] In subsequent cases the Court has accepted that an otherwise illegal state aid may be justified as meeting a service of general economic interest.[69] Notwithstanding the fact that a measure might be justified the CFI has confirmed that such measures are still state aids, and subject to the Treaty rules, including the duty to notify the aid to the Commission.[70] The Commission also has accepted the compatibility of funding public broadcasting services with competition law by reference to Article 86(2) EC.[71]

In addition to the competition rules a public service provider may also infringe the Internal Market rules. Article 86(2) EC has advantages over, and is more flexible than, Article 30 EC which is a fixed list of derogations from the Treaty. It would be virtually impossible for a state to justify the use of a monopoly or exclusive rights under the mandatory requirements of the Court's *Cassis de Dijon*[72] case law since the rules devised by the state creating such monopolies are distinctly applicable and inherently discriminatory.[73] The use of the proportionality principle under Article 30 EC demands that any restrictions on trade must be *indispensable* and closely related to fulfilling the *non-economic* aims the state is seeking to achieve.[74] A crucial limitation of the justifications/derogations under Article 30 EC[75] and the *Cassis* case law[76] is that the state must show that the *principal* aim of its restriction on trade or competition is of a *non-economic* nature.[77] Similarly in relation to the free movement of establishment and services provisions, the Treaty only provides for a justification against discriminatory restrictions on free movement on the grounds set out in Article 46 EC, namely public policy, public security, and public health.[78]

[69] Case C–174/97P, *FFSA* v. *Commission* [1998] ECR I–1303; Case T–106/95, *La Poste* [1997] ECR I–3547.

[70] Case T–106/95, *FFSA* v. *Commission* [1997] ECR II–229; Case T–106/95, *La Poste* [1997] ECR I–3547; Case T–46/97, *SIC* v. *Commission* [2000] ECR II–2125.

[71] Commission Decision of 24 Feb. 1999, N70/98, *Kinderkanal and Phoenix* [1999] OJ C238/3; Commission Decision of 29 Sept. 1999, NN 88/98, *BBC News 24* [2000] OJ C78/6.

[72] Case 120/78 [1979] ECR 649.

[73] Although the Court is beginning to blur the distinction between distinctly applicable and indistinctly applicable rules: Case C–34–36/95, *De Agostini* [1997] ECR I–3843; Case 120/95, *Decker* [1998] ECR I–1831; Case C–158/96, *Kohll* [1998] ECR I–1931.

[74] Case C–189/95, *Criminal Proceedings Against Harry Franzén* [1997] ECR I–5909.

[75] Case 72/83, *Campus Oil Ltd and others* v. *Minister for Industry and Energy and others* [1984] ECR 2752.

[76] This interpretation is drawn from Case 155/73, *Sacchi* [1974] ECR 430, para. 14 where the Court states 'nothing in the Treaty prevents member states, for considerations of public interest, of a non-economic nature, from removing radio and television transmitters, including cable transmissions, from the field of competition by conferring on one or more establishments an exclusive right to conduct them'.

[77] Case 72/83, *Campus Oil* [1984] ECR 2752.

[78] See, e.g., *Decker, supra* n. 73, where Luxembourg attempted to argue that restrictions on obtaining medical services abroad without prior authorization was justified on the grounds of the necessity to protect the equilibrium of the state's social security scheme, the need to guarantee quality medical services and the need to maintain a balanced hospital service with equal access. The first justification was seen as being economic in nature and rejected by the Court. The second and third justifications were held to be within the scope of the public health derogation in Art. 56 EC but in this case were not justified. See also Case T–266/97, *VTM* v. *Commission* [1999] ECR II–2329.

Indistinctly applicable measures may be justified on grounds of the 'general good' but again the Court has been fairly rigorous in setting out the conditions which must be satisfied and its application of proportionality.[79]

Initially it seemed that Article 86(2) EC might be used by the Member States when subject to the rules of secondary Community law, particularly where the Community was attempting to liberalize certain sectors. The existence of public service commitments certainly influenced the initial liberalization of the telecommunications sector.[80] The CFI has taken a tougher stance on the proportionality principle when it has been raised in the context of sectors undergoing liberalization. *Air Inter*[81] was an appeal against a Commission Decision[82] taken under powers granted under Regulation 2408/92 on access of Community air carriers to intra-Community air routes.[83] The Commission had decided that exclusive rights granted to Air Inter over certain French air routes were incompatible with the Community rules relating to liberalization of the air sector. Thus the French Government was obliged to grant access to such routes to private competitors in the market. On appeal to the CFI, it was argued that the exclusive rights granted to Air Inter fulfilled a service of general economic interest. It was argued that the restriction on competition was justified within the meaning of Article 86(2) EC to prevent cream-skimming of profitable routes at the expense of less profitable routes. The public service constituted the opening up of a large number of French cities and regions in the context of regional development, based on a cross-subsidy of tariffs, which enabled Air Inter to finance about twenty unprofitable domestic air routes.

The CFI interpreted Article 86(2) EC strictly, moving away from the *Corbeau*[84] position and back to the original stance taken in *Sacchi*,[85] arguing that Article 86(2) EC can apply only when the application of the competition rules *obstructed* the performance of the tasks entrusted to Air Inter. The mere fact that such performance might be *hindered* or *made more difficult* was not sufficient to attract the protection of Article 86(2) EC. The CFI found that Air

---

[79] These can be summarized as: the conditions must be applied in a non-discriminatory manner; they must be justified by imperative requirements in the general interest; they must be suitable for securing the attainment of the objective which they pursue; and they must not go beyond what is necessary to attain the general interest. See Case C–55/94, *Gebhard* [1995] ECR I–4165.

[80] This is seen in one of the earliest of the Directives liberalizing telecommunications. Recital 18 of Commission Directive 90/388 on competition in the markets for telecommunications services [1990] OJ L192/12 states: '[Article 86(2) EC] allows derogation from the application of [Articles 81 and 82 EC] where such application would obstruct the performance, in law or in fact, of the particular task assigned to the telecommunications organizations. This task consists in the provision and exploitation of a universal network, i.e. one having geographical coverage, and being provided to a service provider or user upon request within a reasonable period of time. The financial resources for the development of the network still derive mainly from the operation of the telephone service. Consequently, the opening-up of voice telephony to competition would threaten the financial stability of the telecommunications organizations. The voice telephony service, whether provided from the present telephone network or forming part of the ISDN service, is currently also the most important means of notifying and calling up emergency services in charge of public safety.

[81] Case T–260/94 [1997] ECR II–997, paras. 134–141.

[82] Commission Decision 94/291 [1994] OJ L127/32.

[83] [1992] OJ L240/8.

[84] *Supra* n. 59.

[85] *Supra* n. 54.

Inter had not provided sufficient economic evidence to show the restriction on competition was justified.

In this ruling the CFI places closer scrutiny on the *way* in which the alleged public service is being provided. In particular the use of proportionality brings into play the idea that the unprofitable routes might be subsidized by means less restrictive of competition than the exclusive rights granted on the lucrative air routes.[86] The outcome of this case is essentially pro-competitive: to grant access to the lucrative, profit-making air routes to a private competitor, thus opening up the protected sector to competitive market forces but also obliging the French state to consider alternative means to finance its public interest goals.

In contrast to *Air Inter*, a more generous role for Article 86(2) EC is seen in its use as a defence to allegations that the free movement rules have been infringed by exclusive monopolies. The issue appeared in the infringement action taken by the Commission in the gas and electricity monopoly rulings.[87] The infringement action was a political move, designed to counteract the resistance by some Member States to the liberalization of the utilities sector.[88] The Commission argued that exclusive rights to gas and electricity supply were incompatible with Articles 28, 29, and 31 EC.

While there is a Treaty-based defence to an infringement of Articles 28 and 29 EC in Article 30 EC and the *Cassis de Dijon* mandatory requirements principle there is no Treaty-based defence to an infringement of Article 31 EC.[89] The Court accepted that it was possible to invoke Article 86(2) EC as a defence or justification for the creation of certain exclusive rights which infringed the free movement of goods provisions.[90] It was incumbent upon the Member State to argue the justification that all the conditions of Article 86(2) EC existed. These infringement actions are rather unsatisfactory from the point of view of developing a normative dimension to the application of Article 86(2) EC to the free movement provisions. The Court did not rule on the incompatibility of the exclusive rights with the free movement rules, arguing that the Commission had not addressed the economic arguments put forward by the Member States in defence of the exclusive rights.[91] What is useful, from the public service dimension, is that the Court does not ask that the Member States show that the

---

[86] For example, by the use of state subsidies which are compatible with Art. 73 EC.

[87] *Supra* n. 65.

[88] Gas and electricity services were subsequently partially liberalized by Directives based upon the Internal Market legal base of Art. 95 EC: Directive 96/92 [1996] OJ L27/30 (electricity) and Directive 98/30 [1998] OJ L204/1 (gas). The Lisbon Summit of Mar. 2000 concluded that further liberalization of these sectors was crucial for the development of the new EU economy but no timetable was set and the Member States have, to date, resisted attempts at further liberalization of this sector. The Commission's attempt to set deadlines at the Lisbon follow-up summit in Stockholm, Mar. 2000: COM(2001)79 was not greeted with enthusiasm.

[89] The idea of using Art. 86(2) EC to defend a state measure contrary to Art. 31 EC was discussed (and favoured) as long ago as 1972 by Roemer AG in Case 82/71, *SAIL* [1972] ECR 146.

[90] Cf. Case 72/83, *Campus Oil Ltd and others* v. *Minister for Industry and Energy and others* [1984] ECR 2747, para. 19.

[91] A similar message is seen in *Eurovision*, discussed below, n. 98.

fulfilment of the service of general economic interest cannot be provided other than through a system granting monopoly (exclusive) rights.

In the infringement action against the Netherlands[92] Advocate General Cosmos had considered the case from the perspective of Article 28 EC, finding an infringement which could be justified by the public policy ground contained in Article 30 EC.[93] In contrast the Court examined, and rejected, the Commission's contention that Article 86(2) EC could not be used to justify measures that are incompatible with the Treaty rules on free movement of goods. Citing *Corbeau*,[94] the Court held that it was not necessary for there to be a threat to the financial balance or economic viability of the undertaking entrusted with the service of general economic interest:

for the Treaty rules not to be applicable to an undertaking entrusted with a service of general economic interest under Article 86(2), it is sufficient that the application of those rules obstruct the performance, in law or in fact, of the special obligations incumbent upon the undertaking. It is not necessary that the survival of the undertaking itself be threatened.[95]

The Court ruled that the appropriate test was whether it would be possible for the undertaking to perform the particular tasks entrusted to it in the absence of the rights at issue. The tasks should be defined by reference to the obligations and constraints to which the undertaking was subject. The question was then whether the maintenance of exclusive rights was necessary to permit the exclusive rights holder to perform the tasks of general economic interest assigned to it under economically acceptable conditions. Applying this reasoning to the Netherlands it was beyond doubt that the removal of the exclusive import rights would have radical effects upon the organization of the electricity supply industry. The Commission had recognized this fact and had outlined in general terms some possible alternatives to exclusive rights. But the Commission had not taken into account the particularities of the national electricity system nor the question whether alternative organization of the electricity system would have enabled the exclusive rights holder to perform tasks of general economic interest assigned to it in compliance with the obligations and constraints imposed upon it.

While the context of the supply of public services is important here the *function* of the services is also important. Inherent within the judgment is recognition that where public services are provided in the public interest to achieve security of supply or public safety there is a tendency for the state to be cautious and not take the risks which a commercial operator might consider.

It should be noted that, in the context of this infringement proceeding, the burden of proof was with the Commission: the Member State did not have to show positive proof that no other measure could enable those tasks to be performed under the same conditions. The Court noted that this was an area of highly regulated industrial activity and economic complexity. Thus the Court

[92] *Supra* n. 65.   [93] Cf. *Franzén, supra* n. 74.   [94] *Supra* n. 59.
[95] Case 157/94, *Commission* v. *The Netherlands* [1997] ECR I–5699, para. 43.

felt the Commission had focused too closely on the legal considerations and not the factual context of the dispute. It had failed, therefore to provide the Court with sufficient information to decide whether the exclusive rights went further than was necessary to enable the exclusive rights holder to perform the tasks of general economic interest assigned to it. The Court also found that the Commission had not demonstrated how intra-Community trade would be affected by the exclusive rights.

In the French gas and electricity monopoly infringement action special attention was addressed to the particular tasks entrusted to EDF and GDF. These included, *inter alia,* compliance with public service obligations and implementation of national environmental and regional policies. The Commission had argued that the tasks were too general to be particular tasks within the meaning of Article 86(2) EC. France in contrast had defended the exclusive rights, arguing that without them the performance of some or all of the public service obligations would make it difficult or impossible to meet the national policies. The Court ruled against the Commission. In *Almelo*[96] the Court had ruled that an undertaking may be entrusted with the operation of services of general economic interest through the grant of a concession governed by public law. Thus where such concessions have been granted to give effect to the obligations imposed upon undertakings (which by statute have been entrusted with the operation of a service of general economic interest), there were clear links between the public interest to be protected in Articles 30 and 31 EC and the national law, and thus the conditions of Article 86(2) EC would be met. But the Court was not content to leave this ruling at a general level of abstraction. Looking specifically at the public service obligations the Court held that such obligations had to be linked to the subject matter of the service of a general economic interest being provided and should be designed to make a direct contribution to satisfying that interest.

Even where the provisions of Article 86(1) EC are not satisfied, that is the state has not entrusted an undertaking with special or exclusive rights, the objectives behind Article 86(2) EC may be invoked to grant an exemption from Community law. In *Almelo*[97] the Court of Justice used the direct effect of Article 86(2) EC to provide national courts with the possibility of granting an exemption to agreements which fell within Article 81(1) EC. This ruling contrasts sharply with the ruling in *Eurovision.*[98] Here the Commission argued that the provisions of Article 86(1) and (2) EC could not apply since a public authority had not been entrusted with a service of general economic interest. The European Broadcasting Union was merely an umbrella organization to which European public television broadcasters belonged. The EBU was an undertaking for the purposes of competition law and the Commission consid-

---

[96] *Supra* n. 52, para. 47.   [97] Case C–393/92 [1994] ECR I–1477.
[98] Joined Cases T–528, 542, 543 and 546/93, *Métropole* v. *Commission (Eurovision)* [1996] ECR II–689. In Case IV/32.150 *Eurovision* [2000] OJ L151/18 the Commission again grants an exemption to the Eurovision Regulations. The decision has been appealed: Case T–185/00 *Métropole* v. *Commission*, pending.

ered that the internal regulations of EBU constituted agreements where the collective purchasing of certain broadcasting rights infringed Article 81(1) EC. The Commission was prepared to grant an exemption to EBU under Article 81(3) EC. The members of EBU carried out specific tasks of public interest, *inter alia,* the broadcasting of a variety of programmes with a cultural and educational content aimed at the population as a whole. The CFI was not responsive to this approach. The CFI stated that the Commission should undertake a more detailed economic analysis before creating an exemption from the competition rules in this way.[99]

One of the difficulties of applying Articles 81 and 82 in conjunction with Article 10 EC to Member State activity is that there is no possibility of the Member State raising a justification or defence to the action except by reference to Article 86(2) EC. This may be a contributory factor to why the Court has been reluctant to find infringements of these provisions by the Member State and, perhaps, its willingness to address Article 28 EC rather than the competition provisions. Gagliardi has suggested that in the interests of further economic integration the Court should abandon the principle that Articles 81 and 82 EC may be used in conjunction with Article 10 EC against a Member State arguing that the failure to capture such forms of anti-competitive conduct:

keeps the debate concerning the harmonization of state economies out of the reach of the federal government, the only location in which a democratic discussion involving representatives of all states could take place. The threat of antitrust litigation could boost the harmonization discussion forcing states to agree with each other on how they want to plan their economic policies.[100]

In this respect Gagliardi argues that the case law under Article 86 EC would provide a useful foundation for a more generalized Treaty clause controlling state intervention in competitive markets, with the proviso that Member States could defend anti-competitive behaviour on the grounds of 'legitimate interest' for both economic and non-economic reasons.

C.   CREATING A COMMUNITY CONCEPT OF PUBLIC SERVICES
THROUGH REGULATION

From the case law we see that the Member States are concerned that the concept of services of general economic interest coincides closely with notions of the public service as understood at the national level. The difficulty with this approach is that, at the national level, the concept of 'public service' has often been used as a generic term to describe the provision of public goods and

---

[99] For example: a comparison of the investments made by EBU should be carried out, showing that the investments were employed for the fulfilment of the tasks; an examination of whether the undertakings in question had received state aid aimed to finance those tasks and also to verify that EBU was open to all undertakings entrusted with public service functions and, indeed, that it was exclusively open to such undertakings.

[100] Gagliardi, 'United States and European Union Antitrust Versus State Regulation of the Economy: Is There a Better Test?' (2000) 25 *European Law Review* 353–73 at 373.

services by the state.[101] This ambiguity is reflected in the Commission's Communication:

[Public Service] . . . is an ambiguous term since it may refer either to the actual body providing the service or to the general interest role assigned to the body concerned. It is with a view to promoting or facilitating the performance of the general interest role that specific public service obligations may be imposed by the public authorities on the body rendering the service, for instance in the matter of inland, air or rail transport and energy. These obligations can be applied at national or regional level. There is often confusion between the term public service, which relates to the vocation to render a service to the public in terms of what service is to be provided, and the term public sector (including the civil service), which relates to the legal status of those providing the service in terms of who owns the services.[102]

From the case law we see that the term public service is often used interchangeably to describe a wide range of state activity, for example, the duties of *imperium* (judiciary, police, diplomacy etc.[103]) or the economic use of a public sector. The term may also embrace a definite description, for example, as a general concept unifying under the same label different kinds of activities, such as the provision of social security, health care, education, or a public rail network. Equally public service has been viewed as a specific activity, for example, the distribution of a public utility such as electricity across a Member State. The term may also refer to the entity which operates the public service in France, for example, SNCF, EDF. Even within a Member State there may be differences between national, local, and regional supply of a public service. Arguably the Europeanization of the provision of public service obligations in competitive markets has helped to clarify and classify these diverse and diffuse activities.

(i)   Universal Service Obligation

The link reconciling the liberalization process and the defence of public service is seen in the deployment of a new Community concept of 'universal service', developed through soft-law measures adopted by the Commission in the context of sector-specific harmonization and liberalization processes. This in turn has led to more generalized statements attempting to create a normative foundation for the concept. Some of these definitions have now been translated into 'hard law' *obligations*. Thus regulation, not competition, has been used to secure a definition of the 'universal obligation' in Community law.

The notion of a universal service will obviously differ from sector to sector. At the most general level there are two motivating factors driving the concept of a universal service: justice and equal opportunities. Universal service obligations therefore have a role to play in redistributive tasks of the state, allowing

---

[101] See Garcia, 'Public Service, Public Services, Public Functions, and Guarantees of the Rights of Citizens: Unchanging Needs in a Changed Context' in Freedland and Sciarra, (eds.), *Public Services and Citizenship in European Law* (Clarendon Press, Oxford, 1998) 57–82.

[102] *Supra*, n. 1.

[103] See González-Orus, 'Beyond the Scope of Article 90 of the EC Treaty: Activities Excluded from the EC Competition Rules' (1999) 5 *European Public Law* 387–404; Winterstein, *supra* n. 37.

for wealthier consumers to cross-subsidize poorer consumers of the service. Universal service obligations may also be used to create equal opportunities and foster notions of citizenship rights, economic and social cohesion by demanding that all consumers have access to such 'essential services'. The Community has a degree of competence to address such issues, particularly in the provisions of the EC Treaty relating to economic and social cohesion.

The concept of 'universal service' was an important aspect securing the liberalization of the telecommunications sector.[104] In the 1996 Communication, *Services of General Interest in Europe*,[105] the Commission defines universal service as:

The basic concept of universal service is to ensure the provision of high-quality service to all at prices everyone can afford. Universal service is defined in terms of principles: equality, universality, continuity and adaptability; and in terms of sound practices: openness in management, price-setting and funding and scrutiny by bodies independently of those operating the services. These criteria are not always met at national level, but where they have been introduced using the concept of European service, there have been positive effects for the development of general interest services.

In the more recent Communication[106] a 'universal service' is defined in terms of purpose and content, but also as part of the dynamic liberation of markets to competitive forces:

in particular the definition of specific universal obligations is a key accompaniment to market liberalization of service sectors such as telecommunications in the European Union. The definition and guarantee of universal service ensures that the continuous accessibility and quality of established services is maintained for all users and consumers during the process of passing from monopoly provision to openly competitive markets. Universal service, within an environment of open and competitive telecommunications markets, is defined as the minimum set of services of specified quality to which all users and consumers have access in the light of specific national conditions, at an affordable price.[107]

The Commission has taken a functional approach, arguing that a European concept of universal service exists independently of, and is not necessarily coextensive with, the concept of public service at the national level. The evolution of the universal service obligation has a number of recurrent themes across the liberalized sectors.

In the telecommunications sector,[108] Directive 97/33/EC (the 'Interconnection Directive') defines a universal service in Article 2.(1)(g)[109] as:

a defined minimum set of services of specified quality which is available to all users independent of their geographical location and, in the light of specified national conditions, at an affordable price.

---

[104] *Communication From the Commission to the Council and the European Parliament on the Consultation of the Review of the Situation in the Telecommunications Sector*, COM(93)159 final.
[105] [1996] OJ C281/03.   [106] *Supra* n. 1, Annex II, Definition of Terms.   [107] *Ibid.*
[108] Note that in the regulatory reform of the telecommunications sector a new Directive addressing the universal service obligation is envisaged: COM(2000)384.
[109] See also Directive 98/10 [1998] OJ L101/24, Art. 2(2)(f).

Equality of access is also given a prominent role in the definition of a 'universal service'. A substantive definition is seen in Article 8 of Directive 98/10/EC[110] which provides for the provision of specific services for 'disabled users and users with special social needs'. The universal service obligation, therefore, rests on three principles first identified by the Commission in 1993:[111] continuity, equality, and affordability.

Affordability and equality of access principles are also seen in the postal services sector. Partial liberalization of postal services was implemented through a piece of soft law, the Postal Services Notice[112] and a Directive, 97/67/EC.[113] The universal service obligation is found in the recognition that the Member States may create a reserved sector and that they must provide for the permanent provision of a postal service of specified quality at all points in their territory at affordable prices for all users.[114] The Member States are to ensure that users have the right to a universal service as a *minimum* of one clearance and one delivery to the home or premises of every natural or legal person every working day and not less that five days a week.[115] The universal service applies to clearance, sorting, transport, and distribution of postal items in the reserved sector.[116] Underlying the notion of universal obligations here is the fact that the Member States accepted only a partial liberalization of the postal sector and therefore the aim is to ensure that incumbents provide services meeting the needs of customers to the same extent as competitive economic operators would have done. In particular the Commission was concerned that postal operators granted special or exclusive rights would let the quality of service decline and omit to improve service quality. These issues have been dealt with by the Court of Justice in its case law under Article 86(1) EC.[117] Given that the standard for the provision of a public service has now been defined through regulation, a Member State would now have difficulty justifying the anti-competitive behaviour of postal service incumbents who were lagging behind the market.

---

[110] [1998] OJ L101/24.

[111] *Communication on the Consultation on the Review of the Situation in the Telecommunications Services Sector* COM(93)159 final, 21.

[112] *Notice from the Commission on the application of the competition rules to the postal sector and on the assessment of certain State measures relating to postal services* [1998] OJ C39/2. The legality of this Notice is open to question since in the enforcement of the competition rules under Art. 86(3) EC the Commission should only use Directives. See: Joined Cases C–271, 281 and 289/90, *Spain, Belgium and Italy* v. *Commission (Telecommunications Services)* [1992] ECR I–5833; Case C–202/88, *France* v. *Commission (Telecommunications Terminal Equipment)* [1991] ECR I–1264.

[113] [1997] OJ L15/14.

[114] The definition of a universal service remains unchanged in the Commission's new proposal, COM(2000)319 final.

[115] Art. 3(3).

[116] The reserved sector comprises: letters up to 2kg and postal packages of up to 10kg (Member States may increase this limit up to 20kg) and the delivery of postal packets from other Member States up 20kg. As well as registered post and insured postal services (Art. 3(4) and (5)). Attempts to decrease the reserved sector as a result of the Lisbon Summit of Mar. 2000 have not met with much enthusiasm from the Member States: COM(2000)319 final.

[117] See, *inter alia, Corbeau, supra* n. 59, *Höfner, supra* n. 33, Case C–179/90, *Port of Genoa* [1991] ECR I–5889.

Universal service, as a Community concept, and independently of the sector to which it applies, is thus defined in terms of universality, access for all at an affordable price, equality of treatment, access independently of geographical location and continuity, based upon a continuous provision of a defined quality. It is not only geographical penetration but also social penetration that is demanded, leaving the principle of equality to exceed the geographical dimension.[118]

Regulating the universal service in this way introduces the notion of providing *consumers* with a defined service which can only be provided at net cost which an operator could, and might, want to avoid but for the universal service obligation.[119] The very existence of universal obligations seems to imply that the services would not be offered under normal conditions since they would not be profitable. Thus a discussion of universal service obligations also entails the question of financing universal obligations. The traditional means of financing a universal service has been through cross-subsidization between profitable and loss-making activities within an integrated public monopoly and, as we have seen in the *Corbeau*[120] case, has been used by the Court to defend public services from the intrusion of market rules. The ability to use cross-subsidization is lost when public monopolies are liberalized and therefore the Member States are obliged to consider different ways of financing the universal service. State aids, subject to the Community law rules, are one possibility. But the use of public revenues in this way militates against a prevailing philosophy, ingrained into the Member States, to reduce public expenditure.

Another possibility is spreading the costs of universal obligations across the whole of the industry. This option is seen in the telecommunications sector in Directives 96/19/EC[121] and 97/33/EC[122] where a Member State may choose between two mechanisms for spreading the cost of a universal service: either supplementary charges for interconnection with the service provider subject to the universal service obligation or a universal service fund, financed by contributions from the industry in proportion to market activity. This form of cross-subsidization may only be used for the universal service obligations imposed by Community law. Where a Member State chooses to provide more stringent or wider universal obligations the funding of such schemes will be subject to the Treaty rules on competition and state aid. In fact, only two Member States, France and Italy, have chosen to implement funding mechanisms to cross-subsidize the universal obligation in telecommunications, reflecting the lack of consensus on the size and nature of the costs involved in

[118] Sauter, 'Universal Service Obligations and the Emergence of Citizen's Rights in European Telecommunications Liberalization' in Freedland and Sciarra (eds.), *Public Services and Citizenship in European Law* (OUP, Oxford, 1998) 117–43.

[119] Wissenschaftliches Institut für Kommunikationsdienste GmbH, *Study on the Re-examination of the Scope of Universal Service in the Telecommunications Sector of the European Union, in the Context of the 1999 Review—Study for the European Commission DG Information Society*, Apr. 2000 http://www.ispo.cec.be/infosoc/telecompolicy/en/Study-en.htm.

[120] *Supra* n. 59. [121] Art. 1(6) amending Art. 4c of Directive 90/388 [1990] OJ L192/10. [122] Art. 5(2).

providing universal services.[123] In addition to the means of financing universal service obligations further Community law requirements are imposed: for example, the financing of schemes in the telecommunications sector is subject to the requirements of transparency, non-discrimination, and proportionality.[124]

In contrast, where there is partial liberalization in the postal sector the issue is dealt with from a regulatory perspective, obliging the Member States to adopt measures concerning tariffs and transparency of accounts of universal service providers.[125] While regulation defines the principles upon which the universal service can be funded, the Commission has indicated that Article 86 EC will have a role to play where postal services are systematically and selectively offered at a price below the average total cost.[126] Costs and the issue of acceptable levels of cross-subsidization[127] are also difficult and controversial issues to resolve in the postal sector. Both Article 86 EC and the state aid[128] rules have been raised by competitors alleging anti-competitive behaviour by incumbents in the postal services sector.[129]

In addition to creating the normative foundation for the way in which public services are to be delivered in a competitive market the liberalization

[123] *Fifth Report on the Implementation of the Telecommunications Regulatory Package,* COM(1999)537, 16; *Communication on Assessment Criteria for National Schemes for the Costing and Financing of Universal Service in Telecommunications and Guidelines for the Member States on Operation of Such Schemes,* COM(96)608 final. For the postal services obligation see Bishop *et al., Liberalising Postal Services: On the Limits of Competition Policy Intervention,* Centre of European Law, Occasional Papers Series 1, King's College, London.

[124] Art. 4 of Directive 96/2/EC, [1996] OJ L20/59 and Art. 5.1 of the Interconnection Directive 97/33/EC [1997] OJ L199/33; Council Resolution of 7 Feb. 1994 on universal service principles in the telecommunications sector [1994] OJ C48/1; *Commission Statement Concerning the Council Resolution on Universal Service in the Telecommunications Sector* [1994] OJ C48/8.

[125] The principles are: separate accounting for the reserved and non-reserved sectors (Art. 14(2)); costs in the reserved and non-reserved sectors must be distinguished (para. 8.6(b)(vi) *PSN* (*supra* n. 112)) and properly assigned (Art. 14(3)(a)); common costs must where possible be allocated on a direct analysis of the origin of the costs or, where this is not possible, on an indirect linkage to another cost category for which a direct allocation is possible (Art. 14(3)(b)); where direct/indirect costs cannot be so allocated a general allocator must be devised based on the ratio of expenses directly/indirectly allocated to the reserved sectors and competitive services (Art. 14(3)(b)(iii)). Where there are difficulties allocating common costs the price of the reserved sector should be at least equal to the average cost of production (para. 3.4.PSN).

[126] *Postal Services Notice, supra* n. 112, Section 3.4.

[127] Hancher and Buendia Sierra, 'Cross-subsidization and EC Law' (1998) 35 *Common Market Law Review* 901–16. Cf Abbamonte, 'Cross-subsidisation and Community Competition Rules: Efficient Pricing versus Equity' (1998) 33 *European Law Review* 414–33.

[128] UPS, the US express parcels company, has made a number of complaints to the Commission arguing that the Deutsche Post monopoly allows it to cross-subsidize activities in the competitive market and this is tantamount to a state aid. According to UPS the Treaty rules and the principles on repayment of illegal state aid are not sufficient and the only way to handle such alleged subsidization is for incumbents such as Deutsche Post to be split into different undertakings. See Case T–182/98, *UPS Europe SA v. Commission* [1999] ECR II–2857. See also Case T–613/97, *UFEX and others v. Commission,* judgment of 14 Dec. 2000.

[129] Reasons of space have not permitted inclusion of the utilities sector here but similar issues are emerging where the partial liberalization of the sector and the protection of an incumbent, ostensibly on the ground of providing a universal service, are leading to similar problems on the competitive *European* market. See the discussion of the aggressive behaviour of EDF by Taylor and Owen, 'Transforming a Powerhouse', *Financial Times,* 2 Feb. 2001.

process in the European Union also focuses upon *institutional* aspects of the delivery of public services in competitive markets. Thus, there is a requirement for independent bodies in the telecommunications sector. The Postal Services Directive also requires that each Member State shall designate one or more regulatory authorities for the postal sector that are legally separate from, and operationally independent of, the postal operators.

The *leitmotif* of the provisions is the requirement that these authorities are independent. This breaks the link between the previous practice where regulatory responsibilities prior to the liberalization of these markets were vested in the monopoly provider. To continue this practice would allow existing incumbents unsatisfactory control over the new competitors in the market. But one of the major tasks entrusted to the new national regulatory authorities is to ensure compliance with the universal service obligations established in Community law.[130]

The establishment of national regulatory authorities has not been accepted totally. While satisfying the principle of subsidiarity, the diversity of regulatory techniques is not conducive to cross-border trade and a number of calls for pan-European regulatory agencies have been made to further the process of market integration.[131] The Commission has proposed to revisit the issue in the area of telecommunications.[132] The medium-term compromise seems to be the greater *co-ordination* of the activities of national regulatory authorities in the post-Lisbon 'further market-opening' strategy described below. Respect for the recognition of the explicit diversity within the national public service objectives becomes far more difficult to achieve in a federal pan-European agency, and this explains why the *communautaire* aspect of services of general interest set out in Article 16 EC and the Commission's Communication will be an important aspect of setting the standards for delivery of public services in the European market. But equally the significance of Article 16 EC becomes apparent. The process entails further obligations on the European Union as regulator, thus enhancing the political competence of the European Union to define and refine the mode of delivery of public services through competitive markets. This in turn may also pose a threat to the credibility of European Union regulation. Such a development demands new administrative instruments which, at the European Union level, poses a threat, due not only to insufficient resources but also insufficient recognition that policy credibility depends upon effective implementation.[133]

---

[130] Such regulatory authorities also have the power to issue licences to operators in the liberalized sector and to set the conditions for the supply of services.

[131] A previous Commissioner, Bangemann, proposed the adoption of the US model of a Federal Communications Commission. See also *Issues Associated with the Creation of a European Regulatory Authority for Telecommunications*, Report to the Commission, 1997, http://www.ispo.cec.be/infosoc/telcompolicy/ec/Study-en.htm.

[132] 25th Recital to the European Parliament and Council Directive 97/33/EC (Interconnection Directive) [1997] OJ L199/32.

[133] See Majone, 'The Credibility Crisis of Community Regulation' (2000) 38 *Journal of Common Market Studies* 273–302.

(ii)   Article 16 EC and Services of General Economic Interest

The first Treaty amendment to address the wider ideas involved in a *Community* definition of, and commitment to, public service provision in competitive markets is found in Article 16 EC. Duff has argued that '[t]here is no more stark exposure in the Treaty of the division . . . between those who wish to regulate to protect public utilities and those who wish to make them competitive'.[134] A Declaration states that this Treaty provision:

shall be implemented with full respect for the jurisprudence of the Court of Justice, inter alia as regards the principles of equality of treatment, quality and control of such [public] services.

There is also a Protocol on public service broadcasting. The broadcasting media have witnessed a spectacular change in the balance between public and private actors during the 1990s, but only the television and radio sectors have been liberalized at Community level. Nevertheless, despite the Protocol, the defence of the Member States' specific regulation of the general interest is subject to Community law. First of all, it is recognized that the general interest is based upon common values. These have been tested in the Court's case law and have found expression in Community legislation.[135] In the Commission's Communication, the common values are identified as 'freedom of expression and the right of reply, pluralism, protection of copyright, promotion of cultural and linguistic diversity, protection of minors and of human dignity, consumer protection'.[136]

Secondly, the Commission's Communication makes it clear that the competition rules will be applied to this sector for the benefit of *consumers*, not citizens. The Commission is entrusted:

with the task of preventing anti-competitive behaviour to the detriment of the consumers, notably the abuse of dominant positions and, on the basis of merger control, the creation of oligopolistic or monopolistic market structures.[137]

Thus Community interests prevail over national interests.

Finally, both the Protocol and the Commission's Communication place constraints on the remit and modalities of public service broadcasting through compliance with the state aid rules of the Treaty. These rules demand that public funding of public service broadcasters is proportional to the public service remit (which can be defined by each Member State). This entails a scrutiny of whether any state compensation exceeds the net extra costs of the particular task assigned to the public service broadcaster under scrutiny. The Communication refers to the number of complaints received by the Commission

---

[134]   Duff, *The Treaty of Amsterdam* (Federal Trust, Sweet and Maxwell, London, 1997) 84.

[135]   See Woods and Scholes, 'Broadcasting; the Creation of a European Culture or the Limits of the Internal Market?' (1997) 17 *Yearbook of European Law* 47–82; Ladeur, 'European Media Law: A Perspective on the Challenge of Multimedia' in Snyder (ed.), *The Europeanisation of Law* (Hart, Oxford, 2000) 101–23.

[136]   *Supra* n. 1, at 35.   [137]   *Ibid.*

from private, commercial broadcasters, particularly complaining about the use of advertising and its compatibility with public interest goals.[138] Again we see constraints placed upon the Member States. Member States are free to choose how to finance public broadcasting and in principle there is no objection to dual-financing schemes which combine public funds with advertising revenue. But competition on the relevant markets (for example, advertising, acquisition and sale of programmes) must not be affected to an extent which is *contrary to the Community interest.*[139]

Further declarations were adopted on public banks. These note the Commission's view that the competition rules allow the services of general economic interest provided by public credit institutions in Germany and the facilities granted to them to compensate for the costs connected with such services to be taken into account in full.[140] This Declaration has not prevented the Commission from investigating alleged unfair competition by state-controlled banks and suggesting that one of the larger banks, Westdeutsche Landesbank, should be split into separate private and public institutions. The German government has argued that the Commission is attempting to disrupt the established banking structure of Germany and that local-level banks perform a service of general economic interest justifying an exemption from the competition rules.

The wording of Article 16 EC, its legal status, and its exact intention have given rise to speculation. Flynn has described Article 16 EC as a response to the growing intrusion of liberalization and privatization into the sphere of public services.[141] He sees Article 16 EC as a reflexive response by some of the Member States to the encroachment of the market: a protectionist measure. But when Article 16 EC is read in the light of the new institutional design towards public service provision this interpretation of Article 16 EC is difficult to sustain.

Ross[142] argues that Article 16 EC may be seen as a declaration of a new updated endorsement of social objectives shielding certain public service provision from the free market and competition rules. Ross argues that one interpretation which could be placed upon Article 16 EC is that it reinforces the regulatory development of a European concept of public service by developing a *communautaire* obligation to support 'services of general interest' beyond the purely competition law context. In this respect Article 16 EC moves Community law on from merely seeing services of general economic interest as a *derogation* from an *obligation* in Community law.

---

138 Further details can be found in the Commission's *XXIXth Report on Competition Policy 1999*, SEC(2000)720 final, 89ff. See Case T–266/97, *VTM* v. *Commission* [1999] ECR II–2329.

139 *Supra* n. 1, at 36.

140 A further Declaration took note of the claim that the Declaration relating to Germany was equally applicable to organizations having a similar structure in Austria and Luxembourg. It is generally thought that Declarations do not have any legal effect but are merely exhortatory.

141 *Supra* n. 2.

142 Ross, 'Article 16 E.C. and Services of General Interest: From Derogation to Obligation?' (2000) 25 *European Law Review* 22–38.

It is the contention of this article that none of the analyses of Article 16 EC capture the role Article 16 EC is to play in the delivery of public services *through* competitive markets. This contention can be supported by the actual wording of Article 16 EC. Article 16 EC supports Article 86 EC which has been interpreted by the Court in an expansive way to bring even more state activity into the realm of the market-based rules of the Treaty. Article 86 EC has also been interpreted in order to give effect to a number of principles on which the provision of services of general economic interest can be provided in competitive markets. Political events *prior* to the Amsterdam IGC also make it difficult to sustain the arguments made by Flynn and Ross. Attempts by France (supported by Belgium) to resist the liberalization of certain sectors using the legislative base of Article 86(3) EC were rebuffed by the Court,[143] the Commission,[144] and the other Member States when rejecting proposals to insert the promotion of services of a general economic interest into the Treaty.[145]

Political events *post-Amsterdam* also support an alternative reading of Article 16 EC. Services of general interest are being manipulated to further the process of market integration and liberalization. The Lisbon Summit of 23–24 March 2000 addressed Article 16 EC in rather oblique terms. The European Council concluded that it was essential that, in the framework of the Internal Market and of a knowledge-based economy, full account should be taken of the Treaty provisions relating to services of general economic interest, and to the undertakings entrusted with operating such services. The response has been to promote a 'European perspective' on services of general interest on three fronts: making the most of market opening, strengthening European co-ordination and solidarity and developing other Community contributions in support of services of general interest. The new institutional design has been 'explained' by the Commission in a soft-law Communication[146] and has been implemented through regulatory tools.

VI.   Services of General Interest Post-Lisbon

A.   MAKING THE MOST OF MARKET OPENING

The European Council of Lisbon called for an acceleration of liberalization in the sectors of gas, electricity, transport, and postal services. More specifically in relation to the relationship between services of general interest and liberal-

---

[143] Case 202/88, *France v. Commission* [1991] ECR I–1223.

[144] In its Communication, *Services of General Interest in Europe* [1996] OJ C281/12, para. 71, the Commission refutes the idea put forward by France and the CEEP that the then Art. 90 EC (now Art. 86 EC) should be modified since Art. 90 EC, and the way it has been interpreted, guarantees an appropriate balance between national services of general interest and Community rules.

[145] This would have been a new Art. 3(u) EC stating that the activities of the Community would include 'a contribution to the promotion of services of general interest'.

[146] *Supra* n. 1.

ization new regulatory evaluation tools, designed to assess the operation, performance, and competitiveness of general interest services, will be used in order to improve the cross-border delivery of such services and allow their adaptation to technological change. This will be implemented using the precedent set in the telecommunications sector where reviews are conducted on a regular basis assessing the impact of regulatory reform. Such reviews also include the use of Green Papers and public consultation. Most strikingly, the framework and benchmarks for assessing new *consumer* (note, *not* citizen) needs and new public interest demands will be the new economic constitutional tools of the Broad Economic Policy Guidelines[147] together with the Report on their implementation and the 'Cardiff Report', the new annual Commission Communication on Economic Reform Report on the functioning of product and capital markets.[148]

A further theme of market opening has been to extend the basic principle of the Treaty that public and private undertakings should compete on a level playing field. The principle of transparency has been extended to the operation of services of general economic interest in the Community. A new Directive, 2000/52,[149] was adopted by the Commission on 26 July 2000, amending and extending the principle of transparency first introduced in Directive 80/723. Thus the rules relating to the separation of accounts also apply to any undertaking caught by Article 86(1) and (2) EC which receives state aid. Similarly, the Commission has proposed that where sectors have been liberalized (water, energy, transport, and telecommunications) then the provisions of the public procurement Directive 93/38 should not apply.[150]

B. STRENGTHENING EUROPEAN CO-ORDINATION AND SOLIDARITY

The significance of Article 16 EC becomes apparent in its link to European citizenship in the post-Lisbon era. In its Communication the Commission states:

> While Member States retain ample freedom as to the means by which the objectives of solidarity served by services of general interest are to be accomplished, a core common concept of such general interest may be necessary to sustain allegiance to the Union.

The link between public service obligations, consumer rights, and citizenship has been made in the past,[151] and the difficulty in finding sufficient consensus

---

[147] *Supra* n. 15.
[148] COM(1999)10 final of 20 Jan. 1999; COM(2000)881 final of 26 Jan. 2000.
[149] [2000] OJ L193/75.
[150] *Proposal for a Directive of the European Parliament and of the Council co-ordinating the procedure of entities operating in the water, energy and transport sectors*, COM(2000)276, 10 May 2000. See the earlier Communication from the Commission that the impact of telecommunications liberalization has exempted most of this sector from the scope of Directive 93/38/EEC: [1993] OJ C156/3.
[151] Useful discussion is to be found in the European Parliament's attempts to include a catalogue of citizens' rights in the Treaty of Amsterdam; one such right was that of the universal service requirement: EP A3–0254/94, Committee on Economic and Monetary Affairs and Industrial Policy, Report on Public Undertakings, Privatization and Public Services in the European

on universal obligations has acted as a brake on the liberalization process, particularly in the utilities sector. ETUC and CEEP[152] drew up a 'Charter for Services of General Interest' in response to the compromise text of Article 16 EC. Buendia Sierra[153] argues that one of the limitations of Article 16 EC is that the principles that it evokes, 'equal treatment, quality and continuity of services' are working principles created by academics, administrative practice, and national case law. There is very little direct Community case law on what these principles mean. The Charter attempts to define the 'principles and conditions' on which the services of general economic interest shall operate in the European Union.[154] CEEP and ETUC called upon the European Institutions to adopt a 'Charter for Services of General Interest', based on the proposal at the Nice IGC 2000. This did not occur, but the link between citizenship and fundamental rights concepts has been created in Article 36 of the Charter of Fundamental Rights. This addresses *access* to services of general economic interest.[155]

In the Presidency Conclusions at Nice more procedural mechanisms were put in place[156] and the European Council noted the Commission's intention to co-operate with the Member States to discover ways of ensuring greater predictability and increased legal certainty in the application of competitive rules relating to services of general interest. The creation of a pan-European approach to services of general interest is to evolve through what the Commission describes as a 'co-ordination' of monitoring the activities of regulators and operators where there is a sufficient degree of market integration in a particular sector. Thus the evaluation of services of general interest and the effectiveness of regulatory frameworks will take place according to

Community, Rapporteur Roberto Speciale. See also the Resolution adopted: Debates of the EP No. 3–448/243–247, 5 May 1994. Surprisingly little reference has been made to access to public services in the literature criticizing the European Union's approach to Citizenship. One set of essays stands out: Freedland and Sciarra (eds.), *Public Services and Citizenship in European Law* (Clarendon Press, Oxford, 1998).

[152] www.ceep.org. The joint text has a wide range of principles underpinning it: building a balanced European Union; guaranteeing the fundamental rights of citizens; ensuring quality of life for all; strengthening solidarity and combating exclusion; supporting economic development and employment; strengthening social and geographic cohesion; associating citizens in the assessment of services of general interest; ensuring sustainable development; stressing the fundamental responsibility of public authorities; providing a framework for the contractual and transparent management of services of general interest; assisting the accession of candidate countries; using the charter for services of general interest to construct the reference framework for one of the European Union's common values.

[153] *Supra* n. 20, at 333.

[154] These comprise: guaranteeing citizens' rights, promoting jobs for all, sustaining competitiveness, shaping a social market economy, promoting cohesion, modernizing through social dialogue, extending the social dimension to accession countries, and building European public services.

[155] The exact legal status of this Charter was not determined at the Nice IGC but was left to be resolved at a future date.

[156] The Council and the Commission are invited to continue their discussions in the framework of the Declaration Guidelines attached as an Annex to the Presidency Conclusions and the provisions of Art. 16 EC with a Report to the European Council in Dec. 2001. Presidency Conclusions available at http://ue-eu.int/en/info/eurocouncil/index, para. 45.

European criteria based upon economic efficiency, consumer protection, economic, social, and territorial cohesion.

VII. Other Community Contributions In Support of Services of General Interest

A key development in the Europeanization of public services has been the inclusion of a number of values recognized as being in the *public interest* into Community-based policies. The major political challenge rests in the fact that in the European Union the Member States, in principle, retain responsibility for a number of services of general interest, particularly where they relate to welfare and social protection. Thus, a case has to be sustained for a pan-European approach involving:

a systematic effort by all concerned including closer administrative co-operation between Member States, national regulatory authorities, service providers and consumer representatives.[157]

The most sensitive area where the demands of market, political, and economic integration clash head on with the provision of public services is in the area of social protection. The Treaty of Nice has added the 'combating of social exclusion' and the 'modernization of social protection systems'[158] to the list of areas in Article 137 EC where the 'Community shall support and complement the activities of the Member States'. This is to be achieved by 'initiatives aimed at improving knowledge, developing exchanges of information and best practices, promoting innovative approaches and evaluating experiences'. But the new competence is limited since Article 137(2)(a) EC excludes any harmonization of the laws and regulations of the Member States in this field and to this limitation is added the rider:

The provisions adopted pursuant to this Article: shall not affect the right of Member States to define the fundamental principles of their social security systems and must not significantly affect the financial equilibrium thereof.[159]

But the Community road to the modernization of social protection has already been taken through soft-law initiatives and new institutional actors appearing on the European stage employing what has become known as the 'new, open method of co-ordination' of Member States' policies.[160] The battleground has been between the Member States' competence to finance and organize their social protection and the imperatives of Community free market and competition law. The Court of Justice has moderated the use of market integration principles by accepting that the social dimension to market integration is on a

---

[157] *Supra* n. 1, at 24.
[158] New Art. 137(j) and (k) respectively. This is without prejudice to Art. 137(c) EC which covers 'social security and social protection of workers'.
[159] Art. 137(4) EC.
[160] Szyszczak, 'Social Policy' (2001) 50 *International and Comparative Law Quarterly* 175–186.

level footing with the economic dimension. In some circumstances, the social policies of the Community may take priority over the competition policies being pursued.[161] Nevertheless, as the rulings in *Albany* and *Pavlov* reveal, the Member States' experiments to modernize social security provision are not immune from the scrutiny of Community law.

Hervey[162] has questioned whether the principle of social solidarity as developed by the Court protects such threats to the 'European social model'.[163] A number of her concerns have been addressed in the case law. Hervey's first contention is that the Court in *Albany* works on the assumption that Member State social welfare systems or bodies entrusted to provide such systems are not carrying out 'economic' activity since it is assumed that such activities are based on 'social' aims, not the economic goal of profit-making. In *Poucet*[164] the Court argued that compulsory social security schemes are based upon the principle of solidarity precisely because they are not intended to be profit-making: the benefits paid are proportional to the amount of compulsory contributions and thus the Member State is seeking to perform a social function towards its own population. Thus the concept of social solidarity recognized by the Court has strong resonance with French notions of social contract or the German notion of the social market.[165] In *Albany* the pension scheme could be closely identified with Dutch political thinking of social solidarity based upon principles of 'equality, fraternity, with mutual protection and insurance'.[166]

Reading the cases in the way suggested above we reach a different conclusion from Hervey on the role of social solidarity in defining the acceptable level of public services for social welfare provision within the European Union. It has already been pointed out that the classification of 'economic' and 'non-economic' activity used by the Court is predicated upon outdated assumptions and is not a useful way to classify market activity caught by the Community rules. Hervey's analysis confuses the different stages in the Court's reading of Article 86(1) and (2) EC.[167] The Court is deciding *three* questions: first, should the activity be caught by the Treaty rules; secondly, if the activity is caught, the Court then has two options. It may either take an approach similar to the *Cassis de Dijon*-type approach to interpreting the boundaries to

---

[161] See Case C–67/96, *Albany International BV, supra* n. 52, para. 54. Although the Court places the 'social' and the 'economic' on an equal footing in this para. the outcome of the case reveals the dominance of the social value over the economic in this particular instance.

[162] Hervey, 'Social Solidarity: A Buttress Against Internal Market Law?' in Shaw (ed.), *Social Law and Policy in an Evolving European Union* (Hart, Oxford, 2000) 31–47.

[163] It is not clear what Hervey is referring to when she describes the 'European social model' since she herself accepts that '[a] distinctively "European" model is discernible only at a high level of abstraction' (*ibid.*, 43). A better description would be the threat to distinctive national regulatory models of strong social welfare provision embedded in the nation state.

[164] *Supra* n. 32.

[165] See Goodin *et al., The Real Worlds of Welfare Capitalism* (CUP, Cambridge, 1999).

[166] Bennet and Clark, *supra* n. 41, at 32.

[167] This is seen in the assertion that 'the Court seems to have failed to make it clear whether social solidarity is a test for whether the activities of a body fall within the scope of Community law, or whether social security provides a justification or exception from Community law ': Hervey, n. 162 above, 46.

Article 28 EC and balance the public service being offered in an economic context against the need to expose such activities fully to the market, or it may separate this question and decide that the activity ought in principle to be caught by the free market rules but the particular socio-economic context of the activity should allow it to be offered a justification or derogation from the Treaty rules on the limited grounds set out in Article 86(2) EC.

Hervey suggests that the outcome may be the same whichever of the latter two tests is applied 'but the issue has ramifications in terms of the reach of Community law, and in terms of which legal system applies in a particular situation'.[168] This again confuses the two-step process involved in Article 86 EC but also the case law suggests that it does make a difference *where* the proportionality principle is applied. When Article 86(1) and (2) EC are read together it is a balancing process to assess whether the activity infringes the Treaty rules. It may be, for example, that the activity is alleged to have a 'non-economic' function which does not fit into the existing exemptions from Community competence. As we have seen in *Poucet and Pistre* the Court is willing to be creative. Whereas the use of proportionality under Article 86(2) EC alone assesses the means whereby an activity which is economic and found to be anti-competitive may still be justified. This question becomes increasingly important when public services are to be provided by competitive markets. The Court has drawn parallels with the case law under Article 30 EC stating that the objectives to be pursued under Article 86(2) EC must be 'non-economic' in nature.[169] In the context of liberalization and privatization the bright line between 'economic' and 'non-economic' justifications becomes increasingly difficult to sustain.

If one views the Court's case law from this perspective the *Albany* and the later *Pavlov* rulings are not surprising: the crossing of the Rubicon had been accomplished in *FFSA*, some years earlier. Where public services are provided in an economic context, such as the situation in *Albany* and *Pavlov*, or the situations identified by Hervey such as the partial 'privatization' of certain tasks, it is submitted that the Court has not made 'a curious elision of "economic" and "commercial" or "for-profit" activity'.[170] Instead the Court is setting a framework whereby a discussion of how public services which display *national* notions of social solidarity can be provided by *public and private actors* in a competitive market. This task, initially undertaken in the case law concerning the application of Article 86(2) EC, has increasingly taken a legislative, regulatory, and soft-law form and finds Community definitions in the ideas of universal obligation discussed above.

The Europeanization of public services has helped clarify some of the problems by dropping the confusing terminology of 'services of general *economic* interest'. In the Commission's Communications the use of the word 'economic'

---

[168] *Ibid.*

[169] Case 72/83, *Campus Oil v. Minister of Energy* [1984] ECR 2727; Case 52/79, *Coditel v. Ciné Vog* [1980] ECR 881.

[170] *Supra* n. 162, at 44. This blurs the fact that the 'general interest' to be pursued must be of a 'non-economic' nature in order for Art. 86(2) EC to apply.

denotes the activity under scrutiny, rather than the interest which is being protected. Thus the confusion between 'aims' and 'means' is clarified. This distinction becomes important when considering the scope of Member State action to protect 'economic' interests in competitive markets. Under Article 86(2) EC it is the *objectives* of the 'service of general economic interest' which must be of a non-economic nature.[171] The means by which this is achieved may be *economic*, for example, entrusting a body with special or exclusive rights and shielding that body from competition and Internal Market rules. While the Internal Market rules demand a strict application of the proportionality principle, the Court[172] and the Commission have taken a softer approach under Article 86(2) EC. This approach is affirmed in the Commission's Communication:

where such organization, in performing a general interest task, engages in economic activities, application of Community rules to these economic activities will be guided by the principles of this Communication respecting in particular the social and cultural environment in which the relevant activities take place. Moreover, where Community law would apply to these activities, the Commission will also examine, in the light of a more general reflection on the use of its discretionary powers, whether the interests of the Community require it to proceed with regard to these cases, subject to its legal obligations established in the EC Treaty.[173]

A positive aspect of *Albany*, which has been overlooked is that where a social security scheme operating in the economic sphere abuses its dominant position (for example, by failing to adapt to competitive market changes, failing to satisfy consumer interests etc.), the possibility of challenge under Article 86(1) EC may ensure that such schemes are kept under review.

A second shortcoming of the principle of solidarity identified by Hervey is the assumption by the Court that welfare benefits cannot be provided by private market actors. In fact the history of liberalization at the national level reveals a degree of experimentation with public and private and 'quasi-public' actors to provide traditional public services.[174] The idea of using non-market actors to provide public services in the areas of education and health underpins the current Conservative Party's ideas on the provision of public services and public–private partnerships have been part of the New Labour 'Welfare to Work' strategy to redress long-term unemployment. The Court has recognized that the state may 'delegate' its non-economic, social activities as well as its

---

[171] That is a 'social' function to provide a universal service or a supplementary social security scheme. But, as we have shown, the division between 'non-economic' (or social activities) and 'economic activities' is increasingly blurred. Gagliardi goes as far as asserting that, generally speaking, there is no 'bright line' dividing 'social' and 'economic' activities, *supra* n. 100, 372.

[172] See *Corbeau, supra* n. 59 and *Almelo, supra* n. 61, and the electricity and gas monopoly infringement actions, *supra* n. 65.

[173] *Supra* n. 1, para. 30.

[174] Such actors are termed 'hybrid' or a third 'public-service sector': see Freedland, 'Law, Public Services, and Citizenship—New Domains, New Regimes?' in Freedland and Sciarra (eds.), *supra* n. 43. In the context of the Internal Market see Case C–70/95 *Sodemare* [1997] ECR I–3395.

economic activities to other bodies,[175] including private market actors. Such actors may also be immune from the free trade rules.[176] What the Court did recognize in *Albany* was that the Dutch government had sought to use principles of social solidarity based upon equality, fraternity, mutual protection, and insurance as a way of distancing the pension funds from market principles.

But the use of such hybrid actors, existing somewhere between the state and the market, may serve to attenuate Member State power. Thus the Commission accepts that bodies such as trade unions, political parties, churches and religious societies, consumer associations, learned societies, charities, relief and aid organizations normally carry out non-economic activities and would be exempt from the competition rules. An example of this is seen in the *Albany* case itself where the social partners are not caught by Article 81 EC since the decision to establish the supplementary pension fund is taken in the context of a collective agreement encouraged by the EC Treaty.[177] Thus the resonance between the Dutch concept of social solidarity utilizing joint representation in the collective bargaining process and on sector-wide pension boards and the European Union's development of the role of the social partners in markets and society[178] made the agreement resistant to challenge. But, as the Commission points out:

Whenever such organisation, in performing a general interest task, engages in economic activities, application of Community rules to these economic activities will be guided by the principles in this Communication respecting in particular the social and cultural environment in which the relevant activities take place.[179]

Hervey also criticizes the Court for not providing adequate protection to the alleged choice on the part of the Member State to provide a social security system in a certain way.[180] In particular, the Court's concept of social solidarity fails to protect social security schemes from cream-skimming. As we have seen, the Court has addressed cream-skimming from a number of perspectives which provide flexibility and contextual approaches with an affirmation

---

[175] Strict criteria must be met if such bodies are to escape the application of the Treaty rules: *CNSD, supra* n. 17.

[176] See Case 109/92, *Wirth* [1993] ECR I–6447.

[177] Note the criticism of the narrow scope of the exemption in *Albany* by Vousden, 'Albany, Market Law and Social Exclusion' (2000) 29 *Industrial Law Journal* 181–91. Cf. the reluctance of the Court to extend the concept to an agreement made by the liberal professions in *Pavlov, supra* n. 52.

[178] See Clark, 'The Vocabulary of European Integration: Code Words for the New Millennium' [2001] *Environment and Planning*, forthcoming. Cf. *Pavlov* (*supra* n. 52) where the Court was *not* willing to extend the principle of *Albany* to an agreement made by members of a liberal profession to establish a pension fund responsible for managing the supplementary pension scheme. At para. 69 the Court emphasizes that there are no provisions similar to Arts. 136–143 EC encouraging members of the liberal professions to conclude collective agreements with a view to improving terms of employment and working conditions.

[179] *Supra* n. 1, para. 30.

[180] Under Art. 86(2) EC the Court has rarely questioned whether a service is of general economic interest and the Commission's Communication (*supra* n. 1) also claims that Member States retain a wide degree of competence to determine public services.

that justifications can be made out under Article 86(2) EC on purely economic grounds. The Court's approach receives reassurances in the Commission's Communication.[181] In *Albany* the Court respects the structure and integrity of the Dutch social security system, finding the request for market preference a claim too far.

The threat of cream-skimming is not a big issue in state provision of social security schemes. Even in *Albany* the employers did not want to cream-skim the good risks; rather they, like the litigants in *Poucet* and *FFS*, wanted to choose which economic provider to buy their sectoral pension scheme from. Similarly in *Pavlov* the objection was only that the state had made affiliation to two social security schemes compulsory. The Court is treating social solidarity in the same way as universal service obligations by recognizing that where non-state actors are involved they may also be shielded from the competition rules. Rather than posing a threat to the 'European social model' the ruling in *Albany* represents a defence to the integrity of *national* solutions to the crisis in pension provision in Europe.

The greater danger to the Member States' preferences in how to provide for social welfare will surely come through the European Union approach to the regulatory reform or the 'modernization of social protection' described above. The buttress against market law will need to develop through the Court's willingness to question the regulatory reform carried out through European Union processes against the values considered to be inherent in the European, not Member State, approach to the provision of public services.[182] This underlines the attempts by ETUC and CEEP to give a *content* to the scope and values inherent in Article 16 EC and shows why Article 36 of the Charter of Fundamental Rights in the European Union does not satisfy the complex range of issues involved in the provision of public services through competitive markets.

Where there is consensus on a universal service obligation, regulation has been used to determine how to provide and finance that obligation. It is difficult to draw parallels between these activities and social security provision since, at the moment, the core of 'social' state provision of social security varies between the Member States. The involvement of the European Union after the Lisbon Summit may lead to a set of core concepts which must be guaranteed across the European Union, but this will probably continue to emerge through a soft-law discourse.

While access to public service provision is an important aspect of the citizenship and fundamental rights dimension to the provision of public services in competitive markets the more pressing question is how should 'uncompetitive' services be financed? Hervey asserts that the Court has:

---

[181] *Supra* n. 1.
[182] Whether such jurisprudence will even materialize is questionable given the limited availability of standing to public interest groups in the European Union.

not yet sufficiently separated out the ideas of cross-subsidisation, public or not-for profit activity and private, commercial or for-profit activity. The Court's rulings suggest that cross-subsidisation assumes a public not-for-profit provider.[183]

In *Albany* the Court recognizes that schemes operating within the economic domain which display the social solidarity hallmark may be subsidized through a variety of means. But where public revenue is involved other issues may arise, such as the application of the state aid rules. As we have seen, notwithstanding the particular exemptions and justifications in these rules, Article 86(2) EC may also be raised as a justification by the Member State.

The Court has also accepted that Article 86(2) EC may be used to justify cross-subsidization from an 'economic' or competitive sector to finance a non-competitive, or universal service obligation, sector where this is necessary to ensure the economic viability of the undertaking entrusted with providing the public service. Later case law[184] has suggested that a tougher approach may be taken on the proportionality question (that is, could less restrictive means be taken?) particularly where a sector is undergoing liberalization. But equally the Court and the Commission have underlined the point that each case (and sector) must be decided on its individual facts and in the legal, social, and cultural environment in which the cross-subsidization takes place. Thus the crucial issue is how far Article 86(2) EC may be used to justify a wide range of tasks such as security of supply, protection of public health, integrity of the financing of social security schemes which do not fall within the concept of universal service obligations.

VIII. The Synergy Between Regulation and Competition and the Provision of Public Services in Competitive Markets

For the most part a variety of regulatory tools have been employed to ensure the presence of public service obligations in the new institutional design of Europe.[185] But increasingly it has been questioned whether regulation as a tool on its own is sufficient to secure the benefits liberalized markets are supposed to bring. Too much, or too heavy, regulation may stifle competition in the market. It is recognized that the new form of public services in the European Union are not static, either in their definition or the way in which they are to be delivered.[186] A question emerges how expectations of public services will be reconciled with the rapid development of markets. Market forces will increasingly determine what is to be perceived as a service. The regulatory objective is to

---

[183] Cf. the discussion of *Corbeau* (*supra* n. 59), a case decided in the pre-liberalization days of the postal sector.

[184] *Air Inter, supra* n. 81.

[185] Scott, ' Services of General Interest in EC Law: Matching Values to Regulatory Technique in the Public and Privatised Sectors' (2000) 6 *European Law Journal* 310–25.

[186] See European Commission, *First Monitoring Report on Universal Service in the Telecommunications Sector in the European Union*, COM(98)182 final.

provide access to the new markets to develop competition but also access to the benefits of the new markets. Another objective of regulation should be to mediate between clashes of fundamental values, both within and beyond the sphere of the competitive market.

Advances in telecommunications provide an example of a regulatory gap. Public telephone boxes and fixed voice telephony services are becoming redundant as more and more consumers become reliant upon mobile phones. In the year 2000 mobile phone users in Britain doubled to a figure of around 40 million. The resources necessary to meet this demand were intensified by the conditions of the 3G licences granted to telecommunications operators, whereby one of the terms was that mobile phone networks must cover at least 80 per cent of the British population by the year 2007. Thus at least 50,000 base stations must be in place by the year 2003 in order to meet market demand and regulatory conditions. There are currently only 22,500 such stations in place.

There is the potential for clashes of fundamental values inherent within this change of use, driven by the market. To make mobile phone services accessible to a larger number of users there are clashes with individual property rights (the 'NIMBY' protest) and clashes with collective and individual rights to protect health and the environment.[187] These are issues which could be resolved through regulatory techniques, but in Britain a regulatory gap has appeared in that there is a lack of planning guidelines for the telecommunications sector. The issue has been addressed in some areas by local government policy. But some of the issues raised involve scrutiny in the judicial arena, particularly where they raise fundamental and constitutional issues.[188] Thus the extension of a service may work to the detriment of citizens in general but also to the detriment of consumers with regard to other essential services. For this reason Scott[189] has argued against a 'one size fits all' approach to the future regulation of public services in Europe and instead argued that different techniques should be employed according to the context of the public service. It is Scott's submission, however, that the values placed upon a particular public service should be secondary to the issue of what is the most effective technique for securing a particular public service.

We have seen, however, that the development of the concept of public service must also address the *procedural* means whereby conflicting interests, particularly between regulators, providers, consumers, and citizens, can be resolved, or at least mediated. Public services are not value-free. Notions of public service must be connoted to *importance* for a particular society or territory. Public services are seen not only as a social good but also a merit good in the sense that they are recognized as essential components of the effective

---

[187] Stemming from alleged health risks associated with mobile phone use and also health and environmental risks alleged to arise from masts.

[188] The legal tactics adopted by the pressure group, Mast Action UK, not only involve a defence of fundamental substantive rights but also invoke procedural rights (the demand for a fair and impartial hearing, for example) under the Human Rights Act 1998.

[189] *Supra* n. 185.

functioning of a modern democratic society. Therefore, in some circumstances, individual preferences may need to be overridden. There are countless reasons why technological developments and the need to sustain markets may, and indeed should, prevail over individual and community (or collective) preferences. The mobile phone is one example where such fundamental conflicts of interest have not been addressed. One can envisage similar clashes of values emerging in the postal sector: the expectation of a daily, personal postal delivery (the 'snail mail') is being replaced by the expectation of faster forms of communication by Internet services, email, WAP phone etc. The latter expectation is not (yet) regarded as a public service but seems to be a service made by *choice* on the part of the market players developing such services, *choice* on the part of individuals or corporate organizations who have the capacity to pay for it, or a *choice* made on the part of governments willing to pay for, or subsidize, such services.[190] But the element of choice is moulded by preferences shaped by the competitive market: elimination of competition, research and development opportunities, price, availability, and so on.

By introducing the private sphere as the primary (and sometimes the sole) provider of public services a completely new set of questions emerges. The market as well as the state is capable of governing preferences and social values: defining and supplying a *need* for new forms of public service. Regulatory techniques have their limitations, and this is why many of the regulatory tools employed in Europe have an innovative mixture of regulation and competition principles embedded within them.[191] The need to be prescriptive must be balanced against the freedom to innovate, develop, and compete on the market. Thus where the market is capable of disrupting the new institutional design competition law is also employed. Not only must private economic power be controlled through regulation and competition; it must also be accountable.[192] It is within this context that European Union competition law has been obliged to adapt existing principles and concepts,[193] address new questions,[194] and evolve new forms of law-making[195] and new processes and

---

[190] For example, provision of Internet services to other public services such as schools, hospitals, or as part of a regional policy in the case of Scotland and Norway.

[191] Nihoul, 'Competition or Regulation for Multi-Media' (1998) 22 *Telecommunications Policy* 207–18.

[192] See the idea of 'special responsibility' developed in Case 322/81, *Michelin NV v. Commission* [1983] ECR 3461. Amato, *Antitrust and the Bounds of Power* (Hart, Oxford, 1997).

[193] See, e.g., *Notice of 9 December 1997 on the definition of the relevant market for the purposes of Community competition law* [1997] OJ C372/5; and a discrimination concept in the *Notice of 22 August 1998 on the application of the competition rules to access agreements in the telecommunications sector* [1998] OJ C265/2.

[194] Pricing and cross-subsidization would be one example. Another example would be the adequacy or otherwise of the Merger Regulation to control abuses of power on the market. The litigation concerning Microsoft in the USA raises important questions about the European Union's lack of divestiture powers, not only for private forms of power, but also the remit of the competition rules in relation to state power.

[195] Seen particularly in the use of soft-law Communications and Notices.

doctrines.[196] Inherent within the new competition law are a new set of principles relating to a constitutional division of power on the market.

IX. Conclusion

The Europeanization of the provision of public services in the European Union follows the classical process seen elsewhere in the integration process: negative integration techniques employing the constitutional principles of market freedom and competition. This has materialized largely through individual litigation questioning national regulatory regimes. Negative integration is then followed by a political need to plug the regulatory and social gap created by identifying and defending certain *Community* notions of public services: re-regulation in the European Union sphere. The defence of public services acknowledges particular values respected within the Member States, but increasingly we see that the European Union has developed its own agenda which is sometimes in direct competition with national interests.

The regulatory reform of the European market has created a new institutional design where the emergence of new forms of power, both public and private, create challenges for the nation state and the developing polity of the European Union. State power in the market has been replaced by an increase in private power through rapid restructuring in some markets, seen, for example, in the use of strategic alliances in the telecommunications sector. The response from the EU has been in the experimental use of conventional, new, and hybrid forms of regulatory, constitutional, and competition law tools to identify, regulate, and create legitimacy for the new forms of public service provision in the EU. The result is a mixture of traditional and new, regulatory and competition concepts emerging during the 1990s. These concepts not only transcend the traditional public/private divide, the satisfactory reclassification of which continues to elude legal theorists, but reveals a legal framework within which a new synergy is developing between competition law, competition concepts, regulation, and constitutional concepts. This synergy is being used not only to *constrain* public and private power (as well as the new hybrid forms of power) emerging in competitive markets but also to determine the constitutional values underpinning the mode of delivery of services in competitive markets.

The Commission continues to affirm the principle of neutrality in Article 295 EC which allegedly allows the Member States to choose between public and private provision of public services. But such 'neutrality' has been lost to the *Community* interest in the process of liberalization and the fiscal constraints imposed upon public spending, by meeting not only the convergence criteria for EMU but also the economic policy guidelines dictated by the Broad

---

[196] Seen, e.g., in the evolution of a 'refusal to deal' doctrine to testing an 'essential facilities doctrine': Case C–7/97, *Bronner* [1998] ECR I–7791.

Economic Guidelines and other policies largely found in the soft-law discourse. Where a sector has been liberalized, a Member State may no longer have the public resources to compete in competitive markets. Equally a Member State may no longer have an interest in competing on liberalized markets. While the Commission and the Court pay lip service to the freedom of the Member States to define public services much of that freedom is illusory. According to the Commission, the Member States' definition of a public service is subject to control only for 'manifest error'. But Community law has imposed other obligations. For example, the requirement of transparency requires a clear definition of a public service mission entrusted through an act of a public authority. Equally an exclusive right may be incompatible with Community law where it fails to meet demand or where it fails to adapt to technological change.

  The introduction of a universal service obligation was initially intended to soften the Member States' attitudes when considering liberalization. It was the conduit by which public services became an obligtion under Community law principles, rather than a derigation. The European Union has imposed upon the Member States *and* private operators in the market not only a duty to provide certain services but also the terms on which such services should be provided. Liberalization and privatization, however, raise a fundamental question: why *should* the European Union demand the provision of public services? Public services can and, it seems, should be provided in competitive markets controlled by a mix of regulation, competition, and constitutional law principles. The market ought to be the place where consumers and citizens are given freedom of choice.[197] The duty to provide public services has been viewed by some as a restriction on the dominance of economic priorities in competitive markets. But as long as the continued recognition of public services is linked to the requirements of integration it will also form part of a process of restricting individual autonomy in favour of broader European Union 'constitutional' values.

---

[197] Teubner 'After Privatization? The Many Autonomies of Private Law' [1998] *Current Legal Problems* 393–424, 411 describes the use of universal service obligations in the 'privatization' process of Community law as the 'witnessing a strange phenomenon' whereby arcane principles discarded from medieval law obligations are suddenly transposed into the private law relationships of competitive markets.

From Obloquy to Equality:
In the Shadow of Abnormal Situations

NELIUS CAREY*

I. Introduction

'Injustice anywhere is a threat to justice everywhere';[1] this is particularly true in relation to homosexuals[2] who are, it is still widely believed, a group apart, granted a modicum of acceptance if it guarantees their silence and discretion to the point where their identity remains locked in the perpetual cycle of exclusion through intolerance born of ignorance.

In order to give a brief survey of the obstacles faced by homosexuals seeking to be treated on a par with all other humans, it is appropriate to consider this intolerance under the guises of normality, reason, and morality as well as its expression through the medium of homophobic violence.

The following snapshot of normality, dated 1952, has been proffered:[3] '[i]n the background stands a little house, one of a row of little houses in a suburb. In the foreground is the white family that lives in the house: the father, who earns the family's living; the mother, who tends the house and the children . . . who will soon go to school'. Karst continues: 'this picture in the "family values" album obscures much of reality of American life, even in 1952. First, many Americans are missing: rural white families, non-white families, rural and urban; gay and lesbian couples; two-wage earner families; single mothers; the poor.' And for those who do not fall within the snapshot he advises: '[o]utsiders have been expected to adjust their lives to approximate the image of the snapshot'. It is precisely this adjustment that the fight for equality seeks to render defunct.

Karst[4] also pronounces on the notion of reason, status, and order: 'because our definitions of Reason are culturally based, they, too, are subject to the stresses of status anxiety. Members of the group that resort to law for the purpose of maintaining Order—that is, preserving their favoured status

* Ph.D candidate, EUI, Florence. This article is based on a Master's Thesis paper written at the College of Europe, Bruges, under the supervision of Prof. David O'Keeffe.

[1] Martin Luther King, Jr. *I have a dream* (1963), delivered on the steps at the Lincoln Memorial in Washington, DC, on 28 Aug. 1963.

[2] In this article the term 'homosexual' is taken to refer to homosexual men and lesbian women.

[3] Karst, *Law's Promise, Law's Expression, Visions of Power in the Politics of Race, Gender and Religion* (New Haven, Conn., Yale University Press, 1994), 3.

[4] *Ibid.*, at 12.

positions—do not see the clash of cultures as the competition of different brands of Reason. [T]hey see their cultural challengers not only as the authors of Disorder but as the embodiment of an Unreason that must be suppressed. So, an officially defined Reason not only grows out of the prevailing Order of status dominance but reinforces it as well.'

That there is still a very vocal school of thought which denies the claims of equality sought by homosexuals there is no doubt. As an illustration of this, the following is an excerpt from a speech given by Senator Jesse Helms: '[t]hink about it. Homosexuals and lesbians, are disgusting people marching in our streets demanding all sorts of things, including the right to marry each other. . . . What about the rights of human beings born and unborn? What about the rights of women who want to stay in the home doing most important job there is—raising our children?'[5] Another illustration of blind intolerance: '[t]o get the 1990s started with a new spate of witch hunts, the admiral commanding the surface Atlantic fleet issued a message urging officers to be vigilant in rooting out lesbian women. He pointed out that investigations might be "pursued half-heartedly" by local commanders because lesbian sailors are generally "hard-working, career-orientated, willing to put in long hours on the job and among the command's top performers" '.[6]

A longstanding justification for discrimination against homosexuals was that their behaviour was 'unnatural', 'objectively disordered'. Rahman[7] has said that 'the essentialist reading of nature that underwrote normality represents a flaw in the science of sex, and of the Enlightenment thinking from which it derived. It was within this assumption that nature was deployed to underwrite moral distinctions. Perverse sexual practices were thus not only unnatural but also wrong.' The Catechism of the Catholic Church holds that homosexuality, the condition, is a disorder to be tolerated whereas homosexuality, the activity, is a sin and is inadmissible.[8] And, just to show that the world can be at one, it has been noted[9] that: '[i]t seems there is, after all, one matter on which the children of Abraham and their three great religions agree. They may disagree on divorce, abortion, contraception, the divinity of Jesus, as to whether salvation is possible outside their own ranks. But one thing they are sure of homosexuality is bad.'

Karst argues that the main function of sodomy laws today is symbolic, representing 'not only the organised community's disapproval of people of homosexual orientation but the community's devotion to a sharply defined gender line. One person's community-defining moral condemnation is another's community-denying stigma.'

---

[5] During his 1990 re-election campaign; *ibid.*, 18.

[6] Gross, 'Navy is Urged to Root out Lesbians Despite Abilities', *New York Times*, 2 Sept. 1990 in Karst, *supra* n. 2 at 128.

[7] Rahman, 'Sexuality and Rights' in Carver and Mottier (eds.), *Politics of Sexuality Identity, Gender, Citizenship* (London, Routledge, Ecpr Studies in European Political Science 4, 1998) at 87.

[8] *Ibid.*, at p. 152.

[9] McCarry, 'Cardinal leads charge as church leaders condemn gay lifestyle', *Irish Times*, 31 Jan. 2000.

The bombing of a gay pub in London in April 1999 highlighted the issue of homophobic violence.[10] Surveys show that, far from being an isolated event, homophobic crimes occur regularly. The International Lesbian and Gay Association Europe (ILGA-Europe), relying on a survey undertaken by Stonewall,[11] believes that in most of Europe 'it can be very dangerous to identify oneself as gay. Actions as commonplace for heterosexuals as holding hands with one's partner, or kissing one's partner farewell, carry considerable risk.'

Having thus established the intellectual, moral, and societal obstacles to recognizing equality for homosexuals, long expected to fit it, be cured,[12] or disappear, this work aims to demonstrate the pivotal role played by the courts in changing perceptions of equality legally, intellectually, and emotionally in relation to a group 'sadly crippled by the manacles of segregation and the chains of discrimination'.[13] From the analysis of Western case law (Part II) an attempt will be made to show that progress has indeed been achieved for the advancement of the rights of homosexuals where there has been a judicial willingness so to advance. The reaction of the legislature is also of great importance in determining whether society should confirm or contain audacious judicial advances. The situation pertaining in Europe will be given separate consideration (Part III) as it is particularly interesting, in that there are two courts of major importance, in Strasbourg and Luxembourg, often reaching different solutions although a convergence in approaches is possible. Within the Luxembourg case law internal contradictions are discernible. Non-judicial progress and prospects for the future will be considered. As a final point, it should be noted that although the case law considered in Parts II and III is as vast in quantity as it is rich in subtlety, this analysis must sacrifice both in order to give an overall picture of developments.

II.   The Western Approach—An Overview

In this part, Canada, the United States of America, South Africa, and the United Kingdom will be considered to give a general impression of judicial activity and legislative reaction in relation to equality for homosexuals.

A.   CANADA—PROTECTION OF HISTORICALLY DISADVANTAGED GROUPS

Let us begin our overview of the western approach in Canada which has a Charter of Rights, section 15(1) of which is of particular interest for the

---

[10] ILGA, Sexual Orientation Discrimination in MS of the EU and the Accession Countries; see News from ILGA Europe at www.ilga.org.

[11] Mason, A. and Palmer, A., *Queer Bashing: A National Survey of Hate Crimes Against Lesbians and Gay Men* (London: Stonewall (1996)).

[12] The WHO considered homosexuality a psychiatric disorder until 1993.

[13] Martin Luther King, Jr., *supra* n. 1.

purposes of our analysis. It reads: 'every individual is equal before and under the law and has the right to the equal protection and equal benefit of the law without discrimination and, in particular, without discrimination based on . . . sex'. The diverse case law on the interpretation of this section will now be considered; the Court's constant reference to *de facto* discrimination and disadvantage is of particular importance.

One of the early discrimination cases before the Canadian Supreme Court (SC) was *Andrew* v. *Law Society of British Columbia*.[14] This case concerned an allegation of discrimination against a resident of Canada in his failed attempt to gain admission to the British Columbia bar solely because he was not a Canadian citizen. The Supreme Court considered section 15 and, in particular, the term 'discrimination' which the majority defined as 'a distinction which, whether intentional or not but based on grounds relating to personal characteristics of the individual or group, has an effect which imposes disadvantages not imposed upon others or which withholds or limits access to advantages available to other members of society. Distinctions based on personal characteristics attributed to an individual solely on the basis of association with a group will rarely escape the charge of discrimination, while those based on an individual's merits and capacities will rarely be so classed.'

The determination of discrimination, it held, necessitated a two-step test:

(1) the determination of whether or not an infringement of a guaranteed right has occurred; and
(2) whether, if there has been an infringement, it can be justified.

These principles came to be applied in relation to homosexual rights in *Egan* v. *Canada*[15] where, alas, the necessary majority was not achieved for the plaintiff to win. This case concerned the fortunes of N who applied for a spousal allowance at the age of 60 under the Old Age Security Act on the basis that his same-sex partner, E, with whom he had lived since 1948, had turned 65 and was thus in receipt of old age security. His application was rejected on the basis that the relationship between N and E did not fall within the Act's definition of 'spouse' which includes 'a person of the opposite sex who is living with that person, having lived with that person for at least one year, if the two persons have publicly represented themselves as husband and wife'. The couple sought a declaration that the definition of 'spouse' contravened section 15(1) of the Charter. The matter reached the Supreme Court where the majority, in dismissing the appeal, held that the analysis under section 15 involves three steps:

(1) whether the law has drawn a *distinction* between the claimant and others;
(2) whether the distinction results in *disadvantage*, and examines whether the impugned legislation imposes a burden, obligation, or disadvantage on a group of persons to which the claimant belongs which is not

---

[14] [1989] 1 SCR 143.   [15] [1995] 2 SCR 513.

imposed on others, or does not provide them with a benefit which it grants others; and

(3) whether the distinction is based on an irrelevant *personal characteristic* which is enumerated either in section 15(1) or one analogous thereto.

There was unanimity in the view that 'sexual orientation is a deeply personal characteristic that is either unchangeable or changeable only at unacceptable personal costs, and so falls within the ambit of section 15 protection'. The Court split in three ways—the discrimination group, the non-discrimination group, and the discrimination but justification group.[16] The Court, quite logically, found that the singling out of legally married and common law couples as the recipients of benefits necessarily excluded all sorts of other couples living together, whatever reasons these other couples may have for doing so and whatever their sexual orientation. L'Heureux-Dubé J stated: '[T]he presumption that same-sex relationships are somehow less interdependent than opposite-sex relationships is, itself, a fruit of stereotype rather than one of demonstrable, empirical reality'. Not for the first time,[17] the Court had recourse to legislative intent to deny the otherwise reasonable claims. The majority considered that the legislative intention, in passing the impugned legislation, was to accord support to married couples who were aged and elderly. Marriage, it surmised, is 'firmly anchored in the biological and social realities that heterosexual couples have the unique ability to procreate, that most children are the product of these relationships, and that they are generally cared for and nurtured by those who live in that relationship. In this sense, marriage is by nature heterosexual'.

Thus, the distinction provided for in the Act not being unconstitutional, the Court could not oblige the government to treat same-sex and unmarried opposite-sex couples equally in the allocation of benefits. This decision, though quite promising in part, was preoccupied with tradition and legislative intent—such was not to be in the case of *The Attorney General for Ontario* v. *M. and H.*[18] M and H were a same-sex couple whose union came to an end after many years, resulting in several property issues and the question whether M could claim support pursuant to the provisions of the Family Law Act (FLA). To do so she sought to challenge the validity of the FLA definition of 'spouse', which includes a person who is actually married and also either a man and woman who 'are not married' to each other and have cohabited . . . continuously for a period of not less than three years'.

The Supreme Court found section 29 unconstitutional, though temporarily suspending its ruling, relying very much on its decision in *Law* v. *Canada*[19] to interpret discrimination under section 15(1). The latter case established that the inquiry into substantive discrimination is to be undertaken in a purposive

---

[16] Wintemute, 'Discrimination Against Same-sex Couples' [1995] *Canadian Bar Review* 682.

[17] Bamforth, 'Setting the Limits of Anti-discrimination Law: Some Legal and Social Concepts' in Dine and Watt (eds.), *Discrimination Law Concepts, Limitations and Justifications* (New York, Longman, 1996) at 61 ff.

[18] [1999] 2 SCR 3.   [19] [1999] 1 SCR 497.

and contextual manner requiring the court to make the following three broad inquiries:

(1) does the impugned law:

    (a) draw a formal distinction between the claimant and others on the basis of one or more personal characteristics, or

    (b) fail to take into account the claimant's already disadvantaged position within Canadian society resulting in substantively differential treatment between the claimant and others on the basis of one or more personal characteristics? If so, there is differential treatment for the purposes of section 15(1);

(2) is the claimant subject to differential treatment on the basis of one or more of the enumerated and analogous grounds? or

(3) does the differential treatment discriminate in a substantive sense, bringing into play the purpose of section 15(1) in remedying such ills as prejudice, stereotyping, and historical disadvantage?

Analysing the impugned legislation the Court noted that the Act 'draws a *distinction* by specifically according rights to individual members of unmarried cohabiting opposite-sex couples, which by omission it fails to accord to individual members of cohabiting same-sex couples'. It proceeded to consider the nature of same-sex relationships: '[s]ince gay and lesbian individuals are capable of being involved in conjugal relationships, and since their relationships are capable of meeting the FLA's temporal requirements, the distinction of relevance to this appeal is between persons in an opposite-sex, conjugal relationship of some permanence and persons in a same-sex, conjugal relationship of some permanence'. Thus, a formal distinction having been drawn on the basis of a personal characteristic (sexual orientation), it remained to be seen whether actual discrimination occurred.

The Court asked whether the distinction reflected 'a stereotypical application of presumed group or personal characteristics, or which otherwise had the effect of perpetuating or promoting the view that the individual is less capable or worthy of recognition or value as a human being or as a member of Canadian society, equally deserving of concern, respect, and consideration'. Given the pre-existing disadvantage and vulnerability of homosexuals the impugned legislation had the effect of exacerbating the problem and thereby 'demeaning the claimant's dignity . . . such exclusion perpetuates the disadvantages suffered by individuals in same-sex relationships and contributes to the erasure of their existence'. For Bastarache J same-sex couples were capable of meeting all of the statutory prerequisites set out in the FLA, *but for* the requirement that they be a man and a woman. The opposite-sex nature of traditional unions resulted in, the judge felt, an exclusion which suggests that same-sex unions are 'not worthy of recognition or protection'. This constituted a denial of equality within the meaning of section 15 and, in relation to Parliament, he did not shun from holding that there was 'no need to be deferential to the legislative choice in this case. The nature of the interest affected by the exclusion is *fundamental*; the group affected is vulnerable'.

The Court acknowledging that the economic dependency, the *raison d'être* for the FLA, which often exists in opposite-sex couples may not be as common amongst same-sex couples, but the Court could find 'no evidence that the inclusion of same-sex couples, within the scope of the FLA would cause any particular difficulty'. Such inclusion 'would be consistent with *Charter* values of equality and inclusion to treat all members in a family relationship equally and all types of family relationships equally'. So, applying 'but for' and 'why not' logic the Supreme Court made a giant leap forward—it was time for the Canadian government to react.

Following *M* v. *H,* the Modernisation of Benefits and Obligations Act (Bill C–23)[20] was introduced into the House of Commons of Canada's Federal Parliament,[21] its aims to amend sixty-eight federal statutes to extend benefits and obligations to same-sex couples on the same basis as common-law opposite-sex couples. The reason? The Department of Justice[22] noted that the Supreme Court 'has made it clear that governments cannot limit benefits or obligations to opposite-sex common-law relationships'. The Bill uses a new federal concept of 'common-law partner', defined as 'in relation to an individual, . . . a person who is cohabiting with the individual in a conjugal relationship, having so cohabited for a period of at least one year'. For same-sex partners, inclusion in this definition represents a major advance. One benefit covered will be the 'spouse's allowance' under the Old Age Security Act which was denied in *Egan.*[23]

After the first reading of Bill C–23, the Justice Minister decided to include in the bill a definition of marriage—'the lawful union of one man and one woman to the exclusion of all others'—in order to pacify some determined to thwart any move to allow same-sex marriages even if, in essence, the bill aims to provide equality between same-sex couples and common-law couples. Thus, the Court's progress is crystallized by the legislature; the reverse, however, has occurred in South Africa, where the Constitution provides explicit protection for homosexuals, the courts have a reduced influence.

B.   SOUTH AFRICA—STRONG CONSTITUTIONAL PROTECTION

The South African Constitutional Court enjoys a particular advantage when questions of discrimination by reason of sexual orientation are brought before it: the South African Constitution. Kader Asmal[24] has said that only by 'embracing the spirit and values of the Constitution could a united and democratic South Africa be built'. One of the Constitution's most advanced

---

[20] Wintemute, *Lesbian/Gay Law Notes* ISSN 8775–9021 Mar. 2000; see: http://www.qrd.org/qrd/www/usa/legal/lgln.

[21] The Dept. of Justice announced the change on 11 Feb. 2000. This bill was signed into law on 29 June 2000.

[22] See *ibid.*   [23] Wintemute *supra* n. 20.

[24] (South Africa) Independent Online, 21 Mar. 1997 'SA's new constitution spurred by human rights abuses of the past' http://www.iol.co.za.

provisions relates to equality; Article 9[25] thereof reads as follows: '(1) Everyone is equal before the law and has the right to equal protection and benefit of the law.... (3) The state may not unfairly discriminate directly or indirectly against anyone on one or more grounds, including . . . gender, sex, . . . and . . . sexual orientation'.

In *National Coalition for Gay and Lesbian Equality* v. *Minister of Home Affairs*,[26] the Constitutional Court (CC) was asked to consider whether section 25(5) of the Aliens Control Act was unconstitutional as it omitted to give same-sex partners the benefits it extends to 'spouses' in relation to the entry of foreign opposite-sex partners into the country. The rights of equality and dignity were found to be closely related in the present case and it was held that section 25(5) 'reinforced harmful stereotypes' of gays and lesbians. This conveyed the message that gays and lesbians 'lack the inherent humanity' to have their families and family lives in such same-sex relationships respected or protected and constituted an invasion of their dignity. Thus, in the light of the 'open and democratic' nature of South African society based on the principles of human dignity, equality, and freedom, unconstitutional discrimination was found under the rubrics of sexual orientation and marital status.

This decision is not surprising given the court's previous case law. In *National Coalition for Gay and Lesbian Equality* v. *Minister of Justice*,[27] for example, Ackermann J found that several anti-sodomy offences, all of which were aimed at prohibiting sexual intimacy between homosexuals, violated the constitutional right to equality in that they unfairly discriminated on the basis of sexual orientation. This discrimination was presumed to be unfair since the Constitution expressly included sexual orientation as a prohibited ground of discrimination. The Constitutional Court found that homosexuals constitute a 'vulnerable minority' in society and sodomy laws, criminalizing their most intimate relationships, 'devalued and degraded' homosexuals and, therefore, constituted a violation of their 'fundamental right to dignity'. Moreover, the offences criminalized private conduct between consenting adults which causes no harm to anyone else; this intrusion on the innermost sphere of human life violated the constitutional right to privacy. The Court noted that open and democratic societies around the world were increasingly turning their backs on discrimination on the basis of sexual orientation. However, South Africa, it observed, was the first to do so in its national Constitution.

Concurring, Sachs J reiterated the Court's jurisprudence on the centrality of dignity and self-worth to the idea of equality, and said that inequality is established not simply through group-based differential treatment, but through differentiation which 'perpetuates disadvantage'. The Constitution required, he continued, 'that the variability of human beings had to be acknowledged and the equal respect and concern, to which everyone is entitled, be affirmed. At

[25] Constitution of the Republic of South Africa 1996 as adopted on 8 May 1996 and amended on 11 Oct. 1996 by the Constitutional Assembly (Act 108 of 1996).
[26] CCT 10/99 2 Dec. 1999. 2000 (1) BCLR 39 (CC).
[27] CCT 11/98 9 Oct. 1998. 1998 (1) BCLR 1517 (CC).

the very least, what is statistically normal is no longer the basis for establishing what is legally normative'. The scope of constitutional normality 'has expanded to include the widest range of perspectives and to acknowledge, accommodate and accept the largest spread of difference . . . in an increasingly open and pluralistic South Africa'. Even in the absence of exceptionally inclusive measures, such as those in Article 9 above, courts can assure equality as the House of Lords has done in *Fitzpatrick*.

C.   UNITED KINGDOM—JUDICIAL ADVANCES;
LEGISLATIVE INTRANSIGENCE

The case of *Fitzpatrick (A.P.) v. Sterling Housing Association Ltd.*[28] concerned the succession claims of Fitzpatrick on the death of his partner, Thompson, the original tenant of the flat. The crux of the case centred around the issue of whether Fitzpatrick had been living with his partner as 'a spouse', 'as his or her wife or husband' or, alternatively, that he was a member of Thompson's family within the meaning of the Rent Act 1977. Ultimately, the Court found for Fitzpatrick; what is of importance here are the passages in which the Law Lords consider the notion of the family.

Lord Slynn's understanding of (same-sex) relationships was as follows: 'the hallmarks of the relationship are essentially that there should be a degree of mutual inter-dependence, of the sharing of lives, of caring and love, of commitment and support. [I]n *de facto* relationships these are capable, if proved, of creating membership of the tenant's family.' Lord Nicholls spoke of mutual love, affection, and long-term commitment which may, he considered, exist in same-sex relationships. He conceded that, in sexual terms, a homosexual relationship is different from a heterosexual relationship, but he was 'unable to see that the difference was material for present purposes'. He emphasized that the concept underlying membership of a family, for present purposes, was the 'sharing of lives together in a single family unit living in one house' and stressed the necessity for a 'bond of love and affection of a permanent nature; mutual support, financial and emotional, and companionship'.

Lords Hutton and Hobhouse, dissenting, reflected on the limitations of their role: 'the developments for which Fitzpatrick contends involve developments of policy and fall far outside the proper ambit of statutory construction'. Notwithstanding these dissenting views, the majority offered understanding and tolerance in spite of, or, perhaps, thanks to, the absence of major legislative protection for homosexuals; in point of fact, the legislation in relation to homosexuals in the UK forms part of the most conservative voted in Europe in recent decades—section 28[29] which the government is trying to repeal despite continued opposition from the House of Lords.

---

[28]   28 Oct. 1999, *FitzPatrick (AP) v. Sterling Housing Association* [1999] 3 All ER 705.
[29]   S. 28(1) of the Local Government Act 1988 reads: 'A local authority shall not—(a) intentionally promote homosexuality or publish material with the intention of promoting homosexuality; (b) promote the teaching in any maintained school of the acceptability of homosexuality as a pretended family relationship . . . '

No consideration of a western approach would be complete without reference to developments in the United States, a topic which has been reserved for the end of this overview not because it is uninteresting but rather because the case law has been so diverse and the legislative reactions so hasty and divergent.

D.   UNITED STATES—A DIVERGING APPROACH

The US Supreme Court began discussions of equality of the sexes in the 1970s and later progressed to consider sexual orientation. In relation to the former, Justice Brennan was the author of a seminal decision: *Fronterio* v. *Richardson, Secretary of Defense.*[30] Therein, he referred to societal perceptions of 'proper roles' for men and women: '[t]raditionally, such discrimination [against women] was rationalised by an attitude of "romantic paternalism" which, in practical effect, put women, not on a pedestal, but in a cage'. Here, the Court recognizes that the long-held views on who should do what, how one should behave, are not immutable; the Court has the duty to analyse such conceptions under the glare of constitutional rights of equality and non-discrimination—it is precisely this reaction in the face of strongly defined societal roles and even prerogatives that must be applied in relation to other historically victimized groups, notably, homosexuals. As with women in the nineteenth century, today's homosexuals are easily losers in the 'proper roles' game though the cages in question may take on a far more physical nature than those entrapping women in the nineteenth century.

Moreover, Brennan J continued, 'since sex, like race and national origin, is an immutable characteristic determined solely by the accident of birth, the imposition of special disabilities upon the members of a particular sex because of their sex would seem to violate the basic concept of our system that legal burdens should bear some relationship to individual responsibility . . . [a]nd what differentiates sex from such nonsuspect statuses as intelligence or physical disability . . . is that the sex characteristic frequently bears no relation to ability to perform or contribute to society.' For this reason legislation making distinctions, for reasons unrelated to the actual capabilities of individuals, is impermissible. Could the Supreme Court have applied this logic in relation to sexual orientation? Yes, but it has decided, as shall be shown below, not to do this. That said, some progress by the US Supreme Court is evident in *Oncale* v. *Sundower Offshore Services.*[31] In *Oncale* the Supreme Court held that same-sex sexual harassment is as actionable under US law as the more traditional opposite-sex harassment, it violating the Due Process clause of the Fifth Amendment.[32]

---

[30] 411 US 677 (1973). This case concerned unequal treatment between male and female Air Force officers and benefits for their spouses.
[31] 200 US 321, 337 (1998).
[32] It contains no equal protection clause but it does forbid discrimination that is 'so unjustifiable as to be violative of due process'.

In *Bowers, AG of Georgia* v. *Hardwick*,[33] the Georgia statute, criminalizing sodomy between adult males, was challenged; the US Supreme Court, holding the statute constitutional, made it quite clear that:

- the Constitution does not confer a fundamental right upon homosexuals to engage in sodomy;
- against a background in which many states have criminalized sodomy and still do, to claim that a right to engage in such conduct is 'deeply rooted in this Nation's history and tradition' or 'implicit in the concept of ordered liberty' is, at best, facetious;
- the fact that homosexual conduct occurs in the privacy of the home does not affect the result; and
- sodomy laws should not be invalidated on the asserted basis that majority belief that sodomy is immoral is an inadequate rationale to support the laws.

More recently, on 28 June 2000, the Supreme Court confirmed its approach when it handed down its decision in *Boy Scouts of America et al.* v. *Dale*.[34] In this case, Dale had been expelled from the Boy Scouts, after years of exemplary service, when the organization became aware of his homosexuality. The Supreme Court, hearing an appeal from the Supreme Court of Jersey in which Dale was successful, split five to four. The majority found that the ninety-year-old organization had the right to bar homosexual men from becoming troop leaders (the position held by Dale). The relevant part of the Boy Scouts' Oath, which was considerably discussed during the case, related to the pledge that members should be 'morally straight and clean'. The Supreme Court effectively accepted that this provision allowed the Boy Scouts, as a private organization, to enforce its First Amendment right of 'expressive association' and exclude potential and present members on the basis of their sexual orientation. Being a private organization, the Supreme Court held, the Boy Scouts are not subject to anti-discrimination laws. The Supreme Court considered the issue of sexual orientation for its 'message' quality. To be a leader and a homosexual was a message at variance with the organization's principles. Justice Rehnquist, writing for the majority, said: '[w]e are not, as we must not be, guided by our views of whether the Boy Scouts' teaching with respect to homosexual conduct are right or wrong. Public or judicial disapproval of a tenet of an organization's expression does not justify the state's effort to compel the organization to accept members where such acceptance would derogate from the organization's expressive message.' Justice Stevens, writing the dissent noted, *inter alia*, 'it is plain as the light of day that neither of these principles [Boy Scouts' law and oath] . . . says the slightest thing about homosexuality'. Nonetheless, the Boy Scouts remain, thanks to the Supreme Court decision, 'morally straight'.

---

[33] 478 US 186 (1986).   [34] 530 US 640 (2000).

While the US Supreme Court is growing less receptive to requests for the recognition of a wider field of application for equality, such is not the case at the state level. The cases at the state level in which the courts adjudicate on questions of equality for homosexuals are numerous. One of the early cases is *Powell* v. *The State (Georgia).*[35] The plaintiff in this case, who was acquitted of rape and aggravated sodomy, challenged the anti-sodomy provision of which he was found guilty. The Georgia Supreme Court held that while many believe that 'acts of sodomy, even those involving consenting adults, are morally reprehensible, this repugnance alone does not create a compelling justification for state regulation of the activity'. The Court pointed out that 'legislative enactments setting "social morality" are not exempt from judicial review'. It continued by stating that the impugned legislation in so far as it criminalized the performance of private, non-commercial acts of sexual intimacy between persons legally able to consent 'manifestly infringes upon a constitutional provision' which guarantees to the citizens of Georgia the right of privacy. Concurring, Sears J added: '[t]he individual's right to freely exercise his or her liberty is not dependent upon whether the majority believes such exercise to be moral, dishonourable, or wrong. Simply because something is beyond the pale of "majoritarian morality" does not place it beyond the scope of constitutional protection'. To allow the moral indignation of a majority to justify criminalizing private consensual conduct would, he held, be a negation of freedoms often dearly paid for. Majority opinion, he continued, should never dictate a free society's willingness to battle for the protection of its citizens' liberties, lest another attack on constitutional democracy, *via* moral majoritarianism, should be committed.

One of the most potent examples of a court defending a minority coming up against severe reprimand by the majority is in Hawaii in the case of *Baehr* v. *Lewin.*[36] Here, the Hawaii Supreme Court found that there was no fundamental right to marriage, a state-conferred legal status giving rise to certain rights and benefits, for same-sex couples under the Hawaii Constitution. After recalling that sex is a supect categorization it then considered the onus of proof: 'if the government cannot cite actual prejudice to the public majority from a change in the law to allow same-sex marriages . . . then the public majority will not have a sound basis for claiming a compelling, or even a substantial, state interest in withholding the marriage statute from same-sex couples; a mere feeling of distaste or even revulsion at what someone else is or does, simply because it offends majority values without causing concrete harm, cannot justify inherently discriminatory legislation against members of a constitutionally protected class—as the history of constitutional rulings against racially discriminatory legislation makes clear.' On the facts of the case the govern-

[35] 510 SE 2d 18 (1988).
[36] 74 Haw. 530, 852 P.2d 44 (1993). For an analysis of the pre-1999 Hawaii position see Errante 'Le mariage homosexuel aux Etats-Unis: les arrêts des tribunaux de l'Etat de Hawaii et leurs implications au niveau national' in Borrillo (ed.), *Homosexualités et droit, De la tolérance sociale à la reconnaissance juridique* (Paris, PUF, 1998).

ment had failed to present 'sufficient credible evidence which demonstrates that the public interest in the well-being of children and families, or the optimal development of children would be adversely affected by same-sex marriage'. In other words, there was no reason not to allow for same-sex marriage.

The Supreme Court having spoken, the matter was returned to the First Circuit Court where, on 11 December 1996,[37] judgment was entered in favour of same-sex marriage because the sex-based classification was unconstitutional by virtue of being 'in violation of the equal protection clause of the Hawaii Constitution'. Consequently, the defendant was prevented from denying an application for a marriage licence because the plaintiffs were of the same sex. A victory for homosexuals in Hawaii? Unfortunately, not so; the matter may be best explained by referring to the decision of the Hawaii Supreme Court of 9 December 1999.[38] 'The passage of the marriage amendment to the constitution took the matter out of the ambit of the equal protection clause of the Hawaii Constitution, in so far as the amendment sought to limit access to the marital status to opposite-sex couples. In effect, the amendment . . . gave to the legislature the power to reserve marriage to opposite-sex couples.'

The setback had become more serious, traversing the Hawaiian frontiers, long before 1999. On 21 September 1996, to circumvent the constitutional rule that contracts validly passed in one state are to be recognized in all other states, an Act of Congress, the Defense of Marriage Act,[39] was signed by President Clinton confirming, for federal purposes, the heterosexual nature of marriage and the right of states to ignore marriage contracts passed in other states between same-sex partners. In a parallel move, about twenty states have modified state law on marriage to confirm that it can be contracted only between persons of the opposite sex.[40] The Hawaiian experience has indeed been confused in the last decade,[41] the reaction of the Hawaii people, the US Congress, and several states has often been knee-jerk, devoid of serious analysis or debate on the rationale for the continued marginalization of certain American citizens.

But all is not lost. In other American states, progress is ongoing, albeit within the confines of the 1996 Act of Congress. Perhaps one of the most progressive states is Vermont where the Supreme Court has shown an understanding of the plight of homosexuals. In its *Baker* v. *State* decision,[42] the Vermont Supreme Court interpreted the equality clause in its Constitution.[43] The

---

[37] *Baehr* v. *Miike* 74 Haw. 530, (1996).   [38] *Baehr* v. *Miike* 92 Haw. 634.

[39] Pub. L. No. 104–199, 110 Stat. 2419 (1996): 'an Act to define and protect the institution of marriage'.

[40] For example, on 7 Mar. 2000 voters overwhelmingly approved Proposition 22 banning recognition of same-sex marriage in California.

[41] See Errante, *supra* n. 36.

[42] 170 vt. 194 (1999) wherein three same-sex couples challenged the constitutionality of the marriage statutes denying them the right to be issued with marriage licences.

[43] Art. 7 of the Vermont Constitution is clear 'that government is . . . instituted for the common benefit, . . . of the . . . community, and not for the particular . . . advantage of any single person, family or set of persons, who are a part only of that community'.

principal question was, in the words of Amestoy CJ, whether the State may 'exclude same-sex couples from the benefits and protections that its laws provide to opposite-sex married couples?' After acknowledging the 'deeply-felt religious, moral, and political beliefs' held by many *vis-à-vis* the question posed, the Court made it clear that its role lay, not in religious or moral debate over same-sex relationships, but rather in the interpretation of the law and whether or not 'the exclusion of same-sex couples from the secular benefits and protections offered married couples' was contrary to the equality clause. It held that 'the State is constitutionally required to extend to same-sex couples the common benefits and protections that flow from marriage under Vermont law'. The granting of these benefits and protections did not necessarily require the institution of same-sex marriage[44] but some parallel partnership arrangement was essential; the state legislature had to act in accordance with the state's Constitution. The state has, the Court considered, 'a strong interest in promoting stable and lasting families, including families based upon a same-sex couple'. It recognized that, despite innumerable obstacles, many same-sex couples have formed 'lasting, committed and caring relationships' whereby they participate in their communities, raise children, and care for family members, just like married couples. The Court recognized the disadvantages consequent upon denial of access to the advantages of marriage and thus held that an equivalent system allowing them to have practically the same benefits as married couples. It was now time for the Vermont legislature to act.

On 17 March 2000 the House of Representatives passed a bill, 'An Act Relating to Civil Unions',[45] in which it recognizes the right of Civil Union status to same-sex couples; a month later the Senate approved it by a majority of two to one.[46] The General Assembly banned discrimination on the basis of sexual orientation in 1992 and recognized gay and lesbian adoptive couples in 1996. The anti-discrimination and adoption measures influenced the Court which has, in turn, influenced the Legislature—progress gives birth to progress even if it is limited to the state.

In recent decades, the case law of the above western jurisdictions has been quite progressive in relation to homosexual rights. The major Canadian cases have broadly interpreted the notion of equality for homosexuals; the South African Constitution has the benefit of the very comprehensive Article 9 for homosexual plaintiffs seeking justice. The Canadian and South African courts look for a distinction causing disadvantage based on sexual orientation; the reinforcement of harmful stereotypes as well as considerations whether the plaintiff has been devalued and degraded as a result of the distinction. Though

[44] The Court upheld the principle that marriage laws apply to the union of one man and one woman; proposals to confirm this with a constitutional amendment were rejected by the Legislature.

[45] The Vermont Civil Union Law, Act 91, was passed by the Vermont House and Senate, and signed into law by the Governor on 26 Apr. 2000. The law came into effect on 1 July 2000.

[46] Several members of the Houses of Congress who voted in favour this law lost their seats in the subsequent elections in which several groups campaigned actively against the re-election of those who had voted a law against the will, it claimed, of the people of Vermont.

without any strong textual basis on which to work the House of Lords has been very willing to adopt a 'modern' notion of the family unit in the *Fitzpatrick* case.[47]

The liberal US Supreme Court of the 1960s and 1970s has not managed to continue in subsequent decades, the main advances are now coming from state courts.[48] Unfortunately, state efforts risk being overturned or curtailed (by US Congress and state referendum), unlike those of the Federal Court which can only be altered, *de facto*, by the Court itself.

III.   Europe—Two Courts, Two Approaches

Having considered the approach of various western courts, it is now apposite to turn our attention to the very intricate situation pertaining in Europe: intricate due to the multiplicity of jurisdictions competent to consider matters of equality and the heterogeneity of the solutions given. While recognizing the role of national courts, attention here will be concentrated primarily on the catalytic role of the European Court of Human Rights (ECHR) and the European Court of Justice (ECJ) in the recognition of equality for homosexuals. The ECHR has shown itself far more responsive to homosexual calls for equality than the ECJ, due in part to the economic origins of the latter. The future does look positive but there is no room for complacency.

A.   THE COUNCIL OF EUROPE—JUDICIAL ADVANCES

Under the rubric of the Council of Europe, the Convention on Human Rights and Fundamental Freedoms must be considered. In this part, the most pertinent Convention provisions as well as the main case law in this area will be considered.

As in the Canadian Charter there is no mention of sexual orientation as a specific ground for combating discrimination. Like the Canadian Supreme Court, the European Court of Human Rights (ECHR) has proved, particularly in recent times, most enlightened in its approach to homosexual rights. The first major case in which the ECHR was asked to consider laws directly, though not exclusively, affecting homosexuals was *Dudgeon* v. *United Kingdom*.[49] By a quirk of circumstances, an almost identical case was brought before the Court seven years later in *Norris* v. *Ireland*.[50] Perhaps the most straightforward way of looking at these two cases without repetition is to consider the later case from the national decision to the European Court's reaffirmation of the

---

[47] It should, however, be noted that the UK courts were not very willing to assist homosexuals complaining about discrimination they claimed to have suffered when members of the Armed Services. The decisions of the European Court of Human Rights are considered in Part III.

[48] See Schapiro, 'Looking For a Way To Expand Rights? Try State Courts', *Washington Post* Online, 26 Mar. 2000, http://www.washingtonpost.com.

[49] 22 Oct. 1981, Series A no. 45.

[50] 26 Oct. 1988, Series A no. 142; the Irish courts' proceedings are reported at [1984] IR 37.

decision as laid down in *Dudgeon*. Norris complained about national legislation criminalizing certain homosexual practices between consenting adult
men. The very same legislation, in force in Northern Ireland, had been condemned by the ECHR in *Dudgeon*; but the Irish Supreme Court found that neither the Convention nor *Dugdeon* was 'in any way relevant' to the *Norris* case.
The Supreme Court, by a three-to-two majority, considered the impugned legislation to be consistent with the Constitution and that no right of privacy
encompassing consensual homosexual activity could be derived from 'the
Christian and democratic nature of the Irish State' so as to prevail against the
operation of such sanctions.

The majority held that the targeting of homosexual males and not females
or heterosexuals was not discrimination contrary to the constitutional principle of equality. Having weighed the restrictions of the plaintiff's freedoms of
expression and association and his suffering because of the legislation, on the
one hand, against the Christian nature of the state, the immorality of the deliberate practice[51] of homosexuality, the damage that such practice causes to the
health of citizens, and the potential harm to the institution of marriage, on the
other, the Court felt confident that Norris could not succeed in his claims.

McCarthy and Henchy JJ both found the impugned legislation inconsistent
with the Constitution because, in their opinions, criminal sanctions are only
for immoral acts endangering the common good, which was not the case here.
However, it was noted, *per* Henchy J, that Norris stood apart from the average
victim of his orientation in that he chose not a vow of silence but rather the
'public espousal of the cause of the male homosexual'; such behaviour, he felt,
may be thought to be 'tinged with a degree of that affected braggadocio which
is said by some to distinguish a "gay" from a mere homosexual'.[52] McCarthy J
noted[53] that 'there have been many male homosexuals who were happily married an obvious example in Irish history is Oscar Wilde whose conviction was
under the 1885 Act'. A case of happily ever after? Not surprisingly, Norris, following in Dudgeon's footsteps, went to Strasbourg, in search not of sympathy[54]
but justice.

The ECHR considered that, in substance, the circumstances in the *Norris*
case were the same[55] as those which gave rise to *Dudgeon*, concerning as it did
identical legislation. In *Dudgeon*, the central issue was that the plaintiff 'either
respects the law and refrains from engaging—even in private and with consenting male partners—in prohibited sexual acts to which he is disposed by
reason of his homosexual tendencies, or commits such acts and thereby
becomes liable to criminal prosecution'. With respect to Norris, the 'very existence of this legislation continuously and directly affected his private life'.[56]

---

[51] Thereby introducing the defence of 'accidental practice' of homosexuality?
[52] *Supra* n. 50 (IR), at 70.   [53] *Ibid.*, 92.
[54] Henchy J (dissenting) referred to the applicant's 'fear of prosecution or of social obloquy'.
[55] Unlike Dudgeon, Norris was not the subject of any police investigation but this did not materially alter matters as the interference with respect for his private life was not dependent upon
such an investigation.
[56] Series A no. 45, 18, para. 41.

The Court thus found that the impugned legislation interfered with Norris's right to respect for his private life under Article 8,[57] first paragraph.

The ECHR, having accepted that the conditions 'in accordance with the law'[58] and 'legitimate aim'[59] were satisfied, considered whether the impugned legislation was 'necessary in a democratic society' for the aim pursued; the criteria—'whether the interference in question answers a pressing social need' and is 'proportionate' to the legitimate aim pursued. In the context of the protection of morals, the Court reiterated its previous case law for determining what is 'necessary in a democratic society', i.e. whether a 'pressing social need' respecting the principle of proportionality existed. The Court saw no reason not to apply this case law in the context of Article 8. The Court was adamant, even in relation to questions of morality, that a state cannot be afforded unfettered discretion; to allow otherwise, it reasoned, would run counter to the wording of Article 19.[60] The Court recalled that, as in *Dudgeon*, not only the nature of the aim of the restriction but also the nature of the activities involved affects the scope of the margin of appreciation. The present case concerned a most intimate aspect of private life. Therefore, particularly serious reasons had to be shown before interference on the part of public authorities could be legitimate for the purposes of Article 8(2). Faced with an absence of evidence which would 'point to the existence of factors justifying the retention of the impugned laws' and applying the above criteria, the ECHR held that, as regards Ireland, a 'pressing social need' mandating criminal sanction for such acts could not be shown. In relation to the issue of proportionality the 'detrimental effects' of the legislation on the private life of homosexuals far outweighed the justifications of morality adduced by the state. Thus, the criminalization of homosexual acts simply because the very idea caused offence without any 'pressing social need' could no longer be accepted.

One of the most recent decisions and, undoubtedly, one of the great illustrations of the recent advances made by homosexuals is that of *Lustig-Prean and Beckett* v. *UK*; *Smith and Grady* v. *UK*,[61] in which the ECHR was asked to consider the expulsion, following harsh investigation, of four homosexual members of the British Armed Forces in accordance with a Ministry of Defence policy. The Divisional Court and the Court of Appeal[62] rejected judicial review applications of their administrative discharge. Pleading, in

---

[57] '(1) Everyone has the right to respect for his private and family life, his home and his correspondence. (2) There shall be no interference by a public authority with the exercise of this right except such as is in accordance with the law and is necessary in a democratic society in the interests of national security, public safety or the economic well-being of the country, for the prevention of disorder or crime, for the protection of health or morals, or for the protection of the rights and freedoms of others.'

[58] Interference is derived from the very existence of the impugned legislation.

[59] The protection of morals.

[60] Whereby the ECHR must 'ensure the observance of the engagements undertaken by the High Contracting Parties'.

[61] *Smith and Grady* v. *United Kingdom* (2000) 29 EHRR 493 and *Lustig-Prean and Beckett* v. *United Kingdom* (2000) 29 EHRR 548.

[62] For an outline of these cases before the UK, courts see Skidmore, 'Sexuality and the UK Armed Forces' in Carver and Mottier (eds.), *supra* n. 7.

principal, violations of Articles 8, 14 and, secondarily, breaches of Articles 3, 10, and 13, the four former members of the British Armed Forces took the matter to Strasbourg.

The Court considered the investigations, the detailed interviews relating to the sexual orientation and practices of the applicants, to have been exceptionally intrusive and offensive for the four whose professional record was 'exemplary'.[63] It noted that the administrative discharges had a profound effect on the applicants' careers and prospects and considered the absolute and general character of the blanket policy, which admitted of no exception, to be striking. In relation to the Report of the Homosexual Policy Assessment Team (HPAT) on which the UK government placed great reliance, the Court found that the views expressed therein 'were founded solely upon the negative attitudes of heterosexual personnel towards those of homosexual orientation' and as the expression of a 'predisposed bias' on the part of the 'heterosexual majority' and as such was insufficient to justify the policy. In relation to the Divisional Court's acceptance of the HPAT[64] justification it has been said: 'it is clear that the more widely held a belief is, however erroneous and unsubstantiated it may be, the more the Ministry is entitled to take it into account in the decision-making process'[65]—the ECHR was not impressed. The ECHR emphasized the fact that the policy was 'not based on a particular moral standpoint and that the physical capability, courage, dependability and skills of homosexual personnel were not in question'. While the Court accepted, without concrete evidence, that 'certain difficulties could be anticipated with a change in policy', it suggested that a strict code of conduct and disciplinary rules could be produced to combat such difficulties. Interestingly, the ECHR declared itself unable to ignore 'widespread and consistently developing views or the legal changes in the domestic laws of Contracting States in favour of the admission of homosexuals into the armed forces of those States'.

In relation to Article 8(2), which provides for justification for interference, the ECHR accepted that the requirement 'in accordance with the law' was met and that the 'legitimate aim' criterion was fulfilled in the sense of 'the interests of national security' and 'the prevention of disorder'. Whether the policy was necessary in a democratic society could be answered in the affirmative only where a 'pressing social need' was being defended and being so in a proportionate manner. On the facts of the case, the Court underlined the link between the notion of 'necessity' and that of a 'democratic society', the hallmarks of the latter including 'pluralism, tolerance and broadmindedness'. While recognizing that it is for the national authorities to make the initial assessment of necessity the ECHR retained the power to determine whether

---

[63] As found by the Div. Ct.

[64] The Report collected views such as 'heterosexuality could be easily undermined if gays and lesbians were allowed to serve. [T]he very fact that a heterosexual has shared a room . . . with a homosexual leaves them open for accusation or suspicion.' Tony Banks MP asked: 'shall we allow racists and sexists to determine policy in Britain?': see Carver and Mottier (eds.), *supra* n. 7, at 53–4.

[65] Carver and Mottier (eds.), *supra* n. 7; it is noted that the Div. Ct. accepted the equal misery test.

reasons given for the interference are relevant and sufficient. The wide margin of appreciation afforded to Contracting States was, the Court deemed, qualified, especially where the restrictions concern 'a most intimate part of an individual's private life'; in such circumstances there must exist 'particularly serious reasons' before Article 8(2) may be successfully invoked. Assertions of a risk to operational effectiveness must be 'substantiated by specific examples'.

The continuation of investigations after admissions of homosexuality for (a) medical, security, and disciplinary reasons; and (b) in order to verify that the four were not simply trying to leave the armed forces, were, respectively, unjustified within the meaning of Article 8(2) and contrary to the express wish of the four to remain in the armed forces; their participation in the investigations was the result of the absence of any real alternative. Having considered in great depth the applicability of Article 8, the Court did not consider it necessary to determine whether there was discrimination under Article 14 in conjunction with Article 8.

In relation to a possible violation of Article 3[66] alone or in conjunction with Article 14, the Court did not exclude that treatment grounded upon a predisposed bias on the part of a 'heterosexual majority against a homosexual minority' as in the present case could, in principle, fall within the scope of Article 3. However, the distress and humiliation suffered did not reach the threshold of severity required by Article 3, alone or in conjunction with Article 14.[67] The Court refused to rule out that the silence imposed on the applicants as regards their sexual orientation, together with the consequent and constant need for 'vigilance, discretion and secrecy', could result particularly from the 'chilling effect' of the blanket ban. Moreover, if continued, such silence could constitute an interference under Article 10,[68] but as this plea was subsidiary to the principal issue it was not discussed.

The Court found a violation of Article 13 as the threshold at which the domestic courts could find the policy of the Ministry of Defence irrational had been placed so high that it effectively excluded any consideration by the domestic courts of the question whether the interference with the applicants' private lives had answered a 'pressing social need' or was proportionate to the national security and public order aims pursued by the Government. In brief, a victory for homosexuals, the UK Government had to accept the ruling and promise change.

In relation to marriage the ECHR has decided in *Rees*[69] that 'the right to marry guaranteed by Article 12[70] refers to "traditional marriage between persons of the opposite biological sex". This appears also from the wording of the

[66] 'No one shall be subjected to . . . degrading treatment or punishment'.
[67] Art. 14 reads: 'The enjoyment of the rights and freedoms set forth in this Convention shall be secured without discrimination on any ground such as sex . . . or other status'.
[68] Art. 10 (1): 'Everyone has the right to freedom of expression . . .'.
[69] *Rees*, Series A, No. 31, 17 Oct. 1986, 14.
[70] Men and women of marriageable age have the right to marry and to found a family, according to the national laws governing the exercise of this right.

Article which makes it clear that [it] is mainly concerned to protect marriage as the basis of the family.'[71] The Commission had made it clear in other decisions that the relationship between homosexual partners did not fall within the private and family life protections of the ECHR despite 'the modern evolution of attitudes towards homosexuality'.[72]

In more recent times, however, in the case of *Salgueiro da Silva Mouta* v. *Portugal*,[73] the Court has taken a different approach, a more liberal stance, to homosexual rights in the context of family life. Salgueiro, a Portuguese national, brought a case before the ECHR to contest the decision reached by the Lisbon Court of Appeal, which gave two reasons in its judgment for granting parental responsibility for his daughter to her mother, namely, the interest of the child and the fact that the applicant was homosexual and living with another man. The ECHR noted from the outset that, under the case law of the Convention, Article 8 applied to decisions concerning granting parental responsibility for a child to one of the parents on a divorce or separation.

In its decision the Lisbon Court of Appeal, finding no sufficient reasons for depriving the mother of parental responsibility, went on to consider the nature of the father's existence, though without pretending to reach any definitive conclusions: '[t]hat the father, who considers himself homosexual, wishes to live with another man is a reality we must accept. It is notorious that society has grown more and more tolerant as regards these situations . . . the child must live in . . . a traditional Portuguese family [and] it is unnecessary to examine whether or not homosexuality is an illness or a sexual orientation towards people of the same sex. Either way, it is an abnormality and children must not grow up in the shadow of abnormal situations.'

The ECHR considered that these passages 'were not simply clumsy or unfortunate, or mere *obiter dicta*; they suggested that the applicant's homosexuality had been decisive in the final decision' and, thus, amounted to a distinction dictated by factors relating to the applicant's sexual orientation that it was not permissible to draw under the Convention. That conclusion was supported by the fact that, when ruling on the applicant's contact rights, the Court of Appeal had discouraged the applicant from behaving during visits in a way that would make the child aware that he was living with another man 'as if they were spouses'. The Court reiterated that a difference of treatment is discriminatory within the meaning of Article 14 if such a difference has no objective and reasonable justification, i.e. that the treatment did not pursue a legitimate goal and where there was no proportionality between the means employed and the aim pursued.

While it admitted that the protection of health and the children were indeed legitimate goals the circumstances of which Salgueiro complained did not sat-

---

[71] Van Dijk, 'The Treatment of Homosexuals under the ECHR', in Waaldijk and Clapham (eds.), *Homosexuality: A European Community Issue* (London, Martinus Nijhoff, 1993).

[72] Jessurun d'Oliveria, 'Lesbians and Gays and the Freedom of Movement of Persons' in *ibid.*

[73] Case n. 33290/96 *Salgueiro da Silva Mouta* v. *Portugal* (21 Dec. 1999).

isfy the tests of legitimacy and proportionality; the means employed for the stated aims were not proportionate to the aims pursued. The Court therefore held that there had been a violation of Article 8 taken together with Article 14 and, as a consequence, it was unnecessary to rule on the allegation of a violation of Article 8 alone.

Thus far, great progress has been made by the Court. 'Widespread and consistently developing views' in relation to homosexuals have influenced the Court. As in South Africa, the hallmarks of a democratic society—pluralism, tolerance, and broadmindedness—have been given consideration. The possibility of relying on Articles 3, 10, and 13 has not been ruled out and, finally, the family rights of homosexuals have begun to be acknowledged. The ECJ is not, as yet, as eager to make such far-reaching references to rights.

B. THE EUROPEAN UNION—THE COURT OF JUSTICE'S INCONSISTENT APPROACH

The EU is being considered after the Council of Europe because, by virtue of Article 6(2) TEU, the EU is expected to respect the fundamental freedoms as they result from the Convention. The interpretations of the ECHR on the meaning of the Convention should thus represent very persuasive authority when the ECJ is considering fundamental rights issues. The economic roots of the Union have been very evident in its discrimination and rights provisions. The first explicit recognition of human rights came with the Maastricht Treaty in Article F (now Article 6) which declares that:

1. The Union is founded on the principles of liberty, democracy, respect for human rights and fundamental freedoms, and the rule of law . . .
2. The Union shall respect fundamental freedoms as guaranteed by the ECHR . . . and as they result from the constitutional traditions common to the Member States . . .
3. The Union shall respect the national identities of its Member States.

In considering the case law of the Community courts, attention will be focused primarily on the decisions of the court in *P*, *Grant* and *D*; the cases of *P* and *Grant* being indicative of the Court's incoherence in relation to minority rights and its illogical application of tests which seem to depend more on possible political and economic implications than the vindication of the rights of the individual. The fact that the Union started out as an economic entity not directly concerned with notions of citizenship will be readily noted when analysing the ECJ's attempts to come to terms with cases dealing specifically with issues concerning the rights of citizens and not merely the economic rights of individuals. *P* gave great hope to homosexuals in that their claims to equality seemed, *a priori*, far stronger than those of transsexuals, a group granted hardly a modicum of protection in many Member States. However, as shall be shown, *Grant* and *D* seem to head in the opposite direction. The distinction between 'sex' and 'gender' is important. Denys[74] makes it as follows:

[74] Denys, 'Homosexuality: a non-issue in Community law?' (1999) 24 *ELRev.* 419.

'whereas sex relates to the biological difference between men and women, gender relates to the sociological dimension of sex, to the traditional roles corresponding to either of the sexes'.[75] This distinction underlies the apparent incoherence of the ECJ.

In *P* v. *S and Cornwall County Council*,[76] P informed her employer that she intended to undergo gender reassignment to change her physical sex from male to female. Her employer decided to terminate her employment. P brought an action before the Truro Industrial Tribunal, which subsequently referred a number of questions to the ECJ concerning the application of the 1976 Directive to gender assignment. The UK Government propounded the 'equal misery' argument—if all transsexuals[77] are treated equally badly, then there is no discrimination. Advocate General Tesauro argued that P should win by reason of the notions of equality and fundamental personal rights.[78] The law cannot, he said, 'cut itself off from society as it actually is, and must not fail to adjust to it as quickly as possible. Otherwise, it risks imposing outdated views and taking a static role. In so far as the law seeks to regulate relations in society, it must, on the contrary, keep up with social change.'

The ECJ, holding that Article 5(1) of Directive 76/207[79] precluded the dismissal of a transsexual for a reason related to gender reassignment, referred to the principle of equal treatment for men and women, non-discrimination on the basis of sex and the principle of equality. It found that P had suffered unfavourable treatment 'by comparison with persons of the sex to which he or she was deemed to belong before undergoing reassignment surgery'. Barnard has remarked that '[i]f the ECJ is genuinely taking a step towards recognizing the moral dimension of rights then it could be argued that *P* v. *S* marks a move away from the perception of an individual's right to participate in the Community venture as a market citizen, *homo economicus*, towards their rights as Union citizens, a shift by the ECJ away from the culture of the market to the culture of the Union.'[80] Though a positive step forward, the Court did have recourse to notions of comparators; this, in itself, was not entirely consonant with the decision in *Dekker*[81] where the ECJ seemed to be moving away from the need for a comparator in every case of sexual discrimination.

The Court did recall that, in accordance with existing jurisprudence, 'the right not to be discriminated against on grounds of sex is one of the fundamental rights which the Court has a duty to ensure . . . the principle of equality . . . is one of the fundamental principles of EC law', concluding that to

---

[75] Denys, 'Homosexuality: a non-issue in Community law?' (1999) 24 *ELRev.* 419, at 424.

[76] Case C–13/94, *P* v. *S and Cornwall County Council* [1996] ECR I–2143.

[77] Male to female, female to male.

[78] Flynn, 'Case Note on P v. S and Cornwall County Council' (1997) 34 *CML Rev.* 367.

[79] '[M]en and women shall be guaranteed the same conditions [governing dismissal] without discrimination on grounds of sex': [1976] OJ L39/40.

[80] Barnard, 'P v. S Kite Flying or a New Constitutional Approach?' in Dashwood and O'Leary (eds.), *Principle of Equal Treatment in EC Law* (London, Sweet & Maxwell, 1997).

[81] Case C–177/88, *Dekker Stichting Vormingscentrum voor Jonge Volwassen* [1990] ECR I–3941; the ECJ held that discrimination based on pregnancy was direct discrimination based on sex incapable, due to the uniqueness of the condition, of comparison with any male condition.

tolerate such discrimination would be 'tantamount, as regards such a person, to a failure to respect the dignity and freedom to which he or she is entitled, and which the Court has a duty to safeguard'. Optimism, palpable following *P*, was quenched in Grant v. *SWT*[82] where travel concessions, not extended to unmarried partners of the same sex, were at issue. Grant alleged a breach of Article 119 EC; a reference was made to the ECJ to clarify the precise import of Community law. To the consternation of many, ignoring the Advocate General's 'modern interpretation' of discrimination based on sex, the *Toonen* report, and the interpretative potential of Article 119,[83] the ECJ concluded that 'refusal to supply travel concessions to same-sex partners of employees, where such concessions were provided for opposite-sex partners, whether married or unmarried, was not discrimination prohibited under Article 119'.

If in *P* the return of the 'comparator' was discernible, its presence in *Grant* was overpowering; the Court's reasoning is grafted onto this notion. Maybe, with the benefit of hindsight, *P* has proved to have been 'merely a temporary breach in the ringfence of the traditional notion as to the applicability of Community discrimination law'.[84] To whom should Grant and her female partner be compared before one may determine whether or not there has been discrimination? Counsel for Grant argued that a comparison with a male employee who has a female partner[85]—the latter would indeed receive travel concessions whereas Grant's partner did not—a clear case of discrimination?

On this occasion the UK Government's espousal of the equal misery approach was accepted by the ECJ: '[s]ince the condition imposed by the undertaking's regulations applies in the same way to male and female workers it cannot be regarded as constituting discrimination directly based on sex'. Sexual orientation is revealed as a sex-based characteristic; as Winemute comments,[86] 'distinctions based on sexual orientation necessarily involve distinctions based on the sexes of individuals. The comparator taken used by the Court should be consistent—*P* and *Grant*[87] are in conflict'. In choosing a comparator, if one is necessary, surely the one affording greatest protection should be favoured? In *Grant* the Court reached the conclusion that fundamental rights offered little protection to homosexuals; in effect, they were not deserving of equal treatment and respect in the Union. As Barnard[88] points out, the Court, in comparing Grant to a homosexual male, was 'taking into account gender "plus" considerations: gender plus sexuality' in that it took account not only of the sex of Grant but also that of her partner. But, to compare Grant to a

---

[82] Case C–249/96, *Grant* v. *SouthWest Trains* [1998] ECR I–621.

[83] Brems, 'Case note on Grant' [1998] *CJEL* 141 at 150.

[84] Connor, 'Community Discrimination Law: No Right to Equal Treatment in Employment in Respect of Same Sex Partner' (1998) 23 *ELR* 378 at 383.

[85] I.e. unmarried.

[86] Bell, 'Shifting Conceptions of Sexual Discrimination at the Court of Justice: From P v. S to Grant v. SWT' [1999] *ELJ* 63.

[87] Guiguet, 'Le droit communautaire et la reconnaissance des partenaires de même sexe' [1999] *CDE* 537 *passim*.

[88] Barnard, 'Some are More Equal than Others: the Decision of the Court of Justice in Grant v. South-West Trains' Vol. 1 [1998] *The Cambridge Yearbook of European Legal Studies* 147.

heterosexual male and thereby find discrimination in that his female spouse would receive benefits that Grant's female partner would not, is also problematic. Such a comparison requires, as Barnard notes,[89] two changes: biological sex and sexual orientation. The intractable question of the appropriate comparator remains. The ECJ has adopted a cost-effective equal misery comparator; Wintemute has another approach. In the following tables he explains the importance of carefully choosing the comparator before determining whether or not there has been discrimination:[90]

Table 1.   Discrimination based on sexual orientation

Victim	Reference person
Female lesbian	Female heterosexual
Gay Male	Heterosexual male

Table 2.   Discrimination based on sex (correct analysis)

Victim	Reference person
Female lesbian	Heterosexual male
Gay Male	Heterosexual female

Table 3.   Discrimination based on sex (traditional approach)

Victim	Reference person
Female lesbian	Gay male
Gay Male	Female lesbian
Traditional analysis—there is no discrimination based on sex	Correct analysis—the discrimination based on sex is clear

	Do we allow the choice of a same-sex partner?[91]	Do we allow the choice of partner of the opposite sex?[92]	Do we allow the choice of a female partner?[93]	Do we allow the choice of a male partner?[94]
Male	No	Yes	Yes	No
Female	No	Yes	No	Yes

---

[89] *The Cambridge Yearbook of European Legal Studies* 147, at 153.
[90] Wintemute, 'Libertés et droits fondamentaux des personnes gays, lesbiennes et bisexuelles en Europe', in Borrillo, *supra* n. 36, 194.
[91] Gay men and lesbian women compared.
[92] Heterosexual men and heterosexual women compared.
[93] Heterosexual men and female lesbians compared.
[94] Female heterosexuals and gay men compared.

In relation to *Grant*, Wintemute gives a compact table:[95]

Table 4.   Discrimination based on the choice of partner

	Cohabitant—choice of female partner	Cohabitant—choice of male partner
Male employee	Advantage granted	Advantage not granted
Female employee	Advantage not granted	Advantage granted

With this comparison between same-sex and opposite-sex couples the distinction, based on sexual orientation and not on sex, is shown. Instead of comparing the couples, one compares the treatment of men who choose a partner of a given sex with the treatment of women who choose a partner of the same given sex. Thus, it is clear, recourse to comparators may give any number of results depending on the outcome sought. Could it not be argued that the greater cause of justice would be served if equal advantage rather than equal misery resulted from a given test? Or does the equal misery approach ensure that those outside the club of normality are to remain there but, while outside, are to be treated equally *inter se*? Following this approach equality fast becomes a means of protecting normality. Normality, in turn, becomes a vicious circle wherein only those who define its parameters are included and where all others, arriving later on in the construction of normality, are simply powerless. Must one attempt to redefine the circle when new strata of society wish to join the club or must one tell those, long excluded, that the choice is simple: fit in as we do or else do not bother complaining that it is cold outside?

As Bell[96] points out, the Court in *Grant* failed to consider that the trend in developments is away from non-recognition, and in favour of equal treatment: legal recognition of same-sex partnerships or marriage is under discussion in nearly all European countries. It is also true that recognition of same-sex partners exists in Denmark (1989), Norway (1993), Sweden (1994), Iceland (1996), The Netherlands (1997), and France (1999),[97] Belgium (2000), The Netherlands (2001 civil marriage), Germany (2001) and Finland (2001). This recognition, with some specific exceptions, allows same-sex couples to enjoy the same rights, benefits, and obligations as opposite-sex couples. A brief glance at Canada, America, and South Africa would have, largely, confirmed this trend. While ignoring the very weak ECHR case law or Member States' protection for transsexuals in the *P* case, the ECJ nonetheless placed great weight on the ECHR's (formerly) restrictive case law in relation to homosexual family

---

[95] Borrillo, *supra* n. 36.   [96] Bell, *supra* n. 86.
[97] For an excellent survey of homosexual partership laws see IGLA World Legal Survey: http://www.ilga.org.

rights and non-discrimination protection in *Grant*. The greater protection accorded by the ECJ to transsexuals is, therefore, 'curious'. But why this dichotomy?

The answer may be found in the revelation by the Advocate General that transsexuals constitute 'a fairly well-defined and identifiable group' whereas the number of homosexuals in the EC of twelve Member States could number up to 35 million.[98] Though, in principle, the mere statistics should not affect the findings of law, it is undoubtedly true that numbers are likely to be a relevant factor in the Court's analysis. The underlying policy decisions of the Court seem to have focused on the potential future impact of a decision in favour of Grant as opposed to considering her cause on its own merits—disadvantage suffered by reason of sexual orientation. The ECJ, in *Grant*, was unimpressed with the progressive approach of the Human Rights Committee which, it noted, is not a judicial institution and which has only stated 'without giving specific reasons [that] in its view the reference to "sex" in Articles 2, paragraph 1,[99] and 26[100] is to be taken as including sexual orientation'.[101]

In the recent case of *Kreil*[102] the ECJ highlighted its continued assurance of equality for women and reiterated the fundamental nature of the equal treatment principle.[103] In brief, the ECJ acknowledges the fundamental nature of human rights when it does not endanger the gender line; this is confirmed by the CFI in *D* v. *Council*.[104] Here the CFI, in following the Commission's approach, considered the Court was under no duty to refer to the laws of the Member States in interpreting and applying the Staff Regulations for Officials, in particular as regards the consequences for a person living with a partner of the

[98] Tatchell, *Europe in the Pink, Lesbian and Gay Equality in the New Europe* (Tatchell Gay Men's Press, 1992) at 79, where he estimates that of the 820 million inhabitants of Europe, 80m are predominantly or exclusively gay, with a further 120m estimated to be bisexual for all or part of their lives. Others would be less generous in their estimates: it is recognized that accurate statistics on the prevalence of homosexuality in society are difficult to obtain. The Kinsey Report (1957) estimated that approximately 10 per cent of the (US) population is predominantly homosexual; others would suggest that homosexuals might occupy only 1 per cent of the population; see, for example, Seidman and Rieder, 'A Review of Sexual Behaviour in the United States', *American Journal of Psychiatry*, Vol. 151, March 1994, p. 339. In any event, precise figures are not a prerequisite to the claims of equality advanced by homosexuals since principles of equality should apply, by definition, to everyone and not just a group occupying a given minimum percentage of the population.

[99] 'Each State Party to the present Covenant undertakes to respect and to ensure to all individuals within its territory and subject to its jurisdiction the rights recognized in the present Covenant, without distinction of any kind, such as . . . sex, . . . or other status'.

[100] 'All persons are equal before the law and are entitled without any discrimination to the equal protection of the law. In this respect, the law shall prohibit any discrimination and guarantee to all persons equal and effective protection against discrimination on any ground such as . . . sex . . . or other status'.

[101] *Toonen* v. *Australia*, Communication No. 488/1992, UN Doc CCPR/C/50/D/488/1992 (1994). Toonen claimed to have been a victim of violations by Australia of the ICCPR.

[102] Case C–285/98, *Kreil* v. *Germany* [2000] ECR I–69 (concerning the exclusion of women from certain sections of the army).

[103] Cf Case C–273/97, *Sirdar* v. *The Army Board and Secretary of State for Defence*, [1999] ECR I–7403 where the Court ruled, *inter alia*, that it may be permissible to bar women from the Army in specific circumstances, in the case of special fighting units such as the Royal Marines.

[104] Case T–264/97. Judgment of 28 January 1999.

same sex. D argued that the Council was under a legal obligation to recognize his registered partnership, this the Court did not do because the notion of marriage in the Staff Regulations, open to autonomous interpretation (i.e. no need to refer to Member States' laws), was confined to its traditional meaning. The Court referred to the ECHR which limits Article 12 to 'traditional marriages between two persons of the opposite biological sex'. Thus, it follows, the Court reasoned, that, 'in the present state of law in the EC, stable relationships between two persons of the same sex are not to be assimilated to relationships between married persons'.

The Court referred to *Grant* to confirm that, 'despite the recent evolution of attitudes towards homosexuality, stable homosexual relationships' could not fall within 'family life' as traditionally understood. *Grant* was to provide further inspiration for the Court in relation to the plea by D that there was direct discrimination based on sex; the equal misery test was applied—no discrimination was found. Therefore, the Council was not required to extend the household allowance to an official living with a partner of the same sex under a status recognized by Swedish law.[105] The logic of almost automatically referring to *Grant* is not wholly obvious. Contrary to Grant who was legally single and without specific obligations towards her partner, D is, under Swedish law, obliged to fulfil duties towards his partner akin to those expected of one spouse towards the other. Therefore, to group Grant and D together simply because of their orientation without reference to the differences between the two cases, was unfortunate and, partly at least, responsible for the disappointing decision.

Scappucci[106] has exposed the Court's decision in *D* to the glaring light of reason. First, she notes that the CFI made it clear that modifications to the Staff Regulations[107] which specifically refer to discrimination by reason of sexual orientation could not be used by D. In effect, the Court decided to consider the notion of 'marriage' and 'spouses' in the Staff Regulations as opposed to considering D's case from the civil status angle. Referring to its previous case law, the Court concluded that notions such as 'marriage' and 'spouses' could not be applied to a couple of the same sex. D argued that his being considered as 'not married' violated the 'uniqueness and immutability of his civil status'. This attempt to use marriage as the barometer by which to judge 'registered partnership' is inappropriate. Instead, the Court should have treated the new notion of 'registered partnership' which extends to same-sex couples, in a 'totally new'[108] manner. Scappucci has rightly criticized the Court's restrictive analysis as it put, she argues, the whole case in a 'wrong perspective'. The fact that one already engaged in a registered partnership in Sweden cannot 'marry' someone else is an important fact, albeit one overlooked by the Court. It should be noted that the CFI decision was appealed to the ECJ by both D, and the Swedish government. The Court's decision, handed down on 31 May 2001,

---

[105] *Grant, supra* n. 82, points 34 and 35 considered.
[106] Scappucci, 'Court of First Instance Refuses to Recognize Swedish "Registered Partnership" Rights and Duties' 6 *European Public Law* 355.
[107] [1998] OJ L113/44.   [108] Scappucci, *supra* n. 106 at 362.

rejected all arguments advanced in favour of allowing D to have his registered partnership under Swedish law recognized for the purposes of staff regulations.[109]

In relation to the freedom of movement guaranteed to all citizens of the EU, do D and similarly placed individuals not find that this freedom carries with it an important qualification: civil status is liable to change as one moves outside one's home state? Member States still retain the authority to define civil status for their citizens—for example, the conditions laid down for 'traditional' marriage and divorce vary from state to state—there is no Community norm and, as such, an individual should not need to make reference to EC law to confirm his or her civil status. For D to have been declared 'unmarried', as he was by the Council in refusing his application for household entitlements for his partner, is clearly at odds with the reality of D's civil status in Sweden.

Why does *P* v. *S* go in one direction while *Grant* and *D* head in another? Apart from the economic and numerical arguments expounded above, Denys[110] explains that whereas changing one's sex does not challenge as such the 'stereotypical depictions of male and female behaviour/conduct' the arguments of *Grant* and *D* were calling into question the ordained roles of men and women in society; this the Court could simply not fathom. Of course, one cannot argue that transsexuals will not encounter difficulties. As Wintemute puts it, '[t]ranssexual[s] . . . gay[s] . . . and men in skirts, all experience direct sex discrimination because they challenge particular aspects of traditional social sex roles. It is only the degree of their departure from those roles, and the (non-transsexual, heterosexual, dress-code-conforming) majority's acceptance of the aspects of those roles they challenge, that distinguishes them from the female bricklayer and the male secretary.'[111] Others contend that the disappointment with the post-*P* decisions is due to the 'heightened expectations'[112] that it created, the Court being faced with the difficulty of reconciling its protection of rights with the real limitation of the legislative texts on which its decisions must be based. As Harrison[113] points out, 'the Court will avoid making far-reaching decisions which challenge important institutions such as marriage and the family'. But the obvious retort is that equality between men and women also has implications for traditional notions of the family.

Of course, abandoning the notion of the comparator is a possibility; in relation to pregnancy[114] (heterosexual) 'man being the measure of all things' is no longer in the ascendant. The rigid circle has been broken but can it be further

---

[109] Joined Cases C–122/99P *D* v. *Council* and C–125/99P *Kingdom of Sweden* v. *Council* 31 May 2001.

[110] *Supra* n. 74 at 424.

[111] Wintemute, 'New Kinds of Direct Sex Discrimination' (1997) 60 *MLR* 334, at 359.

[112] Mancini and O'Leary, 'The New Frontiers of Sex Equality Law in the EU' (1991) 16 *ELRev.* 331 at 353.

[113] Harrison, 'Sexual Orientation Discrimination', in Hervey and O'Keeffe (eds.), *Sex Equality Law in the European Union* (London, Wiley & Sons, 1996) at 280.

[114] Case C–177/88, *Dekker, supra* n. 81.

dismantled? Who or what should change in society—the circle or the homosexual not quite therein? It is clear from the case law that the Community Courts are unwilling to cross the gender line—this may perhaps explain the success of P, a transsexual, and the failure of both Grant and D—homosexuals trying to have their unorthodox lifestyles recognized. Considerations of pluralism and tolerance, which formed a main part the case law in Part II, are lacking before the ECJ—Grant and D would have won in most of the countries and states there considered. The ECHR is more in tune with developments—a conflict for the Citizens of Europe?[115]

While it can be convincingly argued that D was the victim of an unduly restrictive approach taken by the Community Courts for the reasons highlighted above, the Community Courts have become, in recent times, more adamant that the Treaty is to be followed to the letter. As an illustrative example of this new wave, the recent case of *Germany* v. *European Parliament ('tobacco advertising')*[116] deserves mention. In essence, Germany argued, *inter alia*, that incorrect legal bases for Directive 98/43/EC were relied upon. The ECJ made it clear, in paragraph 83, that the provisions of the Treaty used as legal bases for the Directive (Articles 110a(1), 3(c), 7(a)) are 'intended to improve the conditions for the establishment and functioning of the internal market. To construe [Article 100a(1)] as meaning that it vests in the Community legislature a general power to regulate the internal market would not only be contrary to the express wording of the provisions cited above but would also be incompatible with the principle embodied in Article 3b of the EC Treaty (now Article 5 EC) that the powers of the Community are limited to those specifically conferred on it.' It is in the context of this trend that the need to boost the legal bases on which homosexuals can ensure that they do not meet with discrimination by reason of their sexual orientation are so important.

C.   EUROPE—POLITICAL PROGRESS, CHARTERS AND PROTOCOLS

In recent times, advances[117] have been achieved and, as a consequence, a more legally secure future for homosexuals is foreseeable though, of course, not necessarily inevitable. In 1994, the *Roth Report* on equal rights for homosexuals and lesbians in the EC was published. In particular, it referred to anti-discrimination measures in employment and social matters (such as adoption)—the proposals met with sufficient opposition to reduce them to a call on the Commission to propose a recommendation to the Council. Since

[115] Canor, 'Primus inter pares. Who is the Ultimate Guardian of Fundamental Rights in Europe', (2000) 25 *ELRev.* 3.

[116] Case C–379/98, judgment handed down on 5 Oct. 2000.

[117] See Wintemute, *supra* n. 20, *passim*. Also, at a national level, it should be noted, for example, that the UK Government is now reacting to the Lustig-Prean and Smith decisions of the ECHR and still hopes to repeal section 28. Also, the possibility of same-sex couples adopting has been mooted. In September 1935 in Germany, a harsher, amended version of paragraph 175 (originally enacted in 1871), came into effect, punishing a broad range of 'lewd and lascivious' behaviour between men. On 8 December 2000, the German Parliament apologized for the 'harm done to homosexual citizens up to 1969 in their human dignity . . .' because of paragraph 175.

then, the rights of homosexuals have received much consideration. At its meeting of 27–28 July 1999, the Committee of Ministers of the Council of Europe issued the text of an optional Draft Protocol No. 12 to the ECHR which aimed to supplement the existing non-discrimination Article 14, which applies only to discrimination in relation to other Convention rights, by creating an independent right to be free from discrimination,[118] the list of grounds in Article 1 of the Protocol being identical to that in Article 14 ECHR.

On 26 January 2000 the Parliamentary Assembly adopted its Opinion No. 216 (2000) on the Draft Protocol[119] in which the Assembly recommended, *inter alia*, that discrimination on the grounds of 'sexual orientation' should be added to the Protocol; it constituting, declared Mr Jurgens, a most 'insidious and obnoxious' form of discrimination. He also considered that 'lesbians and gay men are still victims of severe discrimination in some . . . European countries and only express recognition of sexual orientation could protect them'.[120] Several months later, however, such efforts were reduced to nought. In Rome, on 4 November 2000, Protocol No. 12 to the ECHR was opened for signature by the European Human Rights Ministers.[121] Efforts to include an express reference to sexual orientation failed because, as noted in the Explanatory Report,[122] inclusion of such was 'considered unnecessary from a legal point of view since the list of non-discrimination grounds is not exhaustive, and because inclusion of any particular additional ground might give rise to unwarranted *a contrario* interpretations as regards discrimination based on grounds not so included.' Express reference was made to the ECHR's decisions such as *Salgueiro da Silva* in which the Court found that sexual orientation did fall within the ambit of Article 14.

Also, in January 2000, *The EU against discrimination compendium*, in which preparatory measures aimed at combating and preventing discrimination in accordance with Article 13 EC were detailed, was published.[123] In February 2000, the Commission held a conference on combating racism at the European level with the participation of Member States, the European Parliament, civil society, and others, in which the use of Article 13 EC to combat all forms of discrimination provided for therein was discussed.[124] In March 2000, the European Parliament[125] adopted its report and resolution on the respect for human rights in the EU in 1998–99,[126] wherein it called for the granting of equal rights to non-married couples, including same-sex couples, as currently existing for married couples; it also condemned the continuing social and legal discrimination of gays and lesbians. On 24–25 March 2000 a special meeting of the Council of Ministers was organized in Portugal to consider the Commission's

---

[118] http://www.coe.fr/cm/dec/1999/677bis/42.htm.
[119] http://stars.coe.fr/ta00/eopi216.htm.
[120] http://stars.coe.fr/verbatim/200001/e/0001261500e.htm.
[121] Press Service of the ECHR. It has been signed by 25 states (including 10 EU Member States).
[122] ECHR Explanatory Report on Protocol No. 12, point 20.
[123] http://europa.eu.int/comm/dg05/fundamri/docs/com016_en.pdf.
[124] 'Politicians and civil society send out a strong message against all forms of discrimination': see http://europa.eu.int/comm/dg05/fundamri/news/discrimination_en.htm.
[125] http://inet.uni2.dk/~steff/news.htm.
[126] EP document A5–0050/2000.

anti-discrimination package.

In the context of Treaty developments, Amsterdam has brought with it, *inter alia*, the very promising anti-discrimination Article, Article 13, which states: '[w]ithout prejudice to the other provisions of this Treaty and within the limits of the powers conferred by it upon the Community, the Council, acting unanimously on a proposal from the Commission and after consulting the European Parliament, may take appropriate action to combat discrimination based on sex... or sexual orientation'. It was drafted with the aim of furthering the human side of the EU. However, it 'stands out as conspicuously and deliberately neutered, lacking any express statement of principle which could be seen as implicitly addressing an obligation to Member States'.[127] Flynn goes on to refer to the subordinate character of Article 13 in relation to other Articles such as Article 12, which reads 'without prejudice to any special provisions'. Also, he criticizes the absence of provisions allowing for positive discrimination in favour of historically disfavoured groups[128] and its silence on the issue of indirect discrimination. Moreover, the use of its empowering measures is in no way mandatory.

In the context of EU citizenship it has been asked:[129] 'to what extent are lesbian and gay people European citizens in the real sense of the term? To what extent, in other terms, are they not, from various standpoints, still second-class citizens?' A sense of belonging to a Union is conceptually problematic for those frustrated with their continued alienation resulting from their second-class status; can the Union afford to ostracize a sizeable minority of its citizens? One could wonder whether any of these measures proposed above, few of which are concrete, will actually assure equality for homosexuals. Regard should be had to the willingness of the various non-European jurisdictions considered and the potential for the ECJ[130] to reanalyse the arbitrary function served by the comparator in its non-discrimination analysis. A reason for judicial restraint could be the 'need for prudence in asserting even a correct principle against a democratic process not ready for it'.[131]

In this context it is apt to consider the recent adoption of the Charter of Fundamental Rights of the European Union.[132] In the Presidency Conclusions following the Nice European Council meeting,[133] the European Council welcomed the joint proclamation, by the Council, the European Parliament, and the Commission of the Charter. In the Charter, non-discrimination by reason of sexual orientation is specifically mentioned in Article 21. Article 21(1) reads: '[a]ny discrimination based on any ground such as sex, race, colour, ethnic or

---

[127] Flynn, 'The Implications of Article 13 EC—after Amsterdam, Will Some Forms of Discrimination be More Equal than Others?' (1999) 36 *CMLRev.* 1127 at 1133.

[128] As in South Africa.

[129] Tanca, 'European Citizenship and the Rights of Lesbians and Gay Men', in Waaldijk and Clapham (eds.), *supra* n. 71.

[130] Harrison, *supra* n. 113 at 280: ' it would be naïve for advocates of the gay cause not to accept that the Court will be influenced by attitudes to homosexuality within the Member States, by the political climate in the other Community institutions'.

[131] Sunstein, 'Leaving Things Undecided' (1996) 109 *Harvard Law Review* 6 at 97.

[132] 2000/C 364/01.　　　　　　　　　　　　[133] 7, 8, 9 Dec. 2000.

social origin, genetic features, language, religion or belief, political or any other opinion, membership of a national minority, property, birth, disability, age or sexual orientation shall be prohibited'. In accordance with the Cologne Conclusions,[134] the precise force of the Charter is as yet undefined: will it remain a solemn declaration of the Member States or will it be incorporated into the Treaties? Time will tell.

This inclusion of sexual orientation could pave the way for the ECJ to head down the path leading to Canadian- or Vermont-like decisions requiring the legislature to act to protect same-sex couples.

IV. Conclusion

The sincere commitment of all branches of Canadian government to respect homosexuals trying to live ordinary lives with the benediction of the state and, hopefully, in time, all spectra of society should serve as an inspiration to other countries while the judicial story in America, with the Defense of Marriage Act, highlights the limits that may be put on judicial advances considered too liberal. The South African constitution was drafted with the willingness to learn from other legal systems' experiences. The insertion of a non-discrimination clause on the basis of sexual orientation was the crystallization of the progressive approach and thus homosexuals in South Africa have a far more direct and automatic right to justice than elsewhere. In relation to non-discrimination the focus is on whether or not there was a difference of treatment, an affront to dignity.

While the ECJ is still locked in the comparator dilemma, so well expounded by Wintemute, the societal and financial implications are given heavy, albeit unspoken, consideration, revealing the latent fears of Luxembourg to venture too far down the federalist path by forcing reform from above. There are moves afoot in the EU and the Council of Europe to create substantial equality for minorities. Bamforth considers equality as the least problematic means of ensuring legal protection of gays and lesbians even if this notion 'often institutionalises a partial (heterocentric) view of the world as the moral norm'.[135]

It is important to consider why discrimination cases ever come before the courts; why national governments have not seen fit to interpret equality in its fullest sense and thereby allow for a government-led change of public opinion. It is, alas, common for recalcitrant governments, particularly in Europe, to leave contentious reform to the 'least dangerous branch' preferably from a foreign tree—hence talk of 'Europe' forcing change. The courts have helped to move the debate forward, but they can only modify the law and change soci-

---

[134] Conclusions of the Presidency of the Cologne European Council, 3 and 4 June 1999, Annex IV. The question of integration of the Charter into the Treaties is now to be considered, given that the Charter has been solemnly proclaimed.

[135] Bamforth, *Sexuality, Morals and Justice: A Theory of Lesbian and Gay Rights Law* (1997) reviewed by Moran (2000) *MLR* 137.

etal opinion to a certain point; society must also contribute to this process.

While it is 'notorious' that society has grown more and more tolerant it has far to travel before it reaches equality for homosexuals, a group long condemned to social obloquy. As shown, the court and, to a lesser extent, the legislature have tried to move society down this path of tolerance; they have tried to question the notion of normality or, more precisely, abnormality with the aim of according respect and dignity to those who choose to live in a manner considered not to be consonant with views of the 'moral majoritarian'. One could ask whether the abnormality lies in the fact of belonging to a minority group, fighting for equality, or in the firmly held conviction that a social majority holds the monopoly of normality by the very force of its numbers and that the numerically inferior group should really fall into line or lose the rights of equality. Wherein lies the abnormality?

The Defeat of the European Tobacco Advertising Directive: A Blow for Health

DEVIKA KHANNA*

I. Introduction

On 5 October 2000, the European Court of Justice decided to annul the Tobacco Advertising Directive.[1] In so doing, it sent out a clear message that the Community is not legally competent to adopt harmonizing regulatory measures which are primarily health-oriented, even where there is clearly the political will on the part of a majority of Member States to do so. This legal and political triumph for Germany, and a number of UK-based tobacco companies who raised the challenge, marked a significant stage in a ten-year struggle by health protagonists to ban tobacco advertising in Europe. From 1989 when the original proposal for such a Directive was made, to 1998 when the Common Position was finally adopted, the ban was made progressively more and more comprehensive.

This article examines many of the interesting points raised by the saga, focusing in particular on the role of interest groups in promoting and opposing the Directive. By analysing the industrial forces behind much of the lobbying against the measure, as well as the input from pro-health organizations, mainly non-governmental groups, it explores the various channels of access of these groups, both public and private, to the EU law- and policy-making process.

Focusing next on the subject matter of this controversy, and the successful judicial challenge to the Directive, the article looks at the reasons for the downfall of this particular European health initiative, before moving on to consider possible ways forward for the EU to adopt legitimate regulatory measures in the field of health.

It will be seen that as well as influencing the debate surrounding the adoption and downfall of this Directive, the choices made by the various parties involved reflect a wider tension, abundantly evident in the field of health, between respecting the constitutional limits of the Community and finding workable solutions to the challenges of the day.

* This paper is based on research carried out at the European University Institute, Florence. I would like to thank Professor de Búrca for her inspiration and support.

[1] Directive 98/43/EC on the approximation of the laws, regulations and administrative provisions of the Member States relating to the advertising and sponsorship of tobacco products [1998] OJ L213/00.

II. Choose a Measure

Directive 98/43/EC owes its origin to a 1984 Communication by the Commission to the Council, namely the 'Cooperation at Community level on Health Related Problems'. Within the framework of the 'Europe Against Cancer' programme,[2] initiated in 1989, the Council made a resolution calling for an examination of ways in which tobacco use might be reduced, suggesting rules on advertising and sponsorship.

The original proposal for such a Directive was made in 1989.[3] It was fairly modest in its aims and scope in that it prescribed only partial harmonization, and was mainly concerned with restricting the advertising of tobacco products in publications intended for under 18-year-olds. Following a suggestion in Council debate that a total ban would be easier to implement, the draft was amended in 1990,[4] 1991,[5] and 1992.[6] This was despite an opinion[7] written for the European Parliament (EP) suggesting that a comprehensive ban would be *ultra vires*. The wider 1992 version sought to prohibit all direct advertising with the exception of that in special tobacco sales outlets, as well as indirect advertising, i.e. the advertising of non-tobacco products using a tobacco brand name (for example, Davidoff perfumes, Camel boots, Marlboro clothing). The modified proposal was also extended to cover the free distribution of tobacco products. Perhaps unsurprisingly, the draft provoked strong reactions. The Legal Service to the Council advised that the Directive could not be adopted on the basis of Article 100a (Article 95 EC)[8] or on any other Treaty provision. The opinion of the Economic and Social Committee (ESC), given a few months after the publication of the 1992 draft, similarly advised that it should be withdrawn. It gave two reasons for this opinion: that voluntary codes would be more in keeping with the tradition, culture, and practice of the tobacco industry, and that the draft did not respect the very recently adopted principle of subsidiarity. Those voting against the opinion of the ESC included representatives from the Consumers Interest Group, which felt that the Commission's proposal should have been endorsed, bearing in mind the seriousness of the health risks associated with smoking. Criticizing the views of the majority, it warned: '[d]oubts should not be cast over health protection and particularly the fight against cancer . . . to serve the specific interests of certain industrialists, manufacturers and dealers or advertising circles and media'.

---

[2] [1986] OJ C184/19

[3] COM(89)163 final/2—SYN 194, 18 Apr. 1989, Proposal for a Council Directive on the advertising of tobacco products in the press and by means of bills and posters.

[4] COM(90)147 final—SYN 194, 19 Apr. 1990, Amended Proposal for a Council Directive on the authorised advertising of tobacco products in the press and by means of bills and posters.

[5] COM(91)0111–C3–0268/91—SYN 194, 11 Feb. 1992, Amended proposal for a Council Directive on advertising for tobacco products.

[6] COM(92)196 final—SYN 194, 30 Apr. 1992, Amended proposal for a Council Directive.

[7] [1992] OJ C67/35.

[8] New Treaty numberings are in brackets.

This shows an express recognition of the clash of interests, apparently prevalent also within the EU committee structure. The result of this clash was the stalling of the proposal to ban tobacco advertising, such that it was not until June 1998 that the Common Position was finally adopted.[9]

All Member States voted in favour of the Directive apart from Austria and Germany, which voted against it, and Denmark and Spain, which abstained. The scope of this final version was even more extensive than the 1992 draft since it also covered sponsorship, yet most of references to the protection of health found in the recitals to the 1992 version were no longer included.

It is interesting to note that despite mounting pressure during this period of promulgation, subsequent drafts of the Directive were made progressively more and more radical. This could be attributed to the aforementioned opinion of the Council that a more inclusive ban would be more effective, or at least more difficult to subvert. Alternatively, it could speak for the scale of activity of the anti-tobacco lobby and/or a growing awareness of the devastating effects of tobacco use.

Directive 98/43/EC, as adopted jointly by the EP and Council following the co-decision procedure, was based on Articles 57(2) (Article 47 EC) and 66 (Article 55 EC), and Article 100a (Article 95 EC). Its aims, as stated, were to harmonize fully the rules on tobacco advertising in view of the fact that partial harmonization would not resolve the problems arising from the divergences in national legislation, and would not therefore guarantee the unhindered operation of the internal market, taking as a base a high level of public health protection.

The first recital to the Directive noted that differences exist between national laws on the advertising and sponsorship of tobacco products. Because such advertising and sponsorship transcend national borders, barriers to the movement of the products which serve as the media for such activities, and the exercise of freedom to provide services in the area, as well as distortions to competition, are likely to arise, thereby impeding the functioning of the internal market.

The second recital introduced the possibility for Member States to take action to guarantee the protection of health of individuals.

Article 3(1) of the Directive sought to prohibit all forms of advertising and sponsorship of tobacco products and Article 3(4) banned any free distribution of such products. Communications between professionals in the tobacco trade, advertising in sales outlets or in publications published and printed in non-member countries, and not principally intended for the Community market, were excluded from the scope of the Directive under Article 3(5).

Article 3(2) dealt with so-called diversification products. The Directive prohibited the use of the same names for tobacco products and for other products and services as from 30 July 1998. Brand names already used in good faith prior

---

[9] Lesny, 'Tobacco Proves Addictive: The EC's Stalled Proposal to Ban Tobacco Advertising', (1993) 26 *Vanderbilt Journal of International Law*, 149–78.

to the entry into force of the Directive were to be distinguished from their use for tobacco products.

Article 5 of the Directive permitted Member States to lay down stricter requirements in the name of public health protection.

Article 6(3) covered the deadline for implementation. This was generally to be no later than three years after the entry into force of the Directive (Article 6(1)). However certain periods of delay were available. These were one year in respect of the press, two years in respect of sponsorship, and until 1 October 2006 for existing sponsorship of events or activities organized at world level provided the sums devoted to the latter were decreased in the interim period. The latter clause was included primarily to appease the Formula One lobby, since motor racing relies heavily on sponsorship from tobacco companies.

II. Choose a Channel

A. INTEREST REPRESENTATION IN THE EU

Prior to considering the specific interest groups lobbying for and against this measure, it is necessary to examine the various channels of access to the EU law- and policy-making process available to them. As Keith Middlemas notes,[10] '[n]othing in the EU is as monolithic as it seems, no choice or decision is free from the competition between different players at different orders at every stage and level'. Indeed, within the EU, interest organization has been viewed from a variety of perspectives including the increasing prominence of the individual firm,[11] direct firm organizations now accounting for one third of all Euro-business groups,[12] weak Euro-groups,[13] direct membership associations,[14] transnational pluralism,[15] and ad-hoc coalitions which form over specific issues.[16]

In order to assess the effectiveness of the various interest groups operating in various forms, in various ways, and at various levels, it is useful to examine the stages at which influence may be brought to bear.

[10] Middlemas, *Orchestrating Europe: The Informal Politics of the European Union 1973–1995* (Fontana, London, 1994).

[11] Coen, *The Large Firm as a Political Actor in the European Union. An Empirical Study of the Behaviour and Logic* (European Union Institute, Florence, 1996).

[12] Cowles, 'Transcending Business Representation: The Mobilisation of Big Business in the 1980s', presented at the Annual Meeting of the American Political Science Association, Washington, DC, 1993.

[13] McLaughlin, Jordan, and Maloney, 'Corporate Lobbying in the EC', (1993) 31 *Journal of Common Market Studies* 191–212.

[14] Greenwood, *Representing Interests in the European Union* (Macmillan, London, 1997). See also Greenwood and Webster, 'Are Business Associations Governable?', European Integration online papers (2000), Vol. 4, No.3. http://www.eiop.or.at/eiop/texte/2000–003a.htm.

[15] Streeck and Schmitter, 'From National Corporatism to Transnational Pluralism: Organised Interests in the Single European Market', (1991) 19 *Politics and Society* 133–64.

[16] Pijenburg, 'EU lobbying by ad hoc Coalitions: an Explanatory Case Study' (1989) 5 *Journal of European Public Policy*, 303–21.

There may be seen to be three key stages in the shaping of European law and policy: the policy development stage, the policy decision stage, and the policy implementation stage.[17] Each is marked by the simultaneous work of several bodies and institutions, so that interest groups need to be well organized to achieve their goals. As Greenwood notes, participating in European affairs therefore involves addressing subnational, Member State, and supranational tiers of authority. There are various points of access to EU policy- and decision-making and the legislative process is generally very long, on average between twelve and fifteen months, though almost ten years in the case of Directive 98/43/EC. At the first stage, the Commission develops a proposal for a piece of legislation, which it then addresses to the Council of Ministers. In order to increase the likelihood of the Council approving a proposal, the Commission works with a range of advisory committees to ensure that its views are fully informed. It is however normally up to the Commission to decide whether advice is needed and, if so, which forum it will use. This discretionary power, coupled with the fact that the Commission alone has the right of legislative initiative, makes it the foremost institutional target for interest representation at European level. Furthermore, research suggests that more influence can be brought to bear at the early stages of the policy-making process. It is generally considered that the second most important institutional target is the European Parliament because of its ability to amend proposed legislation. On the other hand, it is considered more difficult to shape a policy outcome via the Council of Ministers, since issues have already been shaped by this stage of policy development. However the exact balance of power and importance attached to lobbying the EP and Council will vary depending on the particular legislative procedure prescribed.

As mentioned above, the legal basis of the Tobacco Advertising Directive, then Article 100a (Article 95 EC), prescribed the co-decision procedure. Since this procedure gives the EP an effective veto, it raised its importance as an institutional target for lobbyists. Analysis of the impact of such new legislative procedures indicates how the role of the EP has been transformed since the Single European Act. As a result, the EP has come to regard itself as the legitimate representative of the European people, and in this capacity it has been eager to be involved in issues which attract a lot of public attention. Indeed as Kohler-Koch[18] points out, the EP depends on the external support of the European public to strengthen its own role *vis-à-vis* the other Community organs. This has led some commentators to claim that the most effective way to lobby is 'you don't lobby the EP—you lobby the Commission and the Council is via the Parliament'. The structural openness of the EP is in part due to the fact that MEPs work under severe time restraints. As well as having to

---

[17] Pedler and Schaefer, *Shaping European Law and Policy. The Role of Committees and Comitology in the Political Process* (European Institute of Public Administration, Maastricht, 1996), 169–210.
[18] Kohler-Koch, 'Organized Interests in the EC and the European Parliament', European Integration online papers (1997), Vol. 1, No. 9 http://eiop.or.at/eiop/texte/1997–009a.htm.

travel between Brussels, Strasbourg, and their home country, MEPs are not well staffed and lack adequate bureaucratic back-up. Middlemas, noting that MEPs are habitually eager to be involved in issues which makes their voices heard, confirms that since they lack the necessary support structure, they may be prepared to accept the well documented and fully prepared cases offered by lobbyists. One such Brussels lobbyist quoted in the *Economist* put it slightly differently: 'MEPs are lonely people . . . they are flattered when you take an interest in them. You give them information about an issue that helps them look and sound good . . . cultivating them is an investment in the future.'[19]

The tobacco lobby's unsuccessful call to the EP to 'protect the integrity of the EC Treaty'[20] by rejecting the Common Position shows how the tobacco industry has attempted to use the changes in institutional balance to its own advantage. Thus one can see how the institutional and structural characteristics of the political system lead to the evolution of a particular type of interest mediation, which in turn shapes European policy-making. This shows how institutional bargaining can determine the extent to which different players are able to participate in the decision-making process. The sheer cost alone of maintaining a campaign for the duration of the time taken to convert the policy initiative into a policy decision in this case was undoubtedly a major deterrent, especially to groups with limited lobbying funds. However this should not lead one to conclude that success is contingent on financial backing and persistence. In the case of the tobacco industry, for example, their effort was so great that its excesses may have ended by creating a strong adverse reaction. Middlemas describes the evolution of lobbying strategies as a sort of corporate Darwinism that rapidly separates the 'fittest', most astute lobbying firms from the rest. As in nature however, this struggle can lead to excesses and abuses: '[t]he short-lived, extremely expensive and in the end counter-productive onslaught on MEPs by tobacco companies . . . has become a byword on how not to employ lobbyists.'

B.   INTEREST REPRESENTATION THROUGH THE NATIONAL ROUTE

Despite the 'growing army of Euro-lobbyists',[21] it is vital not to ignore the fact that the national stage remains important for interest groups who must seek to understand the traditional channels of representation, as well as how their national governments are geared for working in Europe. As Mazey comments: 'EC lobbying is a multi-lateral operation which requires interest groups to coordinate national and EC-level strategies, since national politicians remain important allies within the Council of Ministers and are usually influential in determining the manner in which EC legislation is to be implemented'.[22] Thus,

---

[19] 'The Brussels lobbyist and the struggle for ear-time', *The Economist*, 15 Aug. 1998,
[20] Report prepared by the Confederation of European Cigarette Manufacturers, 'A Step Too Far. A Call to the EP to Protect the Integrity of the EC Treaty', Apr. 1998.
[21] Buchan, *Europe the Strange Superpower* (Dartmouth, Aldershot, 1993).
[22] Mazey and Richardson (eds.), *Lobbying in the EC* (Oxford University Press, Oxford, 1993).

even though European Commission officials are often easier to establish contact with than officials in some national administrations, the national route remains the tried and tested way for many interest groups. The aforementioned Formula One lobby, working to convince the UK Government to push for a longer transition period for sporting events organized at world level, underlines the importance of the national route. National lobbying also remains important for smaller firms and public interest groups who may not have the resources to lobby in Brussels. Even a group like ASH (Action on Smoking and Health), well known in the UK, is predominantly national in its organization, and to some degree in its outlook, and it considers its resources insufficient to have a representative stationed in Brussels. The danger for such groups is that they will focus too much on the national scene and so miss other key opportunities to effectuate policy change. As Greenwood notes: '[i]nterests which have become over-reliant on the national route take unnecessary risks of decisions bypassing them, or becoming reactive to events rather than seeking to manage them in the first instance'.

C.   COMPLEX BUT RESPONSIVE?

This resulting omnipresence of interest groups does nothing to clarify the already complex policy-making process. This could lead one to expect a degree of remoteness of some interest groups from EU policy-makers. Nevertheless, such a system of multi-level governance involving the diffusion of state authority, upward to supranational and downward to subnational and regional levels, is thought to offer the potential of opening up a greater number of new access points to affected interest groups than is possible under either purely national or purely supranational arrangements. In such a way, it has been hypothesized that the European system of multi-level governance which is emerging might assure increased responsiveness of political decision-making to hitherto marginalized interests.[23] In this light, the many access points to the various Community institutions at all stages leading to the adoption of the Tobacco Advertising Directive can be seen in various ways: first, as giving less powerful players, in particular the many non-governmental organizations (NGOs) involved in lobbying in favour of the ban, an opportunity to be involved in the legislative process. Alternatively, the existence of so many exploitable access points could mean that the potential for big business to engage in overkill was heightened. Either suggestion supports the actual outcome of the legislative process, i.e. the adoption of the Directive, albeit after so much deliberation. The aforementioned omnipresence of interest groups raises the issue of the need for a system of accreditation which also touches on a broader set of concerns, relating to transparency and accountability.

---

[23] Gerstenberg and Sabel, *Directly Deliberative Poliarchy: An Institutional Ideal for Europe* (Academy of the 11th EUI Law Session, European University Institute, Florence, 2000).

IV.   Choose Tobacco

This section will explore the industrial forces behind much of the lobbying against the Directive. It will look primarily at the tobacco industry and its alleged excesses before moving on to consider the role of cross-sectoral groups and other groups representing the interests of tobacco growers, the advertising industry and Formula One.

A.   THE TOBACCO INDUSTRY

The tobacco industry is an oligopoly, made more cohesive by the fact that recent years have seen a considerable increase in the amount of regulation affecting the presentation, sale, and use of its products. For this reason, the industry has proved itself to be extremely strong in its opposition to such health control measures, often being heavily criticized in the process for its alleged excesses. Despite this, the industry has striven to maintain a positive corporate image. All of the tobacco 'giants' have websites detailing their openness and commitment to the Community. Philip Morris for instance boasts contributing money to various causes, among them research into AIDS and help for battered women.[24] A cynical reader might ask why they are not contributing to the harm they are promoting, by funding cancer research for example. Also for public relations reasons, and to have an effective base from which to influence European legislation, all of the major tobacco companies have offices and personnel stationed in Brussels. Much is unknown about the success of the industry's various attempts to skew the decision-making process in Europe.

In the USA, however, it is well recognized that health is one of the most heavily lobbied policy areas, with special interests spending millions of dollars to influence the debate. It is also common knowledge that Philip Morris is the single largest soft-money donor to US Republican Party Committees.[25] In addition the industry has spent in the region of $120 million on federal lobbying activities.

Equally disquieting is evidence uncovered by a recent investigation co-ordinated by the World Health Organization[26] showing how the tobacco industry has systematically attempted to undermine anti-smoking initiatives at a global level. The report shows how the industry has often hidden behind a range of ostensibly independent organizations and concludes that '[s]cientists and policy makers need to understand that they function in an environment

---

[24] http://philipmorris.com/tobacco_issues.
[25] $8.1 million since 1989, source: http://www.commoncause.org/publications/price3.
[26] WHO, *Tobacco Company Strategies to Undermine Tobacco Control Activities* (WHO, Geneva, 2000).

that is heavily influenced by covert industry efforts to subvert the normal decision-making process'.

B. COLLECTIVE ACTION

As well as lobbying individually, tobacco companies are also represented collectively by organizations pursuing common goals. These organizations operate at different levels, recognizing the need to adopt a multi-pronged approach to lobbying within a multi-level polity.

(i) The Confederation of European Cigarette Manufacturers (CECM)

CECM was actively involved in lobbying against the Directive, most notably in its calls to the European Parliament to reject the Common Position in 1997.[27] In that vein, the Confederation produced various documents, culminating in a book, published in 1999. Edited by Professor Torsten Stein, the book, *The European Ban on Tobacco Advertising*,[28] contains a collection of opinions commissioned from professors and legal practitioners from around Europe. Not surprisingly, all reach the same conclusion supporting the tobacco industry's own view regarding the illegality of the Directive.

(ii) The Tobacco Manufacturers' Association (TMA)

A good example of a national organization, also interested in European affairs, is the TMA, an industry-financed organization based in London. Set up in 1915, the TMA is backed by industry suppliers, securities analysts, advertising agencies, management consultants, distributors, wholesalers, retailers, and importers and exporters. The TMA functions as a trade association, delivering factual information to a range of organizations whose business interests depend on such resources. TMA's databank is drawn from over 10,000 domestic and international sources and is updated to give daily, weekly, monthly, quarterly, half-yearly, and yearly reports. Thus it is able to 'provide its supporters with a single, consistent source of economic, legislative, regulatory, trademark, brand and statistical data, market by market and company by company'.[29]

As well as the powerful individual firms and collective groups, the tobacco industry is also represented by cross-sectoral business organizations such as the European Round Table of Industrialists (ERT).

C. THE AGRICULTURAL LOBBY

The interests of tobacco growers are often seen to be synonymous with those of the tobacco industry save for the natural tension between buyers and sellers over

---

[27] CECM, *supra* n. 20.
[28] Stein (ed.), *The European Ban on Tobacco Advertising: Studies concerning its compatibility with European Law* (Nomos, Baden-Baden, 1999).
[29] http://www.tma.org/tma_about/Default.htm.

crop prices. The International Tobacco Growers Association (ITGA) was set up in 1984 to represent growers' interests. Despite World Bank indications that supply-side approaches to tobacco control are flawed,[30] and that declining demand for tobacco will affect tobacco producers gradually, the group has nevertheless had much influence in the past. Among others, it has lobbied ambassadors and the Food and Agriculture Organization (FAO) in order to reduce the impact of tobacco control. As the BSE[31] crisis showed, such agricultural lobbies can hold considerable sway in the EU. However, in the case of the ITGA, it is doubtful whether it now has as much power as it enjoyed in the past, partly as a result of the aforementioned WHO report which showed it to be a front organization for the tobacco industry, and also because the industry has begun to lose favour with the farmers themselves. This is certainly the case in the southern states of the USA, where tobacco growers are struggling to make a livelihood, as quotas are cut and as tobacco companies fail to offer anything by way of compensation. Such discontentment could lead to what was a concern of the tobacco industry all along, namely to ensure tobacco growers stick to politics and do not seek to use the global organization to gang up on manufacturers.

D.   THE ADVERTISING ASSOCIATION (AA)

Also tracing the developments of the Tobacco Advertising Directive with special interest was the AA. A federation of twenty-six trade associations and professional bodies, the AA represents the interests of advertising agencies, the media, and their supporting services, an industry with a combined worth of some £15 billion in the UK alone. The Advertising Association organizes events to discuss the threat from Europe to its members' business interests. Its former deputy director, Lionel Stanbrook, and current director of public affairs, Sara Soltani, also meet with European parliamentarians as part of the Association's lobbying process against what it sees as a growing tide of anti-advertising sentiment at EU level. Stanbrook voiced concern that the advertising industry is becoming an easy target for European legislators: '[t]hey are looking for easy solutions for social difficulties'. He went on to say, 'these issues are too complex to blame advertising. Alcohol consumption has actually risen in France since drink ads were banned there.'[32]

A study undertaken by DTZ Pieda Consulting on behalf of the Tobacco Manufacturers' Association,[33] estimates that £39,000 expenditure supports one full-time equivalent job in the advertising and sales promotion sector. Thus it concludes that the ban would threaten 1,500 such jobs in the UK. The inclusion of such data in a report financed by the Tobacco Manufacturers'

[30] Chaloupka *et al.*, *Curbing the Epidemic: Governments and the Economies of Tobacco Control* (World Bank, Washington, DC, May 1999).
[31] Bovine Spongiform Encephalopathy, commonly known as 'mad-cow disease'. See www.europa.int/comm/food/fs/bse.
[32] 'Screening out the kids', *FT Weekend*, 20 Nov. 1999.
[33] DTZ Pieda Consulting, 'Impact of the European Advertising Ban', (DTZ Pieda Consulting, London, Dec. 1998).

Association shows the possibility for co-operative exchanges between the various affiliated interests opposing the Directive.

The Advertising Association has also lobbied the UK government, claiming that its former plans to implement the Directive ahead of schedule were at odds with its stated objective of 'minimizing' the effect of the ban on this business sector. The Association therefore urged that, at the very least, the Government should agree not to implement the Directive ahead of schedule, in order to give those most affected by the ban, especially the smaller undertakings which rely heavily on tobacco advertising, time to readjust. Mention should be made however of those highly successful advertising agencies, such as Abbott Mead Vickers, which for ethical reasons choose not to run any tobacco advertising accounts. Instead the Department of Health and Health Education Authority feature on the company's client list.[34]

E. THE FORMULA ONE LOBBY

The inclusion of this group within the section dealing with the interests opposing the making of Directive 98/43/EC is perhaps slightly ambiguous. Although there is considered to be a 'natural fit' between Formula One and the tobacco industry since both appeal to 'a similar consumer group',[35] supporters of Formula One have not consistently opposed the Directive as one might expect. Indeed, Max Mosley, President of the *Fédération Internationale de l'Automobile* (FIA) originally pledged to end tobacco sponsorship by 2002, four years ahead of the deadline for implementation laid down by the EU Tobacco Advertising Directive. More recently, on the eve of the European Court of Justice's decision regarding the fate of the Directive, the FIA announced that, whatever the outcome, it would phase out tobacco sponsorship within the time limit set by Article 6 of the Directive. This could point to the fact that Formula One no longer wishes to be associated with the negative perception of the tobacco industry by continuing to oppose the ban, not least since new offers of sponsorship have been forthcoming.[36] Though these new sponsors are not likely to offer the same level of funding as the tobacco industry, the Formula One lobby seems to have accepted the inevitable, by welcoming these new providers of funding. Furlong[37] notes that the Formula One lobby was not so easy to appease when a similar advertising ban was under discussion in Australia. Although in the EU, the opposition from the Formula One lobby was not as staunch as one might have expected, the FIA did manage to secure an extended period of implementation for sports events organized at world level, which were to be given until 2006 to comply with the Directive. This created a

---

[34] www.amvbbdo.co.uk/clients/clients.html.

[35] UK Select Committee Report on the Health Risks of Smoking, (Benson and Hedges).

[36] The Prost Grand Prix team has announced the end of its association with Atladis ('Gauloises Blondes') and new deal with Interbrew ('Stella Artois'). The Williams team is to replace Rothmans with BMW as its prime sponsor.

[37] Furlong, 'Tobacco Advertising and the Sponsorship of Sports' (1994) 22 *Australian Business Law Review*, 159–89.

political furore for the British Labour Party which received (and later returned) a $1.7 million donation from motor racing mogul Bernie Ecclestone, before pushing for the extended implementation period for Formula One. UK government Ministers were also criticized for their role in helping to secure this exemption.

V. Choose Health

This section will consider the national and international pressure to adopt a tobacco advertising ban in an attempt to curb what has been dubbed a tobacco epidemic. It will examine the role of non-governmental groups and international organizations, predominantly the World Health Organization, though reference will also be made to the World Bank's contribution to the debate. It should also be noted that there seems to be public support for such tobacco control initiatives, related to increased citizen awareness of tobacco-related mortality.

A. PUBLIC AND MEDIA SUPPORT

The survey, 'Attitudes to Smoking', taken from a consultation paper issued by the UK Government,[38] shows strong public support for tobacco control programmes. Sixty-one per cent of respondents thought that tobacco advertising should not be allowed at all. Fifty-five per cent disapproved of tobacco sponsorship of sporting events, while 61 per cent disapproved in the case of sponsorship of pop concerts and 57 per cent in the case of arts events. At least four-fifths of those interviewed were in favour of smoking restrictions at work, in restaurants, and in other public places. Although these figures represent the views of sections of the British public only, it cannot be denied that attitudes to smoking, in the developed world at least, have changed considerably in recent years. Gone are the days when tobacco companies could claim that their products were the chosen brand of sportsmen, famous actors, or childhood superheroes. This is no doubt due to a raised awareness of the negative health consequences of smoking, and with the negative image of the tobacco industry, both messages being supported by the mass media. The *Financial Times* recently reported that today 'we are witnessing the early signs of a shift in public consciousness'[39] as regards the use and promotion of tobacco. The media play a major role in this shift in consciousness.

Iyengar[40] believes that the media set the public agenda, which, in turn, sets the policy agenda. Thus, by structuring public discourse, the press plays an

[38] UK Government, 'Draft Regulatory Assessment (Consultation Document) on the Implementation of Directive 98/43/EC', *ONS Omnibus*, Nov./Dec. 1996.

[39] Matthiessen, 'Global Corporate Power—Resist If You Can', *Financial Times*, 29 May 1999.

[40] Iyengar, *Is Anyone Responsible? How Television Frames Political Issues* (Chicago University Press, Chicago, Ill., 1991).

instrumental role in determining our social priorities. As a result, tobacco control will be effective only if the public, as well as the pro-health organizations, perceive it as a problem. The media must therefore print the message that tobacco use causes disease and death as often as possible. However, it is not merely the volume or frequency of news that determines an issue's ascension onto the policy agenda since the content of what is written is also crucial. Thus reports must be framed in the right way to produce a powerful message that relates to people's values and reasoning.

Such advocacy campaigns to build public support for initiatives like the Framework Convention on Tobacco Control share certain elements, identified by the framers of the Convention.[41] These are: strategic analysis and planning for advocacy; building a base of scientific support for policy change by translating the science of tobacco and health into persuasive arguments for appropriate tobacco control policy; organizing and developing broad and deep citizen alliances; building formal coalitions of organizations and informal networks of individual advocates, sometimes called 'grass roots' organizing; lobbying, a form of direct advocacy involving meeting with, and seeking to persuade, government policy-makers; and finally media advocacy, as mentioned above, a form of indirect advocacy based on building strategic alliances with the media in order to build popular understanding and support for tobacco control policy, which, in turn, puts pressure on policy-makers.

Non-governmental organizations are also involved in engaging the media to influence policy-makers to curb tobacco use.

B.   ACTION ON SMOKING AND HEALTH (ASH)

Based in the UK, ASH is a good example of a national pro-health group which lobbied in support of the Directive. It is a non-profit-making legal action and educational organization, 'fighting for the rights of non-smokers against the many problems of smoking. ASH uses the tremendous power of the law to represent non-smokers in courts and legislative bodies and before regulatory agencies'.

Though its income is limited compared to that of some national health organizations, ASH has emerged as a major spokesperson in matters of tobacco policy. Nevertheless, it is stressed that ASH is a national organization, working predominantly with health organizations in the United Kingdom.[42] Many of these specialist groups provide medical expertise, while ASH lends its prowess in public relations to get the message across to policy-makers and to the general public. ASH has twelve regional offices in the United Kingdom, though ASH in London appears to have limited knowledge of their work. In relation to influencing EU policy, this fragmentation and lack of co-ordinated resources

---

[41] http://www.tobacco.who.int/en/advocacy/.
[42] The British Medical Association, the British Heart Foundation, Cancer Research Fund, Imperial Cancer Research, No Smoking Day, QUIT, the Health Development Agency, and various University faculties.

is likely to be disadvantageous. Though it does work with pan-European groups, such as the European Network of Smoking Prevention, ASH has no representatives stationed in Brussels. In addition, as of last year, it no longer has an international campaign manager. It is suggested that ASH's emphasis on being a national organization runs counter to what should be recognized as a global problem which transcends national borders. It seems that, by attaching greater importance to European and global tobacco control developments, ASH could become even more effective than it is at present. It would also encourage the formation of global or pan-European networks of local groups active in the field, allowing for highly effective local–global synergies. The Internet is undoubtedly vital in this respect and ASH's move to make executive summaries of important documents available in five other European languages is to be welcomed. However, communicating with ASH representatives about their work in Europe, it seemed that knowledge of the system and commitment to the cause had distinctively national limitations. Furthermore, staff did not feel comfortable discussing issues of interest representation and lobbying strategies for fear of their work being subverted by the tobacco industry. It would be unfortunate if recent reports of the tobacco industry's dirty tricks, as uncovered by the recent WHO report,[43] were to cause organizations like ASH to retreat and abandon their commitment to transparency. Although everybody working in the field must guard against being manipulated by the industry, it would seem preferable for such pro-health groups openly to work together beyond the confines of the nation state and to learn from each other's experiences. Covert strategies will do nothing to promote an environment in which the exchange of information and formulation of a united anti-tobacco front will emerge.

C.   INTERNATIONAL NON-GOVERNMENTAL COALITION AGAINST TOBACCO (INGCAT)

A good example of an international group, which joins together NGOs from around the globe in the fight against tobacco, is INGCAT. According to Dr Karen Slama, co-ordinator of INGCAT, '[b]y joining together vast numbers of citizens and organizations, we have the power to challenge the relentless and ruthless behaviour of the tobacco transnationals'.

Each NGO working through INGCAT has a distinctive role to play in tobacco control, a unique and complementary role based on its constituency. The strength of its pro-health interest is evident from its founding and current members.[44] Among these members, national NGOs have been pioneers in

---

[43] WHO, *supra* n. 27.

[44] Founding members are the International Union against Cancer, the International Union against Tuberculosis and Lung Disease, and the World Heart Federation. Current members include the American College of Chest Physicians, the American Lung Association, the Danish Lung Association, the European Respiratory Society, and the Swedish Heart and Lung Foundation. Associate members include the British Medical Association, the International Union for Health Promotion and Education, and the National Centre for Tobacco Free Kids.

tobacco control, through health education and influencing public opinion through advocacy for legislative measures. International NGOs have also been in the forefront; the International Union against Cancer, the UICC, was the first to launch a tobacco control programme. In 1967, the American Cancer Society and other American NGOs took the initiative and organized the first World Conference on Smoking and Health. It was after the ninth such conference held in Paris in 1994 that INGCAT was formed. The year 2000 saw the eleventh conference, held in Chicago, USA.[45] Its objectives were to increase the number of organizations and individuals engaged in the fight against tobacco, and to promote policies and strategies to create societal, political, and economic change conducive to reducing tobacco use on a global scale. INGCAT seeks to mobilize NGOs all over the world to support the WHO Director General, Gro Harlem Brundtland, in her endeavour to ensure that governments take immediate and strong action.

D. THE WORLD HEALTH ORGANIZATION (WHO)

The WHO's involvement in the field has given tobacco control sustained global leadership. One may also consider the EU to have played an active role in putting the matter higher on the international agenda, albeit that on this occasion its competence in the field of health was shown to be sadly lacking. Such organizations can also give smaller groups around the world the confidence to speak out and pursue anti-tobacco policies. The seriousness of the challenge perceived by the WHO is reflected in the fact that in implementing the Framework Convention on Tobacco Control (FCTC), it will seek to use its Treaty-making powers under Article XIX of its Constitution, for the first time. Set within the context of WHO's Tobacco Free Initiative, the FCTC promises to be the world's first set of multilaterally negotiated rules devoted entirely to a public health issue. Furthermore, WHO claims that the FCTC is no ordinary convention, but potentially 'a public health movement'. The biggest anticipated benefit of the Convention is that it will act as 'a pathfinder and co-ordination vehicle' allowing 'national public health policies, tailored around national needs to be advanced without the risk of being undone by transnational forces'.[46]

The FCTC now has the financial and political support of a record number of fifty states, some of which, like Brazil, depend quite heavily on tobacco production. It also involves the European Union and a number of NGOs. The general objectives of the FCTC are: protecting children and adolescents from exposure to, and use of, tobacco products and their promotion; preventing and treating tobacco dependence; promoting smoke-free environments; promoting healthy tobacco-free economies, in particular stopping smuggling;

---

[45] INGCAT, *Together Against Tobacco. NGO Mobilisation Process*, presented at the 11th Conference on Smoking and Health, Chicago, Ill., 2000.
[46] For more information on the Framework Convention on Tobacco Control see http://www.who.int/toh/ftct/.

strengthening women's role in tobacco control; enhancing the capacity of all Member States in tobacco control, improving knowledge, and information exchange at national and international level; and protecting vulnerable communities. There are then certain specific protocols dealing with various issues such as pricing, smuggling, advertising and sponsorship, package design, labelling, and agricultural diversification. Despite recent concerns about the enforceability of international agreements, such conventions can have a real impact on the behaviour of states. By establishing review mechanisms, they may help to focus pressure on states by opening them up to public scrutiny. They may also create legal rules enforceable in domestic courts and provide leverage for national policy-makers to pursue the treaty's goals. The behaviour of private actors can also be affected as is shown by the pledge by the International Automobile Federation (FIA), which confirmed just twenty-four hours before the ECJ's verdict that tobacco sponsorship would be phased out between now and 2006. FIA director of campaigns Richard Woods said '[a]s nations world-wide ratify the Convention, international motor sport will face an increasingly limited tolerance of tobacco advertising and sponsorship'.[47]

E.   THE PHARMACEUTICAL INDUSTRY

The pharmaceutical industry is a new arrival in the anti-tobacco arena. The main advantage of such collaboration between the health lobby and the private sector is that greater financial support for tobacco control is now available. For instance, conferences can be organized which serve the interests of both the health groups and the pharmaceutical companies as a mechanism for exchanging new information. From the point of view of the pharmaceutical industry, working with the NGO community gives credibility to its message about addiction, and about its smoking cessation products.

However, despite the obvious advantages to both the NGO community and the pharmaceutical industry of working together on tobacco issues, there is a risk that collaboration could lead to the latter exerting undue influence on the agenda of NGOs. If this happens, there is a danger that tobacco control in the third world, where the pharmaceutical companies do not market their nicotine replacement drugs, will take a back seat. This is obviously problematic since this is exactly where tobacco control initiatives need to focus most. To exemplify this, it has been said that if the world were a village of 1,000 people, made up of 584 Asians, 150 Europeans, 124 Africans, eighty-four Latin Americans, fifty-two North Americans, and six Australians and New Zealanders, then of the 229 smokers in the village, 115 would be Asian, as opposed to only twenty-eight Europeans. This gives some indication of the scale of the tobacco epidemic in Asia and the rest of the developing world. The documents released as part of the aforementioned Minnesota trial settlement reveal that the tobacco industry is keen to further exploit these markets.

---

[47] 'Sport in tobacco rethink', *BBC Sport*, 5 Oct. 2000.

Hence there is a need for ethical guidelines to be established to ensure transparency and independence of decisions from the private sector. A move which NGOs would no doubt welcome would be for these pharmaceutical companies which offer financial support to their activities to establish independent funds for tobacco control outside their marketing departments.

F.   INFUSING THE DEBATE WITH ECONOMIC ANALYSIS

The World Bank has lent legitimacy to the arguments of the lobby supporting initiatives such as the Tobacco Advertising Directive by illustrating the economic incentives for tobacco regulation. In 1993 the World Bank's Development Report, *Investing in Health*,[48] called for an end to the latter's support of the tobacco industry. Drawing on the findings of a research team from the University of Cape Town, South Africa, the World Bank report assesses the expected consequences of tobacco control for health, for economies, and for individuals, and demonstrates that the economic fears that have deterred policy-makers from taking decisive action for so long, are largely unfounded. In response to its findings, the report outlines different measures to curb tobacco use. First, there are measures to reduce demand including raising taxes, banning advertising, launching counter-advertising campaigns, and running cessation programmes. Raising taxes is effective, especially among young people who are more sensitive to price rises than smokers in higher age categories. The tobacco industry, on the other hand, maintains that raising taxes is not an effective way to reduce consumption, and will lead to an increase in smuggling. The World Bank however estimates that a price rise of 10 per cent on a pack of cigarettes would reduce demand by about 4 per cent in high-income countries and by about 8 per cent in low- and middle-income countries. As regards the introduction of comprehensive bans on advertising and promotion, the report shows that they can reduce demand by around 7 per cent, according to econometric studies in high-income countries. Finally in this category of interventions designed to reduce demand are nicotine replacement therapy (NRT) and other cessation programmes which have proven efficacy. The World Bank's endorsement of such products is obviously a bonus for the pharmaceutical lobby.

The other type of government intervention suggested would focus on reducing the supply of tobacco, through for example prohibiting tobacco, enforcing crop substitution, imposing trade restrictions, introducing import bans, and the like. However, the report questions the efficacy of such measures, since the law of the market dictates that if one supplier is shut down, another gains an incentive to enter the market. The conclusion of the report is two-fold; it advocates the adoption of a 'multi-pronged approach' tailored to individual country needs, including tax increases, advertising bans, and wider access to cessation programmes. Secondly, it points to the need for global solutions to cross-border tobacco control issues.

[48] World Development Report, *Investing in Health* (World Bank, Washington, DC, 1993).

The annulment of the Tobacco Advertising Directive was an obvious setback for the pro-health, anti-tobacco policies which the aforementioned groups are struggling to achieve. The reasons for the downfall of the Directive at the judicial stage after such a long and controversial period of promulgation will now be examined.

VI.   Choose a Ground for Annulment

It was to be expected that the Directive would be the subject of a legal challenge once the political routes had been exhausted by the plethora of interest groups discussed above. However, the Court of First Instance was able to dismiss the applications of various non-state actors in the *Salamander* cases[49] on the basis that they failed to satisfy the test of *locus standi*. The Federal Republic of Germany, a 'privileged applicant' under Article 137 EC (Article 230), brought the challenge that was eventually to lead to the annulment of the Directive.[50] The case was subsequently joined with another, brought by a number of tobacco companies and referred by the UK High Court under Article 177 EC (Article 234).[51]

In the joined proceedings, seven grounds of nullity were pleaded: (1) inappropriate legal basis, (2) infringement of the fundamental right to freedom of expression, (3) breach of the principle of proportionality, (4) breach of the principle of subsidiarity, (5) infringement of the obligation to state reasons, (6) infringement of Article 222 of the EC Treaty (Article 295 EC) and/or infringement of the fundamental right to property, and (7) breach of Articles 30 and 36 of the EC Treaty (Articles 28 and 30 EC).

This section will analyse the strengths of these various arguments and evaluate the reasoning of the Advocate General, who delivered his opinion on 15 June 2000, and that of the Court, delivered on 5 October 2000.

A.   THE COURT'S RULING

The Court's analysis focused on assessing whether the Directive could be said to have an internal market rationale to justify its basis on Article 57 (Article 47(2)), Article 66 (Article 55) and Article 100a (Article 95). This led to a reconsideration of the scope of the then Article 100a. It was given a narrower reading than previously, the Court declaring that it is only a basis for measures intended to improve the conditions for the establishment and functioning of the internal market, and not for those seeking merely to regulate it. While admitting that disparities between national laws were likely to give rise to

---

[49] Judgment of CFI (Third Chamber) 27 June 2000 in Joined Cases T–172/98 and T–175/98 to T–177/98.
[50] Case C–376/98, *Federal Republic of Germany* v. *Council and Parliament* [1999] ECR I–50.
[51] Case C–74/99, *R.* v. *Secretary of State for Health and Others, ex parte Imperial Tobacco and Others* [2000] ECR I–8599.

obstacles to free movement in some instances, as in the case of print media,[52] the Court denied that this was true for static advertising on posters, parasols, ashtrays, and the like. Furthermore, the Court pointed to the fact that the Directive did not ensure the free movement of products in conformity with its provisions, most notably diversification products mentioned in Article 3(2) of the Directive. This, and the fact that Article 5 of the Directive permitted Member States to lay down stricter requirements as they deemed them necessary to ensure the protection of health, led the ECJ to the conclusion that, by prohibiting the advertising and sale of goods and allowing Member States to adopt even stricter restrictions, the Directive in no way purported to improve the functioning of the internal market.

On the question of eliminating distortions to competition, the Court applied the *de minimis* rule and held that other than in the case of Formula One sponsorship, the Directive could not be said to have an appreciable effect on competitive conditions in the EU.[53] Furthermore it was held that the Directive would eliminate the market for the products and services concerned, rather than equalizing competition. This reasoning, also given by Advocate General Fennelly in his opinion, ignores the possibility that elimination is just regulation taken to an extreme and so is one sure way to achieve a level playing field, thereby improving the functioning of the internal market. Facilitating the circulation of print media or the development of pan-European advertising and marketing strategies could be given as examples in this case. In sum, the judgment is brief and rather negative in substance. The Court said what would not count as an internal market measure and implied that the Directive was at any rate a disguised health measure, drawing attention to the fact that the national laws it sought to harmonize were predominantly health-oriented.[54] Furthermore, apart from stating that other Treaty bases could not be used to circumvent paragraph 4 of the then Article 129 which precludes harmonization in the field of public health, the ECJ did not positively discuss what Article 129 does allow. The Court therefore seemed to be mainly concerned with underlining the limits to competence, though disappointingly, references to subsidiarity were few.

So the ECJ upheld the pleas alleging that on the basis of the then Articles 100a, 57(2), and 66 the Community was not competent to adopt this measure. It did not therefore consider the other pleas, before annulling the Directive in its entirety.

These other pleas and the response of Advocate General Fennelly to them will now be summarized for the sake of completeness.

B.　CENTRE OF GRAVITY

In its discussion of competence, the ECJ implied that the Directive was a health measure but did not consider whether it could be said legitimately to

---

[52] Para. 97 of the judgment.　　　[53] Para. 109 of the judgment.
[54] Para. 76 of the judgment.

pursue more than one aim. The respondents in the case argued that the Directive pursued three aims indissociably: (1) to provide an equal opportunity for suppliers of products and services to operate in each Member State; (2) to remove barriers to trade; and (3) to provide for protection of public health. They claimed that the broad nature of the prohibition stemmed from the obligation under the then Article 100a(3) to take as a base a high level of health protection.

In response, Advocate General Fennelly stated that while it is theoretically possible for a measure to pursue more than one aim, as in the *Titanium Dioxide* case,[55] where the court must apply the centre of gravity test, this was not possible here. His dubious reasoning was that the centre of gravity test is only applicable where a dispute relates to which of two legal bases should have been used, and not in cases such as this where he considered it impossible to conceive of a dual legal basis.

C.   SUBSIDIARITY

The Advocate General's interpretation of the principle of subsidiarity was also disappointing. To recap, the principle embraces three ideas: that the Community is only to take action where the objectives of that action cannot be sufficiently achieved by the Member States; that the action can therefore be better achieved by the Community by reason of the scale or effects of the proposed measure; and that if the Community takes action, then this should not go beyond what is necessary to achieve the objectives of the Treaty. In the past, the ECJ has avoided having to give a determinate ruling on the justiciability of the principle, enshrined in Article 3b of the Treaty (Article 5 EC). It has been said that 'the true worth of the principle [of subsidiarity] will be known only once some busybody Directive has been challenged in the European Court and the judges have ruled on where Brussels stops and the nations are to be left alone'.[56] The Tobacco Advertising Directive promised to be the 'busybody' to clarify a principle that has gained much attention but still remains the subject of much uncertainty. Unfortunately the opportunity was not taken, the ECJ maintaining its passivity towards the principle. Though considered by some to be the most sensible course of action in the past,[57] this no-answers approach could exacerbate constitutional confusion in the EU, as Member State demand for a clearer demarcation of competences increases.

Following Advocate General Léger in the *Deposit Guarantees* case,[58] Advocate General Fennelly argued that the Community has exclusive competence under the then Articles 100a and 57(2) such that subsidiarity is not applicable. This is a highly contentious point, as was raised by Germany in the

[55] Case C–300/89, *Commission* v. *Council* [1991] ECR I–2867.
[56] 'Survey: the European Community', *The Economist*, 11 July 1992, 14.
[57] Emiliou, 'Subsidiarity: an Effective Barrier Against "the Enterprises of Ambition"?' (1992) 17 *European Law Review*, 383–407.
[58] Case C–233/94, *Germany* v. *Parliament and Council* [1997] ECR I–2405.

Deposit Guarantees case, since it is tantamount to entrusting to the Community exclusive competence in virtually all fields of activity provided the easily-invoked internal market rationale is present.

D.　PROPORTIONALITY

Though the ECJ did not make explicit reference to the principle of proportionality, it is clear from its analysis of the Directive's legal basis that it considered the general nature of the prohibition to be unwarranted. Advocate General Fennelly was also of the opinion that the Directive went beyond what was necessary or appropriate and recommended that this should be an alternative ground for annulling the Directive. This was despite a report presented by the respondents showing the benefits of such a ban,[59] and an admission by Advocate General Fennelly himself that a 6.9 per cent reduction in consumption could potentially 'correspond to saving thousands of lives'.

E.　FREEDOM OF EXPRESSION

As a basic principle of Community law[60] enshrined in Article 10 of the European Convention on Human Rights (ECHR), freedom of expression has been invoked in the past to protect commercial expression[61] and freedom of the press.[62] The applicants in this case drew on relevant decisions of the US Supreme Court[63] and Canadian Supreme Court[64] which gave precedence to freedom of expression. However the respondents pointed to Article 10(2) of the ECHR which permits restrictions on freedom of expression in the name of public health. Furthermore the Court in the *BSE* case[65] ruled that the onus of providing evidence that the measure in question will achieve the public interest invoked is less where that public interest is public health protection. For this reason the Advocate General did not suggest that this was a ground for annulling the Directive as a whole. In his opinion, only Article 3(3) of the Directive, which provided that an undertaking could not use the brand name, trade mark or other distinguishing feature of any product or service for a tobacco product unless it had been marketed in a similar way prior to the entry into force of the Directive, should be annulled on this ground. This was because of the provision's restrictive nature and because its purported benefits were considered tenuous.

---

[59] Saffer and Chaloupka, *Tobacco Advertising: Economic Theory and International Evidence*, NBER Working Paper Series, No. 6958.

[60] Cases C–260/89, *ERT* [1991] 1999 I–2925 and C–386/95 *Familiapress* v. *Bauer Verlag* [1997] ECR I–3689.

[61] Case C–260/89, *ERT* [1991] ECR I–2925.　　　[62] Case C–386/95, *Bauer* [1997] ECR I–3689.

[63] *Virginia State Bd. of Pharmacy* v. *Virginia Citizens Consumer Council* 425 US 748 (1976).

[64] *R.J.R. MacDonald* v. *Canada* (1994) 1 SCR 311.

[65] Case C–180/95, *United Kingdom* v. *Commission* [1998] ECR I–2265.

F.   REASONING

Likewise here, the Advocate General advised annulling only part of the Directive, Article 3(3)(a) for lack of adequate reasoning.

The final annulment of Directive 98/43/EC was obviously a political as well as a legal victory for Germany and the tobacco and advertising industries. However it may prove to be only a temporary reprieve, in that the door has now been left open for the Community legislature to redraft the impugned measure. In this way the outcome may be seen as part of an ongoing political–judicial dialogue rather than a unidirectional decision. It is also clear that national governments and the World Health Organization are still keen to achieve the aims of the Directive. In the former case, this is likely to lead to stronger measures; the UK Government plans to enact a tobacco advertising and promotion ban which will contain penalties for non-compliance, including fines of up to £5,000 and three months' imprisonment. This ongoing commitment to the government's promise to reduce smoking also reflects a growing awareness among citizens of the need for tighter control on tobacco use; the debate surrounding the annulled Tobacco Advertising Directive has no doubt added to this.

The clear political will for such a measure, at least from a majority of Member States, stands in stark contrast to the apparent lack of concern at Amsterdam to give the Community legislature explicit competence in the field of health similar to that granted in the field of environmental protection at Maastricht. This is no doubt linked to the fact that health policy, and the provision of health services, is so deeply ingrained in national social systems that Member States are reluctant to redefine the boundaries of competence through Treaty revision. Instead, they appear to prefer the flexibility to act in isolated areas, as here, where the nature of the problem necessitates transnational action. However the ECJ in this case has reaffirmed the need for clear jurisdictional lines, confirming that the EU has not yet reached the stage in its constitutional development where the legislator can dispense with the need to find clear competence to underpin every policy initiative. This process, relying on intricate Treaty revision, slows progress in fields such as health, and makes the EU less responsive to transnational challenges such as tobacco control. The following section will trace the continuing evolution of the Community's health mandate, and will suggest ways forward for health initiatives in light of the ongoing disparity between constitutional and political reality.

VI.   Choose Life

A.   HEALTH POLICY PAST AND PRESENT

The Single European Act and the emergence of a Citizen's Europe enabled the Community Institutions to tackle new concerns, including health protection, alongside the traditional economic aims of the Community established in the Treaty of Rome. However, despite the major impetus from the Treaty on European Union, the EU still has no general competence in the field of public health. Although Article 30 (Article 28 EC) provides that the activities of the Community include 'a contribution to the attainment of a high level of health protection', that contribution is explicitly limited by Article 129 (Article 152 EC) to support for co-operation between Member States and co-ordination of national policies. Such measures are commonly known as 'incentive measures'. European-level action is to target specified areas of need, namely the prevention of diseases, especially major health scourges, research into their causes and transmission, and the provision of information and education on health. Thus tobacco control could be seen as falling within the area to which Community action should be directed. Article 129 (Article 152 EC) also provides that health protection requirements are to form a constituent part of other Community policies.

Article 129 (Article 152 EC) thus establishes a flanking policy, i.e. an area in which Community action is limited to co-ordination and where harmonization of national laws is explicitly excluded. Member States are obliged to liaise with the Commission and to help in the co-ordination of policies in areas identified as requiring some Community input. Article 129 (Article 152 EC) is therefore a compromise solution for those Member States unwilling to grant the EU any express mandate in the field of health and those who recognized the need for transnational action. At the time of ratification of the Maastricht Treaty, it was seen as setting the limits to EU-level activity in the field of health which had proceeded in the past without such a legal base, and which could otherwise have continued to expand unchecked. The competence of the Community in the field of public health was set out in detail in a 1993 Council Resolution on future action in the field.[66] It reiterated that, as a rule, public health policy is the responsibility of Member States, and established four criteria for Community action. First, there must be a significant health problem for which preventive action is viable. The proposed activity must supplement or support other EC policies, such as the operation of the internal market. It also established that EC activities are to be consistent with those of international organizations, such as WHO.[67] Finally, the resolution provided that the aim of the Community action must be such that it could not sufficiently be achieved by Member States acting alone. This incorporates the principle of subsidiarity in that proposed activities have to be demonstrably better when co-ordinated at European rather than national level.

A subsequent Commission action programme[68] refocused Community health policy towards health promotion in a number of priority areas,

[66] [1993] OJ C174/11.
[67] McKee, Mossialos and Bekker note the desirability of EC co-operation with other international organizations concerned with health in 'The Influence of European Law on Health Policy' (1996) 6 *JESP* 263–86.
[68] COM(94)202 final.

including cancer, acknowledging the need for global multiannual programmes in such cases where repercussions are felt beyond national frontiers,
and call for international responses.

The Treaty of Amsterdam has gone some way to extending the scope of
Article 129 (Article 152 EC) though arguably not far enough. Under the new
Article 152 of the EC Treaty, the Community is empowered to adopt measures
aimed at ensuring, as opposed to merely contributing to, a high level of human
health protection. Among the areas for co-operation, the new Article specifies
more general causes of danger to human health, and ways to improve health
generally, in addition to major disease prevention which has been the focus
before now. Nevertheless, the scope of the Article still limits Community
action to 'incentive measures' and excludes the possibility of harmonization.

A Communication from the Commission last year[69] detailed a proposal for
the adoption of a programme of Community action in the field of public
health, to begin this year and run until 2006. The Commission considers this
programme to be a key initiative which will provide significant added value,
while fully respecting the responsibilities of Member States for the organization and delivery of health services and medical care, as maintained in the
Treaty of Amsterdam.

Among other things, the programme will address health determinants,
including tobacco use. Reference is made to the proposal for the new
Directive[70] to strengthen and update the measures on tobacco control,
adopted by the Commission in November 1999. It contains revised provisions
on the content of cigarettes and product labelling, introduces a limit on the
nicotine and carbon monoxide content of cigarettes, and proposes restrictions
on product description and tobacco additives. The Commission has also
stressed the importance of openness and transparency throughout the programme. It therefore intends to set up a European Health Forum as a consultative mechanism to ensure that the Community's health strategy pursues its
stated aims, and that the public is kept informed. This Communication and
the new public health framework represent an unprecedented commitment
to public health, which now seems to have earned a higher place on
the Community's policy agenda. However, one could claim that this
Communication does not go far enough, and that the lack of explicit competence prevents the Community from taking decisive measures to combat the
single largest preventable cause of death in the EU.

B.   THE FUTURE FOR HEALTH

This section will consider a possible way to break the deadlock between, on
the one hand, having the political will to adopt such measures as the Tobacco
Advertising Directive, and, on the other hand, the continuing reluctance of
Member States to give the Community a general competence in the field of

---

[69] COM(2000)285 final, May 2000.   [70] COM(99)594 final, 16 Nov. 1999.

health. It is proposed that one such way would be to draw a clear distinction in EU competence between health promotion (or prevention of disease), which often benefits from transnational information exchange and policies, and health provision, which is necessarily a matter of concern for individual Member States. Though the tendency to treat health promotion and health care provision co-operatively is understandable, it is suggested that this is what makes the idea of harmonizing measures so controversial. It is therefore necessary to underline the distinction between the two in order that the Community may pursue legitimate policies in the former, and so play its part in the global fight against tobacco-related disease and other health scourges. It is clear that Member States are opposed to the idea of pooling national health care resources, given the enormous divergence in national systems and the absence of any consensus on a European welfare system. In addition, it is recognized that any reorganization in such circumstances would be very difficult to achieve.

For these reasons, Community measures in the field of health have indeed focused on horizontal initiatives to provide information, education, and training. Though the aforementioned Communication on the adoption of a programme of Community action in the field of public health from 2001 to 2006 goes some way to putting health higher on the policy agenda, it is contended that it does not go far enough. Thus in the name of clarity, and to avoid any repetitions of this saga, it is recommended that Member States should discuss this option of giving the Community explicit competence to enact harmonizing as opposed to incentive measures where the nature of the problem demands it. This could still be made dependent on unanimous voting in Council in order to calm any concerns about surging supranationalism. It is surprising that this matter has not been raised so far, especially when one observes the dynamic and largely consensual evolution of Community competence in other related fields such as the environment. Not only would it lead to more effective solutions to transnational problems, but by giving the Community legislature an express mandate to act, it would also protect the democratic integrity of the Community legal order based as it is on the principle of enumerated powers.

However, as this article has highlighted, decisive action is all the more difficult where policies offend powerful and determined interests like the tobacco industry. On other occasions, legislation in areas in which the Community legislator has no explicit competence has been based on a 'generous' reading of a particular Treaty Article without being challenged. The recent example of the Race Directive[71] shows that where there is the political will, the Community can enact unprecedented 'hard' law of very extensive scope in a previously contentious policy area, and at record speed. However, such speedy progress is less likely in the field of tobacco control because national governments will not necessarily be seeking to curb the activities of an industry which pays huge

---

[71] Directive 2000/43/EC of 29 June 2000 implementing the principle of equal treatment between persons irrespective of their racial or ethnic origin [2000] OJ L180/00.

sums in tax, is a generous donor to party funds, and which after all markets a legal product. For this reason, even if the Community did have the necessary mandate to pursue harmonizing policies in the field of health, unanimity is very likely still to be a stumbling block for such anti-tobacco policy initiatives. This highlights the value of the work of WHO and other NGOs in exposing unsavoury tobacco industry practices. In this way it may become too politically embarrassing for national governments to liaise with the tobacco industry in the future or for policy-makers to succumb to tobacco industry lobbying.

One hundred million people[72] are expected to die over the next decade if tobacco use continues unchecked. As a responsible social actor on the global stage, the EU has to choose the role it is going to play in helping to control this epidemic. To allow powerful interests to thwart such an occasion would be regrettable and would undermine the very social identity the Community has tried so hard to construct since the Single European Act. However, pursuing such policies by manipulating existing Treaty bases is damaging to the fabric of the EU constitutional order and represents a failure to acknowledge health promotion initiatives as a Community concern in their own right. The lack of a firm legal basis also makes such legislation an easy target for those who oppose it. Furthermore it is now clear that where a piece of legislation becomes heavily politicized, as in the case of the Tobacco Advertising Directive, any blurring of jurisdictional lines will not stand up to challenge.

The defeat of the Directive was a significant blow for health. One would hope that it may at least prompt the Community to question the influence of lobbyists, review its competence in the field of health and give more weight to the principles of subsidiarity, transparency and accountability.

---

[72] INGCAT, *supra* n. 46.

Locating EC Environmental Law

DONALD MCGILLIVRAY* AND JANE HOLDER**

I. Introduction

From its initial absence from the EEC Treaty, both formally and in practice, environmental policy has moved to centre stage in the EC Treaty. In certain key respects, this development has been further strengthened by judgments of the European Court of Justice and by the European Union's international action in this field. Most recently, the Treaty of Amsterdam has altered the objectives of the Community, making the promotion of the core environmental concept of 'sustainable development' a central objective of the revised EC Treaty.[1] In short, environmental law has now become a structured and embedded body of Community law, a development further reinforced by the extent to which, as a discipline, environmental law is now firmly on the European academic map.[2]

The purpose of this article is to examine this evolution, locating environmental law within the development of EC law more generally. In this context, however, we also consider the use of environmental law to further other objectives of the EU. Our focus, therefore, is the development and application of certain principles with an environmental heritage—sustainable development, integration, and subsidiarity—the current centrality of which in the EC Treaty tells a story of the absorption of the ideas and language of environmental policy into the core of the EU's constitution and policy-formation processes: the 'ecologization' of European governance.[3] We also identify the application of

* Birkbeck College, University of London.

** University College London. Thanks are due to Darren Abrahams for research assistance, and to the European University Institute who supported a period in Florence researching for this article. Thanks also for comments received following presentations of aspects of this work to the participants in the Environmental Law Section of the SPTL at the annual conference in Leeds, Sept. 1999, and to staff and students at the Department of Land Economy, Cambridge, Apr. 2000, and to Sue Elworthy and Joanne Scott for detailed comments.

[1] Art. 2 EC.

[2] See: Krämer, *EC Environmental Law* (Sweet and Maxwell, London, 1999); Kiss and Shelton, *Manual of European Environmental Law* (2nd edn., Grotius, Cambridge, 1997); Scott, *EC Environmental Law* (Longman, London, 1998); Winter (ed.), *European Environmental Law: A Comparative Perspective* (Dartmouth, Aldershot, 1996); Jans, *European Environmental Law* (2nd edn., Kluwer, Dordrecht, 2000), Chalmers, 'Inhabitants in the Field of EC Environmental Law' in Craig and de Búrca (eds.), *The Evolution of EU Law* (Oxford University Press, Oxford, 1999), and the *Yearbook of European Environmental Law* (OUP, Oxford), the first volume of which was published in 2000.

[3] Although the precautionary principle is similarly undergoing a mainstreaming process, so far this change has been reflected only in policy rather than Treaty amendments. See Art. 174(2) EC and *Communication from the Commission on the Precautionary Principle*, COM(2000)1.

concepts from the Community's traditional core areas of competence in social and economic matters to the environmental field, most notably citizenship, which has been tagged as an example of the 'mainstreaming' of environmental policy.[4]

In considering these legal cross-currents, and law's part in furthering and strengthening ideas and values via principles, the main theme is the extent to which recent developments in EC environmental law pose new challenges to legal doctrines and to institutional structures which at present are only uneasily accommodated within existing frameworks. This issue is to be addressed because most early, 'first-generation', Community environmental legislation arose immanently in response to economic law, flanking the market alongside social law, and its accommodation within EC law, legislatively and in judgments of the Court of Justice,[5] proved to be, on the whole, relatively unproblematic.[6] A central reason behind the smoothness of this evolution was the emergence of Community *environmental* law, that is, law aimed at the improved management of the environment and of natural resources and firmly anthropocentric in orientation, rather than the emergence at EC level of what might be termed *ecological* law, stressing the inter-relationship of humans and their natural environment.[7]

The more recent borrowing of principles with an environmental heritage suggests that environmental law is further embedded in the EU's legal core. However, in this process the principles undergo some change in their role and content. Similarly, elements of citizenship may be 'greened', but not without significant broadening of the concept. In this sense, environmental law at EC level reflects many of the inherent limitations in regulating for positive environmental change, such as adequate representation of environmental interests and the capture of environmental values in decision-making.[8] However,

[4] Chalmers, *supra* n. 2, 674.

[5] Case 91/79, *Commission* v. *Italy* [1980] ECR 1099; Case 92/79, *Commission* v. *Italy* [1980] ECR 1115; Case C–240/83, *Procureur de la République* v. *Association de Défense des Brûleurs d'Huiles Usagées* [1985] ECR 531.

[6] On the evolution of EC environmental law and policy generally see Rehbinder and Stewart, 'Legal Integration in Federal Systems: European Community Environmental Law' (1985) 33 *American Journal of Comparative Law* 371; Rehbinder and Stewart, *Environment Protection Policy* (de Gruyter, Berlin and New York, 1985); Sands, 'European Community Environmental Law: The Evolution of a Regional Regime of International Environmental Protection' (1991) 100 *Yale Law Journal* 2511; Jans, *supra* n. 2 chap. 1; Elworthy and Holder, *Environmental Protection: Text and Materials* (Butterworths, London, 1997); chap. 5; Chalmers, *supra* n. 2. In addition to general coverage, there is useful work disaggregating the factors behind individual Member States agreeing to this development: see especially Golub, 'British Sovereignty and the Development of EC Environmental Policy' (1996) 5 *Environmental Politics* 700.

[7] For a strong view of 'ecological law', and a useful overview of the differences between environmental and ecological law see Wilkinson, 'Using Environmental Ethics to Create Ecological Law' in Holder and McGillivray (eds.), *Locality and Identity: Environmental Issues in Law and Society* (Ashgate, Aldershot, 1999). See also *infra* n. 36.

[8] See generally Robinson and Dunkley (eds.), *Public Interest Perspectives in Environmental Law* (Wiley Chancery, London, 1995); Stone, *Should Trees Have Standing?, and Other Essays on Law, Morals and the Environment* (25th anniversary edn., Oceana, Dobbs Ferry, NY, 1996); Holder and McGillivray, *supra* n. 7; Bell and McGillivray, *Ball and Bell on Environmental Law* (Blackstone Press, London, 2000), esp. chap. 2; and see also Section VI below.

there are also limitations specific to the EC context, notably the inadequacy of an environmental agenda within undeveloped areas of EC law such as citizenship, notwithstanding that the EC provides, in principle, a forum for the mediation of a range of conflicts relating to the balancing of environmental and other interests, primarily trade. We conclude that we may be entering a phase in which some of the limits of EC environmental law are being reached, and significant challenges to an 'environmental' approach emerging.

The article is broadly structured in three parts. In the next section, we outline what is meant by the European environment, as the subject of the body of Community environmental law. We examine the idea that '*the* European environment' (the working term of the European Environment Agency) is contestable[9]—the environment is, after all, a many-faceted, variable, and uncertain thing—and consider the part played by law in the construction of this idea by highlighting various legal representations of the environment. The most important, for the purposes of this article, is the idea of the European environment as a common natural heritage which has currency as representative of a united and integrated Europe. Thereafter, the following three sections consider those principles and concepts with an environmental heritage, and the impact of their upward march within the EC Treaty regime. Finally, in what is a necessarily more speculative section, we consider some of the issues which arise when Community environmental law is examined under the lens of EU citizenship.

II.   The Nature of 'the European Environment'

'The European environment' is the central term of reference of the European Environment Agency. The Agency has, for example, recently attempted to assess the state of the European environment coupled with predictions about its future quality.[10] The environment, as portrayed in these reports, is a cluster of 'environmental issues'.[11] Prime amongst these is the quality of air, water, and soil. Considerable importance is also placed on the relationship between environmental quality and human health, an emphasis reflected in the

---

[9] See, similarly, Bankowski and Christodoulidis, 'The European Union as an Essentially Contested Project' (1998) 4 *European Law Journal* 341.

[10] These report that production and consumption look set to increase, with resultant increases of pollution and waste. The forecast, using a baseline, 'business as usual' scenario shows continued pressure on Europe's environment: European Environment Agency, *Environment in the European Union at the Turn of the Century* (EEA, Copenhagen, 1999). See also the previous 'Dobris' and 'Dobris II' assessments (*Europe's Environment: the Dobris Assessment* (EEA, Copenhagen, 1995) and *Europe's Environment: the Second Assessment* (EEA, Copenhagen, 1998). Prior to the EEA, a number of less sophisticated reports were prepared by the Commission.

[11] European Environment Agency, *Environment in the European Union at the Turn of the Century, supra* n. 10, 2. This Report provides an assessment of the 'development of environmental quality in the EU in the near future, i.e. 2010'. The forecasts of environmental quality in various sectors, e.g. greenhouse gases and climate change, hazardous substances, soil degradation, and 'water stress' are summarized by means of icons, showing either smiley faces, non-smiley faces, or frowns. Each of the sectors listed above is portrayed by a 'frown'.

judgments of the European Court of Justice which we discuss below. This suggests that this environment—its boundaries, characteristics, inhabitants—is a given. This essentialist idea, however, belies considerable complexity and uncertainty. For example, many different environments exist—urban,[12] wilderness, the indoor environment even[13]—and the environment may be understood or experienced on different scales (spatial and temporal)[14] with the added capacity to change, albeit slowly.[15]

The terms of reference and methodology of the European Environment Agency are limiting, particularly its apparent failure to capture more complex, extended understandings of environment, shaped by, for example, culture and tradition.[16] Arguably, it is through appreciation of such understandings that a real and recognizable change in the quality of 'the environment' may be engendered.[17] Short of this, the approach taken continues to emphasize quantitative data, along which lines the Agency has recently published its first set of environmental indicators,[18] a precursor to their elevation in the Community's Sixth Environmental Action Programme, published by the Commission in January 2001.[19] It is worth stressing that the indicators being advanced at Community level go beyond the environmental media of air and water and traditional environmental sectors such as waste management, ozone depletion, and climate change to encompass indicators relating to the key sectors of the economy singled out for priority treatment in the Fifth Action Programme, *Towards Sustainability*:[20] agriculture, energy, transport, and industry (tourism being the one, notable, exception) and their integration. Nevertheless, the indicators are still environmental in the sense that they do not reach beyond environmental issues to try to capture more general 'sustainable development' indicators, the position, for example, recently taken in the UK (although these may be criticized as going too far in the direction of subjective 'quality of

[12] Although see *Commission Communication on Sustainable Urban Development in the European Union: A Framework for Action*, COM(1998)605 final.
[13] On the indoor environment see Shove, 'Threats and Defences in the Built Environment' in Elworthy *et al.* (eds.), *Perspectives on the Environment 2* (Avebury, Aldershot, 1995).
[14] On spatial scales and environmental thought see Harvey, *Justice, Nature and the Geography of Difference* (Oxford University Press, Oxford, 1996).
[15] For example, as a result of climate change: see Moore, Chaloner and Stott, *Global Environmental Change* (Blackwell, Oxford, 1996), chap. 7; Wilkinson, 'Plants on the Move' 119 *New Scientist* (1999), 1 (Inside Science).
[16] A more tentative, but possibly more valuable, meaning may be suggested: ' "Environment" is . . . whatever surrounds or, to be more precise, whatever exists in the surroundings of some being that is relevant to the state of that being at a particular place and time. The "situatedness" of a being and its internal conditions and needs have as much to say about the definition of environment as the surrounding conditions themselves, while the criteria of relevance can also vary widely': Harvey, *supra* n. 14, 118.
[17] For example, Macnaghten and Urry, *Contested Natures* (Sage, London, 1998).
[18] *Environmental Signals 2000*, available at http://themes.eea.eu.int/binary/s/signals2000.pdf.
[19] See further *infra* n. 74. Community environmental law has been based on Environmental Action Programmes since 1973.
[20] COM(92)22 final, and see Council Resolution of 1 Feb. 1993 on a Community programme of policy and action in relation to the environment and sustainable development [1993] OJ C138/1.

life' indicators and thus unduly relegating ecological considerations[21]). A more general difficulty with indicators, of course, is that even where there is agreement on the factors to be measured, there is always likely to be debate about what level of danger any particular category should be placed in; like the concept of safety, they have a necessarily subjective quality.[22]

There are also difficulties with the idea of *a* European environment. 'Europe' is not an identifiable bioregion (a discrete natural region defined according to the lay of the land[23]) and the physical boundaries of Europe are not settled, quite simply because of the accession of new Member States, and the variability of the European Economic Area and the European Agreements. The future accession of Central and Eastern European states in particular will radically alter the territory of the EC (and is likely to multiply the sorts of environmental problems which followed the reunification of Germany[24]). There is also an element of extraterritoriality: for example, the European Environment Agency includes Norway (and other states) within its scope, recognizing that for some purposes the 'European environment' extends eastwards to Belarus.[25]

The legal representation of the environment in the EC Treaty and secondary legislation is similarly limited and partial, in terms of its content and reach. Most significantly, the EC pursues, through law, an anthropocentric agenda for environmental protection, so that the focus of EC environmental law is on protecting the health of humans and certain 'useful' or valued animals (whales, seal pups, and certain other (fur-producing) mammals[26]) rather than protecting the environment for its own sake. This is seen by the legal marginalization of the issue of eutrophication of waters, when compared to the

[21] See *Quality of Life Counts* (Department of the Environment, Transport and the Regions, London, Dec. 1999), which includes crime statistics alongside indicators relating to air and water quality and other 'environmental' indicators, following on from *A Better Quality of Life: A Strategy for Sustainable Development in the United Kingdom* (Cm 4345, TSO, London, 1999).

[22] See e.g. the dispute over whether the UK indicator for greenhouse gas emission reductions should be at 'green' (*Quality of Life Counts, supra* n. 21) or 'red' (UK Round Table on Sustainable Development, *Indicators of Sustainable Development* (UKRTSD, London, May 2000)).

[23] According to ideas of bioregionalism, the jurisdictions of national and supranational governments match poorly with these areas, and so make environmental governance difficult. That 'Europe' is not a single bioregion should create similar difficulties, however, in a contradictory fashion, European environmental policy has relied on the fit between the transboundary nature of environmental pollution and cross-border controls for its legitimacy.

[24] For example, see the Commission Opinion on the motorway which intersects the Trebel and Recknitz Valley [1995] OJ C178/3, discussed in Nollkaemper, 'Habitat Protection in European Community Law: Evolving Conceptions of a Balance of Interests' (1997) 9 *Journal of Environmental Law* 271. The European Environment Agency report, *Environment in Europe at the Turn of the Century, supra* n. 11, documents the likely environmental effects of EU enlargement. Some accession countries have more environmentally sustainable economic activities and also more extensive areas of natural habitats. In the transition to EU membership there is a danger that 'their' environment will suffer if they follow the same development path of the existing members.

[25] On 14 Feb. 2000 negotiating directives were adopted in Council under which all accession states are admitted to the European Environment Agency: on the negotiations see http://org.eea.eu.int/news.shtml.

[26] See, e.g. Council Directive 83/189/EEC on seal pups [1983] OJ L91/30, Council Regulation 348/81/EEC on the import of whales and other cetacean products [1981] OJ L39/1, and Council Regulation 3254/91/EEC on leghold traps [1991] OJ L308/1.

emphasis placed on safe drinking water.[27] And, more generally within water policy, a 'suitable for use' formulation has been the rule, combined with standards for various water uses, rather than rights or entitlements to clean water.[28] This is particularly striking in the case of the Habitats Directive,[29] in which the destruction of a habitat for 'development' is provided for, so long as certain procedural requirements are fulfilled.[30] This demonstrates clearly the institutional strains at work which force the Commission, and Court of Justice, to fit environmental problems into a human welfare framework.

   The heritage of the anthropocentric agenda in the EC is in the emphasis on the 'Human Environment' in the Stockholm Declaration of the United Nations Conference in 1972 which prompted action on the part of the European Economic Community.[31] The constraints of Article 235 of the EEC Treaty[32] (a legal base for Community action on the environment before 1986) also contributed to this.[33] Legal measures adopted under this Article were to attain 'in the course of the operation of the common market one of the objectives of the Community'. In the case of environmental measures, this objective was interpreted as improving the living and working conditions of the peoples of Europe. 'Purer' environmental objectives which were expressed in some of the

[27] Although a balance between these two concerns was placed on a legislative footing by the adoption of Council Directive 91/676/EEC on the protection of waters against pollution caused by nitrates from agricultural sources [1991] OJ L375/1.

[28] See, e.g., the emphasis in Council Directive 91/271/EEC [1991] OJ L135/40, on urban waste water treatment, on dispersal rates. This extends to the judgments of the Court of Justice, in which it has interpreted directives with an 'environmental' objective in such a way as to suggest that their primary focus is human health. For example, in Case C–298/95 *Commission* v. *Germany* [1996] ECR I–6747, Council Directive 78/659/EEC on freshwater fish waters [1978] OJ L222/1, was interpreted in such a way since the species of fish covered were edible, notwithstanding that there is no authority for this in the Directive and that the Directive is classified by the EC as a conservation measure (see http://europa.eu.int/eur-lex/en/index.html). Arguably, the preamble is one of the first examples (at least in Community water law) where the ecological foundations for a Directive are stressed ahead of, or at least alongside, competition concerns.

[29] Council Directive 92/43/EEC on the conservation of natural habitats and of wild flora and fauna, [1992] OJ L206/7.

[30] See Art. 6 of *ibid*. This compares with a stricter approach to habitat protection under Council Directive 79/409/EEC on the conservation of wild birds [1979] OJ L103/1, the key provision of which (Art. 4(4), first sentence) is now repealed by the Habitats Directive.

[31] Declaration of the United Nations Conference on the Human Environment (Stockholm, 1972), Principle 1: 'Man has the fundamental right to freedom, equality and adequate condition of life, in an environment of quality that permits a life of dignity and well being . . .'.

[32] See discussion of ex Art. 235 EEC (now Art. 308 EC) as an 'elastic clause' in Weiler, 'The Transformation of Europe' (1991) 100 *Yale Law Journal* 2403, 2443–7.

[33] The Single European Act 1986 inserted a Title on the Environment in the EC Treaty. The Single European Act was concerned with environmental protection because of the distorting effects of differing national environmental laws on competition and intra-Community trade. A further influence was the likelihood of environmental harm caused by increased transportation, industrial restructuring, and enhanced economic growth accompanying fulfilment of the internal market. Environmental policy, alongside social policy, came to be regarded by the Commission as a 'flanking' policy to complement the internal market. See Haigh and Baldock, *Environmental Policy and 1992* (IEEP, London, 1992). We see, therefore, a non-linear development of EC environmental law—i.e. a corrective mechanism for the excesses of economic development. This may be compared with the more marginal use of 'free-standing' measures such as the Wild Birds Directive, Seal Pups Directive etc. prior to the insertion of the Environment Title in the EC Treaty 1986.

early policy documents, action programmes, and legislation[34] were therefore fitted within the constraints of, in policy terms, a conservative European Economic Community. Whilst former Article 235 EEC (now Article 308 EC) has been regarded generally as an all-embracing legal base, 'a true locus of expansion',[35] in the environmental field it restricted the type and content of legislation.

The anthropocentric orientation of EC environmental law and its practical expression in legal instruments underlie the philosophical and political distinction between 'environmentalists' who adopt a technicist and often managerial stance towards the environment and 'ecologists' who view human activities as embedded in nature, and bioregions as determinative of action, government, and law.[36] Although the distinction between the two extremes is often exaggerated, it is important to recognize that, in its purpose, content, and scale, EC environmental law is an implicit rejection of ecological thought. For example, from such an ecological perspective there are gaps in the scope of the substantive law, most notably in areas such as remedying the problem of historically contaminated land[37] in marked contrast to air and water quality (the subjects of numerous directives). A conclusion is that EC environmental law acts on those areas of the environment which are perceived as least economically vital, typically nature conservation. Added to which is the importance of Member States' control over land as a symbol of sovereignty, and energy, as representative of a state's self-sufficiency.[38]

The scope of EC environmental law may also be illustrated by its jurisdictional reach. This is undeniably global:[39] the Community has entered eighteen multilateral environmental agreements and led action in certain fields of international law, for example, the protection of tropical rainforests[40] and ozone depletion.[41] Such involvement has in many cases justified EC action in

[34] For example, the Directive on wild birds, particularly the sixth recital: 'whereas the conservation of the species of wild birds naturally occurring in the European territory of the Member States is necessary to attain, within the operation of the common market, of the Community's objectives regarding the improvement of living conditions, a harmonious development of economic activities throughout the Community and balanced expansion, but the necessary specific powers to act have not been provided by the Treaty;'.

[35] Weiler, *supra* n. 32.

[36] See further Dobson, *Green Political Thought* (2nd edn., Routledge, London, 1995), chap. 1.

[37] The recent Council Directive 99/31/EC on landfill [1999] OJ L182/1, does not address historic land contamination, and Council Directive 80/68/EEC on the protection of groundwater [1980] OJ L20/43, which extends to indirect discharges to groundwater from disposal or tipping, only applies prospectively (Art. 5). The Commission's 1996 waste strategy expressed the view that remediation of such sites should be a matter primarily for the Member States (COM(96)399).

[38] Both of these areas, land development, or town and country planning, and energy persist in requiring unanimity in the Council, as do primarily fiscal measures (Art. 175(2) EC). Community competence is only implied through the statement of this fact in the Treaty. The recently adopted directive on strategic environmental assessment of plans and programmes will impact upon the structure of decision-making in Member States' land development systems (see further text *infra* at n. 105).

[39] See Art. 174(1) EC (ex Art. 130r(1)).

[40] Council Regulation 3062/95/EC on operations to promote tropical rain forests [1995] OJ L327/9.

[41] Council Regulation 3093/94/EC [1994] OJ L333/1.

the form of legal instruments, sometimes in excess of what the original agreement required, and even though the EC may not have been a signatory to the agreement, for example the Convention on International Trade in Endangered Species (CITES).[42] However, the legal competence of the EC in the international arena has been hampered by 'trade' crises provoked by its environmental legislation.[43]

Nevertheless, deference to borders still characterizes much of EC environmental law. Because of its strong ties to land, nature conservation policy, for example, is distinctly 'Eurocentric'.[44] This means that protection is more fully enjoyed by wild birds within the Union's borders than without, even though, ecologically, such an approach is incoherent to the extent that species do not enjoy similar levels of protection outside the EU.[45] And within the EU, the protection of wild birds rests upon their inclusion in the Directive on wild birds.[46] The Habitats Directive is similarly, and exclusively, directed towards protection of European habitats.[47] This orientation has been addressed by the European Court in the context of its case law on the Wild Birds Directive,[48] and also at national level in an important ruling on the reach of the Habitats Directive that 'European territory' is to be interpreted as reaching beyond territorial waters.[49]

In summary, European environmental law contributes to the construction of its subject by defining 'the environment' and drawing its boundaries; in this process it universalizes its subject matter. It also plays an important symbolic role in the process of European integration because the environmental agenda corresponds well with the idea of the EU 'as a polity which transcends state

---

[42] Council Regulation 338/97/EC [1997] OJ L61/1.

[43] See Chalmers, *supra* n. 2, 659 and Cheyne, 'International Agreements and the European Legal System' (1994) 19 *European Law Review* 581, 594. See also Chalmers, 'External Relations and the Periphery of EU Environmental Law' in Weiss, Denters, and de Waart (eds.), *International Economic Law with a Human Face* (Kluwer, The Hague, 1998).

[44] It should be noted that the 1979 Convention on the Conservation of European Wildlife and Natural Habitats, which in many respects the Directive gives effect to, allows non-European states to be a party.

[45] There is the possibility of funding for projects in designated 'third countries' under the LIFE programme, two phases of which ran from 1992 to 1999. A third phase has yet to be adopted. 'LIFE-Third countries' is open to non-member states bordering on the Mediterranean and the Baltic Sea, other than the associated central and eastern European countries. Only 5% of the general LIFE budget (which from 1996–9 was 450m EURO) is annually earmarked for non-member states' projects. See generally http://europa.eu.int/comm/life/home.htm.

[46] See *supra* n. 30.   [47] See *supra* n. 29.

[48] Case C–169/89, *Criminal Proceedings Against Gourmettière Van den Berg* [1990] ECR I–2143 at 2165. The ECJ held that the Netherlands could not ban local sales of birds killed legally in other Member States if the Directive did not specifically protect them. This 'localist' approach was, however, not fully adopted by Van Gerven AG. See further Farber, 'Stretching the Margins: The Geographic Nexus in Environmental Law' (1995–96) 48 *Stanford Law Review* 1247. The Birds Directive provides further examples of the practical and jurisdictional reach of EC environmental law: see Case C–202/94 *van der Feesten* [1996] ECR I–355 (and commentary by Chalmers, 'Environmental Law' [1996] *Yearbook of European Law* 587–8.

[49] *R.* v. *Secretary of State for Trade & Industry, ex p. Greenpeace (No. 2)* [2000] 2 CMLR 94; [2000] Env. LR 221. The EC issues in this case will not form part of a preliminary ruling to the ECJ.

boundaries'.[50] The EU may thereby be considered to be a 'natural' arena for environmental policy. The origin of this idea is in the *sine qua non* of European environmental law, the transboundary nature of pollution. This 'natural law' thrusts environmental problems into the supranational realm, from which follows co-operation. This may be seen in the case of climate change, the regulation of transboundary effects of development projects and the establishment of the Natura 2000 network in relation to biodiversity conservation. In recognizing the irrelevance of borders in such cases, the 'environment' acts as a symbol for the advantages of joint action in Europe.

EC environmental law has now developed the idea of shared ownership of the European environment. This is a more complex but possibly firmer foundation for environmental law than the regulation of transboundary pollution. It has found expression not merely in legislation but also in judgments of the Court of Justice. The shift towards a more inclusive, less functional premiss for environmental law may first be seen in cases in which the Court's interpretation of air quality Directives had the effect of giving individual citizens a right to clean air.[51] This has been lauded as the first stirrings of a public environmental 'trust',[52] although in a limited form for enforcement purposes rather than as part of a broader citizenship agenda.[53] Since then, the Court of Justice in *Lappel Bank* has reinforced that the Wild Birds Directive accords special protection to species constituting 'a common heritage of the Community'. [54] This aspect of the Directive was found to be capable of subjugating the national interest element of land use.[55] Recognizing this, the Court sought to deny the significance of territoriality rather than affirming it as in previous cases.[56] In this respect, the Court pursued an ecological objective, but this is not the general approach of the EU. More important is the Court's broadening of the language of the Directive, which speaks of 'such species . . . constitut[ing] a common heritage'. The Court may here reflect a widening of the language of commonality found in the preamble to the Habitats Directive ('the threatened habitats and species form part of the *Community's* natural heritage'[57]) and more broadly the absorption of the concept of 'commons' from international environmental law. In *Lappel Bank*, the Court spoke the language of integration—of common ownership of a Europe without borders in a real sense and

---

[50] Walker, 'Sovereignty and Differentiated Integration in the European Union' (1998) 4 *European Law Journal* 355, at 359.

[51] Council Directive 779/80/EEC on sulphur dioxide and suspended particles [1980] OJ L229/30. See, e.g., Case C–361/88, *Commission* v. *Germany* [1991] ECR I–2567.

[52] Gray, 'Equitable Property' (1994) 47 *Current Legal Problems* 157, 206–7.

[53] See further Section VI below.

[54] Case C–44/95, *R.* v. *Secretary of State for the Environment, ex p. RSPB* [1996] ECR I–3805 ('Lappel Bank') at para. 23. The ECJ recounted the third recital of the Birds Directive which declares that migratory species 'constitute a common heritage' and that 'effective bird protection is typically a trans-frontier environment problem entailing common responsibilities'. See also Case C–339/87, *Commission* v. *Netherlands* [1990] ECR I–851 in which the Court similarly speaks of 'common heritage'.

[55] Case C–44/95, *supra* n. 54, *per* Fennelly AG.

[56] Case 169/89, *Van den Berg* [1990] ECR I–2143, discussed *supra* at n. 48.

[57] Emphasis added.

common responsibilities. This idea, in law, of shared ownership, or an environmental '*jus humanitatis*',[58] of the European environment, is central to its legitimating force. The Court appears reluctant, however, to refer to commonality in relation to other environmental resources.[59] This may be indicative of the problematic limits of a shared ownership approach to integration, some of which are addressed by recourse to the principle of sustainable development.

III.   Sustainable Development

Following the Treaty of Amsterdam, the international principle of sustainable development now forms part of the Community's *raison d'être* in Article 2 EC: '[d]etermined to promote economic and social progress for their peoples, taking into account the principle of sustainable development and within the context of the accomplishment of the internal market'. The principle has also been added to the Treaty on European Union so that amongst the objectives of the Union is now listed: 'to promote economic and social progress and to achieve balanced and sustainable development'.[60] The principle therefore provides a foundation for EC action in general rather than a more limited field of application, the formation of environmental law and policy.

The principle of sustainable development can be traced to the 1972 United Nations Conference on the Human Environment in Stockholm, but gained currency in the Report of the World Commission on Environment and Development (the 'Brundtland Report') which defined it as 'development that meets the needs of the present without compromising the ability of future generations to meet their own needs'.[61] The inclusion of sustainable development in the EC Treaty thereby introduces for the first time an intergenerational element into EC law. The centrality of the principle in the Union's treaties may be seen primarily as a response to the Member States adopting sustainable development as a guiding principle in national legislation and policy documents, thereby discharging their obligations under international law.[62] It is also a testament to the persistent and effective lobbying by bodies such as Greenpeace International, the Institute for European Environment Policy, the

---

[58] De Sousa Santos, *Toward an New Common Sense: Law, Science and Politics in the Paradigmatic Transition* (Routledge, London, 1995).

[59] Joined Cases C–164/97 and C–165/97, *Parliament* v. *Council* [1999] ECR I–1139, para. 16: 'the natural heritage represented by forest ecosystems'. See also Council Resolution of 15 Dec. 1998 on a forestry strategy for the European Union [1999] OJ C56/1 which eschews the use of 'common heritage' language.

[60] Art. B of Title 1 of the TEU.

[61] World Commission on Environment and Development (The Brundtland Report), *Our Common Future* (Oxford University Press, Oxford, 1987), 8. On the evolution of sustainable development as a legal concept see Jewell and Steele, 'UK Regulatory Reform and the Pursuit of Sustainable Development' [1996] *Journal of Environmental Law* 283; Elworthy and Holder, *supra* n. 6, chap. 4; Alder and Wilkinson, *Environmental Law and Ethics* (Macmillan, Basingstoke, 1999), 136–40 and chap. 6; Kiss and Shelton, *supra* n. 2, chap. 2.

[62] Most notably, in the Declaration to the 1992 Rio 'Earth Summit' and in Agenda 21.

European Environmental Bureau, Friends of the Earth, and the World Wide Fund for Nature.[63]

Although its firm position in the EC legal order suggests some consensus about its meaning and significance, sustainable development is a deeply contested concept.[64] This is not least because of the 'business as usual' philosophy, expressed in the Brundtland Report,[65] and close association with 'environmental modernization' in which an efficiency-oriented approach is pursued, and economic and environmental interests are purportedly integrated into decision-making in such so-called 'win-win' solutions. In other words, this is an approach which sees environmental protection as less of a threat to the economy than an opportunity, and advocates the integration of environmental factors and interests into broader decision-making,[66] so far at the cost of a more overtly ecological approach. The principle of sustainable development thereby provides a continued link with economic priorities, even at a time when the Treaty[67] and certain judgments of the Court of Justice portray a decoupling of environmental policy from its traditional economic base.[68] This economic orientation of the principle may be seen in the continued retention in the EC Treaty of terminology derived from the Treaty on European Union ('sustainable growth').[69] This points to Community

[63] These organizations presented proposals for strengthening the environmental dimension of the EC Treaty in *Greening the Treaty II: Sustainable Development in a Democratic Union, Proposals for the 1996 Intergovernmental Conference*, May 1995, available at www.asser.nl/EEL. See further Haigh, 'Introducing the Concept of Sustainable Development into the Treaties of the European Union' in O'Riordan and Voisey (eds.), *The Transition to Sustainability: The Politics of Agenda 21 in Europe* (Earthscan, London, 1998). See also Christie, *Sustaining Europe: A Common Cause for the European Union in the New Century* (Demos/Green Alliance, London, 1999).

[64] See Beckerman, 'Sustainable Development: Is It a Useful Concept?' (1994) 3 *Environmental Values* 191; Jacobs, 'Sustainable Development, Capital Substitution and Economic Humility: A Response to Beckerman' (1995) 4 *Environmental Values* 57; Daly 'On Wilfred Beckerman's Critique of Sustainable Development' (1995) 4 *Environmental Values* 49; Redclift, *Sustainable Development: Exploring the Contradictions* (Routledge, London, 1989). On justice dimensions in particular see Dobson (ed.), *Fairness and Futurity: Essays on Environmental Sustainability and Social Justice* (OUP, Oxford, 1999) and Dobson, *Justice and the Environment: Conceptions of Environmental Sustainability and Dimensions of Justice* (OUP, Oxford, 1998).

[65] Brundtland Report, *supra* n. 61, 8: 'aspects of technology and social organization can be both managed and improved to make way for a new era of economic growth'.

[66] For a more thorough account see Hajer, *The Politics of Environmental Discourse: Ecological Modernisation and the Policy Process* (Clarendon Press, Oxford, 1995).

[67] For example, the inclusion of broad social policy objectives such as the anti-discrimination principle in Art. 13 EC (ex Art. 6a). This may be compared with the narrowly drawn principle of equality in Art. 119 of the original Treaty of Rome (now Art. 141 EC) on equality between men and women in matters of pay for work.

[68] For example, Case C–44/95 ('*Lappel Bank*'), *supra* n. 54, in which the ECJ held that economic considerations cannot influence the decision to designate an area for special protection for the purposes of the Wilds Birds Directive. See also Case C–371/98 *R. v. Secretary of State for the Environment, Transport and the Regions, ex p. First Corporate Shipping Ltd* [2001] 1 CMLR 19, that economic considerations must be precluded when Member States draw up lists of candidate special areas of conservation under Art.4(1) of the Habitats Directive, *supra* n. 29. See also nn. 79 and 85 below.

[69] 'Sustainable and non-inflationary growth' is no longer expressly linked to or qualified by 'respecting the environment'. Also, the separate task of promoting the development of economic activities must now be 'sustainable' as well as harmonious and balanced. A new task of promoting

adherence to the 'weak' version of sustainable development generally preferred by governments of the Member States. In other words, sustainable
development provides an environmental example of the familiar combination
of the aspirational and the pragmatic which has characterized the evolution of
Community law more generally.

Legal definitions of the concept of sustainable development as a matter of
European law are few, and the term is not directly defined in the EC Treaty.
However, recent proposals on supporting environmental integration in developing countries attempt to put some flesh on the bones. Thus, the proposal to
replace the Regulation on environmental measures in developing countries in
the context of sustainable development[70] provides that: ' "sustainable development" means the improvement of the standard of living and welfare of the
relevant populations *within the limits* of the capacity of the ecosystems by
maintaining natural assets and their biological diversity for the benefit of present and future generations'.[71] This approach elevates the notion of environmental limits in a quite different manner from that taken in the EC Treaty,
which speaks instead of one objective of Community environmental policy
being the 'prudent and rational use of natural resources'.[72] It is evident that different aspects of sustainable development are being played out in different
contexts in what appears to be a quite deliberate manner.[73]

Short of the Treaty itself fleshing out what sustainable development, or 'sustainability', is, the Court of Justice has declined to look to such guidance as is
found in the Community's environmental action programmes, most recently
Towards Sustainability.[74] And, in cases in which issues of sustainability are at
their core, for example on the interpretation of the Directive on environmen-

a 'high level of environmental protection and improvement of the quality of the environment' is
also inserted.

[70] Council Regulation 722/97/EC [1997] OJ L108/1, which refers to 'sustainable development'
without directly defining it.

[71] Amended proposal for a European Parliament and Council Regulation on measures to promote the full integration of the environmental dimension in the development process of developing countries COM(2000)55 final, Art. 2 (emphasis added).

[72] Art. 174(1) EC.

[73] See also ACP–EU Partnership Agreement (the Cotonou Agreement), 23 June 2000, Art. 1.

[74] See *supra* n. 20. In Case C–142/95P, *Associazone agricoltori della provincia di Rovigo and
Others* v. *Commission* [1996] ECR I–6669 the ECJ held that this action programme does not lay
down any legal rules of a mandatory nature but provides merely a framework for the defining
and implementing of Community environmental policy: 'For each of the main issues, long-term
objectives are given as an indication of the sense of direction or thrust to be applied in the pursuit of sustainable development, certain targets are indicated for the period up to the year 2000
and a representative selection of actions is prescribed with a view to achieving the said targets.
These objectives and targets do not constitute legal commitments but, rather, performance levels or achievements to be aimed at now in the interests of attaining a sustainable development
path', point 12, Summary, Fifth Action Programme. It is unlikely that the advancement of mea-
surable indicators under the 6th Environmental Action Programme ('Environment 2001: Our
Future, Our Choice', COM(2001)31) will alter matters, since this generally anticipates their use as
measuring progress, not stipulating targets. Importantly, the Court was not asked, and did not
take the opportunity to explore, the extent to which *Towards Sustainability* (64–70) looks to a
broad range of instruments (economic, procedural, information-based etc.) as necessary to
achieve sustainability.

tal assessment,[75] the Court of Justice has adopted a purposive approach, referring to the necessity of interpreting the Directive so as to confer a high level of environmental protection, but has failed to explain this in terms of 'operationalizing' sustainable development.[76] This may be compared with the approach adopted by the International Court of Justice,[77] and to some extent the approach of the Commission at a policy level.[78] However, Advocate General Léger's opinion in *First Corporate Shipping*[79] represents something of a development in terms of the Court of Justice's conceptualization of sustainable development. The opinion aligns the aim of the Habitats Directive with sustainable development. Drawing on the Directive's preamble (which describes the Directive as making a contribution to the general objective of sustainable development) the Advocate General considers that sustainable development 'emphasises the necessary balance between various interests which sometimes clash, but which must be reconciled'. This assists in reaching the conclusion that in deciding which sites to propose or when defining the boundaries of such sites for the purposes of the Habitats Directive, the Commission (in agreement with the Member States) must assess the interests concerned, ascertaining whether human activities in the area may be reconciled with the objective of biodiversity conservation. Although the Court decided the case without resort to fleshing out its understanding of sustainable development, the end result may be a shift away from its case law on the Wild Birds Directive which consistently held that only objective ornithological criteria could be used in designating bird habitat sites for protection.[80]

The apparent lacuna in the Court of Justice's handling of the principle may be explained by its relatively recent addition to the Union Treaties[81] and its close identification with policy formation, rather than as a justiciable source of rights. It is indeed policy-making that sustainable development is likely further to influence, for example in the direction of an overarching 'First

---

[75] Council Directive 85/337/EEC on the assessment of the effects on the environment of certain public and private projects [1985] OJ L175/40, as amended by Council Directive 97/11/EC [1997] OJ L73/5.

[76] For example, Case C–72/95, *BV Aannemersbedrijf PK Kraaijeveld and Others* v. *Gedeputeerde Staten van Zuid-Holland* [1996] ECR I–5403.

[77] For example, *New Zealand* v. *France*, [1995] ICJ Rep. 288, dissenting opinions of Judges Koroma, Palmer, and Weeramantry. Judge Palmer advocates the recognition of environmental limits, including the calculus of risk via such mechanisms as environmental assessment, 'otherwise the paradigm of sustainable development enhanced by the world at the Rio Conference cannot be achieved' (para. 68). See also *Case concerning the Gabcíkovo-Nagymaros Project (Hungary/Slovakia)* (1998) 37 ILM 162 *per* Judge Weeramantry, who argues that sustainable development is not merely a *concept* but a recognized *principle* of customary international law, albeit one which suggests procedural rather than substantive obligations.

[78] See generally *Towards Sustainability, supra* n. 20, s. 7.   [79] See *supra* n. 68.

[80] See Case C–57/89, *Commission* v. *Germany* [1991] ECR I–883 ('*Leybucht Dykes*'); Case C–355/90, *Commission* v. *Spain* [1993] ECR I–4221 ('*Santoña Marshes*'); Case C–44/95 *R.* v. *Secretary of State for the Environment, ex p. RSPB* (*Lappel Bank, supra* n. 54). It is notable that under the Birds Directive, designation is a task solely for the Member States.

[81] Although a key aspect of the principle, the integration principle, included in the Environment Title since 1986, may be seen as a precursor to sustainable development. See Section IV below.

Sustainable Development Strategic Forum' embracing also the development of a Sixth EU Environmental Action Programme.[82]

IV. Integration

An imperative of sustainable development is the integration of environmental protection requirements into the social and economic dimensions of other policy areas. This suggests the desirability of recognizing existing connections and fostering interrelations between Community institutions and the Member States, to reduce the possibility of the environment being discounted or marginalized in decision-making. Whilst integration provides a template for the development of the European Union as a whole, and integration clauses in the EC Treaty refer to areas other than environmental policy,[83] it has particular significance in the environmental field. This is because of the environmentalists' argument that environmental protection requirements should necessarily form part of all areas of life.[84] Integration therefore provides a mechanism whereby the linkages between the social, economic, and environmental spheres, identified by sustainable development, may be acted upon.[85]

Even in the absence of an integration principle, the Community has for some time been regarded as a space for the important integration of valued objectives. Most notably, there were relatively early attempts at integrating environmental considerations into regional policy, although these are still the subject of fierce criticism.[86] However, the central locus of integration has been through the Court of Justice holding environmental protection to be a mandatory requirement justifying restrictions to the free circulation of goods under Article 28 EC (ex Article 30) where indistinctly applicable measures are taken.[87] The judicial creation of mandatory requirements has overcome some of the limitations inherent in Article 30 EC (ex Article 36) of the Treaty which, despite pressure for change at the pre-Amsterdam Intergovernmental Conference (IGC), continues to exclude environmental protection objectives from its list of justifiable prohibitions. A glimmer of hope for the reinterpretation of what are essentially sanitary and agricultural protections, however, can be seen in

[82] As proposed by the European Consultative Forum on the Environment and Sustainable Development (the European Commission's 'stakeholders' advisory forum on environment and sustainability).

[83] For example, consumer protection (Art. 153(2)), public health (Art. 152(1)) and culture (Art. 151(4)).

[84] For example, the central concern of the Brundtland Report, *supra* n. 64, was the increasing globalization of various crises (environmental, developmental, energy, etc.), and the connections between them. As it memorably put it: 'They are all one'. This, of course, can be taken more narrowly than stronger theses relating to the connectedness of all life, on which see most famously Commoner, *The Closing Circle* (Cape, London, 1972).

[85] This has been explicitly recognized by Léger AG, see *supra* n. 68: 'Integration of the environmental dimension is thus the basis of the strategy of sustainable development . . .'.

[86] See generally Scott, *supra* n. 2, chap. 7.

[87] Case 302/86, *Commission* v. *Denmark* [1988] ECR 4607 ('*Danish Bottles*'). More recently see Case C–389/96, *Aher-Waggon GmbH* v. *Germany* [1998] ECR I–4473.

Bluhme.[88] There, the Court of Justice held that a national legislative measure prohibiting the keeping on a Danish island of a species of bee other than the native subspecies must be regarded as justified, under Article 30 EC, on the ground of the protection of the health and life of animals, thus elevating bio-diversity conservation through protection of the life of potentially affected species. However, the judgment goes further still by allowing trade-related protection for local colonies of species regardless of whether such a colony may be deemed a distinct species or subspecies. So long as the population affected has characteristics distinguishing it from others, this makes it worthy of protection, not merely from a scientific perspective but perhaps also for its cultural significance. Cases such as *Bluhme* highlight that the Court at least provides a unified forum for the resolution of conflicts between trade and environment, even if its rules on standing still serve to exclude environmental voices[89] and the *actual* resolution of trade and environmental objectives remains elusive.[90]

A more certain approach to integration, less reliant on litigation which continues to favour trade-related interests,[91] may flow from the application of a legal principle of integration, the heritage of which is in the Environment Title of the EEC Treaty,[92] inserted by the Single European Act 1986. This was subtly strengthened by the Treaty on European Union 1992.[93] The Treaty of Amsterdam further enhanced the principle by elevating it to a general principle of the EC Treaty, banishing any view that it applied only to 'other [explicitly mentioned] Community policies', and explicitly twinning it with sustainable development.[94] Although undoubtedly strengthened over time (suggesting

---

[88] Case C–67/97, *Criminal proceedings against Bluhme* [1998] ECR I–8033. For a useful review of the case law to *Bluhme* see Temmink, 'From Danish Bottles to Danish Bees: The Dynamics of Free Movement of Goods and Environmental Protection—a Case Law Analysis' (2000) 1 *Yearbook of European Environmental Law* 61.

[89] Sands, 'The European Court of Justice: An Environmental Tribunal?' in Somsen (ed.), *Protecting the European Environment: Enforcing EC Environmental Law* (Blackstone, London, 1996). See further pages 166–8 below.

[90] On which see most notably the insertion, under the Treaty of Amsterdam, of the requirement that measures under the internal market environmental guarantee should not amount to 'an obstacle to the functioning of the internal market', and criticism of the nebulousness of this: Macrory, 'Legal Issues of the Amsterdam Treaty: The Environment' in O'Keefe and Twomey (eds.), *Legal Issues of the Amsterdam Treaty* (Hart Publishing, Oxford, 2000); Sevenster, 'The Environmental Guarantee After Amsterdam: Does the Emperor have New Clothes?' (2000) *Yearbook of European Environmental Law* 291.

[91] Harding, 'Who Goes to Court in Europe? An Analysis of Litigation against the European Community' (1992) 17 *European Law Review* 105; Harding and Swart (eds.), *Enforcing European Community Rules: Criminal Proceedings, Administrative Procedures and Harmonization* (Dartmouth, Aldershot, 1996); Chalmers, *supra* n. 2; Jans, *infra* n. 92.

[92] Art. 130r(2) EEC: 'Environmental protection requirements should be a component of the Community's other policies'.

[93] Art. 130r(2) EC Treaty: 'Environmental protection requirements must be integrated into the definition and implementation of other Community policies'.

[94] Art. 6 EC: 'Environmental protection requirements must be integrated into the definition and implementation of the Community's policies and activities referred to in Art. 3, particularly with a view to promoting sustainable development'. See further Macrory, *supra* n. 90.

that it has been seen as increasingly significant, or, perhaps, in need of clarification), the forms of integration have diversified, differing in application and scope. These can be broadly identified as concerning internal Community institutional structures and procedures, related to which is the integration of policy and the promulgation of integrationist legislation, typically utilizing 'horizontal' or cross-media measures.

A legal analysis of the principle, however, suggests that integration is a procedural requirement.[95] Although not purely exhortatory,[96] neither is it clearly justiciable.[97] And, although the legal status of the principle of integration has been debated in disputes over the legal base of a measure,[98] questions remain whether the principle may constrain Community activities which fail to reflect the integration concept, or requires positive steps to be taken.[99] Beyond limited hard legal effect, therefore, the elevation of the integration principle in the EC Treaty has been felt most at the policy and institutional level. Thus, it has imposed an obligation on the part of the Directorates-General to consider environmental protection requirements as part of their respective policy areas. Triggered by the Cardiff European Summit,[100] there is an expanding number of discussion documents that pertain to 'integrate' the environment into other policy areas. These adopt either a bilateral approach to integration (i.e., the integration of 'the environment' into a specific sector),[101] or, increasingly, a multilateral approach whereby more complex and complete patterns of co-operation are evolving.[102] Elsewhere, it has led to a range of institutional developments such as designated environmental liaison officials in other Directorates-General, in effect a lukewarm version of the Greening Government initiative in the UK.[103]

[95] Hession and Macrory, 'The Legal Duty of Environmental Integration: Commitment and Obligation or Enforceable Right?' in O'Riordan and Voisey (eds.), *The Transition to Sustainability: The Politics of Agenda 21 in Europe* (Earthscan, London, 1998).

[96] The conclusion of the ECJ in Case C–62/88, *Parliament* v. *Council* [1990] ECR I–1527 ('*Chernobyl I*') was that the integration principle in its pre-Maastricht version implies that 'all community measures must satisfy the requirements of environmental protection' has been taken as hinting at 'more than a mere enabling provision' (Hession and Macrory, *supra* n. 95).

[97] Notwithstanding the Opinion of Cosmas AG in Case C–321/95P, *Stichting Greenpeace Council (Greenpeace International) and others* v. *Commission* [1998] 3 CMLR 1 who was prepared to find that the integration principle was capable of direct effect, although the ECJ was silent on this point. Contrast transport policy: Case C–13/83, *Parliament* v. *Council* [1985] ECR 1513.

[98] For example, in Case C–300/89, *Commission* v. *Council (Titanium Dioxide)* [1991] ECR I–2867 the ECJ considered that the principle of integration implied that 'a Community measure cannot be covered by Art. 130s merely because it also pursues objectives of environmental protection'.

[99] Hession and Macrory, *supra* n. 95.

[100] See *The Cologne Report on Environmental Integration: Mainstreaming of Environmental Policy*, SEC(99)777.

[101] For example, *Strengthening Environmental Integration within Community Energy Policy*, COM(98)571 final, *Indicators for the Integration of Environmental Concerns into the Common Agricultural Policy*, COM(2000)20 final, *Single Market and Environment*, COM(99)263 final.

[102] *Partnership for Integration—A Strategy for Integrating Environment into European Union Policies*, COM(98)333 final.

[103] Van Calster and Deketelaere, 'Amsterdam, the Intergovernmental Conference and Greening the EU Treaty' (1998) 7 *European Environmental Law Review* 12 at 18. On 'Greening Government' see Bell and McGillivray, *supra* n. 8, 154–6.

Legislation with an avowedly integrationist intent has ensued. One recent example is Regulation 1257/99 on support for rural development[104] which, by strengthening agri-environmental measures, attempts to integrate environmental concerns into the Common Agricultural Policy under the Agenda 2000 reform process. However, such reforms should perhaps be seen as performing a legitimating function for the purpose of excluding, or 'green-boxing', agricultural grants and subsidies from the purview of the World Trade Organization. A further category of integrationist measure relates not to the internal procedures of the Community institutions, but rather aims more fully to integrate decision-making in the Member States. The Directive on environmental assessment is an early example. A more fully developed approach to assessment is taken in the recent adoption of a Directive on strategic environmental assessment, involving also assessment of plans and programmes but, notably, not policies.[105] In similar vein, attached to the Treaty of Amsterdam is a Declaration[106] that 'the Commission undertakes in its proposals, and that the Member States undertake in implementing those proposals, to take full account of their environmental impact and of the principle of sustainable growth', although this falls some way short of a requirement that impact assessment be carried out and is notable for its reference to 'growth' rather than 'development'.

Elsewhere, the Directive on integrated pollution prevention and control offers an example of the advantages and potential scope of an integrated approach.[107] As well as rejecting a media-based approach to pollution control, which is itself the antithesis of an integrated approach, the Directive reflects a recognition that integrated pollution control requires the regulation of 'inputs' as well as 'outputs', namely energy and natural resources, giving it certain qualities relating as much to environmental resource management as to environmental protection.[108] The inclusion of agricultural processes within the Directive's scope further suggests some progression towards a more holistic approach to the environment. A similarly holistic approach is also evident in the recent Water Framework Directive, which links water quality and quantity objectives.[109]

---

[104] [1999] OJ L160/80.

[105] Parliament and Council Directive 2001/42/EC on the assessment of the effects of certain plans and programmes on the environment [2001] OJ L197/30, recital 4 of which notes that 'environmental assessment is an important tool for integrating environmental considerations into the preparation and adoption of certain plans and programmes which are likely to have significant efects on the environment in the Member States, because it ensures that such effects of implementing plans and programmes are taken into account during their preparation and before their adoption'.

[106] Declaration 12 of the Treaty of Amsterdam, strengthening Declaration 20 of the Treaty of Maastricht.

[107] Directive 96/61/EC [1996] OJ L257/26.

[108] Beckwith and Thornton, *Environmental Law* (Sweet and Maxwell, London, 1997), 142.

[109] EP and Council Directive 2000/60/EC establishing a framework for community action in the field of water policy [2000] OJ L327/1.

There has therefore been much action in terms of documentation and some notable examples of directives taking an integrationist approach.[110] But, taking a broad view, there are few identifiable, 'hard' consequences of the principle in terms of decision-making. The decision to proceed with the completion of the internal market, without any rigorous examination of the likely effects on the environment, [111] is one example, such that the policy decisions on the bolsters to the single market, such as the trans-European network, may be seen as examples of profound 'disintegration'.[112] Perhaps most significant is research that suggests that the moves towards greater integration of policy areas can actually lead to marginalization of the environmental agenda, and non-environmental interests and considerations influencing environmental interests as much as vice versa.[113] Arguably, the proliferation of integration duties may weaken the concept such that the environment loses any distinctive legal status in the Treaty.[114]

V. Subsidiarity

The third principle we consider in the context of the greening of EU governance is subsidiarity, a version of which was included in the Environmental Title following the Single European Act[115] before the principle gained more general currency at Maastricht. Like other provisions of the SEA relating to the environment, however, the insertion of a subsidiarity-type provision in the SEA confirmed and legitimated existing practice, in this case entrenching (albeit to a limited extent) an existing sensitivity to questions of scale. Thus, the First Environmental Action Programme referred to five possible levels of action—local, regional, national, European, international—and the need 'to establish the level best suited to the type of pollution and to the geographical

[110] See also, despite its voluntary nature, Council Regulation 1836/93/EEC on environmental management and audit [1993] OJ L168/1, and calls for guidance, rather than legislation, on integrated coastal zone management (see now Communication from the Commission to the Council and the European Parliament on 'Integrated Coastal Zone Management: A Strategy for Europe' (COM(2000)547) and a proposal for a European Parliament and Council Recommendation concerning the implementation of Integrated Coastal Zone Management in Europe (COM(2000)545), both at http://europa.eu. int/comm/environment/iczm/home.htm).

[111] Klatte, 'The Principle of Integration After 25 Years of Community Environmental Policy' (1999) 3 and 4 *Law and European Affairs* 370.

[112] Sheate, 'From Environmental Impact Assessment to Strategic Environmental Assessment: Sustainability and Decision-Making' in Holder (ed.), *The Impact of EC Environmental Law in the United Kingdom* (Wiley, London, 1997). See also Commission Opinion (EC) 96/15 [1996] OJ L6/14 and draft Opinion of 27 Apr. 1995 [1995] OJ L178/3 on the dissonance between transport and nature conservation objectives.

[113] Baldock *et al.*, *The Integration of Environmental Protection Requirements into the Definition and Implementation of Other EC Policies* (IEEP, London, 1992).

[114] Macrory, *supra* n. 90, 174–5.

[115] 'The Community shall take action relating to the environment to the extent to which the objectives . . . can be attained better at Community level than at the level of individual Member States'.

zone to be protected'.[116] Of course, for some Member States at least, the initial insertion of a subsidiarity-type provision into the EEC Treaty was to prevent an undesirable extension of Community competence rather than anything with wider impact.[117]

As with the version of subsidiarity originally contained in Article 130r(4) of the EEC Treaty, the more general subsidiarity provision inserted at Maastricht reflects a concern with the appropriate level of decision-making, again juxtaposing Community and Member State action using the language of effectiveness as its true measure.[118] Necessarily this has implications for values related to processes rather than outcomes.[119] Thus while there are a number of provisions of EC environmental law which require or promote a measure of public involvement, a difficulty is that this occurs against a background in which procedural values are fundamentally downplayed.[120] A further implication is that the approach in Article 5 EC (ex Article 3b), which conspicuously eschews the citizen-centred approach to subsidiarity taken in Article 1 of the TEU (ex Article A), blocks out an important conceptual space for the ecological citizen, avoiding consideration of the local or the 'domestic' as worthy of Treaty-based protection.[121] In any event, the fluid boundaries of environmental law, and in particular moves to integrate environmental concerns into other policy sectors, pose a particular challenge to the idea of a strict division between exclusive and shared competence.[122] This is further complicated by the difficulty, in the environmental sphere as elsewhere, of drawing sharp distinctions between the local and the global and all points in between.

In addition, continuing attention to effectiveness of outcome clashes not merely with other valuable aspects of regulation, such as process values, but also with the realities of existing EC environmental law. Many new environmental measures move away from traditional 'command and control' regulation and are difficult to judge on normal 'effectiveness of outcome' grounds. Recent amendments to the Directive on environmental impact assessment, for example, retain its procedurally-focused mechanisms based on preventing adverse environmental impact at source, although the Directive is not directly

---

[116] Whether this takes 'situatedness' seriously must be doubted.

[117] Golub, *supra* n. 6, 714.

[118] de Búrca, 'Reappraising Subsidiarity's Significance after Amsterdam', Harvard Jean Monnet Working Paper 7/99. See here also Protocol 30 to the EC Treaty on the application of the principles of subsidiarity and proportionality.

[119] See generally Scott, *supra* n. 2, 15–23 and *passim*. It is notable that incisive reports on environmental law have come from the Court of Auditors: see e.g. Special Report No. 3/98 concerning the implementation by the Commission of EU policy and action as regards water pollution [1998] OJ C191/2.

[120] For example, neither the Directive on landfill (*supra* n. 37) nor the proposed Directive on environmental liability contains provisions for public participation (in relation to the latter, this may be contrasted with the US 'Superfund' rules concerning contaminated land).

[121] Cross, 'Subsidiarity and the Environment' (1995) 15 *Yearbook of European Law* 107. On citizenship generally see Section VI below.

[122] For example, in relation to environmental protection and external trade. For a more general overview of the problem of ascribing exclusive competence see de Búrca, *supra* n. 118.

assessed against this objective, either quantitatively or qualitatively.[123] On the other hand, while the economic costs and benefits of taking action at EC level are captured in the Commission's *fiches d'impact*, political values grounded on more aspirational environmental objectives may in practice prove to be over-riding.[124]

Because subsidiarity-type concerns related to 'who does what' have always influenced environmental policy, Treaty-based provisions have impacted most in relation to 'what it is they actually do', conflating subsidiarity with pressures towards deregulation.[125] While the pace of new environmental legislation undoubtedly slowed following completion of the internal market, and some inert proposals were, for the time being, withdrawn, the greatest impact has been the subtle reorientation of new proposals towards greater flexibility. This is seen most clearly in the exercise of discretion, primarily at national level, and both legislatively and judicially: changes to the form and intensity of legislation, and a greater willingness to apply and interpret this flexibly and to bolster this approach through a preference for decentralized enforcement methods.[126] Nevertheless, the general endurability of existing EC environmental legislation and proposals for new law is striking. Central to this have been the pre-existing twin sensitivities to issues of scale in decision-making, as well as leaving the details of the balancing of environmental and other objectives to the Member States.[127]

Specifically, many directives in areas identified post-Maastricht for simplification, especially those relating to air and water quality standards, have been renewed or are close to revision, albeit subject in differing respects to subsidiarity. For example, there has been some shift in the Directive on drinking water quality towards regulating only for essential quality and health-

[123] *Supra* n. 75. See COM(93)28, and the criteria for assessment contained in the Protocol on the Application of the Principles of Subsidiarity and Proportionality, *supra* n. 118. See also other information-based provisions on freedom of access to environmental information (Council Directive 90/313/EEC [1990] OJ L158/56), eco-labelling (Council Regulation 880/92/EEC [1992] OJ L99/1) and energy labelling (Council Directive 92/75/EEC [1992] OJ L297/16) and environmental management and audit (see *supra* n. 110).

[124] See, e.g., the action of the Parliament in rejecting the conclusions of the *fiche d'impact* in relation to the proposed Directive on landfill (*supra* n. 37) that the Directive should not apply to rural areas, discussed in Froud, Boden, Ogus, and Stubbs, *Controlling the Regulators* (Macmillan, Basingstoke, 1998), discussed in Lange, 'Economic Appraisal of Law-making and Changing Forms of Governance' (2000) 63 *MLR* 294 at 298.

[125] Flynn, 'Subsidiarity and the Rise of "Soft Law" in EU Environmental Policy: Beyond Who Does What, to What it is they Actually do?' [1997] *European Policy Process*, Occasional Paper No. 40.

[126] See generally Scott, *supra* n. 2, chaps. 1 and 2.

[127] '[G]enerally the principle of subsidiarity has been complied with in Community environmental legislation' van Brinkhorst, 'Subsidiarity and European Community Environment Policy: A Panacea or a Pandora's Box?' (1993) 2 *European Environmental Law Review* 16 at 20. See also Jans, *supra* n. 2, 11. Compare the remarks of Leon Brittan: 'Environmental policy should be the first target for subsidiarity', 'Subsidiarity in the constitution of the EC', Robert Schuman Lecture, 11 June 1992 (EUI, Florence, 1992), quoted in Golub, *supra* n. 6.

related parameters, while Member States are to be given greater flexibility in monitoring water quality.[128] Current proposals to amend the Directive on bathing waters may, for the first time, make distinct provision for different waters, for example fresh and coastal waters, or colder northern and warmer southern waters.[129] This approach would take differences in environmental assimilative capacities seriously while, in theory, providing for common minimum health and amenity standards. And in relation to air quality, the adoption of the Directive on ambient air quality assessment and management[130] has put to rest concerns that the Community had, by the mid-1990s, abandoned, at least temporarily, recourse to quality objectives in this sector in favour of emissions standards, seemingly because of the greater flexibility afforded by process-based controls.[131]

In addition, controversial provisions of existing directives in these key policy areas have, for a range of reasons, endured. These include the background presence of international commitments or exhortatory standards, such as the role of World Health Organization standards in guiding drinking water and air quality law, but probably also include the impact of the precautionary principle acting to entrench existing provisions of environmental legislation which might not otherwise remain. Finally, renewed commitment to existing policy areas involves little risk of losing symbolic capital. Similarly, new legislation has been adopted, or proposals remain active, in every key area where, post-Maastricht, at least some Member States were actively hostile to the development of EC environmental law.[132] Notable here are the adoption of Directives on packaging waste and landfills,[133] and on strategic environmental assessment[134] and proposed legislation relating to environmental liability.[135] Even a Directive on zoo animals has emerged, albeit one concerned with the contribution of zoos to public education about biodiversity

---

[128] See Council Directive 98/83/EC [1998] OJ L330/32, replacing Council Directive 80/778/EEC [1980] OJ L229/11 as from 25 Dec. 2003 (longer periods are given for bromate, lead, and trihalomethane).

[129] See COM(94)36, amended proposal COM(97)585. For the latest proposals see COM (2000) 860 is not precluded. A separate directive on bathing water by adoption of the Water Framework Directive, mentioned *supra* n. 109.

[130] Council Directive 96/62/EC [1996] OJ L296/55.

[131] Krämer, *supra* n. 2, 206. The air quality sector in particular is notable for some quite radical approaches to standard-setting and national discretion: see especially Council Directive 88/609/EEC on large combustion plants [1988] OJ L336/1, as amended, and comment by Scott, *supra* n. 2, 40.

[132] See, e.g., the so-called 'hit lists' drawn up by the larger Member States, discussed in Axelrod, 'Subsidiarity and Environmental Policy in the European Community'(1994) 6 *Journal of International Environmental Affairs* 115; Wils 'Subsidiarity and EC Environmental Policy: Taking People's Concerns Seriously' (1994) 6 *Journal of Environmental Law* 85.

[133] Respectively, EP and Council Directive 94/62/EC on packaging and packaging waste [1994] OJ L365/10, and see *supra* n. 37.

[134] See *supra* n. 105.

[135] COM(2000)66 final.

conservation rather than welfare concerns,[136] illustrating continuing ambiguities in the Community's involvement in animal welfare matters.[137]

While generalizations are problematic, some trends seem to emerge. First, minimum harmonization remains the preference, while the scope for Member States to maintain or adopt higher national standards will, in practice, increase.[138] Linked with this, genuinely 'framework' directives have yet to emerge, although the Framework Water Directive has this characteristic, at least for new areas of regulation. (Whilst its pursuit of water quality of 'good ecological status' may prove elusive, its problematic approach combining emissions and quality standards[139] is unlikely to see any weakening of existing provisions.) A continued use of framework directives in the sense of 'umbrella' directives providing a general basis for more detailed controls, however, can be seen in the air quality sector, with 'daughter' directives finally emerging.[140]

Secondly, discretion at implementation persists, although procedural constraints may be attached. Time-limited derogations to particularly affected Member States continue to be used, while central regulatory terms are left undefined or intentionally vague.[141] More generally, a narrow view of taking local environmental conditions into account is emerging more explicitly, even if this is within procedurally constrained parameters.[142] This approach looks

[136] Council Directive 1999/22/EC relating to the keeping of wild animals in zoos [1999] OJ L94/24, implementing in part the 1992 UN Convention on Biological Diversity. Krämer attributes the change of emphasis to a complete change of position by the UK, *supra* n. 2, 147. The earlier proposals focusing on welfare considerations were on the verge of being watered down into a Council Recommendation, a draft of which appeared at COM(95)619. See also the resolution of the Parliament trying to prevent this downgrading [1995] OJ C89/234.

[137] For example, Council Directive 91/629/EEC laying down minimum standards for the protection of calves [1991] OJ L340/28; various 'welfare' inspired measures on whales, seal pups, and leghold traps are noted *supra* n. 18. See also Art. 9(5) of Council Regulation 338/97/EC [1997] OJ L61/1, which transposes welfare provisions in the CITES Treaty. Under Protocol 33 and Declaration No. 24 to the Amsterdam Treaty, regard for animal welfare is limited to CAP, transport, internal market, and research, and the exclusion of EC environmental policy indicates that this provision applies only to domestic, not wild, animals.

[138] Especially, Art. 95(4)–(9) EC, which now time-limits the Commission to respond to requests to exceed harmonization standards. Notably, the Directive on packaging waste, adopted under ex Art. 100a, explicitly allows Member States to set higher recycling and recovery targets, and allows certain states to set lower targets, an interesting use of legal rather than financial flexibility measures (see Art. 175(5)EC). Art. 95 EC should be contrasted with Art. 176 EC (ex Art. 130t) which, post-Amsterdam, continues to authorize measures to maintain or introduce more stringent protective measures.

[139] Howarth, 'Accommodation without Resolution? Emission Controls and Environmental Quality Objectives in the Proposed EC Water Framework Directive' (1999) 1 *Environmental Law Review* 6.

[140] Also in this context, Directive 96/61/EC on Integrated Pollution Prevention and Control, *supra* n. 107, is notable; this is a framework directive in the sense that daughter directives must be agreed for certain categories of installations and polluting substances on the basis of information exchange between the Member States (Art. 18(1)). See, e.g., COM(97)604 on aqueous discharge from incineration of hazardous waste.

[141] For example, the meaning of 'municipal' waste in the Directive on landfill, *supra* n. 37.

[142] See the IPPC Directive, *supra* n. 107, which allows performance standards to be determined with regard to firms' 'geographic location and local environmental conditions', subject to meeting any relevant environmental quality standards, see further Scott, 'Flexibility, "Proceduralization", and Environmental Governance in the EU' in de Búrca and Scott (eds.), *The Changing Constitution of the EU: From Uniformity to Flexibility?* (Hart Publishing, Oxford, 2000).

to physical environmental features rather than situatedness or 'closeness to the citizen'. Further, a divergence is emerging in relation to measures requiring the designation of sites and the application of protective regimes there, an approach traditionally seen as something of a halfway house between emission and target standards. The Court of Justice continues to deliver fairly strongly worded judgments on the designation of conservation areas, including important judgments on the *sufficiency* of a Member State's overall designation.[143] However, this approach tends to be followed where designation does not entail the 'preservation' of such areas, but allows economic considerations to be weighed when deciding on questions of land use. By contrast, where designation 'matters', the Court has, at least in certain situations, shown a certain measure of flexibility towards Member State discretion.[144] Finally in this context, there is a continued resistance to transferring inspection and day-to-day enforcement powers to the EC level, in part because of the loss of symbolic capital involved[145] but no doubt also for the more pragmatic reason that EC-level inspection and enforcement may simply be too challenging a task. Instead, the onus has so far been placed on other mechanisms and institutions such as the role of the European Environment Agency (in gathering information) and the EC Network for the Implementation and Enforcement of Environmental Law (IMPEL) (which promotes the exchange of information and expertise between regulators with a view to developing greater consistency in enforcement). There is the prospect, however, of a Recommendation on minimum criteria for environmental inspections which would require Member States to draw up plans covering both routine monitoring of industrial activities regulated under Community environmental law, and non-routine follow-up inspections.[146]

Thirdly, there has been less resort to a widening of the range of regulatory instruments than the Fifth Action Programme perhaps envisaged. Although market-based instruments have emerged in relation to vehicle emissions and

---

[143] Case C–3/96, *Commission* v. *Netherlands* [1998] ECR I–3031.

[144] Contrast Case C–225/96, *Commission* v. *Italy* [1997] ECR I–6887 (shellfish waters) with Case C–293/97, *R.* v. *Secretary of State for the Environment and Minister of Agriculture, Fisheries and Food ex p. Standley and Metson* [1999] ECR I–2603 (designation of nitrate vulnerable zones). In the latter, the ECJ held that 'Community law cannot provide precise criteria for establishing in each case whether the discharge of nitrogen compounds of agricultural origin makes a significant contribution to the pollution. . . . The Directive may thus be applied by the Member States in different ways' (paras. 38 and 39).

[145] Chalmers, *supra* n. 2, 679. In particular, enforcement of the Directive on environmental impact assessment (*supra* n. 75) proved contentious: see Kunzlik, 'Environmental Impact Assessment: The British Cases' (1995) 4 *European Environmental Law Review* 336; Williams, 'The European Commission and the Enforcement of Environmental Law: an Invidious Position' [1994] *Yearbook of European Law* 351. As the Commissioner responsible at the time (Carlo Ripa di Meana) remarked, 'Whenever we discussed subsidiarity in the commission, I saw Delors glaring at me', in Grant, *Delors: Inside the House that Jacques Built* (Nicholas Brealey, London, 1994), at 108.

[146] Conseil 99/409, Brussels, 13/14 Dec. 1999, available at www.asser.nl/EEL/index4.htm. As with IMPEL, however, the proposed criteria would only apply to industrial activities, not environmental law more generally.

fuel quality,[147] where voluntary agreements with the car industry have also been negotiated by the Commission,[148] the wider use of economic instruments remains a vision rather than a reality.[149] Again for reasons related to symbolic capital, proposals for a carbon/energy tax, and revised proposals for an energy products tax, have stalled.[150] A resurrection in response to the demands of climate change seems unlikely, with the flexibility of emissions trading, either between the Member States or, more likely, individual companies, emerging.[151]

Finally, subsidiarity as a legal concept both fails to resolve fundamental issues about the allocation of responsibility and, as importantly, neglects to frame the kinds of questions that determine such decisions.[152] While there have been improvements in the direction of wider public consultation on certain proposals, experience has been mixed.[153] And current proposals continue to downplay public involvement after implementation, generally by adopting a technocratic approach to what are wider issues.[154] As Chalmers points out, opportunities for public participation in the key Directives on IPPC and environmental impact assessment come in only after the process of industry self-review has taken place,[155] which broadly parallels approaches elsewhere, for example under the Works Council Directive.[156]

VI.   Citizenship

In this section, we consider the extent to which EC environmental law may be conceptualized within a framework drawn from the EU's nascent attempt to carve out a European concept of citizenship.[157] Although much of the present EU concept of citizenship is a loose construction of free movement and equal

---

[147] See, e.g., the Commission statement attached to Directive 98/70/EC relating to the quality of petrol and diesel fuels [1998] OJ L350/58.

[148] COM(98)495 final (European manufacturers); COM(99)446 final (Japanese and Korean manufacturers).

[149] Amongst current proposals see the draft Framework Water Directive, *supra* n. 109, concerning 'full-cost' water charging; and proposals for an integrated products policy. Markets may, however, emerge in response to EC environmental legislation, as has been the case, at least in the UK, with the market in packaging waste recovery notes following implementation of the Directive on packaging waste, *supra* n. 133 and generally Bell and McGillivray, *Ball and Bell on Environmental Law* (Blackstone Press, London, 2000), 201. There is the prospect of an emissions trading system emerging within the EC, as provided for under the 1997 Kyoto Protocol to the 1992 UN Framework Convention on Climate Change.

[150] See COM(92)266 final, as amended, and COM(97)30. See also *supra* n. 38.

[151] COM(2000) 87.   [152] de Búrca, *supra* n. 106.

[153] See, e.g., the conference in Sept. 1993 on future directions for drinking water: see Richardson, 'EU Water Policy: Uncertain Agendas, Shifting Networks and Complex Coalitions' (1994) 3 *Environmental Politics* 139, 140, and contrast the 'Auto-Oil' programme.

[154] For example, the Landfill Directive, *supra* n. 37, and proposals on environmental liability (*supra* n. 135).

[155] Chalmers, *supra* n. 2, 681.   [156] Council Directive 94/45/EC [1994] OJ L254/64.

[157] On citizenship in an EC environmental law context see Cross, *supra* n. 121, and Macrory, 'Environmental Citizenship and the Law: Repairing the European Road' (1996) 8 *Journal of Environmental Law* 219.

treatment rights,[158] we examine the extent to which EC law has begun to construct the EC 'environmental' citizen by the use of existing approaches and incremental development of generally-accepted citizenship claims. Attempts to develop the European environmental citizen, notably in relation to public participation, have often been driven by the need for greater enforcement of existing EC environmental law, long-recognized as a serious weakness.[159] Furthermore, bolder proposals in this area, such as the formal entrenching of environmental 'rights' at the EU level, are addressed only at one understanding of the 'environmental' citizen. By contrast, a more radical conception of 'ecological' citizenship may be advanced.

A.   'ENVIRONMENTAL' CITIZENSHIP

On the surface, there is little within the present formulation of citizenship as a concept of EU law that touches upon human–environment relations. At best, perhaps, citizenship suggests a restricted, residual view either of the 'market citizen',[160] or of a political citizen enjoying political rights through bonds of residence and not mere nationality. On either approach, the interaction between the EU citizen and his or her environment is either indirect, through the market, or through a specific place- or nation-centred participation in political life. We can, however, consider EC environmental law by looking at various tendencies suggested by the concept of citizenship.[161]

Environmental law continues to eschew a full-blown rights perspective,[162] and the Environmental Title of the EC Treaty continues to speak of 'protecting the quality of the environment'[163] rather than adopting a rights-based discourse as found elsewhere in the Treaty in relation to social and economic policy.[164] Similarly, the environmental action programmes have never emphasized rights in the way that, for example, consumer policy has.[165] Environmental policy remains more programmatic in character, based generally on duties of result owed by the Member States. Attempts during the last

---

[158]   Ex Art. 8a–e EC, now Arts. 18–22 EC, described as 'an embarrassment', 'an empty gesture', 'little more than a cynical exercise in public relations', and ultimately 'a failure of the imagination': see Weiler, 'The Selling of Europe: the Discourse of European Citizenship in the IGC 1996', *Harvard Jean Monnet Working Paper* 3/96.

[159]   See *Implementing Community Environmental Law: Commission Communication to Council and Parliament*, COM(96)500 final.

[160]   Everson, 'The Legacy of the Market Citizen' in Shaw and More (eds.), *New Legal Dynamics of the European Union* (Oxford University Press, Oxford, 1996). On this, see, e.g., the problematic eco-labelling and energy labelling regimes, *supra* n. 150.

[161]   Shaw, 'The Interpretation of European Union Citizenship' (1998) 61 *MLR* 293.

[162]   Despite its partial origins in the Stockholm Conference, and Principle 1 of the Stockholm Declaration, *supra* n. 31.

[163]   Art. 174(1) EC (ex Art. 130r(1)).

[164]   For example, Art. 141 (ex Art. 119) on equal pay for equal work.

[165]   Reich, 'The Recognition of Fundamental Rights in the Areas of Consumer and Environmental Protection by the EC' in Kye (ed.), *EU Environmental Law and Policy and EU Consumer Law and Policy: Converging and Diverging Trends* (Kluwer, Dordrecht, 1995). There was no mention of 'environmental rights' in the first three environmental action programmes.

IGC, both by Sweden and the Commission, to see a right of all citizens to a healthy environment inserted into the EC Treaty were unsuccessful,[166] although pressure for such a change may have been bought off only by the insertion of the new integration principle.[167]

Grounding substantive environmental citizenship rights was again raised in the context of the latest IGC by environmental NGOs,[168] and featured in discussion over the Charter of Fundamental Rights.[169] However, it must be doubted whether a legal right to environment as formulated will operate at anything more than a policy level or provide anything more than symbolic capital. While the European Court of Human Rights has, in extreme cases, worked creatively with the European Convention on Human Rights to provide remedies for flagrant instances of environmental injustice, it has done so necessarily within existing categories of the protection of rights and freedoms.[170] It remains to be seen whether abstractly-formulated 'rights' in the context of the environment are useful, not least in relation to issues such as climate change and biodiversity conservation. By contrast to human-constructed concepts such as freedom of trade or the right to equal treatment and freedom from discrimination, the environment is both a social construct and a practical reality; necessarily, our interaction with the environment, in its infinite variety of forms and qualities, means a balancing of complex economic, social, and ethical issues in the setting of environmental standards.[171] As discussed above, so long as the objective is the integration of environment and economics through sustainable development, this requires resolution or balance, rather than the 'trump' character of rights.

Legislatively, there appears to be a modest expansion of procedural rights. While access to EU documents is now provided for at Treaty level,[172] revisions

---

[166] Jordan, 'Step Change or Stasis? EC Environmental Policy after the Amsterdam Treaty' (1998) 7 *Environmental Politics* 227.

[167] Macrory, *supra* n. 90. See Section IV above.

[168] Birdlife *et al.*, *Greening the Treaty III: Institutional Reform, Citizens' Rights and Sustainable Development. Proposals for the 2000 Intergovernmental Conference* (at www.asser.nl/EEL).

[169] See the right to respect for the environment contained in the European Parliament's Draft Constitution of the EU (adopted 1994), in the Parliament's Imbeni Report on Union Citizenship for the European Parliament's Committee on Civil Liberties and Internal Affairs (Doc. A3–0437/93, 21 Dec. 1993), and in the Bindi Report on European Citizenship for the European Parliament's Institutional Affairs Committee (DOC A3–0300/91). See now Art. 37 of the Charter of Fundamental Rights: 'A high level of environmental protection and the improvement of the quality of the environment must be integrated into the policies of the Union and ensured in accordance with the principle of sustainable development'. On previous attempts see Lanaerts, 'Fundamental Rights to be Included in a Community Catalogue' (1991) 16 *European Law Review* 367.

[170] See *Lopez Ostra* v. *Spain* (1995) 20 EHRR 277, *Guerra* v. *Italy* [1998] 26 EHRR 357. But contrast unsuccessful cases not involving property rights, e.g. *LCB* v. *UK* (1999) 27 EHRR 212.

[171] Royal Commission on Environmental Pollution, 21st Report, *Setting Environmental Standards* (Cm 4053, TSO, London, 1998). For specific criticism of environmental rights see Macrory, *supra* n. 158; Miller, *Environmental Rights: Critical Perspectives* (Routledge, London, 1998); Eleftheriades, 'The Future of Environmental Rights in the EU' in Alston (ed.), *The European Union and Human Rights* (Oxford University Press, Oxford, 1999).

[172] Art. 255 EC. See also Decision of 21 Mar. 1997 [1997] OJ C282/5, which governs access to documents emanating from the European Environment Agency.

to key directives such as on environmental impact assessment[173] and the control of major accident hazards[174] show an incremental enhancement of rights to information and participation. In the case of the latter, for example, Member States are now required proactively to publicize information relating to the more hazardous installations covered. Moreover, access to information (rather than merely access to documents) for any natural or legal person who so requests it follows the approach taken in the Directive on environmental information.[175] However, there is no fundamental change of approach from this Directive, namely to view procedural rights as facilitating enforcement, or at best enhancing transparency, rather than providing anything more freestanding.[176] These developments do little to challenge the framing of the EC's democratic difficulties primarily as questions of the balancing of power between the institutions rather than as about the relationship of 'citizens' to these institutions.[177]

There are some signs of a greater role for citizen-type involvement in EC decision-making, such as the emergence of limited attempts to foster an environmental civil society through EC funding for environmental NGOs operating at the European level.[178] Again, though, such funding may primarily assist the Commission, at least indirectly, in its enforcement role. In the same vein, the recent White Paper on Environmental Liability foresees a role for environmental NGOs, but only as a surrogate enforcement agency, generally where official action is not forthcoming.[179] Where environmental NGOs have been given participatory rights at the level of EC decision-making, in practice these may be drowned out by the sound of industrial voices enjoying considerable numeric and other advantages.[180] Eventual implementation of the recently concluded 1998 Århus Convention on Access to Information, Public Participation in Decision-Making and Access to Justice in Environmental Matters, though, may alter this significantly, providing a procedural complement to the more substantively-oriented but less environmentally-relevant

---

[173] See *supra* n. 75.

[174] Council Directive 96/82/EC [1997] OJ L10/13 ('Seveso II').

[175] *Ibid.*, Art. 20(1). See also Directive 90/313/EEC, *supra* n. 123, Art. 3.

[176] The Information Directive can also be seen as serving to correct the sub-optimal provision of information by the market; information is thus promoted as an alternative regulatory mechanism in itself. See generally Heyvaert, 'Access to Information in a Deregulated Environment' in Collier (ed.), *Deregulation in the European Union: Environmental Perspectives* (Routledge, London, 1998). We doubt whether this does more than further underscore the 'market citizen' model.

[177] de Lange, 'Paradoxes of European Citizenship' in Fitzpatrick (ed.), *Nationalism, Racism and the Rule of Law* (Dartmouth, Aldershot, 1995) 97 at 99; Armstrong, 'Citizenship of the Union? Lessons from Carvel and the Guardian' (1996) 59 *MLR* 582 at 588.

[178] Council Decision 97/872/EC [1997] OJ L354/25, which applies for the years 1998–2001. It should be noted, though, that Commission support for environmental NGOs has gone on for longer than this measure, albeit often indirect through the staging of conferences etc.

[179] See *supra* n. 135.

[180] See in particular Council Directive 96/61/EC, *supra* n. 95, Art.16(2).

European Convention on Human Rights (ECHR). But so far, the environmental citizen is generally a passive voice in EC environmental law and policy.[181]

Perhaps the most interesting tangible developments in relation to environmental citizenship are taking place at judicial level. It is notable that the report of the European Court of Justice to the 1996 Intergovernmental Conference (IGC) specifically linked citizenship with its earlier creation of directly effective rights, suggesting that citizenship is to be seen substantively rather than merely in terms of procedural guarantees of political participation.[182] As with legislative action, however, the underlying concern with ensuring greater enforcement is being reflected in a drift away from the view that Community legislation will be reviewable under the direct effect doctrine only where there is detriment to an individual right. Thus, in two cases concerning the Directive on environmental assessment, the Court has held that what matters is the obligation on the Member State (or its competent authorities or even its courts) to take all the appropriate measures to ensure that the Directive is faithfully implemented in practice and that any discretion that a Member State has is not unduly exceeded. In the *Kraaijeveld* case,[183] a case concerning the lack of assessment for the construction of Dutch dykes, the Court held that the Member States' discretion in implementing the Directive in practice did not preclude judicial review of the question whether this discretion had been exceeded, and the courts could be obliged to set aside national legislation going beyond the limits of that discretion where they were bound to review the legality of national decision-making on their own motion. National authorities must then take all the measures necessary to ensure compliance with the Directive. Writing extra-judicially about *Kraaijeveld*, at least one member of the Court (Judge Edward) has tried to make it clear that this did not mean that the Court found this part of the environmental assessment directive to be directly effective, or confer individual rights (thus ruling out *Francovich* claims). In the more recent *Bozen* case,[184] the Court was asked to consider a challenge to a decision not to require an impact assessment for redevelopment at Bolzano airport. The project would have changed the use of the airport from military to civilian and cargo flights, requiring some new development and intensifying effects from things like noise. The Court followed the *Kraaijeveld* case in holding that the key test in relation to such projects was whether they were likely to have significant environmental effects because of their size, nature, or location, and did not explore the issue whether the appli-

[181] See COM(2000)155: 'working for the citizen' (para. 3). But see now the proposal for a Parliament and Council Directive providing for public participation in respect of the drawing up of certain plans and programmes relating to the environment and amending Council Directives 85/337/EEC and 96/61/EC, COM(2000)839 [2001] OJ C154/123.

[182] Report of the Court of Justice (and Court of First Instance) on Certain Aspects of the Application of the Treaty on European Union, May 1995, discussed in de Búrca, 'The Quest for Legitimacy in the European Union' (1996) 59 *MLR* 349.

[183] *Supra* n. 76.

[184] Case C–435/97, *World Wildlife Fund and Others* v. *Autonome Provinz Bozen and Others* [2000] 1 CMLR 149.

cants had any right to bring the case. Thus, while not holding that the Directive conferred directly effective rights on individuals where an authority in a Member State had exceeded its discretion, the Court provided a remedy for the applicants by, in effect, looking to the legality of the national decision-making procedure and the extent to which this, if unchecked, would detract from the effective implementation of the Directive.

Opinions differ on what is happening here. For some, following Judge Edward's lead, the Court is constructing a new remedy through which non-implementation of directives can be checked without opening up the possibility of state liability claims (termed by one commentator 'public law effect').[185] For others, the better view would probably be to see this as an expansion of the direct effect doctrine.[186] In practical terms, however, the result is little different; the notion that individual right must be infringed for a provision to be directly effective, and further that a right based on the protection of human health, or compensation for economic loss arising from environmental 'harm', must be at stake (as against, say, 'interests' relating to nature conservation[187]) would seem to be being replaced by judicial mechanisms which look more towards the administrative duty that has been breached rather than the personal interests at stake.[188] What is clear is that concerns about non-implementation of Community environmental law have driven the Court of Justice away from a narrow, rights-based, citizenship-type agenda, expanding at the same time the environmental citizen although still from an enforcement perspective.

A possible motivation behind the Court of Justice's approach appears to be self-interest in preventing an expansion in the workload of the Court in new areas. This is seen most notably in relation to the test for 'direct and individual concern' in Article 230 EC (ex Article 173), which the Court of First Instance and Court of Justice continue to interpret restrictively against individuals and environmental organizations, an interpretation which, perversely, operates so that the more widespread the environmental harm the stronger is the bar on

---

[185] Scott, *supra* n. 2, 157.

[186] Hilson and Downes, 'Making Sense of Rights: Community Rights in EC Law' (1999) 24 *European Law Review* 121. This argues that direct effect can be established so long as *effet utile* is at stake. This work provides a challenging critique and persuasive basis for laying a doctrinal foundation to the important normative issues at stake in relation to diffuse, impersonal interests such as those relating to the environment.

[187] For an overview of the case law see generally Hilson, 'Community Rights in Environmental Law: Rhetoric or Reality?' in Holder (ed.), *supra* n. 112.

[188] In this sense, mirroring developments in environmental judicial review at the national level; see *R. v. Somerset County Council, ex p. Dixon* [1998] Env. LR 111. At national level, there has also been welcome recognition that the extent to which directives cannot be directly effective because they sought to be applied horizontally between individuals must be given a restricted understanding in those 'tripartite' (or 'indirect horizontal effect') situations where an individual seeks to enforce a procedural environmental right against a Member State which leads to negative consequences for another individual: see *R. v. Durham CC, Sherburn Stone Company Ltd & Secretary of State for Environment, Transport and the Regions, ex p. Huddlestone* [2000] 2 CMLR 313 and comment by Stallworthy, 'Challenging Public Authorities: Consequences for Third Parties and the Limits of Direct Effect' (2000) 2 *Environmental Law Review* 102.

legal recourse before the European Court.[189] The dilemma might also be seen as an attempt on the part of the Court of Justice to fit broad environmental concerns ('of general interest') into a tightly defined legal category, originally drawn up with the protection of discrete and individualized financial interests in mind. Nevertheless, the dissonance between seeking greater involvement of individuals and groups in the legislative process, whilst privileging the rights of only some of these participants in relation to the judicial interpretation or protection of the deals struck, is striking, and of doubtful consistency with the requirements of the Århus Convention.[190] Outside direct effect, the Court of Justice continues to be conspicuously inactive in the creative development of the procedural and participatory protections for individuals and groups seen elsewhere.[191] In practice, a further, related, difficulty, is that while a significant proportion (around one third) of ongoing enforcement action by the Commission relates to the environment, the Court is called upon comparatively rarely to rule on preliminary references in environmental matters, and when it does so these tend to be in cases brought by commercial rather than environmental concerns.[192] This has clear implications for the positive development of EC environmental law.

B. TOWARDS 'ECOLOGICAL' CITIZENSHIP?

Like citizenship generally, environmental citizenship has tended to be conceptualized in terms of the claiming of entitlements in the public sphere. These may be procedural rights of the kind discussed above, or more substantive rights to an environment of a 'clean', 'decent', or 'healthy' quality, framed anthropocentrically for humans.[193] Theoretically, the exercise is often seen as expanding citizenship claims outwards from civic, political, and social rights to 'third-generation' solidarity or collective rights such as environmental rights. Because EC law is an implicit rejection of ecological thought, however, an ecological perspective on citizenship arguably leads not to a 'mainstreaming' of EC environmental law but rather provides a 'disruptive challenge to traditional notions of citizenship', one which looks 'outside the city, beyond the public, and further afield than the nation-state'.[194]

[189] Case C–321/95P, *Stichting Greenpeace Council, supra* n. 97. See also Case T–461/93, *An Taisce and WWF* v. *Commission* [1994] ECR II–733, and generally Krämer, 'Public Interest Litigation in Environmental Matters Before European Courts' (1996) 8 *Journal of Environmental Law* 1. To date Art. 232 (ex Art. 175) has never been used in an environmental context.

[190] Especially Art. 9(3).

[191] For example, the International Court of Justice, *supra* n. 76. These developments have largely been through dissenting opinions. The *Greenpeace* judgment, *supra* n. 97, suggests thinly-concealed differences of judicial opinion which might better be brought to the surface.

[192] Jans, presentation at the conference *Sustaining Environmental Law*, Imperial College, London, 10 Oct. 1998.

[193] Notable here is the European Council's Dublin Declaration on 'the Environmental Imperative' (June 1990), which endorsed the right to a clean and healthy environment for the citizens of the European Union.

[194] Dobson, 'Ecological Citizenship: A Disruptive Influence?', paper presented at the University of Reading, 24 Nov. 1998, 19 and 20.

Various possibilities flow from taking an ecological citizenship perspective which, taking a duties-centred perspective, is not based on a contract between the state and its members.[195] Rather, we may consider EC environmental law as positing a conception of ecological citizenship wedded to the nation-state neither in space nor in time, nor wholly concerned with activities in the public sphere. Clearly, such an ecological citizenship poses a challenge even to the conceptions of citizenship that can be derived, immanently, from existing political, economic, and social rights at EU level.

Initially, a duties-based approach is increasingly being pursued by commentators frustrated at attempts at ascribing environmental rights (and also 'rights to the environment' itself).[196] Moreover, duties-centred approaches can be found in some national constitutions of Member States, including duties both on individuals (for example, the Spanish Constitution) and on government (for example, the Dutch Constitution)). From an ecological perspective, a duties-based approach emphasizes a degree of virtue, and an attitude towards the natural environment, and avoids any necessary connection with rights. By definition, environmental duties, owed across physical and spatial borders, cannot be based on reciprocity.[197]

As far as law is concerned, three issues emerge in relation to duties. We may ask to whom a particular duty is owed, since this will be important for enforcement. Who has the correlative right to any duty placed on either the Commission or the Member States? In *Enichem Base*, for example, the Court of Justice held that the Commission, not the Member State, had the correlative right in respect of reporting obligations in the Waste Framework Directive.[198] However, it has been queried whether the same approach should be taken in a situation similar to that in the *Stichting Greenpeace* case, at least if the geographic nexus is sufficient to establish a right.[199] Further, there may be greater flexibility in relation to transposing duties than rights; an obligation to prohibit an environmentally-damaging activity can generally be transposed either by criminal, civil, or administrative mechanisms, and even within any of these categories there will generally be flexibility as to the degree of obligation, for example, as between strict or fault-based liability. Finally, EC law can, directly or indirectly, regulate or stimulate private behaviour. There is, after all, much in the belief that 'from an ecological point of view, good citizenship is

---

[195] On the traditional link between citizenship and state see O'Leary, *European Union Citizenship: Options for Reform* (Institute for Public Policy Research, London, 1996), 10 (citizenship as the 'internal reflection of state membership'); Preuß, 'Problems of a Concept of European Citizenship' (1995) 1 *European Law Journal* 267; Dahrendorf, 'The Changing Quality of Citizenship' in van Steenbergen (ed.), *The Condition of Citizenship* (Sage, London, 1994), 18.

[196] See, e.g., Miller, *supra* n. 171.

[197] Dobson, *supra* n. 194.

[198] Case C–380/87, *Enichem Base* v. *Comune di Cinisello Balsamo* [1989] ECR 2491. Member States' compliance levels with reporting obligations are generally very poor. See, e.g., Wilkinson, *The State of Reporting by the EC Commission in Fulfilment of Obligations Contained in EC Environmental Legislation* (Institute of European Environmental Policy, London, 1994).

[199] See further Hilson and Downes, *supra* n. 186.

learnt in private, not in public'.[200] At least in so far as there is freedom in the domestic sphere (for example, consumption and disposal) good ecological behaviour may be learnt in the private realm. EC law may further this aspect of ecological citizenship to the extent that such areas (waste; product labelling) are sites of legitimate EC involvement.

In relation to space, loosening the bonds between the citizen and the nation state poses many of the same issues as the subsidiarity and flexibility debates, namely the legitimate extent of involvement in environmental and related affairs across Member State borders.[201] Some strides have been made here, such as the revised Directive on environmental impact assessment which requires public consultation within other Member States which may experience significant environmental effects from developments outwith their borders.[202] There is also some judicial support for the sufficiency of a geographic nexus in relation to enforcement proceedings under Article 230 EC.[203] Here, it may be noted that there is little citizenship-type involvement in relation to the external aspects of EC environmental law where, to take trade as an example, a centralized approach prevails and, in cases where science is not the determinative discourse, a centralized view of institutionalized caution may dominate.[204] In general terms, there is much of an ecological nature that could usefully emerge from a European public space.[205]

A further approach is through the concept of a common European natural heritage, discussed above. Although complex, the development of this concept may parallel the case of the free movement of persons in so far as there is evident a similar process of freeing legal action from an economic trigger in the interests of higher, aspirational ideas of citizenship arising from deeper integration in Europe. In a similar manner, we can see the flourishing of a more autonomous body of environmental law which, although bounded by economic considerations, is not attached umbilically to the single market. Ideas of a common natural heritage in Europe, whose articulation is symbolic and marginal to the conservation directives it underpins,[206] ought therefore to elevate the relationship between community and environment to a higher

---

[200] Dobson, *supra* n. 194, 20. Dobson makes an additional point that the virtues of care and compassion, which he considers necessary to ecological citizenship, are also principally learnt in the private realm.

[201] This dimension need not necessarily be approached through concepts of citizenship but doing so with regard to implied citizenship duties is more fruitful; Weale, 'Citizenship Beyond Borders' in Vogel and Moran (eds.), *The Frontiers of Citizenship* (Macmillan, Basingstoke, 1991), 155.

[202] *Supra* n. 75, Art. 7, implementing the 1991 'Espoo' Convention on Environmental Impact Assessment in a Transboundary Context. This strengthens the limited transboundary notification provisions in the original directive. See also the 'Seveso II' Directive, *supra* n. 161, Art. 13 (information on safety measures).

[203] Case C–321/95P, *Stichting Greenpeace Council*, *supra* n. 97, *per* Cosmas AG.

[204] See, e.g., the *Communication from the Commission on the Precautionary Principle*, COM(2000) 1.

[205] Drawing on Weiler, *supra* n. 158.

[206] On wild birds and habitats, see *supra* nn. 30 and 29 respectively.

plane, in the process creating a more direct connection between individuals and the environment. Without suggesting that such an approach is free from difficulties, articulated and generally accepted ecological duties,[207] owed non-specifically across space and time, may avoid some of the difficulties inherent in what has been coined the 'psychic spillover' justification to EC environmental law, whereby issues of 'mere' concern to citizens in one Member State may justify regulating action in other Member States.[208]

VII. Conclusion

According to the Treaty, and increasingly in practice, sustainable development now provides the organizing idea, or central reference point, not just for environmental law and policy but for all Community activities. Further legal principles (integration primarily, but also precaution and subsidiarity) elaborate and give further expression to it. From a legal point of view, the process of 'mainstreaming' sustainable development and the other associated principles may lead to the application of legal doctrines and principles from social and economic policy areas to the environmental field. However, invoking law for environmental protection still raises problems peculiar to it. The broader issue is that, whilst locating principles of environmental law within mainstream EC law may provide a functional fit with the requirements of sustainable development, the essential and unique quality of environmental concern and thought may be lost, not the least of which are concerns relating to process and to identity which even the evolution of a type of European 'environmental' citizenship may neither capture nor replace.

---

[207] Reaching agreement on what such duties are would require public consent, indicating the connections between public and private in this respect.

[208] See Wils, *supra* n. 132; for critique see Scott, *supra* n. 2.

Reflections on the Future of the Judicial System of the European Union after Nice

P.J.G. KAPTEYN*

I. Introduction

It must be seriously doubted whether, in a Union partly deeper, partly diversified, and, above all, expanded to comprise twenty-five or more Member States, the administration of justice will be able to continue to fulfil the three fundamental requirements which the Court of Justice and the Court of First Instance (CFI) formulated in 1999 in their discussion paper on the future of the judicial system of the European Union.[1] They were:

—the need to secure the unity of Community law by means of a supreme court;
—the need to ensure that the judicial system is transparent, comprehensible and accessible to the public;
—the need to dispense justice without unacceptable delay.

In the last ten years, the importance of Community law in determining the rights and obligations of Member States, of the institutions, and of Community citizens has grown tremendously. This development necessarily creates problems for the Community judicature. There has been a considerable rise in the number of direct actions. In addition, there has been an alarming growth in the number of references for preliminary rulings. These developments not only make proceedings more protracted and threaten to undermine the proper functioning of the referral system. They seriously prejudice the proper administration of justice, especially in proceedings for preliminary rulings; the sheer volume of cases with which the Court of Justice and the CFI have to grapple also presents a long-term threat to the quality of their decisions. More and more frequently, the Court of Justice, in particular, is finding itself deprived of the opportunity of concentrating on its essential task, namely to ensure consistency in the interpretation and application of Community law.

* Judge of the Court of Justice 1990–2000 and President of the Judicial Section of the Dutch Council of State 1984–1990. He is presently teaching European law at the Faculty of the Humanities of the University of Amsterdam. This article is an expanded and updated version of a speech delivered at King's College London (Centre of European Law) on 13 Nov. 2000.

[1] 'The Future of the Judicial System of the European Union', available on the Internet website of the Court. http//curia.eu.int/en/ at 17.

The problems I have just highlighted can only intensify in the future. The advent of the third stage of EMU and the entry into force of the Treaty of Amsterdam will lead in the near future to a further increase in the number of cases coming before the Court of Justice and the CFI. I have in mind the provisions of the Amsterdam Treaty relating to asylum and immigration policy, judicial co-operation in civil matters, and co-operation in the fields of justice and home affairs with a view to promoting security and combating crime. In addition, the forthcoming geographical expansion of the Union will reinforce this trend in the longer term.

It should, therefore, greatly be welcomed that the Member States, urged by the two Community courts, adopted at the Intergovernmental Conference (IGC) in Nice a series of organizational measures in order to enable the Union's judicial system to deal with an increasing workload. But do the modifications in the EC Treaty and the Statute of the Court of Justice to be introduced after Nice sufficiently satisfy the three fundamental requirements I mentioned? And are additional measures needed to ensure the proper functioning of the system in the next decades? The answers to these questions should be based on an analysis of the two most important functions of the administration of justice within the Union, in order to ascertain how responsibility for the exercise of those functions can be shared out amongst the existing judicial bodies and any bodies to be set up in future.

II.   Reorganization of Judicial Functions in the Two Spheres

It is apparent that, as regards Community law and (in so far as it falls within its area of competence) other law of the European Union, the European judiciary has a double function. In the first place, the Court of Justice, assisted by the CFI,[2] adjudicates in disputes, brought before it by way of direct actions, concerning the legality of acts of the institutions and Member States. In the second place, the Court of Justice and the national courts work together, on references for preliminary rulings, with a view to ensuring the uniform application of the law in the Member States.

A.   ALLOCATION OF JUDICIAL FUNCTIONS IN THE CASE OF DIRECT ACTIONS

First of all, some observations should be made on the allocation of functions in the case of direct actions.

In any future system, it will be essential for the legality of the acts, or inaction, of the institutions and bodies of the Community and the Union, and their

---

[2] In the Nice treaty the CFI's function of 'assisting the Court of Justice' is not mentioned anymore. According to the new Art. 220 both courts are mentioned on an equal footing. This can be explained, at least partially, by the fact that, according to this Treaty, the CFI will sometimes adjudicate at final instance, i.e. in appeal against decisions given by judicial panels.

liability for unlawful acts, to be open to judicial adjudication by way of direct action. It is clearly appropriate that this task should be assigned to the CFI and the corresponding workload of the Court of Justice reduced as far as possible. This is wholly in line with the aims of the act by which the CFI was created. It was established, *inter alia*, in order to enable the Court of Justice, with a view to maintaining the quality and effectiveness of judicial review in the Community legal order, to concentrate on its fundamental task of ensuring uniform interpretation of Community law.[3]

In order to ensure uniformity in the interpretation and application of the law, it is necessary, however, to maintain the possibility of bringing appeals, limited to points of law, against judgments of the CFI. In this connection it is fortunate to see that, following a suggestion to this end by the Court of Justice, the new Article 225(1) EC makes it possible to introduce a filtering system. It provides that the Statute will determine not only, as up to now, under which conditions, but also *within which limits* a right to lodge appeals to the Court of Justice on points of law will exist. A filtering system will enable the Court of Justice to hear and determine appeals only if they raise important questions concerning legal uniformity or judicial protection.

However, channelling all direct actions towards the CFI is not an entirely straightforward matter. The question arises whether the function of the CFI as an administrative court should not be restricted to review of the legality of administrative acts of the Union or of the Member States in the implementation of Community law and other European Union law. Jurisdiction should then be reserved to the Court of Justice to adjudicate on constitutional issues, for example in cases requiring a decision on the legality of provisions of national or Community legislation. But to draw a clear dividing-line between administrative and constitutional issues and to allocate them respectively to the CFI and to the Court of Justice is simply not feasible. This is sufficiently demonstrated, in my view, by the academic writing on this question.[4]

Nevertheless, to compel parties, in disputes between Member States and institutions, or between one institution and another, to pursue proceedings in two different forums in succession where the issue involves the classic constitutional question about the division of powers, under the Treaties, between Member States and the Community or between one institution and another would seem a poor idea. Given the importance of issues of this kind, the tendency should always be for them to be litigated before the Court of Justice. For that reason, provision should be made for the possibility of prorogation, so that such disputes may, by agreement between the parties, be brought directly before the Court.

---

[3] See the recitals in the preamble to Council Decision 88/591/ECSC, EEC, and Euratom of 24 Oct. 1988 establishing a CFI of the European Communities [1988] OJ L319/1.

[4] See Due, 'A Constitutional Court for the European Communities', and Jacobs, 'Is the Court of Justice of the European Communities a Constitutional Court?', in Curtin and O'Keefe (eds.), *Constitutional Adjudication in European Community and National Law, Essays for the Hon. Justice T.F. O'Higgins* (Butterworth (Ireland) Ltd., Dublin, 1992), 3 ff, and 25 ff.

A reallocation along these lines of judicial functions between the Court of Justice and the CFI in the case of direct actions seems not to be excluded by the Nice Treaty. Up to now the CFI has only had jurisdiction in the case of direct actions brought against an institution by natural and legal persons. Article 225(1) of the Nice Treaty drops this limitation. It 'shall have jurisdiction to hear and determine at first instance actions or proceedings referred to in Articles 230, 232, 235, 236 and 238, with the exception of . . . those reserved in the Statute for the Court of Justice. The Statute may provide for the CFI to have jurisdiction for other classes of action or proceeding.'

Article 51 of the new Statute for the Court adopted in Nice[5] maintains the existing situation. But the text of the new Article 225(1), enables the Council to extend the CFI's jurisdiction to cases and proceedings brought against an institution by other institutions or by Member States under the just-mentioned Articles of the EC Treaty. According to the Declaration on Article 225, annexed to the Final Act of the IGC, the Court and the Commission are invited to give overall consideration as soon as possible to the division of jurisdiction between the Court of Justice and the CFI, and to submit suitable proposals for examination by the competent bodies as soon as the Nice Treaty enters into force.

It follows that under the rules of the new Treaty an arrangement whereby, subject to the exception just referred to, first-instance proceedings in direct actions become the exclusive preserve of the CFI, coupled with the introduction of a filtering system for appeals against judgments of the CFI, could be envisaged. Such an arrangement would enable the Court of Justice to concentrate more on its essential task of ensuring legal uniformity.

However, the arrangement just envisaged would also mean that the excessive direct-action workload would have to be shouldered by the CFI, which, as matters currently stand, has already reached the limits of its capacity.

One practical way of preventing an accumulation of first-instance cases at the Community judicature might be to increase the number of judges in line with the rise in the number of cases.[6] Whilst the resulting increase in the number of chambers would require additional measures for the co-ordination of judicial decisions, the uniformity of case law would be ensured by the Court of Justice as the court of final instance. However, an unbridled increase in the number of judges and chambers of the CFI would not provide the solution required. Co-ordination measures would impose an excessive burden, which might well cause unacceptable delays in the disposal of cases or might go

---

[5] The new single Statute will replace the Statutes for each of the three Communities.

[6] The proposals submitted by the ECJ and the CFI to the Council with regard to the new intellectual property disputes (to be found at the Court's website) provide for the addition of six judges to the current fifteen judges. The principle of such an increase seems to have been accepted by the Council, but the difficulty of how to allocate the six judgeships to nationals of the Member States has still to be resolved. As for the composition of the CFI, it should be noted that the only condition imposed by the new Art. 224 of the Nice Treaty is that it shall comprise 'at least one judge per Member State'.

awry, thereby necessitating, in too many cases, the intervention of the Court of Justice in order to ensure judicial uniformity.

For the time being, however, those problems do not arise. An increase in the number of judges and chambers would appear to be an appropriate way of adapting the capacity of the CFI to the number of cases brought before it.

Yet, even at present, it is necessary to consider whether a Community judicature consisting of a Court of Justice and a CFI needs to be supplemented as regards certain classes of direct actions. These actions concern frequently recurring disputes in well-defined, specific areas of Community law. Staff cases and actions relating to the Community trade mark are existing examples. In the latter area, actions may be brought, first, before the CFI against decisions of the Boards of Appeal of the Office for Harmonization in the Internal Market (Trade Marks and Designs), which is established in Alicante.[7] Over the next few years the number of actions in this area may rise from a few dozens to several hundred a year.

As regards staff actions, the Court of Justice and the CFI have proposed to the Intergovernmental Conference (IGC) the establishment of an independent board to reconsider in a sort of administrative appeal the institutions' decisions in staff cases.[8] It was expected that, even if this step cannot considerably reduce the number of cases brought before the CFI, it may at least simplify the way in which this category of cases is handled.

The thinking of the Court of Justice and the CFI went further than this, however, since they contemplate the creation of panels having judicial powers in certain specific areas, envisaging the sort of '*contentieux de masse*', or litigation *en bloc*, which is expected in relation to the Community trade mark. Consequently, what is contemplated here is the creation of judicial bodies administering Community law at a level beneath the CFI.

The possibility of creating judicial panels, hearing and determining 'at first instance certain classes of action or proceeding brought in specific areas' has been adopted by the IGC, even in the case of staff actions (new Article 225a EC). It must be regretted that in the latter case the creation of a board of independent persons to reconsider the decisions with regard to staff members, in a less formal way than feasible for a judicial panel, seems now to be ruled out.[9] This was certainly not the intention of the two courts when making their proposal.

Establishing judicial panels at a level beneath the CFI means the introduction of a three-tiered system of judicial review. The lengthening of the judicial

---

[7] See Regulation 40/94 on the Community trade mark [1994] OJ L11/1. See also the proposals mentioned in *supra* n. 6.

[8] The proposed creation of an independent board to hear staff cases would oblige staff members to bring their complaint to such a panel before lodging an appeal with the CFI. There are divergent opinions within the Trade Mark Office on whether the independent Boards of Appeal of that Office, in making their determinations, act as a part of the administration or as true courts of law.

[9] In a Declaration on the new Art. 225a, the Court of Justice and the Commission are invited to prepare a draft decision creating such a judicial panel.

process that may result from such a system is hardly acceptable and serves no useful purpose. The IGC has, of course, been aware of this problem. It has tried to devise a system in which the desirability to avoid as much as possible excessively protracted judicial procedures could be reconciled with the need to secure the unity of Community law.

The possibility for an applicant to take a case higher up has been restricted along two lines. In the first place, decisions of the judicial panels are subject to a right of appeal to the CFI on points of law only, unless the decision establishing the panel provides for a right of appeal also on matters of fact (new Article 225a EC). In the second place, decisions given by the CFI on appeal may only *exceptionally* be subject to review by the Court of Justice (*'faire l'objet d'un réexamen'* in the French text), where there is a serious risk of the unity or consistency of Community law being affected (new Article 225(2) EC). It is left to the Statute to determine the nature of such a review and the conditions under which it may occur. According to its new Article 62 the first Advocate General,[10] where he considers that such a risk exists, may propose, within one month after the delivery of the CFI's decision, a review by the Court of Justice. Whether there will be a review has to be decided within the same time limit by the Court.

Leaving aside for the moment a number of questions concerning the exact nature of this new procedure, it seems highly doubtful that such a review, by reason of its exceptional character, can be a suitable and effective means of securing the unity of Community law. It seems that the IGC has been more concerned by restricting the rights of applicants to have their cases heard by a higher court than by the necessity to assure a uniform interpretation of Community law. Moreover, by introducing the idea that an appeal against the CFI's judgment may be restricted to points of law, the Nice Treaty charges the CFI with the task of securing a uniform interpretation of Community rules as applied by judicial panels and substitutes it in this domain for the Court of Justice. In fact, the Treaty is likely to create two courts of last resort within one judicial institution, the Court of Justice of the EC.

In my view panels may serve a useful purpose as long as their task will be confined to reconsidering decisions taken by the Community administration or other administrative bodies functioning under Community law. They should be in a position to reconcile the parties in a dispute on the basis of the law applicable to it and, if necessary, to modify the administration's decision in conformity with the law and the facts of the case. The operation of panels of this kind may reduce the number of appeals brought before the CFI. As regards

[10] The role of the first Advocate General will be drastically changed by this arrangement. Nowadays the other Advocates General elect him for one year only so that each of them may in turn occupy this office that for the present consists mainly of assigning the cases to his colleagues. It should be noted in this connection that fortunately the useful office of Advocate General has not been abolished, though such abolition was discussed in Nice. It was decided, however, that Advocates General would not have to submit reasoned opinions where the Court, after hearing them, considers that the case raises no new point of law. Cf. the new Arts. 222 of the EC Treaty and 20 of the Statute.

the intended transformation of the Alicante Boards of Appeal into judicial panels, they are, though composed of independent persons, too closely linked to the Trade Marks Office to be given judicial status. It is precisely this link that enables them to play their role as administrative boards of appeal with the authority and expertise to revise decisions of the Office and its various bodies.

There are, in my mind, no compelling reasons for introducing judicial panels administering Community law at a level beneath the CFI. Moreover, the measures taken by the Nice Treaty to avoid the disadvantages of the resulting three-tiered judicial system endanger the unity of Community law and make it less transparent and comprehensible to the public.

Proposals for the introduction of specialized courts in well-defined, specific areas of Community law at the level of the Court of First Instance do not encounter such objections and offer a better approach. The decisions of these tribunals, like those of the CFI, should be subject to a right of appeal to the Court of Justice, if need be, through a filtering system. It is interesting to note that the Commission recently provided, in the context of its proposals concerning a Community patent, for the setting-up of a Community court for intellectual property cases as a subdivision of the Court of Justice.[11] It is proposed that this new court should have jurisdiction in respect of disputes concerning counterfeit or pirated goods and the validity of Community patents.

This initiative induced the IGC to adopt a new Article 229a EC, authorizing the Council, acting on a proposal from the Commission and after consulting the European Parliament, to confer jurisdiction on the Court of Justice in disputes relating to the application of secondary law creating Community industrial property rights. According to the Declaration on this Article it does not prejudice the choice of the judicial framework which may be set up to deal with such disputes. It is regrettable that the Nice Treaty does not contain a general authorization to set up, within the Community judicature, specialized courts in specific areas of Community law. Such an authorization should have been more appropriate in view of possible developments in the future.

B. ALLOCATION OF JUDICIAL FUNCTIONS WITHIN THE FRAMEWORK OF THE PRELIMINARY RULING PROCEDURE

The other key function in the administration of justice in the European Union is co-operation between the Court of Justice and national courts within the framework of the preliminary ruling procedure. Even now, the exercise of this key function is being put under pressure by the steadily increasing number of references for preliminary rulings. The long delays in processing references undermine the proper working of the preliminary ruling system. The situation may be somewhat alleviated, temporarily, by the amendments to the Rules of Procedure of the Court of Justice which entered into force on 1 July 2000, in

---

[11] Proposal for a Council Regulation on the Community Patent, Doc. 500PC0412.

particular through the introduction of a simplified procedure for answering 'straightforward' questions. But the long-term prospects are far from rosy, given the Treaty of Amsterdam and the forthcoming geographical enlargement of the Union.

In the long run, therefore, it is inevitable that fundamental changes will have to be made to the system of references for preliminary rulings. In its discussion paper, the Court of Justice considers four possible structural changes to the system.

The first of those possibilities, imposing a restriction limiting the national courts empowered to make references to the Court of Justice was categorically rejected.[12] Such a restriction would have the effect of jeopardizing the uniform application and interpretation of Community law throughout the Union. It could deprive individuals of effective judicial protection and jeopardize the uniform application and interpretation of the most important parts of Community law.[13] In that regard, it is regrettable that, in the areas of asylum and immigration policy, judicial co-operation in civil matters, and police and judicial co-operation in criminal matters, such a restriction already exists or has been rendered possible as a consequence of the Treaty of Amsterdam (see, respectively, Article 68 of the EC Treaty and Article 35 of the Treaty on European Union).[14]

A second possibility would be the introduction of a filtering mechanism enabling the Court of Justice to select the questions to be answered by reference to specific criteria, such as the importance of the question from the standpoint of legal uniformity or legal protection throughout the Union.[15] However, such a mechanism cannot be reconciled with the idea of judicial co-operation that underlies the preliminary ruling procedure, if only because of the deterrent effect it would have on national courts that were considering making a reference. It is as if a party to a marriage were to say to his or her spouse that, henceforth, only important topics were to be discussed between them.

A third possibility would be to transfer to the Court of First Instance (or, where appropriate, to a specialized tribunal adjudicating in its field of specialization) part of the case-load in preliminary ruling proceedings.[16] However, that raises the question how to prevent discrepancies between the case law of the CFI and that of the Court of Justice.[17] If there were to be a right to appeal in

---

[12] *Supra* n. 1, 22–3.

[13] Curtin and van Ooik, *Revamping the European Union's Enforcement systems with a view to Eastern Enlargements*, Working Document 110 (Oct. 2000) of the Dutch Scientific Council for Government Policy (WRR), 95 and 96.

[14] Recently, Rasmussen, 'Remedying the Crumbling EC Judicial System', (2000) *CMLRev.* 37: 1071–112, at 1106–7, has argued in favour of generalizing the system of Art. 68 EC. He considers 'the cut-off of lower courts' competence to dialogue freely with the Community's judiciary' to be in line with 'the orientation of overall Union politics' seeming 'to be one of renationalization or centifugalism'. My observations in this contribution are not written in such a perspective.

[15] *Supra* n. 1, 23–5.   [16] *Ibid.*, 25–6.

[17] Rasmussen, *supra* n. 13, is not troubled by this difficulty, postulating (at 1103) 'that it does not make a great difference whether it is the same court which from time to time changes its mind in

the ordinary way to the Court against a preliminary ruling given by the Court of First Instance, it would result in the proceedings being prolonged to an unacceptable degree.

It is not to be wondered that the IGC, having decided to make it possible to transfer to the CFI jurisdiction with regard to questions referred for a preliminary ruling under Article 234 EC, in specific areas, has not introduced such a right of appeal. It has, however, tried to avoid the occurrence of discrepancies between the case law of the two courts by other means. According to the new Article 225(3) EC, the CFI, where it considers that the case requires a decision on principle likely to affect the unity or consistency of Community law, may refer the case to the Court of Justice for a ruling. Moreover, its preliminary rulings may *exceptionally* be subject to review by the Court of Justice, where there is a serious risk of the unity or consistency of Community law being affected.

The review procedure (the *'réexamen'*, to quote the French text) to be followed in the latter case is the one laid down in Article 62 of the Statute. We have already touched on this procedure in a situation where the CFI exercises appellate jurisdiction with regard to decisions given by judicial panels. Due to its exceptional character, its value as a suitable and effective means of securing the uniformity of interpretation and application of Community law by the Court of Justice is highly doubtful.

However, the fact that the procedure fails this test would be of less importance if the power of the CFI to give preliminary rulings was confined to certain specific areas, like judicial co-operation in civil matters,[18] and police and judicial co-operation in criminal matters. In such areas uniformity of Community law poses no constrictive problems, since they have little or no connection with (the rest of) Community law. Subject to such conditions, a transfer to the CFI of power to give preliminary rulings would not raise insuperable problems when it came to guaranteeing legal uniformity.

The use of the term *'réexamen'* in the French text of the second and third paragraphs of the new Article 225 EC clearly indicates that it is not an appeal in the ordinary sense. Moreover, as appears from the Declaration on Article 225(3), when the Court of Justice decides to review a decision of the CFI, it should act under an emergency procedure. But the exact nature of the review procedure has yet to be defined in the Statute as has been acknowledged by the IGC in the Declaration on Article 225(2) and (3) the IGC annexed to the Final Act of the Nice Treaty.

---

different cases, or whether it is the legal opinions of two distinct jurisdictions which declare different legal "truths" in the same case'. This may be an acute academic observation, but one may wonder whether national judges would readily endorse it when faced with conflicting decisions of the two courts in the same kind of case.

[18] For example, the Council Regulations 1347/2000, of 29 May 2000, on jurisdiction and the recognition and enforcement of judgments in matrimonial matters and in matters of parental responsibility for children of both spouses [2000] OJ L160/19 and 44/2001, of 22 Dec. 2000, on jurisdiction and recognition and enforcement of judgments in civil and commercial cases [2001] OJ L012/1).

According to this declaration the provisions to be drafted should in particular deal with three questions: (1) the role of the parties in proceedings before the Court of Justice, in order to safeguard their rights, (2) the effect of the review procedure on the enforceability of the decision of the CFI, and (3) the effect of the Court of Justice decision on the dispute between the parties. The only conclusion about the nature of the procedure that one can infer from the declaration is necessarily a vague one: the kind of review procedure envisaged may result in a decision of the Court of Justice affecting the rights of the parties concerned and may have consequences for the enforceability of the CFI's decision under review.

The concern about the rights of the parties to the dispute seems to indicate that the Conference had in mind a review by the Court of Justice resulting in a new decision, delivered at short notice and superseding the CFI's decision under review. Only in such circumstances could the rights of the parties be affected. In such a case the decision of the Court of Justice would bind the parties. The enforcement of CFI's decisions should then be suspended as long as the Advocate General might propose a review procedure and, if such is the case, pending the decision of the Court of Justice on the question whether or not to open the procedure. If the Court decides to engage a review procedure the CFI's decision should, of course, not be enforceable pending the outcome of this procedure.

On the other hand, the text of the declaration does not rule out the adoption of a construction that excludes a situation in which the rights of the parties in the dispute underlying the decision under review are not likely to be affected. That would mean the introduction of a sort of appeal 'in the interest of the law' to be initiated by the first Advocate General. It does not affect the judgment that gave rise to the appeal. Such an appeal, though then to be initiated by the Commission, Council, or Member States, was mooted as a panacea to enable the Court of Justice to secure the uniformity of law within the Community during the 'travaux préparatoires' of the IGC.

The Hoge Raad der Nederlanden (Netherlands Supreme Court) correctly observed, in the opinion on the preliminary ruling procedure presented during the preparatory phase of the IGC, that this kind of appeal cannot be reconciled with the nature of that procedure. As that opinion convincingly states:

[a] right of appeal in the interest of the law does not prejudice any rights acquired by the parties. The preliminary ruling procedure does not directly affect the position of the parties. A preliminary ruling merely operates to provide the national court with guidance, and it does not really appear feasible to prohibit such a court from taking into account the possibility of an appeal against such a preliminary ruling. It is to be feared that litigants would find it difficult to understand the reasons for such a prohibition. Moreover, it is quite conceivable that, where the Court of First Instance has given a preliminary ruling, the national court will follow that ruling even though it has been set aside in the meantime by the Court of Justice.

These arguments should, I hope, convince the competent Community bodies not to take this route. All efforts should be directed at constructing a review procedure that, notwithstanding its emergency nature, offers the parties concerned a fair chance of being heard by the Court of Justice before the latter, in an emergency procedure, either confirms the CFI's decision or substitutes it by its own decision.

We should now turn to the fourth possibility suggested by the Court of Justice It is the creation or designation, in each Member State, of decentralized judicial bodies responsible for answering preliminary questions from courts within their area of jurisdiction. The Court of Justice recognizes that this would be a radical change of the preliminary ruling system. It was aware of the fact that any decentralization of the preliminary ruling procedure to regional or national level would pose a serious threat to the unity of Community law, one of the cornerstones of the Union that will be even more vital and vulnerable after the future enlargements. It considers, however, that the risks entailed in decentralization could be reduced. The decentralized judicial bodies would have to have the possibility of referring the questions to the Court of Justice. There would also have to be a possibility of appealing to the Court of Justice 'in the interest of the law', in accordance with detailed procedures to be laid down, against preliminary rulings given by those judicial bodies.

It will be clear from the above that my view on this possible restructuring, which I base in particular on the considerations set forth in the Hoge Raad's opinion, is that a right of appeal in the interest of the law is not a sound way of ensuring uniformity of case law. Nevertheless, I do believe that it could be possible, without having to introduce such a right of appeal, to devise a decentralized arrangement that would substantially reduce the risks mentioned.

Where, in a Member State, justice is administered in several stages, courts of first instance, when they consider it desirable to seek a preliminary ruling on a question, should address them to specially established chambers of the court having jurisdiction (*in abstracto*) at final instance to hear and determine disputes of the type concerned. Those supreme courts should be empowered either to refer the questions to the Court of Justice, if they consider that the proceedings raise points of general interest for the uniformity or development of Community law, or to answer the questions themselves. The answer should be given in the form of a non-binding opinion[19] on which the parties should subsequently have the opportunity of submitting observations in the proceedings pending before the court seized of the case at first instance, before that court gives its judgment. Higher courts hearing appeals against that judgment should still be empowered or obliged, as the case may be, to refer questions to the Court of Justice for a preliminary ruling.

The French experience with the so-called '*avis contentieux*' shows that it is perfectly feasible to insert such a procedure into a national judicial system.

---

[19] Since the enactment of the Law of 15 Dec. 1987 and the Law of 15 May 1991 the French Conseil d'Etat (Council of State) and Cour de Cassation (Court of Cassation), respectively, have been empowered to give rulings in that form on questions referred to them by lower courts. In relation to such '*avis contentieux*' (opinions in contentious proceedings): see Vincent *et al., La justice et ses institutions* (3rd edn., Dalloz, Paris, 1991), paras. 448–II and 406.

Though it seems preferable from a Community point of view to charge a chamber of the court competent to hear the case at final instance with the task of delivering non-binding opinions to a court asking for it, other solutions should not be ruled out. The task could be entrusted to a chamber of one of the higher courts having jurisdiction in such cases, if it is not feasible in a national judicial system to designate a chamber of the highest court to this end.

There is no reason to fear that this procedure will reinforce the tendency of courts of first instance to make no effort to answer questions of Community law themselves, but to leave it to judges 'who know better'. On the contrary, such a procedure might encourage those courts to keep themselves less aloof from matters of Community law in order not to irritate the higher court by the inanity of their questions. A court higher up in the national judicial hierarchy is in a better position to show its irritation in this respect than the Court of Justice, whose concern it is to be as co-operative as possible in order not to discourage future, less trifling referrals.

The proposed arrangement tends to introduce in this way a filtering system with regard to preliminary questions *at the national level* which offers numerous advantages compared with the introduction of such a system at the Community level. The procedure takes place entirely within the national legal sphere. There is no need for translations into other languages. It is also considerably more straightforward for the designated chamber of the higher court to form a view of the factual and national legal context in which the preliminary questions arose. That may facilitate a swift and useful answer. On the other hand, if the higher court considers, at first glance, that a referral to the Court of Justice is to be preferred, it can always decide so. Consequently, the dialogue between the Court of Justice and national courts of first instance is not cut off in cases requiring decisions of principle likely to affect the unity or the development of Community law. Finally, the existing preliminary rulings system is maintained for national courts adjudicating at higher instance, since the opinion delivered has no binding force.

I am under no illusion about the time being ripe for acceptance of such a system and for the requisite provisions to be enacted in the EC Treaty. Nevertheless, I think that such 'decentralization' of the preliminary ruling procedure could usefully form a topic for discussion in the continuing debate on the necessary restructuring of the judicial system of the European Union.

Finally, even when it is not at first sight a question of modifying treaty provisions, it seems appropriate to add some observations with regard to the lately much-criticised *CILFIT* decision.[20] As is well-known, this decision lays down under which conditions national courts against whose decisions there is no judicial remedy under national law are allowed, notwithstanding the strict obligation imposed upon them by the wording of Article 234,[21] not to refer. It

---

[20] Case 283/81, *CILFIT* v. *Ministry of Health* [1982] ECR 3415, see, in particular, the harsh criticism by Rasmussen, *supra* n. 13, at 1107–10.

[21] Rasmussen, *ibid.*, at 1107–8 seems not to be aware of the fact that CILFIT mitigated this strict obligation resulting from the wording of Art. 234, last para., when he postulates that '*CILFIT* was

cannot be denied that these conditions are often considered as being of a needlessly restrictive nature and are, moreover, for this reason, not always respected in practice. Indeed, one may wonder whether it is really necessary to oblige them to refer to the Court, as sometimes is bound to happen, rather detailed questions concerning, for example, the interpretation of a certain term or phrase used in a specific provision of a directive that does not in any way involve the interpretation of primary Community law.

In view of the prospective entry of a whole series of new Member States it seems, however, untimely to relax these conditions. Nevertheless, in the long run, it would be advisable to explore possibilities of giving these courts more freedom to decide whether it is necessary to refer to the Court of Justice questions of interpreting the provisions, for instance, of directives, when those questions can be answered without the need of treaty interpretation. More and more, Community legislation is extending to areas outside the hard core of the common market law. In such areas, like social (Article 137 EC) and environmental (Article 175 EC) policies, a divergence of interpretation is, to a certain degree, tolerable without creating a distortion of competition or a deflection of trade. Why should one not trust the wisdom of the highest courts of the Member States to ask for a preliminary decision, on their own initiative, whenever the interpretation of a specific provision of a directive diverges in various countries to such an extent that a ruling by the Court is needed to re-establish uniformity of interpretation? It is not, however, a matter for the Court to bring about such modification of the Treaty duty of the highest courts to refer. It is a question that could only be settled by an amendment of Article 234 EC.

III. Composition of the Court of Justice and Procedure for the Appointment of its Members

No examination of the future of the judicial system of the European Union would be complete if it did not also include consideration of the question whether there is scope for improving the existing rules governing the composition of the Court of Justice and the appointment of its members. Hitherto, the number of judges and advocates general has been increased with every enlargement of the Community. If that tradition is maintained, the Court of Justice may in due course number twenty-five or more judges and eleven or more advocates general. The Court of Justice has already on two occasions raised the problems attaching to the increase in the number of judges, first of all in the preparatory discussions leading to the enactment of the Treaty of Amsterdam and latterly in its discussion paper, but without adopting, or being able to adopt, a position on this delicate point.

representative of on the one hand, the Court's ambition to have a say in as many cases as possible and, on the other, a certain belief that the national judiciaries would do harm to the unity of Community law', adding that '(t)he intention behind . . . *CILFIT* was to generate a substantial increase in the number of cases arriving at the Court'.

In outlining the dilemma, I can do no better than to quote the words of the Court of Justice itself:

On the one hand, any significant increase in the number of judges might mean that the plenary session of the Court of Justice would cross the invisible boundary between a collegiate Court of Justice and a deliberative assembly. Moreover, as chambers would hear the great majority of cases, this increase could pose a threat to the consistency of the case-law.

On the other hand, the presence in the Court of Justice of members from all the national legal systems is undoubtedly conducive to harmonious development of Community case-law, taking into account concepts regarded as fundamental in the various Member States and thus enhancing the acceptability of the solutions arrived at. It may also be considered that the presence of a judge from each Member State further enhances the legitimacy of what is the supreme judicial body of the Community.[22]

One should not underestimate, however, the importance, for the purposes of ensuring the uniformity and development of the law, of limiting the number of judges. With fifteen judges, it is still possible to foster solid co-operation and to cope with the disadvantages caused by the changes that take place every three years in the composition of the Court of Justice. The members see and speak to each other more or less every day, in hearings, in deliberations, and in the inner precincts of the Court of Justice. Meetings are held twice a week between the members of the small (eleven members) or large (fifteen members) 'Plenum' of the Court of Justice, at which solutions to new questions of law and the draft judgments dealing with those questions are discussed intensively. Thus, all the judges are kept up to date on the broad outlines of the case law. As a result, serious co-ordination problems hardly, if ever, arise.

As was to be expected, most of the delegations at the IGC were in favour of maintaining the tradition of increasing the number of judges with every enlargement and even to incorporating it as a matter of principle in the EC Treaty. Accordingly the new Article 221 EC says that the Court of Justice shall consist of 'one judge per Member State'. As a counterpart, to keep the system workable, the internal organization of the Court is modified in anticipation of the situation that will arrive with an increased membership. To this end, following the example of the European Court of Human Rights, a Grand Chamber is to be established.

After the entry into force of the new Article 221 of the Nice Treaty the Court of Justice shall sit in chambers or in a Great Chamber and only exceptionally in full Court. According to the rules of Article 16 of the Statute sitting as a *full Court* is obligatory in a number of very uncommon cases. They concern requests to take disciplinary measures against, or to remove from office, the European Ombudsman and members of the Commission or of the Court of Auditors. Moreover, the Court itself may decide so when it considers a case

---

[22] 'Report of the Court of Justice on Certain Aspects of the Appliction of the Treaty on European Union', Weekly Bulletin on the Activities of the Court and the Court of First Instance No. 15/95, at 18.

before it of exceptional importance. The Court sits in *Grand Chamber* when a Member State or an institution that is party to the proceedings so requests.

It is surprising to see that there is no rule permitting the Court of Justice to sit in Grand Chamber if it deems it necessary in view of the importance of the case it has to decide. Probably this is a *lapsus* that has to be redressed. It is hardly conceivable that the Court should be deprived of the right to assign cases to the Grand Chamber. If so, the only choice left in the absence of a request to that end from a Member State or an institution, would be assigning a case it deems important either to a chamber of five or to the full Court. Be that as it may, it is beyond doubt that the IGC intended the Grand Chamber to take over the role of the full Court.

The Grand Chamber consists of eleven judges. Taking into account that the IGC took the decision to fix this number in view of the future enlargement of the membership of the Court of Justice, the intention is probably to keep it so or, at any event, not to increase it beyond thirteen or fifteen judges. The Grand Chamber will be presided over by the President of the Court. Members *ex officio* are the presidents of the chambers of five judges. The judges will hence-forth elect these presidents from among their number not for one year, but, like the President of the Court, for three years. They may be re-elected once. Manifestly, the IGC has wanted to create a more or less permanent core among the membership of the Grand Chamber in order to further the consistency of the case law.

The Nice Treaty guarantees thus that after the enlargement of the European Union all the legal systems and legal cultures prevailing in the Member States will be represented among the judges. This is, of course, important for the legitimacy of the judgments, even though a certain perspective needs to be maintained here.[23] In recent years, over 70 per cent of the Court's judgments and other decisions emanated from chambers in which the representation of the legal system concerned is a matter of pure chance. This has never created any legitimacy problems.

Moreover, a paradox arises here. Upon the enlargement of the Union to twenty-five or more Member States, representation of all the various legal systems among the judges will inevitably lead to a situation in which the Grand Chamber, having a composition much more limited in terms of its membership and thus not representing all those systems, will decide all the more important cases. This formation will preside, therefore, over the further development of the jurisprudence of the Court.

With the present number of fifteen judges, the Grand Chamber will still resemble the existing '*Petit Plenum*' of eleven judges, presided over by the President of the Court. The only difference is the permanent presence of the presidents of the two chambers of five. This will mean that there will be eight rotating places in the Grand Chamber available for the remaining twelve

---

[23] See, in this connection, Koopmans, 'The Future of the Court of Justice of the European Communities' [1991] *Yearbook of European Law*, 15 at 25–6.

judges not holding the office of president of a chamber of five. Consequently, they can rather frequently participate in the Grand Chamber. After the enlargement, however, in a Court with twenty-five or more judges and with four or five chambers of five, only six or five places in the Grand Chamber are available to be assigned by turns to the remaining twenty or nineteen judges not holding the required presidential office. As a result first-class and second-class judges are created, with those sitting for three or even six years in the Grand Chamber (the President of the Court and the presidents of the chambers of five) adjudicating on important cases and those sitting in chambers deciding cases of lesser importance.

In these circumstances I am bound to wonder whether a court of fifteen judges, coupled with a rotation system guaranteeing that every Member State should have in turn a judge on the bench, would be in a much weaker position, in terms of acceptability and legitimacy of its decisions, than a Court functioning along the lines laid down in the Nice Treaty. For the purposes of reflecting the idea of representation of all legal cultures, it should then be sufficient, in my opinion, that the *whole* Court (including, therefore, the advocates general) would consist of one member per Member State.

Finally, a few brief words on the appointment procedure. The way in which appointments are made at present appears to me to be unsatisfactory. What basically happens is that each Member State proposes a candidate and by common accord of the governments of the Member States the judges and advocates general are appointed for a term of six years. If any screening of the candidates takes place, it remains hidden from view. In practice, this means that the candidates who are proposed are appointed.

Such an appointment procedure does not offer a proper institutional guarantee of their impartiality and qualities. The IGC has missed the opportunity to improve the procedure in this respect. In view of the prospective enlargement of the Union to a region of Europe where, at least in some countries, after decades of totalitarian rule, the value of independent judicial opinions is not yet firmly embedded in the minds of politicians and sufficiently distinguished from the promotion of national interests, it should be regretted that nobody has paid attention to this issue.[24]

To provide that guarantee, a number of proposals have been made. The one which goes furthest is that of Koopmans, who suggests that, out of the candidates put forward by the governments, thirteen judges eventually be chosen by an authoritative body consisting of 'the most senior members of the bench in each of the legal systems of the Member States. . . . In this way, a European Judicial Council, solely competent for appointments, could be developed.'[25]

---

[24] That there is some reason for concern in the context of an enlarged membership is evident from a press conference given by the President of the European Court of Human Rights on 28 Oct. 2000. He considered it necessary to call upon the 41 States that have ratified the European Convention to 'respect the Court's judicial independence, particularly in respect of the election of judges' (for the text of the press release, see (2000) *Nederlands Tijdschrift voor de Mensenrechten* (Dutch Human Rights Review), 1296.

[25] *Supra* n. 16, 26.

A less far-reaching proposal has been made by the '*Groupe de réflexion sur l'avenir du système juridictionnel des Communautés européennes*' (Study Group on the future of the judicial system of the European Communities).[26] It proposed to retain the existing system but suggests the setting-up of an advisory committee composed of highly qualified independent jurists to determine the judicial competence of the candidates proposed.

Regrettably, it is most unlikely that such proposals will find acceptance in the foreseeable future. However, it may still be possible to improve the existing system in at least two respects. First, it would be desirable to extend the term of office from six years to nine or twelve years, without any possibility of re-appointment. This would offer two advantages. It would prevent the situation (which, alas, happens quite often) whereby judges who are well settled in are replaced after only six years. In addition, it would stop a judge who wishes to be considered for re-appointment after six years from having to approach his government, thereby obviating a situation which cannot easily be reconciled with his independent status.

Consideration might also be given, at least at national level, to consulting on the nominations an independent committee composed of representatives of the highest national courts. The Netherlands Government recently adopted, and applied, internal rules concerning recommendations for appointments to European judicial bodies from such a committee whereby, *inter alia*, a similar advisory procedure is followed.[27]

There is also the question of the desirability of letting national parliaments or the European Parliament have a first say in the appointment of members of the Court of Justice and of the Court of First Instance. Involving national parliaments in the nomination process would, however, accentuate the national character of the appointments even more strongly than is already the case. It would clearly be preferable to involve the European Parliament in the appointment procedure.[28] However, that proposal is open to the objection that the Parliament may appear as applicant in inter-institutional proceedings concerning its powers under the Treaty.[29] One may wonder whether, in those

[26] See the Internet website of the Commission http://www.europa.eu.int/en/comm/sj/rap due.pdf.

[27] This procedure for nomination of candidates for European courts of justice has been made public in answer to a parliamentary question in appendix 7 to the annex to the Dutch Hansard of the Upper Chamber of the States-General, Handelingen I 1999/2000.

[28] See the procedure laid down with regard to the appointment of members of the Strasbourg Court in Art. 22 of Protocol No 11 to the European Convention on Human Rights. In 1993 the European Parliament adopted the Rothley report (European Session Document A3–0228/93) proposing that judges at the Court should be elected by the Parliament. On 9 Feb. 1994, a resolution was adopted, requiring consultation of the Parliament upon judicial appointments (cf. Brown and Jacobs, *The Court of Justice of the European Communities* (5th edn., ed. Neville Brown and Kennedy, Sweet & Maxwell, London, 2000), 48–9.

[29] See the third para. of Art. 230 of the EC Treaty, enshrining the case law of the Court of Justice, according to which the Parliament may bring actions for annulment of measures where the purpose of such actions is to protect its prerogatives. The new Art. 230 of the Nice Treaty will put the Parliament on the same footing with the other institutions with regard to bringing actions for annulment.

circumstances, it is capable, as an interested party in such conflicts, of acting with sufficient impartiality in relation to appointments. Be that as it may, the involvement of the European Parliament could help to counterbalance the national character of the present appointment procedure.

The conclusion, therefore, is that, as regards the composition of both the Court of Justice and the Court of First Instance, it is important, in two respects at any rate, for the existing rules to be altered. The term of office should be extended to nine or twelve years, without the possibility of re-appointment, and the Member States should be required to put forward their recommendations after consulting an independent committee on which their highest courts of law are represented.

Whether provision should also be made for participation by the European Parliament is, I think, open to doubt in present circumstances. However, there would seem to be some merit in giving the Parliament some say once its power as co-legislator is so consolidated that it no longer needs to appear in inter-institutional proceedings to defend its prerogatives.

Protecting Legitimate Expectations in European Community Law and in Domestic Irish Law

GAVIN BARRETT*

I. Introduction

The doctrine of legitimate expectations is one which has been of growing importance in Irish law in recent years. It would perhaps be more accurate to say the *doctrines* of legitimate expectations, since there are now two bodies of law concerning legitimate expectations in Irish law. One of them is the form of legitimate expectations which has recently attracted attention in various jurisdictions throughout the common law world. It has attained a particular prominence in Ireland since the famous decision of the Supreme Court in *Webb* v. *Ireland*[1]—the case concerning the discovery of the Derrynaflan hoard of early Christian treasure. It is not easy to give this doctrine an uncontroversial title. It can scarcely be called the 'Irish' doctrine of legitimate expectations, since it shares the characteristic of being an integral part of Irish law with another— second—doctrine of legitimate expectations which we shall see presently. Neither does it seem permissible (at least at this point of this article) to term this the 'common law' doctrine of legitimate expectations, since equity lawyers have tended to claim the doctrine as further proof that equity is not past the age of childbearing.[2] Thus for the purposes of this article (and for want of a better name) it is intended to refer to this doctrine by the rubric of the 'domestic' doctrine of legitimate expectations. I am conscious of the potential even of this name to mislead, for, if the truth be told, this doctrine is not completely 'domestic' to the Irish legal system as such—merely more so than the second doctrine.

* Ph.D., Barrister-at-Law, Lecturer in the Law of the European Union, University College Dublin. An earlier version of this article featured as a chapter in Breen, Casey and Kerr, *Liber Memorialis: Professor James C. Brady* (Roundhall, Dublin, 2001). My thanks are due to Prof. Takis Tridimas, Prof. Jim Casey and Oonagh Breen for their valuable suggestions, to John O'Dowd and Tony Kerr for calling my attention to some recent judgments and to Madeleine Coumont de Bairéid for her invaluable help in transforming this essay from a well-nigh illegible scrawl into an immaculately typed manuscript.

[1] [1988] IR 353. This point involves a certain irony since the more correct view is that the Supreme Court's reliance on the doctrine of legitimate expectations in *Webb* was not justified by the facts of that case. (See further text at n. 174, *infra*.)

[2] Brady regarded the recent emergence of the doctrine as 'further evidence of equity's vital role in the modern legal system' (see Brady 'Aspiring Students, Retiring Professors and the Doctrine of Legitimate Expectations' (1996) 31 Ir. Jur. (ns) 133 at 133).

Although the point is not always made in Irish case law, this first doctrine of legitimate expectations is really the product of the whole common law tradition, being the fruit of the intellectual exertions not merely of Irish judges, lawyers, and academics, but of those of their colleagues in other jurisdictions such as Canada, Australia, and New Zealand and above all, England. Nevertheless, it is still true to say that in formulating and applying this doctrine, Irish judges tend to rely to a far greater extent on domestic Irish authorities than on those emanating from any other jurisdiction. In sum, therefore, the claim is not so much that the doctrine is purely domestic, but rather merely that its development has been *more* domestic than that of the second doctrine.

What of the second doctrine of legitimate expectations in Irish law? This second doctrine forms just as much part and parcel of Irish law as the doctrine which I have somewhat arbitrarily styled the 'domestic' doctrine. This second doctrine is the general principle of European Community law of legitimate expectations. Its standing as part of Irish law is unquestionable,[3] and indeed it should be noted that this latter doctrine was relied upon—albeit unsuccessfully—in at least one case before the Irish courts which predated the recent upsurge in cases concerning the domestic doctrine.[4] For the purposes of clarity, this second doctrine will be referred to in this article as the 'Community law' doctrine of legitimate expectations.

The objective of this article is the examination of both of these doctrines. The analysis of each requires examination of a similar range of issues, including the question of what makes an expectation or privilege reasonable or legitimate; the question whether expectations protected by the respective doctrine are procedural (so that the protection extends only as far as, for example, an expectation of a fair hearing and being allowed to put one's case) or if they can also be substantive in nature (so that an expectation of receiving a privilege or benefit sought will be protected); and the issue of what factors will give rise to a legitimate expectation (such as a promise or undertaking given, some long-established practice, or a set of rules or guidelines which may give rise to an expectation that a certain result will follow). Other questions which have been felt to merit attention in this article include the issue of the extent to which an absence of misconduct on the part of an individual is seen as a prerequisite to the application of each doctrine; and how the process of balancing the inter-

---

[3] Thus s. 2(1) of the European Communities Act 1972 (as amended by s. 2 of the European Communites Act 1992) provides that 'from the 1st day of January 1973, the treaties governing the European Communities and the existing and future acts adopted by the institutions of those Communities and by the bodies competent under the said treaties shall be binding on the State and shall be part of the domestic law thereof under the conditions laid down in those treaties.' Note also the words of the ECJ in the landmark case of *Costa* v. *ENEL* (Case 6/64) [1964] ECR 585 at 593:

'By contrast with ordinary international treaties, the EEC Treaty has created its own legal system which, on the entry into force of the Treaty, became an integral part of the legal systems of the Member States and which their courts are bound to apply.'

[4] *Smith* v. *Ireland* [1983] ILRM 300. This case was first brought to light by Delany in 'The Doctrine of Legitimate Expectation in Irish Law' (1990) 12 *DULJ (ns)* 1 at 5.

ests of the administration on the one part, and the administration on the other manifests itself in the application of the European Community law principle and the domestic principle, respectively. The time spent in answering such questions is well spent, for such doctrines constitute a subject of study of some importance. It is perhaps stating the obvious to point out that in an era in which the role of government has expanded to encompass authorizing, licensing, financing, administering, and delegating a vast array of human activities, any doctrine which is concerned with the rights of individuals and companies interacting with the state is obviously likely to be of correspondingly increased significance.[5] Furthermore, in so far as the erstwhile 'zone of immunity' around governmental activities has been contained or is being reduced[6]—and it seems fair to say that the attribution of immunity to governmental activities seems increasingly less tolerable as their scope has become increasingly broad—doctrines such as those which form the subject of this article have had a significant role to play, and seem likely to continue to do so. They thus constitute an important element of Irish administrative law. Beyond providing a brief introduction, the approach has been adopted of looking at the two doctrines consecutively (an approach which may be of assistance to readers whose main interest is confined to one or other doctrine). It should be noted that the emphasis placed in this article on individual issues in the foregoing enumeration varies with the doctrine being examined, since so too do the emphases in the relevant bodies of case law. Hence, to take one example, the question whether there can be such a thing as substantive legitimate expectation has been a major difficulty in the case of the domestic doctrine, but has provoked relatively little controversy in so far as concerns the Community principle of legitimate expectation.

A. THE COMMUNITY LAW PRINCIPLE AND THE DOMESTIC PRINCIPLE:
RULES WITH A COMMON CONCEPTUAL ORIGIN

The Community law and domestic doctrines of legitimate expectations are distinct but in many respects similar bodies of rules, emanating as they do from the same conceptual wellspring. As Delany has pointed out:

while the origins of the principle of legitimate expectations in European Community law and the doctrine of legitimate expectations in English law owe little or nothing to each other, the preconditions for their operation have many common features and they both seek to ensure the protection of expectations legitimately created, whether by the institutions of the European Communities or by various types of government authorities or administrative bodies.[7]

---

[5] See on this point Baldwin and Horne 'Expectations in a Joyless Landscape' (1986) 49 *MLR* 685 at 685–6.
[6] See here de Smith, Woolf, and Jowell, *Judicial Review of Administrative Action* (5th edn., Sweet & Maxwell, London, 1995) at 9 and Delany, 'Significant Themes in Judicial Review of Administrative Action' (1998) 20 *DULJ (ns)* 73 at 73.
[7] Delany, *supra* n. 6, at 6. For 'English' one may read 'Irish' or, more precisely, 'domestic Irish' without damage to the accuracy of the statement.

Thus the two doctrines have in common 'an attribution of legal consequences to reliance by private parties upon the conduct or representations of public authorities'.[8]

It has been said of the Community principle of legitimate expectations that it may be invoked by any individual who is in a situation in which it appears that the conduct of the administration has led him to entertain reasonable expectations or justified hopes.[9] Such a definition seems appropriate whether one is discussing either the Community principle or the domestic doctrine.[10] Another observation which also applies both in the relation to the community principle and the domestic is that:

the expectations which a person can derive from a policy are not merely a matter for factual analysis. They will depend on a normative view of the expectations which an individual can be said to derive from the original policy, combined with an interpretative judgment as to whether the legislative framework will, in some way, be jeopardized by holding the administration to the original policy, even in relation to those already accepted by it.[11]

Further examples of similarities between the Community principle and the domestic doctrine may be discerned from the text below, but one should not make the mistake of overlooking some differences between the Community and the domestic doctrines. Without delving too much into topics which form the substance of the remainder of this article, one difference which may be pointed out, for example, is that the relative importance of the Community principle in the Community legal system and that of the domestic doctrine within the Irish system have not been the same to date. Schwarze has asserted that 'European Community law is primarily made up of rules of administrative law, drawn in particular from the area of law governing the management of the economy' and observed that 'the European Community, already described by the European Court of Justice as a Community based on law, could more precisely be termed a Community based on administrative law'.[12] There may be an element of overstatement here, but it is certainly true to say that, to date, administrative law principles have played a vastly more significant role in the Community legal system than have administrative law principles in the domestic Irish legal system. Furthermore, within the Community law system of administrative law, the Community law principle of legitimate expectations

---

[8] Wyatt 'European Community Law and Public Law in the United Kingdom' in Markesinis (ed.), *The Gradual Convergence* (Clarendon Press, Oxford, 1994) 188 at 194–5.

[9] Vaughan, *Law of the European Communities* (Butterworths, London, 2000) at para. 1266 relying on the words of the ECJ in cases such as *Mavridis* v. *European Parliament* (Case 289/81) [1983] ECR 1731 at para. 21 and *Van den Bergh en Jurgens* v. *Commission* (Case 265/85) [1987] ECR 1155 at para. 44.

[10] *Cf*, however, *Fakih* v. *Minister for Justice* [1993] 2 IR 406 discussed in the text, *infra*..

[11] Craig 'Legitimate Expectations: A Conceptual Analysis' (1992) 108 *LQR* 79.

[12] Schwarze 'Sources of European Administrative Law' in Martin (ed.), *The Construction of Europe—Essays in Honour of Emile Noël* (Kluwer, London, 1994), 183 at 183. The description by the Court of the Community as one based on law has been applied by the Court in a number of cases, among them *Parti écologiste 'Les Verts'* v. *European Parliament* (Case 294/83)[1986] ECR 1339 at para. 23 of the Court's judgment.

has enjoyed a more prominent and long-established role than has the domestic principle in domestic Irish administrative law. (The number of cases in which the doctrine of legitimate expectations has been invoked before the European Court of Justice now runs into the high hundreds.[13])

Of course, the Community law principles of legitimate expectations can be relied upon not alone before the European Court of Justice but, in an appropriate case, before Irish courts as well. Furthermore (albeit only to a limited extent) these Community law principles have found a quite different use, in that an element of cross-fertilization has occurred between the two doctrines. More specifically, some of the judgments of the European Court of Justice concerning the Community doctrine of legitimate expectations have been relied upon by Irish courts in reaching conclusions on the scope of the domestic doctrine.[14] However, for the most part, the Community law principle has remained a relatively unexplored concept both in academic writings and in judgments emanating from Irish courts to date. The first part of the article therefore is primarily dedicated to an examination of the Community law principle. The domestic doctrine will returned to in the second part.

II. The Community Law Principle of Legitimate Expectations

It may perhaps be an unexpected feature of a regime so influenced by the laws of the civil law jurisdictions that Community administrative law (and, within it, the general principles of Community law, and within these again, the legal rules relating to the principle of legitimate expectations) is largely constituted by judge-made law.[15] The legal principles here have been created 'on an

---

[13] See Usher, *General Principles of EC Law* (Longman, London, 1998) at 52. Note also that Schwarze dedicates over 300 pages of his seminal volume *European Administrative Law* (Office for Official Publications of the European Communities/ Sweet and Maxwell, Luxembourg, 1992) to a chapter entitled 'Legal Certainty and Protection of Legitimate Expectations'.

[14] See text, *infra*. Note that in his concurring judgment in *Wiley* v. *Revenue Commissioners* [1993] ILRM 482 at 493, a case which concerned the domestic concept, O'Flaherty J. had regard to authorities both on the domestic doctrine and on the Community law doctrine of legitimate expectation. Hamilton J (as he then was) did the same in *Carbery Milk Products Ltd.* v. *Minister for Agriculture and others* (1988–1993) 4 ITR 492 (judgment of 23 Apr. 1993). This seems acceptable only in so far as it is borne in mind that two distinct, albeit extensively conceptually overlapping, doctrines are being dealt with, something which seems to have been done in the judgment of Fennelly J. in *Glencar Exploration plc and Andaman Resources plc* v. *Mayo County Council* (Supreme Court decision of 19 July, 2001), in which the learned judge, in making reference both to domestic jurisprudence and that of the European Court of Justice, referred to the independent recognition of the doctrine of legitimate expectation in the Irish and the UK courts. (See p. 29 of the judgment of Fennelly J.). On a more general note, Schwarze has observed that:

'today a prolific interaction between Community law and national law is developing: law traditions common to the Member States have provided a basis and an inspiration for the Community's legal order. Community law in turn is now beginning to inspire national laws.'

(See *supra* n. 12 at 194).

[15] It is interesting, however, to note that this is also true of French administrative law and the approach of the Conseil d'Etat in that jurisdiction. See Bell, Boyron, and Whittaker, *Principles of French Law* (Oxford University Press, Oxford, 1998) at 28–9. Note that Community administrative

incremental, *ad hoc* basis in the light of the concrete needs of the cases under consideration'.[16] The unwritten nature of the rules at issue here gives rise to the advantage of flexibility, but has also created an element of uncertainty as to some of the applicable legal norms.

A. THE PROVENANCE OF LEGITIMATE EXPECTATIONS IN EC LAW: GENERAL PRINCIPLES OF COMMUNITY LAW

In the legal system of the European Community, the rule that legitimate expectations are to be respected is an example of what are known as general principles of Community law. General principles of law have been described as a source of Community law.[17] They are an unwritten source of law—a concept which exists in the Community legal system just as in others—hence the observation of the European Court of Justice that 'the fact that a principle is not mentioned in written Community law is not sufficient proof that it does not exist'.[18] A 'principle' in this sense means a general proposition of law of some importance from which concrete rules derive, and in which those rules find their justification.[19] General principles of law have a number of functions. For example, they constitute the particular response of the European Court of Justice to the problem that in the Community legal system (as in every other) it is impossible for legislation or other written sources of law to provide an answer to every question which comes before the courts.[20] A system is therefore needed in Community law—again, as in every other legal system—to perform a gap-filling role, and general principles perfom this function—the same role as that fulfilled, for example, in common law systems by the myth of the common law or, for example, in Irish constitutional jurisprudence by rights derived from, *inter alia*, Article 40.3 of the Constitution.[21] Thus—to use Hartley's vivid phrase—general principles are what the European Court uses:

law is not entirely unwritten. Within certain policy areas, such as the competition and anti-dumping regimes, special codes of administrative procedure have been developed (see Schwarze, 'Developing Principles of European Administrative Law' [1993] *PL* 229 at 230–1).

[16] *Ibid.*, 229.

[17] See generally in relation to general principles, Tridimas, *The General Principles of EC Law* (Oxford University Press, Oxford, 1999) and Usher, *General Principles of EC Law* (Longman, London, 1998).

[18] See the judgment of the ECJ in *Officine Elettromeccaniche Ing. A. Merlini v. High Authority* (Case 108/63) [1965] ECR 1 at 10.

[19] Tridimas, *supra* n. 17, at 1, where the same writer, applying distinctions first posited by Dworkin, observes that 'rules, because of their specificity and concrete character, stipulate answers. Principles do not set out legal consequences that follow automatically from them. A principle states a reason which gives arguments in one direction but does not necessitate a particular result.'

[20] Hartley, *The Foundations of European Community Law* (4th edn., Oxford University Press, Oxford, 1998) at 130.

[21] It has been said that more use is made by the ECJ of general principles of law than is made by other international tribunals.

to cloak the nakedness of judicial law-making: the idea is that, if a ruling can be shown to be derived from a principle of sufficient generality as to command common assent, a firm legal foundation for the judgment will be provided.[22]

The importance of general principles has not decreased with the ever-increasing number of legislative measures adopted by the Community (which might themselves have been expected to fill 'gaps' in the Community legal order). Instead the use of general principles has increased both in terms of the areas of Community law in which they have been applied and the extent of the requirements which they have been held to impose. This increase in their importance has come about because—apart from their role as a source of principles to plug the gaps in the written corpus of Community law—general principles fulfil at least two other major roles. Their second function is to operate as guidance on how Treaty provisions and secondary legislation (i.e., acts which are adopted by the Community institutions in order to implement the Treaties) ought to be interpreted. This role stems from the fact that, as Tridimas has observed:

they express constitutional standards underlying the Community legal order so that recourse to them is an integral part of the Court's methodology . . . Once it is accepted that the general principles embody constitutional values, they may bear determinative influence on the interpretation of written rules, irrespective of the existence of gaps.[23]

The end effect of interpretation in the light of general principles is often to ensure the validity of the relevant secondary Community legislation. This task has been described as the most frequent use to which general principles of Community law are put.[24]

The third role of general principles of Community law is to control the actions both of Community institutions and of national authorities. This control is exercised in one of three ways.

The first is that general principles act as criteria for determining the legality (and hence validity) of acts both of the Community institutions and of the Member States (including, it should be noted, that of legislation).[25] In other words, the general principles are a vital element in the process of judicial

---

[22] Hartley, *supra* n. 20, at 130.

[23] Tridimas, *supra* n. 17, 10. Somewhat ironically, as that writer points out, when general principles are used in this way, written Community law may be interpreted in such a way as to *leave* gaps which then need to be filled by recourse to general principles—something which happened in the *Chernobyl* case (*Parliament* v. *Council* (Case C–70/88) [1990] ECR I–2041), where the Court read what is now Art. 230 (formerly Art. 173) of the Treaty in the light of principles such as effective judicial protection and institutional balance so as to establish the existence of a procedural gap in the Treaty, *viz.*, the lack of a provision establishing the right of the European Parliament to bring an action.

[24] Usher, *supra* n. 17 at 122. If this observation is accurate, the point involves a certain irony, since it is clear that general principles are most often invoked by litigants in order to obtain the annulment of Community measures under Art. 230 (formerly Art. 173) or Art. 234 (formerly Art. 177). See Tridimas, *supra* n. 17, 19.

[25] See, for a case concerning Community secondary legislation, e.g., *Hauer* v. *Rheinland-Pfalz* (Case 44/79) [1979] ECR 3727, and for a case concerning national legislation, see, e.g., *Zuckerfabrik Franken GmbH* v. *Germany* (Case 77/81) [1982] ECR 681.

review in Community law. Questions of legality can come before the Court in a number of ways: (a) in a direct action for annulment aimed at challenging the validity of a measure; (b) if a so-called plea of illegality is raised (i.e., if, in the course of proceedings concerned with something else, the argument is raised that a particular act should not apply because it is invalid[26])—either in a direct action before the Court of Justice or else in the course of national proceedings, and the preliminary reference procedure is employed so as to bring the matter before the Court of Justice;[27] or (c) in the context of claim for damages.[28]

The Court of Justice has pointed out that a violation of a principle (in the case in question legitimate expectations) 'does not automatically mean that the disputed measure is void'.[29] Rather, the remedy awarded will depend on the circumstances of the case.[30] *Semble*, however, that it is only in exceptional cases that a finding of illegality will not result in a declaration of invalidity.[31]

The second method of control of Community institutions and national authorities flows from (and to some extent overlaps with) the first. General provisions (such as legitimate expectations) operate as guidance on how powers granted by Community law ought appropriately to be exercised. As Vaughan has pointed out, the obligation to comply with the general principles of Community law follows from the fact that a failure to do so may lead to an annulment of the exercise of power in question.[32]

The third method of control of Community institutions lies in the fact that breach of general principles of Community law may in certain circumstances give rise to a right to damages on the part of the offended individual. This possibility emerged in *CNTA* v. *Commission*,[33] a case which involved the principle of legitimate expectations. Here, liability was imposed on the Community because the Commission had violated the legitimate expectations of a trader by failing to allow a transitional period before abolishing a system for com-

---

[26] See generally Hartley, *supra* n. 20, at 327–9 and at chap. 14.

[27] There have been numerous instances of the ECJ holding a Community measure to be invalid on a preliminary reference from a national court because the measure in question breached a general principle of Community law. A prominent example is the *Mulder* case (Case 120/86) [1988] ECR 2321 in which a Community measure (a Council Regulation) was held invalid because it breached the principle of the protection of legitimate expectations.

[28] As to which, see the text *infra*.. See generally here, Usher, *supra* n. 17, at 123 ff.

[29] *Mavridis* v. *European Parliament* (Case 289/81) [1983] ECR 1731. See also *Ruckdeschel* v. *Hauptzollamt Hamburg–St. Annen* (Joined Cases 117/76 and 17/77) [1977] ECR 1753 and *Moulin Pont-à-Mouson* v. *Office Interprofessionel des céréals* (Joined Cases 124/76 and 20/77) [1977] ECR 1795, where the finding that a subsidy which was provided for the manufacture of *quellmehl*, but not for what was held to be the comparable product of starch) was held to have infringed the principle of equality.

[30] The Court has suggested that in certain circumstances a breach of a principle would instead justify the award of damages if the person concerned had suffered injury as a result. (See further the text, *infra*.) (See also Schwarze *European Administrative Law* (Office for Official Publications of the European Communities/ Sweet and Maxwell, 1992) at 953).

[31] See Tridimas, *supra* n. 17, 20–1, where he offers some useful guidance to the approach which the ECJ will adopt regarding this issue where violations of the principle of equality on the part of a Community measure are established.

[32] Vaughan, *supra* n. 19, para. 1209 at n. 2.   [33] Case 74/74 [1975] ECR 533.

pensatory amounts applicable to rape and colza seeds, so that even seeds changing hands under already existing contractual arrangements now failed to attract the compensatory amounts. A number of limitations should be noted here. First, and perhaps self-evidently, a prerequisite to the obtaining of damages for breach of one's legitimate expectations will be the existence of a causal connection between loss suffered and the breach of the relevant expectation.[34] Secondly, the *CNTA* judgment itself is a good illustration of the point that, in general, a limit will be placed on the damages recoverable for breach of the principle of legitimate expectations. Compensation will be limited to the positive damage suffered as a result of the expectation. It will not extend to compensation for any loss of profit which results from the disappointment of the expectation.[35] Thirdly, not just any breach of a general principle will suffice to give rise to liability in damages. Where questions of economic policy are concerned, only a sufficiently serious or flagrant breach of a general principle will suffice to give rise to liability in damages. Thus there are instances of a claimant succeeding in having a measure declared invalid on the basis that it violates the general principle of legitimate expectations, and yet failing to obtain any damages in respect of loss caused by this breach.[36]

B.   LEGITIMATE EXPECTATIONS AS A GENERAL PRINCIPLE OF COMMUNITY LAW

The origins of the Community doctrine of legitimate expectations are to be found in the legal systems of the Member States rather than in the Treaties. The concept of legitimate expectations seems to be one which exists in all of the Member States of the Community, although the exact content of the doctrine may vary from state to state.[37] It is also an approach to problem-solving which has featured in the jurisprudence of the European Court of Human Rights as well as in European Community law.[38] In the European Community context,

---

[34] See *Héritiers d'Edmond Ropars and others* v. *Council of the European Union* (Case T–429/93), judgment of the CFI (First Chamber) of 21 June 2000 and *Tromeur* v. *Council of the European Union and Commission of the European Union* (Case T–537/93), judgment of the CFI (First Chamber) of the same date, two of the most recent cases to come before the Court concerning legitimate expectations, both of which involved claims for damages somewhat similar to those at issue in the earlier case of *Mulder II* (discussed in the text *infra*) in which damages had been awarded for breach of the claimant's legitimate expectations. In *Ropars* and *Tromeur*, both claimants were unsuccessful, however, the claimants—unlike Mulder—having been unable to demonstrate the existence of any intention to resume milk production which had been frustrated by a Commission Regulation.

[35] See further on this point *August Töpfer & Co. GmbH* v. *Commission* (Case 112/77) [1978] ECR 1019.

[36] The famous *Mulder* saga, discussed in part in the text *infra*, is a case in point. A good discussion both of the issues here and of the issues which arose in the *Mulder* cases is to be found in Usher, *supra* n. 17, at 128–32.

[37] Schwarze, *supra* n. 13, at 874–937; Craig 'Substantive Legitimate Expectations in Domestic and Community Law' (1996) 55 *CLJ* 289 at 304.

[38] See, e.g., the judgment of the European Court of Human Rights in *National Provincial Building Society and others* v. *United Kingdom* [1997] STC 1466, a decision commented on in Oliver, 'A Negative Aspect to Legitimate Expectations' [1998] PL 558.

the principle of legitimate expectations has been described as requiring public authorities to exercise their powers over a period of time in a manner which
ensures that 'situations and relationships lawfully created under Community
law are not affected in a manner which could not have been foreseen by a
diligent person'.[39]

In so far as the protection of legitimate expectations in Community law is
concerned, it has, as Nolte has observed, the reputation of being 'made in
Germany', with legal writers having tended to ascribe its origins (at least in the
way in which it is commonly formulated) to the German law doctrine of protection of legitimate expectations or '*Vertrauensschutz*' (a doctrine the importance of which vastly increased in the German legal system in the 1950s, as a
result of decisions of administrative courts of the *Länder*, the reasoning in
which was later confirmed by the Federal Constitutional Court, the
Bundesverfassungsgericht).[40] While it can occasionally be difficult to determine the precise provenance of principles endorsed by the European Court of
Justice,[41] it is certainly true to say (as Schwarze has observed) that the
Opinions of the Advocates General tend to be particularly marked by those
legal systems with which they are personally familiar, and that the Opinions of
Advocates General Roemer and Reischl in the *Westzucker* and *Isoglucose* cases
are clearly modelled on the German case law on '*Vertrauensschutz*'.[42] In both
of these cases, the Opinion of the Advocate General was followed by the Court
in its judgment.[43]

The Court has not always clearly distinguished in the language which it has
used between legitimate expectations and the related principles of vested
rights and legal certainty.[44] However, in so far as the relationship between the

[39] See the opinion of Cosmas AG in *Duff and others v. Minister for Agriculture and Food, Ireland, and the Attorney General* (Case 63/93) [1996] ECR I–569 at 582.

[40] See in particular the decision of the Oberverwaltungsgericht Berlin (1957) 72 DVBl 505–6, the Bundesverfassungsgericht at (1981) 59 BverfGE 128, 164–7, and generally Nolte, 'General Principles of German and European Administrative Law—A Comparison in Historical Perspective' (1994) 57 *MLR* 191 in particular at 203 ff. See also Usher 'The Influence of National Concepts on Decisions of the European Court' (1975–6) 1 *EL Rev.* 359 at 363–4; Tridimas, *supra* n. 17, at 15–16; and Charlesworth and Cullen, *supra* n. 18, at 122. The extent of reliance on German law concepts has been ascribed by both Nolte and Tridimas to a combination of (a) jurisprudential reasons (such as what has been described as a parallel search for legitimacy on the part of both the German and Community legal orders in the post-war years—in the former case occasioned by the crisis of legitimacy associated with the abuses of the Nazi regime, in the case of Community law occasioned by the need to establish a novel and unprecedented legal order); and (b) practical reasons (such as, for example, the German nationality of one of the first two Advocates General to the ECJ, Roemer AG).

[41] See here Lagrange AG in *Hoogens v. High Authority* (Case 14/61) [1962] ECR 511 at 570.

[42] See *Westzucker v. Einfuhr- und Vorratsstelle für Zucker* (Case 1/73) [1973] ECR 723 and *Amylum v. Council* (Case 108/81) [1982] ECR 3107 and see generally Schwarze, *supra* n. 13, at 939–40.

[43] In contrast, Schwarze has observed the influence of English legal thinking in the Opinion of Warner AG in *Commission v. Council (Officials' Salaries)* (Case 81/72) [1973] ECR 575. Note, however, that in this particular case the Court did not follow the Opinion of the Advocate General in its judgment.

[44] See *Westzucker v. Einführ- und Vorratsstelle für Zucker* (Case 1/73) [1973] ECR 723 first noted in this context in Usher, 'The Influence of National Concepts on Decisions of the European Court' (1975–6) 1 *EL Rev.* 359 at 364.

principles of legitimate expectations and vested rights is concerned, it may be noted that the decision of the European Court of Justice in *Commission* v. *Council (Officials' Salaries)*[45] has been described as the *locus classicus* of legitimate expectations in Community law in particular because the case did *not* appear to involve the protection of any 'established rights' but rather merely that of an expectation.[46] In this case, the European Court of Justice held that a 1972 Council Decision to apply for a period of three years a particular system for calculating Community staff salaries was binding—and this prevented the valid adoption by the Council of a subsequent Regulation departing from its terms. In reaching this decision, the Court took account of the particular relationship which existed between the employer and the staff and expressly relied upon 'the rule of protection of the confidence that the staff could have that the authorities would respect undertakings of this nature'.[47]

As for the relationship between the principles of legitimate expectations and legal certainty,[48] the concepts appear to be linked. Indeed it is sometimes said that the principle of legitimate expectations springs from that of legal certainty.[49] Schwarze has written that legitimate expectations 'appears to be an expression . . . of legal certainty, which is equal in rank in the hierarchy of rules' and has summarized the position in the following terms:

the overall impression is that although the European Court of Justice in certain individual cases applies the principles of legal certainty and of the protection of legitimate expectations separately from each other, it nevertheless assumes that, in theoretical terms, there is a close correlation between the two with one being derived from the other. Here, legal certainty in many cases is used as a legal principle based on objective criteria, whilst the recognition of legitimate expectations serves to protect subjective rights.[50]

This view now finds support in judgments of the Court of Justice in which the Court has described the legitimate expectations principle as the corollary of the principle of legal certainty.[51]

[45] Case 81/72 [1973] ECR 575. [46] Usher, *supra* n. 44, at 364.

[47] It should be explained that the French term '*protection de la confiance légitime*' was originally translated into English as 'protection of legitimate confidence'. Fears that the use of the word 'confidence' would cause confusion led to the use of the expression 'legitimate expectation' becoming the preferred label for the doctrine, however. See Opinion of Warner AG in *Einführ- und Vorratsstelle Getreide* v. *Mackprang* (Case 4/1975) [1975] ECR 607 at 622 (cited in Usher, *supra* n. 24, at 54). (It may be noted in passing that it is a frequently encountered obstacle to easy comprehension of the general principles that what may effectively be the same principle is sometimes given several names in the jurisprudence of the Court. See Usher, *supra* n. 17, at 8–9.

[48] This is a principle which at its most basic requires that legal rules (both Community rules and national rules in areas covered by Community law) be brought to the attention of those whom they affect and be clear and predictable as regards their effects so that persons affected are capable of knowing with certainty from when their legal position is affected and thus be able to plan their actions accordingly.

[49] Edward and Lane, *European Community Law: An Introduction* (2nd edn., Butterworths, London, 1995) at para. 154. The first author, it should be noted, is a judge of the ECJ. Charlesworth and Cullen refer to legitimate expectations as a 'sub-principle' of legal certainty: *supra* n. 18, at 126.

[50] Schwarze, *supra* n. 13, at 946 and 947, respectively.

[51] See here, e.g., the judgment of the ECJ in *Duff and others* v. *Minister for Agriculture and Food, Ireland, and the Attorney General* (Case 63/93) [1996] ECR I–569, discussed in the text, *infra*.

Whatever its origins, the principle of legitimate expectations is now 'undeniably part of Community law'.[52] Indeed in the case of *Töpfer* v. *Commission* the Court went so far as to state that, by virtue of the principle of legitimate expectation forming part of the Community legal order, failure to respect a legitimate expectation would be a breach of the Treaty within the meaning of Article 230.[53] The large number of cases in which the doctrine is invoked has already been adverted to. From the original invocation of the concept of legitimate expectations in the reasoning of the Court of Justice in staff cases, the principle has spread to cases concerning other areas of law, most prominently concerning agriculture. The basic features of the doctrine were laid down in cases decided through the 1970s and 1980s.[54] Legitimate expectations is by now one of the principles of Community law which is most often relied upon before the European Court of Justice.[55] It must be gainsaid, however, that it is undoubtedly also the case that it is often raised in cases where it seems clear that it will not succeed as an argument. Indeed—perhaps somewhat paradoxically, notwithstanding the widespread reliance on the principle by litigants—it must be said that it is only very seldom that the protection of legitimate expectations has ultimately benefited any of them.[56] Success stories, as Sharpston has observed, are rare,[57] and the Court, while continuously emphasizing the need to protect the individual's legitimate expectations in individual cases, often goes on to conclude those same cases by deciding that no legitimate expectation was raised on the facts, or, if one was, that it was not violated in this particular case.[58] The large number of decisions of this kind may be due to the fact that the Court is aware of the consequences of its rulings and does not wish to reach decisions which would place undue strain on the Community institutions unless a significant injustice has been done. Several commentators have noted the difficulty in discerning any clear pattern to those few cases in which the litigant does succeed in pleading breach of legitimate expectations, although certain points about the doctrine have gradually become much clearer.[59] The point should be made, however, that inconsistent results are not always the product of incompatible reasoning. By its very

---

[52] See Opinion of Lenz AG in joined Cases 63 and 147/84 [1985] ECR 2857 at 2865.

[53] Case 112/77 [1978] ECR 1019. Note that protection for the legitimate expectations of individuals or firms is sometimes provided for in Community legislation. See, e.g., Art. 5(2) of Council Regulation 1697/79 of 24 July 1979 on the post-clearance recovery of import duties or export duties which have not been required of the person liable for payment on goods entered for a customs procedure involving the obligation to pay such duties. This was discussed in *Unifrigo Gadus Srl and CPL Imperial 2 SpA* v. *Commission of the European Communities* (Joined Cases T–10/97 and T–11/97) [1998] ECR II–2231.

[54] Tridimas, *supra* n. 17, at 6.

[55] See here Usher, *supra* n. 17, at 52 and 125, and Tridimas, *supra* n. 17, at 169.

[56] Schwarze, *supra* n. 13, at 950.

[57] Sharpston, 'Legitimate Expectations and Economic Reality' (1990) 15 *EL Rev.* 103 at 132.

[58] Schwarze, *supra* n. 13, at 1171. Sharpston, *supra* n. 57, at 160, has commented that the Court has a tendency to begin by formulating a broad principle on which it seems as though traders may successfully rely; and then to go on to whittle down its potential applicability so that in the end, the trader loses.

[59] See, e.g., Schwarze, *supra* n. 13, at 949 and Sharpston, *supra* n. 57, at 160.

nature as a principle (as opposed to a concrete legal rule[60]) the protection of legitimate expectations tends to provide arguments in a particular direction, rather than *necessitating* any particular result—as Tridimas has observed:

principles incorporate a minimum substantive content and guide the judicial inquiry on that basis. They provide strong arguments for a certain solution, they may even raise a presumption, but rarely do they dictate results in themselves.[61]

Furthermore, the somewhat ubiquitous nature of general principles in the case law relating to various fields of Community law should not distract us from another reality—which is that there is a good deal of relativity involved in their application. The reality is that they do not establish universal, inflexible standards. Rather, they 'are used to protect diverse interests and entail varying degrees of judicial scrutiny depending on the context in which they are applied'.[62]

C.   EXAMINING THE COMMUNITY DOCTRINE OF LEGITIMATE EXPECTATIONS: WHAT IS A 'LEGITIMATE' EXPECTATION FOR THE PURPOSES OF THE COMMUNITY PRINCIPLE?

The principle of legitimate expectations in Community law is a public law principle: the kind of legitimate expectations protected by Community law arise only in relation to laws[63] or administrative acts of Community institutions or national authorities.[64] As Sharpston has noted:

such legitimate expectations can only be generated in a regulated environment and arise, indeed, out of the presence of such regulation. In a completely non-regulated economic environment, there would be no administrative authorities to raise producers' and traders' hopes in the continuance of a particular pattern of regulation.[65]

As if to underline this point, the majority of cases concerning the Community principle have arisen in highly regulated economic sectors such as agriculture and steel.[66] It may be added that in practice the principle usually applies in situations concerning an individual decision. However, as some of the cases discussed in the present text demonstrate, it can also apply in respect of the exercise of more broadly applicable powers.[67]

---

[60] See n. 19 above in relation to this distinction, which was made by Dworkin in *Taking Rights Seriously* (Duckworth, London, 1978) at 24 ff., and which has been applied to the area of general principles by Tridimas, *supra* n. 17, at 1–2.

[61] *Supra* n. 17, at 2.   [62] Tridimas, *supra* n. 17, at 349.

[63] See in this regard, e.g., the *Staff Salaries* case (*Commission* v. *Council* (Case 81/72) [1973] ECR 575, discussed by Tridimas, *supra* n. 17, at 12–13.

[64] Contrast the general principles of equality and proportionality, both of which enjoy a dual function, operating not alone as principles of public law, but also as principles which play a role in areas which are the substantive concern of Community law, such as free movement. (Note that the latter principle is capable of binding private parties, be they natural or legal persons). The dual role of these principles has led to some divergences in the case law concerning each. See generally Tridimas, *supra* n. 17, 5–6 and chaps. 2 and 3.

[65] Sharpston, *supra* n. 57, at 104.   [66] *Supra* n. 57, 108.

[67] See, e.g., *Commission* v. *Council (Officials' Salaries)* (Case 81/72) [1973] ECR 575 (discussed in the text *supra*).

Trade, of course, takes place in an environment of constantly changing factors such as prices, and the fact and level of demand or supply. The question therefore arises why changes in the regulatory environment are not simply regarded as another factor the risk of which should be borne by the producer or trader. The answer seems to be that, in a sense, the principle of legitimate expectations can be regarded as representing the Community legal system's choice as to the appropriate degree of play to be allowed to various countervailing forces. On the one hand, economic policy dictates that there are many factors which a trader should accept as a 'risk of the game', including to some extent, the risk of changes in market regulation, and further requires some degree of freedom on the part of regulatory bodies so as to enable them to respond effectively to market changes. On the other hand, it is also clear that there is a degree of legal certainty without which any forward planning of economic activity by traders or producers will be rendered excessively difficult. In other words, there is a point at which the potential for shifting of regulatory goalposts discourages participation in the market to the ultimate detriment of society.[68] Thus 'if the regulatory authorities are perceived as too arbitrary, or too given to making sudden and frequent changes to the regulatory framework, certain types of business will vote with their feet, if necessary, and move elsewhere'.[69] The general principle of legitimate expectation shows where the Community legal system draws a line in the sand between these two sets of interests. Careful note should be made of the point, however, that it is not *market* uncertainty that the trader or producer is intended to be protected or insured from by the Community doctrine, but rather *regulatory* uncertainty.

One case illustrating some of the above considerations is *Duff and others* v. *Minister for Agriculture and Food, Ireland, and the Attorney General*.[70] Duff and his fellow small farmers were induced to borrow money and develop their farms. They made their plans under the Irish implementation of a 1972 Community Directive,[71] making investments which could be justified only by increasing their output and selling it at a price which would give a reasonable return. These plans needed a period of time to be put into effect. However, before their plans yielded profits, the Council introduced the milk superlevy system,[72] and Duff and his co-litigants were given reference quantities (i.e. milk production quotas) based only on their pre-development output—with the result that, having incurred heavy expenditure, they could not now get an outlet for the sale of their increased milk production. They argued that this sit-

---

[68] It will be noted that the factors weighing in one direction or the other are both economic and legal. As Sharpston has observed, 'for both legal reasons (an estoppel-type argument) and economic reasons (sometimes the economic agent should be able to rely on the administration not changing the rules in the middle of the game), a doctrine of legitimate expectations is attractive': Sharpston 'European Community Law and the Doctrine of Legitimate Expectations: How Legitimate and For Whom?' (1990) 11 *J Intl. L Bus.* 87 at 89.

[69] Sharpston, *supra* n. 57 at 106.   [70] Case 63/93 [1996] ECR I–569.

[71] Community Directive 72/159/EEC of 17 Apr. 1972 on the modernization of farms [1972] OJ L96/1.

[72] The rules governing this system were set out in Regulation EEC/856/84 [1984] OJ L90/10.

uation violated their legitimate expectations and, more particularly, that the 1972 Directive had been a signal that they could increase their milk production and would receive a special reference quantity. The Court of Justice rejected this argument, however, holding that:

the principle of the protection of legitimate expectations may be invoked as against Community rules only to the extent that *the Community itself* has previously created a situation which can give rise to a legitimate expectation.

Neither the Community rules on development plans, nor the terms or purpose of those plans, nor the context in which the plaintiffs in the main proceedings adopted their development plans indicate that the Community created a situation providing producers who were implementing a development plan with reasonable grounds to expect that a special reference quantity . . . would be allocated and that they would therefore be exempted in part from the restrictions established by the additional levy scheme.[73]

Unfortunately for them, therefore, Duff and his co-litigants fell on the wrong side—if perhaps only just—of the line drawn by the European Court of Justice. For, to paraphrase a comment in the Opinion of Advocate General Slynn in the *Mulder* case,[74] in order to rely successfully on the principle of legitimate expectations, one must establish a situation which 'crosses the line between what is merely "hard business luck" and what is unreasonable treatment'. In *Duff*, the Court implicitly took the view that this case fell into the former category. Thus Duff and his co-litigants were to be regarded as indirect victims of a change in the market situation (which the Community rule-making bodies had to be free to respond to) rather than as victims of unreasonable treatment by the Community legislature. Put another way, Duff *et al.* were expected to foresee the possibility of unfavourable market trends and the need of the Community institutions to react to such trends.[75]

D. FACTORS WHICH GO TOWARDS MAKING AN EXPECTATION 'LEGITIMATE' IN COMMUNITY LAW

A number of factors may be derived from the case law of the Court of Justice—which is not always as clear as the following description may suggest—as necessary in order to justify the protection of a legitimate expectation. Summarized, and somewhat roughly grouped, these are as follows:

(i) Conduct Justifying the Expectation

Some conduct on the part of the Community or of a Member State justifying legitimate expectations is required. A mere expectation that the Community

---

[73] Emphasis added.

[74] Case 120/86 [1988] ECR 2321. The claimants ultimately fared better in the Irish Supreme Court, albeit on different grounds. See *Duff* v. *Minister for Agriculture (No. 2)* [1997] 2 IR 22 and the subsequent High Court judgment in the same case by Laffoy J of 25 Mar. 1999 in which the quantum of damages was assessed.

[75] See also the similar case of *Cornée and others* v. *COPALL and others* (Case 196/88) [1989] ECR 2309. *Finsider SPA* v. *Commission* (Joined Cases 63 and 147/84) [1985] ECR 2857 is also analogous.

institutions will act in a particular way is thus not enough (probably because the Court does not wish to assume the role of dictating policy choices to Community institutions—or to allow litigants to do so).[76]

The conduct required on the part of the Community or Member State may take a number of forms. It may consist of (i) an instrument conferring benefits; (ii) a consistent administrative practice (which will obviously be used to justify a legitimate expectation in the continuation of a situation which already exists); or (iii) written or oral statements or representations.

A good example of (i) an *instrument conferring benefits* giving rise to legitimate expectations[77] is provided by legislative provisions which require that special account be taken of certain situations or persons. Such provisions— provided the interests protected are specific and well-defined enough—can create legitimate expectations that these persons or situations will be so treated absent an overriding public interest. A case involving this phenomenon was *Sofrimport Sarl v. Commission*.[78] This concerned Regulation 2707/72, which gave the Commission power to take protective measures regarding the importation of certain goods. The Regulation contained a provision, however, which laid down that account should be taken of the special position of goods in transit—a measure obviously intended to ensure that traders would not be excessively prejudiced by any protective measures taken by the Commission. In 1988, the Commission took protective measures under Regulation 2707/72.[79] It suspended all licences for the importation of apples from Chile (such licences being necessary to engage in this trade). The instrument which the Commission used to effect this suspension, however,[80] made no special provision for goods in transit. The applicant company, which held such a licence and whose goods were already in transit when the suspending measure was adopted, therefore brought an action for annulment. The Court of Justice duly annulled the protective measure, holding that the failure of the Commission to make any special provision for goods in transit was a violation of the claimants' legitimate expectations.

The normal rule, however, is that legitimate expectations will not be created in a situation which can be altered by a Community institution exercising its discretionary powers—including its power to legislate. This is a point which applies with particular force in regulating areas which involve constant attention so as to enable a flexible response to market change.[81] It is worth noting, in this context, the observation by Usher that in the famous milk quota cases (such as *Mulder*[82]) 'the expectation that was protected was not that the rules

---

[76] See, e.g., *Compagnie Industrielle et Agricole du Comté de Loheac and others v. Council and Commission* [1977] ECR 6456.

[77] On which see generally Vaughan, *supra* n. 9, at paras. 1287–1300.

[78] Case C–152/88 [1990] ECR I–2477.   [79] [1972] OJ L291/3.

[80] *Viz.*, Regulation 962/88 [1988] OJ L95/10.

[81] *Pesquerias v. Commission* (Joined Cases C–258 and C–259/90) [1992] ECR I–2901 and *Climax Paper Converters v. Council* (Case T–155/94) [1996] ECR II—877 and see Usher, *supra* n. 24, at 58–9.

[82] See *Mulder v. Minister van Landbouw en Visserij* (Case 120/86) [1988] ECR 2321; *Mulder and others v. Council and Commission* ('*Mulder II*') (Joined Cases C–104/89 and C–37/90) [1992] ECR I–3061. These cases are discussed in the text *infra*.

would remain unchanged when the outgoers returned to milk production, but that they should not be penalised compared with the producers for having participated in a Community scheme'.[83]

In so far as draft legislation is concerned, the form which draft legislation takes will give rise to no legitimate expectation that in its ultimate form the legislation will be the same or similar. This is because the possibility always exists that legislation will be amended during the process leading to its adoption, and the Court has not permitted the law-making powers of the Community institutions to be prejudiced by the recognition of legitimate expectations which are grounded in how legislation appears in its draft form.[84]

As regards (ii) legitimate expectations engendered by *consistent administrative practices*, a good example of this is provided by *Ferriere San Carlo SpA* v. *Commission*,[85] where the claimant company, which had been fined by the Commission for selling steel in excess of a delivery quota was held to have had a legitimate expectation of the continuation of the Commission's general practice in the previous two years of allowing over-quota sales which had been made for the purposes of running down stocks. A 1983 general decision extending the life of the steel quota system was held not to have clearly indicated a modification of the previous practice. Nor had the company been individually informed of a modification of the practice in good time before the sale was made. The Commission decision to fine the company was therefore annulled by the Court. The *San Carlo* case seems to illustrate the point that where a consistent administrative practice is adopted by an authority, producers and traders are entitled to expect continued adherence to that practice, unless and until the authority indicates (whether by legislative provision or by individual warning) that this will no longer be the case.[86]

The exercise on one occasion of a discretion will not, of course, be regarded as constituting a consistent practice.[87] Nor will a legitimate expectation be deemed to have been raised where an individual is effectively on notice that an alteration of the relevant practice is imminent. (It should be explained that it is often the case that changes in the law at European level are preceded by

[83] Usher, *supra* n. 17, 59.

[84] See *Driessen en Zonen* v. *Minister van Verkeer en Waterstaat* (Cases C–13 to C–16/92) [1993] ECR I–4751, where the Court held that no basis for any legitimate expectation existed merely by virtue of the publication of a proposal by the Commission for a regulation on structural improvement in inland water transport which provided for transition rules less strict than those ultimately adopted. Note, however, that it is not always the case that rules which have not yet entered into force are incapable of giving rise to legitimate expectations. In *Opel Austria* v. *Council* (Case T–115/94) [1997] ECR II–39, a legitimate expectation was held to exist that the Council would not introduce measures contrary to the European Economic Area Agreement once the Community had deposited its instruments of approval of the Agreement and the date of entry into force of the Agreement was known.

[85] Case 344/85 [1987] ECR 4435.

[86] See also *Decker* v. *Caisse de Pension des Employés Privés* (Case 129/87) [1988] ECR 6121 and *Italy* v. *Commission* (Case 14/88) [1989] ECR 3677. There can be no legitimate expectation in the continuance of an illegal practice, however. See, e.g., *United Kingdom* v. *Council* (Case 68/86) [1988] ECR 855.

[87] See, e.g., *Holtbecker* v. *Commission* (Case T–20/91) [1992] ECR II–2599.

discussions between the Commission and producers or traders likely to be affected by the alteration. These negotiations may be regarded as having alerted these parties that a change in the existing system is imminent.[88]) Finally, a word may be added in so far as the effects of administrative *inactivity* are concerned. There is no expectation that any decision-making process will have a particular result and, normally, the mere fact that a long time is taken in reaching a decision will *not* give rise to a legitimate expectation as to the eventual outcome of that decision.[89] Nor will the passage of time while negotiations are under way with the authority in question give rise to legitimate expectation.[90] On the other hand, in certain limited circumstances, the passage of time accompanied by inactivity may give rise to a claim of legitimate expectation of the continuation of the *status quo*—such as where past conduct of the administrative authority has given reasonable grounds to the individual concerned to believe that the authority now regards a particular situation as lawful.[91]

In so far as concerns (iii), *written or oral statements or representations*, these can take the form of information given, statements made, or pledges undertaken. In essence, however, what is looked for in order to support a legitimate expectation is a precise or specific assurance to the individual concerned.[92] Thus in *Delauche* v. *Commission* [93] it was held by the Court that mere general statements by the Commission to the effect that the number of women with positions of responsibility should be increased would not give rise to any legitimate expectation on the part of the claimant that she would be promoted.

---

[88] See here Sharpston, *supra* n. 57, at 147 and, by the same writer, *supra* n. 68, at 99.

[89] See *Epichiriseon Metalleftikon Viomichanikon kai Naftiliakon AE* v. *Council* (Case C–121/86)[1989] ECR 3919 and *Continentale Produkten-Gesellschaft* v. *Hauptzollamt München-West* (Case 246/87) [1989] ECR 1151. See more generally, Vaughan, *supra* n. 9, at para. 1282. Contrast the decision, concerning the domestic doctrine, of Hamilton P in *Ghneim* v. *Minister for Justice*, a case dealt with in n. 190 *infra*.

[90] See here Sharpston, *supra* n. 57, at 159.

[91] The administrative authority must, however, be aware of all the material facts of the situation. See generally *Rijn-Schelde-Verolme Maschinefabrieken en Scheepswerven NV(RSV)* v. *Commission* (Case 223/85) [1987] ECR 4617. In *Grogan* v. *Commission* (Case 127/80) [1982] ECR 869 inaction on the part of the Council in rectifying exchange rates which were used to calculate the pensions of retired Community staff—resulting in the prolonged application of a supposedly temporary system which was more favourable to certain pension recipients—was held to give rise to a legitimate expectation on the part of the applicant (a retired Irish Commission official) that suitable transition arrangements (involving a more gradual reduction of the pension) be introduced. Tridimas has described this case and others like it as an 'aberration' and it may be that the reasoning of the Court was influenced by the nature of the benefit involved. See Tridimas, *supra* n. 17, at 195–7.

[92] Silence on the part of a Community institution in response to an assertion by an individual that he or she has an entitlement will not give rise to a legitimate expectation. See *Chornel* v. *Commission* (Case T–123/89) [1990] ECR II–131.

[93] Case 111/86 [1987] ECR 5345. See also *Van den Bergh en Jurgens* v. *Commission* (Case 265/85) [1987] ECR 1155 where frequent public statements by the Commission to the effect that Christmas butter schemes were an inappropriate means of achieving lasting cuts in butter stocks were held not to give rise to a legitimate expectation that no further scheme would be organized by the Commission, partly because they involved no specific undertaking never to institute such a scheme again.

And in *Lefebvre and others* v. *Commission*,[94] letters addressed to the applicants were held not to give rise to any legitimate expectation, since the undertaking made in the letters—*viz.*, to take into account the position of small and medium-sized enterprises in formulating a particular legislative proposal relating to bananas—could not be regarded as a precise assurance.

Even precise or specific assurances by Community officials not to apply the law will not give rise to a legitimate expectation.[95] Nor will acts of national authorities which breach Community law, at least where the Commission has declared that these acts violate Community law.[96] In this regard, it should be noted that where a document is inaccurately completed, the initial reaction of the national authorities to that document (for example, in accepting it) will not normally give rise to a legitimate expectation.[97] The Court has also been unsympathetic to attempts by individuals or companies to rely on the legitimate expectations principle so as to ensure the continuance of erroneous calculations of entitlements by Community institutions which have previously led to traders making profits.[98]

(ii) The Requirement of an Expectation

Secondly (and perhaps somewhat self-evidently) in order for the principle of legitimate expectation in Community law to apply, an expectation must have been generated. The requirement of the existence of this expectation is a subjective test in the sense that the expectation must be a concrete one which was

---

[94] Case T–571/93 [1995] ECR II–2385.

[95] See *Thyssen* v. *Commission* (Case 188/82) [1983] ECR 372 which involved an alleged promise by senior Commission officials not to impose a fine on Thyssen if it exceeded its sales quota. Although the Court held that no legitimate expectation of not being fined had been aroused since 'no official can give a valid undertaking not to apply Community law', it did recognize that Thyssen had been misled by reducing the size of the fine to a token amount and ordering the Commission to bear its own costs: *FRUBO* v. *Commission* (Case 71/74) [1975] ECR 563. Cf., however, *Usines de la Providence* v. *High Authority* (Case 29/63) [1965] ECR 1591 where liability in damages was created on the part of the ECSC High Authority by the making of promises by its officials to make unlawful payments over a period of time, because this demonstrated a lack of care on the part of the High Authority.

[96] *Land Rheinland-Pfalz* v. *Alcan Deutschland* (Case C–24/95) [1997] ECR I–1591. See generally here, Usher, *supra* n. 17, at 63. This point is obviously an important one in the field of state aids, as to which see generally Sharpston, *supra* n. 57, at 132 to 133. Vaughan has gone so far as to assert that 'a wrongful act on the part of a Community institution or one of its officials, or a practice of a Member State which does not conform to Community rules, may never give rise to a legitimate expectation under Community law': *supra* n. 9, at para. 1283, and note the authorities cited at nn. 1–3). See in this regard, e.g., *Hauptzollamt Hamburg-Jonas* v. *Firma P. Krücken* (Case 316/86) [1988] ECR 2213 and *Hauptzollamt Krefeld* v. *Maizena GmbH* (Case 5/82) [1982] ECR 4601 and *Alois Lageder SpA* v. *Amministrazione delle Finanze* (Joined Cases C–31 to 44/91) [1993] ECR I–1761. A parallel can be drawn here with the unwillingness of national courts to apply the domestic doctrine of legitimate expectations to allow it to legitimize *ultra vires* action on the part of administrative authorities, i.e., by giving effect to promises to act or refrain from acting in a way which is *ultra vires* the body in question. See on this point Hogan and Morgan, *Administrative Law in Ireland* (3rd edn., Roundhall Sweet and Maxwell, Dublin, 1998) at 865.

[97] *Van Gend en Loos NV and Expeditiebedrijf Wim Bosman BV* v. *Commission* (Joined Cases 98/83 and 230/83) [1984] ECR 3763, *Unifrigo Gadus and CPL Imperial 2 SpA* v. *Commission* (Joined Cases T–10/97 and T–11/97) [1998] ECR II–2231.

[98] *Firma August Töpfer & Co.* v. *Commission* (Case 112/77) [1978] ECR 1019.

genuinely held by an individual (who must not have acted in a way inconsistent with his holding this expectation[99]) but the standard required is objective in certain other respects.[100] An expectation is not legitimate unless a prudent individual would have had it. Thus if an expectation allegedly created by the conduct of an administrative authority is unreasonable or incapable of fulfilment, then it will not be regarded as a legitimate expectation for the purposes of Community law.[101] Nor will an expectation be regarded as legitimate if its subsequent frustration was foreseeable. Vaughan has summarized the position in relation to this objective element of the legitimate expectations principle by observing:

> no legitimate expectation can be claimed if a change in the law is foreseeable or if frequent changes in the position is a characteristic feature of a given economic situation; if a prudent and discriminating trader could have foreseen the adoption of a Community measure likely to affect his interest (which may arise where legislation provides for its future amendment); if a decision may be subject to review in accordance with the legislation on the basis of which it was adopted; or if the situation can be altered at any time by decisions taken by the Community institutions within the limits of their discretionary powers.[102]

One of the most important elements to note here is that in deciding whether the legitimate expectations of an individual have been breached, regard will be had to the knowledge and information which ought to be available to the prudent and informed business person.[103] The standard applied is what a well-informed, experienced trader would have anticipated. A high level of awareness of market realities is therefore presupposed. Thus 'if the underlying economic situation and the regulatory situation are plainly out of step with one another, an economic agent cannot have a reasonable—let alone legitimate—expectation that sudden regulatory changes will not be made'.[104] The prudent trader is also aware of the rules governing the relevant market sector, so that any expectation which conflicts with those rules will not be regarded as legitimate.[105] A high level of monitoring of Commission activities is also an

---

[99] In *Alpha Steel Ltd.* v. *Commission* (Case 14/81) [1982] ECR 749, the claimant firm failed in its attempt to plead that legitimate expectations on its part had been created by a particular Commission decision regarding steel quotas, since it had brought an action seeking the annulment of the decision in question.

[100] Schwarze, *supra* n. 13, at 951.

[101] *San Marco Impex Italiano SA* v. *Commission* (Case T–451/93) [1994] ECR II–1061. It should be noted that it may be reasonable to hold a belief which is in actual fact erroneous. See Sharpston, *supra* n. 57, at 158.

[102] Vaughan, *supra* n. 9, at para. 1285, and the case law cited therein, in particular *Sociedade Agro-Pecuària Vicente Nobre Lda* v. *Council* (Case 253/86) [1988] ECR 2725, which concerned legislation which made specific provision for the possibility of future changes. Note also the comment in *Delacre and others* v. *Commission* (Case C–350/88) [1990] ECR I–395 at 462 that 'traders cannot have a legitimate expectation that an existing situation which is capable of being altered by the Community institutions in the exercise of their discretionary powers will be maintained'.

[103] See, e.g., *Delacre and others* v. *Commission* (Case C–350/88) [1990] ECR I–395.

[104] Sharpston, *supra* n. 57, at 120.

[105] Illustrated by *Compagnie Continentale France* v. *Council* (Case 169/73) [1975] ECR 117 (where knowledge of the UK's Act of Accession to the European Economic Community was

attribute of the prudent trader,[106] as is awareness of the latest contents of the Official Journal.[107] One might quibble with the standard of knowledge expected. It is not always clear that such a level of knowledge is likely to be reached in practice—by small economic operators in particular. On the other hand, as Sharpston has commented, 'the logic is unassailable: a trader should not be able to place himself in a better position by not taking care than he would have been in had he exercised all due care'.[108] Further, one should be aware in this context and in others (as the Court of Justice undoubtedly is) that the doctrine of legitimate expectations entails serious consequences for a far wider range of persons than merely a particular claimant when it is deployed against the Community legislative or administrative organs. As Usher has observed, 'the exercise of legislative and administrative discretion may be subject to severe constraints in situations where a legitimate expectation has been created'.[109]

The standards of reasonableness and foreseeability will vary according to the circumstances of the case—context counts for much in setting the required standard of knowledge and awareness. As the Court stated in the *Duff* ruling:

it is settled case-law that in the sphere of the common organization of the markets, whose purpose involves constant adjustments to meet changes in the economic situation, economic agents cannot legitimately expect that they will not be subject to restrictions arising out of future rules of market or structural policy . . .[110]

To take one example, the policy area of agriculture—*or*, more accurately, the various Community financial mechanisms and systems which operate in agriculture-related fields—has as its subject matter a volatile market where

---

expected of a French trader) Cf. *Cambo Ebro Industrial SA* v. *EU Council* (Case T–472/93) [1995] ECR II–421 (where awareness was expected of the possibility that Community intervention prices for Spanish sugar might change sooner than a transitional period for price alignments provided for in the Spanish Act of Accession). See also *Blackman* v. *European Parliament* (Case T–33/89) [1993] ECR II–249 (no legitimate expectation stemmed from the failure of the Community administration to bring insurance rules which were publicly available to the attention of the claimant). Cf., however, *Oryzomyli Kavallas* v. *Commission* (Case 160/84) [1986] ECR 1633, where a series of factors combined to make obtaining knowledge of the relevant rules practically impossible, and see generally Usher, *supra* n. 17, at 60–1.

[106] See, e.g., in this regard the case of *Continentale Produkten-Gesellschaft Erhardt-Renken GmbH* v. *Hauptzollamt München-West* (Case 246/87) [1989] ECR 200 where it was held that a prudent and informed trader would be aware that an anti-dumping investigation was under way, and therefore aware that anti-dumping duties could be imposed, when entering into contracts with suppliers.

[107] Seen in *Union Nationale des Coopératives Agricoles de Céréales and others* v. *Commission and Council* (Case 95/75) [1975] ECR 1615 in which the Court distinguished unfavourably the legitimate expectations of claimants who had entered into contracts after the publication in the Official Journal of a regulation modifying the method of calculating monetary compensation amounts *vis à vis* the expectations of those who had entered into such contracts prior to publication.

[108] *Supra* n. 57, at 150.   [109] *Supra* n. 17, at 57.

[110] *Duff and others* v. *Minister for Agriculture and Food, Ireland, and the Attorney General* (Case 63/93) [1996] ECR I–569.

change has been described as the normal state of affairs.[111] (In practice, a good proportion of the legitimate expectations cases which have come before the Court have been brought in this area.) Here, not only is it the case that the Court of Justice usually gives the Community institutions wide freedom to manœuvre in managing the market, and is therefore little inclined to impose restrictions on them via the legitimate expectations principle,[112] but the Court has also firmly adhered to the position that speculative undertakings (by which is meant attempts to take advantages of weaknesses in the Community system to make a profit, rather than actions in the normal course of business) will be entered into at the trader's own risk.[113] In this way, the Court has refused to allow the legitimate expectations principle to be used to make Community institutions in effect the insurers of last resort for such activities.

An area in which the Court, for understandable reasons, has shown itself, if anything, to be even less inclined to allow the doctrine of legitimate expectations to be deployed is that of the Community's external trade relations.[114] A restrictive approach has also been adopted in the field of anti-dumping, at least in any cases with policy implications.[115]

(iii)   Reliance on the Expectation

Thirdly, in order for the general Community law principle of legitimate expectations to be successfully invoked, the individual must have acted on the basis of the expectation, or at least have refrained from acting on the basis of it. Merely hoping that the existing situation will continue will not result in entitlement to protection under the principle of legitimate expectation.[116] Nor will an alteration in one's position which is due to factors other than the expecta-

[111] Sharpston has observed that 'the inexpert do not play in this market which provides considerable opportunities for speculative gains—and also losses': *supra* n. 57, 118.

[112] *Ibid.*, 108. Some idea of the Court's approach can be gained from its observation in *Merkur* v. *Commission* (Case 97/76) [1977] ECR 1063 that liability in respect of losses suffered by traders as a result of measures adopted in relation to the monetary compensatory amounts system would be imposed on the Community only were the Commission to abolish monetary compensatory amounts in a particular sector with immediate effect and without either giving notice or adopting transitional measures—and, even then, only in the absence of an overriding public interest. See also Usher, *supra* n. 17, at 59. Although stringent, these criteria appear to have been met in the earlier case of *Comptoir National Technique Agricole* v. *Commission* (Case 74/74) [1975] ECR 533.

[113] See, e.g., *Pardini* v. *Ministero del Commercio con l'Estero* (Case 338/85) [1988] ECR 2041; *Einführ- und Vorratstelle für Getreide und Futtermittel* v. *Firma C. Mackprang* [1975] ECR 607. See further here Hartley, *supra* n. 20, 145–6.

[114] See *OHG Firma Werner Faust* v. *Commission* (Case 52/81) [1982] ECR 3745; *Edeka Zentrale AG* v. *Germany* (Case 245/81) [1982] ECR 2745. In these cases, the entry into a commercial agreement between the Community and China was held to have the result that no informed trader was entitled to expect that existing patterns of trade would be respected—so that no legitimate expectations were violated subsequently by what amounted to an almost complete prohibition of mushroom imports from Taiwan at very short notice by the Commission.

[115] See further Sharpston, *supra* n. 57, 116–18.

[116] See further *ibid.*, 158. Craig has asserted that:

the case law of the ECJ indicates that the individual must be able to point either to a bargain of some form which has been entered into between the individual and the authorities, or to a course of conduct or assurance on the part of the authorities which can be said to generate the legitimate expectation.

tion (which would be shown to be the case, for example, if the individual altered his or her position before the conduct raising the expectation occurred).[117]

(iv) Absence of Misconduct

A fourth factor, reflecting the point that nobody can rely on a situation caused by his or her own violation of Community law may be stated in negative terms. This is that no legitimate expectation will be given to any individual or firm where the conduct of the Community or national administrative body results from a failure on the part of that individual or firm to provide timely or accurate information about a state of affairs.[118] It has further been held that a manifest breach of the relevant rules by a party seeking to rely upon the principle of legitimate expectations will prevent any such reliance.[119]

(v) A Weighing Up of Interests

Finally, in each case there will be a weighing up of the interests of the person in having his or her legitimate expectations protected against the public interest in having the relevant public authority free to act in whatever way it deems most appropriate.[120] This aspect is one of the ways in which the Community doctrine most closely resembles the domestic doctrine in Irish law under which a public body will be entitled to change its position where objective considerations exist which justify it in so doing.[121]

(See Craig, 'Substantive Legitimate Expectations in Domestic and Community Law' (1996) 55 *CLJ* 289 at 307). Insofar as an alteration in the claimant's position is required this will be the case even when the expectation relied upon has been generated by consistent behaviour by an administrative body. Sharpston has observed that:

> legitimate expectations are most likely to be created as a result of discussions with the administration which put the administration on notice that a trader intends to avail himself or herself of a particular provision and which lead the trader to commit himself or herself reasonably and irrevocably to a particular course of action. If possible, therefore, the competent authorities should be duly notified.

Sharpston, *supra* n. 68, at 102.

[117] See *Agazzi Léonard* v. *Commission* (Case 181/87) [1988] ECR 3823 and see generally authorities cited by Vaughan, *supra* n. 9, at para. 1301.

[118] See, e.g., the judgment of the CFI in *Unifrigo Gadus Srl and CPL Imperial 2 SpA* v. *Commission of the European Communities* (Joined Cases T–10/97 and T–11/97) [1998] ECR II–2231 (where the competent national authorities were misled by incorrect declarations made by an exporter to the effect that particular consignments of cod originated in Norway).

[119] See, e.g., *Eugénio Branco Lda* v. *Commission* (Case T–142/97) [1988] ECR II–3567 in which it was held that a recipient of European Social Fund assistance who had not implemented a training programme in accordance with the conditions to which a grant of assistance by the Commission had been made could not rely on the principle of protection of legitimate expectations with a view to securing final payment of the full amount of assistance initially granted. See also, e.g., *Sideradria* v. *Commission* (Case 67/84) [1985] ECR 3983 and *Industrias Pesqueras Campos* v. *Commission* (Case T–551/93) [1996] ECR II–247 and see Usher, *supra* n. 24, 61–2.

[120] See Craig, *supra* n. 116, at 307; Schwarze, *supra* n. 13, at 953.

[121] See, e.g., *Egan* v. *Minister for Defence* (unreported judgment of Barr J, High Court, 24 Nov. 1988) ('new situation' created by numerous applications for early retirement from air corps); *Council of Civil Service Unions* v. *Minister for the Civil Service* (the 'GCHQ' case) [1985]

As regards the Community principle of legitimate expectations, perhaps one of the most useful examples of this weighing up of interests took place at each stage in the course of the famous *Mulder* series of judgments.[122] The facts which gave rise to the *Mulder* cases stemmed from the need of the Community to cut milk production. Under a scheme with this objective, which was introduced by a 1977 Regulation,[123] producers were permitted to cease production of milk for a period, in exchange for which they received a premium for the non-marketing of milk. *Mulder* took advantage of this scheme, agreeing in 1979 to cease production for a period of five years. Subsequently, further measures to control Community milk production were introduced. Thus in 1984, the milk superlevy system was created. Under a Regulation of that year,[124] milk producers were given milk quotas based on the previous year's production (i.e. that of 1983). Mulder, having ceased to produce milk for the previous five years, now decided that he wanted to resume production in 1984. However, he could obtain no quota from the Dutch authorities, because he had produced no milk at all in 1983.

In practical terms, what this meant was that the bargain Mulder had entered into with the authorities in 1979 was now being used to exclude him entirely from engaging in milk production. Mulder therefore sought the annulment of the 1984 Regulation, arguing that he had an expectation of being allowed to re-enter the market and resume production under the same conditions as those which had obtained when he had entered the arrangement in 1979.

The European Court of Justice held that a producer who had voluntarily ceased production could not expect to resume production under the same conditions on re-entering the market. Rather, such an individual should be aware that the rules relating to the market might change during the period and he or she could not expect to be exempt from these changes. However, Mulder was not without legitimate expectations. The Court held that:

> where such a producer, as in the present case, has been encouraged by a Community measure to suspend marketing for a limited period in the general interest and against payment of a premium he may legitimately expect not to be subject, upon the expiry of his undertaking, to restrictions *which specifically affect him precisely because he availed himself of the possibilities offered by the Community provisions.*[125]

More specifically, there had been nothing in the 1977 instrument to indicate that taking up the bargain which it offered might entail a complete bar to resuming milk production. The Court therefore held that such an effect frus-

---

AC 319 (considerations of national security justified departure from previous practice). Note also the balancing of interests carried out by Sedley J in *R. v. Minister for Agriculture, Fisheries and Foods ex p. Hamble (Offshore) Fisheries Ltd.* [1995] 2 All ER 714.

[122] *Mulder* v. *Minister van Landbouw en Visserij* (Case 120/86) [1988] ECR 2321; *Mulder and others* v. *Council and Commission ('Mulder II')* (Joined Cases C–104/89 and C–37/90) [1992] ECR I–3061.

[123] Council Regulation 1078/77 of 17 May 1977 [1977] OJ L131/1.

[124] Council Regulation 857/84 of 31 Mar. 1984 [1984] OJ L90/13.

[125] Para. 24 of the judgment of the ECJ, *supra* n. 121, emphasis added.

trated the producer's legitimate expectations that the effect of the 1977 arrangements would be limited. In consequence, the 1984 Regulation was annulled.

The key to understanding cases like *Mulder*[126] is that, as Tridimas has observed:

the underlying rationale of the judgments is that those who repose faith in the authorities must not suffer as a result. This is the material criterion which distinguishes them from other cases where the Court refused to intervene to remedy hardship suffered by individual milk producers.[127]

A case of the lattter kind, it may be noted in passing, was *Dowling* v. *Ireland*,[128] a reference to the Court of Justice from the Irish Supreme Court concerning a farmer who produced no milk in 1983 for a rather different reason from that of Mulder. He had earlier suffered a heart attack and, because of his ill health, was unable to resume work until 1984. Unfortunately for Dowling, 1983 was chosen by Ireland as the reference year for the purpose of the additional levy scheme, and he therefore obtained no reference quantity, being unable to show evidence of any milk deliveries in the reference year. The Court of Justice held that his legitimate expectations had not been violated. As Advocate General Jacobs observed, 'Mr. Dowling's legitimate expectation of returning to milk production at the end of his conversion period was not frustrated by the Community provisions in question but rather by his ill health during 1983'.[129]

The first *Mulder* case is illustrative of a number of other points examined elsewhere in this article—the fact that the Community principle of legitimate expectations extends to the protection of substantive rights, and additionally the regard which is had in establishing what is a legitimate expectation to the factors which ought to be within the ken of the prudent and informed trader. It is also illustrative of the balance which the Court seeks to achieve between the interest of the public and those of the individual. The Court's judgment made it clear that the Community legislature *was* free to alter the rules governing the milk market—but not to the extent of excluding entirely from the market those producers who availed of the earlier scheme. In other words, as Usher has put it:

the expectation that was protected was not that the rules would remain unchanged when the outgoers returned to milk production, but that they should not be penalised compared with other producers for having participated in a Community scheme.[130]

---

126 See also *Spagl* v. *Hauptzollamt Rosenheim* (Case C–189/89) [1990] ECR I–4539.
127 *Supra* n. 17, at 190, emphasis added.   128 Case C–85/90 [1992] ECR I–5305.
129 See Opinion of Jacobs AG, *supra* n. 129, at 5323.
130 Usher, *supra* n. 17, 59. In this regard, note the observation by Tridimas, *supra* n. 17, at 189, that there is a link between the concept of legitimate expectations and that of equal treatment. The close inter-relationship between the various principles of law is underlined by the same writer in his observation that 'the principle of legitimate expectations may need to give way to overriding public interests. That assessment entails a balancing exercise which involves considerations of proportionality': *supra* n. 17, 351.

Or, to put it another way, the outgoers had a legitimate expectation that an agreement to suspend production of milk temporarily would not be turned into a permanent prohibition from engaging in this commercial activity.

Further examples of the kinds of balancing of interests which can occur in cases concerning legitimate expectations were provided by subsequent cases concerning essentially the same factual scenario. Following the first *Mulder* case,[131] another Regulation was adopted by the Council in 1989,[132] granting a quota to those farmers who found themselves in a situation similar to that of Mulder, with this quota being based on 60 per cent of the quantity of milk produced in the year before they took part in the agreement to cease production. This Regulation was challenged in turn before the Court on the basis that it violated producers' legitimate expectations because the figure of 60 per cent was too low.[133] Here again, the Court of Justice upheld the challenge. The Court took the view that it *had* been lawful for the Community legislature to seek to ensure that producers who availed themselves of the 1977 scheme gained no advantage over producers who had not. The hands of the Community legislature were therefore not tied to the extent that such producers had to be restored to the situation which they had been in in 1977. Some regulatory response to a changing market environment was permitted, and these producers could not escape that merely by virtue of having availed themselves of the 1977 arrangement. However, the Court took the view that the quota reduction which had now been applied to the former category of producers had been excessive, being over twice the size of the highest quota reduction applied to those who had not availed themselves of the 1977 scheme. Here again, the claimants were effectively being penalized merely for having participated in a Community scheme. The Court therefore annulled the offending Regulation.

The final balancing exercise between public and individual interest—albeit one of a somewhat different nature—was yet to come. Subsequent to the above-mentioned cases, yet another Regulation was adopted, giving the relevant producers an improved quota. Mulder, however, now brought a claim for damages against the Council and Commission under what is now Article 288 (formerly Article 215) of the EC Treaty in respect of his losses during the period before which this final Regulation was introduced.[134] When the matter came before the Court in *'Mulder II'*, the Court acknowledged that both the 1984 Regulation denying Mulder any quota at all and the 1989 Regulation which had introduced the 60 per cent rule had indeed violated the claimant's legitimate expectations. However, the Court was willing to award damages only in relation to the former violation. This was because of the Court's application of

---

[131] And also that in the similar case of *Von Deetzen* v. *Hauptzollamt Hamburg-Jonas* (Case 170/86) [1988] ECR 2355.

[132] Council Regulation 764/89 [1989] OJ L84/2.

[133] *Spagl* v. *Hauptzollamt Rosenheim* (Case C–189/89) [1990] ECR I–4539; *Pastätter* v. *Hauptzollamt Bad Reichenhall* (Case C–217/89) [1990] ECR I–4585.

[134] *Mulder and others* v. *Council and Commission ('Mulder II')* (Joined Cases C–104/89 and C–37/90) [1992] ECR I–3061.

the rule that in a legislative field such as the one in question which was characterized by need for the exercise of a wide discretion, the Community could not incur liability unless the institution concerned had manifestly and gravely disregarded the limits on the exercise of its powers.[135] The Court felt that in adopting the 1989 Regulation the Community legislature *had* taken account of the higher public interest—*viz.,* the higher public necessity of not jeopardizing the fragile stability that obtained in the milk products sector—without gravely and manifestly disregarding the limits of its discretionary power in this area. It had got the balance wrong, and had violated the claimant's legitimate expectations for a second time, but on this occasion its behaviour did not give rise to liability in damages, although (as has already been seen) it was sufficient to have the offending measure annulled.[136]

E.   THE COMMUNITY PRINCIPLE OF LEGITIMATE EXPECTATIONS
AND THE ISSUE OF RETROACTIVE LEGISLATION

One area in which particular difficulties are encountered in balancing the interests of the administration on the one hand and the expectations of individuals or businesses on the other has been that of retroactive legislation. A distinction is generally drawn between 'true' retroactivity or retroactivity *stricto sensu*—which is where a rule is adopted which applies to events which have already taken place—and 'apparent' retroactivity, which concerns the immediate application of new rules to acts or transactions which are in progress (for example, where new quota rules are imposed with immediate effect, thereby affecting the goods delivery of which was agreed under a contract signed prior to the new rules coming into effect).[137] Many cases concerning the Community doctrine involve issues of apparent retroactivity, for 'a person may have planned his or her actions on the basis of one policy choice

---

[135] In contrast, however, in relation to policy areas in which a Community institution or Member State has considerably reduced or even no discretion, mere infringement of the law may be sufficient to establish the existence of a sufficiently serious breach. See now *Laboratoires pharmaceutiques Bergaderm SA* v. *Jean-Jacques Goupil*, judgment of the ECJ of 4 July 2000.

[136] The facts which gave rise to the *Mulder* saga are still resulting in cases coming before the ECJ at the time of writing. Two of the latest cases to come before the Court, *Héritiers d'Edmond Ropars and others* v. *Council of the European Union* (Case T–429/93), judgment of the CFI (First Chamber) of 21 June 2000, and *Tromeur* v. *Council of the European Union and Commission of the European Union* (Case T–537/93), judgment of CFI (First Chamber) of the same date, both of which involved claims for damages somewhat similar to those at issue in *Mulder II*. Both were unsuccessful, however, the claimants having been unable to demonstrate the existence of any intention to resume milk production at the time of the expiry of their undertakings not to market milk pursuant to Regulation 1078/77 [1977] OJ L131/1. As is noted in the text *supra*, the cases are thus illustrative of a perhaps self-evident prerequisite to the obtaining of damages for breach of one's legitimate expectations—the existence of a causal connection between loss suffered and the breach of the relevant expectation.

[137] 'Apparent' retroactivity is sometimes called secondary retroactivity (as distinct from 'primary'—i.e., true—retroactivity. See *Bowen* v. *Georgetown Hospital* 488 US 204 (1988) cited in Craig, *'Substantive Legitimate Expectations in Domestic and Community Law'* (1996) 55 CLJ 289 at n. 46). It has also been referred to variously as 'material retroactivity', 'quasi-retroactivity', and 'immediate application'.

made by the administration, and seek redress when the chosen policy alters, even though this alteration is only prospective and not retrospective'.[138]

One issue which arises which concerns *apparently retroactive rules* is that of transitional measures. For a failure to adopt such measures—or, put another way, the immediate application of a new law—may violate the legitimate expectations of an individual or trader, creating an entitlement, in an appropriate case, to damages.[139] On the other hand, the chances of a legitimate expectation of transitional arrangements being held to exist depend very much on the market which is being discussed.[140] Overall, it may be said that it is generally more difficult to establish that the adoption of apparently retroactive legislation involves the violation of some legitimate expectation than that the enactment of truly retroactive legislation does so.[141] This is to be expected, since the impact of apparently retroactive legislation on pre-arranged events is, by definition, of a lesser order at the time when that legislation comes into force. The general position is encapsulated in Sharpston's observation that:

the European Court has . . . tended to reject arguments for transitional measures, citing variously the overriding public interest, a reasonable fear that making a transitional period available would destroy the whole point of the change in legislation and its oft-repeated tenet that prudent traders should have realised that change was imminent.[142]

Truly retroactive laws are looked upon in principle with disfavour from both a legal and an economic standpoint. Viewed in legal terms, they are felt to be a threat to the rule of law, which requires that situations ought to be judged in the light of legal rules which obtain when they occur so that individuals and businesses may plan their affairs in awareness of what the legal consequences of their actions will be.[143] From the economic viewpoint, they tend to have a negative effect on business and investor confidence in legal systems in which they are allowed. If truly retroactive laws are to be permitted at all in the Community legal system it is therefore obvious that they can be allowed only under the most strictly controlled circumstances. In its case law, the European Court of Justice has ruled out the retrospective imposition of criminal liabil-

---

[138] Craig, *supra* n. 116, at 305.

[139] As was held to be the case in *CNTA SA* v. *Commission* (Case 74/74) [1975] ECR 533.

[140] See *Firma Gebrüder Dietz* v. *Commission* (Case 126/76) [1977] ECR 2431 where the ECJ refused to hold that an international sugar trader had any legitimate expectation that transitional arrangements be provided for when alterations—which stemmed from currency fluctuations—were made in the Community system laying down the rules governing monetary compensation amounts for such traders. The attitude seems to have been that such changes were foreseeable in a situation of fluctuating exchange rates and it was up to the traders themselves to take measures to protect themselves against any consequent changes.

[141] See here, e.g., Tridimas, *supra* n. 17, at 180.

[142] Sharpston, *supra* n. 57, at 144. See, e.g., *Merkur Aussenhandel GmbH* v. *Commission* (Case 97/76) [1977] ECR 1063; *IFG-Interkontinentale Fleischhandelsgesellschaft mbH* v. *Commission* (Case 68/77) [1978] ECR 353; *Hans Spitta & Co.* v. *Hauptzollamt Frankfurt am Main-Ost* (Case 127/78) [1979] ECR 171; and *Firma Anton Dürbeck* v. *Hauptzollamt Frankfurt am Main-Flughafen* (Case 112/80) [1981] ECR 1095.

[143] See generally here chap. 3 of Waldron *The Law* (Routledge, London, 1990).

ity.[144] However, the rule is not so rigid in non-criminal cases, where it has been held that:

although in *general* the principle of legal certainty precludes a Community measure from taking effect at a point in time before its publication, it may *exceptionally* be otherwise where the purpose to be achieved so demands and where the legitimate expectations of those concerned are duly respected.[145]

These conditions are sometimes met—indeed, far from as infrequently as one might imagine.[146] One of the most prominent examples of this happening was in the *Isoglucose* cases,[147] the factual basis of which concerned the introduction by regulation of production quotas for isoglucose, a natural sweetener which competed with sugar. Isoglucose manufacturers succeeded in having the original regulation declared void by the Court of Justice for procedural reasons not relevant in the present context.[148] The Council's response was to adopt a new regulation reintroducing the production quotas and making them retrospective so as to cover the interregnum brought about by the Court's judgment. When the isoglucose producers brought a challenge against this latter regulation in turn, seeking to have it declared void, the Court applied the above-quoted test to uphold the new regulation, notwithstanding its retroactivity. The Court felt that the legitimate expectations of the isoglucose producers (who were a limited number of traders who were very well informed both about the isoglucose market and about likely legislative developments) had been respected in this case, since they had many reasons to expect that the system would be retrospectively reimposed. The *Isoglucose* cases seem to indicate that if it is a reasonably foreseeable likelihood that a forthcoming measure will have retroactive—or, for that matter, immediate—application, affected

---

[144] See here *R.* v. *Kent Kirk* (Case 63/83) [1984] ECR 2689 where the Court observed that the principle that penal provisions may not have retroactive effect 'takes its place among the general principles of law whose observance is ensured by the Court of Justice'. See para. 22 of the Court's judgment.

[145] *Racke (Firma A.)* v. *Hauptzollamt Mainz* (Case 98/78) [1979] ECR 79 at para. 20 (emphasis added). See also, e.g., *Weingut Gustav Decker KG* v. *Hauptzollamt Landau* (Case 99/78) [1979] ECR 101; *Diverinste SA* v. *Administration Principal de Aquanas e Impuestos Especiales de la Junquera* [1993] ECR I–1885; and *Road Air BV* v. *Inspecteur der Invoerrechten en Accijnzen* (Case C–310/95) [1997] ECR I–100. Notwithstanding the tenor of the above-cited statement in *Racke*, it has been observed that 'in general, a claim that a measure which has retroactive effect is incompatible with Community law is not easy to succeed [with]. In the majority of cases, the Court has rejected such claims': Tridimas, *supra* n. 17, 173. Cases in which the validity of retroactive legislation has been upheld include *SAFA* (Case C–337/88) [1990] ECR I–1 and *Parliament* v. *Council* (Case C–259/95) [1997] ECR I–5303. See also the *Isoglucose* cases discussed in the text *infra*.

[146] See *supra* n. 145.

[147] *Amylum* v. *Council* (Case 108/81) [1982] ECR 3107; *Roquette Frères* v. *Council* (Case 110/81) [1982] ECR 3159; *Tunnel Refineries* v. *Council* (Case 114/81) [1982] ECR 3189. The approach taken by the ECJ in *Amylum* (which was confirmed in *Fedesa and others* (Case C–331/88) [1990] ECR I–4023) involved the upholding of legislation which was truly retrospective in respect of a long period.

[148] See, e.g., *Roquette Frères SA* v. *Council* (Case 138/79) [1980] ECR 3333 where the Court declared Regulation 1293/79 [1979] OJ L162/10 void because the obligation (at that time laid down in Art. 43 EC) on the Council of Ministers to consult the Parliament before making a regulation in this field had not been respected. See also *Maizena* v. *Council* (Case 139/79) [1980] ECR 3393.

traders may not be able to claim that any legitimate expectation has been breached. To be contrasted with the *Isoglucose* cases is the case of *Firma Meiko-Konservenfabrik* v. *Germany*,[149] which concerned an attempt by the Commission to change retrospectively the rules concerning qualification for certain financial assistance to sweet cherry producers. This was done by imposing a requirement that certain contracts be forwarded to national authorities by a now expired date. The result was that the applicants were deprived of the opportunity of qualifying for the aid in circumstances which (unlike those in the *Isoglucose* cases) the Court held could not reasonably have been anticipated. The legislation was therefore held invalid by the European Court of Justice, *inter alia*, because the legitimate expectations of the applicants had been breached.[150]

It should be noted that clear and unequivocal reasons will be required to be given in order to justify retrospective effect.[151] Thus where regulations are not expressly stated to be retroactive and, in addition, reasons given for this retroactivity, the test set down in these cases will be used to avoid a retroactive interpretation. Again, if the factual reasoning offered for the retroactivity is defective, there will be no need to demonstrate a violation of legitimate expectations in order to have retrospective legislation annulled.[152]

III.   An Adolescent Cousin? The Domestic Doctrine of Legitimate Expectations in the Light of the Foregoing

A.   INTRODUCTION—THE ORIGINS OF THE DOMESTIC DOCTRINE

The domestic doctrine of legitimate expectations—described judicially as involving the question 'whether in all the circumstances it would be unfair or unjust to allow a party to resile from a position created or adopted by him which at that time gave rise to a legitimate expectation in the mind of another

---

[149] Case 224/82 [1983] ECR 2539. Other cases in which the ECJ held purportedly retroactive legislation invalid include *Agricola Commerciale Olio* v. *Commission* (Case 232/81) [1984] ECR 3881; *Savma* v. *Commission* (Case 264/81) [1984] ECR 3915; and *Crispoltoni I* (Case C–368/89) [1991] ECR I–3695.

[150] Sharpston, *supra* n. 57, at 143, has applauded this decision since 'no ordinary degree of economic caution would have sufficed to warn [the traders] of the likelihood, the nature or the detail of the retroactive change subsequently introduced and thus to invalidate their expectations in the aid scheme as originally established'. On the occasional restriction by the ECJ of the 'retrospective' effect of its own judgments in deference to the legitimate expectations of those who have acted on the basis of what was previously generally understood to be the law: see Mengozzi, *From the Treaty of Rome to the Treaty of Amsterdam* (2nd edn., Kluwer, Deventer, 1999) at 208–11.

[151] See, e.g., *Diverinste SA* v. *Administration Principal de Aquanas e Impuestos Especiales de la Junquera* (Joined Cases C–260/91 and C–261/91) [1993] ECR I–1885 where the Court held a regulation invalid because the regulation's statement of reasons (which merely made the point that the regulation's provisions were being introduced as a matter of urgency in order to avoid speculation) did not make it possible to review the question of whether the retrospective effect was justified. See also *Ilford* v. *Commission* (Case 1/84) [1984] ECR 423.

[152] *Savma* v. *Commission* (Case 264/81) [1984] ECR 3915.

that the situation would continue and might be acted upon by him to his advantage'[153]—has had a striking rise to prominence in the case law since the 1980s. The writers of the leading Irish text on administrative law have observed that 'apart from the doctrine of proportionality, there is, perhaps, no other principle which has so rapidly given rise to so much litigation or which has so quickly become embedded in the fabric of the legal system'.[154] The origins of the domestic doctrine in common law systems have occasionally been ascribed to European Community law.[155] If this is true at all, however, it seems to have been so at most only at a subconscious level. The doctrine was cited for the first time in a common law context in Lord Denning's judgment in *Schmidt* v. *Secretary of State for Home Affairs*,[156] a case which preceded UK accession to the (then) European Economic Community in 1973 by some years. The concept of legitimate expectations was, according to Lord Denning, one which 'came out of my own head and not from any continental or other source'.[157] From these beginnings, its use has spread across the common law world, including to Ireland.[158]

It has been accurately observed that the English and Commonwealth case law appears to have developed with little explicit reference to European parallels, but in this jurisdiction at least, there has been some degree of reference to European Community law authorities. The extent of their influence on the domestic doctrine should not, at the same time, be overestimated, but it is

[153] Barr J in *Cannon* v. *Minister for the Marine* [1991] ILRM 261.

[154] Hogan and Morgan *Administrative Law in Ireland* (3rd edn., Round Hall Sweet and Maxwell, Dublin, 1998) at 858. Chap. 15 of this book contains an outstanding analysis of the domestic doctrine of legitimate expectations. See also by the former writer, 'Judicial Review—the Law of the Republic of Ireland', in Hadfield *Judicial Review: A Thematic Approach* (Gill and Macmillan, Dublin, 1995) 316 at 348–55.

[155] See here, e.g., the recent judgment of 19 July 2001 of Keane CJ (with which three of the remaining four judges of the Supreme Court agreed) in *Glencar Exploration plc and Andaman Resources plc* v. *Mayo County Council* in which the learned Chief Justice asserted that the doctrine seemed to derive from the jurisprudence of the European Court of Justice. See further Mackenzie Stuart, 'Recent Developments in English Administrative Law—the Impact of Europe?' in Capotorti (ed.), *Du Droit International au Droit de l'Integration: Liber Amicorum P. Pescatore* (Nomos, Baden-Baden, 1987) at 417 where Mackenzie Stuart describes legitimate expectations 'as a novelty in English law which lacks discernible English parentage'. He continues 'to find the true ancestry one does not have to go far beyond the channel' (quoted in Hogan and Morgan *supra* n. 154, at 859). For an apparently contrasting opinion, see the judgment of Fennelly J in *Glencar Exploration* (a judgment—like that of the Chief Justice—with which three of the remaining four judges of the Supreme Court agreed) in which Fennelly J, after noting some decisions of the European Court of Justice, observed that the doctrine of legitimate expectations had 'come to be recognized independently' in the Irish and UK courts (although, somewhat confusingly, he also referred to the 'proximate origins' of the doctrine in EC law.)

[156] [1969] 2 Ch. 149. This was followed by his dissenting judgment in *Breen* v. *Amalgamated Engineering Union* [1971] 2 QB 179 which also made reference to legitimate expectations.

[157] In a letter to C. Forsyth quoted by that writer in 'The Provenance and Protection of Legitimate Expectations' (1988) 47 *CLJ* 238 at 241.

[158] See the judgment of Costello J in *Tara Prospecting Ltd* v. *Minister for Energy* [1993] ILRM 771 at 783. See regarding developments in other jurisdictions, e.g., France, 'Legitimate Expectations in New Zealand' (1990–1991) 14 *NZULR* and Hlophe, 'Legitimate Expectation and Natural Justice: English, Australian and South African Law' (1987) 104 *SALJ* 165. In relation to the Canadian courts see, e.g. the recent decision on the Canadian Federal Court of Appeal in *Apotex Inc.* v. *Canada* (Attorney General) (2000) 188 DLR (4th) 145.

probably fair to say that the existence of a parallel doctrine may well have acted in a certain measure as a consolidating influence in so far as the domestic doctrine is concerned.[159] Perhaps because of the early involvement of Lord Denning in the establishment of the doctrine in English law, the domestic doctrine of legitimate expectations is sometimes said to be an equitable doctrine. Indeed in *Webb* itself, Finlay CJ went so far as to assert that the doctrine of legitimate expectations 'is but an aspect of the well-recognized equitable concept of promissory estoppel (which has been frequently applied in our courts), whereby a promise or representation as to intention may in certain circumstances be held bending on the representor or the promisor'.[160] This was a statement which was later relied upon by Barr J in *Cannon* v. *Minister for the Marine*, where he held that 'the concept of legitimate expectations being derived from an equitable doctrine, must be reviewed in the light of equitable principles'.[161] And yet the more correct view would seem to be that the domestic doctrine of legitimate expectations involves 'equity' only in the sense that it is used to promote fairness. (The same point, however, can also be made—and indeed has been—about the Community principle[162]). The case for the domestic doctrine being either an aspect of promissory estoppel or indeed that it derives from that body of rules known as 'equity' seems far from having been convincingly made out. Indeed, fair arguments to contrary effect can be made.[163] In the first place, legitimate expectations is a public law doctrine—in other words, a doctrine which is directed at protecting the individual against unfair administrative decision-making.[164] Secondly, it is a doctrine the appli-

---

[159] Here see both the High Court judgment of Murphy J in *Duff* v. *Minister for Agriculture* [1997] 2 IR 22 and the observations of Hamilton J in *Carbery Milk Products Ltd.* v. *Minister for Agriculture* (1988–93) IV Irish Tax Reports 492 and more recently the judgments (particularly that of Fennelly J) in *Glencar Exploration plc and Andaman Resources plc* v. *Mayo County Council* (Supreme Court decision of 19 July, 2001). For a recent UK case in which careful regard was had to the Community law principle of legitimate expectations in determining the scope of the domestic doctrine see the judgment of the Court of Appeal (delivered by Lord Woolf MR) in *R.* v. *North East Devon Health Authority ex p. Coughlan* [2000] 3 All ER 850.

[160] *Webb* v. *Ireland* [1988] IR 353 at 384. Contrast the recent express acceptance by Fennelly J in *Daly* v. *Minister for the Marine* (Supreme Court ruling of 4 Oct. 2001, *nem. diss.*) that 'there is a distinction between the doctrine of legitimate expectations and promissary estoppel'. (See judgment of Fennelly J at p. 21 thereof.)

[161] [1991] ILRM 261at 266. See more recently the High Court decision of O'Sullivan J in *Daly* v. *Minister of the Marine* (judgment of 25 Feb. 1999) where the learned judge observed that 'it is clear and not disputed that the relief granted on the basis of legitimate expectations is an equitable remedy'. See regarding the Supreme Court decision in the same case, n. 164 below.

[162] See, e.g., Tridimas, *supra* n. 17, at 352 where he ascribes the frequency with which the ECJ disagrees with its own Advocate General in cases involving the general principles of Community law to the fact that the ECJ uses 'general principles of law to exercise an equitable jurisdiction'.

[163] See for a list for some such arguments, Hogan and Morgan, *supra* n. 154, at 897–900.

[164] See *O'Reilly* v. *Mackman* [1983] 2 AC 237 at 275 and see the list of authorities cited by Hogan and Morgan, *supra* n. 154, at 860 n. 11. See the very recent unanimous ruling of the Irish Supreme Court in *Daly* v. *Minister for the Marine* (judgment delivered 4 Oct. 2001) in which Fennelly J observed that 'legitimate expectations constitutes an accepted part of the principles of administrative law applied by our courts through the vehicle of judicial review. It is concerned essentially to see that administrative powers are not used unfairly.' (See judgment of Fennelly J at p. 21 thereof). Elsewhere in his judgment Fennelly J correctly, it is submitted, described the 'essence of the doctrine' as 'fairness', although somewhat confusingly, in doing so quoted from an earlier

cation of which appears to be capable of being denied on the basis of policy considerations relating to good administration which post-date the facts of the case.[165] Thirdly, it requires no existing contractual (or other similar) relationship in order to apply.[166] Fourthly, unlike promissory estoppel, legitimate expectations act as a sword as well as a shield, in that legitimate expectations may give rise to a cause of action in respect of which a court will award damages.[167] These are all factors which appear to distinguish it from promissory estoppel. (In any case, it should not be forgotten that, for better or for worse, the traditional rule is that there is no place for estoppel in public law.[168])

judgment in which it was stated that the concept of legitimate expectations, 'being derived from an equitable doctrine, must be reviewed in the light of equitable principles'. (See judgment at pp. 15–16 thereof.) Similarly, notwithstanding the distinction drawn by Fennelly J between legitimate expectations and equitable estoppel, he nonetheless makes reference to a judgment of Denning J regarding equitable estoppel (*Amalgamated Property Co.* v. *Texas Bank* [1982] QB 84) in asserting that 'in cases involving violation of legitimate expectations, the Court may have to furnish "such remedy as the equity of the case demands". (See judgment at p. 29.) See also on the public law role of the doctrine of legitimate expectations, the recent High Court decision of Carroll J in *Coonan* v. *Attorney General and Ireland* (judgment of 31 Jan. 2001). An appeal from this ruling was later dismissed by the Supreme Court without any decision as to the exclusively public law nature of the doctrine being felt to be necessary (judgment of 29 May 2001). Note that the public law remedies are discretionary. In *Abrahamson* v. *Law Society of Ireland* [1996] 2 ILRM 481, McCracken J distinguished the doctrine of legitimate expectation from that of promissory estoppel, by observing, *inter alia*, that the latter doctrine 'is usually, although not exclusively, related to matters of private law rather than public law'.

[165] See text *infra.*.
[166] Cf. however, the judgment of Kelly J in *Glencar Exploration* v. *Mayo County Council* (unreported High Court judgment of 20 Aug. 1998) where he asserted that 'there was no legitimate expectation such as is contended for and *even if there was, damages would not be available as a remedy in respect of it because of the absence of a contractual or similar relationship between the parties*' (see 66 of the judgment, emphasis added). The only support adduced by Kelly J for this proposition was his assertion that the cases in which damages have been awarded such as *Webb* and *Duggan* were 'distinguishable from this case because the applicants there were in long-term contractual or equivalent relationships with the respondents and the wrongs done were akin to a breach of contract. There is no such equivalent relationship between the parties to this litigation'. With respect, the facts of *Webb* did not involve any such relationship, but rather (as Finlay CJ described it in his judgment in that case) a 'transaction' whereby a hoard of treasure was deposited in the National Museum and accepted on behalf of the State. *Duggan* is also a poor authority, since, properly viewed, the facts of that case probably did not raise an issue of legitimate expectations at all. See further n. 175 below. In neither *Webb* nor *Duggan* was any suggestion made that the award of damages for breach of a legitimate expectation was conditional on the existence of a 'long-term contractual or equivalent relationship'. Nor was this suggestion endorsed by the Supreme Court on appeal in the *Glencar Exploration* case itself (Supreme Court decision of 19 July 2001). See text *infra*.
[167] Damages were awarded by the Sup. Ct. in *Webb* v. *Ireland* [1988] IR 353 and in the High Court case of *Duggan* v. *An Taoiseach* [1989] ILRM 710, in both cases purportedly for violation of legitimate expectations. The judgment of McCracken J in *Abrahamsom* v. *Law Society of Ireland* [1996] 2 IRLM 481 also indicates that damages may be awarded for breach of an individual's legitimate expectations (see 498 thereof). See also *Glencar Exploration plc* v. *Mayo County Council* (High Court judgment of Kelly J of 20 Aug. 1998). Neither of the two Supreme Court judges who delivered judgments on appeal in this case (viz., Keane CJ and Fennelly J) deemed it necessary to express an opinion either way on this point. See text *infra*.
[168] See in this regard the judgment of Costello J in *Tara Prospecting* v. *Minister for Energy* [1993] IRLM 771 at 789. See also his judgment in *Hempenstall and others* v. *Minister for the Environment* [1994] 2 IR 20. This point is referred to again in the text *infra*, and further authorities are cited there.

Rather than in equity, the rationale for creating a doctrine of legitimate expectations lie in the fact that it is in the interest of good administration that these interests be shielded. This is a view which finds support in the recent judgment of the Court of Appeal in *R.* v. *North East Devon Health Authority ex parte Coughlan*,[169] where Lord Woolf MR described the doctrine of legitimate expectations as 'a distinct application of the concept of abuse of power'. Thus France has observed that:

legitimate expectations finds its origin in procedural impropriety, and in particular is most often seen as being the means by which the potential strait-jacket of rights and privileges is broken. The great developments of *Ridge* v. *Baldwin*[170] and subsequent cases were seen to be imperilled by the idea that the imposition of the requirements of natural justice might be restricted to situations where there was present an established interest or right.[171]

Similarly, Baldwin and Horne have attributed the basis of the legitimate expectations doctrine to:

the notion that statutory powers are not given to public bodies to be exercised capriciously. Reasonable and fair action thus involves a modicum of consistency. Certain types of actions will create legitimate expectations on this basis.[172]

As is the case with the Community principle of legitimate expectations, the case law concerning the domestic doctrine is far from entirely consistent. In the case of the domestic doctrine, this is probably for a number of reasons. First, as was observed by McCracken J in *Abrahamson* v. *Law Society of Ireland*, 'it is only to be expected that in an evolving concept there will be contradictory judgments'.[173] Secondly, it must be acknowledged that there has been a tendency in some cases to use the language of legitimate expectations in order to bring about an outcome which is consonant with the requirements of justice, when, properly analysed, the case does not raise an issue of legitimate expectations at all. The prime example of this is the Supreme Court decision in the *Webb* case itself, which, it is submitted, has been correctly characterized as a private law case involving the application of the principles of promissory estoppel, with any reference to notions of legitimate expectations having been superfluous.[174] *Webb* is not by any means the sole example of this phenome-

---

[169] [2000] 3 All ER 850. Lord Woolf gave the judgment of the whole Court of Appeal (Sedley and Mummery LJJ concurring with his opinion).

[170] [1964] AC 40.   [171] See France, *supra* n. 145.

[172] Baldwin and Horne, *supra* n. 5, at 702. In *Fakih* v. *Minister for Justice* [1993] 2 IR 406 at 423 O'Hanlon J described the doctrine of legitimate expectations as a 'manifestation of the duty to act fairly', although he also quoted the observations made by Finlay CJ in *Webb* v. *Ireland* [1988] IR 353 (quoted in the text *supra*), without making any criticism of them. See also the judgment of Lord Diplock in *Council of Civil Service Unions* v. *Minister for the Civil Service* [1985] 1 AC 374 at 408–9 to which reference is made by Keane J (as he then was) in *Pesca Valentia Ltd.* v. *Minister for Fisheries* [1990] 2 IR 205.

[173] [1996] 1 IR 403 at 422.

[174] [1988] IR 353. See Hogan and Morgan, *supra* n. 154, at 872 and 889. See now the judgment of Keane CJ in *Glencar Exploration plc and Andaman Resources plc* v. *Mayo County Council* (judgment of 19 July 2001 with which three of the other four judges of the Supreme Court concurred) in

non, however.[175] A third reason why there are inconsistencies in the case law is that there has been an element of retrenchment from the broadest interpretations of the legitimate expectations doctrine by many judges, perhaps in trepidation of what are felt to be its unclear implications.[176] This topic will be returned to in the text below.

B. FACTORS WHICH GO TOWARDS MAKING AN EXPECTATION 'LEGITIMATE' UNDER THE DOMESTIC DOCTRINE

Some examination of the factors which go towards making an expectation 'legitimate' in Irish law may be worthwhile.[177] We may begin with the observation that upholding legitimate expectations has generally been taken to require the protection of more than merely enforceable legal rights.[178] But

which the Chief Justice asserted that *Webb* 'proceeded on the basis that the facts in that case gave rise to a sustainable claim based on promissary estoppel, rather than on the doctrine of legitimate expectations . . .'. Note also the observation by Fennelly J in the same case (in a judgment concurred in by three of the other judges of the Supreme Court) that the above-quoted words in *Webb* were 'clearly not intended to convey that the doctrine of legitimate expectation is coextensive with promissary estoppel. It clearly is not.' (See p. 23 of Fennelly J's judgment.)

[175] Another prominent case in which the legitimate expectations doctrine was used as the basis of the decision when the facts would not seem to have given rise to such an issue is the High Court decision in *Fakih* v. *Minister for Justice* [1993] 2 IR 406, which is examined below. See also, e.g., *Duggan* v. *An Taoiseach* [1989] ILRM 710, a High Court decision to the effect that two civil servants had a legitimate expectation to continue in posts to which they had been appointed for a certain period, when it could have been decided on the point that the executive had no power to suspend the operation of the Farm Tax Office where they worked(since it was established by a statute and the government cannot, acting alone, alter a statute). In *Conroy* v. *Garda Commissioner* [1989] IR 140, a retired Garda was held to have had a legitimate expectation that he would receive a full pension, when the doctrine of legitimate expectations seemed inapplicable on the facts. *Conroy* really seemed to raise issues of innocent misrepresentation. See Hogan and Morgan, *supra* n. 154, 885 and 887. *Kenny* v. *Kelly* [1988] IR 457 (in which a declaration was granted to the applicant that she was entitled to a place in the Arts School in University College Dublin in 1987, on foot of representations made to her by an official in the university admissions office) is a judgment which is clearly based primarily on the doctrine of promissory estoppel. The last line of the judgment ('whichever legal approach is adopted, the applicant is entitled to a declaration . . .') seems to indicate that subsidiary reliance was placed on the doctrine of legitimate expectations. This is certainly how the case was interpreted by Brady (*supra* n. 2, at 134–7). It can be argued (although the point is far more debatable here) that the case was an inappropriate one for the application of the doctrine of legitimate expectations (and indeed for the grant of a declaration) since it is not clear that it involved a public law issue. (Indeed Barron J himself acknowledged that the public law/private law divide had raised its head here by observing that the case could have been an appropriate one for an order under O. 84, r. 26(5) of the Rules of the Superior Courts 1986 that proceedings should continue as if they had been begun by plenary summons, had such a timely implication for such an order been brought). See however, on the public law/private law divide and the difficulties which it raises, Hogan and Morgan, *supra* n. 154, at chap. 14.

[176] See O'Hanlon J's observation in *Fakih* v. *Minister for Justice* [1993] 2 IR 406 at 423 where he observed that legitimate expectations 'may have some of the characteristics of the "unruly horse" which were associated with the plea of public policy'. See also the similarly unenthusiastic equine analogy drawn by the same judge in *Association of General Practitioners Ltd.* v. *Minister of Health* [1995] 1 IR 382 at 393–4 where he expressed the fear that if the domestic doctrine were 'allowed its head' uncertainty in contract law and property law, *inter alia*, could result.

[177] See generally Delany, *supra* n. 4, 1 at 6–8.

[178] In *Glencar Exploration plc and Andaman Resources plc* v. *Mayo County Council* (decision of the Supreme Court of Ireland of 19 July 2001) Fennelly J (whose judgment was concurred in by

there has been some judicial discussion of whether the word 'legitimate' is so broad as to be merely a synonym for 'reasonable' or whether it signifies a concept which is somewhat narrower in meaning. Initial indications pointed in the direction of the words 'legitimate' and 'reasonable' being interchangeable.[179] Lord Diplock, in the *GCHQ* case expressed a preference for the use of the description:

a 'legitimate expectation' rather than a 'reasonable expectation' in order thereby to indicate that it has consequences to which effect will be given in public law, whereas an expectation or hope that some benefit or advantage would continue to be enjoyed, although it might well be entertained by a 'reasonable' man, would not necessarily have such consequences.[180]

The same general approach seems to have been adopted by Blayney J in his High Court judgment in *Wiley* v. *Revenue Commissioners*,[181] in which he observed of the applicant (who had asserted that he had a legitimate expectation to certain excise duty repayments) that:

at best, all he could have believed was that he had a good chance of getting it because he had got it twice before. And no doubt that would have been a reasonable belief. But it fell far short of being a legitimate expectation.[182]

The terms 'legitimate' and 'reasonable' are occasionally used interchangeably by the Irish courts.[183] For the sake of terminological clarity, however, it is probably better to adhere to the distinction drawn by Lord Diplock. It should be understood that drawing this distinction is a question of labelling, however, not of substance.[184] In other words, it offers no conceptual guidance on what constitutes a legitimate expectation, telling us no more than that a legitimate

three of the other four members of the Supreme Court) rejected the contention that an expectation that a public authority would act within the law would be enough to bring the appellant in that case within the scope of the doctrine of legitimate expectations, observing that if it were, the doctrine would be almost meaningless and would duplicate the ordinary right, for example, to seek judicial review of administrative action.' (See p. 28 of his judgment.) *Attorney General of Hong Kong* v. *Ng Yuen Shiu* [1983] 2 AC 629. The suggestion in at least one Australian case that the doctrine added little if anything to the concept of a right was one which was never taken up in this hemisphere. See the judgment of Barwick CJ in *Salemi* v. *MacKellar (No. 2)* (1977) 137 CLR 396 cited in Delany, *supra* n. 177.

[179] See the judgment of Lord Fraser in *Attorney General of Hong Kong* v. *Ng Yuen Shiu* [1983] 2 AC 629.

[180] *CCSU* v. *Minister for the Civil Service* [1985] 1 AC 374 at 408–9.

[181] [1989] IR 350 at 355. This judgment was appealed unsuccessfully to the Supreme Court. See for that Court's judgment [1993] ILRM 482.

[182] For further examples of cases in which the applicants had what appear to have been perfectly reasonable expectations which were nonetheless held not to involve situations of legitimate expectations, see, e.g, *Egan* v. *Minister for Defence* (High Court judgment of Barr J. of 24 Nov. 1988) and the judgment of Costello J in *Gilheaney* v. *Revenue Commissioners* [1998] IR 150.

[183] See, e.g., the judgment of Finlay CJ in *Webb* v. *Ireland* [1988] ILRM 565 at 384 and that of Hamilton P in *Duggan* v. *An Taoiseach* [1989] ILRM 710 at 727.

[184] Hence the observation by France, *supra* n. 145, at 142 that 'the distinction seems simply an attempt to stress that a legitimate expectation is a reasonable expectation that will be given judicial protection. This is circular and unhelpful, particularly when it is remembered that remedies are discretionary.'

expectation is a reasonable expectation in relation to which judges will be prepared to exercise their discretion to grant a remedy. However, as with the Community principle of legitimate expectations, it is possible to garner from the case law some idea of the elements which the courts will require to be present before the domestic doctrine of legitimate expectations will be deployed in favour of an individual or business whose expectations have been disappointed.[185]

(i)   Conduct Justifying the Expectation

We may begin here by noting that, as is the case with the Community principle, some conduct on the part of an administration justifying a legitimate expectation will normally be called for.

In the case of the domestic doctrine, however, the requirement of conduct justifying an expectation does not always seem to have been seen as an absolute one throughout the common law world—at least in so far as concerns legitimate expectations as to the *procedure* by which a decision will be taken. There have been a number of decisions of the UK courts in which it has been decided that a particular interest is important enough that an applicant should not be refused it without having some procedural rights afforded to him.[186] Indeed this is the context in which legitimate expectations first emerged as a concept in the common law. Here, the rights did not depend on any promise or practice by the decision-making body.[187] These cases are few in number, however, and date from an early period in the evolution of the domestic doctrine.

The conduct normally required for the purposes of the domestic doctrine bears strong similarities to that required under Community law in order to engage the Community principle of legitimate expectations. Hence the conduct may consist of:[188]

> (i)   an express or implied undertaking to behave in a particular way in exercising a power;[189]

---

[185] It is perhaps stating the obvious to point out that an applicant may be held to have had a legitimate expectation in a particular case which falls short of all that the applicant is contending for. See *Cannon* v. *Minister for the Marine* [1991] 1 IR 82. The result in such a case may be that the expectation is not regarded as having been disappointed, with the result that the applicant does not succeed.

[186] As in *Schmidt* v. *Secretary of State for Home Affairs* [1969] 2 Ch. 149 and *McInnes* v. *Onslow-Fane* [1978] 1 WLR 1520. Note the observation by Lord Denning at 170 of *Schmidt* that 'it all depends on whether he has some right or interest, or, I would add, some legitimate expectation, of which it would not be fair to deprive him without hearing what he has to say'. See also Craig, 'Legitimate Expectations: A Conceptual Analysis' (1992) 108 *LQR* at 82–3.

[187] See here Singh, 'Making Legitimate Use of Legitimate Expectations' (1994) 144 *NLJ* 1215 at 1215.

[188] See here Baldwin and Horne, 'Expectations in a Joyless Landscape' (1986) 49 *MLR* 685 at 702.

[189] As in *Webb* v. *Ireland* [1988] ILRM 565 where the promise was express (although see n. 174, *supra*, regarding the status of *Webb* as a precedent on the doctrine of legitimate expectations). See now the judgment of Fennelly J in *Glencar Exploration plc and Andaman Resources plc* v. *Mayo County Council* (delivered 19 July 2001 with three of the four remaining four Supreme Court judges concurring) in which he stated that the High Court judge from whose decision the case had been

(ii) the adoption of a consistent practice. In other words, if a practice continues for a sufficiently long period of time, this may be regarded as justifying a legitimate expectation that this practice will continue.[190] The logic here appears to be that such prior behaviour will have some kind of precedent value, or, put otherwise, that such a pattern of conduct in the past will be taken as amounting to a representation that others in a similar situation will also have legitimate expectations.[191] The latter analysis was clearly that which Barr J had in mind in *Egan* v. *Minister for Defence*[192] when he held that there was no legitimate expectation that the plaintiff—an officer in the air corps—would be granted early retirement, enabling him to take a civilian job. Barr J based his decision on his view that 'such a practice, however firmly entrenched it may have been in the life of the permanent defence force, did not amount to an implied promise or representation . . . made by the Minister to the officer corps . . . that permission to retire would be granted in every case as of course';[193]

(iii) the publication of rules or policies which it is known by the authority will be relied upon. In this case, the relevant public body will have set out the criteria for the application of policy in a certain area, an appli-

---

appealed was right, in determining whether the appellants had a legitimate expectation, to have sought 'something in the nature of an undertaking or promise or representation express or implied addressed to or applicable to the appellants'. (See judgment of Fennelly J at p. 28.) According to Fennelly J, 'it may be sufficient that the claimant belongs to a class or group of persons affected by an act which is accompanied by or implies an intention to follow an identifiable course of conduct by the public authority. See also, regarding express or implied undertakings e.g., *Attorney General of Hong Kong* v. *Ng Yuen Shiu* [1983] 2 AC 629 and *R.* v. *Liverpool Corporation ex P. Liverpool Taxi Fleet Operators' Association* [1972] 2 QB 299.

[190] See here, e.g., *Eogan* v. *University College Dublin* [1996] 2 ILRM 702; *Egan* v. *Minister for Defence* (High Court judgment of Barr J, 24 Nov. 1998); *Wiley* v. *Revenue Commissioners* [1989] IR 350 (High Court) where Blayney J took the view that the doing of something on two occasions only could not constitute a practice. Compare *Holtbecker* v. *Commission* (Case T–20/91) [1992] ECR II–2599 as regards the Community law principle. See also *Council of Civil Service Unions* v. *Minister for the Civil Service* [1985] 1 AC 374 (the '*GCHQ*' case) where, were it not for the exigencies of national security, the applicants would have been held to have had a legitimate expectation that unions and employees would be consulted in relation to certain matters, such right having arisen by virtue of consistent practice. Note Lord Fraser's observation that 'legitimate expectations, or reasonable expectations may arise either from an express promise given on behalf of a public authority or from the existence of a regular practice which the claimant can reasonably expect to continue'. See [1985] 1 AC 374 at 401. See also *HTV* v. *Price Commission* [1976] ICR 170 (which involved a practice of interpreting a so-called 'Price Code' in a particular manner, and the Court of Appeal decision in *R.* v. *Inland Revenue Commissioners ex p. Unilever* [1998] STC 681. Hogan and Morgan, *supra* n. 154, at 880 also refer to the case of *Ghneim* v. *Minister for Justice* (reported in the *Irish Times* of 2 Sept. 1989) where Hamilton J was of the view that a delay of a year and a half in reaching a decision whether the applicant should have permission to stay in Ireland beyond the date stipulated in his entry visa (for the purposes of facilitating the completion of his studies in Ireland) could give rise to a legitimate expectation. Contrast the effect of delay in reaching a decision for the purposes of the Community law principle of legitimate expectations (as to which see text at n. 89 above ff.).

[191] Singh, *supra* n. 187, 1215.   [192] High Court decision of Barr J, 24 Nov. 1988.
[193] See judgment, *supra* n. 182, at 15.

cant will have relied on these criteria, and the public body will now be seeking to apply different criteria.[194]

(ii)   The Requirement of an Expectation

Again, as is the case with the Community law principle, a subjective expectation on the part of the individual concerned is required before the domestic doctrine of legitimate expectations will apply. Forsyth has drawn attention to the 'self-evident and fundamental' and yet 'often overlooked' point that:

whether an expectation exists or not, is simply a question of fact: what did the person concerned actually expect? If that person did not in fact expect anything then, even if others did expect something, that person's expectation, being non-existent, cannot be protected.[195]

The existence of a subjectively held expectation will not suffice in and of itself to make an expectation a legitimate one, however. As is the case with the Community law doctrine, certain further objective requirements concerning the nature of the expectation must be met. Hence the reference by Fennelly J in *Glencar Exploration plc and Andaman Resources plc* v. *Mayo County Council* to the requirement, in order that the doctrine of legitimate expectations might apply, that a representation 'must be such as to create an expectation *reasonably entertained*', and the requirement, referred to by Keane CJ in his judgment, that the complainants be deprived of 'some benefit which they *reasonably* expected to receive'.[196] The issue of whether the protection afforded by the domestic doctrine goes further than the protection of mere procedural (as opposed to substantive) legitimate expectations—a controversy which has largely passed the Community doctrine by[197]—is a subject which has some relevance to this heading. It is a topic examined in the text below.

Other requirements which may be dealt with under this rubric include the limitation that there cannot be a legitimate expectation of something which would be *contra legem*,[198] or, more specifically, a legitimate expectation of anything which would be contrary to the requirements of the Constitution.

---

[194] As in, e.g., *R.* v. *Secretary of State for the Home Department ex p. Khan* [1984] 1 WLR 1337. An Irish case involving this situation, although an unsatisfactory one, is *Fakih* v. *Minister for Justice* [1993] 2 IR 406.

[195] Forsyth, *supra* n. 157, at 376. The point seems to have been overlooked in *Fakih* v. *Minister for Justice* [1993] 2 IR 406. A more deliberate (but no less incorrect) overlooking of this requirement occurred in the Australian High Court case of *Minister of Ethnic Affairs* v. *Teoh* (1995) 128 ALR 353. The assertion in this case that personally entertaining an expectation is unnecessary and that it is enough that the expectation be reasonable was described by Forsyth as wrong and confusing legitimate expectations with the duty to act fairly.

[196] Emphasis added. Both Supreme Court judgments (with each of which three of the four other Supreme Court judges agreed) were delivered on 19 July 2001.

[197] A point which was alluded to by Woolf J in *R.* v. *North East Devon Health Authority ex p. Coughlan* [2000] 3 All ER 850 where he observed that 'this is not a live issue in the common law of the European Union, where a uniform standard of full review for fairness is well established'. See para. 63 of his judgment.

[198] Cf. however the judgment of Hamilton P (as he then was) in *Conroy* v. *Garda Commissioner* [1989] IR 140. Compare the position in Community law, dealt with in the text above at n. 95 ff.

The *contra legem* point is exemplified by the rejection by the Supreme Court of the appellant's case in *Wiley* v. *Revenue Commissioners*, for this rested in part on the Court's view that recognizing the contended-for legitimate expectations (of a recipient of excise duty) would have required the respondent statutory authority to take a decision which would have been *ultra vires*.[199]

The point as to expectations which run contrary to the requirements of the Constitution is exemplified in the High Court judgment in *Pesca Valentia Ltd.* v. *Minister for Fisheries*, where Keane J (as he then was) rejected any idea that the plaintiffs had a legitimate expectation that no legislative changes affecting in a fundamental way their right to fish would be adopted, observing:

no such 'estoppel' could conceivably operate so as to prevent the Oireachtas from legislating or the executive from implementing the legislation when enacted.[200]

In this regard, it should be noted that the principle of the separation of powers will operate as a more important restraint on the operation of the domestic doctrine than will be the case in so far as concerns the Community principle of legitimate expectations. In other words, the Community principle is a more powerful one, capable of prevailing against legislative intent, either at Community or, within certain limits, at national level. In part, this is due to the fact that the separation of powers principle is generally of more limited application at Community level in any case.[201] But, in part, it is also due to the higher status of the doctrine in Community law. General principles of Community law rank more highly in the hierarchy of Community legal norms than does Community legislation, which has the effect that such legislation can be and has been held invalid by the European Court of Justice by reason of its failure to respect legitimate expectations or any other recognized general principle of Community law. Nor should it be forgotten that *national* legislation which comes within the scope of Community law (and this means national laws which either apply Community law norms or which constitute theoretically permissible derogations from Community law standards) may be held inapplicable on the ground that it violates general principles of Community law—including the principle of legitimate expectations.[202] In contrast, reliance on the domestic doctrine of legitimate expectations against

---

[199] See on this point e.g. the judgment of Finlay CJ at 488. Note also the observation by Lord Woolf MR at para. 64 of his judgment in *R.* v. *North East Devon Health Authority ex p. Coughlan* [2000] 3 All ER 850 that it was 'axiomatic that a public authority which derives its existence and its powers from statute cannot validly act outside those powers'.

[200] [1990] 2 IR 205 at 323. The decision of Keane J on this point is discussed by Hogan and Morgan, *supra* n. 154, at 883–4.

[201] Thus, e.g., the powers of the primary 'executive' organ of the Community—the Commission—stretch across the legislative, executive, and judicial fields of government. See for an examination of this area Craig and de Búrca, *European Union Law: Text, Cases and Materials* (2nd edn., Oxford University Press, Oxford, 1998) at 49–56.

[202] See generally here cases such as *Klensch* v. *Luxembourg Secretary of State for Agriculture* (Case 202/85) [1986] ECR 3477; *R* v. *Kent Kirk* (Case 63/83) [1984] ECR 2689; *Wachauf* v. *Germany* (Case 5/88) [1989] ECR 2609; and *Elliniki Radiophonia Tileorassi AE* v. *Pliroforissis and Kouvelas* (Case C–260/89) [1991] ECR I–2925. See further Craig and de Búrca, *supra* n. 200, at 317–31 and Usher, *supra* n. 17, at 132–7.

Irish legislation (or indeed against executive acts which comply with the legislation authorizing them at the expense of the reasonable expectations of individuals) will continue to be precluded unless, or until such time as, the principle of legitimate expectations is accorded the status of a constitutional principle in Irish law.[203] Hence, for example, had the facts of the *Mulder* case occurred in a purely domestic Irish context, and involved a series of domestic statutes rather than European Community regulations, then the invocation of the domestic doctrine –at least in the form in which it has been recognized to date by Irish courts—would have availed the individual concerned naught.

(iii) Reliance on the Expectation

Is an element of detrimental reliance by an individual on the undertaking necessary? In Community law, as we have seen, the answer is 'yes'.[204] There is authority in favour of the view that the approach under the domestic doctrine is the same.[205] The approach is not entirely uncontroversial. Hogan and Morgan, although they agree that expectation depends on prior knowledge, have argued that detrimental reliance on the expectation is not needed since the interests of consistency, good administration, and equal treatment which underlie the doctrine may require that the decision-maker abide by its previous practice.[206] It may be gainsaid, however, that, given that the essence of the doctrine of legitimate expectations is the attainment of a balance between fulfilling the need of the individual for fairness and legal certainty on the one hand, and the need to assure sufficient flexibility to decision-makers to carry out their task on the other, it is difficult to see what unfairness is being inflicted on an individual by changing a policy on which in any case he has not placed any reliance. The most recent pronouncements of the Irish Supreme Court now indicate that one or other of two situations must be the case. Either the representation must form part of a transaction definitively entered into or a relationship between a person/group and a public authority *or else* the person or group must have acted on the faith of the representation. These alternative requirements, first advanced on a 'provisional' basis in the judgment of

---

[203] On such a possibility, see Hogan and Morgan, *supra* n. 154, at 214ff.

[204] See text, *supra* at 000.

[205] *Garda Representative Association* v. *Ireland* [1989] ILRM 1; *Cosgrove* v. *Legal Aid Board* [1991] 2 IR 43. Note also *Daly* v. *Minister for the Marine* (High Court decision of O'Sullivan J of 25 Feb. 1999) where it appeared to work to the applicant's disadvantage that finding him to have the legitimate expectation he claimed would have made him 'the beneficiary of an unpaid for advantage which cost him nothing'.

[206] Hogan and Morgan, *supra* n. 154, 869–98. See also *Attorney General of Hong Kong* v. *Ng Yuen Shiu* [1983] 2 AC 629 where there appears to have been no detrimental reliance and yet the doctrine of legitimate expectations was applied. *Fakih* v. *Minister for Justice* [1993] 2 IR 406 involved a conscious purported application of the doctrine of legitimate expectations by O'Hanlon J in the absence of detrimental reliance (see in this regard in particular p. 423 of the judgment) but the case is not a very strong authority. *Fakih* has been described as probably having really involved an application of the principle that it is in the interests of good and orderly administration that, in the absence of good reasons to the contrary, that an administrator should be bound to agreed procedures (Hogan and Morgan, *supra* n. 154, 869). This seems an accurate characterization, since the facts of the case did not show even advance knowledge of any applicable procedures on the part of the applicants, let alone any detrimental reliance.

Fennelly J in the Supreme Court decision in *Glencar Exploration plc and Andaman Resources plc* v. *Mayo County Council*[207] were confirmed in the unanimous decision of the Supreme Court delivered by the same judge in *Daly* v. *Minister for the Marine*[208] in which, on the one hand Fennelly J observed that 'an expectation may be legitimate and cognisable by the courts even in the absence of the sort of action to the claimant's detriment that forms part of the law of estoppel', but on the other hand observed that a representation made by a government department 'did not tend to alter the disadvantage of the applicant (*sic.*) On the contrary, it constituted a gratuitous or fortuitous and uncovenanted benefit. This is not the sort of interest that the doctrine is designed to protect.'[209]

(iv) Absence of Misconduct

Although the relevance of misconduct is not a point which seems to have attracted as much attention in the context of the domestic legitimate expectations doctrine as it has in Community law, it should be noted that in so far as the domestic doctrine is invoked for the purposes of obtaining public law remedies, declarations, or injunctions, these remedies are all discretionary. Lack of utmost good faith, or of full disclosure on the part of the applicant, may therefore result in a denial of relief,[210] as may any conduct of the applicant which is not considered satisfactory by the court.[211]

(v) A Weighing Up of Interests

Perhaps the most obvious point to make about the domestic doctrine of legitimate expectations is that it, like its parallel principle in Community law, involves a balancing exercise. For both doctrines involve balancing, on the one hand, the interest of the individual in securing the optimum level of fairness and certainty in decision-making in public law matters (and indeed the societal interest in according an individual or business this degree of fairness) and, on the other hand, the societal interest in maintaining maximum flexibility on the part of decision-makers to react to the changing needs of circumstance. There may be instances where the public interest in a fresh exercise of a discretion will outweigh the injustice suffered by an individual (or business) who has relied on an earlier representation that the discretion will be exercised in favour of a particular result.[212] The process of attaining a balance between the

---

[207] Judgment delivered on 19 July 2001. (See p. 30 thereof.) Three of the four Supreme Court judges involved in deciding the case agreed with Fennelly J's judgment.

[208] Judgment of 4 Oct. 2001.   [209] See judgment of Fennelly J at p. 21 thereof.

[210] See, e.g., *Cork Corporation* v. *O'Connell* [1982] ILRM 505.

[211] *Ex parte Fry* [1954] 2 All ER 118; *Fulbrook* v. *Berkshire Magistrates Court* (1970) 69 LGR 75.

[212] Hence the observation by Fennelly J in delivering his judgment in the Supreme Court decision in *Glencar Exploration plc and Andaman Resources plc* v. *Mayo Council Council* (delivered 19 July 2001, with three of the other four Supreme Court members concurring) that the requirements which had to be met in order to establish a legitimate expectation were 'qualified by considerations of the public interest including the principle that freedom to exercise properly a statutory power is to be respected'. (See p. 30 of judgment.) See also Lewis, 'Fairness, Legitimate Expectations and Estoppel' (1986) 49 *MLR* 251 at 252.

sometimes competing interests of consistency and flexibility in policy manifests itself in a number of ways. Thus, for example, a necessary and sometimes explicit part of the application both of the domestic doctrine of legitimate expectations and of the Community principle will be an examination of whether some overriding public interest has justified the change of policy which is alleged to have violated an expectation.[213] In so far as the domestic doctrine is concerned, there has been controversy on where this balancing act should be carried out: should it go to the issue of whether there is a legitimate expectation,[214] or should it come into play only after the legitimacy of the expectation has been established?[215] It is not intended to attempt to resolve this debate here. Suffice it to point out that whichever view is correct, a balancing process is involved.[216]

In the context of the domestic doctrine, one way in which it has been sought to establish the boundary between what we may roughly call private and public interest has been the approach of some judges of denying legitimate expectations a substantive aspect and asserting that it is capable only of affecting the procedure by which decisions are reached.

The Procedure vs. Substance Debate

Forsyth has observed that:

expectations divide broadly into two groups: *procedural expectations*—where procedural justice of one form or another is expected—and *substantive expectations*—where a favourable decision of one kind or another is expected.[217]

Put simply, therefore, the distinction between procedure and substance is the difference between the process by which a decision-maker uses to reach a conclusion and the conclusion itself. Although 'substantive due process' is said to be a concept which is gaining increasing acceptance, the idea has met with uneven levels of acceptance in the context of the domestic doctrine of legitimate expectations—principally due to a reluctance on the part of the

---

[213] See here concerning the domestic doctrine Craig, 'Legitimate Expectations: A Conceptual Analysis' (1992) 108 *LQR* 79 at 97 and concerning the Community doctrine see, e.g., Schwarze, *supra* n. 13, at 952–3

[214] A view adopted by Sedley J (as he then was) in *R. v. Ministry for Agriculture, Fisheries and Foods ex p. Hamble* [1995] 2 All ER 714.

[215] A view advocated by Craig. See, here and on this point generally, Craig, *supra* n. 116, at 300 to 304.

[216] In the case of the domestic doctrine, it may be that further potential for disagreement lies in the as yet apparently unresolved question of whether the departure from the previous representation has to be objectively justified or merely justified in the view of the decision-maker, (or somewhere between these two extremes—e.g., justified in the view of the decision-maker, which view must be reasonable). See on this point Singh, *supra* n. 187, at 1216.

[217] Forsyth, 'Wednesbury Protection of Substantive Legitimate Expectations' [1997] *PL* 375 at 376. Similarly, Craig has taken the concept of procedural legitimate expectations to denote 'the existence of some species of process right, whether in the form of natural justice, fairness or a related idea of consultation' and the concept of substantive legitimate expectations to refer to where the applicant seeks 'a particular benefit or commodity, whether this takes the form of a welfare benefit, a licence or one of the myriad other forms which such claims can assume'. See Craig, *supra* n. 116, at 290.)

judiciary to be seen to interfere excessively in the operation of other branches of government.[218]

There is no doubt that the doctrine of legitimate expectations can be relied upon in order to secure procedural rights.[219] The outcome here is that the relevant decision may still go against the person affected, but it will be required to follow a procedure which is fair. Thus 'at the least, a legitimate expectation will normally be protected by the imposition of obligations of procedural fairness. The content of the fairness requirement will vary according to the circumstances.'[220] It should be noted that even a substantive expectation may be afforded procedural protection by the courts.[221]

A conservative view of the legitimate expectations doctrine is that it affords no more than procedural protection. Viewed in this way, the doctrine of legitimate expectations can be described as being about no more than achieving an acceptable middle ground between a general obligation to consult prior to the taking of a decision, and the total freedom to change policy.[222] The clearest statement of the conservative position by an Irish court to date has been that of Costello J in the High Court case of *Tara Prospecting* v. *Minister for Energy* where, after reviewing the authorities, he came to the following conclusions in the context of a challenge to the exercise of a ministerial discretion. They are of general interest and hence worth quoting at length:

(1) There is a duty on a minister who is exercising a discretionary power which may affect *rights* or *interests* to adopt fair procedures in the exercise of the power. Where a member of the public has a *legitimate expectation* arising from the minister's words and/or conduct that (a) he will be given a hearing before a decision adverse to his interests will be taken or (b) that he will obtain a benefit from the exercise of the power then the minister also has a duty to act fairly towards him and this may involve a duty to give him a fair hearing before a duty adverse to his interests is taken. There would then arise a correlative right to a fair hearing which, if denied, will justify the court in quashing the decision.

(2) The existence of a legitimate expectation that a *benefit* will be conferred does not in itself give rise to any legal or equitable right to the *benefit itself* which can be enforced by an order of *mandamus* or otherwise. However, in cases involving public authorities, other than cases involving the exercise of statutory discretionary powers, an equitable right to benefit may arise from the application of the principles of promissory estoppel to which effect will be given by appropriate court order.

---

[218] See Delany, *supra* n. 6, at 75. On the topic of a constitutional right of substantive due process, see by the same writer 'The Doctrine of Legitimate Expectation in Irish Law' (1990) 12 *DULJ (n.s.)* 1 at 19–20.

[219] See here, e.g., the judgment of Costello J in *Tara Prospecting* v. *Minister for Energy* [1993] ILRM 771.

[220] France, *supra* n. 158, at 142. France gives the example of *Daganayasi* v. *Minister of Immigration* [1980] 1 NZLR 355, where the New Zealand Court of Appeal held that the complainant had a legitimate expectation not alone to make submissions on her proposed deportation, but also the right to see reports held by the Minister who was making the decision.

[221] See, e.g., *Administrator, Transvaal and others* v. *Traub and others* 1989 (4) SA 731. Note also the observations of Costello J to this effect in *Tara Prospecting Ltd.* v. *Minister for Energy* [1993] ILRM 771 at 788.

[222] To adapt phraseology first employed by France, *supra* n. 158, at 141.

(3) In cases involving the exercise of a discretionary statutory power the only legitimate expectation relating to the conferring of a benefit that can be *inferred* from words or conduct is a conditional one, namely, that a benefit will be conferred provided that at the time the minister considers that it is a proper exercise of the statutory power in the light of current policy to grant it. Such a conditional expectation cannot give rise to an enforceable right to the benefit should it later be refused by the minister in the public interest.

(4) In cases involving the exercise of a discretionary statutory power in which an explicit *assurance* has been given which gives rise to an expectation that a benefit will be conferred no enforceable equitable or legal right to benefit can arise. No promissory estoppel can arise because the minister cannot estop either himself or his successors from exercising a discretionary power in the manner prescribed by parliament at the time it is being exercised.[223]

As exemplified by the judgment of Costello J in *Tara Prospecting,* Irish courts have often refrained from advancing beyond the procedural aspect of legitimate expectations and holding that legitimate expectations can give rise to substantive, rather than merely procedural fairness.[224] Instead, driven by concerns that administrative discretion might be fettered[225]—or that, as a judge in another jurisdiction has put it 'that it will entail curial interference with administrative decisions on the merits by precluding the decision-maker from ultimately making the decision which he or she considers most appropriate in the circumstances'[226]—there has been a frequent (though far from universal) tendency to draw back from taking the step of upholding substantive legitimate expectations.

On the one hand, such concerns demonstrate an awareness of the reality that the doctrine of substantive legitimate expectations threatens to overwhelm the traditional approach that there is no room for estoppel in public

---

[223] [1993] ILRM 771 at 788–9.

[224] See in this regard also the judgment of Shanley J in *Eogan* v. *University College Dublin* [1996] 1 IR 390, where the doctrine is quite clearly regarded as having procedural implications only. Note also *Fakih* v. *Minister for Justice* [1993] 2 IR 406, where O'Hanlon J upheld the right of the applicant asylum-seekers to rely on the doctrine of legitimate expectations so as to have their claims for asylum determined by reference to procedures set out in a letter sent to the representative of the UN High Commissioner for Refugees by an official of the Department of Justice. However, O'Hanlon J noted 'I accept that the legal status of applicants, or the question of their legal entitlement to remain in Ireland, are not governed in any way by the terms of the letter and that it is of benefit to the applicants only in relation to the manner in which their claims to rights of asylum are to be processed'. See [1993] 2 IR 406 at 424. See also the earlier High Court decision of Keane J in *Pesca Valentia Ltd.* v. *Minister for the Fisheries and Forestry* [1990] 2 IR 305. Such judgments repeat sentiments also expressed in English cases such as *R.* v. *Secretary of State for Health ex p. US Tobacco International Inc.* [1992] 1 All ER 212 and *Findlay* v. *Secretary of State for the Home Department* [1995] AC 3187.

[225] The argument that a public body should not fetter its own judgment is sometimes put in terms of the *ultra vires* rule, the argument here being that if a public body fetters its own discretion, it will be held to have acted beyond its powers. Craig has criticized the merits of this *ultra vires* approach as a comprehensive framework for looking at the question of substantive legitimate expectations, describing it as failing to take any account at all of another value recognized in our legal system—that of legal certainty. See Craig, *supra* n. 116, at 299.

[226] Mason CJ in *Attorney-General for New South Wales* v. *Quin* (1990) 170 CLR 1 at 23.

law.[227] On the other hand such a conservative approach to the doctrine of legitimate expectations reduces the domestic doctrine of legitimate expectations to a shadow of what it could be and goes against the increasing tendency on the part of the courts to ensure not only that fair procedures are adhered to, but also that a fair result or outcome is arrived at.[228] Even the European Court of Justice—famously slow in practice to allow reliance on the Community principle of legitimate expectations—has never applied such a restrictive approach to the principle of legitimate expectations in Community law. Its ruling in the *Mulder* case is a case in point. In that case, what Mulder sought was what the justice of the case seemed to clearly demand—*viz.*, substantive relief. Those who would advocate the confinement of the scope of the domestic doctrine to the vindication of procedural rights alone would have denied Mulder relief, had his case arisen in a domestic Irish context, and had he sought to rely on the domestic doctrine of legitimate expectations instead of the Community principle. It is submitted that such an approach is not to be preferred. On the contrary, taking such a restrictive view of the domestic doctrine arguably either clears the way for unreasonable and unfair decisions or puts an undesirable degree of pressure on a court confronting such decisions to prevent them by recourse to other doctrines which fetter discretion to an extent similar to that which it would supposedly be objectionable for the legitimate expectations doctrine to fetter it—for example, *via* judicial review for unreasonableness,[229] or *via* the notion of contracts or agreements being entered

---

[227] Hence the assertion (quoted in the text above) by Costello J in *Tara Prospecting Ltd.* v. *Minister for Energy* (which concerned the exercise of a ministerial discretion) that 'no promissory estoppel can arise because the Minister cannot estop either himself or his successors from exercising a discretionary power in the manner prescribed by parliament at the time it is being exercised'. See [1993] IRLM 771 at 789. It should be noted that Costello J was, however, prepared to countenance the application by the principles of promissory estoppel 'in cases involving public authorities, other than cases involving the exercise of statutory discretionary powers'. See also in relation to this estoppel point the judgment of Costello J in *Hempenstall* v. *Minister for the Environment* [1993] IRLM 318. See further Singh, *supra* n. 187, at 1215 where he cites as cases in support of the no-estoppel rule: *Maritime Electric Co. Ltd* v. *General Dairies Ltd.*[1937] AC 610; *Southend-on-Sea Corporation* v. *Hodgson* [1962] 1 QB 416; and *Western Fish Products* v. *Penwith District Council* [1981] 2 All ER 204. Note also Lewis's description of the House of Lords as having paid 'lip service' to the principle that estoppel did not apply to public bodies' in its judgment in *R.* v. *Inland Revenue Commissioners ex p. Preston* [1985] 2 WLR 836 (Lewis, 'Fairness, Legitimate Expectations and Estoppel' (1986) 49 *MLR*, 251 at 252). Finally, by way of contrast it is interesting to note Schwarze's description of the judgment of the ECJ in *Nakajima All Precision Co. Ltd.* (Case C–69/89) [1991] ECR I–2069 as having integrated the legal argument of estoppel into already existing legal concepts and notices at Community level, 'in particular those of legal certainty and the protection of legitimate expectations'. See Schwarze, *supra* n. 13, 192.

[228] See here Delany, *supra* n. 6, 75–7.

[229] See here e.g., *R.* v. *Inland Revenue Commissioners ex p. Unilever* [1996] STC 681 and *R.* v. *Secretary of State for the Home Department ex p. Hargreaves* [1997] 1 WLR 906. Both of these decisions are analysed in Forsyth, *supra* n. 157, and Foster. 'Legitimate Expectations and Prisoners' Rights: The Right to Get What You Are Given' (1997) 60 *MLR* 727. See now the judgment of the Court of Appeal (delivered by Lord Woolf MR) in *R.* v. *North East Devon Health Authority ex p. Coughlan* [2000] 3 All ER 850 where the concept of legitimate expectations is distinguished from that of unreasonableness and the view taken that both legitimate expectations and *Wednesbury* unreasonableness are categories of abuse of power. See para. 81 ff. of Lord Woolf's judgment.

into to exercise statutory powers in a particular way, or of promissory estop-pels operating.[230]

Not all judgments of the Irish courts have viewed the domestic doctrine of legitimate expectations as confined to ensuring protection for procedural rights. The seminal Supreme Court judgment in *Webb* v. *Ireland*[231] is one in which the opposite approach was adopted. In this case Finlay CJ described the effect of the unqualified assurance give by the director of the national museum to Webb as being 'that the State cannot now go back on the assurance. It must be given effect to in the effect of a monetary award of an amount which is rea-sonable in the light of all the relevant circumstances.' However, the authority of this judgment is lessened by the fact that no real consideration was given in *Webb* to the question now at issue: *viz.*, whether the doctrine of legitimate expectations can operate to protect substantive expectations or whether it should be confined to procedural expectations. Furthermore, the judgment of the Chief Justice is arguably even further weakened because of its almost cer-tainly incorrect characterization of legitimate expectations as an aspect of promissory estoppel.

Webb was expressly followed by Hamilton P in the High Court case of *Duggan* v. *An Taoiseach*,[232] where the learned judge held that 'if a person establishes that he has a legitimate expectation of receiving a benefit or privi-lege, the courts will protect his expectation by judicial review as a matter of

---

[230] In *Gilheaney* v. *The Revenue Commissioners* [1998] IR 150, a case in which a decision not to promote the applicant was challenged, Costello J acknowledged that a statutory provision (s. 17 of the Civil Service Regulation Act 1956 which empowered the Minister for Finance to enter into 'arrangements' for the purpose of, *inter alia*, fixing the terms of employment and of promotion of civil servants) involved the possibility of a minister entering into arrangements even with a serv-ing civil servant whose original appointment had been the result of the exercise of a statutory power and was not contractual. However, Costello J noted the further power conferred on the Minister by the same statutory provision to vary and cancel arrangements made for the promo-tion of a civil servant, and held that 'this [latter] discretionary power cannot be fettered by con-tract. This means that the only *intra vires* contract which could be entered into was one which allowed the respondents to vary or cancel its terms and I can find no evidence of an intention to enter into such an unusual contract.'

In the subsequent case of *O'Leary* v. *Minister for Finance* [1998] 2 IRLM 321, however, (which concerned the same statutory provision) it was held by Quirke J on the facts that a s.17 contract had been created 'on the basis of an understanding that generally it is not in the interest of the public service that the statutory powers [i.e. to vary or cancel it] would be exercised'. Apparently taking the view that the doctrines of legitimate expectations, estoppel, and contract all applied, Quirke J went on to hold 'I am satisfied that Mr. O'Leary has a legitimate expectation that he will receive the benefits of the contract into which he entered with [the Minister] and that the latter is estopped from denying Mr. O'Leary the benefits arising from the contract or "arrangement" (and the exercise of the statutory power by the first respondent)'. Thus a combination of contract, estoppel, and legitimate expectations was used to prevent the Minister resiling from an arrange-ment reached with the applicant. In other words, they were used to fetter a ministerial discretion. Quirke J seemed to feel that the doctrines of estoppel and legitimate expectations alone sufficed, holding 'I make no finding as to whether or not the first named respondent has in fact exercised his statutory power to cancel or vary the terms of the benefit which was conferred upon Mr. O'Leary. If he has not done so, then contractual rights against [the Minister] may also be vested in Mr. O'Leary but in my judgment it matters little because I see no reason why contractual rights should not co-exist with rights arising out of the doctrine of "legitimate expectation" or the equi-table concept of promissory estoppel'. See [1998] 2 IRLM 321 at 343.

[231] [1988] IR 353.   [232] [1989] IRLM 710.

public law'.[233] Again, as in *Webb*, an award of damages was made to the applicants (who, in this case, were civil servants who had been disappointed in their expectation that temporary promotions to a higher grade would be made permanent). Again, however, as in *Webb*, no real consideration was given to the procedural/substantive legitimate expectations issue now being discussed.[234]

In the two further High Court decisions, *Kelly* v. *Kenny*[235] and *O'Leary* v. *Minister for Finance*,[236] the doctrine of legitimate expectations was also invoked as a ground for holding the applicant to be entitled to a substantive benefit. In both cases, however, alternative grounds for finding the existence of this entitlement were relied upon.[237] Once again, no thought seems to have been devoted to the question whether the doctrine of legitimate expectations could actually give rise to substantive as opposed to merely procedural rights.

One case in which the procedural/substantive issue was clearly at the forefront of the deciding judge's mind, however, was the High Court case of *Abrahamson* v. *Law Society* where, after considering a number of authorities such as *Tara Prospecting*, McCracken J asserted that:

> where the legitimate expectation is that a benefit will be secured, the courts will endeavour to obtain that benefit or to compensate the applicant, whether by way of an order of mandamus or by an award of damages, provided that to do so is lawful.[238]

Abrahamson is probably the strongest authority that exists in favour of the existence of a substantive aspect to the doctrine of legitimate expectations in domestic Irish law.[239] Overall, however, it must be said that there is, relatively speaking, a regrettable dearth of reasoned analysis by Irish courts on this issue. At least equally regrettable, in this writer's view, however, is the fact in so many Irish cases a highly restrictive approach has been exhibited towards the notion of substantive legitimate expectations.

The issue is one which has attracted considerable judicial attention in other common law jurisdictions. In these jurisdictions (as may be expected) the existence of procedural legitimate expectations has frequently been acknowledged.[240] In some cases this has been accompanied by a refusal to acknowl-

---

[233] [1989] ILRM 710 at 727.

[234] The above-quoted statement by Hamilton P in *Duggan* was adopted by Blayney J in the subsequent case of *Wiley* v. *Revenue Commissioners* [1989] IR 350 at 355 but again with no real consideration being given to the procedural/substantive legitimate expectations issue. The Supreme Court judgments in the same case were much less sympathetic to the idea of substantive legitimate expectations. See [1994] 2 IR 160.

[235] [1988] IR 457 (judgment of Barron J).   [236] [1998] 2 ILRM 321 (judgment of Quirke J).

[237] *Viz.*, in *Kelly*, the ground of promissory estoppel, and in *O'Leary*, both the ground of promissory estoppel and that of contract.

[238] [1996] 2 ILRM 481 at 498.

[239] It is worth mentioning at least in passing, however, that where Irish courts have dealt with decision-making which does not involve the exercise of a statutory discretion, a similar less inhibited approach has been adopted to the idea of what in effect has seemed to amount to the vindication of substantive legitimate expectations. See *Latchford* v. *Minister for Industry and Commerce* [1950] IR 33 and *Staunton* v. *St. Lawrence's Hospital* (unreported High Court judgment of 21 Feb. 1986). Both of these cases are discussed in Hogan and Morgan, *supra* n. 154, at 890–3.

[240] See, e.g., *Attorney-General of Hong Kong* v. *Ng Yuen Shiu* [1983] 2 AC 629, and *Re Findlay* [1985] AC 318.

edge the existence of substantive legitimate expectations.[241] In other cases, however, a very different view has been taken. Thus some decisions seem to be situated a least some distance along the road of recognizing substantive legitimate expectations.[242] Others are unambiguously in favour of the concept of legitimate expectations giving rise to substantive rights.[243] The most recent decisions in other jurisdictions paint a picture which differs markedly from the approach of the courts in the Irish Republic. Hence, notwithstanding the conservative approach previously adopted by the House of Lords in cases such as *In re Findlay*,[244] *Council of Civil Service Unions* v. *Minister for the Civil Service* (the *'GCHQ'* case),[245] and *Hughes* v. *Department of Health and Social Security*,[246] the English Court of Appeal has now moved unambiguously in the direction of accepting the existence of legitimate expectations in its carefully reasoned judgment in *R.* v. *North East Devon Health Authority ex parte Coughlan*.[247] Given the influence which previous decisions of the English courts have had on the development of the doctrine of legitimate expectations in the common law world, the decision in *Coughlan* is likely to prove something of a turning point. Certainly, in his recent Northern Ireland High Court decision in *Re Treacy and Another*,[248] Kerr J (although finding no legitimate

---

[241] See, e.g., the English case of *R.* v. *Secretary of State for Transport ex. p. Richmond upon Thames LBC* [1994] I WLR 74, the Canadian cases of *Re Canada Assistance Plan* (1991) 83 DLR (4th) 297; *Furey* v. *Conception Bay Centre Roman Catholic School Board* (1993) 104 DLR (4th) 455; the New Zealand cases of *Bradley* v. *Attorney General* [1988] 2 NZLR 454; *Khalon* v. *Attorney General* [1996] 1 NZLR 458; and the Australian case of *Minister for Immigration and Ethnic Affairs* v. *Teoh* (1995) 183 CLR 273 although *cf.* the earlier Australian case of *Attorney-General for New South Wales* v. *Quin* (1990) 170 CLR 1. Note also the dicta of Ralfph Gibson LJ in *R.* v. *Secretary of State for the Home Department ex. p. Mowla* [1992] 1 WLR 70 at 88–9.

[242] For example, *R.* v. *Secretary of State for the Home Department, ex p. Khan* [1984] 1 WLR 1337 (legitimate expectation held to have been created that only criteria laid out in a Home Office circular would be regarded as relevant when an application to adopt a child from overseas was being processed). This judgment can be contrasted with the Irish High Court judgment of O'Hanlon J in *Fakih* v. *Minister for Justice* [1993] 2 IR 406 (as to which see *supra*). See also *R.* v. *Secretary of State ex p. Ruddock* [1987] 1 WLR 1482 (where Taylor J, in a case concerning telephone tapping, held that the legitimate expectations doctrine imposed a duty to act fairly. This duty was not, as the respondent had argued, confined to the mere right to be heard—a right which was clearly not going to apply anyway in a case which involving a decision to intercept telephone messages—even if most of the cases involved this latter right).

[243] See *R.* v. *Ministry for Agriculture, Fisheries and Foods ex p. Hamble (Offshore) Fisheries Ltd.* [1995] 2 All ER 714; *R.* v. *Secretary of State for the Home Department ex p. Ruddock* [1987] 1 WLR 1482. See the New Zealand case of *Bradley* v. *Attorney General* (1988) 7 NZAR 193 (where Smellie J held that the plaintiff had a legitimate expectation 'that in due course he would be promoted'). And note the early (albeit dissenting) judgement of Lord Denning in *Breen* v. *Amalgamated Engineering Union* [1971] 2 QB 175.

[244] [1985] 1 AC 318 (legitimate expectation of a prisoner seeking parole envisaged at most as being of a particular type of hearing (*viz.*, an individual hearing)). See the judgment of Scarman J in [1985] AC 318 at 388.

[245] [1985] AC 374 (trade union held to have had legitimate expectation to be consulted in advance of an instruction which prohibited workers at GCHQ from belonging to a trade union).

[246] [1985] AC 776 (where what was at issue were retirement ages and the House of Lords seemed unsympathetic to the idea of taking legitimate expectations beyond issues of procedural fairness). See in particular here the judgment of Lord Diplock [1985] 2 WLR 866 at 875.

[247] [2000] 3 All ER 850 and see also the note thereon by Elliot in (2000) 5 *JR* 27.

[248] [2000] NI 330. Cf. the judgment of Evans, JA in the Canadian Federal Court of Appeal in *Apotex Inc.* v. *Canada* (2000) 188 DLR (4th) 145 at 183, in which, in a very brief paragraph, he

expectation had arisen on the facts of this case) paid careful regard to *Coughlan* and expressly refused to accept that the courts in Northern Ireland have set their face against the concept of substantive legitimate expectations.

It is to be hoped that the Irish courts will arrive at a position on legitimate expectations similar to that adopted by the Court of Appeal in *Coughlan*. It has been observed that the restrictive definition of the doctrine adopted in some cases (*viz.*, confining the domestic doctrine to questions of procedural impropriety) is sometimes achieved by 'the definitional device of limiting the description of the actual expectation'.[249] Yet it is clear that the interest of the individual in a situation where he or she has been led to believe that a discretion will be exercised in a particular way by a public authority will normally relate to the substantive question of how that discretion is exercised, and not to the question whether he or she will be consulted if the authority decides to go back on its word. Assuming that securing fairness in decision-making is the ultimate objective of this doctrine, why should it be regarded as fair to frustrate a legitimate expectation that something will be done but unfair to frustrate a legitimate expectation that a hearing will be granted before the final decision is made?

In this regard, Craig has made the point that the cogency of the 'no fettering' argument is overstated. Policies must be allowed to develop, and in this sense:

it is correct to say that they cannot be fettered. Once cannot therefore ossify administrative policy, which may alter for a variety of reasons, including experience gleaned from the operation of the previous policy, change of political outlook, or new technological developments. Nevertheless the 'no fettering' theme must be kept within bounds. Where a representation has been made to a specific person, or where conditions for application of policy in a certain area have been published and relied on, then the public body should be under a duty to follow the representation or the published criteria. This does not prevent it from altering its general policy for the future, but is should not be allowed to depart from the representation or pre-existing policy in relation to an individual who *has* relied, unless the overriding public interest requires it, and then only after a hearing.[250]

The same writer has observed that:

in the case of changes of policy the court would not be preventing the agency from adopting a new substantive policy . . . nor would it be dictating the content of that policy. It would be deciding that if legitimate expectations really could, both practically and normatively, be held to have been generated by the earlier policy, then that policy should continue to apply to the relevant individuals in circumstances where the public interest was not thereby jeopardized.[251]

appears to reject the approach of the English Court of Appeal and to take the view that the doctrine does not have a substantive aspect.

[249] France, *supra* n. 158, at 137.

[250] Craig, *supra* n. 186. It is on the basis of this logic that Craig welcomed decisions such as that of the Court of Appeal in *R. v. Secretary of State for the Home Department ex p. Khan* [1984] 1 WLR 1337 where a broad approach was adopted to the meaning of legitimate expectations.

[251] *Supra* n. 186, at 95. A further fear which sometimes receives judicial expression is that legitimate expectations may enable bodies to extend their powers by making representations which

There are weighty arguments which await an appropriate degree of consideration in a judgment of an Irish court. However, it is submitted that it would be an undesirable emasculation of the domestic doctrine were it (unlike its counterpart in Community law) to be confined to mere surface formalities, leaving decision-makers in the public law field free to disregard in the most unfair manner solemn undertakings which have been given by them. The objective of securing fairness in decision-making—the origin of the domestic doctrine—arguably demands more than a doctrine conferring only procedural benefits—a doctrine which has been rightly derided by one commentator as merely giving the individual or business the right to get what they are given.[252] As Delany has argued, 'clearly for the doctrine to be of real value it must extend beyond an expectation of being heard; procedural guarantees will not always adequately depend and vindicate substantive legitimate expectations'.[253] Cases like *Abrahamson, Treacy,* and *Coughlan* may be read as indicating that in the courts of both Ireland and the United Kingdom, the tide is turning or has already turned in favour of substantive legitimate expectations. Perhaps a further indication of a sea-change here is provided by the recent decision of the Irish Supreme Court in *Glencar Exploration plc and Andaman Resources plc* v. *Mayo County Council.*[254] In this case both Keane CJ and Fennelly J (with whose judgments all remaining judges of the Supreme Court concurred) noted the controversy regarding the existence of substantive legitimate expectations, but found it unnecessary for the purposes of the case before the Court to express an opinion either way on the point. It is of interest, however, that although given the opportunity, neither judge chose to endorse the views of Costello J in this regard as expressed in *Tara Prospecting* v. *the Minister for Energy,*[255] which, as we have seen, were strongly unfavourable to the notion of substantive legitimate expectations. Indeed, the judgment of Fennelly J contains strong hints that the opposite approach (*viz.* in favour of the existence of substantive legitimate expectations) is to be preferred, and Fennelly J described a passage from a judgment of the European Court of Justice in which a substantive remedy for breach of legitimate expectations was envisaged, as one which accorded 'due weight to the competing imperatives of private justice and public policy'.[256] It is submitted that this is an approach favoured not

could then be held to bind them. One solution to this is to adopt the position that a legitimate expectation would not be created if the relevant representation was outside the powers of the relevant public body or the relevant officer of that body. For a discussion of this point see Craig, *supra* n. 186, 87–9.

[252] Foster, *supra* n. 225. Hence the comment of Deane J in *Australian Broadcasting* v. *Bond* (1990) 170 CLR 321 at 366 to the effect that 'it would be both surprising and illogical if fair procedures involved mere surface formalities and left the decision-maker free to make a completely arbitrary decision' and the observation by Cooke J in *Daganayasi* v. *Minister for Immigration* [1980] 2 NZLR 130 that 'fairness need not be confined to procedural matters'. In relation to both of these comments see further Delany, *supra* n. 6, at 77.

[253] Delany, *supra* n. 6, at 22.   [254] Supreme Court decision of 19 July 2001.

[255] [1993] ILRM 771.

[256] *Tomandi* v. *Amminisitrazione della Finanze dello Stato* (Case 84/78) [1979] ECR 801 at para. 20 thereof, referred to by Fennelly J at p. 29 of his judgment.

only by authority, but by the interests of justice, and an approach for which precedent exists in that field of Irish law which is comprised of European Community law.

IV. Conclusion

Fifteen years ago, Baldwin and Horne observed that:

to create a new property in the public interest state is not to attack the discretions that govern the enjoyment of governmentally-created wealth. It is however, to demand that those discretions should be used fairly and reasonably and not exceeded or abused.

In Britain the new property has arrived, albeit in struggling fashion. The courts have taken some steps on the procedural front to protect those affected by largesse but they have not gone far enough.[257]

If one substitutes 'Ireland' for 'Britain,' the validity of the above statement seems to hold good for the present day state of law in this jurisdiction, at least in so far as the domestic doctrine of legitimate expectations is concerned. So too does the authors' call on the courts to construe statutes in a manner that respects public and private interests to keep discretionary powers within their proper bounds and to eschew restrictions on the notion of legitimate expectations that owe more to formalism or legalism than to life's realities. Arguably, the most significant contribution which could be made in this respect is the acknowledgment and proper development by the Irish courts of the substantive side of the domestic doctrine of legitimate expectations. In this regard, as in others, much useful guidance is to be found in the wealth of jurisprudence which has now accumulated in respect of the principle of legitimate expectations in Community law, a principle which in several respects provides stronger protection for the individual or business than does its domestic Irish law cousin.[258] Although the domestic doctrine of legitimate expectations has certainly consolidated its presence in the landscape of Irish administrative law in the last decade or so, there is a telling ring to the observation by Tridimas that:

the expanding presence of Community law in the area of remedies and the higher standards introduced by the Court have led in many a case to reverse discrimination . . . the situation where claims based on purely domestic law are treated less favourably than claims based on Community law. Such reverse discrimination flies in the face of justice.

---

[257] Baldwin and Horne, *supra* n. 5, at 710.

[258] It is instructive in this regard to note the importance attributed by Lord Woolf in his judgment in *R. v. North East Devon Health Authority ex p. Coughlan* [2000] 3 All ER 850 to the position adopted by the ECJ in relation to the concept of substantive legitimate expectations (note in particular paras. 77 and 79 of the judgment). See also in this regard the influence of Community law jurisprudence in the judgment of Fenelly J in the *Glencar Exploration plc and Andaman Resources plc v. Mayo County Council* (Supreme Court Decision of 19 July 2001. See in particular p. 29 thereof.) This is proof, were any needed, of the potential for useful cross-fertilization between the national and Community law ideas in this area of the law.

That is particularly so since often the intrinsic value of Community rights which enjoy superior protection is less than the intrinsic value that rights governed by domestic law possess.[259]

It is submitted that the problems underlined by criticisms such as this require some judicial reaction. It will therefore be interesting to see what developments and refinements come about in the coming years in the case-law which emanates from the courts of the Irish Republic regarding the domestic doctrine of legitimate expectations.

[259] Tridimas, *supra* n. 17, 354–5.

SURVEYS

The Institutional Law of the European Union in 2000

KIERAN ST C BRADLEY*

I. Introduction

Another year, another Treaty, though this time round a successful outcome of the intergovernmental conference ('IGC') was anything but a foregone conclusion, and Mr Prodi's remarks that the chances of a positive result were fifty-fifty were less an horatory admonition to the troops on the eve of battle than a realistic assessment of the situation. There was something approaching consensus after the event, possibly for very diverse reasons in different camps, that the existing Treaty reform process was wholly unsuitable, though the modification of the formal process for Treaty revision never made it onto the IGC agenda. That said, the IGC did largely complete the limited agenda set for it at Amsterdam, agreeing notably on the composition of the Commission and the carve-up of Council votes now and after enlargement, and adding for good measure some urgently-needed reforms of the Community's judicial system and a loosening-up of the rules for recourse to Community/Union flexibility. Agreement was also reached on an authochthonous fundamental rights Charter for the Union, though this was probably faciliated by the Charter's non-binding character.

Institutional matters kept the Courts as busy as ever. In a millennial judgment which reflects the spirit of the political times, the Court struck down the Parliament-Council directive banning tobacco advertising for failing to respect the division of competences operated by the Treaty; the Court also warned the institutions against circumventing clear Treaty limitations on Community competence. For the first time ever, it fined a Member State for

* Member of the Legal Service, European Parliament; visiting lecturer, College of Europe Natolin (2000–2001). The views expressed are personal, and should not be taken as representing those of any institution, member of an institution or service with which the author is or has been associated. Only current numbering of EC Treaty Articles is used throughout; square brackets are used to indicate that the original reference was to the previous numbering.

failing to comply with an old infringement judgment, while the Court of First Instance (CFI) ordered the European Investment Bank to pay over a million Belgian Francs in damages for refusing outright to comply with one of its judgments in a staff dispute. A specimen of that most rare and exotic of proceedings, the infringement action between two Member States, was spotted during the year, though the result of the case may discourage further specimens from taking flight. The question whether national bodies of various denominations, characteristics, and functions can refer requests for preliminary rulings exercized the Court a great deal during the year, on one occasion on the motion of the referring court itself; in the end, the Court proved as generous in its judicial decisions in this regard as it had in its submissions to the IGC. The role and functions of the Advocate General were examined in a landmark order, which affirms the specificity of the Community's legal and judicial order, including as regards its fundamental rights protection; the CFI had the opportunity to remind the institutions that officials have fundamental rights too. The Court finally aligned the conditions for liability of institutions and Member States under Community law. Exceptionally, the major judgments in the area of access to documents and transparency generally were handed down by the Court of Justice, though the CFI consolidated its much-praised case law in this regard. By not appealing in a staff case, the Court of Auditors will find itself complying with a CFI judgment materially identical to one annulled by the Court of Justice.

Meanwhile over at the European Parliament, various individual MEPs and minority political (non-)groups litigated with the majority of the institution on matters ranging from the defence of the independent exercise of their parliamentary and ancillary duties (yes) to the necessity to submit a request in order to belong to the parliamentary pension scheme (apparently not); Parliament's headlong rush to conspicuous financial virtue hit the buffers when the application of its decision to bring in the anti-fraud office, OLAF, was suspended. The first legal action against the Ombudsman was ruled manifestly inadmissible, though there are others in the pipeline. The Council overhauled its rules of procedure again, only a year after the last revision, while the Commission amended its rules in anticipation of the outcome of the IGC. Both the Court of Justice (twice) and the CFI amended their rules too, with a view to speeding up their procedures and taking judicial notice of certain twentieth-century technologies.

II. Case Law

A.   JUDICIAL REVIEW OF LEGISLATION

(i)   The Tobacco Advertising Directive

Probably the most significant single judgment handed down by the Court during the year was that in Germany's action to challenge the 1998 Tobacco

Advertising Directive.[1] Purportedly with a view to eliminating the barriers to intra-Community trade in advertising products and associated services which arise from the differences in national legislation, and to ensuring equal conditions of competition, Directive 98/43[2] in effect banned all forms of advertising and sponsorship of tobacco products; an exception was allowed, under certain conditions, for *bona fide* 'diversification products', which use brand names also associated with tobacco products.[3] Germany challenged the validity of the Directive on the grounds that it could not be based on Article [95 EC], that it infringed the Treaty provisions on the freedom to provide services, on the free movement of goods, and on the duty to provide reasons for legally binding measures, as well as breaching the principles of proportionality and subsidiarity, and the fundamental right to freedom of expression. The validity of the Directive had also been challenged on essentially identical grounds before the High Court of England and Wales, which had referred a series of questions for a preliminary ruling.[4]

In the result, the Court dealt only with the question of the legal basis of the Directive, and in particular the reliance on Article [95 EC]. The main points of the Court's analysis[5] may be summarized as follows:

—while harmonizing measures based, for example, on Article [95 EC] may have an impact on the protection of human health, '[other] articles of the Treaty may not . . . be used as a legal basis in order to circumvent the express exclusion of harmonisation laid down in Article [152(4)(c) EC]';

—Article [95 EC] does not provide the Community with a general power to regulate the internal market; such an interpretation 'would not only be contrary to the express wording of [this provision and Articles 3(1)(c) and 14 EC] but would also be incompatible with the principle embodied in Article [5 EC] that the powers of the Community are limited to those specifically conferred on it';

—'a measure adopted on the basis of Article [95 EC] must genuinely have as its object the improvement of the conditions for the establishment and functioning of the internal market'; if an abstract risk of disparities in the national rules or of a distortion of conditions of competition were sufficient to justify recourse to this provision, 'judicial review of compliance with the proper legal basis might be rendered nugatory'; in particular, if this provision did not require that distortions of competition be at least appreciable, rather than merely remote or indirect, 'the powers of the Community legislature would be practically unlimited'.

---

[1] Case C–376/98, *Germany* v. *Parliament and Council* [2000] ECR I–8419.

[2] [1998] OJ L213/9.

[3] The makers of a number of such products challenged the directive before the CFI: see n. 10 below.

[4] Case C–74/99, *The Queen* v. *Secretary of State for Health, ex p. Imperial Tobacco and Others* [2000] ECR I–8599.

[5] This largely follows the comprehensive Opinion of Fennelly AG , though in some respects the Court is more severe on the bicephalous Community legislator.

Regarding the contested directive itself, the Court held that:

—while a ban on tobacco advertising in print media could be justified on the basis of Article [95 EC] in order to ensure free movement of these products, such a prohibition could not be justified for the numerous other forms of tobacco advertising covered by the directive;

—the directive does not ensure the free movement of diversification products which comply with its provisions, as it does not contain any provision guaranteeing such free movement, and the Member States may in any case adopt stricter provisions on advertising and sponsorship on grounds of health protection;

—advertising agencies and producers of advertising media in Member States which impose fewer restrictions on tobacco advertising are at a disadvantage compared to their competitors in other Member States, but these distortions are not of such magnitude as to justify a Community prohibition, such as those caused, for example, by differences in production costs;

—while differences in national rules regarding sponsorship do give rise to distortions of competition which could justify a Community prohibition on certain forms of sponsorship, these are not such as to justify a blanket ban on tobacco advertising;

—moreover, the directive would not so much eliminate appreciable distortions of competition, as 'generalise [the] restriction of forms of competition by limiting, in all Member States, the means available for economic operators to enter or remain in the market'.

The Directive could not therefore validly be based on Articles [95 EC, 47(2) EC and 55 EC], and was annulled. Although ruling that 'a directive prohibiting certain forms of advertising and sponsorship of tobacco products could have been adopted on the basis of Article [95 EC]', the Court refused to annul the contested directive only partially, as this 'would entail amendment by the Court of provisions of the Directive . . . [which] amendments are a matter for the Community legislature'. As a result of this judgment, the Court held that there was no need to answer the question put by the English High Court in *Imperial Tobacco*.

The judgment is significant particularly because it is the first occasion on which the Court has annulled, at the suit of a Member State, an act of (Council/Parliament) legislation as *ultra vires* the purported legal basis.[6] At a time when the distribution of regulatory competences between the Community and the Member States, and the mechanisms for ensuring respect for that distribution,[7] are more than ever at the centre of the debate on the

---

[6] For earlier attempts, see, e.g., Cases C–84/96, *United Kingdom* v. *Council* ('working time directive') [1996] ECR I–5755, and C–268/94, *Portugal* v. *Council* ('Indian co-operation agreement') [1996] ECR I–6177.

[7] A persuasive case for the ECJ being vested with what has been termed 'judicial *Kompetenz-Kompetenz*' is made by Weiler and Haltern in Slaughter *et al.* (eds.), *The European Courts and National Courts: Doctrine and Jurisprudence* (Hart Publishing, Oxford, 1998).

future of integration, the judgment serves as a signal to the national constitutional courts that the Court of Justice can be trusted to carry out its vested role of restraining the legislative activities of the Council and Parliament, even if it did not—indeed, it was not invited to do so—rule that the Directive was outside the competence of the Community, as distinct from that of the legislator.[8] In the circumstances of this particular case, recourse to Article [308 EC] as an alternative legal basis would probably be excluded as a matter of political fact, because of the unanimity requirement;[9] if the Court's 'no circumvention' admonition were taken at face value and applied generally, then such recourse would be excluded as a matter of law too. In making its strongest affirmation of Community judicial review, however, the Court was careful to display a certain restraint, in particular by refusing to sever the clauses which could validly have been based on Article [95 EC] *et al.* from the remainder of the condemned text.

The annulment proceedings by the tobacco advertisers and holders of diversification marks before the Court of First Instance fared rather less well.[10] The CFI began by recalling that, for such an action to be admitted, an applicant must show direct concern in the sense that 'the measure must directly affect his legal situation and leave no discretion to the addressees'. It held that a directive does not impose obligations on individuals, and cannot be relied upon as such against him; in particular, the obligations identified in *Interenvironnement Wallonie*,[11] being based on [Article 10 EC], may not be extended to individuals. In the present case, the Directive was found not to impose any obligations on the applicants and, in any case, it left the Member States with a margin of discretion as regards its application. The Court also rejected the arguments that if their action were not admitted, the applicants would not be guaranteed adequate legal protection in the national courts against the effects of the Directive, and that a reference for a preliminary ruling was less effective than a direct annulment action: 'such a circumstance, even if proved, could not entitle the Court to usurp the function of the founding authority of the Community in order to change the system of legal remedies and procedures established by [Articles 230 EC, 234 EC and 235 EC]'. A trifle po-faced, considering it had quoted *Les Verts* in the previous paragraph, the Court added that '[that] circumstance can certainly not allow an action for annulment brought by a natural or legal person which does not satisfy the conditions laid down by the fourth paragraph of Article [230 EC] to be declared admissible'. As though to soften the blow, however, the Court did allude to the

---

[8] Weiler, 'The Transformation of Europe' (1991) 100 *Yale Law Journal* 2403, 2447, reprinted in the same author's *A Constitution for Europe* (Cambridge University Press, Cambridge, 1999), 10, 57; the Court has nonetheless shown its mettle in other procedural settings, particularly in the external relations field, notably in Opinion 2/94 [1996] ECR I–1759.

[9] Though it was rumoured that subsequent change of government almost brought about a change of heart.

[10] Joined Cases T–172/98 and T–175/98 to T–177/98, *Salamander AG and Others* v. *Parliament and Council* [2000] ECR II–2487.

[11] Case C–126/96 [1997] ECR I–7411, esp. para. 45.

reference requested in *Imperial Tobacco*, and to the possibility of recovering damages for loss occasioned directly by the Directive, before concluding that the right to an effective remedy had been complied with.

Two of the four applicants appealed against the judgment of the Court of First Instance, and maintained their appeal even after the annulment of the contested Tobacco Advertising Directive.[12]

(ii) The Beef Labelling Regulation

The Commission's attempt, under pressure from the European Parliament, to overturn the '*hormones*' judgment and its progeny[13] was thrown out by the Court in the 'Beef Labelling Regulation' case.[14] On the very day in 1997 that Parliament was due to vote on a motion to censure the Commission for its handling of the BSE crisis, it was examining proposals for two of the measures designed to restore public confidence in beef in the shops, one on the identification and registration of bovine animals, and one on the labelling of beef and beef products. In adopting its opinion on the latter, Parliament had opted for Article [95 EC] as the legal basis, in preference to Article [37 EC]; though no such amendment had been adopted to the registration proposal, Parliament's rapporteur managed to convince the Commission to amend the legal basis of that proposal to Article [95 EC] too. Parliament adopted a 'suspended motion of censure', and the Commission duly amalgamated its proposals into a single proposal based on Article [95 EC], which the Council duly adopted on the basis of Article [37 EC].

The Commission, supported by Parliament, argued before the Court that the principal objective of the Regulation was the protection of human health, that 'the authors of the Treaty intended to impose the co-decision procedure for [public health] matters', and that the Treaty had evolved since the '*hormones*' case, particularly with the addition of specific provisions on Community action on human health protection and consumer protection. Pointing out its 'leading role' in the investigation of BSE and protecting the citizen from contaminated beef, Parliament added that 'the context in which the contested regulation was adopted, which is an objective factor, makes possible a better determination of the objective pursued by the legislature', and suggested a systematic interpretation of the Treaty, according to which the fact that the Treaty provisions on human health and consumer protection and the internal market all provided for the co-decision procedure 'must be construed as being the expression of the general will of the authors of the Treaty to make the Parliament ... participate in the adoption of acts which are of direct importance for the well-being of citizens', and that to hold against the Commission would 'run counter to the new direction of the Treaty'. In the alternative, both

---

[12] Case C–281/00, *Una Film*, and Case C–313/00, *Davidoff* (respectively, [2000] OJ C259/13 and C302/18).

[13] Case 68/86, *United Kingdom* v. *Council* [1988] ECR 855; of the progeny, see in particular Case C–180/96, *United Kingdom* v. *Council* [1998] ECR I–2265, paras. 120, 121, and 133.

[14] Case C–269/97, *Commission* v. *Council* [2000] ECR I–2257.

the Commission and Parliament trotted out *Titanium Dioxide* to argue that the Regulation should have been based on both Articles [37 EC] and [95 EC], as it simultaneously pursued two inseparable objectives.[15] For its part, the Council argued that the principal purpose of the Regulation was to stabilize beef markets; though it had taken account of the requirements of consumer confidence and the protection of human and animal health, the Council pointed out that the Regulation would guarantee consumers neither that beef on sale presented no health danger, nor that BSE would be eradicated. Somewhat gleefully, it drew the Court's attention to the political background to the Commission's change of heart on the legal basis question, and accused Parliament of using 'an argument based on political necessity rather than on the pre-eminence of law'.

In line with its standard practice, the Court recalled that the choice of legal basis 'must rest on objective factors which are amenable to judicial review' and in particular the aim and content of the measure. 'In this connection', the Court continued, 'the fact that an institution wishes to participate more fully in the adoption of a given measure, the work carried out in other respects in the sphere of action covered by the measure and the context in which the measure was adopted are irrelevant'. Reaffirming the continuing validity of its interpretation of the scope of Article [37 EC], the Court went on to examine the content and then the aim of the contested Regulation; the reversal of the usual order may reflect the fact that the parties all relied primarily on the 'principal purpose/objective' of the Regulation. The Court found that the Regulation concerned the production and marketing of agricultural products and that it is 'essentially intended to attain the objectives of Article [33 EC]'. The application was therefore dismissed.

Full-frontal challenges to well-established case law of the Court are relatively rare, and even more rarely successful, and it is thus difficult to make generalizations concerning the conditions under which they are likely to succeed.[16] One recurring feature, if hardly a necessary precondition, of such judgments is that they are preceded by one or more Advocate General's Opinions recommending a modification of the Court's position; the present case qualified under this criterion, as Advocate General Saggio had concluded in favour of the Commission, though, of course, this is no guarantee that the Court will budge.[17] In the present case, the Commission was unable to show that the previous judgments were in any sense mistaken, in that the Court had misjudged the legal context, or that its earlier position had given rise to undesirable consequences, as in '*Chernobyl*', *Keck and Mithouard*, or *HAG II*.[18] It relied instead on an evolution in the Treaty provisions, to argue that leaving

[15] Case C–300/89, *Commission* v. *Council* [1991] ECR I–2867.
[16] For a brief review of such cases, see paras. 141–146 of the Opinion of Fennelly AG in Joined Cases C–267/95 and C–268/95, *Merck* v. *Primecrown* [1996] ECR I–6285.
[17] See, e.g., Case C–91/92 *Faccini Dori* [1994] ECR I–3325, and *Merck, supra* n. 16.
[18] Respectively Case C–70/88, *Parliament* v. *Council* [1990] ECR I–2041, Joined Cases C–267/91, and C–268/91 *Keck and Mithouard* [1993] ECR I–6097, and Case C–10/89, *HAG GF* [1990] ECR I–3711.

the regulation of public health in respect of agricultural products to the consultation procedure rather than co-decision was an 'anomaly'.[19] It is not clear from the judgment whether the Commission or Parliament also relied expressly on the addition to Article [152 EC] of subparagraph 4(b), which applies the co-decision procedure for the adoption of 'measures in the veterinary and phytosantiary fields which have as their direct objective the protection of public health' since the entry into force of the Amsterdam Treaty; in any case, the Court firmly rejected any such reasoning, and showed little inclination to follow the 'Treaty evolution' line of argument.[20] The Court was, understandably, equally unsympathetic to the type of 'systematic interpretation' of the Treaty in the legal basis context suggested by Parliament, which it has consistently rejected right through from the 'Financial Transparency' case to 'Mauritania Fisheries Agreement'.[21]

(iii)   The 1998 Lawyers' Directive

Though it had occasionally contested decisions of Parliament before,[22] Luxembourg's challenge to the 1998 Lawyers' Directive was the first action it had ever commenced against the primary legislator.[23] The Grand Duchy's principal complaint was that the Directive allowed migrant lawyers to practise the law of the host Member State without prior training, thereby breaching Article [43 EC], both as regards the principle of non-discrimination it contains and the requirements of consumer protection. While the Court did not dispute Luxembourg's contentions that national law 'is not identical or even broadly the same from one Member State to another', or that the institutions must respect the general principle of equality, it was quick to point out that the respective situations of migrant and home-based lawyers are not comparable; the former are subject to a number of restrictions in accordance with the Directive while the latter 'may undertake all the activities open or reserved to the profession of lawyer by the host Member State'. Not only does the Directive contain a large number of consumer protection provisions, but it does not so much abolish the requirement that a lawyer know the national law of the host Member State, as Luxembourg contended, as dispense with the requirement to show advance proof of such knowledge, which can 'in some circumstances' be gradually assimilated through practice. Luxembourg's complaint that the legislator had bypassed the unanimity requirement of the second sentence of Article [47(2) EC] for directives whose implementation entails amendment of

[19]   Case C–269/97, *supra* n. 14, Opinion of Saggio AG , para. 20.

[20]   Oddly, the Court examined the evolution of the relevant Treaty provisions in Case C–209/97, *Commission* v. *Council* [1999] ECR I–8067.

[21]   Respectively Joined Cases 188–190/80, *France, Italy and United Kingdom* v. *Commission* [1982] ECR 2545, paras. 12–14, and Case C–189/97, *Parliament* v. *Council* [1997] ECR I–4741, para. 34 (and paras. 56–57 of the Opinion of Mischo AG).

[22]   Particularly regarding the question of its seat and working places; see, e.g., Joined Cases 213/88 and C–39/89, *Luxembourg* v. *Parliament* [1991] ECR I–5643.

[23]   Directive 98/5, [1998] OJ L77/36; Case C–168/98, *Luxembourg* v. *Parliament and Council* [2000] ECR I–9131.

'existing principles laid down by law', also received short shrift; the Court held simply that the contested provisions of the Directive fell within the scope of either Article [47(1) EC] or the first and third sentences of Article [47(2) EC]. The Court had equally little difficulty in demonstrating the sufficiency of the statement of reasons, which, as required by Article [253 EC], indicated both the general situation which led to the adoption of the Directive, and the general objectives it sought to achieve.

(iv) Proportionality of Commission Measures

The Commission suffered a rare out-and-out condemnation for breach of the principle of proportionality in *Wiedergeltingen*,[24] in which a dairy was one day late in submitting its report to the national authorities on the total quantity of milk delivered to it, and suffered a hefty penalty as a result. Though recognizing the importance of respecting the deadline, the Court held that 'observance of that deadline [was not] absolutely indispensable to [the] smooth operation' of the milk quota scheme, and that the rule was disproportionate in that it failed to allow for any account to be taken of the seriousness of the delay or its impact on the attainment of the objectives of that provision.

B.   COMITOLOGY

(i)   'Mixed' Procedures for the Adoption of Implementing Legislation

The most significant issues regarding the operation of the comitology system decided by the Court during the year were those of the duties of the Member State authorities in a 'mixed' procedure for the adoption of implementing decisions, such as obtains under Directive 90/220,[25] and the possibility for individuals to challenge a Community measure because of irregularities at the national level. Under this Directive, a request for authorization to market a genetically modified product must first be submitted to the competent authority of a Member State; this authority may grant the authorization, unless the authority of another Member State objects, in which case the matter is decided by the Commission, acting under a regulatory procedure type III(a). A negative opinion of the national authority, on the other hand, stops the procedure, though in theory the applicant could re-submit its request to the competent authority of another Member State.

The request at issue in *Greenpeace France*,[26] for the marketing of genetically-modified maize, had first been approved by the competent French authority, the Committee for the Study of the Release of Biomolecular Engineering; however, as the authorities of a number of other Member States had raised various objections, the matter was referred to the Commission which adopted a

---

[24] Case C–365/97, *Molkereigenossenschaft Wiedergeltingen eG* [2000] ECR I–5461.
[25] [1990] OJ L117/15.
[26] Case C–6/99, *Association Greenpeace France and Others* v. *Ministère de l'agriculture et de la pêche* [2000] ECR I–1651; see Mastromatteo (2000) 25 *ELRev.* 425.

decision granting the authorization requested in January 1997.[27] Though the Commission decision had been adopted in rather controversial circumstances,[28] it was the national implementation thereof which gave rise to the proceedings before the French Conseil d'Etat. Greenpeace had applied for the suspension or annulment of the relevant ministerial decree, notably on the ground that the original, favourable, opinion of the French authority, which had launched the procedure, had been based on an incomplete file. The Conseil d'Etat first suspended the application of the implementing decree, largely in application of the precautionary principle,[29] and then referred two questions to the Court of Justice, on whether the national authorities had any discretion not to authorize a product the Commission had authorized, and whether any irregularities such as those alleged by the applicants in the present case would affect the decision of the national authority.

As to the first, the Court emphasized that the authorization procedure provided for close co-operation between the Commission and the national authority considering the request, which must be satisfied regarding the safety of the product to be marketed from the point of view of the environment and human health. In its turn, the Court went out of its way to point out the various respects in which the precautionary principle informed the authorization system. In these circumstances, the Court held that the national authority was obliged to implement a Commission authorization decision unless it had information undermining its previous positive assessment, in which case it was obliged to inform the Commission and the other Member States. The Court answered the second question by acknowledging that irregularities at the national level could indeed affect the validity of the Commission measure: 'the decision of the competent authority is the prerequisite for the Community procedure and . . . may even determine its outcome'. Where such irregularities are brought to the attention of a national court, it is obliged under *Foto-Frost*[30] to refer the matter to the Court of Justice which alone can declare a Community act invalid.

(ii)   Absence of an Obligation to Conclude a Comitology Procedure

In *Bergaderm*[31] the Court applied to a regulatory committee type III(a) its ruling of the previous year before regarding a committee type III(b)[32] that the Commission is not obliged to submit a proposal to the Council where the committee's opinion is either not favourable or not forthcoming. As the Advocate General remarked, '[it] would be absurd if the fact that a particular type of

[27] Commission Decision 97/98/EC [1997] OJ L31/69.
[28] See Bradley, 'Alien Corn, or the Transegenic Procedural Maze' in Van Schendelen, *EU Committees as Influential Policymakers* (Aldershot, Ashgate, 1998).
[29] The suspension decision was widely heralded in France as a major victory for the environmental cause in general and this principle in particular.
[30] Case 314/85 [1987] ECR 4199.
[31] Case C–352/98 P, *Bergaderm v. Commission* [2000] ECR I–5291; the case is further considered below (section II.C(iv)).
[32] Case C–151/98 P, *Pharos v. Commission* [1999] ECR I–1937, para. 27.

measure can only be adopted by a prescribed procedure were held to imply that that procedure, once commenced, must be pursued to the end even if the party proposing the measure wishes to reconsider its appropriateness, or its chances of adoption, in the course of the procedure'.[33]

C. JURISDICTIONAL QUESTIONS

(i) Fining Member States for Non-compliance with Court Judgments

Almost seven years after such a possibility was introduced into the EC Treaty, the Court had to consider the weighty matter of imposing a fine on a Member State for its continued failure to comply with a judgment finding it to be in infringement of its Treaty obligations.[34] In 1992, Greece had been condemned for four separate infringements of the directives concerning the management of waste and toxic and dangerous waste in the Chania area, in each case for failing to apply the directives in practice and for failing to draw up the necessary plans and programmes.[35] In October 1993, the Commission had written to the Greek authorities to remind them of their duty to comply with that judgment, and setting a deadline by which they were to communicate the necessary measures to the Commission; Article [228 EC] proceedings were initiated only in September 1995.

As one might expect in the first judgment of its kind, the Court had to deal with a large number of issues regarding the interpretation of a rather laconic set of Treaty provisions:

—Admissibility
Greece maintained that the procedure, which had in its view been initiated by the letter of October 1993, could not be applied retroactively, i.e. before the Maastricht Treaty had entered into force, and that any fine imposed would contain retroactive elements. The Court simply noted that all the stages of the pre-litigation procedure, which had in fact been initiated in September 1995, post-dated the entry into force of the Maastricht Treaty, and that the relevance of past factors for assessing the fine was a matter to be dealt with in considering the merits of the action.

—The law in force
Conscious that Community law on environmental protection is in a state of constant flux, the Court examined, as a preliminary point and apparently of its own motion,[36] whether the obligations Greece had been found in 1992 to have failed to respect were still in force. Whether or not a defendant Member State could, as a matter of Community law, benefit from the

---

[33] *Ibid.* Opinion, para. 37.
[34] Case C–387/97, *Commission v. Greece* [2000] ECR I–5047 ('*Greece II*').
[35] Case C–45/91, *Commission v. Greece* [1992] ECR I–2509 ('*Greece I*').
[36] Following a suggestion to this effect by Ruiz-Jarabo Colomer AG, in his *Greece II* Opinion, *supra* n. 34, para. 48 ff.

principle of *la loi la plus douce*,[37] any relaxation of the previous obligations would, at the very least, be relevant for the calculation of the amount of any fine, while a periodic payment could no longer be imposed; Advocate General Ruiz-Jarabo Colomer opined that if the original obligations had ceased to exist, there would be no need to rule on the Article [228 EC] proceedings.[38] Here the Court found that the directives in force at the time of the original infringement had subsequently been tightened up in certain respects, and that the relevant provisions had been maintained.

—Establishment of the continuing breach of Community obligations
To establish the existence of the breach, the Court examined in turn the scope of the original obligations at issue in *Greece I*, and Greece's purported subsequent compliance with these; to this end, it admitted in evidence a scientific study jointly produced by the University of Crete and the Institute of Ecological Chemistry, Munich, which, though produced by Greece, was rather damning in its assessment of waste disposal conditions in Chania.[39] The Court nonetheless accepted Greece's argument that no toxic or dangerous waste had been dumped into the local river since 1996, and reminded the Commission of its duty in such proceedings to provide the Court with sufficient evidence to find an infringement. The remaining three complaints, regarding the absence of management plans and non-application of the general waste directive, and the absence of disposal plans for toxic and dangerous waste, were upheld.

—Fixing the penalty
In its memorandum of 21 August 1996 and communication of 28 February 1997,[40] the Commission set out criteria for evaluating the seriousness and duration of a Member State's non-compliance with a Court judgment. The amount of a fine is the product of a fixed sum (500 EUR), a seriousness factor on a scale from one to twenty, a duration factor on a scale from one to three, and a factor **n,** intended to take into account the ability to pay of each individual Member State, and varying from one (Luxembourg) to 26.4 (Germany). In this case, the Commission had proposed to the Court that it impose a daily payment of 24,600 EUR per day. Though it did not contest the method of calculation, Greece pleaded for a reduction in the relevant coefficients.

The Court began by ruling that compliance with judgments finding infringements 'must be initiated at once and completed as soon as possible'. It followed that the Commission could initiate Article [228 EC] proceedings

---

[37] For a recent illustration of the application of such a national rule in a Community context see Case C–319/97, *Kortas* [1999] ECR I–3143, para. 16; see also Case C–341/94, *Allain* [1996] ECR I–4631.

[38] Opinion, *supra* n. 34, para. 48.

[39] Examination of such scientific studies is a normal proceeding in litigation concerning Member State compliance with environmental legislation; for the Wild Birds Directive, e.g., see Case C–3/96, *Commission v. Netherlands* [1998] ECR I–3031, para. 70.

[40] Respectively [1996] OJ C242/6, and [1997] OJ C63/2.

from the expiry of the time-limit it had fixed in its reasoned opinion. The Court approved as being 'transparent, foreseeable and consistent with legal certainty' the Commission's publication of its criteria for calculation, and the inclusion of a factor reflecting the Member State's ability to pay. However, though a 'useful point of reference' the Commission's proposal for a penalty could not bind the Court in any way, nor should the Court treat the proposal as a decision subject to review only for manifest error, a misuse of powers or a breach of the Commission's margin of appreciation, as Advocate General Ruiz-Jarabo Colomer had recommended.[41] In this regard, the Court's reasoning is closer to that proposed by Advocate General Fennelly in his Opinion of 9 December 1999 in other Article [228 EC] proceedings, also against Greece, which were subsequently withdrawn.[42]

The Court noted that 'since the principal aim of penalty payments is that the Member State should remedy the breach of obligations as soon as possible, a penalty payment must be set that will be appropriate to the circumstances and proportionate both to the breach which has been found and the ability to pay of the Member State concerned'. In assessing the amount, the Court added that 'regard should be had in particular to the effects of the failure to comply on private and public interests and to the urgency of getting the Member State concerned to fulfil its obligations'. The failure to ensure safe waste disposal was 'particularly serious', in that it could endanger human health and harm the environment. Equally, the failure to draw up waste disposal plans in each case was deemed serious, and was in no way excused by the adoption of specific measures to reduce the quantities of toxic waste. The duration of the infringements was considerable, even taking as the starting point the date on which the Maastricht Treaty came into force, rather than the date of the first infringement judgment. The Court thus imposed a penalty payment of EUR 20,000 per day from the date of delivery of its judgment until compliance has been effected.

(ii) The Role and Functions of the Advocate General

The status of the Advocate General and his or her role in the functioning of the Court were examined, for the first time in Community legal history,[43] in the Order in *Emesa Sugar*, a far cry from the days when the Court did not deign to acknowledge the existence of this judicial officer in its judgments.[44] Following the delivery of the Opinion in this case, Emesa had applied to submit written observations, relying on the case law of the European Court of Human Rights ('ECtHR'), and in particular on the judgment in *Vermeulen* v. *Belgium*.[45] In that

---

[41] Opinion, *supra* n. 34, paras. 86–95.

[42] Case C–197/98, *Commission* v. *Greece*, removed from the register by Order of the President of the Court of 6 Oct. 2000; exceptionally, the AG's Opinion was published: [2000] ECR I–8609.

[43] This was not, however, the first occasion on which a party had sought to submit comments on the AG's opinion; see e.g., Case C–8/96, *Locamion* [1997] ECR I–7055, paras. 17 and 18.

[44] Order of 4 Feb. 2000 in Case C–17/98, *Emesa Sugar (Free Zone) NV* v. *Aruba* [2000] ECR I–665, reviewed critically by Lawson (2000) 37 *CMLRev.* 983.

[45] Reports of Judgments and Decisions, 1996 I, p. 224.

case, the ECtHR had found that the absence of any procedural possibility for a party to comment on the opinion of the Procureur Général, 'an independent member of the national legal service' (or '*magistrat indépendant*' in the orginal French of the ECtHR judgment) constituted a breach of the right to a fair trial guaranteed by Article 6(1) of the European Convention on Human Rights (ECHR).

The Court took the opportunity to recall the express recognition in Article 6(2) of the Treaty on European Union, as amended the previous year by the Amsterdam Treaty, of its jurisdiction to ensure respect for fundamental rights in the Community legal order. It noted that Advocates General have the same status as judges as regards their qualifications for office, procedure for appointment, and judicial immunity, and, in contrast to putatively equivalent officers in certain national legal systems, are neither 'subject to any authority' nor 'entrusted with the defence of any particular interest in the exercise of their duties'. The Court therefore held that the Advocate General's opinion 'does not form part of the proceedings between the parties, but instead opens the stage of deliberation of the Court'; rather than being the opinion of an out-side authority, it is 'the individual reasoned opinion, expressed in open court, of a Member of the Court of Justice itself'. The Court continued:

[the] Advocate General thus takes part, publicly and individually, in the process by which the Court reaches its judgment, and therefore in carrying out the judicial function entrusted to it.

Though it was not strictly necessary, the Court went on to point out that any such right of reply would cause serious practical difficulties, adding that it could in any case reopen the oral procedure of its own motion, particurly 'if it considers . . . that the case must be dealt with on the basis of an argument which has not been debated between the parties'. This latter, somewhat lim-ited, procedural option would at best provide rather cold comfort to parties disappointed by the Opinion, as the conditions for its application have been defined very narrowly in the case law.[46] Moreover, should the procedure be re-opened, the Advocate General would once again deliver an Opinion on which the parties once again would not be able to comment.

(iii)   Contentious Proceedings between Member States

The finely balanced dispute in *Belgium* v. *Spain* constitutes only the second infringement proceedings initiated by a Member State in accordance with Article [227 EC] in the Community's history to come to judgment.[47] In effect, Belgium was seeking to enforce the preliminary ruling in *Delhaize* v. *Promalvin*,[48] which provided some grounds for considering that the Spanish provisions prohibiting the export of Rioja wine in bulk infringed Article [29 EC]; though supported by four other wine-importing Member States, two other wine-exporting Member States, Italy and Portugal, lined up behind

---

[46] See, e.g., the *Polypropylene* appeals in 1999 (noted in Bradley, (2000) 19 *YEL* 547, 565–7).
[47] Case C–388/95 [2000] ECR I–3123.   [48] Case C–47/90 [1992] ECR I–3669.

Spain, as did the Commission. In the result, the Court took account of 'new information' not available at the time of the earlier judgment, which went to justify the Spanish requirement that Rioja be bottled at the place of production, including the general tendency of Community legislation to enhance the quality of agricultural products, and the necessity to protect the reputation of the product in the minds of the consumer. In an almost lyrical vein, the Court observed that 'quality wine is a very specific product . . . [its] particular qualities and characteristics, which result from a combination of natural and human factors, are linked to its geographical area of origin and vigilance must be exercised and efforts made in order for them to be maintained'. To the doubters who argued that the complex oenological operations which precede bottling, such as filtering, clarifying, and cooling, can be carried out just as well in the importing Member State, the Court replied that 'the best conditions are more certain to be assured if bottling is done by undertakings established in the region of those entitled to use the designation' because of their 'specialized experience' and 'thorough knowledge of the specific characteristics of the wine'. The action was thus dismissed.

(iv)   Strict Respect for Deadlines and Excusable Error

The wisdom of the Court's strict line on respect for imperative time-limits was illustrated by its order in *Austria* v. *Commission*.[49] A Commission state aid decision was delivered to the Austrian permanent representation on 23 February 1999; doubtless through inadvertence, the date of reception was recorded, by hand rather than by date-stamp, as 24 February, and the deadline for submitting the application for annulment duly calculated in accordance with the later date. In reply to the Commission's plea that the application was out of time, Austria sought to rely on the unforeseen circumstance that its carefully-selected personnel had, exceptionally and in breach of the relevant regulations, incorrectly noted the date of reception. After helpfully clarifying the circumstances in which such a plea may succeed, the Court rejected it, essentially on the ground that the error was the responsibility of the staff of the Austrian permanent representation. Austria's reliance on excusable error and equity was no more successful; the Court noted that the authorities in Vienna had failed to ascertain why the date had been added, irregularly, by hand, and recalled that it had no leeway in applying deadlines in the name of any novel principle of equity. No doubt the Court bore in mind that an unscrupulous party might, in similar circumstances, seek to cover up its tardiness by amending *ex post facto* the date from which the deadline to act started to run.

(v)   Liability under Community Law

In *Bergaderm*,[50] the Court of Justice finally made good on the promise it had made four years previously in *Brasserie du Pêcheur*[51] to align the conditions

---

[49] Case C–165/99, Order of 26 Oct. 1999, not reported.
[50] Case C–352/98 P, *Bergaderm* v. *Commission* [2000] ECR I–5291.
[51] Joined Cases C–46/93 and C–48/93 P, *Brasserie du Pêcheur and Factortame* [1996] ECR I–1029.

for Community liability with those which obtain for Member State liability for damage arising from a failure properly to apply Community law. In defining the latter in *Brasserie*, the Court had noted that these 'cannot, in the absence of particular justification, differ from those governing the liability of the Community in like circumstances', adding more generally that the protection of individual rights 'cannot vary depending on whether a national authority is responsible for the damage'.[52] It also justified its rather restrictive approach to compensation in respect of national legislative measures on the basis of that already developed for Community liability in equivalent circumstances.

The Court of First Instance in *Bergaderm* had applied the standard *Schöppenstedt* test of a breach of a superior rule of law for the protection of individuals.[53] The Court of Justice first established that the *Brasserie* test—a 'sufficiently serious' breach of a rule of law intended to confer rights on individuals, and a 'direct causal link between the breach and the damage'—was applicable in the context of Community liability, before simply interpreting the relevant appeal ground as concerning the infringement of 'a rule of law intended to confer rights on individuals'. It also held that, in determining the extent of any discretion enjoyed by the defendant institution, 'the general or individual nature of a measure . . . is not a decisive criterion'. Though it displayed its usual coyness regarding the modification of a rule which had stood undisturbed for the last thirty years, the fact that the Court was sitting in plenary formation to hear a somewhat pedestrian appeal might be taken as indicating that a significant change in the law was intended.

Community liability was also at issue in *Fresh Marine* in somewhat unusual circumstances.[54] Following what it assumed was a breach by the applicant Norwegian company of an undertaking not to undercut Community salmon prices, the Commission adopted regulations imposing anti-dumping and countervailing duties on the company's imports just in time to ruin its chances of selling on the lucrative Christmas market. It transpired, however, that the Commission had in effect unilaterally amended the report concerning the company's exports to the Community during the reference period on the basis of which it had decided to adopt the punitive regulations. While the Commission maintained that the applicant was relying on damage caused by legislative measures, and was therefore required to show a sufficiently serious breach of a higher-ranking rule of law, the Court held that the damage had in fact arisen from the unlawful interpretation of the company's report, which had merely been applied in the adoption of the regulations, and so upheld the claim in damages.

The principal issues in the appeal in *Dorsch Consult*[55] were those of the reality of the alleged damage and the existence of a causal link between this and

---

[52] Joined Cases C–46/93 and C–48/93 P, *Brasserie du Pêcheur and Factortame* [1996] ECR I–1029/4893 P, *supra* n. 51, para. 42.
[53] Case 5/71, *Schöppenstedt* v. *Council* [1971] ECR 975, para. 11.
[54] Case T–178/98, *Fresh Marine Company AS* v. *Commission* [2000] ECR II–3331.
[55] Case C–237/98 P, *Dorsch Consult* v. *Council and Commission* [2000] ECR I–4549.

the conduct of the Community institutions. In August 1990, the Council had adopted a regulation to implement the trade embargo imposed by the United Nations Security Council on Iraq following its invasion of Kuwait; Iraq riposted by freezing the assets and holdings of governments and companies of states which had adopted 'arbitrary decisions' against Iraq. The appellant had claimed unsuccessfully before the CFI that it had suffered financial loss through the non-payment of debts outstanding in its favour against the Iraqi government, relying on liability both for lawful acts, in that its property rights had effectively been expropriated, and for unlawful acts, in that the Council had failed to provide for compensation.

The Court of Justice started by noting that for Community liability 'it is necessary to prove that the alleged damage is real and that a causal link exists between that act and the alleged damage'. It recalled that the burden of proof of damage falls on the applicant, and held that 'the existence of actual and certain damage cannot be considered in the abstract by the Community judicature but must be assessed in relation to the specific facts characterising each particular case in point', and that the appellant had failed to discharge that burden of proof. As the remaining grounds of appeal concerning the reality of the damage, alleging mainly that the lower court had assessed the evidence incorrectly, were also dismissed, the Court did not examine the pleas regarding the causal link, the existence of special and unusual damage, or the possibility of claiming compensation in respect of damage caused by a lawful act.

On the same day as *Bergaderm*, the Court clarified certain aspects of Member State liability in *Haim II*.[56] In *Haim I*, the Court had ruled that the German authorities had acted wrongly by refusing, in 1988, to take into account the applicant's practical experience in rejecting his request for registration as a dentist in a social security scheme.[57] In the present case, the applicant was suing for the loss of earnings during the period between the contested decision and his eventual registration.

The first issue was whether an independent public-law body, as well as the Member State, could be held liable in such circumstances. Recalling its ruling in *Konle*[58] that 'it is for each Member State to ensure that individuals obtain reparation for loss and damage caused to them by non-compliance with Community law', the Court went on to hold that it was not necessary that the State itself be liable, and that Community law did not oppose liability being imposed on either 'territorial bodies with a certain degree of autonomy or . . . any other public-law body legally distinct from the State'. Regarding the discretion enjoyed by the authority responsible, which is central to the characterization of the breach as 'sufficiently serious', the Court held that '[its] existence and scope are determined by reference to Community law and not by reference to national law' and that, in the absence of any such discretion, 'a mere infringement of Community law by a Member State may, but does not

56 Case C–424/97, *Haim* v. *KVN* [2000] ECR I–5123.
57 Case C–319/92, *Haim* [1994] ECR I–425.
58 Case C–302/97, *Konle* v. *Austria* [1999] ECR I–3099.

necessarily, constitute a sufficiently serious breach'. While repeating its almost consistent[59] position that it is for the national courts to apply the rules regarding Community liability to a given set of facts, the Court noted that when the defendant association had refused to register the applicant, the decision in *Vlassopoulou*, which established for the first time the necessity to take account of such experience, had not yet been handed down.[60]

(vi)   Suspension of a Contested Directive

Just three weeks before the deadline for transposing the Directive on the patent protection of biotechnological inventions into national law, the Netherlands, which had already taken annulment proceedings, requested the suspension of the application of the Directive.[61] It also requested the suspension of the Directive until the defendant institutions had presented their observations; this proved to be a pointless tactic as Parliament and the Council submitted these within a week and a half. While the Order sets out the main arguments of the parties on the merits and on the request for an interim suspension, the application turned in the end on the urgency of such a measure. The President noted that the fundamental character of the applicant's ethical objectives did not go to the question of urgency. As regards legal uncertainty, the President pointed out that 'some forms of legal uncertainty are inherent in any legal challenge to the validity of an act', and that the suspension would cause a similar degree of legal uncertainty in the other Member States, especially those which had already transposed the Directive. No irreparable damage had been shown and, indeed, the President underlined that the Dutch authorities were themselves able to deal with the various problems raised. Nor could the applicant Member State rely on its own delay in complying with its Community obligations to demonstrate the existence of serious and irreparable damage. In the absence of proven urgency, the application was refused.

(vii)   Compliance by Institutions with Court Judgments

The obligations which arise for an institution under Article 233 EC to comply with judgments of the Community judicature, *in casu* a ruling of the Court of First Instance (CFI) which had been appealed, were once again under the spotlight during the year. In *Hautem* v. *European Investment Bank*, the Bank had taken the view that it would be 'at the very least premature, if not contrary to the proper adminsitration of justice' to comply with a 1999 judgment of the CFI upholding a complaint by the applicant against a decision removing him

---

[59] In the absence of particular justification, Case C–392/93 *British Telecom* stands out as an apparent anomaly: [1996] ECR I–1631, para. 41.

[60] Case C–340/89, *Vlassopoulou* [1991] ECR I–2357; the Court also acknowledged that it had applied the principle in this judgment when deciding *Haim I*.

[61] Case C–377/98 R, *Netherlands* v. *Parliament and Council* [2000] ECR I–6229; the application was made on 6 July, the written procedure was finished on 17 July, the oral hearing was held on 18 July, and the Order handed down on 25 July.

from his post, and ordering the Bank to pay him arrears of salary.[62] The CFI noted that the Bank had not applied for a suspension of the earlier judgment, as no such suspension would have been granted in the absence of irreparable damage, and that it had no intention to comply with the judgment until the appeal had been decided.[63] Describing the Bank's conduct as a '*de facto* stay of execution', the CFI noted that only the Court of Justice could adopt interim measures in such circumstances: 'that is a prerogative which the EIB cannot arrogate to itself'. The fact that a reasonable period for compliance had not yet expired was nullified by the Bank's stated refusal to comply, nor could it rely on any alleged uncertainty regarding the legal status of its employees, on which the CFI had ruled, following the judgment in *Mills* v. *EIB* of the Court of Justice.[64] Unsurprisingly in the circumstances. The CFI went on to hold that the Bank's refusal to comply with the earlier judgment was 'unlawful conduct capable of rendering the Community liable'; as this conduct would 'adversely affect the confidence that litigants must have in the Community judicial system' and had 'placed the applicant in a prolonged state of uncertainty and anxiety' regarding his employment position, the Bank was ordered to pay the relatively modest figure of EUR 25,000 by way of non-material damage.

The Court of Auditors may find it rather more difficult to comply with the judgment in *Busacca and Others*[65] than the Bank in *Hautem*. As in *Chvatal and Others* and *Losch* v. *Court of Justice*,[66] the applicants had applied to their institution to be included on a list of those requesting to be considered for early retirement following the 1995 accessions. As the termination-of-service scheme had been limited by the relevant Council regulation to officials of the European Parliament, the requests had in each case been refused; however, the refusal was in turn annulled by the CFI as the regulation discriminated arbitrarily between objectively similar situations, and because the Council had failed to reconsult either Parliament or the Staff Regulations committee before adopting the contested regulation. The Council, which had intervened in *Chvatal* but not in *Busacca and Others*, appealed against both sets of judgments.

The Court of Justice upheld the appeal in *Chvatal*, on the ground that termination-of-service measures 'do not have their legal origin in the Staff Regulations and therefore do not constitute a standard event in the careers of the persons concerned'.[67] It followed that the institution could not grant such termination of service in the absence of a proper legal basis, which could only

---

[62] Case T–11/00 [2000] ECR-SC II–1295; the previous case was Case T–140/97 *Hautem* v. *EIB* [1999] ECR-SC I–A–171 and II–897.

[63] Art. 53 of the EC Statute of the Court provides that appeals shall not have suspensive effect.

[64] Case 110/75 [1976] ECR 955; this establishes beyond reasonable doubt that the Bank's relations with its staff are contractual (para. 22).

[65] Case T–164/97, *Busacca and Others* v. *Court of Auditors* [1998] ECR-SC I–A–565 and II–1699.

[66] Cases T–154/96 [1998] ECR-SC I–A–527 and II–1579, and T–13/97 [1998] ECR-SC I–A–543, and II–1633, hereinafter for convenience '*Chvatal*'; see Bradley, (2000) 18 *YEL* 477.

[67] Joined Cases C–432/98 P and C–433/98 P, *Council* v. *Chvatal and Others and Losch* [2000] ECR I–8535, judgment of 5 Oct. 2000, not yet reported in ECR.

have been provided by the contested regulation: 'even if that regulation were unlawful . . . that circumstance could not have the effect of providing a legal basis for the requests of the officials' excluded from the scheme. The Court annulled the CFI judgements in these cases and dismissed the officials' complaints.

The situation was quite other in *Busacca and Others*,[68] where Article 49 of the EC Statute constituted a formidable obstacle to the admissibility of the Council's appeal; this provides that in staff disputes institutions may appeal only CFI judgments to which they were not party where they had intervened at first instance, as the Council had in *Chvatal*. The Council argued that the restriction on the institutions' right to appeal in staff cases was limited to those concerning individual decisions, and that legal clarity would suffer if its appeal succeeded in *Chvatal* but failed in the present case.

The Court would have none of it. As regards the first, it held that '[the] nature of a dispute . . . must be assessed in the light of the subject-matter of the action', not the pleas relied on; the success of the officials' complaints can in any case lead only to the annulment of a series of individual decisions. As regards the second, the Court merely noted that the inapplicability of a regulation in accordance with Article [241 EC] 'is binding only between the parties to those proceedings'.

The cases illustrate vividly the strict line the Court applies on the admissibility of appeals, both *ratione personae* and *ratione materiae*.[69] Moreover, in *Chvatal*, the Court rejected the converse argument to that of the Council in *Busacca*, where the respondents had argued that admitting the appeal 'would be tantamount to allowing [the Council] to call into question the binding authority of the judgment in *Busacca*'. The Court found that the conditions for the admissibility of an appeal 'are assessed in relation to the case at issue and that alone'. It also refused in the same judgment to examine the Council's plea, most vehemently urged at first instance,[70] that the failure to reconsult the Staff Regulations committee did not amount to an infringement of an essential procedural requirement, on the ground that the CFI had acted erroneously in ruling on this matter in the first place. Finally, one can only wonder why the Court of Auditors did not itself lodge an appeal, or why the Council intervened in only two of the three relevant actions before the CFI; the *Busacca* judgment at first instance, though substantively discredited, is law and must now be complied with. One awaits with interest the next stage of the saga.[71]

---

[68] Case C–434/98 P, *Council* v. *Busacca and Others* [2000] ECHR I–8577, judgment of 5 Oct. 2000, not yet reported in ECR.

[69] See, e.g., the order in *ADT Projekt* [1999] ECR I–6467 (noted in Bradley, (2000) 19 *YEL* 547, 564).

[70] Bradley, *supra* n. 65, at 490.

[71] Before the appeal had been decided, Chvatal and other had initiated proceedings contesting the failure of the administration of the ECJ to comply with the CFI judgment in their case: Case T–115/00 [2000] OJ C211/22.

(viii) Preliminary Rulings

The interpretation and application of the notion of 'court or tribunal' for the purposes of Article [234 EC] continued to divide the Court and its Advocates General during the year.[72] In *Gabalfrisa and Others*, the Court examined of its own motion the question whether a Spanish Tribunal Económico-Administrativo ('TEA') could be so considered, before concluding that such a body satisfied the five standard criteria: permanence, compulsory jurisdiction, *inter partes* procedure, operation under the rule of law, and independence.[73] It thus declined to follow Advocate General Saggio who had strongly argued that the TEA is neither sufficiently independent of the adminstration, of which it is a part, albeit organizationally separate, nor are its proceedings *inter partes*; he considered its proceedings typical of an administrative appeal to challenge an act, rather than a judicial form of action. The Court held that the *inter partes* requirement was not absolute, and in any case was here satisfied, and that the legal separation of the TEAs from the operational departments of the tax authority ensured them 'the character of a third party in relation to the departments which adopted the decision forming the subject-matter of the complaint and the independence necessary for them to be regarded as courts or tribunals'.

The Court was similarly open to the suggestion in *Abrahamsson and Anderson* that the Swedish Appeal Committee for Institutes of Higher Education was competent to make preliminary references under this provision.[74] Advocate General Saggio was unconvinced that the independence of Committee members was sufficiently protected by the legal provisions governing their dismissal, notwithstanding any indications to the contrary in *Köllensperger*;[75] in his view, a general duty of non-interference was insufficient to guarantee the absolute independence of the Committee which required clear provisions in the primary interest of the litigants themselves. The Court held that the Swedish Constitution guaranteed the Committee 'a status separate from the authorities which adopted the decisions under appeal and the necessary independence'.[76]

On one occasion, the Court had to deal with an undated 'application in the interests of the law', referred by the Court of Appeal, Paris.[77] The Court of Justice noted that though the form of the reference was unusual, it had no

---

[72] For earlier examples see Case C–54/96, *Dorsch Consult* [1997] ECR I–4961, and the Opinion of Tesauro AG, and Case C–134/97, *Victoria Film* [1998] ECR I–7023, and the Opinion of Fennelly AG, in this case.

[73] Joined Cases C–110/98 to C–147/98 [2000] ECR I–1577.

[74] Case C–407/98, *Abrahamsson and Anderson* v. *Forelqvist* [2000] ECR I–5539

[75] Case C–130/97 [1999] ECR I–551; in this judgment the Court also declined Saggio AG's recommendation to declare the reference inadmissible.

[76] See also Case C–195/98, *Österreichisher Gewerkschaftsbund* [2000] ECR I–10497, where the Austrian Oberster Gerichtshof itself asked whether in the particular national proceedings it qualified to submit a request under Art. 234 EC; both Jacobs AG and the Court replied in the affirmative.

[77] Case C–116/00, *Laguillaumie* [2000] ECR I–4979.

competence to verify whether the order for reference had been adopted in accordance with the applicable national rules. The request for a preliminary ruling was then ruled inadmissible on *Telemarsicabruzzo* grounds,[78] and in particular the referring court's failure to provide any information on the factual background to its request or on the reasons for the choice of provisions of Community law whose interpretation was at issue.

In *Schlebusch*, the Court refused to 'amend' a reference by a national supreme court to a provision of Community law which clearly did not apply in the circumstances of the case.[79] The Court held that the referring court, 'which could not be unaware of the date of the contested decision' had made its reference 'with full knowledge of the facts' and that 'it is not for the Court of Justice but the national court to ascertain the facts which have given rise to the dispute and to establish the consequences which they have for the judgment which it is required to deliver'. By happy coincidence, the provision referred to was identical to that which applied in the present case, and the Court was therefore able to provide the ruling requested.

D. PROCEEDINGS IN THE INSTITUTIONS

(i)   Application of the OLAF Agreement in Parliament

Shunned at its inception by the Court of Auditors, the Community's high priests of fiscal rectitude, the interinstitutional agreement on internal investigations by OLAF,[80] the anti-fraud office, continued to prove controversial in its application. In November 1999, Parliament adopted a decision modifying its rules of procedure with a view to requiring members to co-operate fully with OLAF, and obliging them to report any matter giving rise to a suspicion of fraud, corruption, or illegality either to the President of Parliament or to OLAF directly. Seventy-one MEPs, led by Mr Willi Rothley,[81] not only instituted proceedings for the annulment of the decision, but also requested an interim injunction to prevent its application, principally on the ground that it would undermine their independence and affect the free exercise of their political mandate.[82]

The interim procedure[83] was marked by a slightly surreal exchange between the President of the Court of First Instance and Parliament's highest political authorities, following a proposal at the oral hearing by the former for a friendly settlement, whereby Parliament would undertake not to permit any search of a member's office in his or her absence or without his or her consent. Understandably in the circumstances, Parliament's agents sought instructions

[78] Joined Cases C–320 to 322/90 [1993] ECR I–393.
[79] Case C–273/98 [2000] ECR I–3889.
[80] [1999] OJ L136/15; the agreement was not signed by either the Court of Auditors or the ECJ.
[81] No stranger to legal and political controversy, Mr Rothley served for many years as rapporteur on the proposal for a directive on the patent protection of biotechnological inventions, and is currently rapporteur on the statute of MEPs.
[82] Case T–17/00 *Rothley and Others* v. *Parliament*, pending.
[83] Case T–17/00 R [2000] ECR II–2085.

from the President of Parliament, who is ultimately responsible within the institution for the conduct of litigation; in a letter to the Court some days later, she simply 'confirmed the positions adopted by the agents in the course of this procedure'. With what could be construed as barely disguised exasperation, the President of the Court requested Parliament to indicate clearly whether or not it would warn members of any proposal to search their offices by OLAF; this elicited the response, this time from Parliament's Conference of Presidents,[84] that no new answer was necessary, as the President's previous letter had been clear. No friendly settlement was forthcoming.

The applicants' request still had to surmount the hurdles of manifest inadmissibility, a *prima facie* appreciation of its possible merits, and the requirement of urgency. Recalling that decisions which only concern Parliament's internal organization are immune from judicial review, the President held that, in requiring members to co-operate with OLAF and inform the Office of suspected irregularities, the contested decision had legal effects with respect to members which did not concern the exercise of their parliamentary mandate or ancillary political activities. In particular, the President was concerned that OLAF enquiries could undermine the parliamentary immunity accorded members by the 1965 Protocol on privileges and immunities of the EC. On this basis, the President concluded that direct and individual concern could not be excluded, as Parliament might be obliged to take account of the particular situation of members and the specific interest that they be able to carry out their activities completely independently. He also referred to the 'complete system of judicial protection' to which the Treaty aspires according to *Les Verts et al.*,[85] as though hinting at the possible need to take an expansive interpretation of Article 230 EC. The possible breach by Parliament of the same Protocol was taken as establishing a *prima facie* case on the merits. Parliament's contention that OLAF agents would not in any case be able to enter members' offices in their absence or without their consent was contradicted by the Director of OLAF, who had been invited to the oral hearing. The President had little trouble in finding that the application of the decision would cause serious and irreparable harm and that the urgency of the interim injunction was justified.

The proceedings are noteworthy in a number of respects. In the first place, seventy-one members, led by a veteran German Socialist, is a substantial minority in both numerical and political terms, whereas almost all the previous 'political' actions against Parliament before the Community judicature have been initiated either by minority political groups—the French ecology party in the early 1980s, and since then the French *Front National*—or

---

[84] Comprising the President and the chairmen of the political groups (Art. 23, Parliament's rules of procedure).

[85] Case 294/83, *Les Verts* v. *Parliament* [1986] ECR 1339; Case 314/85, *Foto-Frost* [1987] ECR 4199; and Case C–2/88 Imm. *Zwartveld and Others* [1990] ECR I–3365; his remarks stand in marked contrast to the views of his colleagues in *Salamander and Others, supra* n. 10.

individual members seeking vindication of their financial rights.[86] The subtext of the *Rothley* proceedings is, however, the protection of parliamentary minorities, and indeed individual members, in general from politically-motivated investigations, or even the fear of political witchhunts, such as are alleged to have occurred in some Member States. They also reflect both the erosion of the politics of the consensus which had normally characterized decisions concerning Parliament's functioning up to recent times, and the increasing juridification of political relations in the Community. One novel feature was the intervention, in what might otherwise be considered an internal dispute, of the Commission and, even more surprising, the Council, in support of Parliament, though their combined authority did not make any difference in this instance.

(ii)   Justiciability of an Alleged Failure to Act by the Ombudsman

Apart from being the first legal proceedings against the European Ombudsman, the case of *Associazione delle cantine sociali venete* is of more general interest.[87] Following the refusal by the Commission to give them access to a number of documents, the applicants, an association of Italian wine producers and co-operatives, submitted a complaint to the Ombudsman in June 1997; in December 1998, the applicants called upon the Ombudsman to take a position on the complaint, in accordance with Article [232 EC]. Failing a reply, they initiated Article [232 EC] proceedings against both the Ombudsman and Parliament on 27 April 1999; four days later, the Ombudsman notified the applicants of the results of his inquiry into the complaint. While the Ombudsman was content to request the CFI to hold that there was no need to give judgment, Parliament argued that the proceedings were manifestly inadmissible, on the grounds that, as the Ombudsman was neither an institution nor part of an institution, no Article [232 EC] proceedings were available against him, that the measures he adopts have no legal effect, and their non-adoption cannot constitute a failure to act, that the applicants had not invited Parliament to act, and that in any case Parliament had manifestly no power to intervene in a dispute between the applicants and the Commission. While submitting themselves to the wisdom of the court on the matter of whether it should come to judgment or not, the applicants vigorously contested Parliament's view on the admissibility of their action, largely on the ground that the Ombudsman was Parliament's creature, but also relying on the reference in the Commission's access to documents rules to a complaint to the Ombudsman as a 'means of recourse' to challenge a refusal of access to documents.

---

[86] For a slightly surprising example of the latter, see Joined Cases T–83/99 to T–85/99, *Ripa di Meana and Others* v. *Parliament* [2000] ECR II–3493.

[87] Order of 22 May 2000 in Case T–103/99, *Associazione delle cantine sociali venete* v. *European Ombudsman and Parliament*, not published in ECR; given that this is the first proceeding against the Ombudsman to be decided by the Community judicature, one might have thought that the decision merited publication.

Though clearly unable to come to judgment on an action which was so fundamentally flawed, not to say warped, from most possible procedural angles, the CFI did not take the line of least resistance and simply rule that there was no need to do so. Instead it held that, in order to rule on whether it should come to judgment, and to decide on the costs, it had first to rule on the admissibility of the action. Without any particular difficulty, the CFI held this to be inadmissible, as the Ombudsman was not an institution; for good measure, it went on to find that, even if he were considered an organ of Parliament (a question it left open), the Ombudsman's report on a complaint could not be the subject of Article [232 EC] proceedings, notwithstanding the description of such a complaint as a means of recourse.

In so holding, the CFI corrected, in principle if not in fact, a substantive injustice committed against Parliament in similarly perverse legal proceedings in 1993.[88] By ruling that it did not need to come to judgment in, rather than declaring manifestly inadmissible, the action for failure to act initiated by the *Liberal Democrats*, the Court of Justice implicitly accepted that Parliament had failed to comply with its legal obligations until after the action had been commenced, which was, after all, the main issue in contention between the parties. The reasoning followed by the CFI here, that admissibility precedes a finding that there is no need to decide, is clearly correct; before the Court can decide whether it need come to judgment on an action, it must have an admissible action on which to decide. That the CFI was aware of the issue of principle involved is demonstrated by the fact that it did not even need to make such a ruling in order to decide on costs; Parliament had omitted to ask for costs against the applicants.

(iii) 'Internal Guidelines' and Member States' Rights

In *Spain* v. *Commission* [89] the Court upheld, albeit indirectly, the Commission's prerogatives in the implementation of the Community budget. Spain, supported by Italy and Portugal, all major beneficiaries of the structural funds, had attacked the Commission's 1997 internal guidelines for the application of financial controls to the operation of the relevant funds, on the ground that there was no legal basis for the measure. The Court, however, sided with the Commission's view that the guidelines did not affect the legal situation of the Member States: 'in principle, internal guidelines have effects only within the administration itself and give rise to no rights or obligations for third parties'. There was nothing in the Treaty to prevent the Commission adopting guidelines for its own departments for the purpose of exercising the powers it had been granted under the legislation applicable; indeed, they assisted the Commission in ensuring equal treatment of the Member States and transparency in the decision-making process. The fact that the Member States were consulted at various levels before the guidelines were adopted was a reflection

---

[88] Case C–41/92, *The Liberal Democrats* v. *Parliament* [1993] ECR I–3153; see Bradley, in Bradley and Feeney, (1994) 13 *YEL* 384, 391–3.
[89] Case C–443/97 [2000] ECR I–2451.

of the partnership principle underlying the financial management of the funds. As they only indicated the intention of the Commission to follow a particular line of conduct, the guidelines did not produce legal effects, and the annulment action was dismissed as inadmissible.

(iv) Authentication of Commission Decisions—Over and Out

The last act of the 'authentication saga' was played out during the year when the Court rejected the Commission's appeals in *ICI* and *Solvay* ('Soda ash').[90] Whereas the appellants in the 'Polypropylene' cases had sought to raise the non-existence of the Commission decisions just days before the CFI was due to give judgment, in 'Soda ash' the applicants had been able to raise this issue before the oral procedure in their annulment proceedings before the CFI, which prompted the Court to investigate the matter of its own motion after awaiting the outcome of the appeal in *BASF and Others* (Soda Ash).[91] In the Soda Ash appeal, the Commission argued that the CFI had erred in admitting the new plea by the respondents, had misinterpreted the purpose of authentication, and had incorrectly failed to consider whether the alleged defect relied on affected the interests of the addressee of the contested decision.

In a brief judgment, largely following the approach proposed by Advocate General Fennelly, the Court held that it was the Commission which had misinterpreted *BASF*: 'it is the mere failure to authenticate an act which constitutes the infringement of an essential procedural requirement and it is not necessary also to establish that the act is vitiated by some other defect or that the lack of authentication resulted in harm to the person relying on it'. Furthermore, '[if] the Community court finds, on examining the act produced to it, that the act has not been properly authenticated, it must of its own motion raise the issue of infringement of an essential procedural requirement . . . and . . . annul the act vitiated by that defect'. The Court also rejected the series of rather sophistical arguments of the Commission to the effect that authentication could be carried out after the notification of the act: Commission texts should, it held, be authenticated within a short period after their adoption and '[at] the very least it is indispensable for authentication to precede notification because otherwise there would always be a risk that the notified text would not be identical to the text adopted by the Commission', which would undermine the very purpose of the authentication requirement. In the light of these findings, the Court did not have to deal with the other Commission pleas. While this is clearly correct, the Court omitted expressly to mention that it had ruled, in paragraph 46, on the Commission's third plea.

---

[90] Case C–286/95 P, *Commission* v. *ICI* [2000] ECR II–2341 and Joined Cases C–287/95 P and C–288/95 P *Commission* v. *Solvay* [2000] ECR II–2391.

[91] Respectively Cases C–199/92, P *Hüls* v. *Commission* [1999] ECR I–4287 and the other 'Polypropylene' appeals decided on 8 July 1999, and C–137/92 P, *Commission* v. *BASF and Others* [1994] ECR I–2555.

(v) Freedom of Expression of Community Officials

It is far from obvious from the text of the second paragraph of Article 17 of the Community Staff Regulations that freedom of expression is a fundamental right enjoyed 'in particular' by Community officials, as the CFI observed in *Cwik*.[92] Under this provision, an official may not publish 'any matter dealing with the work of the Communities' without prior permission, which may be refused only 'where the proposed publication is liable to prejudice the interests of the Communities'. The applicant had been refused permission to publish the written text of a presentation he had, with the Commission's authorization but not acting on its behalf, made at a conference some months previously. The refusal was based, first, on the menace to the Community's interests arising from the expression by an administrator of non-managerial status acting in a personal capacity of a view different from that of the Commission services,[93] and, secondly, because certain other officials had some doubts regarding the quality of the article.[94]

Presumably drawing inspiration from the judgment of the ECtHR in *Vogt* v. *Germany*,[95] though it was not mentioned, the CFI held that Article 17 of the Staff Regulations reflected a fair balance between the guarantee of a fundamental right and the protection of a legitimate objective of general interest. It followed that restrictions on the right of expression were permitted only if the concrete circumstances so required, and only in so far as they could be justified. The CFI held that the mere fact that the official's views differed from those of the institution did not in itself constitute a threat to the Community's interests, and that to limit the freedom of expression to the mouthing of official positions would render this fundamental right nugatory. The CFI rejected as 'manifestly unfounded' the defendant's arguments based on the alleged risk of confusion regarding the Commission's position or the reduction in its margin for manœuvre; the absence of any such risk was demonstrated by the fact that the Commission had authorized the applicant to make the presentation in the first place. As the Commission did not rely before the CFI on the quality of the text as a reason for rejecting authorization, the Court did not rule on this aspect of the refusal.

The existence and extent of the freedom of expression of Community officials, an issue so long hidden from view like a shameful secret, has come to assume a new importance in recent years, particularly in the light of the actions of Mr Van Buitenen, whistle-blower, and Mr Connolly, author and EMU critic. While the CFI's upbeat assessment of the guarantees for the exercise of this most fundamental of political freedoms may not be shared by all of

---

[92] Case T–82/99, *Cwik* v. *Commission* [2000] ECR-SC II–713, para. 50.

[93] The Commission had argued before the CFI that the college of Commissioners had not adopted an official policy line on the contested matter, but the CFI sharply rejected this evidence (paras. 65 to 67).

[94] It appears that the official's function was to explain aspects of economic and monetary union to visitors' groups and at conferences.

[95] Judgment of 26 Sept. 1995, series A, vol. 323.

those most directly concerned, the Court's willingness to subject the decisions of the institutions to substantive review, and to ensure that the 'fair balance' is respected in fact, will surely be welcomed by the beleaguered Community civil service. That said, the absence of clear implementing rules, particularly regarding the duties of the institutions in this regard,[96] creates a situation of considerable legal uncertainty which can, in some circumstances, affect the very substance of the right. Little wonder that the European Ombudsman investigated this very subject.

(vi)   The Justiciability of a Commissioner's Declaration

In its order in *France* ('British beef imports'),[97] the Court ruled that a simple declaration by which a Commissioner announced the conclusions of a report by a scientific committee did not constitute a statement of position of the institution, and did not therefore provide evidence of a Commission decision refusing to modify the date from which France was obliged to admit beef imports from Great Britain. Nor did the sending of a letter of formal notice in the framework of infringement proceedings provide such evidence. In the absence of any act which could be annulled, the Court declared the action manifestly inadmissible.

E.   TRANSPARENCY/ACCESS TO DOCUMENTS

(i)   The Fundamental Right to the Objectively Justified Disclosure of Data

Potentially the most far-reaching judgment in the area of transparency during the year arose in the unlikely framework of a dispute concerning support payments for arable crop production.[98] The applicants had been fined for sowing land which was eligible for set-aside, though the Ministry of Agriculture, relying on the national provisions on the protection of data, had refused to provide them with the necessary information on the previous use of the land; the applicants had challenged that decision before the national courts. The Court acknowledged that the Member States were under an obligation, according to the aid payments legislation, to protect the data they hold; however, it pointed out that the measures they take must be proportionate to the objective sought, and not undermine the effectiveness of the set-aside scheme. That scheme depended on aid applicants being able to provide complete and accurate information, and they thus had an essential and legitimate interest in being able to procure this. In deciding whether or not to disclose the information 'the competent authority must balance, on the one hand, the interest of the person who provided the information and, on the other, the interest of the person who has need of that information in order to meet a legitimate objective'. The deci-

---

[96] Thus, e.g., in the absence of any more specific provision, the institution may sit on a publication request for four months, in accordance with Art. 90(1) of the Staff Regulations, though this could hardly count as good administration.
[97] Case C–514/99, *France* v. *Commission* [2000] ECR I–4705.
[98] Case C–369/98, *Ex parte Fisher* [2000] ECR I–6751.

sion must be taken with the fundamental rights of the interested parties in mind; to this end the Court referred to Directive 95/46 on the protection of individuals with regard to the processing of personal data[99] as providing 'criteria that are suitable for application by the competent authority in making that assessment', as this 'adopts, at Community level, the general principles which already formed part of the law of the Member States in the area in question'. While paying lip-service to the competence of the national court to decide the issue, the Court gave a clear indication that there was nothing in the case-file to indicate that the applicants were pursuing anything but an essential and legitimate interest, or that disclosure would adversely affect 'any interest whatever of the owner of those data or his fundamental rights or freedoms'.

The importance of the ruling resides in the fact that the Court did not hesitate to apply the principle of transparency to areas of Community law other than public access to documents held by the institutions. In doing so, it employed a balancing requirement similar to that already developed by the CFI in *Carvel and Guardian Newspapers* v. *Council* and its subsequent case law on the application of discretionary exceptions.[100] Moreover, the Court applied this reasoning to the Member States in their application of Community law generally, not just those areas governed by rules specifically dealing with the disclosure of information, notwithstanding its express recogition that the agricultural legislation at issue here left the matter to the Member States. It is also rather novel to see the Court refer, as its source of inspiration for the content of fundamental rights in Community law, to a piece of Community legislation rather than either the constitutions of the Member States or international instruments in this area, particularly given that the deadline for transposing the Directive had not yet expired at the material time.

(ii)   The 'Court Proceedings' Exception and the Fundamental Right to a Fair Trial

In *Van der Wal*, the Commission had sent letters to various national courts in the framework of its 1993 Notice on co-operation in the application of what are now Articles 81 EC and 82 EC, and noted that fact in the relevant annual competition policy report. The applicant, a Brussels-based competition lawyer, had requested copies of three letters. The request was refused on the ground that this would be detrimental to the protection of the public interest (court proceedings). The refusal was upheld by the CFI which took the view, based largely on its interpretation of the right to a fair trial guaranteed under Article 6 of the ECHR, that the Commission was obliged to refuse access to documents it had drawn up for the sole purpose of a particular court case, as only the national court can decide on disclosure of documents submitted to it during the course of proceedings.

---

[99] [1995] OJ L281/3.
[100] Case T–194/94 [1995] ECR II–2765; for the later case law, see, e.g., Travers, (2000) 35 *Irish Jurist* 164, and Bradley, (1999) 35 *CDE* 283.

Both the applicant and the Dutch government, which had intervened in the earlier proceedings, appealed, in the event successfully.[101] The Court overturned the lower court's interpretation of Article 6 ECHR; in particular, it held that neither this provision, nor the constitutional traditions of the Member States, justified the conclusion that 'a court hearing a dispute is necessarily the only body empowered to grant access to the documents in the proceedings in question'. The independence of national courts in this context was sufficiently safeguarded by the Commission decision on public access to documents, and judicial review of decisions taken under that measure. The Court next examined the type of documents which could be supplied under Commission cooperation with national courts, noting that some were already in the public domain, in which case the Commission was obliged to take a decision on an individual basis on their release, while others contained legal or economic analyses, in which case the national rules on the disclosure of expert evidence would apply. The fact that 'national law may preclude the disclosure of those documents . . . is . . . not enough to exonerate the Commission entirely from its obligation to disclose those documents. In so far as they are held by the Commission, such documents fall within the scope of Decision 94/90, which provides for the widest public access possible. Any exception to that right of access must therefore be interpreted and applied strictly.' In concrete terms, the Commission must properly examine such requests for access, consulting, if need be, the national court in case of doubt whether disclosure would be allowed under national law. The Court therefore annulled both the judgment at first instance and the Commission's refusal in the present case.

This is the first appeal from a CFI ruling in an access to documents case to come to judgment. The Court's approach to the extent of the citizen's right to access—'the widest public access possible'—and to the interpretation of the mandatory exceptions appears to be even more rigorous than those adopted heretofore by the CFI, though very much in line with the Court's own case law on the only other related legislative measure, Directive 90/313 on access to information on the environment.[102]

(iii) Reliance on More than One Mandatory Exception to Justify a Refusal of Access

In *Denkavit Nederland BV*[103] the CFI confirmed that an institution may rely jointly on two mandatory exceptions at once. The Commission had refused access to a report of an inspection visit to pig farms in the Netherlands on the ground that the procedure in the framework of which the inspection had taken place was not completed at the time of the decision refusing access. While the fact that the document concerned an inspection was not in itself sufficient

---

[101] Joined Cases C–174/98 P and 189/98 P [2000] ECR I–1; see Davis (2000) 25 *ELRev.* 303.

[102] [1990] OJ L158/56; see Cases C–321/96, *Mecklenburg* [1998] ECR I–3809 and C–217/97, *Commission* v. *Germany* [1999] ECR I–5087.

[103] Case T–20/99, *Denkavit Nederland BV* v. *Commission* [2000] ECR II–3011.

justification for the refusal,[104] the Court held that 'the Commission could properly form the view that the inspection work that had to be carried out . . . required that the report . . . be withheld so as to preserve the climate of mutual trust essential to the smooth conduct of that procedure'. In the light of this finding, the Court did not have to examine the Commission's reliance on commercial secrecy, where the defendant institution was on rather shakier ground.[105] Though not at issue in these proceedings, the Community's transparency rules appear to have influenced the application of the national provisions on access to documents, as the national authorities 'founded their refusal of the applicant's request . . . on instructions received from the Commission'.[106]

(iv)   The Necessity for a Document-by-document Examination of a Request

The Council's failure in *Kuiler*[107] to carry out a document-by-document examination of whether access to certain asylum policy reports should be granted to a university researcher was sharply rebuked by the CFI. The Court repeated its ruling in *Svenska Journalistförbundet*[108] that the institution 'is obliged to consider, in the case of each document to which access is sought, whether, in the light of the information available [to it], disclosure is likely to undermine one of the facets of public interest protected by the first category of exceptions'. Given that the Council's refusals were identically worded despite the variety of the reports at issue, the Court could find 'no evidence' that the Council had examined each document, despite its protestations to the contrary. Furthermore, the Council was not entitled simply to ignore the reasons given by the applicant in his confirmatory application casting doubt on the reasons given for the first refusal. Having annulled the Council decision because of its unsatisfactory statement of reasons, for good measure the CFI also annulled it for failing to examine the possibility of giving the applicant partial access to the passages not covered by the public interest exception relied upon (international relations).

(v)   The Democratic Motivation for Transparency Rules

In factual circumstances somewhat reminiscent of the *Interporc* affair,[109] the Commission had in *JT's Corporation* refused access to various categories of documents concerning, directly or indirectly, the importation of textiles from Bangladesh which the applicant had requested in order to be able to dispute post-clearance demands for customs duty.[110] Access to the internal Commission documents and correspondence it had sent to the Bangladesh

---

[104] The Court was careful to cite *Van der Wal, supra* n. 100.
[105] The applicant's claim that it could have had partial access to the report was eminently plausible.
[106] Para. 26 of the judgment; see also Case C–223/98, *Adidas* [1999] ECR I–7081.
[107] Case T–188/98, *Kuiler* v. *Council* [2000] ECR II–1959.
[108] Case T–174/95, *Svenska Journalistförbundet* v. *Council* [1998] ECR II–2289, para. 12.
[109] Case T–92/98, *Interporc* v. *Commission* [1999] ECR II–3521.
[110] Case T–123/99, *JT's Corporation* v. *Commission* [2000] ECR II–3269.

government was refused for the protection of the public interest, in that they concerned the Commission's inspection and investigation tasks. Access to the Bangladesh government's responses was refused under the authorship rule, while the request regarding reports or summaries concerning the operation of the GSP scheme for textiles from Bangadesh was considered too unspecific.

The applicant's complaint was ruled inadmissible as regards the last category of documents, as the Commission had left open the possibility of access. On the other hand, the CFI admitted the complaint regarding a particular mission report of which the applicant had received a partial version from the UK customs authorities, as it had not had full access thereto. The CFI also ruled that the applicant could rely in its reply on *Hautala*, though it had not been able to do so in its initial application: '[that] judgment merely clarifies the scope of the right of access as laid down by the Code of Conduct, by specifying that the exceptions to that right must be interpreted in the light of the principle of the right to information and the principle of proportionality'.

On the merits, the Commission's refusal of access to its internal documents was annulled as it had 'reasoned by reference to categories of documents and not on the basis of the actual information contained in the documents in question' and had therefore 'not assessed specifically whether the exception concerning the protection of the public interest genuinely applies to the whole of the information contained in those documents'. Moreover, the Court found that much of the information requested was merely descriptive and factual, disclosure of which 'clearly [would] do no harm to inspection and investigation tasks'. The Court rejected as 'irrelevant' the Commission's arguments that the national court could ask it to produce the documents and that the right of access of a party in national legal proceedings was a matter for national law, referring in particular to *Van der Wal*.[111] It also found that the Commission had failed to provide a proper statement of the reasons for which it had rejected access to these documents, as it had reasoned 'exclusively on the general characteristics of the categories of documents requested'.

More significantly, the Court rejected the Commission's reliance on the confidentiality of customs information based on the Community's rules on co-operation between the Member States on customs matters: '[the] Code of Conduct . . . sets out an essential right . . . with the aim of making the Community more transparent, the transparency of the decision-making process being a means of strengthening the democratic nature of the institutions and the public's confidence in the administration'. It therefore held that such rules 'cannot be interpreted in a sense contrary to Decision 94/90', though in any case Regulation 1468/81 provided that the confidential character of customs information could not impede its use in legal proceedings.

After these robust affirmations, the CFI went on to uphold the Commission's reliance on the authorship rule as regards the documents emanating from the

---

[111] Joined Cases C–174/98 P and C–189/98 P, *supra* n. 100.

Bangladesh government, in the absence of a higher rule of law prohibiting its application. The Commission's reasoning in this regard was also found to be sufficiently clear.

F. INTERNATIONAL RELATIONS LAW

(i) WTO Agreements: Direct Effect (Again) and Jurisdiction of the ECJ

The possibility of direct effect for provisions of the WTO Agreements, and particularly Article 50(6) of TRIPs, continues to exercise the national courts, and hence the Court of Justice. In *Christian Dior*,[112] as a follow-up to *Hermès*,[113] the Court was questioned on the scope of its own jurisdiction to interpret this provision and the extent, if any, of the direct effect of Article 50(6). The Court recalled that, as the WTO Agreement is a mixed agreement, it has jurisdiction to define the Community's obligations and *pro tanto* to interpret TRIPs, in particular to assist national courts in protecting rights arising under relevant Community legislation, or on *Dzodzi*[114] grounds, to prevent possible differences of interpretation. It added that, as 'Article 50 of TRIPs constitutes a procedural provision which should be applied in the same way in every situation falling within its scope and is capable of applying both to situations covered by national law and to situations covered by Community law', both the national and Community courts should interpret it uniformly. This jurisdiction is thus not restricted to situations covered by trade-mark law. As regards direct effect, the Court simply referred to its ruling in *Portugal* v. *Council*[115] that 'the WTO Agreement and the annexes thereto are not in principle among the rules in the light of which the Court is to review measures of the Community institutions', before concluding that 'the provisions of TRIPs . . . are not such as to create rights upon which individuals may rely directly before the courts by virtue of Community law'. The Court went on to point out, however, that in a field to which TRIPs applies and where the Community has already legislated, such as trade marks, 'the judicial authorities of the Member States are required by virtue of Community law [to apply national rules] as far as possible in the light of the wording and purpose of Article 50 of TRIPs'.[116] No such obligation obtains on the other hand where the Community has not legislated, and it falls to the national courts to 'specify in detail the interests which will be protected under TRIPs as "intellectual property rights" and the method of protection', as long as this is effective and does not lead to distortions of, or restrictions on, international trade.

---

[112] Joined Cases C–300/98 and C–392/98, *Christian Dior and Van Dijk* [2000] ECR I–11307.

[113] Case C–53/96, *Hermès* v. *FHT* [1998] ECR I–3603.

[114] Joined Cases C–297/88 and C–197/89 [1990] ECR I–3763.

[115] Case C–149/96 [1999] ECR I–8395, para. 47; the judgment is roundly criticized by Griller, (2000) 3 *JIEL* 441.

[116] Jacobs AG has observed that he finds it 'difficult to understand why Community law governs the effects of Article 50 of the TRIPs agreement . . . in situations concerning national trade marks' (Opinion in Case C–89/99, *Schieving-Nijstat and Others* v. *Groeneveld*, judgment of 13 Sept. 2001, not yet reported).

(ii) The Obligation to Denounce Prior International Agreements which are Incompatible with the Treaty

Unlike certain other Member States charged by the Commission with having failed to adjust or denounce merchant shipping agreements with third countries,[117] as required by Council Regulation 4055/86, Portugal put up a fight, though with no greater degree of success.[118] The Court began by recalling its previous ruling that, where it is possible, denunciation of an agreement is a duty. It was unimpressed by the argument that the disintegration of the Federal Republic of Yugoslavia justified Portugal's inaction: 'the existence of a difficult political situation in a third State . . . cannot justify a continuing failure of the part of a Member State to fulfil its obligations under the Treaty'. The principal point at issue, however, was the interpretation of Article [307 EC]. Portugal had argued that denunciation would be a duty only in exceptional circumstances, and not where it would involve a disproportionate disregard of the Member State's foreign policy interests. The Court held that this provision is general in scope, and that its purpose is 'to make it clear, in accordance with the principles of international law . . . that application of the EC Treaty is not to affect the duty of the Member State concerned to respect the rights of third countries under a prior agreement and to perform its obligations thereunder'. As the agreement concerned in each case allowed denunciation, recourse to this procedure did not encroach on the rights of the third State. The Court also held that 'the balance of foreign-policy interests of a Member State and the Community interest is already incorporated in Article [307 EC] in that it allows a Member State not to apply a Community provision in order to respect the rights of third countries . . . [and] to choose the appropriate means of rendering the agreement concerned compatible with Community law'.

(iii) Relations with Entities not Recognized by the Community under International Law

The highly sensitive issue of the importation of citrus fruit from the northern part of Cyprus also came up before the Court for a second time during the year. In *Anastasiou I*, the Court had refused to recognize that phytosantiary certificates issued by the 'Turkish Republic of Nothern Cyprus' complied with the relevant 1976 Directive on the protection of plants from harmful organisms.[119] Nothing daunted, the exporters arranged to have their fruit inspected and certified during a brief call to a Turkish port, much to the chagrin of exporters from the Republic of Cyprus who sought to have this practice too declared incompatible with the Directive in proceedings before the United Kingdom courts. In *Anastasiou II*,[120] the Court, after a very detailed examination

---

[117] See, e.g., Case C–170/98, *Commission* v. *Belgium* [1999] ECR I–5493, and Joined Cases C–171/98, C–201/98 and C–202/98, *Commission* v. *Belgium and Luxembourg* [1999] ECR I–5517.

[118] Cases C–62/98 and C–84/98, both *Commission* v. *Portugal* [2000] ECR I–5171 and 5215; Reg. 4055/86 [1986] OJ L378/1.

[119] Case C–432/92 [1994] ECR I–3087.   [120] Case C–219/98 [2000] ECR I–5241.

of the wording and scheme of the Directive, concluded that it did not preclude the certification of the fruit by a non-member consignor country other than the country of origin, to wit, Turkey. The importation of fruit required both a certificate of compliance with the phytosanitary regulations of the importing country and inspection on entry into the Community. The consideration that it was in practice impossible to ensure that non-member country checks were as rigorous as Community checks is equally applicable to countries of origin and consignor countries. In order to ensure that the objectives of the Directive were achieved, and to avoid importation on the basis of worthless certificates of convenience, the Court restricted the possibility of certification to 'non-member countries from which the plants were exported to the Community after having entered the territory of those countries and having remained there for such time and under such conditions as to enable the proper checks to be completed'.

(iv) Miscellaneous Commercial Policy Matters

The proceedings in *Polo/Lauren* posed a novel question of principle concerning the scope of the Community's commerical policy competence.[121] The applicant, a company with its registered office in New York whose products enjoy a certain international stature[122] persuaded the local customs authorities in Linz, Austria, not to release a number of T-shirts bearing its famed trade mark on suspicion that the goods were counterfeit or pirated. However, the lower courts refused to issue an order prohibiting the consignor from marketing the goods and allowing Polo/Lauren to have them destroyed, on the ground that the goods were in transit from Indonesia to Poland, and that the counterfeit goods regulation applied only to goods which could come onto the Community market, or at least affect that market. The Court disagreed, noting that the 'Regulation is . . . expressly designed to apply to goods passing through Community territory'. On the question of the Community's competence to regulate such activities, the Court merely referred to *Opinion 1/94*,[123] where it had recognized that the regulation was a commercial policy measure, adding that in any case the external transit of goods could have an effect on the internal market, particularly if the goods were fraudulently brought on to the market, and that such external transit is but a legal fiction.

The right of a consumer organization to be considered an 'interested party' for the purposes of the Community's basic anti-dumping regulation was at issue, and not for the first time, in *BEUC* v. *Commission*.[124] In the present case, the Commission had initiated an investigation regarding importations of unbleached cotton fabrics; as this was not a product sold at retail level, and the

---

[121] Case C–383/98, *Polo/Lauren* v. *PT. Dwidua Langgeng* [2000] ECR I–2519.

[122] As recounted by Ruiz-Jarabo Colomer AG (Opinion, para. 3), though it may be regretted that one of the few literary works cited before the Court during the year should be his reference to the slightly repulsive *American Psycho*.

[123] *WTO Agreement* [1994] ECR I–5267.

[124] Case T–256/97 [2000] ECR II–101; see the earlier, inconclusive, proceedings between the same parties, Case T–84/97 [1998] ECR II–795.

applicant did not represent consumers of such products, the Commission took the view that the applicant was unable to provide the Commission with 'quantifiable information that sufficiently reflects the Community interest . . . nor . . . to add to the information which the Commission receives from other parties'. The CFI started by holding that the Commission was right, in line with *Nakajima*,[125] to interpret the basic Community regulation in the light of the WTO Antidumping Code. On the other hand, in granting rights to organizations to participate in the adoption of anti-dumping measures, the Community legislator had not adopted any distinction based on whether products are sold at retail level or not; all that is required is 'an objective link between the party's activities, on the one hand, and the product under investigation, on the other', which the Commission must decide on a case-by-case basis. The blanket exclusion of consumer organizations was not therefore justified.

The importation of unbleached cotton fabrics was also at the origin of *Eurocoton*, where the applicants were challenging the non-adoption by the Council of a proposal for a regulation imposing a definitive anti-dumping duty on such imports.[126] The proposal had not garnered the support of even the simple majority required for its adoption, and hence the provisional duties lapsed. In its defence, the Council argued that there had been no act at all. The CFI agreed; the fact that a regulation imposing such duties was open to judicial review did not mean that the failure to adopt such a regulation constituted a reviewable act: 'no provision of the EC Treaty requires the Council to adopt . . . anti-dumping duties' nor is any right to the adoption of a regulation conferred on the applicants. The CFI also examined whether the WTO Antidumping Code required the Council to adopt such duties, though it is far from clear that any such breach could be relied upon by individuals. Both the action for annulment and that for damages were rejected.

Extramet's charmed life as a complainant against Community anti-dumping measures[127] came finally to an end during the year, when the Court rejected an appeal by its successor company, *Industrie des Poudres Sphériques* ('IPS').[128] Following *Extramet II*, the Commission had resumed the investigation procedure, which led once again to the adoption of a definitive anti-dumping duty on imports of calcium metal, and annulment proceedings, this time unsuccessful, before the CFI. On appeal, the Court held that the Commission was entitled to reopen the investigation on the basis of a different reference period without initiating a new anti-dumping proceeding, as the annulment of the previous regulation in *Extramet II* did not affect the initiation of that proceeding, and the Commission was under a duty to carry out an

---

[125] Case C–69/89, *Nakajima All Precision* v. *Council* [1991] ECR I–2069, para 29.

[126] Case T–213/97, *Eurocoton and Others* v. *Council* [2000] ECR II–3727; Eurocoton had submitted the initial complaint in Case T–256/97, *BEUC, supra* n. 123, para. 7.

[127] See Case C–358/89, *Extramet Industrie* v. *Council*—admissibility (*'Extramet I'*) [1991] ECR I–2501 and merits (*'Extramet II'*) [1992] ECR I–3813.

[128] Case C–458/98 P [2000] ECR I–8147.

investigation on the basis of the most recent information available. As IPS had been given the opportunity to comment on the memorandum on the assessment of injury a month before the publication of the relevant notice, no breach of its right to a fair hearing had been established, and the appeal was therefore rejected.

III. Other Institutional Developments

A. THE POLITICAL INSTITUTIONS

(i) Interinstitutional Agreements

The year 2000 saw the conclusion of several important interinstitutional agreements. Of these, the most far-reaching in political terms was the Framework Agreement between Parliament and the Commission adopted on 5 July.[129] While purporting not to affect the powers and prerogatives of the two signatory institutions, the agreement imposes a large number of obligations on the signatories, and particularly on the Commission, for example, regarding the presence of Commissioners at parliamentary committee meetings, or concerning the prior information of Parliament in writing before the Commission takes 'any legislative initiative or significant initiative or decision'. Furthermore, despite the principle of collegiate responsibility, Parliament and the Commission agree that 'each Member of the Commission shall take political responsibility for action in the field of which he or she is in charge', and the Commission accepts that its President must 'consider seriously' whether or not to invite a Commissioner who had lost Parliament's confidence to resign. As well as substantive provisions on dialogue and information flow between the institutions, political responsibility, Commission participation in Parliament's work, and the reform of the Commission, the agreement contains three annexes on legislative proceedings, parliamentary participation in, and information regarding, the conclusion of international agreements, and on the forwarding of confidential information to the Parliament.

It was particularly the last-mentioned annex which provoked twenty-two MEPs to challenge the validity of the agreement in annulment proceedings, largely on the ground that it affected their right to ask questions of the Commission and the latter's duty to respond.[130]

Following a well-entrenched tradition, Parliament and the Commission concluded an agreement, undated but published in October 2000,[131] on the

---

[129] See EP minutes of 5 July 2000, [2001] OJ C121/122–30; see Editorial, (2000) 25 *ELRev.* 333 and Rodrigues (2000) 442 *RMCUE* 590.

[130] Case T–236/00, *Stauner and Others* v. *Parliament and Commission*, pending; on 21 Jan. 2001, the President of the CFI refused to suspend the application of the agreement (Case T–236/00 R [2001] ECR II–15).

[131] [2000] OJ L256/19.

application of the 'Comitology II' decision of June 1999.[132] Apart from abolishing three of the existing agreements on parliamentary supervision of implementing legislation, this specifies the information Parliament is to receive under Article 7(3) of Comitology II, and obliges the Commission to grant it access to committee minutes '[pursuant] to . . . Case T–188/97 *Rothmans* v. *Commission*', though of course the Commission had undertaken a similar obligation in its rules of procedure shortly before this judgment.[133] The agreement provides that resolutions indicating that implementing measures are *ultra vires* the basic act must be adopted in plenary session within a month of the receipt of the final draft, though of course no plenary sessions are held for a period of up to eight weeks during the summer. Not surprisingly, Parliament expresses its support for the objective of bringing pre-Comitology II procedures in line with the 1999 decision, as the failure of Comitology I to deal with the 'cost of the past' was one of Parliament's major criticisms of that decision.

Both this and the Framework Agreement appear to run counter to the spirit of the 'Declaration on Article 10 [EC]' adopted by the Nice IGC, which purports to require the assent of all three political institutions for the conclusion of interinstitutional agreements based on this Treaty provision.[134]

In October, Parliament approved an agreement adopted jointly with the Council and the Commission on financial statements 'aimed at improving financial programming and the availability of recources necessary for implementing programmes',[135] and instructed the committee responsible to prepare the necessary amendments to its rules of procedure. The agreement, somewhat confusingly entitled 'joint statement' in the body of the resolution but 'interinstitutional agreement' in the title, affirms the necessity for the budgetary authority to have 'accurate information about the financial consequences of each new proposal presented by the Commission', and requires the Commission to indicate whether a legislative proposal is compatible with existing financial programming, whether reprogramming of the financial perspectives will be necessary, and the level of human resources required to manage the programme. The institutions also agree to assess the financial implications of new legislative proposals, and of parliamentary and Council readings of these, at their meetings under the 1999 omnibus budgetary interinstitutional agreement.[136] Considering its obvious potential relevance, it is rather anomalous that neither resolution nor statement refers to Article 270 EC on budgetary discipline.

During the year, the Commission submitted a proposal for an agreement between all the institutions and the two Grand Committees to set up an

---

[132] Council Decision 1999/468/EC, [1999] OJ L184/23; see Lenaerts and Verhoeven (2000) 37 *CMLRev.* 645 and Bradley 19*YEL* 547, 591–2.

[133] [1999] ECR II–2463, criticized in Bradley, *supra* n. 131, 554–6.

[134] [2001] OJ C80/77; on the institutional aspects of this Treaty, see section IV.

[135] See also Council Regulation 2040/2000 on budgetary discipline [2000] OJ L244/27.

[136] [1999] OJ C172/1.

advisory group on standards in public life, following a request to this effect made by Parliament in the aftermath of the second report of the independent experts on misfeasance in the Commission of 10 September 1999.[137] The proposal is unusual in that it is intended to cover more than the usual suspects, Parliament, Council, and Commission, though the last such initiative, the OLAF agreement, failed to garner any support outside this charmed circle.[138]

(ii) The Council's Rules of Procedure

In June, the Council adopted a number of further important modifications to its rules of procedures, following the extensive revision carried out in 1999 to take account of the entry into force of the Treaty of Amsterdam.[139] In particular, these:

— limit the number of its formations to the sixteen set out in a list adopted by the General Affairs Council;[140]
— entrust Coreper to ensure the 'consistency of the Union's policies and actions' and respect for certain constitutional principles and rules, including subsidiarity and the distribution of competences amongst the institutions;
— define the duties of its General Secretariat in 'organising, coordinating and ensuring the coherence of the Council's work';
— provide for the drawing up of an exhaustive list of the committees and working groups involved in preparatory work on the Council's behalf;
— relax the procedural requirement from unanmity to qualified majority for case by case decisions to hold public debates, and reflect the Council's agreement to hold 'at least one public debate on important new legislative proposals';
— charge the presidency to ensure the 'businesslike conduct' of its discussions, to check the quorum in case of a vote, and to provide indicative provisional agendas for all the Council meetings during its term of office; and
— reflect the Council's undertaking not to adopt resolutions or declarations (other than statements entered in its minutes on the occasion of the adoption of legislative acts) on matters on which legislative proposals or initiatives have been submitted to it.

It is interesting to see the Council taking a leaf from Parliament's book; the new rules are characterized by a large number of footnoted statements which appear to serve the same purpose as the interpretations adopted by Parliament to its rules and appended thereto in italics.[141]

If the Council started the year in a sunburst of increased transparency, with the inclusion from 1 January on the register of its documents of a list of

---

[137] SEC(2000)2077 final.
[138] See also section II.D(i) above, Case T–17/00, *Rothley and Others, supra* n. 81.
[139] Council Decision 2000/396 [2000] OJ L149/21, replacing Decision 1999/385 [1999] OJ L147/13.
[140] [2000] OJ C174/1.   [141] See Rule 180(5) of Parliament's rules of procedure.

legislative items on the agendas of its meetings and those of its preparatory bodies,[142] it rather blotted its copybook, at least in the eyes of some, by adopting, through the person of its Secretary General, rules on the classification of information, and excluding this information from the Council arrangements for public access to documents. All such information is to be classified on a spectrum from 'Top Secret' to 'Confidential', depending on the degree of harm to the interests of the Community or the Member States which would be caused by its release into the public domain.[143] The catalyst for this initiative was said to be the adoption by the Helsinki European Council of two reports on military and non-military crisis management in the area of security and defence policy, though nothing in the secrecy rules restricts the application of the system to information regarding these matters.[144] Primarily on the grounds that the exclusion of such classified documents from the arrangements on access pre-empted in part the general decision the Council was to take under Article 255(2) EC, and undermined the very substance of the right of access to documents, Parliament initiated proceedings to have the two decisions annulled; the Netherlands is also seeking the annulment of Council Decision 2000/527, for breach of both the substantive and procedural rules of Article 255 EC.[145]

(iii)   Rules of Procedure of the Commission and other Community Bodies

The principal modification to its rules which the Commission adopted in November[146] was the addition of a new Article on the delegation of 'the adoption of management or administrative measures to the Directors-General or Heads of Service', subject to the principle of collective responsibility and any conditions specified in the delegating decision. Delegation of similar powers to individual Commissioners was re-named 'empowerment'; subdelegation by a Commissioner of empowered competences to a Director General or Head of Service is henceforth allowed unless expressly prohibited, where before a specific authorization in the enabling decision was required for subdelegation. A second new Article provides for the recording of the adoption of empowered or delegated decisions in a 'day note' in the minutes of the next Commission meeting. The Commission also adopted, by way of a supplementary measure annexed to the rules, a 'Code of Good Administrative Behaviour for Staff of the European Commission in their Relations with the Public'.[147] Not only should such a move give the Ombudsman a certain satisfaction, and facilitate respect for the Commission's duties under the third indent of Article 21 EC (the right to receive a response from the Community administration), but

---

[142] In accordance with Decision 2000/23/EC [2000] OJ L9/22.

[143] Council Decision 2000/527/EC [2000] OJ L212/9, and Decision 2000/C 239/01 of the Secretary General of the Council [2000] OJ C239/1.

[144] While the USA reached transparency as a reaction to the establishment of a system of classified information, the Community may be said to have adopted a system of classified information in reaction to its transparency rules (on the US situation, see anon, 'Keeping Secrets: Congress, the Courts and National Security Information', 103 *Harvard LR* 906 (1980)).

[145] Case C–387/00, *Parliament* v. *Council* and Case C–369/00, *Netherlands* v. *Council*, both pending.

[146] [2000] OJ L308/26.   [147] *Ibid.*, at 32.

the Commission thereby anticipated the Charter of Fundamental Rights of the European Union solemnly proclaimed at Nice, Article 41 of which provides, in strikingly unqualified terms, for a right to good administration.[148]

The Commission may also have intended to give a good example to other Community institutions and bodies. In fact, Parliament's Bureau had adopted its own 'Guide to the Obligations of Officials and Others Servants of the European Parliament—Code of Conduct' in February 2000.[149] Though mainly taken up with clarifying the obligations of parliamentary officials *vis-à-vis* the institution, the guide lays down a number of provisions on administrative openness, on access to Parliament's documents, the storage of data, and the possibility for members of the public to complain against infringements of these provisions. The Community Plant Variety Office too qualified for the vanguard of public-friendly Community bodies, by adopting its own code of good administrative behaviour. While a commendable initiative, the Office fell rather short of its own desire for speedy administration and to 'ensure the code enjoys the widest possible publicity among members of the public'; though adopted in, and effective from, mid-April, it was not published until just before Christmas.[150]

Parliament did not undertake any major revision of its rules this year. It did publish for the first time in the Official Journal the rules of procedure of COSAC, the Conference of Community and European Affairs Committees of Parliaments of the European Union, which was established in November 1989.[151] Emboldened perhaps by its new-found public profile, in October COSAC used, for the first time, the possibility recognized to it by clause 4 of the Protocol on the Role of National Parliaments of making a submission directly to the Community institutions.[152] The Committee of the Regions also over-hauled its rules.[153]

B.   THE COURT OF JUSTICE AND THE COURT OF FIRST INSTANCE

(i)   The Court of Justice

The year saw the triennial renewal of the Court of Justice, and the turnover of four judges and three Advocates General; the Official Journal announcement also gives the composition of the six chambers of the Court.[154] Mr Rodríguez Iglesias was elected for an unprecedented third term as President by the renewed Court.

---

[148]   [2000] OJ C364/1, at 18.

[149]   This was published by Parliament as a booklet, and is also available on Parliament's website, at http://www.europarl.ep.ec/codex/default_en.htm#A2.

[150]   [2000] OJ C371/14; the European Foundation for the Improvement of Living and Working Conditions turned in a slightly worse performance (Decision 2000/791 of 11 Feb. 2000, published in mid-Dec. [2000] OJ L316/69).

[151]   [2000] OJ C175/1.

[152]   *Agence Europe*, 19 Oct. 2000.

[153]   [2000] OJ L18/22.

[154]   [2000] OJ C316/1.

The Court of Justice amended its rules of procedure on two occasions during the year. Like certain of the modifications to the Council's rules, the amendments adopted in May were primarily designed to improve the expeditious conduct of the Court's business, at a time when Court reform was under examination at the IGC.[155] On the one hand, the Court in effect widened its own discretion not to hold an oral hearing, both in direct actions (including appeals) and in preliminary rulings; whereas before the consent of the parties was required for this course of action,[156] now a party who wishes a hearing to be held must submit an application 'setting out the reasons he wishes to be heard'. It may prove difficult for the Court to prevent a party submitting the substantive arguments he wishes to make at the oral procedure in the application setting out his reasons for requesting a hearing, though such a tactic could, of course, cut both ways. The President of the Court is allowed, under the expedited procedure, to request those submitting observations 'to restrict the matters addressed . . . to the essential points of law raised in the question referred', a provision which could probably with profit be applied generally to preliminary rulings. In adding the necessary provisions to regulate new heads of jurisdiction inserted into the EC Treaty (Article 68(3) EC) and the Treaty on European Union (Article 35(1) and (7) EU) by the Treaty of Amsterdam, the Court went even further, dispensing with the oral hearing unless a Member State, the Commission, or the Council requests that one be held. The Court thereby appears to have deprived itself of the possibility of holding an oral hearing in such matters.

On the other hand, the May modifications allow the Court to improve the quality of the information on the basis of which it reaches its judgments, by asking either the parties (in direct actions) or the national court (in preliminary rulings) for further and better particulars. The latter provision is particularly novel; the Court appears to have been reluctant heretofore to take such a common-sense step on the ground that some of the national judges consider themselves to be *functus officio* once they have made a reference. The modifications allow the Court to issue practice directions regarding both the written and oral phases of the procedure before it, and to establish an accelerated procedure for dealing with preliminary rulings raising 'a matter of exceptional urgency'. A procedure for applying in effect the *CILFIT*[157] dispensation to requests from national courts at all levels is introduced into the rules, which also take account of the renumbering of the EC Treaty. The new rules applied from 1 July 2000.

The Court's quest for efficiency was continued in the November modifications to its rules which entered into force on 1 February 2001.[158] These introduce an expedited procedure, on an application by the parties, for direct actions equivalent to that for preliminary rulings adopted six months

---

[155] [2000] OJ L122/43; on the IGC in general, see section IV below.
[156] In the case of appeals, the party had to show that he had not been able fully to defend his point of view in the written stage: Art. 120, ECJ rules.
[157] Case 283/81 [1982] ECR 3415.   [158] [2000] OJ L322/1.

previously; it is difficult to judge whether the slight difference in the wording of the condition for its application, 'particular urgency [requiring] . . . the minimum of delay' as opposed to 'exceptional urgency', will translate into a real difference in practice. Under this procedure, the President may refuse the second round of written pleadings and interventions, unless he considers these 'necessary'; by way of compensation, parties may be allowed greater flexibility to rely on new arguments during the oral procedure. The Court will henceforth allow the transmission of pleadings by 'telefax or other technical means of communication available to the Court', presumably including e-mail. To avoid the vagaries of faulty receiving fax machines, or of pleadings sent by e-mail to the Court but to the wrong address, the rules require a signed original to be deposited within ten days. The extension on account of distance from the Court's seat in Luxembourg is fixed as ten days for all parties appearing before the Court. It may be regarded as somewhat unfortunate that, in the interests of legal certainty, the Court did not provide expressly for any transitional provisions in this regard. Thus, for example, an American company notified of a negative Commission decision on, say, 15 November 2000, on 31 January 2001 still had two weeks to send in an application for annulment; by the following day, its application was already a week late.[159] The deadline for applying to intervene is cut by half, to six weeks; a party may, on application, be allowed to intervene after the expiry of that deadline, though only orally. In appeals, the appellant has just seven days to justify the submission of a reply to the defence.

(ii)   The Court of First Instance

A week after the Court of Justice's November amendments, the CFI adopted similar rules regarding an expedited procedure in direct actions, and the use of modern means of communication, as well as the renumbering of the Treaty.[160] The CFI gave itself the power to dispense with the reply and rejoinder in all cases, and not just urgent proceedings, where it considers the first round of pleadings is 'sufficiently comprehensive to enable the parties to elaborate their pleas and arguments in the course of the oral procedure'. It also took the opportunity of correcting the slight anomaly thrown up the previous year in *ADT Projekt*, where it was obliged to transmit to an applicant a document it had judged necessary for consideration of the case, despite the Commission's plea that this would breach the obligation of professional secrecy imposed on the institutions by Article 287 EC.[161] A new paragraph 3 added to Article 67 of the rules seeks to ensure that the CFI will take into account only documents on which the parties have been given an opportunity to comment, and that the

---

[159] As of 30 Jan 2001: 15 Nov. 2000, plus 2 months (5th para., Art. 230 EC), plus 1 month (Art. 81(2), and Art. 1, Annex II, ECJ rules) = 16 Feb. 2001; as of 1 Feb. 2001: 2 months (as before), plus 10 days (new Art. 81(2) ECJ rules) = 25 Jan. 2001.

[160] *Ibid.*, at 4.

[161] Case T–145/98, *ADT Projekt* v. *Commission* [2000] ECR II–387, esp. paras. 38–44.

CFI itself will be able to evaluate the necessity to protect the confidentiality of a document before it is, if at all, transmitted to the opposite party.

Just before they entered into force, the CFI published a notice explaining the changes to its rules;[162] to mark their entry into force on 1 February 2001, the Courts published consolidated versions of their rules for information in the Official Journal.[163]

As it has on previous occasions, and in order to comply as far as possible with the principle of the *juge légal* recognized in the legal order of some of the Member States,[164] the CFI published the criteria for assigning cases, along with the announcement of the composition and presidency of its five Chambers in their normal and extended compositions, containing three and five members respectively.[165] State aid cases and those concerning the implementation of trade protection measures may be assigned to any one of the five-judge chambers, while all other cases are dealt with by chambers of three judges, or possibly even a single judge. Only the second and fourth chambers deal with intellectual property cases, being appeals from the Trade Mark Office in Alicante. Other cases are divided into three categories, being staff disputes, competition cases, and other cases, and are allocated according to a rota. Where a plenary formation of the CFI would contain an even number of judges, the least senior judge sits out, unless she or he is judge-rapporteur, in which case the next least senior member does the honours.

IV. Treaty Reform

A. THE TREATY OF NICE

The Treaty of Nice,[166] concluded in the early hours of 11 December 2000 after the usual bleary-eyed horsetrading and brinkmanship, is the first exercise devoted primarily to the composition and functioning of the institutions since the Merger Treaty of 1965. Much of the immediate comment, even from some of the participants, was negative, not to say fiercely hostile; however, when the dust has settled, it will probably transpire to have been a mitigated success, though perhaps not the product of a 'great summit' of the French President's dreams, particularly as, on one view, its major achievement was to shift important areas of constitution-making out of the Treaty and into the Council chamber.

---

[162] [2001] OJ C28/26.

[163] [2001] OJ C34/1 (ECJ) and 39 (CFI); the consolidated rules are also available on the Court's website, http://www.europateam.cc.cec/cj/en/index.htm.

[164] See in particular Case C–7/94, *Gaal* [1995] ECR I–1031, where the ECJ held that this principle did not preclude the panel system it had instituted for its own chambers.

[165] [2000] OJ C259/14.

[166] The version signed on 26 Feb. 2001 is published, for information, in [2001] OJ C80/01 and also as ISBN 92-824-1977-0; references in this section are to the amended EC Treaty unless otherwise stated. See also Cloos, (2001) 44 *RMCUE* 5, Louis, (2001) 76 *JT-Droit Européen* 25, Pescatore (2001) 38 *CMLRev.* 265, Yatanagas, 01/01, Shaw, *European Public Law* 195 (2001) and Bradley, *CMLRev.* (forthcoming). On 7 June 2001, the Nice Treaty was rejected by the Irish electorate in a referendum.

(i)   Reform of the Commission

(a)   Composition   The reform of the composition of the Commission was generally considered one of the most intractable problems the IGC faced, pitting demands for legitimacy from the smaller Member States against the imperative of efficiency in the operation of this institution, defended notably by the larger Member States. The Treaty of Nice seems to have found a generally acceptable compromise. The Commission which takes office in January 2005 will have the same number of members as there are Member States; whatever number this is, it is unlikely to bring the Commission much above the present figure of twenty, unless the 'Big Bang' option of allowing most of the candidates to accede simultaneously is chosen. The five largest Member States (Germany, the United Kingdom, France, Italy, and Spain) will thus 'give up' their second Commissioner, though this privilege was in fact little more than a historical accident, the justification for which disappeared decades ago.[167] Following the accession of the twenty-seventh Member State, the number of Commissioners will be decoupled from the number of Member States. All the Member States will instead partipate in a rotation system for the nomination of one of their nationals to the Commission, which the Council is to lay down acting unanimously, 'based on the principle of equality'. The system must ensure that 'Member States shall be treated on a strictly equal footing as regards determination of the sequence of, and the time spent by, their nationals as Members of the Commission'; in other words, no Member State can have a second turn at nominating a Commissioner until all the others have had their first. The composition of any given Commission, at least as regards the nationality of its members, is to be determined 'automatically', though the Council may vary the number of Commissioners, for example, in function of an increase or decrease in the tasks of the institution, of its own motion, or at the suggestion of an incoming President. The Council must also ensure that each college reflect 'the demographic and geographical range of all the Member States of the Union'. The Treaty will no longer provide that only nationals of the Member States may be Commissioners, though this is unlikely to have any significance in practice.

(b)   Appointment   After Nice, the ordinary Commissioners will be only nominated, not appointed, by the Member States, while the Council, acting by a qualified majority, is vested with the power to appoint both the President and the college of Commissioners, subject to the approval in each case of the European Parliament. The amendment has two slightly surprising, perhaps even unintended, consequences. In the first place, as the two decisions are taken by the Council, albeit at the level of heads of State or Government, they

---

[167] When the Treaties were being drawn up, 6 members was considered too few, given the extent of the functions of the High Authority and EEC Commission, so 9 was chosen instead, with 5 considered sufficient for the Euratom Commission.

are in principle subject to judicial review.[168] The second might be considered of more symbolic than legal significance. While traditionally one could claim that its appointment by the Member States, rather than the Council, showed that the Commission was in no way subordinate to the latter institution, this analysis is no longer valid.

(c)   Reinforcement of the position of the Commission President[169]   As suggested by the Commission itself,[170] the role of the Commission President has been enhanced by the Treaty of Nice. The President has been given a number of new powers regarding:

—the internal organization of the college, subject to the requirement that the Commission act 'consistently, efficiently and on the basis of collective responsibility';
—the structuring of portfolios and their distribution amongst the Commissioners, along with a power to reshuffle portfolios during the Commission's term of office;
—the devolving of duties on Commissioners, who then act under the authority of the President;
—the determination of the number, and appointment, of Vice-Presidents;
—the forced resignation of individual Commissioners.

To a large extent, however, the Treaty amendments regarding the President's powers reflect either current practice or the Commission's rules of procedure, as modified on 29 November 2000,[171] just a week before the Treaty of Nice was adopted. The appointment of Vice-Presidents and the forced resignation of Commissioners may be exercised only with the 'collective approval' of the Commission, a first express Treaty recognition of the principle of collective responsibility of the Commission.[172]

(ii)   Qualified Majority Voting in the Council

(a)   Reweighting of the Votes of the Member States   The reweighting of the votes of the Member States was part of the *quid pro quo* agreed at Amsterdam to compensate 'those Member States which give up the possibility of nominating a second member of the Commission'. The inclusion of this item on the agenda was also justified by the prospect of enlargement, so that the candidate Member States know, at least in principle, where they stand in this regard. Like the new arrangements on the composition of the Commission, the reweighting of Member States' votes also takes effect in phases, the number of which will depend on the number and timing of the future waves of enlargement.

---

[168] By analogy with Case 297/86 *CIDA* v. *Council* [1988] ECR 3531.
[169] On the role of the Commission President before Nice, see Kargiannis (2000) 36 *CDE* 9.
[170] 'Adapting the institutions to make a success of enlargement', 26 Jan. 2000.
[171] [1999] OJ L252/41 and [2000] OJ L308/26; see section III.A(iii), above.
[172] But see section II.(iv), above.

With effect from 1 January 2005, for the purposes of a qualified majority vote, a total of 237 votes are to be distributed amongst the Member States so that, instead of ten votes, the Big Four will each wield twenty-nine votes, Spain will have twenty-seven instead of eight, and all the other Member States will be allocated from thirteen (the Netherlands) to four (Luxembourg) votes, depending on their population. The net result of this exercise is that:

—subject to the majority rule and the demographic safety net (see below), a qualified majority is attained with 169 votes (71.31 per cent), and a blocking minority requires sixty-nine votes;
—the Big Five increase their individual share of the vote (by a whopping 2.2 per cent in the case of Spain, and 0.75 per cent for each of the others), and, of course, their collective share, which rises from 55 per cent to over 60 per cent, while the relative difference between Member States also increases (that between Germany and Luxembourg goes from five to 7.25);
—the United Kingdom, France, and Italy retain parity with Germany, though the traditional Netherlands–Belgium parity is broken;
—a blocking minority can be comprised, for example, of two large Member States plus one medium-sized Member State (with at least twelve votes; at present, two large Member States require either Spain or two other Member States, or three if one of them is Luxembourg), or the eight smallest Member States (unchanged).

Two new rules come into force on that date. For a qualified majority a vote on a Commission proposal, 'at least a majority of the members' of the Council must be in favour; this will kick in only after enlargement, as under the pre-Nice regime at least eight of the fifteen must vote in favour to reach the sixty-two votes currently required. Where the Council is not voting on a Commission proposal, the favourable votes of two-thirds of the Member States is required; this is also no change on the present regime of ten out of fifteen. The second rule is that 'any member of the Council may request verification that the qualified majority comprises at least 62 per cent of the total population of the Union', a rule which will primarily, or perhaps exclusively, benefit Germany.

(b) Extension of Qualified Majority Voting The hopes of those Member States and institutions which wished to see qualified majority voting extended to all remaining policy areas and certain other decisions under the EC and EU Treaties were not realized at Nice, and progress was generally considered rather disappointing in this area. Although about half the Treaty Articles requiring unanimous decision were amended to allow majority voting, unanimity continues to apply for legislation on tax and most social protection measures, and in Title VI of the EU Treaty. Moreover, the link between majority voting and the application of the co-decision procedure which had been urged particularly by the Commission and Parliament was not even discussed at the Conference.

(iii)   Reform of the Judicial System

The two sections of the Treaty concerning the organization of the judicial system, Articles 220–245 and the new single Statute of the Court, are considered by many to be the most coherent and complete set of reforms agreed upon, as well as being urgently required regardless of enlargement.[173]

(a)   Judicial Panels   The Treaty of Nice provides for a new level of Community jurisdiction, 'judicial panels', to be attached to the CFI in the same way as the CFI is presently attached to the Court of Justice. That they are courts by any other name, rather than committees or some hybrid organ, is clear from both their function, to 'exercise in certain specific areas, the judicial competence laid down in this Treaty', and the qualifications for membership of the panels, which are identical to the current qualifications required of CFI judges. The panels will 'hear at first instance certain classes of action or proceeding brought in specific areas', a formulation clearly inspired by Article 11 of the Single Act allowing the establishment of the CFI. While the 'specific area' of competence of each panel will be determined by the Council decision establishing it, two documents attached to the Nice Treaty give a strong hint of the first two likely candidates, and the most direct existing precedent. In a declaration, the Conference asks the Court and the Commission to propose a panel for staff disputes 'as swiftly as possible', while in a unilateral statement Luxembourg undertakes not to claim the seat of the Boards of Appeal of the Trade Mark Office, currently in Alicante, should they become panels.[174] Other candidates, as identified in the Due report,[175] are panels for other intellectual property matters, judicial co-operation in civil matters, police and judicial co-operation in criminal matters, and visa, asylum, and immigration and, depending on the future evolution of competition law, even this, rather large, area.

The EC Treaty leaves the creation of the panels to the Council, acting by unanimity, and allows the Commission as well as the Court of Justice to propose such a decision, with the other institution (and the European Parliament) being consulted in each case. A joint working group, chaired by the registrar of the CFI, and with the participation of representatives of the legal services of the political institutions, has been set up to prepare the proposals for a judicial panel for staff disputes.

(b)   The Court of First Instance   Apart from a number of symbolic changes, such as the upgrading of the qualifications for membership to that of 'ability

---

[173] See, e.g., Rasmussen (2000) 37 *CMLRev.* 1071, and Turner and Muñoz (2000) 19 *YEL* 1.

[174] At present, the members of these Boards are Community officials, at A3 grade, appointed by the Council; a number of them have been to Court to defend their independence (Case T–159/97 R, *Chaves Fonseca Ferrão* v. *Office for Harmonization in the Internal Market* [1997] ECR II–1049; Case T–148/97, *Keeling* v. *Office for Harmonization in the Internal Market* [1998] ECR II–2217).

[175] 'Rapport du groupe de reflexion sur l'avenir du système juridictionnel des Communautés européennes', chaired by Ole Due, former President of the Court of Justice, Brussels, Jan. 2000.

for appointment to high judicial office' rather than mere 'judicial office', the Treaty of Nice makes numerous substantive changes to the role and functions of the CFI:

—It becomes the court of general jurisdiction for all actions for annulment, illegal failure to act, and damages, for staff disputes (if not for long), and for arbitration actions, subject to those classes of action or proceedings in specific areas to be attributed to the judicial panels, and those which are reserved to the ECJ;

—The CFI may be called upon to give preliminary rulings 'in specific areas laid down by the Statute'. This is a truly revolutionary change, given that the splitting of preliminary ruling jurisdiction was one of the proposals the ECJ set its face most firmly against in 1995,[176] though the determination of the 'specific areas' is left to a unanimous decision of the Council. A saving clause allows, but does not oblige, the CFI to refer to the ECJ any case 'requir[ing] a decision of principle likely to affect the unity or consistency of Community law'.[177]

—The right of appeal from judgments of the CFI is moved from the Treaty to the ECJ Statute; while it is preserved intact for now, it can be abolished for any particular form of action by the Council acting unanimously;

—The CFI itself becomes a court of appeal in actions or proceedings against the decisions of the judicial panels, as it already is for the Trade Mark Office; the constituent act of the judicial panel will determine in each case whether this is to be an appeal on a point of law only, such as that exercised by the ECJ over CFI judgments, or whether it is a full appeal including matters of fact.

The first paragraph of Article 224 EC as amended provides that the court 'shall comprise at least one judge from each Member State', though Article 48 of the new ECJ Statute fixes the number at an unqualified fifteen. The second paragraph of Article 224 EC provides for the possibility of permanent Advocates General at the CFI. A reported Council agreement earlier in 2000 to appoint a further six judges to ease the current pressure of work at the CFI, particularly from trade-mark cases which are beginning to make their presence felt, seems to have disappeared without trace.

(c) The European Court of Justice   The ultimate effect of the Treaty of Nice on the functioning of the Court of Justice is to some extent dependent on the use the Council makes of its new powers regarding the lower levels of Community jurisdiction. In any case, the Treaty makes the following amendments concerning directly the Court of Justice.

---

[176] 'Report of the Court of Justice on certain aspects of the application of the Treaty on European Union', Luxembourg, 1995, para. 13. By 1999, the Court's stance had considerably softened ('The Future of the Judicial System of the European Union', Luxembourg, 1999, Chap. IV(3)(iii)).

[177] Art. 225(3), second subpara., EC.

Composition

Article 221 EC as amended will provide that the 'Court of Justice shall consist of one judge from each Member State'; while it is of course legally possible for a future IGC to amend this, as the Member States unceremoniously dumped the 700-member ceiling for the European Parliament at Nice,[178] it is a clear political signal to all concerned, current and future Member States, that the rule of one judge per Member State will be maintained, all suggestions to the contrary notwithstanding.[179] The power of the Council, acting unanimously, to increase the number of judges at the Court's request is, however, abolished, thereby dissipating any lingering, theoretical, danger of 'court-packing'. The number of Advocates General is maintained at eight; this is generally considered to be a definitive figure, though it may still be increased at any time by the Council at the Court's request.

Functioning

The relaxation of the unanimity requirement for the Council approval of the Court's rules of procedure effected by the modified sixth paragraph of Article 224 EC goes some way to meeting a long-standing request by the Court. Only the Court's language régime remains subject to a unanimity requirement, under a proposed amendment to Article 290 EC.

At the same time, the Member States transferred certain arrangements from the Court's rules to the body of the Treaty, making them more difficult to amend, should the need arise. The small plenary, a creature devised by the Court itself to palliate the administrative burden of the requirement that the Court sit in plenary session, is now reborn as the 'Grand Chamber'. This is a chamber of eleven judges, with a quorum of nine, presided over by the President of the Court and containing the Presidents of the five-judge chambers; as the latter are now also to be elected for a three-year term,[180] the Grand Chamber ensures a certain continuity of personnel and jurisprudential consistency. Indeed, as the vast majority of cases will be heard in chambers, and preliminary rulings will in the future be heard by chambers of the Court of First Instance, ensuring such consistency is likely to be the main concern of the Grand Chamber. The Grand Chamber will probably, of practical necessity, need to be constituted for a longer period than the current one year for ECJ chambers, presumably three years, as few plenary cases will in fact be dealt with within a single year. The Court is granted a good deal of discretion in deciding how frequently the Grand Chamber will be called into operation; the Statute requires it to consider matters only 'when a Member State or a

---

[178] Proposed amendment to Art. 189, 2nd para, EC.

[179] In its 1995 report cited above, the Court famously warned against the danger of the plenary formation's '[crossing] the invisible boundary between a collegiate court and a deliberative assembly', though acknowledging at the same time that 'the presence of all the national legal systems within the Court is undoubtedly conducive to the harmonious development of Community case-law' (*supra* n. 175, para. 16).

[180] Art. 16, 2nd and 1st paras., EC Statute; at present the Court's rules provide that Presidents of Chambers are elected for one year (Art. 10(1)).

Community institution that is party to the proceedings so requests', a facility used very sparingly at present for compulsory referral of a case to the plenary formation. Obviously the Grand Chamber will be the normal forum for dealing with novel points of Treaty interpretation and other matters of principle arising for the first time, and for ironing out any possible divergences of interpretation which result from judgments adopted by the smaller chambers.

The full plenary formation, with a quorum of eleven, survives, though it is required by the Statute only for rulings on the divestiture of office of the Ombudsman, Commissioners, or Members of the Court of Auditors. A full plenary formation may also be convened to hear any 'case of exceptional importance'.

Article 222, second paragraph, EC takes up a popular suggestion regarding the possibility for the Court to decide cases without the benefit of an Opinion of an Advocate General, though only where the Court, having heard the Advocate General on the procedural point, 'considers that the case raises no new point of law' (Article 20, fifth paragraph, ECJ Statute).

Remarkably, Article 20 of the new unified 'Statute of the Court of Justice', to replace the separate EC and Euratom Statutes, still provides that the procedure of the Court must include an oral part, which 'shall consist of . . . the hearing of the Court of agents, advisers and lawyers', though in an increasingly large proportion of cases the Court dispenses with the oral hearing.[181]

Jurisdiction

The Court's jurisdiction at first and final instance in direct actions will be restricted to those commenced by Member States, Community Institutions, and the European Central Bank, while its future juridiction at first and final instance in respect of preliminary rulings will depend on precisely what 'specific areas' are transferred to the jurisdiction of the Court of First Instance. On the other hand, the Court's appellate function is likely to grow considerably in volume and importance; in providing that CFI decisions '*may* be subject to a right of appeal', Article 225(1), second subparagraph, EC opens the way to a possible future filtering mechanism, to enable the Court to cope with the volume of such appeals.[182]

Apart from appeals strictly so-called, the Court will have to deal with 'review' of CFI judgments in two areas, preliminary rulings and appeals from judicial panels, in each case 'where there is a serious risk of the unity or consistency of Community law being affected'. Article 62 of the Court of Justice Statute lays down a special procedure for such review; within a month of the decision of the CFI, the First Advocate General proposes to the Court that it review; within a further month the Court must decide whether or not to review. It appears from the wording of the Statute that the First Advocate General's proposal is a *sine qua non* of the operation of the review procedure, and that his or her decision not to propose is final.

[181] See the modifications to the Court's rules adopted in May 2000 [2000] OJ L122/43.
[182] 'The Future of the Judicial System of the European Union', *supra* n. 175, Chap. III(2).

The new review procedure poses a number of more substantive problems which are adumbrated in Declaration No. 13 on Article 225(2) and (3) EC annexed to the Treaty of Nice. This calls upon the Council to define 'the essential provisions of the review procedure' in the Court's statute and, in particular, the role of the parties in such proceedings, the effect of review on the enforceability of the CFI ruling, and the effect of the judgment of the Court of Justice on the dispute between the parties.

B.   THE CHARTER OF FUNDAMENTAL RIGHTS OF THE EUROPEAN UNION

In parallel to the IGC, a grouping originally known mysteriously as 'the Body', and later, no less mysteriously, as 'the Convention', beavered away on the preparation of a Charter of Fundamental Rights for the European Union.[183] The Charter is divided into seven chapters, defining rights concerning the protection of human dignity, classical civil liberties ('freedoms'), equal treatment, social rights ('solidarity'), political ('citizens') rights, and the right to fair legal procedures ('justice'), as well as general provisions, including a safeguard for the existing standard of protection under national or international law, and a prohibition on the abuse of the rights. Unlike the ECHR, the Charter rights are drafted in unqualified terms, with a few general exceptions. The Charter was solemnly proclaimed by Parliament, the Council, and the Commission, but not the Member States, at the European Council in Nice.

Within weeks of its proclamation, the Charter had been relied on before the CFI, which declared it temporally inapplicable in the particular proceedings,[184] and cited by a number of Advocates General.[185]

---

[183] Published for information as [2000] OJ C364; see Vitorino (2000) 3 *RDUE* 499; Fernández Sola, (2000) 442 *RMCUE* 595 and Dutheil de la Rochère (2000) 443 *RMCUE* 674.

[184] Case T–112/98, *Mannesmannröhren-Werke AG* v. *Commission* [2001] ECR II–729, judgment of 20 Feb. 2001, not yet reported in ECR, paras. 15 and 76.

[185] The honours go to Tizzano AG (Opinion of 8 Feb. 2001 in Case C–173/99 *BECTU*, judgment of 26 June 2001, not yet reported), though Jacobs AG was not far behind (Opinion of 22 Mar. 2001 in Case C–270/99 P, *Z* v. *Parliament*, pending).

European Union Employment and Social Policy 1999–2000

CATHERINE BARNARD* AND TAMARA HERVEY**

I. Introduction

At the Lisbon summit in March 2000[1] the Union set itself a new strategic goal 'to become the most competitive and dynamic knowledge-based economy in the world capable of sustainable economic growth with more and better jobs and greater social cohesion'. The Presidency Conclusions elaborated:

Achieving this goal requires an *overall strategy* aimed at:

- preparing the transition to a knowledge-based economy and society by better policies for the information society and R & D, as well as by stepping up the process of structural reform for competitiveness and innovation and by completing the internal market;

- modernising the European social model, investing in people and combating social exclusion;

- sustaining the healthy economic outlook and favourable growth prospects by applying an appropriate macro-economic policy mix.

The modernization of the 'European social model' is a key component of these ambitious strategic goals.

Since our last survey,[2] the employment and social policy of the European Union has been reconfigured (or modernized). It is emerging from a period within which its defining notion could be summarized in terms of a dichotomy between social policy as a 'market correcting' or 'market perfecting' device.[3] Perhaps predictably, the 'new European social model' rejects these rationales as mutually exclusive, and aims to consolidate both within a construction that asserts that social protections (of various sorts) are a key component of competitiveness. This is implicit in the Lisbon Presidency conclusions. The new European social model concerns itself with the need for creating employment

---

* Trinity College, Cambridge.
** University of Nottingham.

[1] Presidency Conclusions, 24 Mar. 2000, paras. 5–7.
[2] Barnard and Hervey, 'EC Social Policy 1995–7' (1998) 18 *YEL* 613–57.
[3] For a history and summary of rationales of European social policy, see Barnard, *EC Employment Law* (OUP, Oxford, 2000), chap. 1; Hervey, *European Social Law and Policy* (Longman, London, 1998), chap. 1 and Barnard, 'EC Social Policy', in Craig and De Búrca (eds.), *The Evolution of EU Law* (OUP, Oxford, 1999).

and giving rights to those in employment, but it also considers the positive impact that social expenditure on health and education, pensions, and social security has on productivity.[4] This is essential for combating social exclusion and increasing social cohesion and solidarity. Therefore, the new European social model is a site for reconciling what used to be conceived of as opposing objectives in the policy agenda[5]—objectives of employment and social rights. This indicates the EU's attempts to find a 'third way'[6] between the 'Anglo-Saxon' model of deregulation, low unemployment, and fewer welfare benefits, and the continental European model of job protection, high unemployment, and generous welfare provision.

Three key documents provide an outline of the contours of the new European social model: the Commission's Communication on the 'Social Policy Agenda',[7] the Guidelines for the Luxembourg Process on employment policy;[8] and the Charter of Fundamental Rights,[9] proclaimed at the Nice Summit in December 2000. According to the Presidency conclusions of the Nice Council, the Charter is to combine in a single text 'the civil, political, economic, social and societal rights, hitherto laid down in a variety of international, European or national sources'. There is, however, some uncertainty whether the Charter will merely achieve such consolidation,[10] or whether it will in effect add to existing legal provisions.[11] In any event, it seems likely that the Charter will bolster the status of the rights contained in it.[12] One of the most striking features of the Charter is that 'social' and 'economic' rights are included on the same footing as 'civil' and 'political' rights. The social rights are mainly contained under Chapter IV, entitled 'Solidarity', and include collective and individual rights in employment law,[13] and rights to social security,

[4] See also COM(2000)379, at 6.
[5] See Addison and Siebert, 'The Social Charter of the European Community: Evolution and Controversies' (1991) 44 *ILRR* 597–625.
[6] See Giddens, *The Third Way: The Renewal of Social Democracy* (Polity, Cambridge, 1998). See also Kenner, 'The EC Employment Title and the "Third Way": Making Soft Law Work' (1999) 15 *IJCLLIR* 33.
[7] COM(2000)379.
[8] See Council Resolution of 15 December 1997 on the 1998 Employment Guidelines [1998] OJ C 30/1.
[9] The process of agreeing the Charter was set in motion at the Cologne summit in June 1999. The Charter was 'solemnly proclaimed' at Nice on 7 Dec. 2000, [2000] OJ C364/1.
[10] For example it contains new rights not previously recognized in the *acquis communautaire*, e.g., Art. 13: 'The arts and scientific research shall be free of constraint. Academic freedom shall be respected.' The Nice Presidency Conclusions state that 'the question of the Charter's force will be considered later'.
[11] Art. 50 provides 'this Charter does not establish any new power or task for the Community or the Union, or modify powers and tasks defined by the Treaties. Art. 51 provides 'Rights recognized by this Charter which are based on the Community treaties or the Treaty on European Union shall be exercised under the conditions and within the limits defined by those Treaties'. But see discussion *infra* at n. 62.
[12] As with any soft law, the Charter may be used by courts in interpreting measures of hard law.
[13] Art. 26 Worker information and consultation; Art. 27 Right of collective bargaining and action; Art. 29 Protection from unjustified dismissal; Art. 30 Right to working conditions respecting health, safety and dignity; limited working hours and paid leave; Art. 32 Reconciliation of work and family life.

social assistance, health care, and other 'services of general economic interest'.[14]

Building on the Presidency Conclusions at the Lisbon summit which emphasized the need to modernize the European social model in order to confront the technological and societal changes facing the European Union, the Commission issued a Communication on the 'Social Policy Agenda'.[15] At the heart of this agenda lies the 'guiding principle' of strengthening the 'role of social policy as a productive factor'.[16] Thus, the new European social model combines 'good social conditions with high productivity and high quality goods and services'.[17] A wide range of actors are expected to help achieve these objectives: 'the European Union institutions, the Member States, the regional and local levels, the social partners, civil society and companies'.[18] In recent years, the role of the social partners has assumed particular importance. In the Social Policy Agenda, the Commission reiterates the view that the 'social partners at all levels should play their full role, in particular to negotiate agreements and to modernize and adapt the contractual framework and contribute to a sound macro-economic policy'. It adds that the 'non governmental organisations will be closely associated with the development of inclusive policies and equal opportunities for all'.[19] Thus, the Commission appears to focus on a new form of governance, 'providing a clear and active role to all stakeholders and actors enabling them to participate in managing the policies associated with this new Agenda'.

The Agenda continues to place considerable emphasis on 'raising the employment rate' to underpin the sustainability and financing of social protection systems and minimize 'the underuse of human resources'. However, this time, the target is more ambitious than the Treaty of Amsterdam: as the Lisbon Summit made clear, the emphasis is on regaining 'the conditions for *full employment*', and not just a high level of employment, as in the Employment Title of the Treaty of Amsterdam. This goal is to be achieved not by harmonization of social policies but through the 'open method of co-ordination' which involves extensive use of soft law measures: 'establishing policy guidelines, setting benchmarks, concrete targets and a monitoring system to evaluate progress via a peer group review'.[20] This open method of

---

[14] Art. 33 Social security and social assistance; Art. 34 Health care; Art. 35 Services of general economic interest. 'Services of general economic interest' are those where it is considered by national public authorities that the service needs to be provided even where the market may not provide sufficient incentives to do so, see Commission Communication on Services of General Economic Interest COM(2000)580. They include services relating to matters such as transport, energy, telecommunications, postal services, radio, and television.

[15] COM(2000)379.   [16] *Ibid.*, 5.   [17] *Ibid.*, 7.   [18] *Ibid.*, 14.

[19] See also Opinion of the Economic and Social Committee on 'The Role and Contribution of Civil Society Organizations in the Building of Europe' ([1999] OJ L329/30): '[c]ivil society is a collective term for all types of social action, by individuals or groups, that do not emanate from the state and are not run by it . . . The participatory model of civil society also provides an opportunity to strengthen confidence in the democratic system so that a more favourable climate for reform and innovation can develop'.

[20] COM(2000)379, at 7.

co-ordination characterizes the Luxembourg process which was set in train by the European Council on 20–21 November 1997, at the so-called Jobs Summit, prior to the Amsterdam Treaty coming into force. Under the 'Luxembourg process' the first guidelines outlining policy areas for 1998 were agreed by the Member States and adopted by the Council of Ministers.[21] The Member States were then obliged to incorporate these guidelines into National Action Plans (NAPs). The guidelines have centred on four main 'pillars'.[22] The first of the pillars is *employability*, which focuses on the prevention of long-term and youth unemployment by means of vocational education and training[23] and active labour market policies including the placement of young workers in work experience schemes and subsidies to employers offering training. Secondly, the *entrepreneurship* pillar attempts to make the process of business start-ups more straightforward, and incorporates steps to revise regulations affecting small businesses. The *adaptability* pillar encourages negotiation over the improvement of productivity through the reorganization of working practices and production processes. The reduction and renegotiation of working time, the flexible implementation of labour standards, and information and consultation over training issues have also come under this heading. The benefits of this approach for both employers and employees were stressed in the Commission's Communication on the Social Policy Agenda, in terms of protecting or improving *quality of work*. Finally, the *equal opportunities* pillar has been concerned with raising awareness of issues relating to gender equality in terms of equal access to work, family friendly policies, and the needs of people with disabilities.[24]

This is not the place to assess the Luxembourg process.[25] However, the framework for the European Union's employment *policy* provides a useful structure within which to assess recent developments in Community employment *law*.[26] This will form the first part of our survey. The second part will consider the *social policy* element of the Commission's Social Policy Agenda.

---

[21] Council Resolution of 15 Dec. 1997 on the 1998 Employment Guidelines [1998] OJ C30/1.

[22] Barnard and Deakin, 'A Year of Living Dangerously? EC Social Rights, Employment Policy, and EMU' (1997) 2 *Industrial Relations Journal European Annual Review* 355.

[23] See Resolution of the Council and Representatives of the Governments of the Member States on the employment and social dimension of the information society [2000] OJ C8/1.

[24] See generally the Commission's 'EQUAL' programme.

[25] See Deakin and Reed, 'The Contested Meaning of Labour Market Flexibility: Economic Theory and the Discourse of European Integration'; and Szyszczak, 'The Evolving European Employment Strategy'; in Shaw (ed.), *Social Law and Policy in an Evolving EU* (Hart, Oxford, 2000); Kenner, *supra* n. 6.

[26] For discussion of the distinction between employment policy and employment law, see Freedland, 'Employment Policy' in Davies *et al.*, *European Community Labour Law: Principles and Perspectives. Liber Amicorum Lord Wedderburn of Charlton* (Clarendon Press, Oxford, 1996).

II. 'Employment Policy'

A. EMPLOYABILITY

The link between the competitiveness of the European economy and the education and training provided to its workforce was first made explicit in Commission thinking in the Delors White Paper on Growth, Competitiveness and Employment.[27] Since 1993, Commission education policy has increasingly focused upon 'lifelong learning', the idea that in a post-Fordist world, the knowledge and skills of members of the workforce must be constantly updated to keep pace with changes in technology, and to respond to new patterns of work, in particular the demise of a 'job for life'. Lifelong learning, then, is presented as one answer to Europe's unemployment problems. Thus the field of education and training provides a clear example of social protection as a 'productive factor' in the European economy. However, given that competence for matters of education and training remains largely at national level, there are (legal, and also practical political) limits to the extent to which the EU institutions may intervene in the field. To some extent, the legal limitations on the Community's competence in the education field have been lifted by the jurisprudence of the European Court of Justice, in opportunistic litigation, mainly brought by free-moving students in tertiary education.[28] Through these cases, and subsequent legislative responses, and Treaty reform, the contours of Community education policy, as part of the free movement of persons, were established.

The Commission communication *Towards a Europe of Knowledge*[29] sets out guidelines for Community action in the fields of education and training for 2000–6. This document makes clear the policy linkage between education as an element of employability, and the pre-existing Community law and policy on education and vocational training, as part of the free movement of persons, or citizenship, provisions.[30] The main thrust of the guidelines is to work

[27] *Growth, Competitiveness and Employment. The Challenges and Ways Forward into the 21st Century.* Bull. EC, Supp. 6, 1993. See Shaw, 'From the Margins to the Centre: Education and Training Law and Policy' in Craig and de Búrca (eds.), *The Evolution of EU Law* (OUP, Oxford, 1999).

[28] See, for instance, Case 39/86, *Lair* v. *Universität Hannover* [1988] ECR 3161, Case C–3/90, *Bernini* v. *Minister van Onderwijsten Wetenschappen* [1992] ECR I–1071; Case 293/83, *Gravier* v. *City of Liège* [1985] ECR 593, Case 197/86, *Brown* v. *Secretary of State for Scotland* [1988] ECR 3205, Case C–357/89, *Raulin* v. *Minister van Onderwijst en Wetenschappen* [1992] ECR I–1027.

[29] COM(97)563 final.

[30] This includes the educational and training rights of migrant workers (Regulation 1612/68/EEC [1968] OJ Spec. Ed., [1968] JO L257/2 Art. 7(2) and (3); Case 39/86, *Lair* [1988] ECR 3161; Case C–3/90, *Bernini* [1992] ECR I–1071); the rights of migrant students (Case 293/83, *Gravier* [1985] ECR 593; Case 197/86, *Brown* [1988] ECR 3205; Case C–357/89, *Raulin* [1992] ECR I–1027); and the mutual recognition of educational and professional qualifications. See further, Shaw, *supra* n. 27, Hervey, *supra* n. 3, chap. 6. Recently, in this field, the Parliament and Council have adopted Directive 99/42/EC [1999] OJ L201/77 completing the mechanism for mutual recognition of professional qualifications further to Directive 89/48/EC [1989] OJ L19/16 and Directive 92/51/EC [1992] OJ L209/25.

towards an 'open and dynamic European education area', within which citizens of the EU are to have the means of constantly updating their knowledge and to acquire skills attuned to developments in the organization and nature of work. The creation of such a 'European education area' is an extremely ambitious scheme, which would require a high degree of harmonization or at least convergence of national education and training provision. However, in spite of this, the Commission has had some modest success in translating its proposals into action.

For instance, the existing and largely successful mobility programmes in education and training (Socrates, Leonardo, and Youth for Europe, along with Tempus) are to be continued for the period 2000–6. Some changes in priorities, in particular an increased focus on lifelong learning[31] and encouraging the use of new technologies, are to be noted. Another example is the '*e*Europe 2002' action plan, concerning harnessing the benefits of the Internet and World Wide Web, elements of which have an educational dimension.[32] The Commission is also acting as a co-ordinator in determining best practice in some educational matters, for instance in evaluating quality in school education.[33] This mode of action reflects the new mechanisms of governance, in particular the 'open method of co-ordination', now applicable in the employment and social policy fields.

B.   ADAPTABILITY/QUALITY OF WORK

Under the pillar of 'Encouraging Adaptability', the 1998 Employment Guidelines[34] provide that the Social Partners are invited to negotiate, at the appropriate levels, agreements 'to modernize the organization of work, including flexible working arrangements, with the aim of making undertakings productive and competitive and achieving the required balance between flexibility and security'.[35] One element of such 'quality of work' is the regulation of work-

---

[31] See also Report for the Commission, *ECTS Extension Feasibility Project* (Jan. 2000) on the feasibility of applying the 'European Credit Transfer Scheme'—a system of recognition of educational 'credits' across the EU—to lifelong learning; Proposal for Decision on a European Year of Languages 2001, COM(99)485 final.

[32] Commission, *e-Learning—Designing Tomorrow's Education* COM(2000)318 final. See also Commission, *Designing Tomorrow's Education: Promoting Innovation with New Technologies* COM(2000)23 final; the 'Netd@ys Europe' initiative (IP/00/1189).

[33] See Council Recommendation 98/561/EC [1998] OJ L270/56; Council Resolution on the 1999 employment guidelines [1999] OJ C69/2; Commission, *Evaluating Quality in School Education, Pilot Project, Interim and Final Report* (May 1998, June 1999); Proposal for Recommendation of Parliament and Council on European co-operation in quality evaluation in school education COM(99)709 final; amended COM(2000)523. This proposal suggests use of the open method of co-ordination for promoting best practice in quality evaluation in school education.

[34] Council Resolution of 15 Dec. 1997 on the 1998 Employment Guidelines [1998] OJ C30/1. See also the Supiot Report, *Transformation of Labour Law in Europe* (EC Commission, Brussels, June 1998), para. 755.

[35] On the various meanings of 'flexibility' in the context of the EU's social law and policy, see Deakin and Reed, *supra* n. 25, at 73–86.

ing time. The much-criticized Directive on Working Time 93/104[36] is now being supplemented by sectoral agreements negotiated by the sectoral social partners[37] and, where negotiations have failed, there is a proposal to extend the provisions of Directive 93/104 to these sectors, as well as to non-mobile workers in the transport industry and to doctors in training.[38]

Another aspect of flexible working arrangements concerns atypical workers. In the past, Community employment law has tended to conceptualize the employment contract along traditional lines, as between employer and full-time, permanent employee. However, in recognition of changing patterns of work, Community law has increasingly begun to cover 'atypical' employment contracts. Key examples are found in Directive 97/81 on part-time work[39] and Directive 99/70 on fixed-term work,[40] both negotiated by the social partners and extended to all workers by a directive. These Directives attempt to reconcile, on the one hand, demand-side needs for numerical flexibility, allowing employers to modulate the numbers employed, and on the other the supply-side (employee) needs for family friendly policies.[41] Both Directives are under-pinned by application of the principle of non-discrimination between atypical and typical workers. The effect of this, however, is that the model against which entitlements are provided remains that of the traditional employment contract.

The purpose of the 1999 agreement on fixed-term work[42] is to 'improve the

---

[36] [1993] OJ L307/18. Barnard, 'Working Time in the UK' (1999) 29 *ILJ* 61 and 'Working Time Regulations 1999' (2000) 30 *ILJ* 167.

[37] See, e.g., Council Directive 99/63/EC concerning the Agreement on the organization of working time of seafarers concluded by the European Community Shipowners' Association (ECSA) and the Federation of Transport Workers' Unions in the European Union (FST) ([1999] OJ L167/33, corrected [1999] OJ L244/64) and European Agreement on the Organization of Working Time of Mobile Staff in Civil Aviation, 22 Mar. 2000.

[38] COM(97)334.

[39] Council Directive 97/81/EC ([1998] OJ L14/9) and extended to the UK by Council Directive 98/23/EC ([1998] OJ L131/10; Consolidated legislation [1998] OJ L131/13). On the background to the legislation, see Jeffery, 'Not Really Going to Work? Of the Directive on Part-time Work, "Atypical Work" and Attempts to Regulate It' (1998) 3 *ILJ* 193.

[40] [1999] OJ L175/143. For the original proposal, see COM(99)203 final. The Member States have until 10 July 2001 to comply with the Directive (see Corrigendum [1999] OJ L244/64). For a discussion of the potential impact of the Directive, see the contributions to the special issue of the (1999) 15/2 *IJCLLIR*. See also Barnard, *supra* n. 3.

[41] See generally, Deakin and Read, *supra* n. 25; on the emerging concept of 'family' in Community law, see McGlynn, 'A Family Law for the EU?' in Shaw (ed.), *supra* n. 25.

[42] The agreement applies to 'fixed-term workers who have an employment contract or employment relationship as defined in law, collective agreements or practice in each Member State' (Cl. 1). Clause 3 provides that a 'fixed-term worker' means a person having an employment contract or relationship entered into directly between an employer and a worker where the end of the employment contract or relationship is determined by objective conditions such as reaching a specific date, completing a specific task, or the occurrence of a specific event. The Preamble to the agreement makes clear that the 'agreement applies to fixed-term workers with the exception of those placed by a temporary work agency at the disposition of a user enterprise'. In addition, Member States, after consultation with the Social Partners, may provide that this agreement does not apply to:

    (a) initial vocational training relationships and apprenticeship schemes;
    (b) employment contracts and relationships which have been concluded within the framework of a specific public or publicly-supported training, integration and vocational retraining programme. (Cl. 2(2)).

quality of fixed-term work by ensuring the application of the principle of non-discrimination; and to establish a framework to prevent abuse arising from the use of successive fixed-term employment contracts or relationships'.[43]

The agreement contains three main rights for fixed-term workers. First, the principle of non-discrimination applies. Clause 4 provides that in respect of the (limited) field of employment conditions, fixed-term workers shall not be treated in a less favourable manner than comparable permanent workers solely because they have a fixed-term contract or relationship, unless justified on objective grounds. Where appropriate, the principle of *pro rata temporis* applies. The term 'comparable permanent worker' means a worker with an employment contract or relationship of an indefinite duration, in the same establishment, engaged in the same or similar work or occupation, due regard being given to qualifications and skills.[44] Where there is no comparable permanent worker in the same establishment, the comparison must be made by reference to the applicable collective agreement, or where there is no applicable collective agreement, in accordance with national law, collective agreements, or practice. The arrangements for the application of this clause are to be defined by the Member States after consultation with the Social Partners, having regard to Community law, national law, collective agreements, and practice. Further, Clause 4(4) provides that period of service qualifications relating to particular conditions of employment must be the same for fixed-term workers as for permanent workers except where different length of service qualifications are justified on objective grounds.

The second element of protection is prevention of abuse of fixed-term contracts. In countries such as the UK there are, at present, no limits on the number of occasions on which fixed-term contracts can be renewed.[45] As a result, Clause 5(1) provides that:

Member States, after consultation with social partners in accordance with national law, collective agreements or practice, and/or the social partners, shall, where there are no equivalent legal measures to prevent abuse, introduce in a manner which takes account of the needs of specific sectors and/or categories of workers, one or more of the following measures:
a) objective reasons justifying the renewal of such contracts or relationships;
b) the maximum total duration of successive fixed-term employment contracts or relationships;[46]
c) the number of renewals of such contracts or relationships.

The third right relates to information. Clause 6 requires employers to inform fixed-term workers about vacancies which become available in the undertak-

---

[43] Cl. 1.   [44] Cl. 3(2).
[45] Although continuity of employment may be implied for the purposes of access to statutory rights, such as the right not to be unfairly dismissed, in certain circumstances.
[46] Member States after consultation with the Social Partners and/or the Social Partners, shall, where appropriate, determine under what conditions fixed-term employment contracts or relationships: (a) shall be regarded as 'successive'; (b) shall be deemed to be contracts or relationships of an indefinite duration (Cl. 5(2)).

ing or establishment by, for example, displaying a general announcement at a suitable place in the undertaking, to ensure that fixed-term workers have the same opportunity to secure permanent positions as other workers. Further, as far as possible, employers must facilitate access by fixed-term workers to appropriate training opportunities to enhance their skills, career development, and occupational mobility.

The two Directives on part-time work and fixed-term work attempt to reconcile 'adaptability' for employers with 'quality of work' for employees. In respect of the twenty-four million people working part-time in the EU there may be a degree of coalescence of interests. From the employer's point of view, part-time work provides the flexibility necessary to meet changing consumer demands and economic trends. From the worker's point of view, it may provide the only access to any employment, or the flexibility to make it easier to combine work with other family responsibilities.[47] Through the principle of non-discrimination, the agreement provides a degree of protection for these workers. However, while part-time work may well represent a positive 'choice' for many workers, those engaged under fixed-term contracts would usually choose, if the choice was available, contracts of indefinite duration,[48] since fixed-term contracts, by their very nature, are insecure and precarious. It is therefore somewhat surprising that both the part-time work and fixed-term work agreements are drafted in a similar manner and are based on the principle of non-discrimination. Thus, it appears that the 'adaptability' element, rather than the notion of 'quality of work', seems to be asserting itself more strongly in this area of Community employment law.

The difference between the two types of work is recognized to a limited extent. The fixed-term work agreement does not contain a clause requiring Member States and the Social Partners to remove obstacles to fixed-term work. Further, the Preamble to the fixed-term work agreement expressly states that 'contracts of an indefinite duration are, and will continue to be, the general form of employment relationship'. However, given the differences between the nature of fixed-term and part-time work, Murray argues[49] that the protection needed by temporary workers is a full-fledged scheme of portability of entitlements which recognizes all relevant working experience, even if undertaken with different employers and with breaks in between, to qualify for employment rights. This, rather than the principle of non-discrimination, would provide security for fixed-term workers which would balance the flexibility offered by fixed-term contracts to employers.

---

[47] Green Paper, *Partnership for a New Organization of Work*, COM(97)127 final, para. 52.
[48] See Delsen, 'Atypical Employment Relations and Government Policy in Europe' (1991) 5 *Labour* 123 and Murray, 'Normalising Temporary Work' (1999) 28 *ILJ* 269.
[49] *Ibid.*

C. EQUAL OPPORTUNITIES

Promoting equal opportunities has always been the key pillar of the EU's employment and social law. Its prominence continues to grow. The Treaty of Amsterdam explicitly introduced equality between men and women as one of the tasks (Article 2) and activities (Article 3) of the Community. At much the same time, mainstreaming[50] has become a major policy issue. In the 1999 Employment Guidelines,[51] the Commission emphasized the need to pursue integration of equal opportunities for men and women into all aspects of employment policies, notably by guaranteeing active employment market policies for the vocational integration of women proportionate to their rate of unemployment and by promoting women in the context of entrepreneurship. The 2000 Guidelines focus on facilitating reintegration of men and women into the labour market after a period of absence.[52] The Social Policy Agenda has also emphasized the need '[t]o promote full participation of women in economic, scientific, social, political and civic life as a key component of democracy. This is not only an issue of rights, but also a major component for promoting social and economic progress. The long-standing commitments on equality between women and men at European level should be broadened and a gender perspective should be mainstreamed into all relevant policies.'

The goal of achieving equality is no longer confined to men and women. A new provision, Article 13 (ex Article 6a), was introduced at Amsterdam to allow the Council to adopt measures to prohibit other types of discrimination. This provides:

Without prejudice to the other provisions of this Treaty and within the limits of the powers conferred by it on the Community, the Council, acting unanimously on a proposal from the Commission and after consulting the European Parliament, may take appropriate action to combat discrimination based on sex, racial or ethnic origin, religion or belief, disability, age or sexual orientation.[53]

A new second paragraph was added to Article 13 EC by the Treaty of Nice. Article 13 (2) allows Council to adopt 'flanking policy' measures, that is, those

---

[50] See further, Beveridge, Nott, and Stephen, 'Addressing Gender in Law and Policy-making' in Shaw (ed.), *supra* n. 25, at 148–52; Beveridge and Nott, 'Gender Auditing: Making the Community Work for Women' in Hervey and O'Keeffe (eds.), *Sex Equality Law in the European Union* (Wiley, Chichester, 1996).

[51] [1999] OJ C69/2.

[52] Proposal for Guidelines for Member States' Employment Policies 2000.

[53] Only 'social origin' was lost from the original list proposed by the Irish Presidency, *The European Union Today and Tomorrow. Adapting the European Union for the Benefit of its Peoples and Preparing it for the Future. A General Outline for a Draft Revision of the Treaties*, Brussels, 5 Dec. 1996, CONF/2500/96. See Bell and Waddington, 'The 1996 Intergovernmental Conference and the Prospects of a Non-Discrimination Treaty Article' (1996) 25 *ILJ* 320; Bell, 'The New Article 13 EC Treaty: A Sound Basis for European Anti-discrimination Law?' (1999) 6 *MJ* 5; Waddington, 'Article 13 EC: Mere Rhetoric or a Harbinger of Change' (1999) 1 *CYELS* 175 and 'Testing the Limits of the EC Treaty Article on Non-discrimination' (1999) 28 *ILJ* 133; Flynn, 'The Implications of Article 13 EC—After Amsterdam, will Some Forms of Discrimination be more Equal than Others?' (1999) 36 *CMLRev.* 1127; Bell, 'Anti-discrimination Law after Amsterdam' in Shaw (ed.), *supra* n. 25.

that involve no harmonization of national laws, in this field, by qualified majority.

Using the powers in Article 13 (1), the Commission introduced a 'package' of four instruments:

1. A Communication on certain Community measures to combat discrimination;[54]
2. A Directive to establish a general framework for equal treatment in employment and occupation (the 'horizontal' labour market Directive);[55]
3. A Directive to implement the principle of equal treatment between persons irrespective of racial or ethnic origin;[56]
4. A Decision to establish an Action Plan to combat discrimination 2001–6.[57]

The horizontal Directive, which applies to all the groups identified in Article 13, excluding sex, race and ethnic origin, and nationality, concerns employment and occupation. The Race Directive is, however, more far-reaching and touches areas at the outer limits of Community competence.[58] This is interesting, given that the governments of the Member States at Amsterdam appeared to be keen to stress that Article 13 EC applies only within the limits of Community competence. It appears that the position of Jorg Haider's Freedom Party in the Austrian government may have contributed to the determination of the governments of the Member States to enact a wide-ranging race discrimination measure.[59] The horizontal Directive applies the principles of non-discrimination to the conditions for access to employment, self-employment, and occupation; access to all types and to all levels of vocational guidance, vocational training, advanced vocational training, and retraining; employment and working conditions, including dismissals and pay; membership of and involvement in an organization of workers or employers, or any other organization whose members carry on a particular profession, including the benefits provided for by such organizations; social protection, including

---

[54] COM(99)564.

[55] COM(99)565, now adopted as Directive 2000/78/EC [2000] OJ L303/16.

[56] COM(99)566, now adopted as Directive 2000/43/EC implementing the principle of equal treatment between persons irrespective of racial or ethnic origin [2000] OJ L180/22.

[57] COM(99)567, now adopted as Decision 2000/750/EC [2000] OJ L303/23. The new Art. 13(2) will presumably allow measures such as this to be adopted by qualified majority in Council.

[58] If the Directive is lawfully enacted on the basis of Art. 13 EC, and Art. 13 EC does not extend the material scope of Community competence, but merely gives power to enact non-discrimination provisions with respect to matters falling within Community competence, then the list of substantive matters covered in the Directive will have to be construed as falling within the scope of Community law. One way to do this might be in terms of the provision in Art. 308 (ex 235) EC, which gives the EU institutions power to take appropriate measures to achieve the objectives of the Community. The objectives of the Community are set out in Art. 2 EC, and include the provision of 'a high level of social protection, [and] . . . the raising of the standard of living and quality of life'. Measures on non-discrimination in, for instance, housing, might thus be conceptualized as concerned with the raising of the standard of living. See recital 9 of the Preamble to the Directive.

[59] Guild, 'The EC Directive on Race Discrimination: Surprises, Possibilities and Limitations' (2000) 29 *ILJ* 416–23.

social security and healthcare; social advantages; education, including grants and scholarships; and access to and supply of goods and services, including housing. This is considerably more ambitious than the existing directives on sex equality which apply to employment and occupation, although the Commission's Social Policy Agenda talks of further strengthening equality rights by making a proposal for an equal treatment directive based on Article 13 in areas other than employment and occupation.

The Treaty of Amsterdam also amended Article 119 (new Article 141) on equal pay: Article 141(1) (ex Article 119(1)) extended the definition of equal pay for equal work by reference to 'or work of equal value'. The new Article 141(3) finally provided an express legal basis for the Council to adopt measures, in accordance with the Article 251 (ex Article 189b) co-decision procedure, 'to ensure the application of the principle of equal opportunities and equal treatment of men and women in matters of employment and occupation, including the principle of equal pay for equal work or work of equal value'. This has provided the legal basis for a proposed modification of the 1976 Equal Treatment Directive.[60] Finally, the new Article 141(4) allows Member States to adopt or maintain positive action measures for the under-represented sex in respect of professional careers.

At the same time equality has assumed considerable prominence in the Charter of Fundamental Rights 2000. Following the model found in many modern Constitutions, Article 20 provides: '[e]veryone is equal before the law'. Article 21 then spells out the meaning of this in terms of anti-discrimination.[61] It provides:

1. Any discrimination based on any ground such as sex, race, *colour*, ethnic or *social origin, genetic features, language*, religion or belief, *political or any other opinion, membership of a national minority, property, birth*, disability, age or sexual orientation shall be prohibited (emphasis added).
2. Within the scope of application of the Treaty establishing the European Community and of the Treaty on European Union, and without prejudice to the special provisions of those Treaties, any discrimination on grounds of nationality shall be prohibited.

The list of grounds on which discrimination is prohibited is longer than the list found in Article 13. This sits uncomfortably with the statement in Article 51(2) that '[t]his Charter does not establish any new power or task for the Community or the Union, or modify powers and tasks defined by the Treaties'.[62]

---

⁶⁰ COM(2000)334 final. The main proposed modifications include defining sexual harassment and including it within the scope of sex discrimination; defining indirect discrimination and genuine occupational qualifications in line with the Art. 13 measures; inclusion of a woman's right to return to her job or an equivalent post after giving birth; and establishment of a framework applicable to independent 'equality commissions' at national level.

⁶¹ See further Barnard, 'The Principle of Equality in the Community context: *P, Grant, Kalanke* and *Marschall*: Four Uneasy Bedfellows' (1998) 57 *CLJ* 352.

⁶² See *supra* n. 11. The extent to which the Charter will alter the existing legal position remains ambiguous. See Verkaik, 'Britain may veto EU's new Human Rights Charter', *Independent*, 8 Feb. 2000; BBC Radio 4 *World at One* interview with Keith Vaz, MP, 12 Oct. 2000; Norman and Parker,

Article 23 deals specifically with '[e]quality between men and women' which must 'be ensured in all areas, including employment, work and pay'. It continues that '[t]he principle of equality shall not prevent the maintenance or adoption of measures providing for specific advantages in favour of the under-represented sex'. In addition, Article 33(2), found in the section on solidarity and not equality, provides: '[t]o reconcile family and professional life, everyone shall have the right to protection from dismissal for a reason connected with maternity and the right to paid maternity leave and to parental leave following the birth or adoption of a child'.

These statements and measures are wholly consistent with the notion that social rights should be seen as an input to growth. At the same time, they recognize that social rights, and equality in particular, have an independent, and not merely functional, value. As the Commission's Social Policy Agenda explains, '[t]o ensure the development and respect of fundamental social rights [is] a key component of an equitable society and of respect for human dignity'. This is reminiscent of the Court of Justice's decision in *P & S* that to tolerate discrimination on the ground of gender reassignment would be 'tantamount, as regards such a person, to a failure to respect the dignity and freedom to which he or she is entitled, and which the Court has a duty to safeguard'.[63] It remains to be seen, however, whether this rights-based definition of equality will prevail in situations of practical application of the detail of employment law. To assess this, we must turn to the measures of Community law concerning the reconciliation of work and family life.

(i) Reconciling Work and Family Life

The most important step taken by the Community towards reconciling work and family life has been the negotiation of the parental leave agreement which was implemented by Directive 96/34.[64] Insufficient time has elapsed to assess the effectiveness of this Directive. Nevertheless, experience from the Nordic countries where parental leave already exists indicates that it is usually the woman who takes the parental leave.[65] This fact was recognized by the Court in *Lewen*,[66] where it said that failure to pay a Christmas bonus[67] to employees

---

'Britain resists binding EU Charter on Rights', *Financial Times*, 12 Oct. 2000; Parker and Burns, 'Charter of Rights "would influence European court" ', *Financial Times*, 13 Oct. 2000; Osborn and White, 'Blair goes with flow on lesser EU issues', *Guardian*, 14 Oct. 2000; Castle, 'Summit endorses move to multispeed Europe', *Independent*, 14 Oct. 2000; Groom, 'Government defends line on Charter of Rights', *Financial Times*, 31 Oct. 2000; Heringa, 'Editorial' (2000) 7 *MJ* 111; White, 'Editorial' (2000) 25 *ELRev.* 97; Eicke, 'The European Charter of Fundamental Rights—Unique Opportunity or Fundamental Distraction?' (2000) 3 *EHRLR* 280. According to the Council at Nice, 'the question of the Charter's force will be considered later'.

[63] [1996] ECR I–2143, para. 22.

[64] [1996] OJ L145/4, amended by Directive 97/75/EC ([1998] OJ L10/24), consolidated [1998] OJ L10/11. See also Council Resolution on the balanced participation of women and men in family and working life 2000/C 218/02 ([2000] OJ C218/3).

[65] Bruning and Plontenga, 'Parental Leave and Equal Opportunities' (1999) 9 *JESP* 195.

[66] Case C–333/97 [1999] ECR I–7243, para. 35.

[67] The Court had held the previous month that a Christmas bonus constitutes 'pay' within Art. 141 in Case C–281/97, *Krüger v. Kreiskrankenhaus Ebersberg* [1999] ECR I–5127.

on parental leave was *prima facie* indirectly discriminatory against women. Such discrimination contravened Article 119 (new Article 141) if the bonus was awarded retroactively for work performed in the course of the year and the woman did not receive an amount proportionate to the time worked. If, on the other hand, the bonus was paid as a way of encouraging those in active employment to work hard and to reward *future* loyalty to an employer then failure to pay such a bonus was not discriminatory since a woman on parental leave was in a 'special situation' which could not be 'assimilated to that of a man or woman at work since such leave involves suspension of the contract of employment and, therefore, of the respective obligations of the employer and the worker'.[68] Article 141 also offers no protection against employers taking periods of parental leave (but not maternity leave) into account to reduce the benefit *pro rata.*[69]

The relationship between Article 141 and Directive 76/207 and measures concerning reconciliation of work and family life (Parental Leave Directive, Pregnancy and Maternity Directive) looks set to remain problematic for the foreseeable future. This is largely because the European Court of Justice has never satisfactorily resolved the issue of the extent to which Community sex equality law requires the promotion of *substantive* rather than merely formal equality.[70] A number of factors—the place of equality in new Articles 2 and 3 EC; the placing of reconciliation of work and family life within the 'equality' rather than the 'adaptability' pillar of the employment guidelines; and the place of equality in the Charter on Fundamental Rights—might suggest that an 'equality'-based interpretation should be placed on the provisions on reconciliation of work and family life. If the Court imports its previous sex equality jurisprudence into this new area of Community legislation, particularly in respect of those on maternity leave, this would imply that the new provisions are to operate on the basis of construction (and protection) of workers with families as in a 'special situation'. The price to pay for such a situation might be comparison with a notional 'typical' worker—one who, male or female, has never taken maternity or parental leave. Until Community law manages to free itself from this construct, neither 'quality of work' nor true 'equality' can be said to be promoted by its provisions.

### (ii)	Affirmative Action

Affirmative action is another example of an area where the Court of Justice vacillates between formal and substantive notions of equality.[71] As we have

---

[68]	See, e.g., Case C–342/93, *Gillespie* [1996] ECR I–475; Case C–218/98, *Abdoulaye* [1999] ECR I–5723 (women could be paid a maternity bonus not payable to new fathers); Case C–249/97, *Gruber* v. *Silhouette International Schmied GmbH* [1999] ECR I–5295; Case C–309/97, *Wiener Gebietskrankenkasse* [1999] ECR I–2865; and Case C–333/97, *Lewen* v. *Lothar Denda* [1999] ECR I–7243, para. 38.

[69]	Case C–333/97, *Lewen* [1999] ECR I–7243, paras. 48–49.

[70]	Fenwick and Hervey, 'Sex Equality in the Single Market: New Directions for the European Court of Justice' (1995) 32 *CMLRev.* 443.

[71]	See further Fredman, 'Affirmative Action and the ECJ: A Critical Analysis' in Shaw (ed.), *supra* n. 25.

seen, affirmative action on the grounds of sex is envisaged both by Article 141(4) and the Charter of Fundamental Rights. The provisions of Article 141(4) appear to codify the Court's decision in *Marschall*,[72] which has been discussed in an earlier survey.[73] This upheld, as compatible with Article 2(4) of the Equal Treatment Directive, a state law which gave preference to a woman in a tie-break situation, so long as the apparently equally-qualified man was considered on his individual merits. The Court recognized that:

even where male and female candidates are equally qualified, male candidates tend to be promoted in preference to female candidates particularly because of prejudices and stereotypes concerning the role and capacities of women in working life and the fear, for example, that women will interrupt their careers more frequently, that owing to household and family duties they will be less flexible in their working hours, or that they will be absent from work more frequently because of pregnancy, childbirth and breastfeeding. For these reasons, the mere fact that a male candidate and a female candidate are equally qualified does not mean that they have the same chances.[74]

This is the closest the Court has come to recognizing a substantive approach to equality. In the earlier case of *Kalanke*,[75] the Court, adopting a narrow procedural approach to equality of opportunity, had said that that a rule which *automatically* gave priority to women when they were equally qualified to men did involve discrimination on grounds of sex. More recently, in *Abrahamsson*[76] the Court reaffirmed this approach. It said that a national rule which gave automatic priority to a person of the under-represented sex who had adequate qualifications but which were inferior in minor respects to those of the person who would otherwise have been appointed, failed to satisfy the requirements of Article 2(4) of the Directive and Article 141(4) EC.[77]

On the other hand, the *Marschall* approach is also reflected in recent case law. In *Baedeck*[78] the Court held that Article 2(1) and (4) of Directive 76/207/EEC did not preclude state rules that encouraged 'fair' participation in the workplace by allocating at least half the places for training in public administration to women, subject to certain safeguards. The Court also considered the legality of the so-called 'flexible result quota' in the state of Hessen ('*flexible Ergebnisquote*'). This is a rule applying in sectors of the public service in which women are under-represented. It gives priority to female candidates where male and female candidates for selection have equal qualifications, if this is necessary for complying with the binding targets in the women's advancement plan, provided that there are no reasons of 'greater legal

---

[72] Case C–409/95, *Marschall* v. *Land Nordrhein-Westfalen* [1997] ECR I–6363.
[73] Barnard and Hervey, *supra* n. 2; Barnard, *supra* n. 61, at 366–72; Barnard and Hervey, 'Annotation of Case C–178/94 *Hellmut Marschall*' (1998) 20 *JSWFL* 333–52.
[74] Paras. 29 and 30.
[75] Case C–450/93 [1995] ECR I–3051.
[76] Case C–407/98, *Abrahamsson* v. *Fogelqvist*, Judgment of 6 July 2000, not yet reported in ECR.
[77] This outcome was not affected by the limited number of posts to which the rule applied nor the level of the appointment.
[78] Case C–158/97, *Badeck* v. *Hessischer Ministerpräsident and Landesanwalt beim Staatsgerichtshof des Landes Hessen*, Judgment of 28 Mar. 2000 [2000] Rec. I–1875 (French edn.).

weight'.[79] The Court said that the priority rule introduced by the Hessen law was not 'absolute and unconditional' in the *Kalanke* sense. It was lawful so long as it guaranteed that candidatures were the subject of an objective assessment which took account of the specific personal situations of all candidates. The Court recognized that capabilities and experience acquired by carrying out work in the home were to be taken into account in so far as they were of importance for the suitability, performance, and capability of candidates. By contrast, seniority, age, and the date of last promotion were to be taken into account only in so far as they were of importance to the job. The family status or income of the partner was immaterial. Further, part-time work, leave, and delays in completing training as a result of looking after children or other dependants could not have a negative effect on the selection process. Thus, the Court seems to allow some (indirect) discrimination against men in the application of the selection criteria. Only if a female candidate and a male candidate could not be distinguished on the basis of their qualifications could the woman be chosen according to the flexible quota.

Perhaps the most interesting aspect of the case concerned the Hessen rule which prescribed binding targets for women for temporary posts in the academic service and for academic assistants where women were equally qualified to the men. These targets required that the minimum percentage of women be at least equal to the percentage of women among graduates, holders of higher degrees, and students in each discipline. The *Land* Attorney noted that this minimum quota system came very close to equality as to results, a principle which had been rejected in *Kalanke*. Nevertheless, the Court said that this rule was compatible with Community law. It pointed out that this system did not fix an absolute ceiling but only one relative to the number of persons who had received appropriate training. It said that this amounted to using an actual fact as a quantitative criterion for giving preference to women. This type of 'roll-over' quota comes very close to achieving 'full equality in practice'. Its success depends, however, on the state developing such policies. For instance, this would not be possible in the UK without substantial amendment of the present positive action provisions.[80]

(iii)   Race Discrimination Directive

Directive 2000/43/EC, based on Article 13 EC, implements the principle of equal treatment by prohibiting both direct and indirect discrimination based on racial or ethnic origin (but not nationality).[81] While racial and ethnic origin

---

[79] These reasons of 'greater legal weight' concern 5 rules of law, described as 'social aspects', which make no reference to sex. Preferential treatment is given, first, to former employees in the public service who have left the service because of family commitments; secondly, to individuals who worked on a part-time basis for family reasons and now wish to resume full-time employment; thirdly, to former temporary soldiers; fourthly, to seriously disabled people; and fifthly, to the long-term unemployed. See generally Barnard, *EC Employment Law, supra* n. 3, at 241–8.

[80] See Barnard and Hepple, 'Substantive Equality' (2000) 59 *CLJ* 562–85.

[81] Art. 1. According to the Commission, this is covered by Arts. 12 and 39 EC.

are not defined,[82] the definitions of direct and indirect discrimination are similar to those found in the context of sex equality.[83] Direct discrimination 'shall be taken to occur where one person is treated less favourably than another is, has been or would be treated on grounds of racial or ethnic origin'. Indirect discrimination, by contrast, shall be taken to occur 'where an apparently neutral provision, criterion or practice would put persons of racial or ethnic origin at a particular disadvantage compared with other persons, unless that provision, criterion or practice is objectively justified by a legitimate aim and the means of achieving that aim are appropriate and necessary'.[84] Originally, the definition of indirect discrimination focused on the adverse affect on an individual person or persons rather than on an individual as a member of a group.[85] The US case law, from which the concept derives, as well as the settled case law of the European Court of Justice, as codified in the Burden of Proof Directive 97/80/EC,[86] makes it clear that the adverse impact must be on members of a group, not simply an individual. The drafts came under much criticism[87] and the definition was changed in the final version. However, despite the omission of 'person' in the singular, the definition still does not make it clear that the disadvantage must be suffered by a group of persons of a particular racial or ethnic origin in comparison with persons not of that group.[88] This interpretation would assimilate the concepts of direct and indirect discrimination, because the former occurs where the effect of the defendant's action is to put an individual at a disadvantage on racial grounds, even without any conscious motivation on the part of the discriminator.[89] A purposive interpretation, in keeping with the decision of the Court of Justice in *O'Flynn*[90] would make the comparison between persons of the same racial or ethnic origin as the complainant and all other persons.

The new definition of indirect discrimination does however have the benefit of moving away from the approach that had developed with respect to sex discrimination, according to which indirect sex discrimination arises where 'a considerably smaller percentage' of women than men can meet the relevant requirement or criterion.[91] This approach led to a tendency to use statistics to show the adverse impact of a requirement or criterion, a practice that is problematic for practical reasons, as it can be difficult or impossible for litigants to find the relevant statistics, and also for conceptual reasons, as it may be

---

[82] Cf. *Mandla* v. *Lee* [1983] IRLR 209.   [83] Art. 2.

[84] Drawing on Case C–237/94, *O'Flynn* v. *Adjudication Officer* [1996] ECR I–2617, para. 18.

[85] This section draws on Barnard and Hepple, *supra* n. 80. For further discussion of the concept of indirect sex discrimination see Hervey, *Justifications for Sex Discrimination in Employment* (Butterworths, London, 1993).

[86] [1998] OJ L14/16, amended by Council Directive 98/52 [1998] OJ L205/66.

[87] See esp. House of Lords Select Committee on the European Union, *EU Proposals to Combat Discrimination*, HL Paper 65, Session 1999–2000, 9th Report, paras. 79–83.

[88] See Race Relations Act 1976, s. 1(1)(b)(i); and see Memorandum by JUSTICE to the House of Lords Committee (*supra* n. 87), 113.

[89] See *Nagarjan* v. *London Regional Transport* [1999] ICR 977.   [90] *Supra* n. 84.

[91] Case 170/84, *Bilka-Kaufhaus* v. *Weber von Hartz* [1986] ECR 1607.

unclear exactly which statistics are relevant, and indeed what constitutes a 'significant' disparity.[92]

The Directive extends the principles contained in Articles 3 and 4 of the Burden of Proof Directive to race. Thus, 'when persons who consider themselves wronged because the principle of equal treatment has not been applied to them establish, before a court or other competent authority, facts from which it may be presumed that there has been direct or indirect discrimination, it shall be for the respondent to prove that there has been no breach of the principle of equal treatment'.[93]

Following the sex discrimination model, while indirect discrimination can be objectively justified, direct discrimination on the grounds of race or ethnic origin can be saved only by reference to an express defence, described as a 'Genuine and Determining Occupational Requirement'.[94] Article 4 provides that:

Member States may provide that a difference of treatment which is based on a characteristic related to racial or ethnic origin shall not constitute discrimination where, by reason of the nature of the particular occupational activities concerned or of the context in which they are carried out, such a characteristic constitutes a genuine and determining occupational requirement, provided that the objective is legitimate and the requirement is proportionate.

Unlike in Directive 76/207, no exhaustive list of derogations is provided but the Commission has suggested that examples of such differences may be found where a person of a particular racial or ethnic origin is required for reasons of authenticity in a dramatic performance or where the holder of a particular job provides persons of a particular ethnic group with personal services promoting their welfare and those services can most effectively be provided by a person of that ethnic group. The Commission does, however, note that these situations will be highly exceptional.

In addition, the Directive permits positive action. Following the wording of Article 141(4),[95] Article 5 provides that '[w]ith a view to ensuring full equality in practice, the principle of equal treatment shall not prevent any Member State from maintaining or adopting specific measures to prevent or compensate for disadvantages linked to racial or ethnic origin'.

The Directive also introduces the innovation that harassment shall be deemed to be discrimination when 'unwanted conduct related to racial or ethnic origin takes place with the purpose or effect of violating the dignity of a person and of creating an intimidating, hostile, degrading, humiliating or

---

[92] For an illustration of this point see Case C–167/97, *R. v. Secretary of State for Employment, ex p. Seymour-Smith and Perez* [1999] ECR I–623, discussed in Barnard and Hervey, *supra* n. 2.

[93] Art. 8.

[94] See the parallels with Genuine Occupational Qualifications (GOQs) found in the British Sex Discrimination Act 1975 and the Race Relations Act 1976; and the *unverzichtbare Voraussetzung* provision of the German *Bundesgesetzbuch*, Art. 611a (1). For further discussion, see Hervey, *Justifications, supra* n. 85.

[95] See text above at n. 71 ff.

offensive environment'. This provision circumvents the weakness of the existing Harassment Recommendation and Code of Conduct[96] by attaching the force of the remedial provisions in the Directive to the anti-harassment provision. Inclusion of harassment within the definition of discrimination appears to move the Community law concept of discrimination nearer to the 'rights-based' notion, enunciated by the Court in *P* v. *S*.[97]

The remedies provisions are found in Chapter II. They envisage the right of victims to a personal remedy against the discriminator as well as the duty on each Member State to lay down rules on penalties for breach of the Directive. Member States must ensure that 'judicial and/or administrative procedures including where they deem it appropriate conciliation procedures, for the enforcement of obligations under this Directive are available to all persons who consider themselves wronged by failure to apply the principle of equal treatment to them, even after the relationship in which the discrimination is alleged to have occurred has ended'.[98] While this reflects Article 6 of Directive 76/207, a new requirement has been added, obliging the Member States to ensure that 'associations, organizations or other legal entities which have, in accordance with the criteria laid down by their national laws, a legitimate interest in ensuring that the provisions of this Directive are complied with, may engage, on behalf or in support of the complainant with his or her approval, in any judicial and/or administrative procedure provided for the enforcement of obligations under this Directive'.[99]

To reinforce the effective legal protection, the Directive contains a provision on victimization. Article 9 provides that 'Member States shall introduce into their national legal systems such measures as are necessary to protect individuals from any adverse treatment or adverse consequence as a reaction to a complaint or to proceedings aimed at enforcing compliance with the principle of equal treatment'. In addition, as with the Burden of Proof Directive, Member States are obliged to ensure 'that the provisions adopted pursuant to this Directive, together with the relevant provisions already in force, are brought to the attention of the persons concerned by all appropriate means throughout their territory'.[100] Member States must also ensure, following the model of Articles 3, 4, and 5 of Directive 76/207, the elimination of discrimination from any legal or administrative provisions, as well as from collective agreements or individual contracts of employment.[101]

Article 11 requires the Member States to take 'adequate measures to promote the social dialogue between the two sides of industry with a view to fostering equal treatment, including through the monitoring of workplace practices, collective agreements, codes of conduct, research or exchange of experiences and good practices'. The European Social Partners have already

---

[96] Commission Recommendation 92/131/EEC of 27 Nov. 1991 on the protection and dignity of men and women at work ([1992] OJ L49/1). See generally Bakirci, 'Sexual Harassment in the Workplace in Relation to EC Legislation' (1998) 3 *IJLD* 3.
[97] See *supra* n. 63.   [98] Art. 7(1).   [99] Art. 7(2). This is subject to national time limits.
[100] Art. 10.   [101] Art. 14.

concluded a Joint Declaration on Racism and Xenophobia in the Workplace adopted in Florence in 1995 and, at national level in certain states, have adopted framework agreements and codes of conduct on combating racial and ethnic discrimination in companies.

Perhaps the most striking feature of the Race Directive is the obligation contained in Article 13 for Member States to 'designate a body or bodies[102] for the promotion of equal treatment of all persons without discrimination on the grounds of different racial or ethnic origin. These bodies may form part of agencies charged at national level with the defence of human rights or the safeguard of individuals' rights'. Not only must an agency be set up but, following the model of the British Commission for Racial Equality, these bodies must have among their functions: providing independent assistance to victims of discrimination in pursuing their complaints about discrimination on grounds of racial or ethnic origin; conducting independent investigations or surveys concerning discrimination; and publishing reports and making recommendations on issues relating to discrimination based on racial or ethnic origin.

(iv) Exclusions From the Equal Treatment Principle

In two cases concerning employment of women in the armed forces, *Sirdar* and *Kreil*,[103] the Court has been concerned with the scope of application of Community (sex equality) law, and with the justification provision in the Equal Treatment Directive, Article 2 (2). The Court held that there is no general exclusion for the armed forces from the scope of Community law. In interpreting Article 2(2) of Directive 76/207/EEC, the Court stressed that, as an exception, it must be construed narrowly and limited to exceptional circumstances. The proportionality principle must be met.

The British Royal Marines exclude women from service on the basis that every Marine, irrespective of his specialization, must be capable of fighting in a commando unit: the requirement of 'interoperability'. Mrs Sirdar, who had been in the British Army since 1983, had served as a chef in the Royal Artillery since 1990. She was notified that she was to be made redundant in February 1995. In July 1994, she received an offer of a transfer to the Royal Marines. However, when the Royal Marines discovered that she was a woman, they informed her that the offer has been made in error. Mrs Sirdar challenged this as contrary to Community law. The industrial tribunal which heard her case referred to the European Court of Justice. The national court wished to know whether policy decisions which a Member State takes during peacetime and/or in preparation for war in relation to employment in its armed forces, where such policy decisions are taken for the purposes of combating effec-

---

[102] The requirement found in earlier drafts of 'independence' of these bodies has been removed. On enforcement mechanisms for sex equality see Beveridge, Nott, and Stephen, *supra* n. 50.

[103] Case C–273/97, *Sirdar* v. *The Army Board* [1999] ECR I–7403 and Case C–285/98, *Kreil* v. *Germany* [2000] ECR I–69.

tiveness, are outside the scope of the Treaty and its subordinate legislation. It also asked whether it made a difference that forces are to engage in close combat with enemy forces in the event of war. In the event that such matters fall within the scope of Community law, what was the position under Article 2(2) of the Equal Treatment Directive?

The German army operates a much broader exclusion of women: women may not be engaged in any post involving the use of arms. Ms Kreil, trained in electronics, applied for voluntary service in the army, requesting duties in weapon electronics maintenance. She was refused, and challenged this refusal. Again the national court referred to the European Court of Justice.

The Court has consistently held that Article 2 of Directive 76/207—as an exception to a general principle—must be construed narrowly and exceptions must be proportionate to their aim.[104] Article 2 (2)—at issue in *Sirdar* and *Kreil*—provides:

This Directive shall be without prejudice to the right of Member States to exclude from its field of application those occupational activities . . . for which, by reason of their nature or the context in which they are carried out, the sex of the worker constitutes a determining factor.

In spite of the general principle that exceptions should be construed narrowly and the requirement of proportionality, the Court adopted a curiously generous interpretation of Article 2(2) in *Johnston* v. *RUC*.[105] In this case, the Court was required to decide whether the policy of the Royal Ulster Constabulary concerning women members and their equipment, in particular the policy that women members of the RUC were not armed, was consistent with Directive 76/207. The effect of this policy was that the plaintiff, Ms Johnston, lost her job, where a man in her situation would not have done so. The Court held that:

the possibility cannot be excluded in a situation characterized by serious internal disturbances that the carrying of firearms by policewomen might create additional risks of their being assassinated and might therefore be contrary to the requirements of public safety. In such circumstances, the context of certain policing activities may be such that the sex of police offenders constitutes a determining factor for carrying them out. If that is so, a Member State may therefore restrict such tasks . . . to men.[106]

The ruling in *Johnston* may be regarded as problematic. It was accepted by the Court that women RUC officers were more likely to be assassinated. But what is the basis for this assertion? There is no biological reason preventing women from using arms as effectively as men use them. Given appropriate training, there seems to be no reason why women should be more vulnerable than men when faced with a situation of internal disturbance. Would public perceptions

---

[104] Case 318/86, *Commission* v. *France (Sex Discrimination in the Civil Service)* [1988] ECR 3559; Case 184/83, *Hofmann* v. *Barmer Ersatzkasse* [1984] ECR 3047; Case 312/86, *Commission* v. *France (Protection of Women)* [1988] ECR 6315.

[105] Case 222/84, *Johnston* v. *RUC* [1986] ECR 1651.   [106] Paras. 36–37.

of women as weaker and more vulnerable constitute a *significantly* greater risk to women, so as to meet the proportionality test?

Sirdar and *Kreil* may be regarded as consistent with the *Johnson* ruling. In the case of *Kreil*, the general rule at issue could not be justified either by reference to the specific nature of the posts in question, or by the particular context in which the activities in question are carried out. Moreover, where women were appointed to the German army, they were given basic training in the use of arms. Therefore the exclusion of women from all posts involving the use of arms was disproportionate. By contrast, in the case of *Sirdar*, the Court found that the proportionality principle might be met. In the light of the function of front-line commandos, the exclusion of women could be justified. The Court explained its decision thus:

the organisation of the Royal Marines differs fundamentally from that of other units in the British armed forces, of which they are the 'point of the arrowhead'. They are a small force and intended to be the first line of attack. It has been established that, within this corps, chefs are indeed also required to serve as front-line commandos, that all members of the corps are engaged and trained for that purpose, and that there are no exceptions to this rule at the time of recruitment.

Thus, service in the Royal Marines may be a 'special case', compared to service in the army in general, just as service in the RUC was a special case, compared to service in the police force in general. The objections raised above with respect to the *Johnston* case apply. There may however be something about the *context* in which the work of the Royal Marines is carried out (the conditions of front-line attacking—a small force, operating in difficult and unsanitary conditions) which does justify the exception from the point of view of personal privacy. This will be a matter for the national court to decide.

III.   'Social Law'

In the Community context, social law has in the past perhaps been something of a 'poor relation' to employment law. However, the contours of the new European social model make it clearer than ever that employment law cannot be seen in isolation from other policy areas with which it has clear structural links. The inter-relationship between social and employment law has been stressed by the reconfigured Article 137 EC, after the Treaty of Nice. This provides a unified list of areas for Community action supporting and complementing national activities, including employment law fields such as health and safety, working conditions, worker consultation and sex equality at work, and social law matters such as social security, social protection of workers, the combating of social exclusion, and the modernization of social protection systems.[107] Competence to adopt, by means of a directive, measures of minimum harmonization is granted for all areas listed except the combating of social

---

[107] This latter is to be without prejudice to the social security and social protection of workers.

exclusion.[108] The co-decision procedure is to be used. However, a number of areas do remain somewhat the 'poor relation' as, in those fields, Council must act unanimously on a proposal from the Commission, and the European Parliament has only consultation rights. These fields[109] include both social and labour law issues, and appear to comprise highly sensitive areas for Community law.

We have already considered the increased interest at Community level in education and vocational training, and noted the importance of the interactions between such soft-law measures and the internal market measures on freedom of movement of workers. The Commission's Social Policy Agenda sees social policy intervention as both a guarantee of rights fundamental to 'European' (as opposed to US) society, and as a productive factor. As investments in human resources, benefits in areas such as health, education, pensions, and social security are to be seen as beneficial to Europe's economy. However, the Commission is clearly of the view that modernization of social protection systems will be necessary to achieve such a beneficial effect.[110] According to the Commission, such modernization is to focus around the guiding concept of the 'quality of social policy', a term which implies a high level of social protection; good social services available to all on the basis of non-discrimination; and guarantees of fundamental social rights. As in the employment context, measures of Community social law may be viewed in terms of their place within this construct.

A.   SOCIAL PROTECTION

In terms of hard law, the Community has so far developed only one element of the non-discriminatory basis of social protection.[111] A prohibition on discrimination on grounds of sex in state social security schemes is found in Directive 79/7/EEC. A significant line of jurisprudence concerns the scope of this provision, and the effect of the exemption provisions contained therein. In determining the material scope of Directive 79/7, the Court asks whether the benefit concerned is 'directly and effectively linked' to one of the risks enumerated in the directive: sickness, invalidity, old age, accidents at work and occupational diseases, unemployment.[112] A distinction is drawn with 'social

---

[108] Otherwise, a clear conflict would have arisen between the procedure under Art. 137 EC (qualified majority voting in Council) and that in Art. 13 EC (unanimity in Council).

[109] Social security and social protection of workers; protection of workers on the termination of their employment contract; worker representation; conditions of employment for nationals of non-member states.

[110] The European Council approved the Commission's approach at the Nice summit: see Presidency Conclusions, paras. 20–21.

[11] It will be interesting to compare the impact of the Race Discrimination Directive, *supra* n. 56, in these fields. The Horizontal Labour Market Directive, *supra* n. 55, explicitly excludes state social security or social protection schemes from its scope.

[112] Case C–243/90, *Smithson* [1992] ECR I–467; Cases C–63 & 64/91, *Jackson and Cresswell* [1992] ECR I–4737; Case C–137/94, *Richardson* [1995] ECR I–3407; Case C–228/94, *Atkins* [1996] ECR I–3633.

assistance' benefits, which are regarded as protecting against the risk of poverty, are usually means-tested, and fall outside the scope of Directive 79/7. The distinction between 'social security' benefits, falling within the scope of Directive 79/7, and 'social assistance', falling outside its scope, is difficult to draw in practice. This has led to a number of challenges, many from the UK, to welfare provisions made on the basis of differential state retirement pension ages. The Court has dealt with each of these by attempting to focus on the 'listed risks' in Directive 79/7. So, for instance, medical prescriptions (risk of sickness) fall within the Directive's scope;[113] housing benefit[114] and travel concessions[115] do not.

The latest significant contribution to this jurisprudence is the ruling in *Taylor*[116] concerning winter fuel payments. Under the UK's social fund winter fuel payment regulations, two categories of persons were entitled to winter fuel payments. These were persons in receipt of income support or income-based jobseeker's allowance (means-tested benefits) who receive one of a number of premiums which are payable only to those who have reached the age of 60, or who live with a person who has reached that age; and men aged 65 and over and women aged 60 and over who were entitled to one of a number of listed benefits, including the state retirement pension. Mr Taylor, aged 62, claimed that he was the victim of unlawful discrimination in that he was denied a winter fuel payment, in circumstances in which, if he were a woman, the payment would have been made.

The Court held that a winter fuel payment—as it is directly and effectively linked to the risk of old age—fell within the scope of Directive 79/7. The derogation in Article 7(1)(a) of the Directive did not apply, as the financial equilibrium of the social security system would not be affected by equalization of such a non-contributory benefit.

The drawing of the distinction between social security and social assistance is an important control on the scope of Community law and its potentially highly disruptive impact on national social security systems. Moreover, in applying the derogation provision in Article 7(1)(a), the Court appears to be careful to ensure that the equilibrium of national schemes is maintained. It will be interesting to see whether this approach is continued in interpreting the relevant provisions of the Race Discrimination Directive. The Court's jurisprudence on the financial equilibrium of social security schemes may be part of the inspiration for the new Article 137 (4) EC, introduced at Nice. This provides that measures adopted under Article 137 'shall not affect the right of Member States to define the fundamental principles of their social security systems and must not significantly affect the financial equilibrium thereof'. Thus the 'quality' of national social security systems is to be maintained.

[113] Case C–137/94, *Richardson* [1995] ECR I–3407.
[114] Case 243/90, *Smithson* [1992] ECR 467.
[115] Case C–228/94, *Atkins* [1996] ECR I–3633.
[116] Case C–382/98, *Taylor* [1999] ECR I–8955.

B.   PENSIONS

As we have noted above, the Commission has shown an increased interest in the modernization of social protection systems. This was endorsed at the Nice summit.[117] In some cases, such as that of pensions, such modernization might involve the use of 'market models', in particular competition between providers of social benefits, in order to promote efficiency. One question which arises in this respect is the extent to which *existing* measures of Community (hard) law—not simply the limited sex equality provisions in Directive 79/7, but the more general law of the internal market and Community competition law—might contribute towards such a modernization process. Moreover, if they do so, how is the Community to protect its social model—and the 'quality' of pension provision—from the 'cold winds' of competition? The Court appears to be addressing this issue in a series of decisions in which 'solidarity' elements of pension arrangements either operate to exclude the arrangement from the scope of Articles 81 and 82 EC, or operate to justify the grant of an 'exclusive right' in terms of Article 86 (2) EC. The emerging meaning of 'solidarity' in this sense appears to relate to measures of social policy (such as pension provision[118]) adopted on the basis that a decent level of social benefits may be efficiently provided for all within a group, where contribution towards the provision of those benefits is made compulsory, irrespective of the possibility that some individuals within that group might find more generous social provision through opting out of the group coverage. The implication of this emerging branch of jurisprudence appears to be that the European model of 'quality of social policy' is to be promoted through protection from the application of Community competition law (and presumably internal market law) to arrangements for such social policy provision.[119]

Such issues arose in *Albany International et al.*,[120] concerning the Dutch system of compulsory affiliation to sectoral pension funds. Albany International (and the other litigants) were ordered to pay contributions to sectoral pension funds. They refused, on the ground, *inter alia*, that their own supplementary pension scheme was more generous than the sectoral scheme. Albany took the view that the national system of compulsory affiliation breached Community competition law in a number of respects, in particular that it constituted an 'abuse of a dominant position' by the sectoral pension funds, contrary to Article 86 EC.[121] According to Article 90 (1) EC,[122] public

[117] See Presidency Conclusions, paras. 20–21.

[118] Although the principles may also apply to other social benefits, such as for instance sickness insurance, see Case C–222/98, *Van der Woude* [2000] ECR I–7111.

[119] For further discussion see Hervey, 'Social Solidarity: A Buttress Against Internal Market Law' in Shaw (ed.), *supra* n. 25.

[120] Case C–67/96, *Albany International*; Case C–115–7/97, *Brentjens*'; Case C–219/97, *Drijvende Bokken*, all [1999] ECR I–5751.

[121] New Art. 82 EC. This provides that '[a]ny abuse by one or more undertakings of a dominant position within the common market or a substantial part of it shall be prohibited as incompatible with the common market in so far as it may affect trade between Member States'.

[122] New Art. 86 EC.

undertakings and 'undertakings to which Member States grant special or exclusive rights' are required to comply with Community competition law. Where such an undertaking is entrusted with the provision of a 'service of general economic interest', those rules apply only in so far as their application does not obstruct the performance of the particular tasks assigned to them.[123]

Following earlier jurisprudence,[124] and the opinion of its Advocate General,[125] the Court confirmed that organizations with sufficient elements of 'solidarity' do not constitute 'undertakings' under Community competition law. By contrast, the pension fund at issue here operated in accordance with the principle of capitalization, the fund itself determined the amounts of contributions and benefits, the amounts of benefits depended on the financial results of the fund and 'in the event of withdrawal from the fund, compensation considered reasonable by the Insurance Board is offered for any damage suffered by the fund, from the actuarial point of view, as a result of the withdrawal', so that, in all these respects, the fund operated in the same way as a private insurance company.[126]

The Court confirmed that the funds occupied a 'dominant position' in the sense of Article 86 EC,[127] but concluded that there was, in this case, no unjustified abuse of that dominant position. Departing from the view of its Advocate General, the Court did not take a '*Corbeau*-type approach',[128] but rather examined first whether there was a breach of Article 90(1) EC, and then considered whether that breach was justified under Article 90(2) EC. The Court held that an abuse would arise 'only if the undertaking in question, merely by exercising the exclusive rights granted to it, is led to abuse its dominant position, or when such rights are liable to create a situation in which that undertaking is led to commit such abuses'.[129] Restrictions on competition *did* derive directly from the exclusive rights conferred on the sectoral pension fund: the system meant that, as the pension benefits available from the fund no longer met the needs of employers, employers wishing to ensure adequate benefits for their employees were required to make separate 'top-up' pension arrange-

---

[123] Art. 86(2) (ex Art. 90 (2)) EC. Art. 86 (ex Art. 90) provides '(1) In the case of public undertakings and undertakings to which Member States have granted special or exclusive rights, Member States shall neither enact nor maintain in force any measure contrary to the rules contained in this Treaty, in particular to those rules provided for in Art. 12 and Arts. 81–89. (2) Undertakings entrusted with the operation of services of general economic interest or having the character of a revenue-producing monopoly shall be subject to the rules contained in this Treaty, in particular to the rules on competition, insofar as the application of such rules does not obstruct the performance, in law or in fact, of the particular tasks assigned to them. The development of trade must not be affected to such an extent as would be contrary to the interests of the Community.'

[124] Case C–41/90, *Höfner and Elser* [1991] ECR I–1979; Cases C–159 & 160/91, *Poucet and Pistre* [1993] ECR I–3395; Case C–244/94, *FFSA* [1995] ECR I–4013.

[125] Paras. 71–87.   [126] Paras. 80–84.

[127] Para. 92, following Case C–179/90, *Porto di Genova* [1991] ECR I–5889.

[128] Following Case C–320/91, *Corbeau* [1993] ECR I–2533, a case concerning postal services—a subject matter not in the social security field—in which the Court held that the provision of special (postal) services could be lawfully prohibited only where the existence of those special (postal) service providers would compromise the economic basis and general equilibrium of the general (postal) service.

[129] Para. 93.

ments. Such employers could not enjoy the administrative efficiency of comprehensive pension cover for their employees from a private insurance company. There was thus a *prima facie* breach of Article 90(1) EC. This breach was, however, *justified*, under Article 90(2) EC. The Court held that the pension scheme at issue did fulfil a 'service of general economic interest' in the Dutch pensions system,[130] and that its exclusive right (to enjoy compulsory affiliation) was necessary for the performance of that service.[131] The fund at issue displayed a high level of solidarity, including elements such as the fact that contributions did not reflect individual risks, there was an obligation to accept all workers without a medical examination, pensions continued to accrue in the event of non-payment of contributions through incapacity for work, the amount of pensions was index-linked in order to maintain their value, and, perhaps most significantly, there was cross-generational, cross-income, cross-undertaking, and activity risk subsidization.[132]

The Court's ruling in *Albany* has been applied in two judgments handed down in September 2000: *Pavlov*[133] and *Van der Woude*.[134] In *Pavlov*, the Court considered the legality in Community competition law of the provisions of Dutch law requiring compulsory membership of a pension fund for self-employed professional medical specialists. Mr Pavlov and four other applicants refused to pay contributions into the fund, on the basis that they should belong to a different fund, that for employees. The Court found that the decision of the relevant professional association to set up an occupational pension scheme and to apply for membership of that scheme to be made compulsory for all professional medical specialists was a decision of an association of undertakings within the meaning of Article 85 (now Article 81) EC. However, the Court went on to find that the decision did not appreciably restrict competition on the common market, as the cost of the supplementary pension scheme, being only one element of the costs of services provided by self-employed professional medical specialists, had only a marginal and indirect influence on the final cost of the services offered by those professionals.[135]

As in *Albany*, in *Pavlov*, the fund itself was held to be carrying on its activities on a sufficiently 'economic' basis to constitute an undertaking within Community competition law.[136] The fund enjoyed 'exclusive rights' in the sense of Article 90 (now Article 86) (1) EC in that membership had been made compulsory by national law. Although the fund occupied a dominant

---

[130] Para. 105.   [131] Para. 111.   [132] Para. 108.

[133] Cases C–180–184/98, judgment of 12 Sept 2000, not yet reported in ECR.

[134] Case C–222/98 [2000] ECR I–7111. This concerns sickness insurance, and will thus be discussed below.

[135] Para. 95.

[136] See paras. 103–116. The Court referred specifically to the operation of the principle of capitalization, the fact that the level of benefits depends on the performance of the fund's investments, and the fact that medical specialists may opt to purchase their basic pension either from the fund or from an authorized insurance company, pointing to a sufficient element of competition with insurance companies (paras. 114–115).

position, the Court found that it had not abused that dominant position, as the exclusive right granted to it was not such as to lead the fund to commit such an abuse. In reaching this conclusion, the Court pointed out that Mr Pavlov was not seeking to arrange his supplementary pension with a competitor insurance company, merely claiming that he should belong to another pension fund. It seems that the Court is not prepared to allow the application of Community competition law in what was essentially an internal dispute concerning the classification of medical specialists as employed or self-employed within the Dutch social security system. Implicit in the judgment was the view that it is not appropriate to apply the ordinary rules of competition to social benefits such as pensions, provided on the basis of 'solidarity'.

Although the schemes at issue were held to be lawful, the Court's rulings in *Albany* and *Pavlov* confirm that, in principle, social insurance schemes may be subject to Community competition law. Thus, it is possible for undertakings administering social insurance schemes to 'abuse their dominant position' in contravention of Article 82 (ex Article 86) EC. Such undertakings would almost certainly be granted 'special or exclusive rights', as otherwise they would not be able to provide the service of universal social insurance, and thus are likely to occupy a dominant position. This is all the more likely if the relevant market is restricted to provision of social insurance of a particular type (for instance, as in *Albany* and *Pavlov*, retirement pensions), to those working in a particular Member State, or a particular economic sector within a Member State. One potential effect of the application of Community competition law in such a case may be an increased risk of 'cream-skimming' activities in pensions markets. Private pension providers must have a sufficient incentive to make a profit. Notwithstanding the possibility of profit-making through increased efficiency, there must be at least a possibility that such providers will seek to enter only the more lucrative parts of the pensions market, for instance by restricting access to lower risk groups. Governments of the Member States may impose regulatory standards on providers of such pensions, in order to counteract such behaviour. Whether these regulatory standards are justifiable will be a question of Community competition law. However, it seems from the Court's approach that the potential for application of competition law—certainly that applied through individual litigation—to such provision, as a driving force for the modernization of social security systems called for by the Commission and others, appears to be limited. In this context at least, it appears that Community law is to be construed in terms of ensuring the protection of 'solidarity', an element of the 'quality of social policy' within the European social model.

C.   HEALTH

Probably the most important EU-level development in the health field in 1999–2000 is the package of public health protection measures introduced by DG Consumer and Health Protection on promoting a 'farm to fork' basis for regulation of food within the EU.[137] In the wake of the BSE and other agricultural crises, this series of measures and proposals aims to restore consumer confidence in the European food industry, and to establish the protection of public health (rather than the free movement of goods) as the core tenet of Community food law. However, as the relationship between these measures and those of social and employment policy is tenuous, these provisions will not be discussed further here. Rather, we will consider the protection of health as a traditional element of social protection, through national health systems and sickness insurance schemes. As with the area of pensions, the potential application of Community law—in particular the law of the internal market and competition law—in these fields has recently been the subject of Court rulings, and also responses by other institutions to those rulings.

In terms of sickness insurance, it was noted above that the Court applied the principles of *Albany International* in *Van der Woude*. This concerned the compulsory affiliation of Mr Van der Woude to a particular sickness insurance scheme, in accordance with the provisions of the applicable collective agreement. Mr Van der Woude calculated that he would be considerably better off were he permitted to transfer to another sickness insurance scheme.[138] He thus sought to have the relevant provisions of the collective agreement declared void as contrary to Community law.

The Court dismissed his claim in a very brief judgment. The collective agreement at issue did not fall within Article 85 (now Article 81) EC, as its nature was that of a collective bargaining arrangement and its purpose was to improve employment and working conditions, by providing employees with the means to meet medical expenses, and reducing the costs of medical insurance for individual employees by providing such insurance on a collective basis.[139] The Court found that there was nothing in the reference to suggest that the health insurers had abused a dominant position in the sense of Article 86 (now Article 82) EC. As in the case of pension provision, it appears that the Court is anxious to ensure that European models of social policy provision through traditional mechanisms of collective bargaining are not undermined by the application of Community competition law. The 'inefficiencies' from the point of view of an individual of a collectively provided sickness insurance scheme are not to be subjected to Community competition law through individual litigation.

Whether the Court will protect the provision of health benefits from the application of the free movement provisions of internal market law seems to be less clear. In 1998, the Court ruled in two references concerning cross-frontier receipt of medical goods and services: *Decker* and *Kohll*.[140] The references involved requests to the Luxembourg social security funds for

---

[137] Commission White Paper on Food Safety, Jan. 2000, and proposed regulation on food law COM(2000) 716.

[138] Para. 14. [139] Paras. 24–25.

[140] Case C–120/95, *Decker* [1998] ECR I–1831; Case 158/96, *Kohll* [1998] ECR I–1931. As *Kohll*, decided on the same day as *Decker*, concerned a very similar issue (receipt of services rather than goods), discussion here is limited to *Decker*.

reimbursement for medical goods or treatment. In *Decker*, the issue concerned a Luxembourg national who bought, on a prescription given by an ophthalmologist established in Luxembourg, a pair of prescription spectacles from an optician established in Belgium. According to national law, treatment abroad would be reimbursed by the social security fund only where prior authorization had been granted. That was not the case in Decker's circumstances, and so authorization was refused. Decker challenged the refusal on the grounds that it breached (then) Article 30 (now Article 28) EC,[141] in that it constituted a hindrance to the free movement of goods within the internal market. The national court took the view that this case fell within the measures on co-ordination of national social security systems, Regulation 1408/71/EEC, not Article 30 (now Article 28) EC. Article 22 of Regulation 1408/71 provides that *authorized* individuals may go to another Member State to receive medical treatment. It does not impose any duty on a Member State to grant authorization to receive medical treatment, at the expense of the responsible Member State's public health funds, in another Member State, except in the unusual situation in which the treatment sought is not available in the responsible Member State.[142]

The Court, citing earlier jurisprudence,[143] stated that 'according to settled case law, Community law does not detract from the powers of the Member States to organize their social security systems'.[144] However, the Court went on to note that 'the Member States must nevertheless comply with Community law when exercising those powers'.[145] The Court found that the fact that the national rules at issue fell within Regulation 1408/71 did not exclude the application of Article 30 (now Article 28) EC.[146] This is in stark contrast to earlier rulings such as that in *Sodemare*[147] where the rules at issue were found to be outside the scope of internal market law. Therefore, the Court had little difficulty in finding that the rules of the Luxembourg social security scheme, by requiring a prior authorization to purchase spectacles from an optician established outside Luxembourg, but no prior authorization to purchase spectacles from an optician established in Luxembourg, constituted a barrier to the free movement of goods, as the national rules are liable to curb the import of spectacles assembled in other Member States.[148] Moreover, with regard to Luxembourg's submission that the national rules were justified by the need to control health expenditure—an argument based on the social solidarity concept—the Court accepted that as spectacles were reimbursed only at a flat

[141] New Art. 28 EC.

[142] See Case 117/77, *Pierek No 1* [1978] ECR 825 and Case 182/78, *Pierek No 2* [1979] ECR 1977. The responsible Member State is normally the state of residence of the person in receipt of the social security benefit. See further Van der Mei, 'Cross-border Access to Medical Care within the EU' (1998) 5 *MJ* 277; Hervey, 'Buy Baby: The European Union and the Regulation of Human Reproduction' (1998) 18 *OJLS* 207–33, at 215–6. Reg. 1408/71 is at [1971] JO L149/2.

[143] Case 238/82, *Duphar* [1984] ECR 523, para. 16; Cases 159 & 160/91, *Poucet and Pistre* [1993] ECR I–637, para. 6; Case C–70/95, *Sodemare* [1997] ECR I–3395, para. 27.

[144] Para. 21.   [145] Para. 23.

[146] Para. 25.   [147] Case C–70/95, *Sodemare* [1997] ECR I–3395.

[148] Para. 36, following Case 8/74, *Dassonville* [1974] ECR 837.

rate, the financial burden on the social security funds was the same as it would have been had the spectacles been bought in Luxembourg. In general, the risk of seriously undermining the financial balance of a national social security system could constitute a justification, but here that risk was not present.[149] The Court therefore found that the national rules requiring prior authorization breached Articles 30 and 36 (now Articles 28 and 30) EC.

The *Decker* and *Kohll* cases establish that, provided that no direct threat is posed to the financial stability of the social security funds, individuals may receive health or welfare benefits from providers in another Member State, and require that their national social security funds meet the cost, at least at the rate at which they would be reimbursed if the benefit were received in the home Member State. Of course, this principle applies only in the case of benefits or social services provided through the mechanism of cash benefits to be spent in the market of social service providers. The principle would not apply where a Member State makes provision through publicly funded services, and health or welfare benefits are free at the point of receipt.

Two distinct pressures on national health systems may arise from the rulings. Difficulties experienced by those Member States whose nationals go elsewhere to receive medical treatment or purchase medical goods[150] are unlikely to affect a Member State where health services are not, in the main, financed through a mechanism of cash benefits. However, a Member State in which professionals have both national health service and privately funded patients[151] might find itself becoming a 'host state', to which patients go to receive medical goods or services. Such host states may experience an unpredictable influx of patients. This may have an impact on national health care provision for nationals, for instance longer waiting lists. Nothing in the *Decker* or *Kohll* judgment appears to provide a mechanism by which such host states may protect the stability of their health service systems, as they may not lawfully refuse treatment to non-nationals as to do so would be discriminatory, contrary to Articles 49 (ex Article 59) and 12 (ex Article 6) EC. Moreover, a Member State that provides a higher standard of service, better value for money, or a greater choice for medical 'consumers' is likely to attract more free movers to receive these services. Perhaps, for instance, Decker wanted to go to Belgium to purchase spectacles because the choice of frames and lenses was greater there. Or perhaps the amount of reimbursement would purchase a higher quality of spectacles on the Belgian market than in Luxembourg. Member States whose medical professions enjoy a high reputation may attract free movers seeking treatment. As a worst case scenario, if such pressures reached extreme levels, there might be a temptation on the part of the national authorities of those states to reduce the quality of service provided, in order to discourage such 'medical tourism': a classic 'race to the bottom'.

---

[149] Paras. 39–40.
[150] In particular, loss of control over supply as a cost containment measure.
[151] As is the case, for instance, with dental professionals in the UK.

The Commission (DG Employment and Social Affairs) has responded to *Decker* and *Kohll* by commissioning a report on the implications of the rulings. This suggests a number of possibilities for EU-level action, including an interpretative communication from the Commission on the judgments, a modification of the authorization procedure in Regulation 1408/71, requirements for provision of information to consumers on medical services and goods available, more general consumer protection in terms of assessment of qualifications of medical professionals, and other quality or safety measures in the health sector, more rigourous enforcement of Community public procurement provisions in the field of medical goods and services, and development of EU 'centres of excellence' for particular medical services, to which fair access for all EU citizens could be ensured. Obviously, many of these are likely to prove too gross an intrusion into national health systems to be acceptable to the governments of the Member States.

A number of pending cases will clarify the contours of the rulings.[152] In the wake of these, and depending on how the Court develops this line of jurisprudence, there may be sufficient support among governments of the Member States for at least a modification to Regulation 1408/71, if not other Community-level provision concerning the relationship between freedom of movement and national health systems, or even capitalizing on the economies of scale that such free movement might allow. However, if the Court follows a similar line to that which it appears to be developing with regard to the application of Community competition law in matters of social protection such as pensions and sickness insurance, national health systems probably have nothing to fear from internal market law.

IV. Conclusion

The contours of the new European social model are emerging. It seems clear that new modes of governance, promoting co-ordination and voluntary convergence of national social policies, will form an important mechanism for elaboration of a multi-level European employment and social law. However, it also seems likely that measures of 'hard' (and enforceable) employment law will continue to be enacted at EU level, using either the social partners, or more traditional legislative routes. The Charter of Fundamental Rights may have a profound effect on social and employment law, but as yet its status remains unclear. There will be a continued need to evaluate provisions of hard law in respect of whether they actually implement and support the 'fine words' of soft-law declarations.

Questions concerning the relationships between labour and social law, on the one hand, and, on the other, internal market and competition law are likely

---

[152] The Advocate General gave his opinion in the first of these, Case C–368/98, *Van Braekel*, on 18 May 2000.

to become more pressing. How to maintain the 'quality' of European social policy, and at the same time modernize social protection systems, especially pensions, will remain a key issue for the governments of the Member States and the EU institutions. In the past, the law (and in particular the rulings of the European Court of Justice) has provided a significant integrative stimulus in the employment and social field. However, it seems that, at present at least, the Court does not seem to be the main motor of integration in the social sphere. Rather, processes of partnership and political participation, involving national authorities, the social partners, the EU institutions, NGOs, and other 'stakeholders', seem to be asserting themselves as a key driving force in developing EU social policy. The new European social model is attempting to respond to the broader picture, including the impact of forces of globalization, changing population profiles, and reconfiguration of the world of work and of the family. Whether a sufficiently strong legal framework to protect the 'quality' of European social policy, and individual rights of workers and citizens, can be promulgated within this process remains to be seen.

The Brussels Convention 1999–2000

Edwin Peel*

I. Matters Relating to Contract

A.   *GIE GROUPE CONCORDE AND OTHERS* V. *THE MASTER OF THE VESSEL SUHADIWARNO PANJAN, PRO LINE LTD AND OTHERS,*[1]
LEATHERTEX DIVISIONE SINTETICI SPA V. *BODETEX BVBA*[2]

Article 5(1) of the Brussels Convention states:

A person domiciled in a Contracting State may, in another Contracting State, be sued:
(1) in matters relating to a contract, in the courts for the place of performance of the
obligation in question.

The European Court of Justice has considered more references for the interpretation of this provision than any other in the Brussels Convention. As a
result, the interpretation of its constituent parts did appear to have reached a
settled basis and one which provided a not unreasonable balance between the
interests of the parties and the sound administration of justice. Nevertheless,
it was necessary to consider two further references in 1999. The first, in *GIE
Groupe Concorde*, may fairly be described as a colossal waste of time and
money, while the result reached by, or forced upon, the Court in the second,
Leathertex, comes close to bringing the operation of the Convention into dis-
repute.

(i)   GIE Groupe Concorde

In *GIE Groupe Concorde*, the vessel *Suhadiwarno Panjan*, flying the
Indonesian flag, was loaded in Le Havre, France, with almost 1,000 cases of
bottles of wine for shipment to the port of Santos, in Brazil. The carrier was a
German firm, Pro Line Limited. It was found on arrival at Santos that some of
the cases were missing and others were damaged. Nine cargo insurers, of
which GIE Groupe Concorde was the lead insurer, indemnified the consignee
for a total of 666,279 FF. The insurers were subrogated to the consignee's rights
and commenced proceedings before the Land and Sea Commercial Court, Le
Havre, against the master and the owner of the vessel, Pro Line Limited, and
the Swedish insurer of the vessel. The Cour d'Appel in Rouen found that the

---

* Keeble College, Oxford.
[1] Case C–440/97, [1999] ECR I–6307, [2000] ILPr. 626 (hereafter '*GIE Groupe Concorde*').
[2] Case C–420/97, [1999] ECR I–6747; [2000] ILPr. 273 (hereafter '*Leathertex*').

French courts lacked jurisdiction under Article 5(1)[3] on the basis that the place of performance of the relevant obligations contained in the contract of carriage was Santos. On the face of it, this was an entirely correct and proper application of Article 5(1), as previously interpreted by the European Court of Justice, but it did not prevent the Cour de Cassation, on appeal, from referring the following question to the Court:

With a view to the application of Article 5(1) . . . must the place of performance of the obligation, within the meaning of that provision, be determined in accordance with the law which, pursuant to the rules on conflict of laws of the court seised, governs the obligation at issue, or should national courts determine the place of performance of the obligation by seeking to establish, having regard to the nature of the relationship creating the obligation and the circumstances of the case, the place where performance actually took place or should have taken place, without having to refer to the law which, under the rules on the conflict of laws, governs the obligation at issue.[4]

Put in such terms, the question referred to the Court seems implicitly to accept the ruling in *De Bloos* v. *Bouyer*[5] that the 'obligation in question' is the obligation upon which the claim is based, i.e. the 'obligation at issue'. The Court had also previously ruled, in *Tessili* v. *Dunlop*,[6] that the 'place of performance' of the obligation in question was to be determined by the law applicable to the contract, as established in accordance with the choice of law rules of the forum, i.e. 'the rules on conflict of laws of the court seised'. Notwithstanding that this ruling had been confirmed as recently as 1994 in *Custom Made Commercial Ltd.* v. *Stawa*,[7] the Court was being asked to reconsider it by the Cour de Cassation.[8] But if this is the issue which was before the Court,[9] there is an initial difficulty in explaining how it should be assessed, and how it was assessed, by the Court.

As acknowledged by Advocate General Colomer in his Opinion,[10] at least some of the criticism made of *Tessili* stems from the fact that it must be applied in combination with the ruling in *De Bloos* that the 'obligation in question' is the obligation upon which the claim is based. This is most obvious when one considers payment obligations. In an action for non-payment, the obligation in question is the obligation to pay. If, in accordance with *Tessili*, the law applicable to the contract determines the place of performance, then two

---

[3] This seems to have been the only basis of jurisdiction available against Pro Line Ltd. (domiciled in Germany) and the insurers of the vessel (domiciled in Sweden).

[4] There is no evidence to suggest that the interpretation put forward by the Cour de Cassation would actually have made any difference to the outcome of the case. The motivation for the reference seems to have been, as much as anything, that the courts should not have had to go to the trouble of ascertaining the applicable law to reach their decision.

[5] Case 14/76 [1976] ECR 1497.

[6] Case 12/76 [1976] ECR 1473.   [7] Case C–288/92 [1994] ECR I–2913.

[8] The right of the national courts to refer settled questions of interpretation to the Court under Art. 234 (formerly 177) EC has been recognized by the Court (see the Judgment in Joined Cases 28–30/62, *Da Costa en Schaake NV and others* v. *Nederlandse Belastingadministratie* [1963] ECR 61), but recognition of the right and the wisdom of exercising it are not at all the same thing.

[9] And there is no mention of the ruling in *De Bloos* in the judgment of the Court.

[10] See para. 57.

'problems' are encountered. First, a different answer may be provided under the laws of different states, i.e. barring any express agreement between the parties, the place of payment may be the place of the debtor's domicile,[11] or the place of the creditor's domicile.[12] Secondly, as is the case with the laws of the Contracting States, the answer provided may more often tend to favour the courts where the claimant is domiciled. *If* such results are thought to be objectionable, they are not due to the operation of *Tessili* alone and it may be argued that it is the ruling in *De Bloos* which should be reconsidered.

In this regard, one may consider the changes which are made to Article 5(1) by the Council Regulation which will soon replace the Brussels Convention.[13] Article 5(1) will be retained in its current form, but it is also laid down in the Article itself that, for contracts for the sale of goods or the provision of services, the 'place of performance of the obligation in question' is the place where the goods/services were delivered or should have been delivered. For example, if a buyer is sued for non-payment, the place of performance of the obligation to pay will not determine jurisdiction. Instead, jurisdiction will be determined by the place of performance of the obligation to deliver the goods. This will avoid the 'problems' with payment obligations referred to above, but this is achieved principally by denying any role as a connecting factor to the payment obligation; not by changes to the way in which the place of performance is determined.[14]

Similarly, in *GIE Groupe Concorde*, the German and UK Governments and the EC Commission advocated that the approach adopted in *Mulox IBC Ltd.* v. *Geels*[15] should be extended to cover all types of contract. In *Mulox*, the Court confirmed that, in individual contracts of employment, the place of performance should be interpreted autonomously and not by reference to the law applicable to the contract. The autonomous place of performance is the place where the employee carries out his obligation to work and, if he works in more than one Contracting State, it is the place where he principally carries out that obligation. However, in contracts of employment, it is appropriate to apply an autonomous interpretation to the place of performance because the Court has also ruled that only one obligation is relevant, i.e. the obligation to work, which is said to be the characteristic obligation of the contract of employment. If a similar approach is to be taken with other contracts, it requires the Court to reconsider not only the ruling in *Tessili*, but also the ruling in *De Bloos*. However, any controversy concerning the correct classification of the obligation in question, and whether the courts should apply the concept of the 'characteristic obligation' to all contracts,[16] was outside the scope of the

---

[11] As under the laws of Germany, Belgium, Spain, and France.

[12] As under the laws of Denmark, Greece, Ireland, Italy, The Nertherlands, and England.

[13] Council Regulation 44/2001 of 22 Dec. 2000 [2000] OJ L12/1. The Regulation comes into force on 1 Mar. 2002 and will be reviewed in full in the 2001 *Yearbook*.

[14] In other cases it may still be necessary to apply *Tessili* to determine the place of performance.

[15] Case C–125/92 [1993] ECR I–4075.

[16] An interpretation which was confined to individual contracts of employment by the Court in Case 266/85, *Shenavai* v. *Kreischer* [1987] ECR 239.

proceedings before the Court. Any assessment of the need to reconsider *Tessili* must therefore be made on the basis that the ruling in *De Bloos* continues to operate.

On that basis, the Court wasted little time in upholding its earlier rulings in *Tessili* and *Custom Made Commercial* that the place of performance must be determined according to the law applicable to the contract and not by reference to any autonomous interpretation, whether along the lines suggested by the Cour de Cassation or otherwise. In doing so, it emphasized the position adopted in *Custom Made Commercial* that, of the various objectives behind the Convention, and Article 5(1) in particular, priority should be given to legal certainty. It is submitted that it was entirely justified in doing so.

The principal reasons for departing from the previous rulings of the Court, as formulated in the Opinion of Advocate General Colomer, may be summarized as follows: the method used in *Tessili* (1) is complex and laborious; (2) is often misapplied, or simply ignored by the national courts as a result, and (3) too often confers jurisdiction on the courts for the place where the claimant is domiciled, contrary to the general rule in favour of the courts for the place where the defendant is domiciled (*actor sequitur forum rei*).[17] The complexity of the methodology employed in *Tessili* is over-stated. For the national courts of the Contracting States the relevant choice of law rules are now to be found in the Rome Convention on the Law Applicable to Contractual Obligations.[18] In principle, this should ensure a degree of uniformity in the determination of the applicable law.[19] If there is any complexity in the choice of law rules themselves, then this is more a question of amending[20] the Rome Convention than disturbing the settled interpretation of the Brussels Convention. True, the national courts may think it premature to delve into choice of law rules for the purpose of determining whether they have jurisdiction[21] and, if a foreign law is found to be applicable, there is a further problem of determining the content of that law.[22] This problem is also open to exaggeration. It can be argued that it is for the party relying on foreign law to prove its content to the satisfaction of the court and, if it fails to do so, the court may proceed on the assumption that any foreign law is the same as the law of the forum.[23] This is the principled answer and surely no case for the rejection of *Tessili* can be based simply on the fact that some national courts have simply failed, or refused, to follow it.[24]

There is greater force in the third argument that recourse to the law applicable to the contract to determine the place of performance may, in practice,

---

[17] As enshrined in Art. 2.   [18] [1980] OJ L266/1.

[19] See para. 30 of the Judgment.   [20] Some would prefer its abandonment.

[21] All the more so if there will be no requirement to return to the question of the applicable law, either because jurisdiction has to be declined, or it is unnecessary for the resolution of the merits.

[22] See para. 37 of the Opinion of Colomer AG.

[23] In some legal systems the circumstances in which the application (and thus the proof) of foreign law is mandatory are more extensive than others: see the survey in Fentiman, *Foreign Law in English Courts* (OUP, Oxford, 1998), chap. IX.

[24] The chief culprits appear to be the French courts: see the decisions referred to in the Opinion of Colomer AG, paras. 46–48, nn. 29–31.

undermine the general rule of *actor sequitur forum rei*. It has been noted earlier that, in the majority of the Contracting States, the place of performance of payment obligations, in the absence of any express agreement of the parties, is the place of the creditor's (i.e. the claimant's) residence or place of business. This would be easier to justify if, in all such cases, there was a close connection between the claim and the claimant's own courts. That is meant to be the justification for allowing the claimant to invoke Article 5(1) to sue the defendant other than in the defendant's own courts, but this objective may not always be fulfilled on the basis of the current interpretation of Article 5(1). It was precisely this concern which was voiced in the reference to the European Court in *Custom Made Commercial* v. *Stawa,* where the Court nevertheless ruled that the legal certainty which is also one of the objectives of the Convention must take priority. Entirely predictably, the same response is given by the Court in *GIE Groupe Concorde* and it is all too easy to see why if one stops to consider the alternative approach which would have to be adopted to deal with the criticisms made of *Tessili*.

The only viable alternative is to subject the 'place of performance' to an 'autonomous interpretation', in line with the majority of the provisions of the Brussels Convention, but what form should this autonomous interpretation take? In *Custom Made Commercial,* Advocate General Lenz suggested that the justification for Article 5(1) should also be made the basis of its interpretation and that the place of performance should refer to the place closest to the subject matter of the contract. This approach also requires a departure from the *De Bloos* ruling, in favour of the 'characteristic obligation'. In effect, this is the approach which is taken in Article 5(1) of the new Regulation,[25] as far as contracts for the sale of goods or the provision of services are concerned.[26] However, the outcome of any general application of this autonomous interpretation to the current Article 5(1) and to other types of contract under the new Article 5(1) would be very hard to predict and would amount to the introduction of a broad-based notion of *forum conveniens* to determine the jurisdiction of the courts. An element of *forum conveniens* may be the objective of Article 5(1), but to elevate it into a criterion for its interpretation runs contrary to the whole scheme of the Convention.[27]

Similar problems of uncertainty also apply to the proposal put forward by Advocate General Colomer in *GIE Groupe Concorde*. In his opinion,[28] 'the place of performance of a contractual obligation means the place designated by reference to the circumstances of the case, taking account of the nature of the legal relationship in question, it being understood that it is presumed that that place is the same as the place where the obligation characterising the legal relationship in question was or is to be performed'. Once again, it should be noted that the latter part of this proposal amounts to a change to the ruling in

---

[25] *Supra,* n. 13.   [26] See text to n. 51 *infra.*
[27] That is not to say that the rules-based scheme of the Convention is in any way superior to a discretion-based scheme.
[28] Para. 109.

De Bloos, notwithstanding Advocate General Colomer's own acknowledge-ment that this was outside the scope of the proceedings in *GIE Groupe Concorde.* As for the test for the place of performance, it would become a factual enquiry and one which is both unpredictable and certain to lead to dif-ferent results in different courts. It is no answer to these objections, as the Advocate General maintains, to say that the same can be said of the 'place where the harmful event occurred' in Article 5(3), but that the Court has not had the 'slightest difficulty' in giving an independent interpretation to this concept.[29] The Court has, indeed, established that the place where the harm-ful event occurred may be either the place where damage occurred or the place of the causal event.[30] Even if it has not been expressly recognized by the Court, it has been shown[31] that this still leaves open the problem of determin-ing just what is the causal event in relation to individual torts.[32] There is a clear parallel here with any autonomous interpretation of the place of performance in Article 5(1). Such an interpretation may be formulated along the lines sug-gested by Advocate General Colomer, but short of references to the European Court dealing with every type of contract, or contractual obligation, the national courts will lack any guidance on the application of this interpretation to the facts of particular cases.

Tessili may not be perfect in some respects, but, in conjunction with the interpretation of other aspects of Article 5(1), it provides a reasonably work-able solution. In most cases, the parties themselves will have specified the place of performance. If they have not done so, it has been suggested by some commentators that there is no alternative but to fall back on the law which governs the contract to fill in the gaps which the parties have chosen to leave.[33] This is all too apparent when one considers what the alternatives may be and the European Court is to be applauded for sticking to its guns, *again,* in resist-ing the attempt to persuade it to depart from its very first ruling on the inter-pretation of the Brussels Convention.

(ii) Leathertex

As noted above, the 'obligation in question', for the purposes of Article 5(1) is the obligation upon which the claim is based.[34] In the event that the claim is based on more than one obligation, the European Court of Justice had sug-gested, in *Shenavai* v. *Kreischer,*[35] that it should be possible to identify a prin-cipal obligation to which all other obligations were ancillary, thus giving

---

[29] Para. 101.   [30] Case 21/76, *Bier* v. *Mines de Potasse* [1976] ECR 1735.
[31] See Briggs, 'Brussels Convention' [1995] *YEL* 512–13.

[32] For example, in defamation the ECJ has ruled that it is the place where the defamatory state-ment was originally produced, an interpretation which would clearly not have been adopted under a number of national laws, which would regard it as the place of publication: Case C–68/93, *Shevill* v. *Presse Alliance SA* [1995] ECR I–415 Cf. Case C–364/93, *Marinari* v. *Lloyd's Bank* [1995] ECR I–2719.

[33] Briggs and Rees, *Civil Jurisdiction and Judgments* (2nd edn., Lloyd's of London Press, London, 1997), at 106.

[34] Case 14/76, *De Bloos* v. *Bouyer* [1976] ECR 1497.   [35] Case 266/85 [1987] ECR 239.

jurisdiction to the courts for the place of performance of the principal obligation (*accessorium sequitur principale*). In the hands of a national court robust and pragmatic enough to find a principal obligation this seemed to solve any of the problems which might be encountered in determining the 'obligation in question'. Indeed, given that it will rarely be the case that a contractual dispute is based on the breach of a single obligation, in practice, the approach suggested in *Shenavai* amounts to a limited[36] application of the 'characteristic obligation'. It was perhaps only a matter of time, however, before a national court would find itself unable to adopt the necessary robust and pragmatic approach. In *Leathertex* it proved to be the Belgian courts that were found wanting.

For a number of years, Bodetex, a Belgian company, had acted as commercial agent for Leathertex, an Italian company, in Belgium and The Netherlands. Having failed to obtain from Leathertex the payment of commission which it alleged was owing, Bodetex regarded the contract as terminated and commenced proceedings in the Rechtbank van Koophandel (Commercial Court), Coutrai. The claim was for the unpaid commission and compensation in lieu of notice. The court found that the claim was based on two obligations—the obligation to pay commission which was to be performed in Italy,[37] and the obligation to give a reasonable period of notice, or compensation in lieu thereof, which was to be performed in Belgium. The Rechtbank van Koophandel does not appear to have considered which of the two obligations was the principal obligation. It proceeded on the basis that, since it had jurisdiction over the claim for compensation in lieu of notice, it had jurisdiction over the whole proceedings given the connection between the obligation to pay compensation and the obligation to pay commission. On the appeal to the Hof van Beroep (Court of Appeal), Ghent, it was held that the two obligations were *of equal rank*, leading to a reference from the Hof van Cassatie. In short, the question referred to the European Court of Justice was whether, in such a case, it was possible for the claim to be heard in full by the court which had jurisdiction under Article 5(1) so far as one of the obligations was concerned. The answer given to that question by the Court is that it was not possible.

This is, of course, an entirely unsatisfactory result. If it needs to be spelled out, it flies in the face of the objectives of the Convention which entail 'the need to avoid, so far as possible, creating a situation in which a number of courts have jurisdiction in respect of one and the same contract',[38] which gives rise to 'the risk of irreconcilable judgments'.[39] Of course, this can be avoided by the claimant bringing his entire claim before the courts for the place where the

---

[36] Limited because the characteristic obligation would have to be at least one of those obligations upon which the claim is based.

[37] In accordance with *Tessili* v. *Dunlop, supra* n. 6, which was once again thought to be the real villain of the piece by Léger AG, notwithstanding that it was the interpretation of the 'obligation in question' which was the principal focus of the reference.

[38] *De Bloos, supra* n. 5, paras. 8 and 9; *Shenavai, supra* n. 35, para. 8.

[39] Case C–125/92, *Mulox IBC Ltd* v. *Geels* [1993] ECR I–4075. See also Case 34/82, *Martin Peters Bauunternehmung GmbH* v. *ZNAV* [1983] ECR 987, para. 17.

defendant is domiciled.[40] To limit the claimant to Article 2 would hinder not only the effective operation of Article 5(1), but also any other provision which may be applicable, but which does not extend to closely related claims.[41] And yet, if one looks at the alternatives, it seems that no other answer could have been given by the Court.

First, it was submitted by the United Kingdom that, in effect, the fault lay with the Belgian courts which should have found that the principal obligation was the obligation to pay commission.[42] The Court rejected a proposal that it should reformulate the question so as to allow for this answer. Any alteration to the substance of the question referred for a preliminary ruling would be incompatible with the Court's function under the Protocol to the Convention and with its duty to ensure that the Governments of the Member States and the parties concerned are given the opportunity to submit observations pursuant to Article 5 of the Protocol and Article 20 of the EC Statute of the Court.[43] This is no doubt correct, but the impression which is left is that this issue could, and should, have been resolved within the confines of the existing interpretation of Article 5(1) at the level of the national court.

Secondly, the Commission submitted that the Court should allow for what may be called 'accessory jurisdiction', i.e. allowing claims to be heard together if there is such a close relationship between the claims that it is advantageous to hear and decide them at the same time in order to avoid the possibility of irreconcilable decisions if they were adjudicated separately. Some instances of accessory jurisdiction are provided expressly by the Convention. Most notably, under Article 6(1), a co-defendant may be sued in the courts for the place where any of the other defendants is domiciled and, under Article 6(2) and 6(3), third parties and defendants to a counterclaim respectively may be sued in the courts which have jurisdiction over the 'original' proceedings or claim. But therein lies the problem. The Court has previously held that there must be a textual basis for any accessory jurisdiction and, as a result, had rejected similar arguments in relation to Article 5(3)[44] and Article 16(5).[45] No textual basis exists in Article 5(1), nor can one be found in Article 22. The latter deals with

---

[40] See para. 41 of the judgment.

[41] A similar stance was, of course, taken in Case C–68/93, *Shevill* v. *Presse Alliance SA* [1995] ECR I–415 in the context of defamation where the claimant relied upon the damage done to her reputation to establish the jurisdiction of the courts. She could do so, but only for the damage which occurred to her reputation within the particular jurisdiction in question. However, one judgment vindicating the reputation of the claimant may be all that is required and the possibility exists that all claims may be heard in the courts for the place where the publisher of the defamatory statement is based (albeit this will often be the same as the place where the defendant is domiciled).

[42] This would, of course, have led to the jurisdiction of the Italian courts and prevented the Belgian courts from hearing the claims made by the Belgian company.

[43] Para. 22. See, in relation to the procedure under Art. 177 of the EC Treaty (now Art. 234 EC), Case C–352/95, *Phytheron International SA* v. *Jean Bourdon SA* [1997] ECR I–1729, at para. 14, and Case C–235/95, *AGS Assedic Pas-de-Calais* v. *Dumon and Froment, Liquidator of Etablissements Pierre Gilson* [1998] ECR I–4531, at para. 26. See also: Case C–295/95, *Farrell* v. *Long* [1997] ECR I–1683, at para. 11.

[44] Case 189/87, *Kalfelis* v. *Schröder* [1988] ECR 5565.

[45] Case 220/84, *AS-Autoteile Service GmbH* v. *Malhe* [1985] ECR 2267.

'related' actions and is concerned with the problems created when two sets of proceedings are taking place in the courts of different Contracting States. It *confers* jurisdiction only incidentally, by allowing for consolidation of the two actions in the court first seised, but only if that court would have had jurisdiction over each of the actions under one of the bases allowed under the Convention.[46]

There are, of course, strong policy arguments in favour of a degree of accessory jurisdiction under the Convention. In *Peters* v. *ZNAV*,[47] the Court noted that: 'multiplication of the bases of jurisdiction in one and the same type of case is not likely to encourage legal certainty and effective legal protection throughout the territory of the Community. The provisions of the Convention *should* therefore be interpreted in such a way that the court seised is not required to declare that it has jurisdiction to adjudicate upon certain applications but has no jurisdiction to hear certain other applications, *even though they are closely related*.' Since, in *Leathertex*, the Court has reaffirmed its view that there must be some form of textual basis which allows for this interpretation, it is disappointing to report that no such provision is included in the amendments which will be introduced by the new Regulation.[48]

Thirdly, the Court might have reconsidered the ruling in *De Bloos* and the interpretation of the 'obligation in question' as the obligation(s) upon which the claim is based. The alternative of conferring jurisdiction on the place of performance of the 'characteristic obligation' would, at least, have the merit of avoiding a multiplicity of proceedings, but at the risk of considerable uncertainty in establishing the 'characteristic obligation' in individual contracts. For that reason, this interpretation has hitherto been confined to individual contracts of employment,[49] and this approach is maintained by the Court in *Leathertex* with little or no debate.[50] The changes to be made to Article 5(1) by the new Regulation will introduce a degree of compromise on this issue. For contracts for the sale of goods or the provision of services, the courts will, in effect, be required to look to the 'characteristic obligation', but certainty is maintained by expressly providing in Article 5(1) that this is the obligation to deliver the goods or provide the services.[51] For all other contracts, the interpretation in *De Bloos* will continue to apply, and rightly so. In conjunction with *Tessili* it will tend to point to the jurisdiction of courts which have a close connection with the claim, but for those cases where this result is not achieved, both interpretations should be adhered to in the interest of certainty.

Lastly, it might be argued that, in cases where the national court is unable to identify a principal obligation, Article 5(1) should have no application at all, leaving the claimant to sue the defendant in the courts for the place where he

---

[46] Para. 38 of the judgment. See also Case 150/80, *Elefanten Schuh GmbH* v. *Jacqmain* [1981] ECR 1671; Case C–51/97, *Réunion Européenne SA* v. *Spliethoff's Bevrachtingskantoor BV* [1998] ECR I–6511, [1998] YEL 704–5.

[47] Case 34/82 [1983] ECR 987, 1003 (emphasis added).   [48] *Supra*, n. 13.

[49] Case 266/85, *Shenavai* v. *Kreischer* [1987] ECR 239.   [50] Paras. 36–37.

[51] Subject to any contrary agreement of the parties.

is domiciled.[52] This argument is not considered by the Court, but it should be rejected. The claimant can sue the defendant in the place of his domicile for all claims, or he may, at least, sue in the place of performance of the individual obligations upon which his claims are based. It would have been better if the Court could have found some acceptable basis for allowing related claims to be heard by a court which has jurisdiction under Article 5(1), but, not having been able to do so, it would go too far to deny the claimant any part of the optional jurisdiction which Article 5(1) is intended to confer.

II. Choice of Court Agreements

A. *TRASPORTI CASTELLETTI SPEDIZIONI INTERNAZIONALI SPA* V.
HUGO TRUMPY SPA[53]
CORECK MARITIME GMBH V. *HANDELSVEEM BV*[54]

The first paragraph of Article 17 states:

If the parties, one or more of whom is domiciled in a Contracting State, have agreed that a court or the courts of a Contracting State are to have jurisdiction to settle any disputes which have arisen or which may arise in connection with a particular legal relationship, that court or those courts shall have exclusive jurisdiction. Such an agreement conferring jurisdiction shall be either—
(a) in writing or evidenced in writing or,
(b) in a form which accords with practices which the parties have established between themselves, or
(c) in international trade or commerce, in a form which accords with a usage of which the parties are or ought to have been aware and which in such trade or commerce is widely known to, and regularly observed by, parties to contracts of the type involved in the particular trade or commerce concerned.

This latest version[55] is the culmination of a process of relaxation of the formal requirements laid down by Article 17, which originally allowed only for agreements in writing or evidenced in writing. This process was necessary principally in order to be sympathetic to the requirements of international trade, which was potentially hampered in its operation and effectiveness by the very strict requirements of the original version. The extent of the relaxation introduced by this process was the subject of the references made to the European Court of Justice in *Trumpy* and *Coreck*. While the judgments in both cases still leave a number of questions unanswered, and some aspects of the rulings are far from convincing, they are both largely consistent with the commercial good sense which led to the changes to Article 17 in the first place.

---

[52] One of several suggestions made in Briggs and Rees, *supra* n. 33, 101.

[53] Case C–159/97 [1999] ECR I–1597 [1999] ILPr. 492 (hereafter '*Trumpy*').

[54] Case C–387/98 [2000] (hereafter '*Coreck*').

[55] Contained in the Convention of San Sebastián of 26 May 1989 (on the Accession of Spain and Portugal) [1990] OJ C189/2. A number of further amendments are made by the new Regulation, *supra* n. 13, none of which are material to the issues before the Court in *Trumpy* and *Coreck*.

(i) Trumpy

In *Trumpy* consignments of fruit were loaded by various Argentinian shippers under bills of lading issued in Buenos Aires on board a vessel operated by a Danish carrier. They were bound for delivery in Savona, Italy, to Trasporti Castelletti ('Castelletti'), an Italian company. As a result of problems which arose during the unloading of the goods Castelletti brought an action in Genoa against Hugo Trumpy ('Trumpy'), an Italian company, in its capacity as the forwarding agent of the ship and the Danish carrier. Trumpy challenged the jurisdiction of the Genoese court on the basis of a jurisdiction clause contained in the bills of lading which provided for the exclusive jurisdiction of the English courts.

On the basis of this very typical set of facts, the Corte Suprema di Cassazione managed to refer no fewer than fourteen questions to the European Court of Justice. The principal focus of those questions was sub-paragraph (c) of the first paragraph of Article 17[56] and, in particular, the earlier version of that provision then in force at the time the claim arose.[57] However, it is hard to disagree with the observation of Advocate General Léger that the Court was, in effect, being invited to review all of its already extensive case law on Article 17. In doing so, it did little more than reaffirm a number of earlier rulings which may be summarized as follows with little or no comment:

1. Although Article 17 will apply only to agreements entered into with the consent of the relevant parties, sub-paragraph (c) makes it possible to *presume* that such consent exists where commercial usages of which the parties are or ought to have been aware exist in this regard in the relevant branch of international trade or commerce.[58]
2. The existence of a usage, which must be determined in relation to the branch of trade or commerce in which the parties to the contract operate, is established where a particular course of conduct is generally and regularly followed by operators in that branch when concluding contracts of a particular type.[59]
3. It is for the national court to determine whether the requisite usage exists, but the Court confirmed that it is not necessary for the relevant course of conduct relied upon to be established in specific countries or, in particular, in all of the Contracting States. Nor is a specific form of

---

[56] The Corte Suprema di Cassazione had found that the signature of the original shipper could not be deemed to imply consent to all of the clauses in the bill of lading, thus ruling out any reliance on sub-paragraph (a) and an agreement in writing, or evidenced in writing.

[57] i.e. the Accession Convention of 1978. It differs from the current version in that it states only that the agreement conferring jurisdiction shall be 'in international trade or commerce, in a form which accords with a usage of which the parties are or ought to have been aware'.

[58] Para. 20, affirming Case C–106/95, *Mainschiffahrts Genossenschaft* v. *Les Gravières Rhénanes Sàrl* [1997] ECR I–911.

[59] Para. 30; *Mainschiffahrts Genossenschaft, supra* n. 58 (in effect now part of the wording of the current version of Art. 17 due to the closing words of sub-paragraph (c)).

publicity required. These are, nevertheless, factors which may be taken into account by the national courts.[60]

4. The fact that a course of conduct amounting to a usage is challenged before the courts—as is often the case with jurisdiction clauses in international trade—is not sufficient to cause the conduct no longer to constitute a usage.[61]

5. The requirement that the agreement shall be in 'a form which accords' with a commercial usage (for example, whether the agreement must be in any particular language or appear in any particular part of the contract) must be assessed solely in the light of the commercial usage of the branch of international trade or commerce concerned, without taking into account any requirements of form which national provisions may lay down.[62]

Two further rulings of the Court in *Trumpy* do, however, call for further comment. First, the Court ruled that there are no limitations on the choice of court allowed to the parties, other than those laid down in Article 17 itself. Thus, there is no need for any objective connection between the relationship in dispute and the court chosen.[63] This is uncontroversial. The whole point of an Article 17 agreement is that the parties should be allowed to choose a particular jurisdiction which may not otherwise have any connection with the dispute and that, in the interest of certainty, that choice should prevail. Any concern that this may operate to the disadvantage of so-called weaker parties, for example, consumers, employees and insured parties, is dealt with by the limitations placed upon choice of court agreements by further provisions of the Convention.[64] No further general limitation should be imposed upon Article 17.

The further implication of this ruling is that 'any further review of the validity of the clause and of the intention of the party which inserted it must be excluded and substantive rules of liability applicable in the chosen court must not affect the validity of the jurisdiction clause'.[65] This is more controversial. The latter prohibition confirms that the court seised may not take account of its mandatory rules in reviewing the validity of a jurisdiction clause. For example, in *The Hollandia*[66] the House of Lords refused to give effect to an exclusive jurisdiction agreement in favour of the Dutch courts, since it was common ground[67] that the Dutch courts would uphold a lower limitation of liability than that which was allowed by the Hague–Visby Rules.[68] If the same situation

---

[60] Para. 30.   [61] *Ibid.*
[62] Para. 38, affirming Case 150/80, *Elefanten Schuh* v. *Jacqmain* [1981] ECR 1671.
[63] Para. 50; Case 56/79, *Zelger* v. *Salinitri* [1980] ECR 89.
[64] Art. 15 (consumers), Art. 12 (insureds), Art. 17, para. 5 (employees).
[65] Para. 51.   [66] [1983] 1 AC 565.
[67] There was an express choice in favour of Dutch law, which continued to apply the earlier Hague Rules.
[68] The jurisdiction clause was, therefore, void under Art. III, para. 8 of the Hague–Visby Rules. According to the House of Lords, the Hague–Visby Rules were given mandatory status by the Carriage of Goods by Sea Act 1971 which provided that they 'shall have the force of law' (s. 1(2)),

should arise now that the Brussels Convention is in force, the English courts would be obliged to decline jurisdiction and give effect to the parties' agreement. It may be that any judgment subsequently given by the Dutch courts could be denied recognition in England on the basis that it would be contrary to public policy, but this possibility must be doubted, given the narrow interpretation placed upon 'public policy'.[69]

The former prohibition goes even further, in that it appears to suggest that, provided the formal requirements of Article 17 have been met, there can be no review of the substantive, or material, validity of the clause. This issue has yet to be considered directly by the European Court of Justice,[70] and it is far from certain that this prohibition could be maintained, if and when it is. A choice of court 'agreement' may well comply with the formal requirements of Article 17; for example, it may be in writing and signed by both parties, but what is to be done if one party alleges that his signature was obtained by fraud, duress, or misrepresentation, so that there is, in substance, no agreement? It is surely no answer simply to say that the (formal) requirements of Article 17 have been met and, in any event, they have not. In no sense, whether by reference to national law[71] or some form of autonomous interpretation,[72] could it be said that the parties 'have *agreed*' upon a choice of court. If a challenge to the substantive validity of a jurisdiction agreement is made it must be open to the court seised to review it, all the more so since there is no basis upon which such a challenge could later provide a defence to the recognition of any judgment subsequently given by the 'chosen' court. It is one thing to say that a national court may not apply rules of its law so as to override an agreement which has been reached, but quite another to expect it to give effect to something which amounts to no agreement at all.

The final ruling in *Trumpy* deals with the fact that neither party to the proceedings was a party to the jurisdiction agreement contained in the bills of lading. The bills were issued to the original Argentinian shipper by the Danish owners of the vessel; the proceedings were between Castelletti, as ultimate consignee, and Trumpy, as agent for the carrier. In accordance with its earlier ruling in *Tilly Russ*,[73] the Court ruled that it is sufficient that the jurisdiction clause is valid under Article 17 *as between the shipper and the carrier*, i.e. the original contracting parties, the parties' nationality being irrelevant for the

---

thus resolving a matter of some academic controversy: Mann, 'Statutes and the Conflict of Laws' (1972–1973) 46 *BYIL* 117; Morris, 'The Scope of the Carriage of Goods by Sea Act 1971' (1979) 95 *LQR* 59.

[69] See the review of the decisions in *Krombach* and *Maxicar* below.

[70] See Case C–269/95, *Benincasa* v. *Dentalkit Srl* [1997] ECR I–3767 which carries the same implication as *Trumpy*. Cf. Case C–214/89, *Powell Duffryn* v. *Petereit* [1992] ECR I–1745 which lends support to the review of material validity in accordance with the substantive law applicable to the putative agreement (contained in the constitution of a German company).

[71] i.e. an 'agreement' in accordance with the substantive law applicable to the putative agreement.

[72] i.e. some form of consensus 'in the light of community law': see *I.P. Metal Ltd* v. *Ruote OZ SpA* [1994] 2 Lloyd's Rep. 560.

[73] Case 71/83, *Partenreederei MS 'Tilly Russ'* v. *NV Haven & Vervoerbedrijf Nova* [1984] ECR 2417.

purposes of that investigation.[74] So far as the parties to the proceedings are concerned, the jurisdiction clause can be pleaded so long as, under the relevant national law,[75] the third party (Castelletti, as the holder of the bill of lading) succeeds to the original contracting party's (the shipper's) rights and obligations. Where sub-paragraph (c) of Article 17 is relied upon, the relevant enquiry therefore is to look at the commercial usage of which the original contracting parties were aware, or ought to have been aware. This makes eminent sense; in particular, it is consistent with the relaxation of Article 17 so as to give effect to the commercial expectations of parties involved in international trade, but it still leaves unanswered one or two further questions which were the subject of the reference in *Coreck*.

(ii)   Coreck

In *Coreck*, consignments of groundnut kernels were carried on a Russian vessel under bills of lading issued by Coreck, a German company and the time charterer of the vessel. The bills of lading called for delivery in Rotterdam and proceedings were commenced there under Article 5(1) by Handelsveem BV, the holder in due course of the bills of lading. Coreck challenged the jurisdiction of the court in Rotterdam on the basis of a jurisdiction clause in the bills of lading in the following terms:

3. Jurisdiction.
Any dispute arising under this Bill of Lading shall be decided in the country where the carrier has his principal place of business and the law of such country shall apply except as provided elsewhere herein.

Clause 3 was followed by a rather complex clause which sought to determine the 'identity of the carrier'. Coreck's challenge led the Hoge Raad de Nederlanden to refer four questions to the Court of Justice.

The Court confirmed the ruling given in *Trumpy* that compliance with Article 17 was to be assessed as between the original contracting parties and that the question whether Handelsveem was bound by the agreement was a matter for the applicable national law. The Court also ruled that determination of the applicable national law was a matter for the national courts and was not one of the interpretation of the Convention.

A number of other issues were also raised by the questions referred in *Coreck* which did not arise in *Trumpy*. First, under the jurisdiction clause the parties had not agreed to the jurisdiction of the courts of a Contracting State as such; they had agreed to the jurisdiction of the courts for the principal place of business of the carrier. Although it might be possible to work out which courts this would mean in the event of a dispute, was this sufficient to comply with Article 17? The Court ruled that it is not necessary for the clause to be formulated in such a way that the competent court can be determined on its wording alone,

---

[74] Paras. 41–42.
[75] For example, in English law, the Carriage of Goods by Sea Act 1992 or now, more generally for other types of contract, under the Contracts (Rights of Third Parties) Act 1999.

i.e. the parties do not need to have chosen the courts of a named Contracting State. It is sufficient that the 'the clause state the objective factors on the basis of which the parties have agreed to choose a court. . . Those factors, which must be sufficiently precise to enable the court seised to ascertain whether it has jurisdiction, may, where appropriate, be determined by the particular circumstances of the case.'[76] Thus, a formulaic choice of court is permissible, but it must be possible to determine with a degree of certainty what that choice amounts to. It must be debatable whether the clause in *Coreck* could be said to satisfy this latter requirement; the 'identity of carrier' clause purported to identify the shipowner as the carrier, but acknowledged that another party, for example, the charterer, might be so identified. It can be notoriously difficult in contracts for the carriage of goods by sea to determine the identity of the carrier where the goods are carried on a chartered vessel. A claimant can find to his cost that he has been pursuing the wrong party and that he is out of time so far as any claim against the real 'carrier' is concerned. It is submitted therefore that the clause used in *Coreck* is too uncertain to satisfy the requirements laid down by the Court and that, in the interest of avoiding the risk of further delay for any claimant, it should be considered invalid under Article 17.[77]

If a formulaic choice of court is allowed under Article 17 this may not necessarily result in the choice of the courts of a Contracting State; for example, in *Coreck*, if the Russian shipowner was found to be the carrier, it would have the effect of conferring jurisdiction on the Russian courts. It may also mean that that both of the original contracting parties, i.e. the shipper and the 'carrier', were not domiciled in a Contracting State. In answer to a question from the Hoge Raad about the applicability of Article 17 in such circumstances, the Court ruled that 'Article 17 . . . only applies if, first, at least *one of the parties to the original contract* is domiciled in a Contracting State and, secondly, the parties agree to submit any disputes to a court or the courts of a Contracting State'. The latter part of this ruling is uncontroversial. If the parties have chosen the courts of a non-Contracting State, whether by reference to a formula or otherwise, Article 17 does not apply and the court seised will be required to give effect to the choice in accordance with its national law.[78] The first part, concerning the domicile of the parties, is far less straightforward.

It will be recalled that, in *Trumpy*, the Court ruled that the nationality[79] of the parties is irrelevant for the purpose of *compliance* with the requirements of Article 17, but this left open how the identity or status of the parties might affect the question *whether* Article 17 applies in the first place. Article 17 gives effect to agreements between 'parties, *one or more of whom* is domiciled in a

---

[76] Para. 15.

[77] Of course, the claimant may still find that he has sued the wrong party as carrier, but he should not have the further delay of having to go to another court to find this out.

[78] Schlosser Report [1979] OJ C59/71, para. 176.

[79] It is far from clear that 'nationality' should have been the appropriate concern, as opposed to domicile which is a far more relevant enquiry under the Convention; it may be that domicile was, in fact, the real concern of the Court.

Contracting State'.[80] If neither party is domiciled in a Contracting State, Article 17 has a more limited role in that it directs that the courts of other Contracting States shall have no jurisdiction unless the court chosen has declined jurisdiction.[81] In *Trumpy*, at least one of the original contracting parties[82] was domiciled in a Contracting State and both of the parties to the proceedings were domiciled in a Contracting State, so that it made no difference which set of parties was relevant to the application of Article 17. In *Coreck*, the Court has ruled that the relevant enquiry is to consider the identity and status of the original contracting parties. This does not look right.

It is submitted that the correct approach to Article 17 is to distinguish between two different references to the 'parties'. The 'parties' referred to in the opening line are the parties to the proceedings, i.e. in *Coreck*, Coreck and Handelsveem; the 'parties' referred to in sub-paragraph (c) are the parties to the original agreement, i.e. in *Coreck*, the shipper and the 'carrier'. Thus, provided one of the parties *to the proceedings* is domiciled in a Contracting State, Article 17 will apply and, in cases of third party succession like *Coreck*, it should be entirely irrelevant that neither of the original parties may be so domiciled. However, if neither party *to the proceedings* is domiciled in a Contracting State, Article 17 will not apply, save to the limited extent referred to above, even if one of the original contracting parties is so domiciled.[83] Most of the jurisdictional rules of the Convention apply to regulate proceedings where the defendant, i.e. a party to the proceedings, is domiciled in a Contracting State. Article 17 operates as an exception to this scheme since it is sufficient that one of the 'parties' is so domiciled, but this must still be taken to refer to the parties to the proceedings. It would be entirely inappropriate for Article 17 to apply to a dispute between, for example, a US claimant and a Japanese defendant, just because one of the original parties to a jurisdiction agreement had been domiciled in a Contracting State.[84] Conversely, if a party to the proceedings is domiciled in a Contracting State and is found to 'have agreed' to the courts of a Contracting State, in accordance with the requirements laid down in *Trumpy* and *Coreck*, the requirements of Article 17 have been met. It should apply on the basis that it is the scheme of the Convention to regulate the jurisdiction of the Contracting States' courts where, in the case of Article 17, either the defendant or the claimant is domiciled in a Contracting State.

---

[80] In this sense it departs from the normal scheme of the Convention under which the rules on jurisdiction apply only where the *defendant* is domiciled in a Contracting State.

[81] Under its national law, since neither the Convention rules in general nor Art. 17 in particular will apply in this case.

[82] The Danish carrier.

[83] If the domicile of the original contracting parties is the relevant enquiry there may also be difficult questions of time involved, i.e. when must the original contracting party have been domiciled in a Contracting State—at the time of the agreement, or at the time proceedings are commenced?

[84] Some provisions, e.g. Art. 16 (exclusive jurisdiction) apply regardless of the domicile of the parties, but only because there are other close connections with one of the Contracting States, e.g. the location of immovable property (Art. 16(1)).

Finally, one of the questions submitted to the Court led it to consider the position if a third party had not 'succeeded' to the rights and obligations of an original contracting party under the applicable national law. It ruled that, in such circumstances, the court 'must ascertain, having regard to the requirements laid down in the first paragraph of Article 17 . . . whether he *actually* accepted the jurisdiction clause relied on against him'.[85] The implication is that a third party is *deemed* to have accepted the jurisdiction clause when he is found to have 'succeeded' to it under the applicable national law, but this does not rule out a finding that the third party could be bound by the jurisdiction clause within the requirements of Article 17 itself. In practice, this may mean, at least for contracts for the carriage of goods by sea, that it is unnecessary to invoke the applicable national law. For example, the applicable national law may well contain provisions that the subsequent holder of a bill of lading succeeds to the rights and obligations of the shipper, including any jurisdiction clause.[86] Such provisions have been introduced principally on the basis that they are in accordance with the commercial expectations of the parties to the various contracts involved in the carriage of goods by sea, i.e. they are in accordance with the usage of this particular branch of international trade or commerce. If that is the expectation of the parties, could it not be said, as between the carrier and the holder of the bill of lading, that the requirements of sub-paragraph (c) of Article 17 have been met without recourse to the applicable national law?

III. Public Policy

A. *KROMBACH* V. *BAMBERSKI*[87]
RÉGIE NATIONALE DES USINES RENAULT SA V. *MAXICAR SPA*[88]

Article 27(1) of the Brussels Convention states:

[A judgment shall not be recognized) . . . If such recognition is contrary to public policy in the State in which recognition is sought.

The scope of this defence to recognition is determined in part by other provisions of the Convention, in particular Article 28(3) and Article 29 which state as follows:

28(3). Subject to the provisions of the first paragraph,[89] the jurisdiction of the court of the State of origin may not be reviewed; the test of public policy referred to in point 1 of Article 27 may not be applied to the rules relating to jurisdiction.

---

    [85] Para. 26 (emphasis added).
    [86] See, e.g., the provisions of the Carriage of Goods by Sea Act 1992.
    [87] Case C–7/98 [2001] ILPr 540 (28 March 2000) (hereafter '*Krombach*').
    [88] Case C–38/98 11 May 2000 (hereafter '*Maxicar*').
    [89] Under which the jurisdictional competence of the judgment court may be challenged if jurisdiction was taken in breach of Sections 3 (exclusive jurisdiction (Art. 16)), 4 (insurance contracts (Arts. 7–12A)), and 5 (consumer contracts (Arts. 13–15)).

29. Under no circumstances may a foreign judgment be reviewed as to its substance.

Since the aim of the Convention is to facilitate the free movement of judgments, the defences to recognition allowed by Article 27, of which public policy is one example, are interpreted strictly.[90] Consequently, so far as public policy is concerned, the Court has previously ruled that it must be invoked only to deny recognition to the judgment of another Contracting State in exceptional cases.[91] According to the Court in *Krombach*[92] and *Maxicar*[93] it follows that while it is a matter for the Contracting States to determine according to their own conceptions of what public policy requires, *the limits* of that concept are a matter of interpretation of the Convention. It was those limits which were tested in the references to the Court in both cases.

(i) Krombach

Mr Bamberski's daughter died during a short visit to Mr Krombach's home in France in 1992. She had felt unwell and an injection was administered by Mr Krombach, who was a doctor. She was found dead the following morning. A preliminary investigation in Germany into Mr Krombach's responsibility for the death was discontinued. Mr Bamberski lodged a complaint in France and an investigation was opened there, as a result of which Mr Krombach was committed for trial. The French Criminal Court founded its jurisdiction on section 689(1) of the French Code of Criminal Procedure, which provided that any foreigner who committed a crime against a French national outside France could be tried under French criminal law. Mr Krombach was ordered to appear in person, but did not attend the hearing. Consequently, the French courts applied their contempt procedure under which defence counsel was prevented from making submissions on his behalf.[94] Mr Krombach was convicted of involuntary manslaughter and ordered to pay 350,000 FF in damages to Mr Bamberski. An application to enforce the order for compensation in Germany led the Bundesgerichtschof to refer a number of questions to the Court, all of which were concerned with the scope of Article 27(1).

The rule contained in section 689(1) of the French Code of Criminal Procedure is equivalent to Article 14 of the French Civil Code, the second part of which provides that a foreigner may be sued in the French courts for obligations contracted by him to French nationals in a foreign country. Under Article 3(2) of the Convention, this provision (i.e. Article 14 of the Civil Code and not section 689(1) of the Code of Criminal Procedure) is not applicable as against persons domiciled in a Contracting State. The fact that the French courts had based their jurisdiction on a ground which was the *equivalent* of one which they were prevented from invoking under the Convention led the Bundesgerichtshof to refer, as its first question, whether this fell within the

---

[90] Case C–414/92, *Solo Kleinmotoren* v. *Boch* [1994] ECR I–2237, para. 20.
[91] Case 145/86, *Hoffmann* v. *Krieg* [1988] ECR 645, para. 21; Case C–78/95, *Hendrikman and Feyen* v. *Magenta Druck & Verlag* [1996] ECR I–4943, para. 23.
[92] Para. 22.   [93] Para. 27.   [94] Art. 630 of the French Code of Criminal Procedure.

meaning of public policy in Article 27(1). The Court ruled that it did not. *Even if* the French courts had exercised jurisdiction on the basis of Article 14 of the Civil Code itself, there could have been no defence to the recognition of the judgment on the grounds of public policy. The provisions of Article 28(3) allow for no other result. In the interests of the free movement of judgments, challenges to the jurisdiction of the court of origin have been greatly circumscribed.[95] For the most part, the court of origin has to be trusted to apply the jurisdictional rules of the Convention correctly, and fairly, but, if it fails to do so, this in itself is not enough to lead to the non-recognition of any judgment subsequently handed down. It is too late to ask if this is too high a price to pay.

The answer to the first question was, therefore, very predictable, but it may be argued that it was the wrong question to ask. It seems that the French courts were, in fact, perfectly entitled to exercise jurisdiction. It is true that the Convention applies to decisions given in civil matters by a criminal court.[96] However, this does not alter the fact that the French courts were entitled to apply their national law (including section 689(1)) to determine jurisdiction in what were *criminal* proceedings.[97] Once seised of the proceedings on this basis, it was then possible to invoke Article 5(4), which states as follows:

As regards a civil claim for damages or restitution which is based on an act giving rise to criminal proceedings, in the court seised of those proceedings, to the extent that court has jurisdiction under its own law to entertain civil proceedings.

Article 5(4) therefore provides an exception to the general rule that the courts of the Contracting States should not invoke their national rules of exorbitant jurisdiction as against a defendant domiciled in a Contracting State. In that sense, it bears comparison with Article 24 under which the courts of a Contracting State may hear applications for 'provisional measures' notwithstanding that the courts of another Contracting State have jurisdiction as to the substance of the matter. As will be seen below,[98] this has led the Court to rule that no judgment may be enforced if it was handed down in the purported exercise of Article 24 and it does not, in fact, amount to a 'provisional measure'. In other words, it seems that a provision which allows for the exceptional application of national rules of exorbitant jurisdiction must not be relied upon beyond the circumstances in which it was envisaged that it should be used. The same may be said of Article 5(4), but the difficulty is that it is very widely drafted so as to allow for any 'civil claim for damages or restitution' which may be added to the criminal proceedings under the relevant national law. That

[95] Of course, this is why a defendant must take any objections in the court of origin, even in cases, like *Krombach*, where it would seem to be self-evident that the court of origin should not be hearing the case.

[96] Case C–172/91, *Sonntag* v. *Waidmann* [1993] ECR I–1963, para. 16.

[97] On the basis that, on their inception, such proceedings do not amount to a 'civil and commercial matter' within the meaning of Art. 1.

[98] Case C–99/96, *Hans-Hermann Mietz* v. *Intership Yachting Sneek BV* [1999] ECR I–2277, reviewed below.

may suggest that it is a provision which is ripe for reconsideration,[99] but no changes are made to it in the new Council Regulation.[100]

Given that either the French courts did have jurisdiction to hear Mr Bamberski's claim, or it did not matter anyway because of Article 28(3), Mr Krombach should, perhaps, consider himself fortunate that the French courts also applied their contempt procedure. This prevented defence counsel from making any submissions on his behalf. According to the Court this was something which could fall within the limits of the concept of public policy. It was necessary to ask whether the recognition of a judgment given in such circumstances would infringe a 'fundamental principle' of the recognizing state. This was further defined as a 'manifest breach of a rule of law regarded as essential in the legal order of the State in which enforcement is sought or of a right recognized as being fundamental within that legal order'. The right to be defended was clearly to be seen as a right which fell within this category.[101]

In the context of the proceedings in *Krombach*, some difficulty is created in this regard by Article II of the Protocol annexed to the Convention. This expressly recognizes the right of a defendant to be defended in criminal proceedings in the courts of a Contracting State if he is neither domiciled there, nor a national of the state, but only if he is prosecuted for an offence committed unintentionally. This implies that where the defendant is prosecuted for an offence committed intentionally, as in *Krombach*, he does not have such a right. The Court had little difficulty, however, in ruling that such an interpretation would run contrary to the fundamental principle of Community law that everyone has the right to a fair hearing. Article II of the Protocol did not therefore preclude a ruling that recognition of the French judgment would be contrary to public policy.

Of course, it may be argued that a court's disregard for the jurisdictional rules of the Convention also amounts to a breach of the right to a fair hearing, but this is precluded by Article 28(3). The practical effect of the Court's ruling in *Krombach* is that a defendant must, at the very least, be given the opportunity of a hearing, in which he could challenge the jurisdiction of the court of origin, either in person or through a lawyer acting on his behalf. If he declines to take this opportunity, or his arguments fall on deaf ears, there appears to be

---

[99] Perhaps by limiting civil claims to the recovery of property taken as part of the crime and excluding claims for damages.

[100] *Supra* n. 13.

[101] It could be derived from the general principle of Community law that everyone is entitled to fair legal process (Case C–185/95 P, *Baustahlgewebe* v. *Commission* [1998] ECR I–8417, paras. 20 and 21; Cases C–174/98 P and C–189/98 P, *Netherlands and Van der Wal* v. *Commission* [2000] ECR I–0000, para. 17), as recognized in the European Convention on Human Rights, Art. 6. More specifically, the European Court of Human Rights (to which a reference was also made in *Krombach*) has ruled in cases relating to criminal proceedings that, although not absolute, the right of every person charged with an offence to be effectively defended by a lawyer is one of the fundamental elements in a fair trial and an accused person does not forfeit entitlement to such a right simply because he is not present at the hearing: judgment of 23 Nov. 1993, in *Poitrimol* v. *France*, Series A No. 277-A; judgment of 22 Sept. 1994 in *Pelladoah* v. *Netherlands*, Series A No. 297-B; judgment of 21 Jan. 1999 in *Van Geyseghem* v. *Belgium*).

nothing in the Convention that will protect him from recognition of the judgment of a court which should not have been hearing his case.[102]

(ii) Maxicar

In *Maxicar*, the defendants, Mr Formen and Maxicar, were ordered by the Cour d'Appel, Dijon, to pay 100,000 FF by way of damages to Renault. The claim was based on the defendants' manufacture and marketing of body parts for Renault vehicles.[103] In an application to enforce the judgment in Italy, the defendants argued that it was based on a breach of Community law, i.e. the principle of free movement of goods and freedom of competition. The Corte d'Appello di Torino referred to the Court of Justice the question whether such a defence fell within the concept of public policy in Article 27(1).[104]

The Court reaffirmed everything that was said in *Krombach* about the limits of the concept of public policy. By disallowing any review of a foreign judgment as to its substance, the Court emphasized that the court of the state in which enforcement is sought cannot review the accuracy of the findings of law or fact made by the court of origin.[105] This also extended to Community law. The defence raised did not therefore fall within the concept of public policy.

If there may be some misgivings after *Krombach* about the powerlessness of the courts to rely on Article 27(1) so as to control misapplications of the Convention rules on jurisdiction, there need be less concern about the need to control misapplications of Community law. The defendant can be expected to take such objections in the court of origin and, if necessary, can ask for a preliminary ruling of the Court of Justice prior to any judgment. As the Court emphasized, it may be appropriate to ask whether, in such cases, the system of legal remedies in each Contracting State, together with the preliminary ruling procedure provided for in Article 177[106] of the Treaty, affords a sufficient guarantee to individuals. It is not appropriate, once judgment has been entered, to allow any alleged misapplication of Community law to undermine the aim of the Convention.[107]

---

[102] Any attempt to commence proceedings for a declaration of non-liability in the courts for the place where the defendant is domiciled to create a defence of *res judicata* under Art. 27(3) seems to be precluded by Art. 21 which prevents a 'second' court from taking jurisdiction in proceedings involving the same cause of action and between the same parties. Notwithstanding this apparent difficulty, it cannot be ruled out that the English courts would attempt to find a solution in the form of an anti-suit injunction: *Turner* v. *Grovit* [2000] QB 345 (where the English courts were, at least, first seised).

[103] The main proceedings were for forgery, but Renault joined the proceedings as a civil party.

[104] There was an issue of admissibility since Renault contended that the Corte d'Appello di Torino had no power to ask the Court to give a preliminary ruling concerning the interpretation of the Convention. It was found to have the power to do so since it was sitting in an appellate capacity and fell within Art. 2(2) of the Protocol to the Convention.

[105] Para. 29; *Krombach, supra* n. 87, para. 36.

[106] Now Art. 234.　　　　　　　　　　　　　　[107] Para. 33

IV.   Enforceable Judgments

A.   *COURSIER V. FORTIS BANK SA*[108]

Article 31 of the Brussels Convention states:

A judgment given in a Contracting State and enforceable in that State shall be enforced in another Contracting State when, on the application of any interested party, it has been declared enforceable there.

Until the ruling in *Coursier* there had been no direct consideration by the Court of Justice of the meaning of 'enforceability' in Article 31.[109] By so considering it in *Coursier*, the Court was required to rule on the dividing line between matters which affect the *enforceability* of a judgment and those which concern only its *execution*. It is submitted that that line was drawn in exactly the right place.

Fortis Bank SA ('Fortis'), domiciled in Luxembourg, granted a loan to Mr and Mrs Coursier, domiciled in France. As a result of their failure to repay the loan, Fortis commenced proceedings in France[110] and obtained a judgment in the sum of 563,282 LF (the 'contested judgment'). Mr Coursier's business—a bar in Rehon, France—was subsequently placed in liquidation, in the context of which Fortis gave notice of its claim. Shortly thereafter the Tribunal de Commerce de Briey closed the liquidation on the ground that there were insufficient assets (the 'insolvency judgment'). The effect of this closure was that the individual claims of creditors could be reinstated only under the conditions specified in Article 169 of Law No. 85–98 ('Article 169'), none of which applied to Fortis. Having proved not to be a successful barman, Mr Coursier then decided to pursue a career as a frontier worker in Luxembourg. By doing so, he generated a salary which Fortis decided it would like to attach, resulting in an application to the Luxembourg courts for enforcement of the contested judgment. Mr Coursier argued that the effect of Article 169 was that the contested judgment was no longer enforceable in France and, under Article 31, could not therefore be enforced in Luxembourg. This, in essence, was the question which was referred to the Court of Justice by the Cour Supérieure de Justice.

The judgment of the Tribunal de Commerce de Briey to close the liquidation could not itself be recognized and enforced under the Convention, since it concerned insolvency[111] and was excluded from the scope of the Convention

---

[108] Case C–267/97 [1999] ECR I–2543, [1999] ILPr. 202 (hereafter '*Coursier*').

[109] Other aspects of Art. 31 have been the subject of rulings in Case 42/76, *De Wolf* v. *Cox* [1976] ECR 1759, and Case 145/86, *Hoffmann* v. *Krieg* [1988] ECR 645.

[110] In accordance with Arts. 13 and 14 of the Convention since the loan amounted to a consumer contract.

[111] A separate Bankruptcy Convention (see [1996] ILM 1223, for the text in English) is not in force. It remained open for signature until 23 May 1996 and was signed by all the Member States, except the UK.

by Article 1(2).[112] It could still, of course, have been recognized under national law, but it seems that, as a matter of Luxembourg law, it could have only strictly territorial effect.[113] In one sense, therefore, the question for the Court was whether a judgment (the insolvency judgment) which was not entitled to recognition either under the Convention, or as a matter of national law, could nonetheless be recognized indirectly by rendering the contested judgment unenforceable within the meaning of Article 31. It ruled that it could not.

According to the Court, the question whether a judgment is *enforceable* in character must be distinguished from the question whether that judgment can any longer be *enforced* by reason of payment of the debt, or some other cause.[114] This distinction may not be easy to draw, but it is both sensible and entirely just. For example, it may be that, under the law of the adjudicating state, the only assets of the judgment debtor which are available to satisfy the debt, for example the matrimonial home, are immune from execution. If the judgment debtor owns other assets in another Contracting State, they should be available for execution and nothing in Article 31 should prevent this outcome. Of course, the effect of Article 169 was that *all* assets of Mr Coursier were immune from execution. The distinction between an unenforceable judgment and one which is enforceable, but which cannot be enforced against any assets, may seem almost illusory. Nevertheless, the effect of Article 169 is not to extinguish the creditor's substantive rights, but rather to prevent any legal action from being taken against the debtor to obtain satisfaction of those rights,[115] i.e. in *Coursier* it still affected only the question whether the contested judgment could be executed. Furthermore, Article 169 is regarded as highly controversial, even in France,[116] and is a provision which appears to have no equivalent in any other Contracting State.[117] It is one thing for it to take effect in France, where bankruptcy proceedings are governed by the principle of territoriality,[118] and quite another for it to acquire an extra-territorial effect under Article 31 of the Convention which it would not otherwise have enjoyed. It is submitted that the Court was correct both in the distinction drawn between enforceability and execution, and in ruling that Article 169 fell within the latter.

---

[112] '[The Convention shall not apply to] Bankruptcy, proceedings relating to the winding-up of insolvent companies or other legal persons, judicial arrangements, compositions and analogous proceedings.'

[113] See para. 23 of the Opinion of La Pergola AG.   [114] Para. 24.

[115] See para. 8 of the Opinion of La Pergola AG.

[116] See Derrida. Godé, and Sortais, *Redressement et liquidation judiciaires des enterprises, cinq années d'application* (3rd edn., Paris, 1991), at 426.

[117] See para. 8 of the Opinion of La Pergola AG.   [118] *Ibid.*, para. 23.

V.   Scope of the Convention and Reinsurance

UGIC, a company domiciled in Canada, entered into a reinsurance contract with Group Josi, a company domiciled in Belgium. The reinsurance contract was brokered by Euromepa, a company domiciled in France. Group Josi refused to satisfy a claim from UGIC, alleging that it had been induced to enter the reinsurance contract by a material non-disclosure.[120] UGIC commenced proceedings before the French courts. Group Josi challenged jurisdiction on the basis that the Convention applied, that it should have been sued in Belgium under Article 2, and that none of the exceptional bases of jurisdiction provided in the Convention conferred jurisdiction on the French courts. UGIC argued that the Convention does not apply where the plaintiff is domiciled in a non-Contracting State and that, therefore, the French courts were free to take jurisdiction under their national law.[121] It was this submission from UGIC which formed the basis of the first question referred to the Court of Justice by the Cour d'Appel, Versailles. The Cour d'Appel also took the opportunity to refer to the Court the question whether the special rules of jurisdiction in the Convention dealing with insurance contracts extended to reinsurance contracts.

In answer to the first question, the Court ruled that Title II of the Convention (i.e. the Convention rules on jurisdiction) is 'in principle applicable where the defendant has its domicile or seat in a Contracting State, even if the plaintiff is domiciled in a non-member country'.[122] This was entirely predictable and the arguments in its favour may be briefly summarized.

First, the general rule of the Convention is that the defendant shall be sued in the courts for the place where he is domiciled.[123] The domicile of the defendant is also the precondition for the application of the exceptions to this general rule laid down in the Convention. If the defendant is domiciled in a non-Contracting State, then the courts shall apply their national law to determine jurisdiction.[124] Thus, the domicile of the defendant is the key to the scope of Title II.[125] The domicile of the plaintiff is irrelevant. Where the domi-

---

[119] Case C–412/98 [2000] ILPr. 549 (hereafter '*Group Josi*').

[120] Euromepa failed to inform Group Josi that other reinsurers were either reducing, or not retaining, their share.

[121] Though Group Josi also argued that, even if French national law applied, the Belgian courts should have heard the claim under Art. 1247 of the French Civil Code.

[122] Para. 61.   [123] Art. 2.

[124] Art. 4. Provided the claim is a 'civil and commercial matter' it still falls within the scope of the Convention as a whole. As such, certain general provisions, e.g. Arts. 21–23 dealing with *lis alibi pendens*, remain applicable and any judgment subsequently handed down will be enforced within the Convention scheme.

[125] Art. 16, which contains rules of exclusive jurisdiction, applies even if the defendant is not domiciled in a Contracting State. This is justified on the basis of 'a particularly close connection between the dispute and a Contracting State': para. 46 of the judgment.

cile of the plaintiff is referred to, it is only to confer an additional, optional, basis of jurisdiction to those applicable on the basis that the defendant is domiciled in a Contracting State.[126]

Secondly, implicit support for the ruling could be found in earlier cases in which the Court has interpreted the rules of jurisdiction laid down by the Convention in cases where the plaintiff had his domicile or seat in a non-Contracting State.[127] Thirdly, the Convention is particularly hostile to rules of jurisdiction which favour the jurisdiction where the plaintiff is domiciled or resident. This is manifested, in part, by Article 3 which prohibits a plaintiff from invoking against a defendant domiciled in a Contracting State national rules of jurisdiction. The interpretation put forward by UGIC would leave open the very real possibility that a plaintiff could remove himself from the Convention and determine the court with jurisdiction by the choice of his domicile.[128]

If the answer to the first question was fairly predictable, it is nonetheless important not to overstate its significance. In particular, it has no direct relevance to the debate which surrounds the correctness of the decision of the Court of Appeal in *Re Harrods (Buenos Aires) Ltd*.[129] In *Re Harrods*, the English courts had jurisdiction under the Convention because the defendant company was domiciled in England. The plaintiff's petition of unfair prejudice was based on the conduct of the defendant company's affairs, which were principally carried out in Argentina, a non-Contracting State. A stay of proceedings in favour of the Argentinian courts was granted. It was held that the courts retain a discretion to stay their proceedings where no other Contracting State is involved on the basis that 'the Convention was intended to regulate jurisdiction as between the Contracting States'.[130]

The decision has been criticized[131] and it has been noted recently at the highest level that the matter *should* be referred to the Court of Justice.[132]

---

[126] Art. 5(2) (proceedings by a maintenance creditor); Art. 8(2) (proceedings by a plaintiff insured); Art. 14(1) (proceedings by a plaintiff consumer). Under Art. 17 a jurisdiction agreement may take effect under Art. 17 provided *one* of the parties is domiciled in a Contracting State, but it will therefore apply if the defendant alone is so domiciled.

[127] Case C–190/85, *Marc Rich & Co. AG* v. *Societa Italiana Impianti PA* [1991] ECR I–3855 (Art. 1(4), Swiss plaintiff (the Lugano Convention is now in force in Switzerland)); Case C–406/92, *The Tatry* [1994] ECR I–5439 (Art. 21, Polish plaintiff (the Lugano Convention is now in force in Poland)).

[128] Para. 50.   [129] [1992] Ch. 72.

[130] Collins '*Forum non Conveniens* and the Brussels Convention' (1990) 106 *LQR* 535. The Court of Appeal overruled *S & W Berisford plc* v. *New Hampshire* [1990] 2 QB 631 and *Arkwright Mutual Insurance* v. *Bryanston Insurance* [1990] 2 QB 649. The fact that the claimant may lose the benefit of a Convention judgment is a relevant factor for the courts to take into account when deciding whether to stay their proceedings in favour of proceedings in the courts of a non-Contracting State: *International Credit and Investment Co. Ltd.* v. *Tai Ping Insurance Co. Ltd.* [1999] ILPr. 302.

[131] Briggs, '*Forum non Conveniens* and the Brussels Convention' (1991) 107 *LQR* 180.

[132] In *Lubbe* v. *Cape Plc* [2000] 1 WLR 1545, 1562 Lord Bingham thought that the answer to the question whether the English courts retain a discretion to stay proceedings commenced in accordance with the Convention was 'far from clear'. Unfortunately, no such ruling will result from *Lubbe*, since, having decided not to stay proceedings in any event, a ruling from the ECJ was unnecessary.

However, the ruling in *Group Josi* in no way renders such a reference unnecessary. It merely confirms that Title II of the Convention must be applied where the defendant is domiciled in a Contracting State, regardless of the domicile of the plaintiff. In *Re Harrods*, it was not in dispute that the jurisdiction of the English courts was to be determined by the Convention and that they had jurisdiction under Article 2. Unlike *Group Josi*, the question was not whether the English courts could instead apply the jurisdictional rules of their national law, but whether they were bound to *exercise* the jurisdiction conferred on them by the Convention. As it happens, in *Re Harrods* the plaintiff (a Swiss company) was not domiciled in a Contracting State,[133] but the availability of the courts' discretion and the exercise thereof was based not on the plaintiff's domicile, but on the fact that no other Contracting State was concerned and the close connections with Argentina.

It might be argued that the ruling in *Group Josi* affirms the mandatory application of Title II when the conditions for its application are satisfied, i.e. when the defendant is domiciled in a Contracting State, and that this *implies* that such jurisdiction *must* be exercised. It cannot be put any higher than that and this is unlikely to be sufficient for the English courts to depart from the *Re Harrods* principle without a further reference to the Court.

The answer to the second question was equally predictable. Articles 7–12a are contained in section 3 which deals with 'jurisdiction in matters relating to insurance'. The basic premiss of these special rules is that additional protection should be given to the insured as the presumptively weaker party. For example, the policyholder, the insured, or a beneficiary may be sued only in the courts for the place where they are domiciled;[134] an insurer may be sued in the courts for the place where he is domiciled,[135] but the policyholder also has the option of suing in the courts for the place where he is domiciled.[136] If section 3 extended to reinsurance, UGIC could have benefited from these special rules since, under Article 8, 'an insurer [Group Josi] who is not domiciled in a Contracting State but has a branch, agency or other establishment in one of the Contracting States shall, in disputes arising out of the operations of the branch, agency or establishment, be deemed to be domiciled in that State'. It is not clear from the reference, but it appears that the Cour d'Appel must have considered the prospect of a submission that Euromepa, domiciled in France, was acting as agent for UGIC.

The presumption that the insured is the weaker party may not always accord with reality and, if anything, there is an argument for further restricting the special protective rules contained in section 3. Not surprisingly, the Court had no hesitation in rejecting any submission that they should be extended to disputes *between a reinsurer and a reinsured* in connection with a reinsurance contract; both parties 'are professionals in the insurance sector, neither of whom can be presumed to be in a weak position compared with the other

---

[133] Both the majority and minority shareholders were Swiss companies (Switzerland is now a party to the Lugano Convention).

[134] Art. 11.   [135] Art. 8(1).   [136] Art. 8(2).

party to the contract'.[137] However, the words in italics are intended to stress that the Court did not exclude from section 3 *all* proceedings in connection with a contract of reinsurance. It seems that it will apply where, under the law of a Contracting State, the policyholder, the insured, or the beneficiary has the option of approaching directly any reinsurer in order to assert his rights under that contract as against the reinsurer, for example in the case of the bankruptcy or liquidation of the insurer.[138] Reinsurers, and those acting for them, should not therefore fall into the trap of thinking that the restrictions on their jurisdictional freedom contained in section 3 are entirely inapplicable to them.

VI. Tenancies of Immovable Property

A. *DANSOMMER AS* V. *ANDREAS GÖTZ*[139]

Article 16(1) of the Brussels Convention[140] states:

The following courts shall have exclusive jurisdiction, regardless of domicile:

(a) in proceedings which have as their object rights *in rem* in immovable property or tenancies of immovable property, the courts of the Contracting State in which the property is situated;

(b) however, in proceedings which have as their object tenancies of immovable property concluded for temporary private use for a maximum period of six consecutive months, the courts of the Contracting State in which the defendant is domiciled shall also have jurisdiction, provided that the landlord and the tenant are natural persons and are domiciled in the same Contracting State.

In *Dansommer*, the Court was asked to do little more than confirm its earlier interpretation of Article 16(1)(a) so far as it applied to tenancies of immovable property. The only difficulty it faced in this regard was to distinguish its earlier unsatisfactory ruling in *Hacker* v. *Euro-Relais GmbH*.[141]

Mr Götz, a German national who was domiciled in Germany, rented from Dansommer, a company domiciled in Denmark, a house in Denmark owned by a private individual resident in Denmark for a two-week holiday. Under the general terms and conditions of the contract between Dansommer and Mr Götz, the price payable included a premium for insurance to cover the costs in the event of cancellation. As required by German law, Dansommer

---

[137] Para. 66. An interpretation supported by the Schlosser Report, [1979] OJ C59/71, at 117.

[138] It might be argued that a teleological interpretation which focuses on the parties and their relative standings could be extended to exclude from section 3 *insurance* contracts where there is an equality of bargaining power between insurer and insured, but this is not possible with the present wording: *New Hampshire Insurance* v. *Strabag Bau* [1992] 1 Lloyd's Rep. 361.

[139] Case C–8/98 [2001] ILPr 410 (27 January 2000) (hereafter '*Dansommer*').

[140] San Sebastián version, which inserted Art. 16(1)(b) to deal with the problem of short-term holiday lets.

[141] Case C–280/90 [1992] ECR I–1111.

also guaranteed reimbursement of the price paid by Mr Götz in the event of insolvency. Dansommer was not under an obligation to provide any other services and was described as having acted as 'intermediary'.[142] After Mr Götz had stayed in the house, Dansommer brought proceedings against him before the German courts. It did so on the basis that it had been subrogated to the rights of the owner of the house. The claim was for damages on the ground that Mr Götz had failed to clean the house properly before his departure and had damaged the carpeting and the oven safety mechanism. The Langericht Heilbronn referred the following question to the Court of Justice: '[i]s Article 16(1)(a) of the Brussels Convention applicable if the tour operator's performance obligation is limited to making available a holiday home and automatic provision of travel cost and cancellation insurance, but the owner and lessee of the holiday home are not domiciled in the same Contracting State?'

It was common ground that, although this was a short-term holiday let, Article 16(1)(b) did not apply because the landlord and tenant were not domiciled in the same Contracting State. The only issue for the Court, therefore, was whether the proceedings had as their object the tenancy of an immovable property within the meaning of Article 16(1)(a). The Court reaffirmed that Article 16 must not be given an interpretation broader than is required by its objective, since it deprives the parties of the choice of forum which would otherwise be theirs and, in some cases, results in their being brought before a court which is not that of the domicile of any of them.[143] Nevertheless, it was fairly clear that the claim did fall within Article 16(1)(a). In *Rösler* v. *Rottwinkel*[144] the Court had earlier ruled that 'proceedings which have as their object tenancies of immovable property' extends to actions for possession, repair, and rent. The claim against Mr Götz clearly fell within the meaning of an action for repair. This interpretation, which conferred exclusive jurisdiction on the Danish courts, was also consistent with the underlying purpose of Article 16. The reason for conferring exclusive jurisdiction on the courts of the *locus rei sitae* is that they are best placed, for reasons of proximity, to ascertain the facts satisfactorily, by carrying out checks, inquiries, and expert assessments on the spot, and to apply the rules and practices which are generally those of the state in which the property is situated.[145] This rationale may be outweighed by the inconvenience to the parties in the case of short-term holiday lets, but the conditions in Article 16(1)(b) which allow for an exception to exclusive jurisdiction had simply not been met in *Dansommer*.[146]

---

[142] Para. 8 of the judgment.

[143] Para. 21. See Case 73/77, *Sanders* v. *Van der Putte* [1977] ECR 2383, paras. 17–18; Case C–115/88, *Reichert and Kockler* [1990] ECR I–27, para. 9; Case C–292/93, *Lieber* v. *Göbel* [1994] ECR I–2535, para. 12.

[144] Case 241/83 [1985] ECR 99. The result in *Rösler* would now be reversed under Art. 16(1)(b).

[145] Para. 27. See *Sanders, supra* n. 143, para. 13; *Reichert and Kockler, supra* n. 143, para. 10.

[146] Nor would they be met under Art. 22(1) of the new Regulation, *supra* n. 13. This now only requires that the tenant must be a natural person, but both the tenant and the landlord must still be domiciled in the same Contracting State.

The application of Article 16(1)(a) to the claim in *Dansommer* seems so obvious that there has to be some explanation both for the reference to the Court and the slightly curious wording of the question referred. That explanation is to be found in the earlier ruling of the Court in *Hacker*.[147] There, the defendant travel agent had sold, as part of a package holiday, the use of a house in the Netherlands. The plaintiff customer commenced proceedings in Germany, where both parties were domiciled, complaining that the house was smaller than advertised and that the holiday had been spoiled. The Court ruled that Article 16(1)(a) did not apply on the unsatisfactory basis that the contract provided many services of which the tenancy was not the 'main object'. There is, of course, an obvious difference between the proceedings in *Dansommer* and those in *Hacker*. In *Dansommer*, having been subrogated to the rights of the house-owner, the tour operator was bringing a claim *qua* landlord for non-repair. In *Hacker*, the customer was bringing a claim for damages for misrepresentation. The former has as its object a tenancy in immovable property, the latter does not. However, the reasoning employed in *Hacker* required the Court to go further and look at the contract between Dansommer and Mr Götz and the services provided therein (for example, the insurance cover) so as to conclude that the 'main object' was the tenancy of immovable property. The Court had little difficulty in going even further than this and concluding that the action concerned exclusively the letting of immovable property,[148] but was it really necessary to have to do so? It has been argued[149] that *Hacker* employs reasoning which will be difficult to apply and which introduces an unwelcome degree of uncertainty, given that violation of Article 16 is a ground upon which non-recognition of a judgment is mandatory.[150] The reference from an 'unsure'[151] Landgericht Heilbronn seems to bear this out. There may well be cases where it is justifiable to focus on the principal part of the claim advanced, so as to avoid applying Article 16(1) where questions of title to land or tenancies arise only incidentally.[152] This was entirely unnecessary in both *Hacker* and *Dansommer*; it is a pity therefore that the Court was only able to distinguish *Hacker* in a way which perpetuates the unsatisfactory reasoning which it represents.

VII.   Consumer Contracts and Interim Relief

A.   *HANS-HERMANN MIETZ V. INTERSHIP YACHTING SNEEK BV*[153]

Articles 13–15 of the Brussels Convention contain special rules of jurisdiction for consumer contracts, aimed at the protection of the consumer. A 'consumer contract' is defined in Article 13(1) as:

---

[147] *Supra*, n. 141.   [148] Para. 33.   [149] Briggs and Rees, *supra* n. 33, at 46.
[150] Art. 28(1).   [151] Para. 14.
[152] For example, trespass; for other possible examples, see Briggs and Rees, *supra* n. 33.
[153] Case C–99/96 [1999] ECR I–2277, [1999] ILPr. 541 (hereafter '*Mietz*').

a contract concluded by a person for a purpose which can be regarded as being outside his trade or profession, if it is—

1. a contract for the sale of goods on instalment credit terms, or. . .
3. any other contract for the supply of goods or a contract for the supply of services, and
   (a) in the State of the consumer's domicile the conclusion of the contract was preceded by a specific invitation addressed to him or by advertising; and
   (b) the consumer took in that State the steps necessary for the conclusion of the contract.

Article 24 of the Convention states:

Application may be made to the courts of a Contracting State for such provisional, including protective, measures as may be available under the law of that State, even if, under this Convention, the courts of another Contracting State have jurisdiction as to the substance of the matter.

Finally, Article 28 states:

(1) . . . a judgment shall not be recognised if it conflicts with the provisions of Sections 3, 4 or 5 of Title II, or in a case provided for in Article 59.
(2) In its examination of the grounds of jurisdiction referred to in the foregoing paragraph, the court or authority applied to shall be bound by the findings of fact on which the court of the State of origin based its jurisdiction.

The principal significance of *Mietz* lies in the further clarification given to the interpretation of 'consumer contracts'. The Court also confirmed its ruling of the previous year in *Van Uden* v. *Deco-Line*[154] on the interpretation to be given to provisional measures in Article 24. The Court decided that it was unnecessary to answer a question on the interpretation of Article 28(2), though this aspect of the ruling needs careful consideration.

Intership Yachting, a company domiciled in the Netherlands, and Mr Mietz, who was domiciled in Germany, concluded in writing in the Netherlands a contract described as a 'contract of sale' for the purchase of a yacht. The yacht was a standard model to which a number of alterations were to be made. The price was 250,000 DM which Mr Mietz agreed to pay in five instalments. Mr Mietz made only part of the payments required. In adversarial interim proceedings in the Netherlands known as the *kort geding*, Mr Mietz was ordered to make an interim payment of 143,750 DM, plus interest. In proceedings to enforce the Dutch judgment in Germany, Mr Mietz sought to rely on Article 28(1) by arguing that the judgment conflicted with section 4 of Title II, i.e. the jurisdictional rules applicable to a consumer contract.

This led the Bundesgerichtshof to refer three questions to the Court of Justice which may be summarized as follows: (1) did the contract between Intership and Mr Mietz qualify as a contract for the sale of goods 'on instalment credit terms' within the meaning of Article 13(1)(1); (2) if it did not, did it qualify as a contract for the supply of goods within the meaning of Article

---

[154] Case C–391/95 [1998] ECR I–7091.

13(1)(3); (3) was Mr Mietz prevented by Article 28(2) from introducing new facts which were necessary to establish that the claim satisfied the additional requirements of Article 13(1)(3)? If the claim did, in fact, concern a consumer contract so as to fall within section 4, the Bundesgerichtshof referred a fourth question whether the Dutch judgment qualified as a provisional measure within the meaning of Article 24. This was necessary because, as the Court accepted,[155] the Dutch courts would still then have had jurisdiction to order provisional measures. Presumably, enforcement would have been allowed on the basis that the exercise of jurisdiction to grant provisional measures only under Article 24 would not 'conflict' with section 4 within the meaning of Article 28(1).

In answer to the first question, the Court ruled that the contract between the parties was not a contract for the sale of goods on 'instalment credit terms'. Payment was to be made by instalments, but there was no 'credit' element. The final instalment was to be paid before possession of the yacht passed to Mr Mietz. It is the need for credit which singles out a 'consumer' requiring the protection provided by the special rules of jurisdiction contained in section 4, and this hardly seemed to apply to Mr Mietz.[156] However, he could still rely on section 4 if the contract was one for the supply of goods and he satisfied the additional requirements laid down in Article 13(1)(3). The Court had little difficulty in answer to the second question in ruling that the contract between the parties was, at the very least, either a contract for the supply of goods or a contract for the supply of services, both of which fall within Article 13(1)(3). If it should be necessary to decide precisely which type of contract it amounted to, this could be left for the national court to determine.

In order to rely on section 4, Mr Mietz still had to satisfy the additional elements of Article 13(1)(3)(a) and (b). Mr Mietz argued that he could do so on the basis that the contract was, in substance, negotiated and entered into during a specialist show in Germany; the contract of sale entered into in the Netherlands was merely formal confirmation. The difficulty faced by the Bundesgerichtshof was that the Dutch judgment contained no information about where the acts preparatory to the conclusion of the contract were performed. It seemed that Mr Mietz was introducing a new argument. If allowed, the Court was asked whether this would infringe Article 28(2). In fact, the Court found it unnecessary to answer this third question because of the answer it had given to the fourth question on the interpretation of Article 24.[157]

---

[155] Para. 45.

[156] The Court was not asked to consider the question whether Mr Mietz satisfied the general requirement of Art. 13 that he should have concluded the contract for 'a purpose which can be regarded as being outside his trade or profession'; it seems that the yacht was intended for private use.

[157] Léger AG was of the opinion that Art. 28(2) did prevent the court of the state applied to from taking into account 'matters of fact other than those that the court of origin has taken into account or could have taken into account if the party putting them forward had not refrained from adducing them before it'.

The question whether an interim payment qualified as a 'provisional measure' within the meaning of Article 24 had been considered by the Court in the previous year in the reference in *Van Uden*.[158] The Court had ruled there that it could qualify if, first, repayment to the defendant of the sum awarded is guaranteed if the plaintiff is unsuccessful as regards the substance of his claim and, secondly, the measure ordered relates only to specific assets of the defendant located or to be located within the confines of the territorial jurisdiction of the court to which application is made.[159] The correctness of this interpretation has already been considered in these pages.[160] In *Mietz*, the Court found that the payment ordered by the Dutch courts did not meet the requirements laid down in *Van Uden* and was not a provisional measure within Article 24. There is nothing controversial in this,[161] but the Court went on to conclude that, as a consequence, the Dutch judgment '*cannot* be the subject of an enforcement order under Title III of the Convention'.[162] It was for this reason that it was unnecessary to answer the third question. Whether or not section 4 applied, the Dutch judgment could not be enforced.[163]

On the face of it the order for an interim payment was a judgment[164] of a Contracting State within the meaning of Article 25 and therefore entitled to recognition and enforcement under Title III. As was seen earlier when considering the decision in *Krombach*, the fact that the court of origin does not, in fact, have jurisdiction under the Convention to hear the claim provides no ground to refuse recognition.[165] The fact that the order did not qualify as a provisional measure within the meaning of Article 24 could have formed the basis of a challenge to the jurisdiction of the Dutch courts, but, under the scheme of the Convention, it seems to provide no ground to deny recognition at the enforcement stage. The only jurisdictional objections which can be raised at that stage are those laid down in Article 28, including a breach of section 4. That is why it seemed necessary to determine whether the contract between the parties was a consumer contract, including whether the Court was allowed to admit new evidence to establish this.

The key to understanding the decision of the Court lies in its observation that 'the question which arises for the court to which application for enforcement is made therefore relates *not to the jurisdiction*, as such, of the court of

---

[158] *Supra*, n. 154.   [159] Para. 42.   [160] [1998] *YEL* 694–8.

[161] The order neither guaranteed repayment, nor was limited to assets within the territorial jurisdiction of the Dutch courts; by definition a judgment which requires enforcement against assets of the defendant located abroad will fail to meet the second requirement laid down in *Van Uden*.

[162] Para. 56.

[163] If that was so, it was, presumably, also unnecessary to answer either the first or the second question. But, perhaps, the answers to those questions were easier.

[164] It was not an *ex parte* judgment and therefore excluded by the interpretation in Case 125/79, *Denilauler* v. *SNC Couchet Frères* [1980] ECR 1553.

[165] The Court quite correctly rejected an argument that Mr Mietz had submitted to the jurisdiction of the Dutch courts, so as to give it jurisdiction over the substance of the matter under Art. 18 by appearing 'in the context of fast procedures intended to grant provisional or protective measures in case of urgency and which do not prejudice the examination of the substance'.

origin, but rather to the extent to which it is possible to seek enforcement of a judgment delivered *in the exercise of* the jurisdiction recognised by Article 24'.[166] In other words, where the court of origin purports to exercise the jurisdiction conferred by Article 24,[167] it must do no more than grant the sort of measures which fall within that jurisdiction; anything beyond that cannot be enforced under Title III of the Convention. It has to be said that there is little in the way of any textual basis for this interpretation, from a Court which usually insists on this requirement, but the end result is very welcome.

The courts of the Contracting States may occasionally flout the jurisdictional rules of the Convention when hearing the substance of the claim, but such cases will be fairly exceptional and it is the price to be paid for the efficient operation of the enforcement regime of the Convention that this does not, of itself, provide any ground for non-recognition.[168] However, Article 24,[169] which allows the courts of Contracting States to exercise jurisdiction even when it is accepted that the courts of another Contracting State have jurisdiction as to the substance of the matter could, if not kept in control, provide very real encouragement to undermine the jurisdictional scheme of the Convention on a regular basis. In one sense, therefore, this aspect of the ruling in *Mietz* may be seen as a partial antidote to the wide interpretation given to the meaning of 'provisional measures' in *Van Uden*.

VIII. Authentic Instruments

A. *UNIBANK A/S V. CHRISTENSEN*[170]

Finally, and in a case which calls for little or no comment, the Court of Justice has ruled that an acknowledgment of indebtedness which is enforceable under the law of the state of origin, but whose authenticity has not been established by a public authority empowered for that purpose by that state does not constitute an authentic instrument within the meaning of Article 50 of the Brussels Convention. Accordingly, Unibank, a bank established under Danish law, could not enforce in Germany three acknowledgments of indebtedness signed by Mr Christensen while he was resident in Denmark.

Authentic instruments may be enforced in the same way as judgments, save that the application may be refused only if enforcement is contrary to public policy in the state in which enforcement is sought.[171] Since, therefore, their

---

[166] Para. 49 (emphasis added).

[167] And, it seems, where it is silent about the basis of its jurisdiction to order provisional measures: para. 56.

[168] Art. 28(3).

[169] There is no change to the wording of Art. 24 (to become Art. 31) of the new Regulation, *supra*, n. 13.

[170] Case C–260/97 [1999] ECR I–3715, [2000] ILPr. 135 (hereafter '*Unibank*').

[171] As it will have been a consensual matter, the other restrictions on the enforcement of judgments are not appropriate.

enforceability can easily be extended beyond the state in which they were entered, the Court held that the authentic nature of such instruments must be established beyond dispute by the involvement of a public authority.[172]

[172] Support for this interpretation was also provided by the Jenard-Möller Report on the Lugano Convention; the wording of the two Conventions was not identical at the material time in *Unibank* but the difference in the wording was immaterial to this issue; the wording of Art. 50 of the Convention has subsequently been amended so that it is now identical to that of Art. 50 of the Lugano Convention.

EC Competition Law 1999–2000

IAN S. FORRESTER, QC AND JACQUELYN F. MACLENNAN*

I. Introduction

In our last review of European competition law developments, written in spring 1999, we predicted that we might in due course realize that we were at the beginning of a new era. And, indeed, two years later the landscape has changed. There are major changes in procedure, constitutional structure and substantive law; and there was a considerable crop of Commission decisions and judgments from the European Courts.

A. PROCEDURALLY WHERE WE WERE

The traditional approach to enforcement of competition by the European Commission was too much dominated by textual analysis of written clauses rather than by economic analysis of business reality. The system as established following the adoption of Regulation 17[1] did not function properly during the 1990s, and sometimes did not function at all. The problem had several elements:

- Article 81(1) (formerly Article 85(1)) was given a broad scope and caught all sorts of agreements, including those which were basically pro-competitive but which contained restrictive clauses. There was little analysis of the merits or seriousness of the restriction, merely a noting of its presence, which entailed the consequent triggering of Article 81(1).
- This meant that thousands of basically desirable agreements were caught by the prohibition of Article 81(1), void under Article 81(2), and finable under Regulation 17. Only an exemption could cure these hazards; and only the Commission could issue an exemption.
- Decisions by the Commission were rare because every decision was a major piece of rule-making, not a mere response to an individual problem. Perfection and comprehensiveness were the goals, not adequacy.

* The authors practise European law in Brussels. Ian Forrester is Visiting Professor in European Law, Glasgow University. Warm thanks are expressed to all those at White & Case, Brussels who provided precious assistance in gathering and summarizing very extensive materials to produce this article.

[1] Council Regulation 17, First Regulation Implementing Arts. 85 and 86 [now Arts. 81 and 82] of the EC Treaty [1956–1962] OJ Spec. Ed. p. 87.

- There was not enough application of the law in a transparent and procedurally predictable manner. Because too many agreements were prohibited, most agreements could not receive an exemption: there were approximately 225 exemption decisions from 1962 to 2000, sometimes only one or two in a year.[2]
- A theoretically necessary but practically unavailable exemption was therefore a source not of legal certainty but of legal uncertainty.
- To avoid this uncertainty, block exemption regulations came to be regarded as black letter, obligatory standards, failure to respect which was dangerous and close to illegal.
- Every intervention by the Commission in a disputed situation was very cautiously considered and elaborately researched. The Commission had to be scrupulously careful and scrupulously neutral in any communication with national courts. Although national courts were the natural ally of the Commission in the enforcement process, they were under-utilized.

The Commission could react to these problems in three ways. It could share more responsibility with the Member States, whose enforcement resources are notionally limitless; or relax its interpretation of Article 81(1) to release basically benign agreements from the difficulties of needing an exemption which was practically unobtainable; or render the taking of decisions very much simpler and quicker, so that an individual decision became no more than an answer to a specific problem rather than a long, public, detailed *ex cathedra* pronouncement of general importance. The reforms have been more radical than expected, taking elements of each of the three options. They are still under debate but appear to be gathering support.

B.   THE PROPOSED NEW SYSTEM[3]

Several procedural innovations will collectively eliminate the procedural *de facto* and *de iure* monopoly of the European Commission. Instead of encouraging the notification of all remotely doubtful agreements by the legal fiction that any caught but unexempted agreement was void and liable to a huge fine, the Commission proposes to eliminate notifications and to share the power to grant exemptions with Member States. The proposals include the following elements:

- There will no longer be a system of notification of agreements to the Commission; companies will be responsible for assessing for themselves the legality and wisdom of their agreements and conduct, without depending upon the Commission's blessing. The Commission justifies

[2] Forrester, *The Modernisation of EC Antitrust Policy: Compatibility, Efficiency, Legal Security*, Robert Schuman Centre Annual Conference on European Competition Law 2000: The Modernisation of EC Antitrust Policy (not yet published).

[3] White Paper on the Modernisation of the Rules implementing Arts. 81 and 82 of the EC Treaty, COM(1999)101 final, [1999] OJ C132/00.

this on the disingenuous ground that eliminating the 'need to notify' will represent a financial benefit in reduced transactional costs to companies, and on the more plausible ground that it will reduce the Commission's own workload.

- There will be a new system of registration whereby companies may provide information to the Commission and seek a ruling from the Commission; this system will not provide immunity from fines, though one may assume that *de facto* truthful and complete communication would make the imposition of fines very difficult.

- The Commission may give informal guidance to companies, but reasoned advice will be issued only in those limited circumstances where there is an unresolved, genuinely new question of interpretation; it is to be hoped that there will continue to be informal advice upon demand.

- The new enforcement structure will treat Article 81 in its entirety as a prohibition rule. Article 81(3) will be directly applicable, which means that national courts, national competition authorities, and the Commission all have power to grant exemptions. The Commission may adopt block exemptions and guidelines to assist in the assessment of agreements and practices. National courts and competition authorities will have power to apply Articles 81 and 82 in full (and those national competition authorities which have not already been empowered to apply EC competition law must be given these powers), within their respective territorial jurisdictions. Only the Commission will have the power to take decisions finding that Article 81 and/or Article 82 does not apply to an agreement or practice in order to establish a new principle or general precedent. National authorities would not have the power to take affirmative decisions blessing an agreement as acceptable under Article 81(1), but would be able to take decisions finding an infringement and removing the benefit of an existing block exemption from a particular case.[4] The law would progress by condemnations rather than by approvals of the benign. We will move from a system of prior authorization, either by administrative decision in a specific case or by 'normative' exemption regulation, to a system based upon a directly-effective exemption.

- In the past, the theory claimed that that which was not approved remained unlawful because it lacked approval; in the future, everything will be allowed which is not prohibited. It will be by prohibitions that the law will advance. Prohibitions have the merit that they are likely to be challenged by those whom they inconvenience. By contrast, affirmative decisions which say 'Article 81(1) does not apply to this agreement' will often never be challenged.

---

[4] A national competition authority might, without either naïvety or prejudice, agree that a practice or agreement notified to it was acceptable and presented no problem to competition. Although no formal decision would be taken, that position, taken on an *ex parte* basis, would be authoritative, would not be tested judicially, and might be based on incomplete knowledge.

- The Commission would have the power to adopt block exemptions without the involvement of the Council.
- The Commission seeks new powers to inspect private houses where records may be held (the houses of directors, managers, or other members of staff) and to summon for interview staff members and other persons to seek information relating to an investigation (not just explanations of documents). The conformity of these powers with the European Convention for the Protection of Human Rights and Fundamental Freedoms is yet to be tested.
- Fines for not supplying information or for supplying incorrect information or refusing to answer questions will be raised to a maximum of 1 per cent of turnover; and periodic penalty payments for such infringement are also to be increased (to 5 per cent of average daily turnover).

C.   CO-OPERATION WITH NATIONAL COURTS AND COMPETITION AUTHORITIES

The Commission proposal for a new Regulation 17 contains a number of provisions relevant for co-operation with national competition authorities (apparently there were some fifty cases of co-operation in 1999 alone[5]—and national courts. These provisions do not provide any guarantees as to the future consistency of national decision-making, and the Commission envisages revision of the existing notices as well as new guidelines on where complaints should be addressed. The intention is that companies will be able to apply directly to national authorities for enforcement of the EC rules. The co-operation with national authorities foreseen is far reaching—particularly the duty to exchange confidential information In the application of their concurrent jurisdiction, national courts are merely requested to make 'every effort' to avoid decisions which conflict with the Commission; or to seek guidance from the Commission where there is a potential conflict; or to seek a preliminary ruling from the European Court; and to suspend a national decision where the Community Courts are adjudicating a Commission decision. The problems inherent in the 'competition network' foreseen in the new system are epitomized and to some extent settled by the Court of Justice's decision in *MasterFoods*,[6] a long-needed decision of great constitutional importance which confirms the pre-eminent position, technically and constitutionally, occupied by the European Commission. Details of the new style of applying the competition rules via block exemptions are set forth below under Legislative Developments.

---

[5] See EC Commission, *29th Report on Competition Policy* (EC Commission, Brussels, 1999), Box 2, 23.

[6] Case C–344/98, *Masterfoods Ltd.* v. *HB Ice Cream Ltd.*, judgment of 14 Dec. 2000.

D. THE COMMISSION'S HANDLING OF COMPLAINTS

Commission officials regularly point out that the number of formal decisions taken is not a fair measure of the institution's productivity. It is also drafter of legislation; co-ordinator of Member State policies; interface with other countries' enforcers, notably the US Justice Department; and keeper of the competitive conscience of the European Commission.

In addition to these well-recognized roles, the Commission is increasingly called upon to adjudicate on quarrels between competitors. In more peaceful times, the Commission's intervention would be lobbied for, and in quite rare cases the Commission would take up the combat. Very often the matter would not be given much priority if the Commission's staff had other preoccupations. Formal rejections of complaints were rather unusual, and judicial challenges to such rejections were even rarer. In the *Automec*[7] cases, the European Courts confirmed that the Commission had the right to set its own priorities and could properly elect not to take up a complaint which presented little interest for the development of the law. However, that has not prevented a sharp growth in the number of controversies where the Commission is sued for having failed to act on a complaint or for having rejected it. One has the impression that the Commission has difficulty in coping with this challenge. Its tradition calls for decisions which are long, thorough, comprehensive reviews of a marketplace and the functioning there of competition. It takes a long time to acquire that level of knowledge; staff have other cases about which to worry; each side offers a non-neutral view of the facts; and there is no formal procedure, like rules of court, which assists the authority to progress a case to conclusion fairly but expeditiously.

The Commission is thus 'damned if it does and damned if it does not'. If it takes too long, it is chastized for inaction. If it intervenes rapidly, it does so on inadequate data. If it rejects a complaint, it may do so without sufficiently considering some argument. The Court of First Instance has been ready to find administrative errors in the Commission's handling of complaints. A particular feature of the jurisprudence covered in this review is the challenges brought to Commission rejections or inactivity with regard to complaints: for example, *Stork* v. *Commission and Serac*,[8] *Florimex*,[9] *Union Française de l'Express*,[10] *Asia Motor France and Others* v. *Commission*,[11] *SODIMA*,[12] *Dalmasso and Others*[13] and *UPS*.[14] As the Commission tries to get control of its

---

[7] Case T–24/90 [1992] ECR II–2223.　　　　[8] Case T–241/97 [2000] ECR II–309.

[9] Case C–265/97 P, *Coöperatieve Vereniging De Verenigde Bloemenveilingen Aalsmeer BA (VBA)* v. *Florimex BV and Others* [2000] ECR I–2061.

[10] Case C–119/97 P [1999] ECR I–1341.　　　　[11] Case T–154/98 [2000] ECR II–3453.

[12] Cases T–190/95 and T–45/96, *SODIMA* v. *Commission*, Joined Cases T–9/96 and T–211/96, [1999] *Européenne Automobile* v. *Commission*, Joined Cases T–189/95, T–39/96 and T–123/96, *SGA* v. *Commission* [1999] ECR II–3617.

[13] Joined Cases T–185/96, T–189/96 and T–190/96, *Riviera Auto Service Etablissements Dalmasso SA and Others* v. *Commission* [1999] ECR II–0093.

[14] Case T–127/98 *UPS Europe SA* v. *Commission* [1999] ECR II–2633.

own agenda, eliminating notifications towards this end, its handling of complaints seems likely to give it little respite from demands for authoritative disposition of controversies between competitors.

The consistency with the European Convention for the Protection of Human Rights and Fundamental Freedoms of the Commission's powers of enquiry and its capacity to impose fines for failure to respond to questions have been challenged in a number of fora and writings.[15] It remains unclear whether the imposition of fines for failing to answer questions is consistent with the privilege against self-incrimination;[16] and whether the procedures by which decisions are taken satisfy the requirements of the Convention with respect to an 'independent and impartial tribunal'. In early cases, the European Courts reacted to such criticisms by stating that respect for rights of the defence and due process was adequately secured in the specific area of competition law to a level equivalent to that guaranteed by Article 6. It was also argued that since EC competition law was not penal, the human rights associated with a criminal investigation do not attach to companies under scrutiny. The latter theory has been made untenable by the judgments of the European Court of Human Rights in *Stenuit* v. *France*[17] and *Bendenoun* v. *France*,[18] following which in *Polypropylene*[19] the applicability of the Convention was not contested. As regards the privilege against self-incrimination which forms part of the rights guaranteed by Article 6, the judgment of the European Court of Human Rights in *Funke*[20] and *Saunders*[21] compelled an appraisal of what the Court of First Instance had said in *Orkem*.[22] The issues were raised in *Siderca* v. *Commission*,[23] settled before arguments, and in *Mannesmann* v. *Commission*,[24] decided in February 2001. It seems probable that further modification of Commission procedures will be necessary before the compatibility of Community procedures with the Convention can confidently be asserted.

F.   THE RECORD OF 1999 AND 2000

(i)   Statistics

In 1999, the Commission took sixty-eight formal decisions under Articles 81, 82, and 86. Not all were published, especially rejections of complaints and deci-

---

[15] For example, Forrester, *Modernisation of EC Competition Law*, 2000 Fordham Corp. L. Inst. 181 (B. Hawk ed. 2000), and other articles published in the same volume.

[16] The *Siderca* case, Case T–8/98, *Siderca SAIC* v. *Commission*, settled shortly before argument, presented a number of these questions, which were further addressed in the recent *Mannesmann* case in Feb. 2001.

[17] Series A No. 232–A (1992).   [18] Series A No. 284 (1994).

[19] Joined Cases T–305–307/94, T–313–315/94 [1999] ECR II–931, and on appeal Joined Cases C–279–280/98, C–283/98, C–286/98, C–297–298/98 [2000] ECR I–9757.

[20] Series A No. 256 (1993).   [21] 1996–VI–No 24 (1996).

[22] Case 374/87 [1989] ECR 3283.   [23] Case T–8/98, *supra* n. 16.

[24] Case T–112/98, Judgment of 20 Feb. 2001.

sions to conduct dawn raids. In 2000 this number was approximately thirty-six (in 1996 it was only twenty-one). The highest fine in the period amounted to a total of EUR 273 million, imposed on the members of the *Trans-Atlantic Conference Agreement* (*TACA*),[25] in a decision taken in 1998 and published in 1999. A total fine of EUR 99 million was imposed in 1999 on a market-sharing cartel between seamless steel tube producers under the Coal and Steel Treaty.[26] The highest fine in 2000 was EUR 110 million, imposed on members of the so-called lysine cartel (also known as the amino acids cartel),[27] and the highest fine on an individual company in 2000 was the EUR 43 million on *Opel*.[28] During 1999, fines for failure to give correct information were imposed on two brewers, *Anheuser Busch*[29] and *Scottish & Newcastle*.[30] 'Symbolic' fines were imposed in two cases in the period: EUR 1,000 was imposed on the organizers of the 1998 World Cup for breach of Article 82 because of their discriminatory ticketing scheme,[31] and Bricolux, a 'family firm', received the same fine for participating in anti-competitive distribution practices.[32] In 2000, a number of decisions under Articles 81 and 82 concerning soda-ash were readopted, reimposing the original fines of EUR 33 million levied on Solvay and ICI in cartel and abuse of a dominant position proceedings.[33]

During 1999 and 2000, fines were imposed as follows:

Lysine cartel (amino acids) [2001] OJ L152/54	EUR 110 million
Seamless steel tube cartel [1999] OJ L95/1 8 December 1999	EUR 99 million
Opel [2001] OJ L59/1	EUR 43 million
JCB, IP/00/1526, 21 December 2000	EUR 39.6 million
FETTCSA [2000] OJ L268/1	EUR 6,932,000
Virgin/British Airways [2000] OJ L30/1	EUR 6.8 million
Nederlandse Federative Vereniging voor de Groothandel op, Elektrotechnisch Gebied (FEG/TU) [2000] OJ L39/1	EUR 6.55 million
Bricolux/Nathan [2001] OJ L54/1	EUR 1,000 (symbolic) and EUR 60,000
Anheuser-Busch and Scottish & Newcastle [2000] OJ L49/37	EUR 3,000 both parties

25 [1999] OJ L95/1.   26 [1999] OJ L95/1.   27 [2000] OJ L152/24.
28 [2001] OJ L59/1.   29 [2000] OJ L49/37.   30 [2001] OJ L49/37.
31 [2000] OJ L5/55.   32 [2001] OJ L54/1.
33 Commission press release, IP/00/1449, 13 Dec. 2000.

1998 World Cup [2000] OJ L5/55	EUR 1,000 (symbolic)
TOTAL for 1999	EUR 112.3 million
TOTAL for 2000 (not including reimposed fines)	EUR 199.6 million

During 1999, the Commission opened a total of 388 new cases: 162 following notification, 149 following a complaint, and 77 on the Commission's own initiative. During 2000, only 297 new cases were opened: 101 following notification, 112 following a complaint, and 84 on the Commission's own initiative. During 1999, the Commission closed 514 cases informally. In 2000, 343 cases were closed informally. Compared to the three previous years, notifications, complaints, and *ex officio* investigations have slightly declined. The Commission's case-load has drifted down from a peak in 1996. At the end of 1999, there were 1,013 cases pending. At the end of 2000, 931 cases were pending.

During 1999, 11 cases applying Articles 81 and 82 were decided by the Court of First Instance and 17 by the European Court of Justice. During 2000, 59 cases were decided by the Court of First Instance and 29 by the Court of Justice. The number of Court cases pending in the competition field has been remarkably stable at between 185 and 205 for about five years.

The Commission received 292 notifications under the Merger Regulation[34] in 1999 (of which 20 were treated by sectoral directorates) and 345 in 2000 (of which 13 were treated by sectoral directorates). In 1999, 270 merger decisions were published (260 Phase I and ten Phase II). For the first time, fines were imposed for failure to provide information or the provision of misleading information. Four fines were imposed in 1999, and one in 2000. The fines imposed in 1999 were EUR 100,000 on Deutsche Post AG[35] (two fines each of EUR 50,000), EUR 40,000 on KLM[36] and EUR 50,000 on Sanofi and Synthélabo.[37] The total of all fines amounted to EUR 190,000. In 2000, the only fine imposed was on Mitsubishi[38] (EUR 50,000 plus a periodic penalty payment of EUR 900,000), a non-notifying party, for failure to provide information.

In summary, there has been a clear reduction in the number of new antitrust cases, due largely to the policy change in the area of vertical restrictions, but a substantial increase in the number of merger cases coming before the Commission.

(ii)   Commission Decisions

(a)   Parallel Trade and Other Horizontal Issues   A striking feature of the formal decisions taken by the Commission over the past two years is the

---

[34] Regulation 4064/89, (1989) OJ L395/1.   [35] [2000] OJ L97/1.
[36] Commission Press Release IP/99/985 of 11 Dec. 1999.
[37] [2000] OJ L95/34.   [38] [2001] OJ L4/31.

continued concentration on parallel trade. There were major condemnations of parallel trade infringements in *Nathan-Bricolux*[39] and, more remarkably, *Opel*,[40] which was fined EUR 43 million for discouraging its dealers from making sales to customers in other Member States. *JCB*,[41] a far smaller company, was fined the comparable sum of EUR 39.6 million for hindering cross-border trade in its construction equipment. Those decisions are imbued with a rhetoric that would have been in tune with the times in 1975 or 1985; and, on the face of it, may not seem easy to reconcile with the new-look competition policy. Evidently, the Directorate General for Competition remains committed to its goal of a Europe where goods flow unimpeded by distribution structures and is prepared to devote its limited decision-taking resources to sending this message out loud and clear. Also, one more in the long series of condemnations of binding constraints upon members of Dutch trade associations was made, this time concerning electrical equipment wholesalers, where the effect was to restrict imports of cheaper equipment: *Nederlandse Federatiëve Vereniging*[42] where fines of EUR 4,400,000 and EUR 2,150,000 were imposed.

Attempts to apply the competition rules appropriately in the UK beer sector were reflected in a disproportionate number of Decisions—*Whitbread*,[43] *Scottish & Newcastle* (a fine was imposed upon two brewers, Anheuser Busch and Scottish & Newcastle for supplying incorrect or incomplete information, contrary to Article 15(1)(b) of Regulation 17).[44] *Inntrepreneur and Spring*[45] The sensitive question of the balance between environmental concerns and competition policy arose in the *CECED*[46] Decision, where the Commission exempted an agreement among domestic washing machine manufacturers to phase out on environmental grounds certain categories of machine. The proper role of environmental concerns in competition law enforcement remains to be clarified.

(b) Cartels Those who operate price-fixing cartels no longer have friends in government, even if they are national champions. Member States rarely accord lobbying protection in such cases. The Commission promised tough action against cartels, and its policy could be seen in operation in a number of Decisions published in 1999, particularly in the area of shipping. In the *TACA*[47] case, fines totalling the record sum of EUR 273,000,000 were imposed on members of a shipping conference, an association of shipowners served by a secretariat which co-ordinated their tariffs. In addition to infringements under Article 81, there were infringements under Article 82 in the form of collective dominance. Fines on a more modest scale were imposed on seven Greek ferry operators for fixing prices on routes between Greece and Italy: there was

---

[39] [2001] OJ L54/1.   [40] [2000] OJ L59/1.

[41] Commission Press Release IP/00/1526, 21 Dec. 2000.

[42] [2000] OJ L39/1. See also Commission Press Releases IP/99/104, of 11 Feb. 1999 and IP/99/457 of 5 July 1999.

[43] [1999] OJ L88/26.   [44] [2000] OJ L49/37.

[45] [2000] OJ L195/49.   [46] [2000] OJ L187/47.

[47] [1999] OJ L95/1.

evidence about ministerial interest in the setting of such rates, but it was not clear that they had actually been imposed by public authority. Fines were also imposed on members of a Far East shipping conference, *FETTCSA*,[48] which had agreed not to grant discounts, and a condemnation without fines was directed at *EATA*,[49] whose members had notified their arrangements on non-utilization of capacity. In the lysine cartel, affecting the animal-feed sector, fines totalling EUR 110 million were imposed on five companies for operating a global price-fixing cartel.[50]

(c)   Joint Ventures: Telecommunications, Broadcasting and Media, Transport, Heavy Engineering   The Commission was, again, active in the fast-converging field of telecommunications, broadcasting media, and the Internet. The Commission, it is now apparent, tends to look at the growing number of alliances and joint ventures in this sector in terms of the degree of competition existing at three levels: infrastructure, access, and content. It authorized the creation of *TPS*,[51] a digital pay-TV satellite platform, after having obtained the removal by its two cable operator associates of their commitment to give the new channels priority access to their cable networks. The Commission granted a negative clearance to *Cégétel+4*,[52] a new telecommunications entrant, and granted an exemption shortly thereafter to *Cégétel*[53] and *SNCF*,[54] who notified their co-operation in a new infrastructure company *Télécom Développement*. A more controversial case was that of *British Interactive Broadcasting/Open*,[55] a joint venture between a satellite broadcaster, a telephone company, a bank, and a hardware provider to develop a digital satellite set-top box: there were major opportunities for foreclosure, but the Commission finally granted an exemption subject to a number of conditions. The *EBU/Eurovision*[56] system for collective bidding to acquire the rights to cover sporting events like the Olympic Games and to exchange signals between public mission broadcasters reached another milestone when a new exemption was granted, replacing that granted in 1993 and subsequently annulled.

In other sectors, two ferry companies, *P&O* and *Stena*[57] were allowed to combine their cross-Channel ferry services, in light of the expected competitive pressure from Eurotunnel and the expected damage to their revenues by the elimination of duty free concessions on tobacco and alcohol in intra-Community travel. A joint venture between *General Electric* and *Pratt & Whitney*[58] to develop and sell Airbus engines was approved even though it would reduce from three to two the number of potential suppliers, on the

---

[48]   [2000] O L268/1.   [49]   [1999] OJ L193/23.
[50]   [2001] OJ L152/54, see also Commission Press Release IP/00/589, 7 June 2000. This decision was not published in 2000 and will be covered in the next review published in *YEL*.
[51]   [1999] OJ L90/6.   [52]   [1999] OJ L128/14.
[53]   [1999] OJ L218/24.
[54]   [1999] OJ L218/24.   [55]   [1999] OJ L312/1.
[56]   [2000] OJ L151/18.   [57]   [1999] OJ L163/61.
[58]   [2000] OJ L58/16.

grounds that it would allow them to bring a better engine more quickly to the market.

(d) Financial Services In the area of financial services, where the Commission has trodden fairly softly in the past, a renewal of an exemption was granted to a group offering protection and indemnity insurance to shipowners (*P&I Clubs*[59]). However, a number of important changes were required to the agreements before the Commission would accept them, and the exemption is subject to important conditions regarding the share of the market held by the members of the group. As a result, detailed reporting requirements have been imposed. In *Dutch Banks*,[60] the Commission applied the judgment of the Court of Justice in the *Bagnasco*[61] case, and found that a uniform inter-bank fee charged by Dutch banks in the implementation of the Giro banking system was not caught by Article 81(1) as it did not restrict trade between Member States (a rare finding for the Commission to make).

(e) Professions The Commission took another decision applying competition law to professional organizations, this time as regards patent agents (*EPI*[62]). The time taken to issue the statement of objections and the Decision, and the remedy granted, reflects the novelty of the area and the perceived sensitivity of the task. Ultimately, the Commission found that various elements in the European Patent Agents code of conduct were restrictive of competition— in particular, provisions prohibiting members from carrying out certain types of comparative advertising and from actively offering their services to former clients of other representatives—but granted an exemption for a very short period (it has already expired) 'so as to give the profession time to adapt its commercial practice and permit an orderly transition which would avoid confusion and allow consumers a fair share of the resulting benefit'. Further activity may be expected in this area.

(f) Sport There was a great deal of press coverage of Commission action in the field of sport, where there was some progress towards a *rapprochement* with the main European sporting combatant, *UEFA*, the continental grouping of national football associations, on the subject of ticketing, multiple ownership of sports clubs, and the power of the sports organization to prescribe where matches shall be played.[63] With respect to Formula One motor racing, and to *FIFA*,[64] however, the atmosphere was still turbulent: FIFA was fined under Article 82 about ticketing arrangements for the football World Cup international championship. The *FIFA* decision may present concern for any '*de facto* monopolist' which is organizing an attractive event for which there is

---

[59] [1999] OJ L125/12.
[60] [1999] OJ L271/28.
[61] Joined Cases C–215/96 and C–216/96 [1999] ECR I–135.
[62] [1999] OJ L106/14.
[63] See Commission Press Releases IP/00/591, 8 June 2000 and IP/99/956, 9 June 1999; [1999] OJ L363/2.
[64] [2000] OJ L5/55.

wide public demand. The Commission has also issued guidance on the general principles it applies in reconciling sport and competition law.[65]

(g)   Dominance   There were robust decisions under Article 82, where the Commission fined *British Airways*[66] EUR 6.8 million for granting to travel agents discounts which did not reflect the volume of their business, but rather the proportion of their business that was directed towards British Airways. Even more confident decisions condemned national airport authorities for the landing fees charged at Finnish, Spanish, and Portuguese airports.[67] The fees ostensibly offered standard levels of discounts, but in reality the biggest discounts were available only to the national carrier. Behaviour in other public services—in particular postal services—came under scrutiny: in *Reims II*,[68] the Commission gave a cautiously-drafted and short-lived exemption to an arrangement whereby the charges levied for delivering cross-border mail were fixed horizontally.

(iii)   Court Judgments
We begin by observing that delays are beginning to damage the valuable contribution made to EC competition law by the European Court of First Instance, as it enters its second decade. There is no doubt that the Court has contributed importantly to the effectiveness of judicial control in factually controversial cases; its case load is increasing; and the pleadings of most parties before it are too loquacious. The Court is itself subject to appeal, so its judgments must to some degree be written defensively. However, we respectfully question the necessity of setting forth the pros and cons of every argument in as much detail as is the Court's tradition. By concentrating on the key points, the Court would save paper and translation time, and make its judgments more agreeable to read. It is not unknown for translation of a finalized but yet undelivered judgment to take nine months. These practical problems must be addressed as accession of new Member States approaches.

(a)   Cartels   Recent cartel cases demonstrate the problems mentioned above. The Court of First Instance had to grapple with some forty appeals in the largest competition case ever—*Cement*,[69] possibly the last of the old generation of cartel cases. That case involved procedural disputes about access to the file, confidentiality, and heated controversy over whether the Greek alleged participants in the cartel had indeed been its victims. The Commission's fact-gathering processes were criticized: the fines were reduced by some EUR 140 million, and the need for the Commission to prove actual participation in the concerted practices found was emphasized. The lengthy *PVC* saga (Cases T–305/94 [1999] ECR II–931 etc.) had another airing in court: the Court of First

[65] Com (1999) 644 final.   [66] [2000] OJ L30/1.
[67] [1999] OJ L69/24, [1999] OJ L69/31 and [2000] OJ L208/36.
[68] [1999] OJ L275/17.
[69] Joined Cases T–25/95, T–26/95, T–30–32/95, T–34–39/95, T–42–46/95, T–48/95, T–50–65/95, T–68–71/95, T–87/95, T–88/95, T–103/95 and T–104/95; [2000] ECR II–491.

Instance was called to review the Commission's second decision fining companies for price-fixing in the PVC sector. The Commission Decision was largely upheld. In an important judgment on the criteria relevant for the assessment of responsibility and imposition of fines, *Polypropylene*,[70] the Court of Justice largely upheld the decisions of the Court of First Instance. Rather late in the day, judicial clarification has been given on the interpretation of the competition provisions of the ECSC Treaty in the *Steel Beams*[71] judgment. The *Cartonboard*[72] appeal, in which the Commission first applied its new approach to 'leniency', finally reached the Court of Justice. A small number of fines were further reduced, and two cases were remitted to the Court of First Instance for the fine to be set on the basis of further information. It is by no means clear today whether it is prudent for a company which fears accusation or has just been accused to approach the Commission and volunteer the whole truth 'warts and all', and the Commission is due to issue a new notice for discussion. The US leniency programme, which offers clearly quantifiable financial advantages, is much more successful.

We may add that, having looked at all the judgments of the Court reviewing fines and all decisions imposing fines, it is very difficult to see economic or moral consistency between them: the most heinous infringement viewed by reference to the level of the fine, is clearly hindering parallel trade. *Volkswagen*[73] was hit with a gigantic fine (EUR 102 million, cut to EUR 90 million by the Court of First Instance), as was *Opel*,[74] albeit to a lesser extent (EUR 43 million); *JCB's* fine[75] was just a little less than *Opel's*. Volunteering the painful truth conferred very little discernible benefit on *Stora*.[76] Medium-sized businesses like those involved in *Nathan Bricolux*[77] were fined many times more than the organizers of the World Cup in France.[78] Those engaged in cartel activity were fined sums ranging from the very moderate to the very severe. There is more explanation in the judgments, but still little pattern and predictability. It is glaringly obvious from the foregoing that the level of fines now imposed by the Commission is high, far higher than the average just a few years ago. Ten years ago, a fine of EUR 2 million for parallel trade infringements was considered appalling; today, a company of any size would be relieved if it was hit by such a fine.

(b) Distribution The Court of First Instance finally issued its eagerly awaited judgment in *Bayer/Adalat*.[79] As promised by the Interim Measures decision, this was indeed a watershed judgment in defining what is unilateral action and what is an agreement with the corresponding potential to fall seriously foul of Article 81(1). The Commission's creativity in finding bilateral

---

[70] C–200/92 *ICI* [1999] ECR I–4399 etc.
[71] Case T–141/94 *Thyssen Stahl* v. *Commission* [1999] ECR II–347 etc.
[72] Cases C–248/98 P etc., [2000] ECR I–9641.
[73] Case T–62/98, *Volkswagen* v. *Commission* [2000] ECR II–27.
[74] [2001] OJ L59/1.   [75] Commission Press Release IP/00/1526, 21 Dec. 2000.
[76] *Supra* n. 72.   [77] [2001] OJ L54/1.
[78] [2000] OJ L5/55.   [79] Case T–41/96 [2000] ECR II–3383.

agreements implied by a unilateral policy has been reined in, to the relief of companies legitimately engaged in profitably marketing their products at different prices in different European countries. However, in its decisions in *Volkswagen*,[80] and the *BASF/Accinauto*[81] appeals, the Court of First Instance accepted the Commission's arguments in the main, reducing Volkswagen's fine a small amount and BASF and Accinauto's fines not at all.

(c)   Mergers and Joint Ventures   The years 1999 and 2000 have seen a number of cases in the area of merger and joint venture co-operation. Commission decisions and general developments regarding the Merger Regulation[82] are outwith the scope of this review. However, there have been interesting decisions of the Court of First Instance in this field which have real relevance for EC competition law generally—particularly as regards the concept of collective dominance in EC law—*Gencor/Lonhro* and *Irish Sugar*.[83] The Court of Justice also ruled on this point in *Compagnie Maritime Belge*.[84] The Court of First Instance delivered other rulings of general importance: on the relevance of a finding of dominance in a Commission decision under the Merger Regulation for Article 82 purposes in *Coca Cola*,[85] where it found that a company which had made concessions in order to obtain a favourable decision could not subsequently challenge that decision, since victory in the appeal would not change the company's legal position; and on the meaning of the concept of 'effect on trade between Member States' in *Kesko Oy*.[86]

(d)   Dominance and Abuse   Some interesting judgments were delivered on collective dominance as noted above; on market definition (*Kish*[87]); and on abusive pricing (*Compagnie Maritime Belge*[88] and *Irish Sugar*[89]). Probably the most important is the Court of First Instance's judgment in *Micro Leader*,[90] a development of the law set out in the *Magill*[91] judgment, away from protecting at all costs the rights of intellectual property rights holders. The suggestion is that hindering transatlantic trade or blocking the imports of trademarked goods from outside the EEA has not yet become an infringement of Article 82.

(e)   Postal Services   In two noteworthy references from Germany, *Citibank*[92] and *GZS*,[93] the Court of Justice gave quite surprising judgments, confirming Germany's right to charge the full internal rate to postage which was actually put into the mail system of another Member State (the Netherlands and

---

[80]   *Supra* n. 73.   [81]   Cases T–175 and 176/95 [1999] ECR II–1581 and 1635.
[82]   *Supra* n. 34.
[83]   Case T–102/96 [1999] ECR II–753 and Case T–228/97 [1999] ECR II–2969.
[84]   Joined Cases C–395 and 396/96 P [2000] ECR I–1365.
[85]   Joined Cases T–125/97 and 127/97 [2000] ECR II–1733.
[86]   Case T–22/97 [1999] ECR II–3775.   [87]   Case T–65/96 [2000] ECR II–1885.
[88]   *Supra* n. 84.   [89]   *Supra* n. 83.
[90]   Case T–198/98 [1999] ECR II–3989.   [91]   Cases C–241 and 242/91 P [1995] ECR I–743.
[92]   Case C–147/97 [2000] ECR I–825.
[93]   Case C–148/97 [2000] ECR I–825.

Denmark), instead of 'terminal dues', i.e. the rate for handling the final stage of international postal services, thereby dissuading companies situated in Germany from taking their mail to another, cheaper, Member State for posting to Germany. The Commission's reluctance to initiate proceedings against post offices was challenged in two cases (*UFEX*[94] and *UPS*[95]).

(f)   Financial Services/Health Funds   In *Bagnasco*,[96] the Court of Justice gave a very restrictive interpretation to 'effect on trade between Member States' to exclude agreements between national banks on interest on repayable loans from the ambit of the EC competition rules, a judgment which was swiftly applied by the Commission in the *Dutch Banks* case.[97] The Court of Justice was called to balance the demands of competition law with social policy and decide whether various pension and health insurance schemes in the Netherlands were justifiable under EC competition law in *Albany and others*,[98] *Pavlov*,[99] and *Van der Woude*.[100]

(g)   Professional Services   As noted above, competition law was applied in this fairly new area by the Commission in a case concerning *European Patent Agents*.[101] In *CNSD*,[102] the Court of First Instance upheld the earlier Commission decision that an agreement on tariffs to be charged by Italian customs agents was contrary to Article 81. A ruling was also made regarding employment agents in *Carra*.[103]

(h)   Environmental and Competition Law Balance   The Court of Justice has currently tipped the balance in the direction of protecting environmental concerns, rather than competition, where this can be justified under Article 86, in an interesting judgment regarding services of general economic interest, *Sydhavnens*.[104]

(i)   Groundhandling Services   The Commission's application of the competition law to various groundhandling services was given forceful backing by the Court of First Instance in *Aeroports de Paris*,[105] affecting the two main airports serving Paris.

(j)   Procedural Issues   Some of the judgments handed down by the Court of Justice have important procedural implications for companies. The Court issued what might, conceivably, be the final judgment in the fifteen-year-long *Woodpulp*[106] procedure. It is now clear that the risk of not joining other

---

[94]   Case C–119/97 P [1999] ECR I–1341.
[96]   Cases C–215 and 216/96 [1999] ECR I–0135.
[98]   Case C–67/96 [1999] ECR I–5751 and others.
[99]   Case C–180–184/98 [2000] ECR I–6451.
[100]   Case C–222/98 [2000] ECR I–7111.
[101]   *Supra* n. 62.
[103]   Case C–258/98 [2000] ECR I–4217.
[105]   Case T–128/98 [2000] ECR II–3929.

[95]   Case T–127/98 [1999] ECR II–2633.
[97]   [1999] OJ L271/28.

[102]   Case T–513/93 [2000] ECR II–1807.
[104]   Case C–209/98 [2000] ECR I–3743.
[106]   Case C–310/97 P [1999] ECR I–5363.

companies in an appeal against a cartel decision is that fines paid under a part of the decision which is subsequently annulled as regards the appellants will not be repayable to the non-appellants. Clearly, there is an incentive for companies fined in a cartel case to participate in an appeal: the chances of a reduction of the fine may be fairly high, and the risk of non-participation is that all is lost. In *Eco Swiss*,[107] at last, the Court of Justice confirmed that an arbitration award could be annulled on the grounds of public policy where the award contravenes the competition provisions of the EC Treaty. The door also seems to have been closed on the *Soda Ash*[108] cases (the *Solvay* and *ICI* procedural *débâcle*, that is the question of the requirements for the proper authentication of a Commission decision). The original decisions, and fines, have now been properly adopted and imposed.[109] In addition, in *Masterfoods*,[110] the Court of Justice has handed down guidance which is likely to be tested to the full in the future complex interactions which can be expected between national courts and the Commission in the exercise of their parallel roles in enforcing EC competition law.

(iv) Legislative Changes

(a) Vertical Restraints Europe's competition law with respect to distribution was probably the most elaborated and prescriptive on earth. The Directorate General for Competition used competition law as a tool to achieve market integration; so-called vertical restraints upon resellers were liable to be very sensitive. On 1 June 2000 a new block exemption, Regulation 2790/1999,[111] entered into force, replacing the three books of the old bible of distribution law—the block exemptions on exclusive distribution (Regulation 1983/83[112]), exclusive purchasing (Regulation 1983/84[113]) and franchising (Regulation 4087/88[114]). The new Regulation is supplemented by detailed 'Guidelines on Vertical Restraints'. Regulation 2790/1999 is intended to cover essentially all types of vertical agreement for the distribution of products and services, including OEM agreements and (a novelty) selective distribution agreements. The intention is that the law should be less formalistic and based instead on the concept of 'significant market power': if the market is sufficiently competitive, then many forms of vertical restraint will pose no threat to competition.[115] A great deal of debate accompanied the drafting process of the new Regulation, particularly on the proper approach to assessing market power. The Regulation provides that the block exemption will not be available where a supplier's market share is above 30 per cent (in the case of

---

[107] Case C–126/97 [1999] ECR I–3055.   [108] Cases C–286–288/95 P [2000] ECR I–3341.
[109] Commission Press Release IP/00/1449, 13 Dec. 2000 [2000] OJ L187/00.
[110] Case C–344/98, judgment of 14 Dec. 2000, not yet reported.
[111] [1999] OJ L336/21.   [112] [1983] OJ L173/1.
[113] [1983] OJ L173/5.   [114] [1988] OJ L359/46.
[115] See 1999 EC Commission *29th Report on Competition Policy*, point 11: 'The new block exemption . . . will effect a shift from the traditional policy, which relied largely on formalistic assessment criteria, towards an approach which focuses more on the economic effects of vertical agreements'.

exclusive distribution agreements, the buyer's market share is considered). The Commission suggests that this will be interpreted fairly flexibly.

A 'black list' of clauses is contained in the Regulation, as is traditional. These are rather salaciously termed 'hardcore restrictions', and where found will immediately take an agreement outside the scope of the block exemption. These include: resale price maintenance (interestingly, fixing maximum prices is specifically not included as a 'hardcore' offence, and price 'recommendations' are still permitted); export bans (including restrictions on passive sales as regards selective distribution); and restrictions on cross supplies in a selective distribution network. Reflecting the basic concern with the potential risk of market foreclosure, non-compete clauses, generally only in so far as they do not exceed five years, are covered by the block exemption. There is no 'white list' of manifestly acceptable clauses. The benefits of the block exemption may be withdrawn where the agreement does not meet the criteria of Article 81(3) even though the enterprise holds a market share below 30 per cent. This mechanism gives the Commission power to act where it considers the cumulative effect of parallel agreements is restricting competition. National competition authorities have also been given the power to withdraw the block exemption where an agreement restricts competition in a national market constituting a discrete geographic market.

Where the 30 per cent market share threshold is surpassed the Commission Guidelines become very important. Logically, the competition concerns increase in ratio to market shares as indicators of market power.

Rather like the effect of GPS navigation systems on the role of the London taxicab driver, much of the 'old knowledge' on distribution is now irrelevant. For example, great energy was poured into the debate over the meaning of paragraph 27 of the Commission Notice on Regulation 1983/83 and Regulation 1984/83,[116] and whether in an exclusive distribution agreement, where a supplier agrees to appoint one reseller for a territory, the supplier could validly refuse to supply other potential resellers in that territory on the basis that he has granted exclusivity to one distributor. It now seems clear that if the block exemption applies, exclusive distribution should mean what it says.

The relaxation of Commission concerns in certain areas of vertical agreements does not extend to the historically particular feature of EC competition law of restrictions on cross-border sales. The degree to which a distribution structure needs to assure the feasibility of parallel trade within the EC and beyond has seen some very important decisions in the period of this review. The Commission had its powers trimmed by the Court of First Instance in *Bayer/Adalat*,[117] and has promised to take a more economics-driven, less clause-driven approach to enforcement. However it still uses its limited resources to take decisions reinforcing its view of the centrality of the prevention of obstacles to cross-border trade.

---

[116] *Supra* nn. 112 and 113.   [117] *Supra* n. 79.

It remains uncertain how the Commission will approach future controversies in the field of exclusive distribution, an area where infringements which were economically and morally quite trivial have been severely condemned. Will it take a clause-driven approach, as in *TEG*,[118] where a fine of 2,000,000 ECU was inflicted on a company which in the course of revising dozens of contracts nevertheless overlooked the presence of an export ban in three of them; the ban had never been enforced, and indeed one of the contracts containing a ban had been lost, and certainly never implemented. Similarly, *Novalliance/Systemform*[119] involved a fine of 100,000 ECUs, a massive penalty for a sole trader. The complaining party was itself in doubtful good faith, and the most likely explanation for the presence of the inflammatory clauses was genuine ignorance of Community law, which was promptly corrected when the company realized its error and before any complaint was made to the Commission. Or will the Commission leave disputes between manufacturers and traders who are refused supplies to be settled by market forces? *JCB*[120] was fined almost as much as *Opel*[121] in 2000, despite the vast disparity in size. The indications are not clear.

(b)   Horizontal Guidelines   Two new block exemptions[122] were adopted in 2000 in the field of specialization and R&D agreements, as well as Guidelines on the applicability of Article 81 to horizontal co-operation agreements.[123] These guidelines cover agreements on R&D, production, marketing, purchasing, as well as standardization and—very topically—environmental agreements. According to the Commission, '[t]he basic aim of this new approach is to allow competitor collaboration where it contributes to economic welfare without creating a risk for competition'.[124] The approach is essentially to assess agreements according to the 'centre of gravity' of the co-operation, and the parties' combined market power. The Commission Guidelines are, again, very detailed and usefully provide a consolidated version of the approach likely to be applied. The block exemptions (which replace the previous Regulations on specialization and R&D) apply below a combined market share threshold of 25 per cent in the case of R&D (an increase of 5 per cent compared to the earlier Regulation) and 20 per cent in the case of specialization.

(c)   Liberalization of Public Services   The Commission continued its inexorable application of competition principles to new, previously 'untouchable' sectors with the adoption of a proposal in 2000[125] to amend the 1997 Directive on Postal Services,[126] and further open the postal services market to competition. This, predictably, has been subject to significant resistance from certain

---

[118]   *Viho/Toshiba* Case No IV/32.879, [1991] OJ L287/39; (1991) 11 YEL 422.
[119]   [1997] OJ L47/11.   [120]   *Supra* n. 41.   [121]   *Supra* n. 28.
[122]   Commission Reg. 2658/2000 on the application of Article 81(3) to categories of specialization agreements [2000] OJ L304/3, and Commission Reg. 2659/2000 on the application of Article 81(3) to certain categories of R&D agreements [2000] OJ L304/7.
[123]   [2001] OJ C3/2.   [124]   *Supra* n. 123.
[125]   COM(2000)319, 30 May 2000.   [126]   Directive 97/67, [1998] OJ L15/14.

Member States. In telecommunications, there were substantial developments with Regulation (EC) No 2887/2000 of the European Parliament and of the Council of 18 December 2000 on unbundled access to the local loop,[127] the draft Commission Directive consolidating existing Directives on competition in the telecommunications markets,[128] and Commission Directive amending Directive 90/388/EEC in order to ensure that telecommunications networks and cable TV networks owned by a single operator are separate legal entities.[129] The Commission also published two Communications: 'The Status of voice on the Internet under Community law, and in particular, under Directive 90/388/EEC—Supplement to the Communication by the Commission to the European Parliament and the Council on the status and implementation of Directive 90/388/EEC on competition in the markets for telecommunications services',[130] and 'Unbundled access to the local loop: enabling the competitive provision of a full range of electronic communication services, including broadband multimedia and high-speed Internet'.[131]

The Commission has been actively monitoring progress in the liberalization of the gas and electricity markets, and developments may be expected in the coming year. In addition, the Commission adopted a Communication on services of general interest in Europe,[132] intended to clarify both the scope and criteria of application of the competition rules to such services.

(d) Transport The block exemption of liner shipping consortia was renewed by Commission Regulation (EC) 823/2000,[133] which will remain in force for five years.

(v) Co-operation between Competition Agencies

An Agreement between the European Communities and the Government of Canada regarding the application of their competition laws, modelled on the up and running EC/US co-operation agreement, was concluded and entered into force in 1999.[134] The possibility of triangular consultation between three agencies therefore becomes a real possibility. We can already observe effective co-operation between Washington and Brussels in important cases, and in rare cases simultaneous enforcement action on both sides of the Atlantic, as well as the giving to the European Commission of 'tips' by national authorities (*Nathan Bricolux*[135]).

---

[127] [2000] OJ L336/4.   [128] [2001] OJ C96/2.   [129] [1999] OJ L175/39.
[130] [2000] OJ C369/3.   [131] [2000] OJ C272/55.
[132] COM/2000/0580 final, [2001] OJ C17/4.   [133] [2000] OJ L100/1
[134] See the report at COM(2000)645 final.   [135] *Supra* n. 39.

II.   Competition Decisions 1999/2000

A.   ARTICLE 81

(i)   Distribution

Obstacles to Parallel Trade

The Commission has devoted much attention to shaping the law regarding distribution. In the early years of this survey we noted its inordinate concentration upon distribution cases as a means of increasing its output of decisions and of pursuing the political goal of market integration. The year 2000 was notable for the Court of First Instance's condemnation of Commission theories in *Bayer/Adalat*[136] (a thunderous statement of basic principles which endorsed the proposition that unilaterally refusing to supply unwelcome orders from parallel traders was not an infringement), while at the same time the Commission pursued a number of old-fashioned parallel trade cases.

(a)   *JCB*[137]   On 21 December 2000, the Commission announced the imposition of a heavy fine of EUR 39,614,000 on JCB, the English manufacturer of excavators, forklift trucks, and other off-highway vehicles. JCB had a strong position in the market for all earth-moving and construction equipment as well as in the market for specific machines such as back-hoe loaders. The infringement was in classic style: low prices in the UK, high prices in France, unwelcome exports from France to the UK to the displeasure of the UK manufacturer and its official network. A complaint was made by an unauthorized French reseller, and the subsequent investigation revealed a variety of pieces of evidence of prohibited agreements and practices restricting sales outside the allotted territory. To make matters worse, a financial penalty had been imposed by JCB on one of its distributors for making unwelcome sales outside its territory. The Commission also found bonuses and fee systems aimed at disadvantaging out-of-territory sales, restrictions on purchases between authorized distributors in different Member States, and some fixing of resale prices and discounts. One controversial question was whether the block exemption regulations on motor vehicles (Regulation 123/85[138] and Regulation 1475/95[139]) extended to all vehicles equipped with four wheels or only to passenger cars. The regulations do not specify, but Commission policy has been made clear in cases concerning motorcycles and industrial vehicles, though not hitherto in a formal decision appealed to Luxembourg. If excavators did not fall within the block exemption Regulation, then JCB could not restrict its exclusive dealers from selling to unauthorized resellers. The Commission evidently regarded the case as presenting serious moral and legal

---

[136] Case T–41/96, *Bayer AG* v. *Commission* [2000] ECR II–3383.

[137] Commission Press Release IP/00/1526, 21 Dec. 2000. Not yet published in the Official Journal.

[138] [1985] OJ L15/16.   [139] [1995] OJ L145/25.

issues, reflected in the very large fine. The fine is in part composed of a sum equal to twice the financial retaliation levied by JCB on its errant distributor, and is influenced by the long duration of the 'very serious' infringement. The decision has been appealed.

(b)   Nathan-Bricolux[140]   This was brought to the Commission's attention by the French competition authorities which 'in the course of investigations carried out in France into the distribution of educational material . . . had come across anti-competitive agreements concerning several Member States'. Nathan was the French supplier, Bricolux and Borgione the Belgian and Italian exclusive distributors whose territorial sensitivities led to fines.

The Commission made its traditional review of what constitutes the relevant market, noting that for educational material robustness is important, eye-catching packaging is not important, and education authority choices shape the volume and composition of educational material.

'In short, these factors indicate that the manufacture and distribution of educational materials in establishments looking after young children is a separate market from identifiable neighbouring markets' [paragraph 19].

'The fact that local authorities have regulatory and budgetary powers in the area of education in most Member States can thus create markets narrower than the national markets. For example, the allocation of powers for education, differences in curricula and cultural habits split the Belgian market between the French and Flemish-speaking communities.'

'Furthermore, although the quality of the products and their educational value is a prerequisite for the development of sales, they must be based on a local commercial presence, in particular for the purposes of on-the-spot demonstration' [paragraphs 25 and 26].

The decision turns up some surprising facts; for example, an Italian six-year-old will attend school for 1,080 hours while the UK child will attend for 773 hours; and a Belgian child will have twice as much artistic activity as a Spanish child. The market share held by Nathan and its subsidiaries seems to have varied from less than 5 per cent to less than 15 per cent.

The practices challenged were essentially the imposition of resale prices on distributors, and co-ordination in price campaigns against undercutting resellers. In 1993, Nathan told Bricolux to pursue similar prices to those set by Nathan in France

There was concertation against La Découverte, a bookseller in Brussels which was obtaining supplies from Vauban, a French bookseller. Vauban was warned to stop poaching on Bricolux's territory:

'As your letter (of 14 April 1995) appears to indicate that you will continue to supply Belgium, we must inform you that we shall flood the town halls and schools of northern France with Nathan and Bricolux catalogues at prices which will without question

140   [2001] OJ L54/1.

ensure that your customers consider your prices to be extortionate. It is for you to decide whether the game is really worth the candle and whether you want a trade war to the finish. Check with Nathan, they will confirm that . . . we have powerful methods of getting our own way' [paragraph 63].

An internal memorandum inaccurately noted: '[u]nfortunately, the European directives prevent us from not supplying them' [paragraph 65].

The decision recites several 'golden oldies' of European competition law, including *Miller*,[141] *Hasselblad*,[142] *BMW* v. *ALD*,[143] *Javico*,[144] *ICI*,[145] *Völk* v. *Vervaecke*,[146] *Lancôme*[147] and others. It found:

'the obligation not to market contract products outside the exclusive territory prevents potential customers, in particular French customers, from benefiting from such lower prices, and restricts competition with local booksellers and with Nathan itself in its capacity as direct distributor to schools. The Belgian schools also ultimately suffer from the restricted competition resulting from the limitation of sales by French distributors either to customers in Bricolux's territory or to Belgian distributors competing with Bricolux that obtain supplies in France for resale in Belgium' [paragraph 85].

'Fixing a resale price level distorts price trends on the market and has the object of restricting competition. On the one hand, a distributor must comply with the contractual commitments which restrict its freedom to define its pricing policing. On the other hand, Nathan is endeavouring artificially to harmonise prices and discounts in relation to those applied in France' [paragraph 88].

However, 'the Commission no longer believes that an obligation not to exceed a maximum resale price, in this case a multiplier of the price charged in France by Nathan for the same products . . . in itself necessarily restricts competition' [paragraph 87].

Arguments about no effect on trade between Member States and the availability of either block exemption (exclusive distribution or vertical agreement under Regulation 2790/1999[148]) were rejected.

The decision contains an interesting and commendably transparent explanation of how fines are set. Bricolux was fined a symbolic amount of EUR 1,000. Nathan, where the fine was stated to be based upon a 'minor infringement', was hit with a fine of EUR 84,000, increased by 20 per cent because the infringement was enforced over three years, and cut by 40 per cent to EUR 60,000 in light of Nathan's co-operation.

It is far from clear that the Commission has renounced its former passion for parallel trade, an enthusiasm which has distorted its priorities for many years.

---

[141] Case 19/77, *Miller International Schallplatten* v. *Commission* [1978] ECR 131.
[142] Case 86/82 *Hasselblad* v. *Commission* [1984] ECR 883; (1984), 4 YEL 401.
[143] Case C–70/93, *Bayerische Motorenwerke AG* v. *ALD Auto-Leasing D GmbH* [1995] ECR I–3439, (1995) 15 YEL 353.
[144] C–306/96, *Javico* v. *Yves Saint Laurent Parfums* [1998] ECR I–1983, (1998) 18 YEL 555.
[145] Case T–13/89, *ICI* v. *Commission* [1992] ECR II–1021, (1992) 12 YEL 626.
[146] Case 5/69, *Völk* v. *Vervaecke* [1969] ECR 295.
[147] Case 99/79, *Lancôme and Cosparfrance Nederland* v. *Etos BV and Albert Heyn Supermarkt BV* [1980] ECR 2511.
[148] [1999] OJ L336/21.

It is also unclear whether the conduct objected to was more than the healthy and normal competitive process of price-setting, price-cutting, and the consequential skirmishes; or whether the efforts of the supplier to deter competition with its appointed resellers were effective or were aimed at hindering cross-border trade as such.

(c) Opel Nederland BV[149] In a statement to the press, Commissioner Monti claimed this decision was 'a clear signal that competition policy serves consumers' interests', since '[t]he right to buy products cheaper in other Member States is one of the main benefits of the Single Market'. The Commissioner's statement implies that Community law gives consumers a general entitlement to be supplied with goods of any description in other Member States. It would have been more accurate to say that while a supplier generally is under no obligation to supply any customer, whether that customer is a local or a foreigner, he is under an obligation not to prohibit any purchaser from exporting to other Member States. Moreover, in the unique case of cars the supplier is obliged, as a condition of retaining the benefit of the block exemption (Regulations 123/85 and 1475/95[150]) for an exclusive and selective distribution system, to deal with end-users from other Member States. Many consumers, especially in Germany, sought to avail themselves of the benefits of the Regulation by purchasing Opel cars in the Netherlands, where car prices before tax were generally substantially lower than in most other Member States. Opel Nederland BV ('Opel'), the Dutch importer of Opel cars, took steps to dissuade its dealers from supplying customers outside the Netherlands. Opel's EUR 43 million fine is less than half the amount levied on Volkswagen for allegedly similar behaviour; it is nevertheless a very severe penalty for conduct which many observers might regard as neither *de facto* nor *de jure* anticompetitive. Indeed, one argument raised by Opel in its defence is that 'it had received conflicting legal advice, and that major competitors had used a comparable . . . policy' (paragraph 192).

The successive block exemption regulations allow manufacturers and importers to prevent their dealers from selling new vehicles to unauthorized resellers who do not belong to the official dealer network, but 'sales to end consumers . . .and sales to other dealers belonging to the same dealers' network must not be restricted' (paragraph 1). However, the Commission received complaints that Opel and its parent company, General Motors Nederland BV ('GM'), were doing just that. A Commission investigation found that in September 1996 Opel's management adopted a decision concerning a strategy which 'comprised, *inter alia*, measures of a restrictive supply policy, a restrictive bonus policy and instructions to dealers to refrain from export sales in general'. These measures took the following forms:

---

149 [2001] OJ L59/1.   150 [1995] OJ L145/25.

—the supplying of dealers . . . was stipulated in such a way that only vehicles needed for sale to customers in the respective contract area were to be delivered and these orders were to be treated with priority,

—the bonus policy introduced in connection with various sales promotion pro-grammes was structured in such a way that sales to foreign end consumers were excluded from the bonus entitlement,

—through the auditing of dealers, their sales activities abroad were inspected. Finally, dealers were repeatedly and urgently instructed to cease carrying out exports in gen-eral. Many dealers expressly undertook to . . . waive such business in future [paragraph 22].

'Directives' annexed to Opel's dealership contract dated 1 January 1997 estab-lished the number of new vehicles which Opel 'reasonably' expected its deal-ers to sell in a given year. These calculations were based on previous sales of Dutch-registered vehicles only, and account was taken of changes in demand patterns only with regard to the Dutch market. Thus, in practice the supply of vehicles to dealers was 'limited to the number of vehicles they were expected to sell to Dutch customers, which would leave them no room for additional export sales'.[151] Opel claimed that dealers 'may have been wrongly advised or brought under an erroneous impression', perhaps by Opel's district managers, that the policy had been introduced to block export sales. (The Commission pointed out that if the district managers were indeed responsible, they were merely putting into effect a policy decided by their supervisors.) Moreover, these were sales targets, not supply calculations (to which the Commission replied that what was at issue was not the sales targets as such, but the fact that supplies were tailored to those targets). Finally, Opel stressed that the restric-tions applied to only twenty-one of Opel's dealers, and suggested that 'product shortage can be invoked as an 'objective reason' possibly justifying such mea-sure'. (But, retorted the Commission, it is hardly likely that a product shortage would apply to all models; and the twenty-one dealers in question were pre-cisely those who had been found 'guilty' of exporting.)

It has long been recognized that bonus schemes, incentive awards, com-missions, and the like can have a powerfully motivating effect on sales efforts, and that a supplier can use these to target conduct which it favours, and restrict competition. 'Bonus payments', the Commission notes, 'are, in addi-

---

[151] At para. 35. The Commission found documentary evidence that Opel's sales staff manager feared these measures were not compatible with the EC competition rules. He sought grounds for hope in 'the pending Bayer [Adalat] case, in which Bayer hindered export through product alloca-tion. . . . If the case does turn out positively (which is not very likely), we could try to limit in the same way orders by Opel dealers who export a great deal, by introducing a limited allocation. In practice, however, this seems to me difficult to realize properly without the allocation being inter-preted as an impediment to export. For models in short supply we would have to be able to prove that we are doing this with complete impartiality.' The Court in fact upheld Bayer's marketing strategy of attacking parallel trading by reducing supplies. The Commission will doubtless argue that Bayer's limits on the volumes of product it made available to particular wholesalers were applied unilaterally within the Bayer organization, while Opel's restrictive supply practices formed part of the contractual nexus binding Opel and its dealers with whom it had a relationship caught by Art. 81(1) and governed by the relevant EC regulations.

tion to the dealer margin, the dealer's most important source of revenue and profit from the sale of vehicles'. An internal memorandum dated 23 May 1996, stipulated 'that the bonuses envisaged within the framework of sales promotion programmes should not be offered for sales abroad, even if the customers were end-consumers' (paragraph 47). Further internal correspondence suggested discussing this strategy with GM Europe 'to make it 'EC legal proof' as much as possible'.[152] In September 1996 Opel decided that vehicles registered outside the Netherlands would not earn their vendors a sales campaign bonus. The legal question is whether denying bonuses in respect of sales which the manufacturer does not favour or wish to encourage (still less to reward) is restrictive of competition. Is awarding a bonus an incentive to reward specific achievement in the local territory, which can be unilaterally withheld in other circumstances? Or does it form part of the normal compensation established by the manufacturer for every sale by any deal, so that withholding it is an anti-competitive act? It is by no means clear that the Commission's posture is correct, but it was very firm. Opel related the decision not to pay bonuses on export sales to a special Dutch automobile tax. For good measure Opel added that the restriction applied only to sales outside Dutch territory and not to sales outside the dealer's territory, and claimed that in any event it did not prevent export sales from taking place. The Commission failed to see the supposed connection between the bonus restriction and the Dutch automobile tax; indeed, it pointed out that Opel had not taken similar action in any of the other Member States which collected comparable taxes.

With regard to other general restrictions on exports, the Commission found evidence that Opel had carried out a long campaign of warnings and direct instructions, backed up by audits, to ensure that dealers did not make export sales. It was indicated that export sales were contrary to the dealers' contracts with Opel, even when they were perfectly legal in terms of EC competition law. Some dealers attempted to justify their practices by pointing out that they had sold to recognized Opel dealers in other Member States, or to end consumers. The majority of the 'exporting dealers' undertook to stop selling abroad.

The decision concludes that the object of all these measures was to restrict intra-brand competition, contrary to Article 81(1), by preventing Opel dealers in the Netherlands from exploiting the competitive advantages they enjoyed over dealers in other Member States. They went beyond legitimate measures to prevent sales to unauthorized resellers, since they also prevented sales to other Opel dealers and individual consumers from other Member States, directly or through authorized intermediaries. The Commission took the opportunity to summarize its interpretation of the rights of European consumers with regard to car purchases, which:

include the right to be able to purchase a motor vehicle within the common market in the Member State where it is offered at the most favourable price. This right included,

---

[152] At para. 50. The Opel document also states with rare elegance that 'Cross-borders sales are a pain in the ass for many [national sales companies] and GME as an organization'.

but is not limited to, new motor vehicles which are offered by the authorized dealers in the volumes and specifications which are required to satisfy the demand of end consumers in the respective contract territory of the dealer.

This right is protected, in practice, by the Community competition rules on parallel trade. In the light of these rules, market partitioning through arrangements concerning restricted supply of motor vehicles to dealers in the distribution network cannot be accepted. Such arrangements have as their object a restriction of competition within the meaning of Article 81 [paragraphs 129 and 130].

The restriction on competition was appreciable owing to the popularity of Opel cars, and it had an appreciable effect on trade between Member States.

The Commission then considered whether Opel's measures might qualify for the block exemption under Regulations 123/85 and 1475/95.[153] The Commission conceded that these Regulations take into account a manufacturer's interest in protecting his selective distribution system, by providing in Article 3(10)(a) that manufacturers and importers may 'forbid dealers to supply contract goods, or corresponding goods, to resellers which are not part of the sales network'. However, Opel had referred 'both in the terminology and in the actual formulation of measures, to exports in general. No distinction was made between sales to . . . resellers outside the Opel distribution network and . . . sales to end consumers, their authorized intermediaries or other contract dealers belonging to the Opel distribution network. In other documents, although these distinctions were made, the measures adopted expressly referred to business which may not be prohibited or restricted under the block exemption regulations' [paragraph 150]. Some dealers had attempted to defend themselves by pointing this out, but to no avail. As for an individual exemption, Opel had not asked for one, and had it done so its request would have been rejected:

Even if it could be assumed that such export restrictions helped to improve the distribution of goods, the end consumer does not share in the resulting benefits. Consumers are prevented from taking advantage of the Single Market and benefiting from the price differences for motor vehicles between the Member States, in that they are restricted in their right to buy goods of their choice wherever they want within the Single Market. The export restrictions adopted by Opel Nederland BV are thus in serious contradiction with the objective of consumer protection, which is, by virtue of Article 81(3), an integral part of the Community's competition rules [paragraph 160].

The large fine was justified not only to redress the wrong done to consumers, but owing to the length of the infringement, its gravity, and the evidence that Opel knew it was breaking the law. As already noted, it is not easy to detect a moral or economic rationale for fining JCB and Opel similar amounts, or for having fined Volkswagen two-and-a-half times as much.

GM and Opel have asked the CFI to annul the decision.[154]

---

[153] *Supra* n. 150.
[154] Case T–368/00, *General Motors Nederland BV and Open Nederland BV* v. *Commission*, [2000] OJ C61/17.

It may be noted that the next version of the block exemption regulation is currently under discussion. The main populist feature of the present one is the obligation upon the manufacturer to ensure the supply of unwelcome end-users from other Member States. There is no ceiling on the number of vehicles which a manufacturer must supply, so in principle the entire car-buying population of, say, the UK could demand to be supplied by Danish distributors or dealers (the pre-tax price there being especially low as tax is especially high). It is not surprising that controversies have arisen, and it remains to be seen whether greater clarity will flow from either the appeal or the drafting of the new rules.

(d) Nederlandse Federative Vereniging[155]   On a number of occasions, most recently in the *Dutch Crane* case,[156] the Commission has had occasion to challenge industry-wide practices in the Netherlands whereby members of a trade association agree, via codes of conduct, gentlemen's agreements, or the like to follow certain patterns of doing business, often involving no dealings with non-members, and imposing duties on members to refrain from certain unwelcome activities, and similar restrictions. In October 1999, the Commission decided that the Dutch association of electro-technical equipment wholesalers,[157] the FEG, and its largest member, Technische Unie (TU), had infringed Article 81(1) by operating a system of collective exclusive dealing and price co-ordination. The decision followed a complaint by a UK distributor of light fittings that it was virtually impossible to sell in the Netherlands without being a member of the FEG. The Commission noted the existence of decisions by the FEG, 'gentlemen's agreements', and concerted practices which prevented the Dutch association of importers from selling to non-members of the FEG. The system ensured that potential price cutters—non-members of FEG—were deprived of their source of supply, and resulted in an artificial price stability in the Dutch market. Unsurprisingly, the Commission found that this restricted competition from suppliers from other Member States, and fines were imposed on the FEG of EUR 4.4 million and on the TU of EUR 2.15 million. Following the ECJ's judgment in *Baustahlgewebe*,[158] the levels of fines imposed were reduced by a small amount to take account of the Commission's admitted responsibility for the length of the proceedings—it took almost ten years for a decision to be adopted.

Foreclosure in the UK Beer Market
(a)   The Commission issued three exemptions and one clearance[159] in the last two years concerning beer supply agreements and leases with public houses

---

[155] [2000] OJ L39/1.   [156] (1995) 15 YEL 330–3.
[157] The Nederlandse Federative Vereniging voor de Groothandel op Elektrotechnisch Gebied.
[158] Case C–185/95-P, *Baustahlgewebe GmbH* v. *Commission* [1998] ECR I–8417.
[159] *Whitbread* [1999] OJ L88/26; *Bass* [1999] OJ L186/1; *Scottish and Newcastle* [2000] OJ L49/37. See also Commission Press Releases IP/99/104 of 11 Feb. 1999 and IP/99/457 of 5 July 1999.

(pubs). In each instance, the principal element in question was the 'beer tie', an exclusive purchasing and non-compete obligation provision which dictates that the lessee will purchase only specified beers and only from the brewer/lessor. Several beer suppliers notified their leases to the Commission after extensive litigation began in the UK over the difference in prices charged to tied lessees and their non-tied competitors. Following Notices in the Official Journal stating that the Commission intended to exempt the leases, the Commission received hundreds of observations from interested third parties. In the *Whitbread* decision, the Commission mentions, perhaps sheepishly, perhaps with a wink, that its services supplemented the observations submitted by Whitbread lessees with visits to three of them at their premises.

In the UK, national brewers typically own retail outlets which they rent to independent landlords, who in turn contract to buy all of their beer requirements from the brewer/lessor. According to the ECJ's jurisprudence, such leases fall within the scope of Article 81(1) if they hinder a competitor's access to the national beer market, especially access to the retail channel, and contribute significantly to foreclosure.[160] Prior to the entry into force of the new Vertical Restraints Block Exemption Regulation,[161] leases containing beer ties were exempted from Article 81(1), subject to certain conditions, by special provisions of the exclusive purchasing block exemption regulation.[162] The Commission granted individual decisions in these four cases because it considered that the form of beer tie commonly used in the UK did not fall within the provisions of the latter Regulation, which requires that the exclusive purchasing obligation pertain only to beers specified in the agreement, whereas the UK leases referred to the brewer's price list, which was subject to unilateral change by the supplier. The scope of the obligation could therefore be easily expanded by the supplier, defeating the Regulation's purpose of limiting the scope to a mutually agreed list of beers.

The Commission defined the relevant product market as 'the distribution of beer in premises for the sale and consumption of drinks' ('on-trade market') (paragraph 97) and the relevant geographic market as the UK because most beer supply agreements are still concluded at national level and conditions vary significantly from Member State to Member State.

The leases were deemed agreements within the meaning of Article 81(1) and contained restrictions in the form of a non-compete provision as well as an exclusive purchasing obligation. The effect of the restrictions was a reduction in both intra-brand and inter-brand competition, as competing suppliers were not able to supply the lessees with the brands that the brewer/lessor sold or other brands of specified types of beer. The Commission nevertheless concluded that the clauses did not have a restrictive effect on competition

---

[160] Case C–234/89, *Stergios Delimitis* v. *Henninger Bräu* [1991] ECR I–935; (1991) 11 YEL 421, 457–9.

[161] Commission Regulation 2790/1999/EC [1999] OJ L336/21.

[162] Commission Regulation 1984/83 [1983] OJ L173/5.

because they did not impede the lessees' ability to offer non-specified types of beer on their premises.

Following the ECJ's two-pronged test laid out in *Delimitis*,[163] the Commission examined whether the leases in question, in conjunction with the various other beer supply agreements, created a cumulative effect which either foreclosed or hindered access to the market, and the extent to which each brewer's network of agreements contributed to any foreclosure, with particular regard to the position of the contracting parties in the market and the duration of the agreements in question.

The beer supply market in the UK experienced significant changes following the UK Monopolies and Merger Commission's Beer Orders issued in 1989.[164] The Orders imposed various changes on the major brewers, including freeing lessees from the tie on non-beer drinks and low-alcohol beers, giving lessees the right to buy one cask-conditioned ale from a different source (a 'guest beer clause'), limiting the number of pubs that could be tied and permitting a loan tie (a loan of money in exchange for exclusivity), to be terminated on three months' notice. Prior to the Orders, approximately 70 per cent of total beer consumption occurred in tied outlets. By comparison, in 1997, the Commission estimated that a maximum of 58 per cent of the on-trade volume was through such tied outlets. The Commission nevertheless concluded that even after the Orders the cumulative effect of the brewers' tying agreements on the possibilities for independent access to the UK on-trade beer market was considerable.

Although the Commission examined other factors relevant to market access, such as acquiring an established brewery or opening new pubs, it concluded that because of licensing restrictions, the decline in overall demand for beer and recent concentration in the beer supply market, the UK brewers' tying agreements had the cumulative effect of hindering independent access to the market.

The Commission considered the market share of each brewer and the amount of beer governed by tying provisions and loan ties at both wholesale and retail level. It also took into account the managed estate of the brewer, even though this part of a brewer's activities does not involve independent operators, as the Beer Orders permit a brewer to lease a managed property or to turn a leased property into a managed one at the end of a lease. The Commission concluded that each of the brewers' networks of agreements individually contributed significantly to the foreclosure of the UK on-trade market.

The question of effect on trade between Member States had to be addressed: beer is relatively costly to transport and relatively low in value for its bulk. Millions of bottles of beer enter southern England from France, reflecting differences in excise duty which the common market is too timid to modify. There were more sophisticated means of measuring an effect on trade between

---

[163] *Supra* n. 160.   [164] *Supra* n. 159.

Member States. The Commission found that the lease agreements affected an appreciable amount of trade between Member States, in that their foreclosing effect hindered both UK and foreign suppliers from gaining independent access to the market. Such restrictions may have the effect of reducing the level of intra-EC trade in beer. The Commission noted, for example, that most foreign producers license their production to UK brewers in order to gain access to their on-trade network.

With regard to the countervailing pro-competitive benefits of the leases, the Commission first noted that the exclusive purchasing and non-compete clauses found in the beer supply agreements did not fall within the scope of the exclusive purchasing block exemption Regulation. Secondly, it recognized that such agreements make beer distribution significantly easier for both the brewer and the lessee: the lessee obtains the benefit of a low-cost entry into the market and the brewer is not required to integrate vertically distribution of its products. Efficiencies result from the ability to plan long-term sales and carry out cost-effective organization of production and distribution. The peculiarity of the UK tie by type of beer was considered to suit exclusive beer supply arrangements in the UK better than the specification provided for in the Regulation, and to facilitate the introduction of foreign beers, as the brewer was not obliged to obtain the consent of all its lessees before adding new beers to its price list.

The Commission paid close scrutiny to whether there were sufficient benefits to offset the appreciable price differences between tied and free pubs. In particular, it was concerned that the brewers might attempt to leverage the exclusive purchasing provision unfairly by raising prices, secure in the knowledge that lessees were unable to turn to other sources of supply. After reviewing whether price differentials were significant in amount and long in duration, the Commission turned to possible countervailing benefits that the lessees received. It highlighted procurement benefits, capital expenditure, and rent subsidies calculated in terms of management, training, marketing, and catering services provided by the brewer to the lessee. The Commission also noted that in individual cases brewers had reduced rents and accepted surrendered leases. Consumers were also found to benefit from the tied leases. The Commission accepted the somewhat boilerplate language offered by the brewers about ensuring the supply of goods of satisfactory quality at fair prices and the freedom to choose between different manufacturers' products, and added that tied leases might also save from closure a local pub that is too small to be run economically by the brewer's own staff. The Commission therefore concluded that the leases and the beer tie fulfilled the conditions of Article 81(3).

(b) Inntrepreneur and Spring[165] Inntrepreneur and Spring separately notified standard tenancy leases for the upstream supply of beer containing

---

[165] [2000] OJ L195/49.

the classic beer tie provisions. The Grand Pub Company ('GPC') was made a party to each of those notifications when it acquired Inntrepreneur and Spring. GPC is a free-standing pub company, not a brewer, which also grants leases containing beer tie provisions. GPC notified the form of leases it has used since its purchase of Inntrepreneur and Spring.

The Commission noted that GPC was not vertically integrated with any UK brewer, and concluded that the relationship between lessor and lessee was economically different from that between brewer/lessor and pub/lessee. After its acquisition of Inntrepreneur and Spring, GPC implemented a policy of 'multi-sourcing' and 'periodic tendering,' meaning that 'brands are sourced on the basis of a diversified portfolio from national and regional brewers' (paragraph 60). It was not committed to take specific volumes from any of the brewers whose beers were on its price list and from 1998–2003 'approximately 98 per cent of the beer throughput will provide an opportunity for third party brewers to tender' (paragraph 60).

The Commission concluded that because brewers both in the UK and abroad could reach the retail market through GPC, the effect of its leases was 'therefore to mitigate rather than reinforce any network effect of brewers' agreements in the [UK] on-trade beer market' (paragraph 61). Such an independent distribution structure reduced foreclosure and could even enhance the competitive structure of the market. The leases therefore did not form part of a brewer's tied network, and the restrictive provisions were deemed to fall outside the scope of Article 81(1).

The exemptions were granted from the date of notification. The duration of the exemption for Whitbread was somewhat longer as it still owned a large leased estate and continued to enter into twenty-year leases with pubs. As Bass and Scottish & Newcastle had either sold off most of their leased estate or were converting it to managed houses, the duration of their exemptions was shorter.

(ii) Shipping Conferences and Maritime Cartels

(a) TACA[166] This case was notable in that it involved the abuse of joint dominance as well as the existence of a cartel. In September 1998, the Commission decided to fine the sixteen parties to the Trans-Atlantic Conference Agreement (TACA) a total of EUR 273 million for having abused their joint dominant position. This fine was higher than the previous record fine of EUR 248 million imposed in 1995 on Europe's cement producers. The Commission also found that the TACA members had entered into a number of agreements contrary to Article 81(1). However, these agreements had been notified to the Commission in 1994[167] and consequently enjoyed immunity

---

[166] [1999] OJ L95/1.

[167] On 5 July 1994 the parties to the TACA submitted an application to the Commission pursuant to Regulation 4056/86 ([1986] OJ L378/4) seeking an exemption under Art. 81(3) in respect of the TACA. Regulation 4056/86 covers agreements which fall within the scope of Art. 81(1) and concern maritime transport services It provides for a block exemption for members of a liner

from fines. The TACA is the successor agreement to the Trans-Atlantic Agreement (TAA), an agreement which was notified to the Commission in 1992 and prohibited by a formal negative Commission decision in October 1994.[168] The TACA came into effect after the TAA was prohibited.

Liner shipping conferences are associations of shipowners served by a secretariat. The shipowners act together to set common or uniform freight rates and agree a common policy on discounts or rebates which may be offered to certain shippers. Depending on the trade concerned, they may share the cargo between themselves in various ways, co-ordinate sailing timetables, pool revenues, and agree measures to combat competition from non-conference competitors. Conference secretariats organize meetings of members of the conference and monitor trade conditions by collecting statistics of trade volumes and prices supplied to the secretariat by the members of the conference. Unlike liner shipping consortia, conferences do not bring about the joint operation of a liner shipping service. Operational issues other than scheduling fall outside the scope of conference activity. It is not uncommon to find one or more consortia operating within a liner conference. The essential feature of conference agreements is that conference members agree to operate under uniform rates. The TACA notified in 1994 provided for agreement by its members on the applicable rate, charges, and other conditions of carriage under its common tariff, which contained a matrix of prices for the carriage of cargo between defined points: twenty-six classes of cargo were defined and a rate was specified for each class. The tariff was published by the TACA and was available to all shippers.

The members of the TACA include some of the world's largest shipping lines, which dominate container trade across the North Atlantic.[169] The number of members of the TAA and the TACA rose from eleven in 1992 to seventeen in 1996. The Commission estimated their combined market share at over 60 per cent. Their customers consist of importers and exporters who ship goods ranging from agricultural produce to electrical white goods and raw materials in containers. The TACA covers eastbound and westbound shipping routes between ports in Northern Europe, the USA, and Canada. Thus the Commission considered that the market for sea-transport services was that for containerized liner shipping between Northern Europe and the USA, using the sea route between ports in northern Europe and ports in the USA and Canada. Not surprisingly, the Commission rejected an argument that the market should also include air freight services.

conference in respect of uniform or common freight rates and certain other conditions Agreements which fall under Art. 81(1) and which concern inland transport services are covered by Regulation 1017/68 ([1968] OJ 175/1). Restrictive agreements which do not concern transport services are covered by Regulation 17 ([1962] OJ 13/204). In the present case, the Commission decided to examine some of the notified activities which fell outside the scope of Regulation 4056/86 under both Regulation 17 and Regulation 1017/68.

[168] [1994] OJ L376/1.
[169] The parties to the TACA are listed in Annex 1 of the Decision.

In the Commission's view, the behaviour of the members of the TACA was very different from that of traditional and legitimate conferences. This was shown not only by practices which were intended to ensure a very high degree of discipline between the parties to the TACA, but also in the methods adopted to extend its scope beyond the shipping lines which are usually members of a conference to include a number of other shipping lines which do not usually operate as conference members. The Commission found that the TACA members had entered into four agreements which were caught by Article 81(1):

- fixing prices charged for the provision of maritime transport services between Northern Europe and the USA;
- fixing prices charged for the provision of inland transport services within Community territory;
- agreeing on the terms and conditions for entering into service contracts with shippers; and
- fixing the prices paid to freight forwarders.

It was not disputed that these agreements were intended to restrict competition between the TACA members within the common market. In this context, the Commission referred to the venerable *Consten and Grundig* cases[170] and stated that:

There is no need to await to observe the concrete effects of an agreement once it appears that it has as its object the prevention, restriction or distortion of competition [paragraph 381].

Thus it was not necessary for the Commission to examine the effect of the TACA on the market in order to establish an infringement. Further, the restriction of competition between TACA members was likely to be appreciable, as was the effect on trade between Member States, owing to their high market share (over 60 per cent) and the large number of containers involved.

Only the first of the four agreements, which concerned price-fixing agreements for transport between northern Europe and the USA, was considered to fall within the scope of the group exemption for liner shipping conferences contained in Article 3 of Regulation 4056/86.[171] The Commission refused to grant individual exemptions for the remaining three agreements on price-fixing for inland transport services and freight forwarding, and the terms and conditions of service contracts. The Commission considered that these agreements would not lead to any improvement in the quality of services and did not allow shippers a fair share of the resulting benefits, and that they contained restrictions of competition which were not indispensable. Thus they did not fulfil the conditions for an exemption under Article 81(3) or Article 5 of Regulation 1017/68.[172]

---

[170] Joined Cases 56/64 and 58/64, *Consten and Grundig* v. *Commission* [1966] ECR 299.
[171] [1986] OJ L378/4.
[172] [1968] OJ L175/1.

With regard to Article 82, in accordance with previous case law on collective dominance, the Commission held that 'the members of the TACA collectively enjoy a dominant position by reason of the fact that they are bound together by a considerable number of economic links which has led to a significant diminution of their ability to act independently of each other'.[173] The parties' market share of over 60 per cent gave rise to a strong presumption of a dominant position, which was confirmed by the fact that they had succeeded in maintaining a discriminatory pricing structure with the purpose of maximizing revenues. A further indication of the TACA's dominant position was the limited ability of its customers to switch to alternative suppliers, thereby making the TACA an unavoidable trading partner. As the Court held in its judgment in *United Brands*,[174] a market share must also be viewed in light of the strength and number of competitors.

The Commission then analysed whether the TACA's members had abused their dominant position. Interestingly, the Commission stated that although some of the TACA's activities could be authorized by a block exemption, this did not prevent Article 82 from being applicable.[175] The Commission found that the TACA members had abused their dominant position in two ways. First, they had restricted individual customers from entering into service contracts (for the carriage of a certain quantity of goods over a fixed period) with individual shipping lines. This restriction had given rise to the largest number of complaints by shippers against the TACA. TACA members openly banned individual service contracts in 1995, and thereafter service contracts were available only on the basis of highly restrictive conditions. Thus TACA members had refused to supply shippers with maritime and inland transport services except on the basis of certain terms which had been chosen by the TACA collectively. The decision's definition of circumstances which may indicate abusive refusal to deal will no doubt be frequently invoked in future:

A refusal to supply can take a number of forms: it can be an outright refusal to supply, a refusal to supply otherwise than on terms which the supplier knows to be unacceptable (a constructive refusal) or a refusal to supply other than on the basis of unfair conditions. Compliance with an agreement to place restrictions on the contents of service contracts amounts to a refusal to supply services pursuant to service contracts otherwise than in accordance with the terms of that agreement and falls into the third of these three categories of refusals to supply. Compliance with an agreement to place restrictions on the availability and contents of service contracts also limits the supply of transport products. Accordingly, such behaviour falls within the scope of Article 86 of the Treaty, and in particular points (a) and (b) thereof, where the supplier in question is in a dominant position [paragraph 553].

The second infringement related to the recruitment of new members. In the notification the parties argued that they had a large number of potential com-

---

[173] At para. 525. See also Case T–102/96, *Gencor Ltd* v. *Commission* [1999] ECR II–753, reviewed later in this survey.

[174] Case 27/76, *United Brands* v. *Commission* [1978] ECR 207.

[175] Case T–51/89, *Tetra Pak* v. *Commission* [1990] ECR II–309.

petitors who exercised an effective competitive restraint, since if the TACA forced prices too high, new entrants would arrive on the market and bring prices back into balance. However, the Commission held that in fact they had committed a second infringement of Article 82 by inducing potential competitors to join the TACA, thereby using their joint dominant position to alter the competitive structure of the market. The Commission referred to the judgment in *Continental Can*[176] as authority for the proposition that the elimination of potential competition may constitute an abuse of a dominant position.

One method used by TACA members to seek to enroll potential competitors was to offer service contracts at high prices to traditional conference members and at lower prices to traditional independents and new entrants. This eliminated not only potential but also actual competitors, in that by becoming members of the TACA they would also become parties to the cartel. This behaviour therefore strengthened the dominant position of the TACA parties by eliminating actual or even potential competition which would otherwise have exerted pressure on the TACA parties. In this context, the Commission noted that between 1994 and 1996, two major Asian liner shipping companies entered the transatlantic market. Both of them did so by becoming a party to the TACA. During the same period, no TACA member left the TACA to operate as an independent transatlantic shipping line, and not a single significant shipping line entered the transatlantic trade as an independent competitor to the TACA. Thus the ultimate purpose of inducing potential competitors to join the TACA was to eliminate price competition by damaging the structure of the market and limiting the supply of transport services.[177]

The fines imposed for the two breaches of Article 82 amounted, as noted above, to a total of EUR 273 million, ranging from EUR 41,260,000 imposed on P&O Nedlloyd, to EUR 6,880,000 imposed on Atlantic Container Line AB and Transportación Maritima Mexicana/Tecomar. The TACA enjoyed immunity from fines for infringements of Article 81(1) from the date of the notification until the Commission's decision. Consequently the decision imposed fines only for the infringements of Article 82. The Commission noted that the infringement relating to service contracts constituted either an absolute refusal to deal or an agreement to deal only under certain conditions. This was considered to be a serious infringement of Article 82, covering part of 1994 and the whole of 1995 and 1996. The larger TACA members were fined more heavily than the smaller ones to reflect the considerable disparity between their sizes. The Commission divided the parties into four groups for fining purposes, according to size based on their worldwide liner shipping turnover. Since the duration of each of the infringements was two to three years, the initial fines were increased by 25 per cent. The Commission saw no reason to

---

[176] Case 9/72, *Continental Can* v. *Commission* [1973] ECR 215.

[177] According to the European Shippers' Council (which represents companies exporting goods), from 1993 to 1995 the TAA and TACA imposed overall price increases in excess of 80 per cent. The US Federal Maritime Commission estimated that the price increases announced by the TACA for 1995 were in the region of US$ 70–80 million as compared to 1994 prices.

adjust the level of fines any further in order to take account of aggravating or attenuating circumstances. It considered that all the TACA parties had participated in the infringements in an equal manner.

The adoption of the decision led several shipping lines to withdraw from the TACA, leaving eight members which at the beginning of 1999 notified a revised agreement with a view to obtaining an exemption under Article 81(3). On 6 May 1999 the Commission published a Notice[178] inviting third parties to comment on the revised TACA, which no longer provides for price-fixing with regard to inland transport. The parties have instead agreed to adopt a 'not-below-cost' rule, by which each line would agree, when providing maritime transport services according to the conference tariff, not to charge a price less than the direct out-of-pocket cost it incurred for inland transport services supplied within the EEA in combination with those maritime services. The Commission has approved this rule but is still examining the maritime aspects of the agreement. If finally approved, the amended TACA will probably be used as a model for the whole liner shipping industry serving Europe.

(b)   Greek Ferries[179]   A complaint by a member of the public led to seven ferry operators being fined EUR 9.1 million by the Commission. The Commission found damning evidence of agreements between the operators to fix prices for roll-on roll-off ferry services and fares for trucks on three routes between Greece and Italy. The evidence included telex messages (discovered during dawn raids) relating to the introduction and calculation of prices. The Commission concluded that the parties had participated in a price-fixing cartel between 1987 and 1994.

Several of the parties argued that the agreements on prices were either required or influenced by Greek shipping law and regulations, and the practice of the Greek Ministry for the Merchant Navy. The Greek Government told the Commission that while it considered services on the Greece–Italy routes to be of public interest and wanted to ensure the viability of the routes and avoid price wars, the Ministry was involved in fixing prices for internal routes only, and not for the international legs of these shipping routes. The fact that the price of the internal portion of the route was fixed inevitably affected the total fare to and from Italy, and the Ministry did encourage operators to keep fares low and annual increases within the limits of inflation. However, Greek law restricted the freedom of companies to fix prices only when this led to unfair competition (derisory and disproportionate fares); the Ministry could then intervene to define upper and lower price levels, but not a specific fare. The Greek authorities strongly denied that they obliged companies to enter into price agreements for international fares.

In light of these explanations and the fact that none of the evidence uncovered by the Commission even mentioned the Ministry or the relevant shipping law on which the parties were attempting to rely, the Commission rejected the

---

[178] [1999] OJ C125/6.   [179] [1999] OJ L109/24. The decision was in fact adopted in 1998.

parties' claim that they were obliged to fix prices on international routes. However, in imposing fines, the Commission recognized that the usual practice in Greece of fixing domestic fares through consultation of all operators may have created doubt whether price fixing of international fares was an infringement or not. It took the possible confusion into account and stated that it had therefore reduced the basic level of fines by 15 per cent.

The Commission noted in its assessment of the case that to fall within the scope of Article 81(1), an agreement need not be intended to be legally binding on the parties; nor were contractual sanctions or enforcement procedures necessary. Trade between Member States had clearly been affected: the importance of the sea routes had increased owing to the problems in former Yugoslavia since 1992, which made it impossible to use the overland routes for trade between Greece and the rest of the EU.

There were mitigating circumstances. The actual impact on the market had been limited, the parties had not applied the specific price agreements in full, they had engaged in limited price competition through discounting, and, encouraged by the Greek Government, their fares were amongst the lowest in the EU. Moreover, the infringement had effects in only a limited part of the Community. Consequently, the Commission concluded that the infringement was serious rather than very serious. The Commission also adjusted the fines to impose greater penalties on larger companies, and increased fines by between 20 per cent and 70 per cent to reflect the duration of the infringement by each company. In addition to the 15 per cent reduction mentioned above, four of the companies received further reductions of 15 per cent to reflect the exclusively 'follow my leader' roles they had played in the cartel. Furthermore, Anek was granted a 45 per cent reduction because documents it had submitted had significantly assisted in confirming the existence of the infringement, while the other companies were awarded a 20 per cent reduction because none of them had contested the factual basis of the Statement of Objections. In contrast, however, the fine imposed on Minoan was increased by 10 per cent because the Commission found the company had been the ringleader of the price-fixing operations and had attempted to thwart the investigations by proposing, in response to the Commission's request for information, that other companies should each reduce different selected fares by 1 per cent in order to camouflage their collaboration on prices. Minoan was fined EUR 3.26 million in total. The other operators, Strintzis, Anek, Ventouris, Karageorgis, Adriatica, and Marlines, were each fined between EUR 1.5 million and EUR 0.26 million.

(c) Europe Asia Trades Agreement[180]   On 30 April 1999, the Commission decided that the 'Europe Asia Trades Agreement' (EATA), an agreement between shipping companies relating to the non-utilization of capacity and the exchange of information which was notified to the Commission in 1992,

---

[180] [1999] OJ L193/23.

infringed Article 81(1). The agreement concerned scheduled maritime transport services for the carriage of containerized cargo from Europe to the Far East. Following indications from the Commission that it was caught by Article 81(1) and could not be exempted under Article 81(3), it was terminated in 1997. The Commission nevertheless issued a decision in order to state the law in this area. No fines were imposed.

The following elements of the agreement were held to infringe Article 81(1):

- The provisions relating to non-utilization of capacity (which were reinforced by financial sanctions against lines carrying more cargo than permitted) enabled the parties to limit or control production, contrary to Article 81(1)(b); and by limiting the volume of liner shipping capacity offered to the market, the agreement increased prices. In view of the very high market shares held by the parties to the EATA and the fact that the same companies were members of another agreement, the Far Eastern Freight Conference (FEFC) which obliged them to operate under uniform or common freight rates,[181] the restriction on competition was clearly appreciable.
- The provisions relating to the exchange of information, whereby the parties to the EATA provided the secretariat on a monthly basis with information including (i) maximum declared capacity; (ii) total actual filled slots; (iii) non-scope cargo lifted; (iv) percentage utilization; (v) forecast capacity for next two months; and (vi) estimated monthly total capacity for next four months. This information, which clearly identified the provider, was forwarded without being aggregated to the other parties to the agreement. The anti-competitive nature of the agreement and the commercial sensitivity of this information were emphasized, in the Commission's view, by the pains the members of the EATA took to maintain confidentiality *vis-à-vis* third parties throughout the administrative procedure.

The Commission commented interestingly on the effect on trade between Member States. It considered that the EATA not only affected exports of goods to third countries,[182] as the members argued, but also had a direct effect on trade between Member States in the markets for the provision of transport and intermediary services, and an indirect effect on trade in goods between Member States. In these markets the restrictions placed on the use of capacity were restrictions on services intended to reduce price competition, and 'influenced and altered trade flows in transport services within the Community which would have been different in the absence of the EATA' (paragraph 166).

The EATA was also capable of affecting trade between Member States because it altered the way in which more efficient service providers might otherwise have behaved (in terms of increasing their share of the business and lowering their prices), and may thus have changed the capacity available at

---

[181] In order to benefit from the block exemption under Regulation 4056/86 [1986] OJ L378/4.
[182] Basing itself on Joined Cases T–24/93, T–25/93, T–36/93, and T–28/93 *Compagnie Maritime Belge Transports and others* v. *Commission* [1996] ECR II–1201, para 205.

ports and deflected trade between ports in Europe. This in turn would have an impact on the supply of ancillary services such as freight forwarders, port services, land transport services, and stevedoring services. Trade between Member States may also have been affected, in that goods which might have been exported to third countries in the absence of the EATA were instead traded between Member States owing to the high price of shipping. Finally, relying on earlier case law,[183] including cases relating to Article 82, and confirming its view that the analysis to be performed under Article 81 and 82 in this regard was identical, the Commission considered that the EATA, which was intended to affect the price of transport services for exported goods, had an indirect effect on trade in goods between Member States, since it may have had an effect on goods exported from Member States to third countries.

The other point of interest in the decision relates to the application of an exemption. The Commission excluded the applicability of Regulation 4056/86[184] on the basis that the EATA did not meet the Regulation definition of a liner conference. Then, in the interests of providing 'increased legal certainty' for a number of companies which had already fallen foul of Community competition law, as well as for other shipping companies, national courts, and competition authorities in the event that a third party sought compensation under national law—and for the purpose of future enforcement action in view of its practice of increasing penalties for recidivists—the Commission considered it should set out its findings as regards the applicability of Article 81(3). Furthermore, although the Commission did not have to analyse the applicability of each part of Article 81(3), as the four conditions are cumulative and once it finds that any one of them is not met it need not look at the others,[185] it nevertheless decided to 'undertake . . . this exercise in the interest of providing greater legal clarity and in order to address the arguments raised by the EATA parties' (paragraph 187). The Commission then 'examined the EATA in its full economic context and, in particular, in the light of all the other restrictions of competition in which the EATA parties were engaging' (paragraph 237), and rejected all the arguments to the effect that the EATA met the conditions of Article 81(3). In particular, with regard to the requirement that the agreement must encourage technical and economic progress, the Commission did not accept that investments would be made in new technology due to the scheme; on the contrary, it thought that more efficient lines were less likely to invest in new technology than would be the case in a more competitive market. The Commission therefore stated that it would agree that capacity regulation led to benefits only if there was a real withdrawal of inefficient or outdated capacity leading to an actual reduction of costs and prices. It found no evidence that the parties' services were in any way improved by the agreements to limit capacity

---

[183] Case 136/86, *BNIC* v. *Aubert* [1987] ECR 4789, (1987) 7 YEL 330; Joined Cases 67/85, 68/85, and 70/85 *Van der Kooy* v. *Commission* [1988] ECR 219; Joined Cases 6/73 and 7/73, *Commercial Solvents* [1974] ECR 223.

[184] [1986] OJ L378/4.

[185] Case T–66/89, *Publishers Association* v. *Commission* [1992] ECR II–1995; (1992) 12 YEL 612.

and exchange information. The Commission also predictably found no evidence that consumers benefited from the EATA; on the contrary, it had given rise to complaints from consumers.

One apparently strong argument of the parties was that the EATA represented the loosest and least restrictive way of ensuring the future viability and stability of scheduled liner services from Europe to Asia. In particular, they argued that if a conference which fixes prices and regulates capacity can be exempted under Article 81(3), an agreement which only regulates capacity must be exemptable. The Commission answered that the EATA had to be seen in context, and since the vast majority of its members were also party to other price regulation agreements, the combined effect of all the agreements had to be considered. It also noted that the block exemption was applicable only if there was effective competition in the market. The parties also argued that if a liner conference comprising all the members of the EATA qualified for a block exemption, an agreement with less extensive co-operation between the parties would not eliminate competition for a substantial part of the services in question, the fourth condition of Article 81(3). The Commission rejected this on the grounds that where the parties had very high market shares, Article 7 of Regulation 4056/86 obliged the Commission to withdraw it if effective competition was absent from the market.

(d)   Far East Trade Tariff Charges and Surcharges Agreement (FETTCSA)[186]
In May 2000 the Commission took another decision in the area of maritime transport. It found that the fifteen parties to FETTCSA had infringed Article 81(1) by agreeing not to discount from published tariffs for charges and surcharges. The agreement had not been notified to the Commission for exemption, as the parties considered it was a 'technical agreement' intended to standardize their offers to customers. They argued that it should benefit from a block exemption under Article 2(1) of Regulation 4056/86.[187] The Commission disagreed, saying that Article 2(1) simply lists certain types of agreement that may not fall within the scope of Article 81(1), and in any event, an agreement not to offer discounts did not have the sole object or effect of achieving technical improvements or co-operation. Some of the parties to the agreement were not parties to the FEFC, which, *inter alia*, regulates tariffs and is entitled to an exemption under Regulation 4056/86. The Commission was concerned that the FETTCSA was extending the FEFC to non-conference lines, and reducing competition overall in the market for shipping services.

The Commission imposed 'moderate' fines of between EUR 134,000 and EUR 1.24 million to 'ensure the necessary deterrent effect of the decision'. This reflected the fact that an agreement not to discount is less serious than a price-fixing agreement, and took into consideration the lack of evidence of the effect of the agreement and the parties' co-operation with the Commission—not to mention the length of the proceedings.

---

[186] [2000] OJ L268/1.   [187] *Supra* n. 171.

(e) Lysine Cartel (Amino Acids)[188]   Fines of EUR 110 million were imposed on five companies for price-fixing worldwide, operating sales quotas, and exchanging sensitive information in the market for lysine (an amino acid used in animal foodstuffs). The Commission considered that this was its most significant case of 2000, at least in terms of the fines levied and the fining policy applied. The case is now on appeal and, interestingly, the Commission has for the first time requested the Court to increase the fines originally imposed.

(iii) Joint Ventures: Heavy Engineering, Shipping, Telecom, Broadcasting, Media, Post, Financial Services, Environment, Professions

(a)   Pratt & Whitney and General Electric[189]   In September 1999 the Commission approved the creation of the Engine Alliance joint venture between Pratt & Whitney (P&W) and General Electric Aircraft Engines (GE) to develop and sell a jet engine for sale to Airbus for use in its A3XX, a new long-range commercial jet aircraft. The new engine may also be used to equip upgraded versions of Boeing's planned B747–400. Rolls-Royce (RR), P&W, and GE are the world's only manufacturers of large jet engines. RR would be able to offer a derivative of one of its existing engines to Airbus for use with the A3XX. The Engine Alliance will be owned and run on an equal basis by P&W and GE, which have shared out the responsibility for different parts of the manufacturing process. P&W will be responsible for the engine's low-pressure system and GE for the core system. The Engine Alliance will also be responsible for the final assembly and sale and marketing of the new engine.

Following publication of an Article 19 Notice,[190] a number of interested third parties submitted observations, which related mainly to the content and wording of the undertakings given by P&W and GE. Some third parties, including RR, believed the indicated thrust range of the new engine had become too wide, creating a risk that the joint venture would reduce competition between the parties in market segments where they currently compete (for example, existing commercial wide-body aircraft).

The Commission concluded that although it might be economically more efficient for the parties to develop the new engine jointly, it would be technologically and economically feasible for them to develop it independently. The creation of the Engine Alliance appreciably restricted competition for the new engine, since it reduced the choice of potential engine suppliers from three to two. As certain potential customers of the new A3XX aircraft were European airlines, the proposed joint venture might affect trade between Member States and was therefore caught by the prohibition in Article 81(1). However, the Commission granted an exemption to the joint venture under Article 81(3), as it would permit P&W and GE to concentrate on specific areas where each had a technological advantage and enable them to develop a new engine fulfilling stricter performance targets than any existing engine, within a shorter time frame and at a lower cost than would otherwise have been possible.

---

[188] [2001] OJ L152/54.   [189] [2000] OJ L58/16.   [190] [1998] OJ C339/3.

Competition would not be eliminated, since a derivative of RR's Trent engine would compete with the new engine.

Since there are only three competitors on the market for large jet engines, it was deemed important that co-operation between P&W and GE should not extend into other market segments where they currently compete and where both have high market shares. The Commission considered there was a risk that the joint venture would provide an incentive in the future for the parties to adapt the new engine for use in other aeroplanes, instead of individually developing new jet engines. This would impair competition between the parties. The exemption was therefore granted on condition that their co-operation remained limited to a specific engine intended exclusively for the A3XX aircraft and any future four-engine Boeing aircraft designed for more than 450 passengers.

In order to allow the Commission to monitor the parties' commercial behaviour, the exemption was made subject to a number of obligations. P&W and GE must notify the Commission of any proposed change of the extent of the joint venture; the Engine Alliance must be an autonomous legal entity whose accounting and auditing records are separate from those of its parents, and must submit its auditing records to the Commission; P&W and GE personnel may not market the new engine, but only act as client contacts; if a customer requests several engines, including P&W's and GE's own engines and the new engine, the terms of sale of the new engine must be negotiated separately; P&W and GE may not disclose the terms of their separate offers to the Engine Alliance or each other; and P&W, GE, and the Engine Alliance must lay down guidelines to avoid sharing competitively sensitive information concerning P&W's and GE's separate engine offers.

In addition to these conditions and obligations, the parties offered a number of undertakings. The joint venture will not request, solicit, or impose conditions of exclusivity in its bids or contracts for the development or supply of the new engine to airframe manufacturers, except for campaigns in which another engine manufacturer has offered to enter into an exclusive agreement. The joint venture will make engine manuals and related technical information available to third parties so they can carry out basic repairs to the new engine. GE will inform the Commission in writing of any purchase orders placed by its subsidiary General Electric Capital Aviation Services (GECAS) for any new aeroplanes powered by the new engine.

The exemption for the joint venture is granted for a period of fifteen years from notification of the agreements until 26 September 2011. The relatively long period is justified by the fact that in the sector concerned investments are typically not recovered in the short or medium term.

(b) P&O Stena Line[191]   In January 1999 the Commission approved the P&O Stena Line joint venture whereby the Peninsular and Oriental Steam

---

[191] [1999] OJ L163/61.

Navigation Company ('P&O') and Stena Line Limited ('Stena') would combine their respective Channel crossing ferry operations. The parties notified the joint venture agreement in October 1996, with a view to obtaining an exemption under Article 81(3). The Commission initially expressed serious doubts whether the joint venture could be cleared under the competition rules.[192] It sent the parties a letter stating its concern that the joint venture could lead to a duopolistic market structure conducive to parallel behaviour by the joint venture and Eurotunnel on the Short Sea tourist market. Moreover, the case posed particular difficulties because of uncertainties about future developments in the market for cross-Channel ferry services, including the effects of the abolition of the duty-free system in July 1999.

However, in February 1998 the Commission published a Notice[193] indicating its intention to exempt the joint venture under Article 81(3), but to limit the duration of the exemption to three years. The Commission held that:

Following detailed examination of the agreement and its likely effects in the market into which new entry cannot be expected, the Commission considers that despite a high degree of concentration in the market after the operation, and despite the significance and the similarity of market shares for both the joint venture and Eurotunnel, the absence of capacity constraints, at least in the short to medium term, and the differences in cost structure of the joint venture and Eurotunnel mean that they can reasonably be expected to compete with each other. The Commission therefore considers that a duopoly would not be brought about by the creation of the joint venture [paragraph 5 of the Notice].

Consequently, in its decision of 26 January 1999, the Commission assessed in detail whether the creation of the joint venture would lead to a duopolistic market structure conducive to parallel behaviour by the joint venture and Eurotunnel.

With regard to product markets, the Commission considered the joint venture was active on two markets: the market for tourist passenger services (passengers and passenger vehicles) on the Channel crossing routes between Dover/Folkestone/Ramsgate/Newhaven and Calais/Dieppe/Boulogne/Dunkirk/Ostend and the Channel Tunnel; and the market for unitized freight services between England and mainland Europe on the Western Channel, Short Sea, and North Sea routes. With respect to the market for Channel crossings, the Commission upheld its findings in the *Night Services*[194] and *Eurostar*[195] decisions and concluded that there are distinct markets for leisure and business travellers, since the latter category values rapidity, comfort, and frequency, while tourists put a higher value on price. Consequently, the assessment of the joint venture was confined to the effects on tourist passengers. The Commission considered that tourists who travelled from the centre of London to Paris or Brussels would be likely to travel by air rather than

---

[192] Commission press release IP/97/511, 11 June 1997.
[193] [1998] OJ C39/21. See also Commission press release IP/97/1008, 19 Nov. 1997.
[194] [1994] OJ L259/20.   [195] [1994] OJ L354/66.

by ferry in the absence of Eurostar, thus excluding the services of Eurostar from the relevant product market. However, Le Shuttle and ferry services were considered as substitutes, since there was evidence that market shares of both the Eurotunnel and ferries would vary in response to relative prices.

The Commission examined whether the parties' co-operation in the joint venture might spill over into their independent tourist passenger services on the North Sea, Western Channel, and Irish Sea. It concluded that due to the number of players in the market and the resulting competition, the parties would be unlikely to be able to raise prices without losing their customers to competitors. The risk of co-ordination was therefore considered to be low.

The creation of the joint venture reduced the number of market players from six to five and increased the combined market share of the two largest operators from 64 per cent (Eurotunnel and P&O) to 82 per cent (Eurotunnel and the joint venture), with three other operators following a long way behind (9 per cent, 8 per cent, 1 per cent). However, the Commission pointed out that market shares had not been stable in the last few years, due in particular to the entry of Eurotunnel onto the market and the end of a pooling agreement. In order to evaluate the actual risk of parallel behaviour, the Commission assessed various factors affecting trade between the joint venture and Eurotunnel:

- The Commission noted that in general parallel behaviour is more likely when transactions are small and frequent, and at prices that are transparent to other operators. These criteria were met with respect to the carriage of tourists' cars, which accounted for 94 per cent or more of tourist vehicles carried. The prices for these transactions resulted from either published brochure fares or promotional fares, both of which were transparent to competitors as promotions were usually advertised and thus capable of being monitored. The remaining percentage was accounted for by bulk sales to larger coach operators; these fares were usually negotiated individually and thus were not transparent, but these sales represented only a small proportion of all transactions. The Commission therefore concluded that the market was relatively transparent.
- The Commission looked notably at spare capacity at critical times of the year. If there was insufficient spare capacity at peak periods, it was more likely that Eurostar and the joint venture would raise prices in parallel than that they would compete for volume. However, it was established that both operators had sufficient spare capacity even in peak periods. The Commission concluded that:

  > [both] operators therefore have incentives to adjust their pricing strategies so as to grow volumes rather than increasing prices. The existence of spare capacity could restrain any attempt by either operator individually to raise prices because its competitor would have the necessary spare capacity at its disposal to carry customers who switch [paragraph 95].

At off-peak times both the joint venture and Eurotunnel were considered to have clear incentives to increase loads, as they reached an annual average capacity utilization of only 54 per cent (Eurotunnel), 43 per cent (P&O), and 39 per cent (Stena). Consequently, the Commission concluded that parallel behaviour would be unlikely, as any price increase would lead customers to switch to a competitor disposing of sufficient spare capacity.

- The Commission noted that in general firms with different cost structures are less likely to act in parallel. It was established that Eurotunnel had lower variable and semi-variable costs than the parties, which might leave Eurotunnel more room to sustain low pricing periods. There would also be scope for further divergence in cost structures in the future, as the market evolved. Eurotunnel was therefore in a position to try to increase market share by under-cutting the ferries, as it had done from May 1996. For these reasons, the Commission concluded that the joint venture and Eurotunnel could be expected to compete with each other rather than act in parallel to raise prices.
- The Commission also examined whether competition would be affected by current or potential competitors to the joint venture and Eurotunnel. It concluded that there would not be sufficient competition from current operators. The directly competing ferry line SeaFrance would not, unlike the joint venture, be in a position to offer a departure every forty-five minutes for eighteen hours a day, and hourly for the remaining six hours, thus allowing for continuous loading, a significant competitive advantage. Hoverspeed's capacity was regarded as too small to compete effectively with the joint venture. Therefore, according to the Commission, there would not be a sufficient probability of effective competition from current competitors after the abolition of the duty-free concessions in 1999, resulting in a loss of income for ferry operators. However, there would be sufficient competition until 1999.

  With respect to potential competition, the Commission concluded that barriers to entry would be high. A minimum efficient scale for Channel crossing services was considered to be three conventional ferries or two fast ferries. Chartering costs were estimated at £5 to £10 million a year for a conventional ferry and between £3.5 and £4 million for a fast ferry, while purchasing costs were approximately £85 million for a conventional ferry. Consequently, new entries by companies not already in the ferry industry could be considered unlikely. Entry barriers would be lower for an existing operator which could add one or two ferries.
- Finally, the Commission was concerned about the effects of the end of the duty-free concessions in mid-1999, as it seemed likely that fare prices could rise by 30 per cent to 40 per cent. According to the Commission, the abolition of duty-free concessions might have knock-on effects on competition between the joint venture and Eurotunnel; passengers deprived of duty-free purchase possibilities and confronted with potentially higher fares might switch to Eurotunnel, which in turn might find its Le Shuttle capacities constrained. Moreover, the extent to which the other ferry operators would be

able after 1999 to compete effectively with the joint venture and Eurotunnel was uncertain.

The Commission therefore considered it appropriate to limit the duration of the exemption to three years between 10 March 1998 and 9 March 2001, to allow for a review once the effects of the abolition of duty-free concessions were clearer.

(c) TPS[196] On 3 March 1999, the Commission authorized agreements creating a new entrant in the French digital pay-TV market, the digital satellite platform Télévision Par Satellite ('TPS'), thus making France the only European market where three digital satellite television platforms (CanalSatellite, AB-Sat, and TPS) coexist with cable television and terrestrial pay-TV. The Commission gave clearance because it considered that the entry of TPS would reinforce the competitive situation, and that the increased pay-TV offer and more advantageous subscription conditions would promote technological progress and benefit consumers.

As well as from its digital pay-TV satellite platform, TPS's programming is also distributed on cable networks in France. TPS planned to position itself on the French pay-TV market as a competitor of two market leaders, Canal+ (4.3 million subscribers) and CanalSatellite (one million subscribers), as well as AB-Sat. The Commission noted the primarily pro-competitive effect of a new operator created by French broadcasters (TF1, M6, France 2, France 3), a telecommunications operator (France Télécom), and a cable operator (Suez Lyonnaise des Eaux). The parties initially contacted the Commission in summer 1996 with a view to notifying the operation under the Merger Regulation.[197] After the Commission had concluded that the parent companies did not have joint control of TPS, the parents notified the operation pursuant to Regulation 17.[198]

The Commission considered that the creation of TPS did not restrict competition, although two clauses limited competitors' access to a certain type of content. However, the Commission concluded that these clauses, which would originally have remained in place for ten years, could be exempted under Article 81(3) for a start-up period of three years. They granted TPS: (i) priority and right of first refusal to broadcast channels and television services edited and controlled by its parent companies; and (ii) exclusive rights to distribute digitally the four general content channels, TF1, France 2, France 3, and M6. The Commission considered that the exclusive availability of these four general-content channels made TPS an attractive product, with the differentiating feature it would need to break into the pay-TV market previously dominated by the Canal + group.

At the Commission's request, the parties limited the scope of the noncompete clause to TPS's core activity. The Commission considered this clause

---

[196] [1999] OJ L90/6.   [197] *Supra* n. 34.   [198] *Supra* n. 1.

ancillary to the creation of TPS for the period of launching the platform. The parties also deleted a clause whereby the two cable operators associated with TPS, France Télécom, and Suez Lyonnaise des Eaux, undertook to give the chains broadcast on TPS priority access to their cable networks and to co-ordinate their offer with that of TPS, a provision which had provoked numerous critical comments from French thematic channels.

Announcing the decision, the Competition Commissioner, Karel van Miert, stated:

The emergence of this new broadcaster on the French market shows that competition in digital pay-TV is possible. Also, it is quite favourable to consumers, who benefit from a wider choice and from more advantageous conditions to subscribe.[199]

(d) Cégétel Decisions On 20 May 1999[200] in *Cégétel + 4*, the Commission granted one of its relatively rare (though becoming more common) negative clearance decisions to agreements restructuring Cégétel SA, a new entrant on the French telecommunications services market, which aimed to enable it to become France's second full-service telecommunications operator, offering a full range of telecommunications services, including fixed voice telephony. Cégétel's activities were to be limited to France. Initially Vivendi (at that time called Compagnie Générale des Eaux) held 100 per cent of Cégétel's shares. Through agreements dated 14 May 1997, British Telecom ('BT'), Mannesmann, and SBC International Inc. ('SBCI') joined the pool of Cégétel's parents. After the operation Vivendi held 44 per cent of Cégétel's shares, BT 26 per cent, Mannesmann 15 per cent and SBCI 15 per cent. The operation proved relatively non-controversial. The Commission received no comments from third parties following the publication of an Article 19 Notice.

The Commission established that the parties' market shares in the fixed telecommunications market segments were negligible. In almost all segments of the fixed telephony market the French incumbent operator, France Télécom, was found to hold a dominant position due to its former legal monopoly. Moreover, the Commission recognized that many companies had recently entered or intended to enter some or all of the French telecommunications market segments. Although BT and SBCI were incumbent operators on their home markets, the Commission considered they were new entrants in France and any other national telecommunications market for fixed voice telephony, which the Commission considered as 'by far the most important' market. Through the restructuring the parent companies would create more effective competition to the incumbent operator in France than any of them could have offered separately. The Commission therefore found that Cégétel's restructuring fell outside the scope of Article 81(1).

The Commission held that the general restriction of competition on the parent companies expressed the shareholders' commitment to Cégétel by guaranteeing that they would each focus their efforts on the French market

---

[199] Commission Press Release IP/99/161, 8 Mar. 1999.　　[200] [1999] OJ L128/14.

through Cégétel. The non-compete clause was therefore regarded as ancillary to the operation so long as the parties retained their influence over Cégétel.

In the mobile telecommunication services sector, three companies provided mobile telephony services in France, France Télécom, SFR (a subsidiary of Cégétel), and Bouygues Télécom. SFR's share of the French mobile telephony market was 38 per cent and France Télécom's 51 per cent. The Commission expressed concern over proposed non-compete provisions which it regarded as possibly restrictive of competition in the mobile market. The parties responded by lifting restrictions on the sale of mobile telephony services by SFR (SIM cards) outside France, and on sales by Mannesmann and BT of their respective national mobile services (D2 and Cellnet) in France. Cégétel was also appointed as exclusive distributor in France of BT's Concert services, consisting of value-added and enhanced international services for big multinational customers. The Commission granted a ten-year exemption for the Concert exclusive distribution agreement, which aimed to facilitate the promotion of Concert services in France and lead to intensive marketing. The Commission considered that the exclusivity would stimulate competition between the different providers of global services in France, and could be considered as the most effective competition for France Télécom's GlobalOne subsidiary in the market for customized packages of corporate telecommunications services.

(e) Télécom Développement[201] Two months later, in July 1999, the Commission again dealt with Cégétel when it decided to authorize the agreements notified in July 1997 between Cégétel and Société Nationale des Chemins de Fer ('SNCF'), the French national railway company, to co-operate through a jointly-owned subsidiary, Télécom Développement ('TD'). Following the parties' modifications to the agreements, the Commission exempted several clauses. TD develops and runs a national long-distance telecommunications network built along the French national railway network. It does not itself provide services for end-users, businesses, or individuals. Rather, it provides: (i) long-distance interconnection services for telecommunications operators; (ii) long-distance transmission capacity, primarily for Cégétel but also for other telecommunications network operators and services providers; and (iii) end-to-end long-distance voice telephony services for distribution exclusively by Cégétel's subsidiaries, 'Cégétel Le 7' (residential market) and 'Cégétel Entreprise' (businesses).

The agreements between SNCF and Cégétel granted TD a 'priority right of access' to deploy its telecommunications network along the railway lines, and provided a guarantee for the arrangement through a penalty clause which remained in force for three-and-a-half years (1997–2000). SNCF also granted TD a non-exclusive right to use public railway land for a period of thirty years.

---

[201] [1999] OJ L218/24.

Rival companies were worried about conditions of access to railway lines for the purpose of installing telecommunications networks. The Commission investigated the matter: its survey confirmed that railway lines, like gas and electricity networks and motorways, are a form of infrastructure that allows the rapid deployment of a national telecommunications network. In such cases the Commission seeks, particularly while competition is in the process of emerging, to avoid a situation in which access to physical infrastructure is restricted by exclusivity agreements or agreements resulting in *de facto* exclusivity, to the detriment of other new operators wishing to enter the telecommunications market. Given the scope of TD's deployment plan, SNCF's capacity for installing telecommunications infrastructure would be close to saturation point for several years. The Commission therefore considered it justifiable to give priority access to TD, provided this did not prevent SNCF from making any spare installation capacity available to other operators.

To ensure that the arrangement did not lead to *de facto* exclusivity, the Commission called for changes to the initial agreements to restrict the 'priority right of access' granted and define clearly the conditions under which it applied. The parties met the Commission's concerns by amending the initial agreements to (i) provide equal treatment for third parties wherever there was no alternative to laying their cables alongside SNCF's railway infrastructures; and (ii) allow SNCF to give other telecommunications operators access to its railway infrastructures, provided these operators did not interfere with the development of TD's network.

The Commission took into account the fact that SNCF and Cégétel were neither actual nor potential competitors. Moreover, by building up its own network and offering long-distance services over the transmission capacity developed by TD, Cégétel would compete more effectively on the French market. The agreements were not likely to affect the competitive position of third parties, in so far as SNCF was not unduly prevented from granting access to its railway infrastructures to other operators.

When it issued the decision the Commission was in the process of examining a number of similar cases relating to the establishment of telecommunications networks along different types of existing facilities (for example, railways, electricity grids, gas pipelines), in Germany, Ireland, Spain, Italy, and the UK. The Commission declared that it would examine the specific characteristics of each case, but the same general principles would remain applicable.

(f) Digital Interactive TV Services: British Interactive Broadcasting/Open[202]
On 15 September 1999, the Commission authorized for seven years as from August 1998, British Interactive Broadcasting Ltd. ('BIB', subsequently renamed 'Open'), a joint venture between BSkyB Ltd., BT Holdings Limited, Midland Bank plc, and Matsushita Electric Europe (Headquarters) Ltd. BIB planned to provide consumers in the UK with digital interactive television,

---

[202] [1999] OJ L312/1.

which had not previously been provided there on a significant scale. In order to provide this service, BIB had to put in place the necessary infrastructure and services to enable companies such as banks, supermarkets, and travel agents to interact directly with the consumer. Among other things, BIB intended to subsidize the retail selling price of digital satellite set-top boxes, an important element of the new service infrastructure.

The Commission considered that BIB would be mainly active in the UK on (i) the digital interactive television services market, and (ii) the technical services market. The following were identified as forming part of BIB's digital interactive television services: home banking, home shopping, holiday and travel services, downloading of games, on-line learning, entertainment and leisure, sports, the motor world, a limited collection of 'walled garden' internet sites provided by a third party and e-mail and public services. The Commission distinguished the digital interactive television services to be offered by BIB from high-street retailing, digital interactive services available via PCs and pay-TV.

The Commission analysed the technical aspects and limitations of both satellite broadcast technology and narrowband telecommunications customer access infrastructure. It confirmed that when the decision was issued, satellites were capable only of one-way communication, and could therefore not provide digital interactive services alone. The traditional twisted pair of copper wires, although capable of two-way communication, were thought at that time to be unsuitable for high-bandwidth services. In combination, however, use of a satellite downlink and a fixed-line uplink enabled a new form of service to be provided to the vast majority of the UK population.

Comparable services had previously been available only via the Internet and personal computers, and the limited penetration of PCs in the UK continued to prevent them from reaching the majority of consumers. However, almost all UK households possessed a TV, and purchasing a BIB/BSkyB digital set-top box would give them access to digital interactive services via the TV screen. In addition, digital interactive services offered a new distribution channel. The Commission therefore concluded that the creation of BIB would contribute to improved distribution of goods and to technical and economic progress.

BSkyB and BT were present in markets closely related to the markets for digital interactive television services and technical services in the UK. While recognizing that they each had the necessary expertise to provide some form of interactive service individually, they argued that by co-operating within BIB they could provide a better service in a shorter time-frame. BT had gained skill and experience in developing and integrating interactive multimedia services through its past interactive television trials.[203] It also had great expertise in providing telecommunications services, which were vital for the operation of BIB's telecommunications return path and its connections with the servers.

---

[203] However, in 1991 a Conservative government had banned BT from offering broadcast TV over its copper lines, in order to protect cable companies as they established their place in the market. The ban was originally to last for 10 years.

BSkyB contributed its experience in set-top box design and operation, together with its knowledge of consumer demand for pay-TV. The Midland Bank contributed its expertise in merchant acquisition and transaction management, and in integrating these services into BIB's infrastructure. Finally, Panasonic contributed its technical expertise, particularly in the area of set-top box design. The Commission agreed that BT's and BSkyB's participation, together with that of Midland Bank and Matsushita, was indispensable to the creation and establishment of BIB as a viable market player.

Conditions: The Commission was concerned that once BIB was created, BT and BSkyB would cease to be potential competitors in the digital interactive television services market. Both had sufficient skills and resources to launch such services, and both could afford the technical and financial risks of doing so alone. The Commission imposed conditions to ensure that (i) competition came from the cable networks; (ii) third parties had sufficient access to BIB's subsidized set-top boxes and to BSkyB's films and sports channels; and (iii) set-top boxes other than those of BIB could be developed in the market.

The Commission also imposed a condition requiring the parties to inform both end-users and their agents for the sale of set-top boxes that a subscription to BSkyB's digital pay television service was not a prerequisite for purchasing a BIB-subsidized set-top box. This ensured that consumers would have the choice of acquiring a set-top box either with BSkyB's pay-TV package or without subscribing to BSkyB's pay-TV offer, and also made sure that the original requirement would not be reintroduced at a later date, and that end-users were provided with accurate information. Further, BT agreed not to expand its cable television interests in the UK and to divest its existing cable TV interests in Westminster and Milton Keynes.

(g) Eurovision[204]   In May 2000, after more than a decade of procedures, the Commission finally granted the European Broadcasting Union ('EBU') a new exemption under Article 81(3) in respect of its 'Eurovision' rules governing the joint acquisition and sharing of broadcasting rights for sports events. The EBU is an association of European broadcasters who mainly provide public service broadcasting. Its conditions for active membership, set out in its Statutes and Guidelines of Interpretation, require the member to offer varied and balanced programming for all sections of the population which can be received by 98 per cent of national households, with at least 30 per cent of all programmes broadcast produced by the member itself.

The notified Eurovision system is a programme exchange system which enables members to obtain coverage, notably of international sports events, on a reciprocal basis. It covers the joint acquisition of TV sports rights, the sharing of jointly acquired TV sports rights, a scheme for non-members to have access to the sporting rights acquired, sub-licensing rules relating to the exploitation of Eurovision rights on pay-TV channels and the exchange of the

[204] [2000] OJ L151/18.

television signal by broadcasters for sporting events. The Eurovision system was first granted a conditional exemption by the Commission in 1993,[205] in response to the EBU's original 1989 notification. However, that decision was annulled by the Court of First Instance in July 1996[206] as a result of objections raised by a number of European television channels. The EBU intervened in support of the Commission, and subsequently appealed the CFI judgment to the ECJ. This appeal was dropped when the Commission granted the new exemption. However, national actions about the EBU by a number of commercial broadcasters, including Métropole Télévision (M6) of France, are continuing.

Following the annulment of the Commission's original decision, the EBU re-activated its request for an exemption under Article 81(3). In its new decision the Commission found that the joint acquisition of rights, the sharing of those rights, and the exchange of the Eurovision signal constituted an appreciable restriction of competition between the EBU members, and of trade between Member States. The Commission rejected the EBU's claim that the relevant market was the acquisition of rights in all sports, irrespective of the national or international character of the event, and suggested that the acquisition of rights for certain events such as the summer Olympics could constitute individual markets. However, the Commission concluded that the Eurovision system led to improved distribution and technical and economic progress because it reduced transaction costs, enabled events to be broadcast by a larger number of broadcasters, and resulted in better coverage of sporting events. Moreover, without the joint acquisition system, smaller members would be unable to obtain television rights to many sporting events. The sharing of rights between EBU members in the same country also improved distribution, as it usually led to almost continuous coverage of major events through alternating of transmissions between such members.

The Commission considered that the joint acquisition and sharing of rights and the exchange of the signal were indispensable to the overall aim of the Eurovision system, and resulted in clear benefits for consumers, particularly in smaller countries. If EBU members negotiated separately for rights, consumers in small countries would probably not obtain those benefits. Competition was not eliminated, because in principle the EBU confined joint bidding to international sporting events, which formed a minority of TV sport, and there was increasing competition from media groups and brokers outside the Eurovision system. Moreover, the EBU's market share had been declining for the last ten years. The system notified to the Commission in 1993 already offered an access scheme whereby non-EBU members would be granted live and deferred transmission rights to jointly acquired Eurovision sporting events on reasonable terms, particularly when the rights were not taken up by EBU members.

---

[205] [1993] OJ L179/32, (1993) 13 YEL 444.   [206] [1996] ECR II–649; (1996) 16 YEL 534.

However, the Commission was concerned that the increasing involvement of EBU members in thematic pay-TV channels would place non-EBU pay-TV operators at an unfair competitive disadvantage. To address these concerns, the EBU introduced and submitted to the Commission in 1999 new sub-licensing rules for the exploitation of Eurovision rights on pay-TV channels. Under these rules, when an EBU member transmits part of a sporting event on its pay-TV channel, a non-EBU member has the right to transmit identical or comparable events on its pay-TV channel, in addition to the rights for live or deferred broadcasting under the 1993 access rules. The new exemption is conditional on respect for the 1993 and 1999 access and sub-licensing rules: the EBU and its members may conclude only agreements for the collective acquisition of rights which comply with the rules governing the granting of access and sub-licensing to third parties or grant more favourable conditions to non-EBU members. Furthermore, the EBU must inform the Commission of any changes to the access and sub-licensing schemes and any arbitration procedures for disputes relating to them.

The exemption was backdated to February 1993, when the EBU, in the course of its first notification, submitted its access scheme for non-members to the Commission. The Commission considered the 1999 amendments to the access scheme were necessary to reflect changes in market conditions but did not indicate that the rules were inadequate from 1993 to 1999. The exemption is valid until 31 December 2005, so that the Commission can reassess the competitive environment before 2006 when bidding for the 2012 Olympics will take place.

(h) Unisource[207] In the last days of 2000, the Commission adopted a decision repeating an exemption decision taken in 1997 regarding the telecoms alliance formed by KPN, Telia, and Swiss Cam and called Unisource.[208] It appears from the press release that the revised scope of the agreement between the parties does not bring it within Article 81(1) (there is no longer any exclusive distribution or non-compete provision).

(i) Reims II[209] This decision concerns the politically delicate issue of liberalization of Community postal services. In 1993 the Commission received a complaint about the system established by the public postal authorities (PPOs) in the Community for 'terminal dues'[210] on cross-border mail under the European Conference of Postal and Telecommunications Administrations (CEPT), a sub-grouping of the Universal Postal Union (UPU) Convention. The complaint argued that the system was contrary to Article 81(1) because it fixed a uniform rate for the delivery of incoming international mail. The

---

[207] [2001] OJ L52/30, see also Commission Press Release IP/01/1, 3 Jan. 2001.
[208] [1997] OJ L318/1. [209] [1999] OJ L275/17.
[210] This term refers to the fees which have to be paid by a postal operator sending cross-border mail to the receiving postal operator to remunerate the costs of handling and delivering the mail in the country of destination.

Commission agreed, but no formal decision was taken. (This was unsuccessfully challenged by the complainant[211] before the CFI,[212] and appealed to the ECJ.[213]) Almost all the PPOs in the EEA then entered into a new agreement (Reims II) to establish a system providing the parties with compensation for the delivery of cross-border mail that more accurately reflected the real costs of delivery and was linked to the quality of the service provided by the PPO delivering the mail. This decision was notified to the Commission.

The Reims II agreement sets out terminal dues for all the parties in a uniform way as a certain percentage of domestic tariffs. In its decision, the Commission found the agreement was caught by the prohibition of Article 81(1). Acknowledging that it was a 'price fixing agreement with special characteristics', the Commission considered that although it did not fix the actual amounts to be paid, but established percentages based on domestic tariffs, it might still in reality fix prices; and although the parties could enter into other agreements on terminal dues, with lower tariffs, in practice the incentive to do so was low. However, the Commission exempted the Agreement under Article 81(3) on the ground that it would encourage the PPOs to improve their services, but only until 31 December 2001 and subject to certain conditions. In particular, the PPOs were obliged to limit increases in terminal dues and grant each other access to their domestic tariffs. They must also establish a transparent cost accounting system as provided for in Directive 97/67,[214] and provide annual reports on domestic tariffs, tariffs for cross-border mail and costs and cross-border mail traffic flows.

It is highly probable that postal services will continue to be the subject of competition law controversies. Public service obligations, a civil service tradition, large numbers of under-trained employees, and sharp competition from courier services for the best business offer a difficult environment for national postal services, which will continue to request approval of special arrangements.

(j) P&I Clubs[215] This case concerned two agreements concluded within the International Group of P&I Clubs ('IG'), which are mutual associations providing protection and indemnity insurance to their shipowning members. In granting an exemption under Article 81(3), the Commission imposed detailed reporting requirements on the parties.

P&I insurance covers contractual and third party liability and injury or death of crew or passengers, collision damage to ships, damage to third party property, environmental damage, damage to cargo etc. Approximately 89 per cent of worldwide tonnage and almost all EU–EFTA tonnage is insured by P&I Clubs

[211] International Express Carriers Conference or IECC, which provided express mailing services.

[212] Case T–110/95, *IECC* v. *Commission* [1998] ECR II–3605, (1998) 18 YEL 582.

[213] Case C–44/98 P, still pending.

[214] Directive 97/67 on common rules for the development of the internal market of Community postal services and the improvement of the quality of services [1998] OJ L15/14.

[215] [1999] OJ L125/12.

which are members of the IG. They offer cover up to approximately EUR 39 billion. The remaining tonnage is insured by small independent P&I mutual associations or maritime commercial insurers, or is not insured against P&I liabilities at all.

One of the two agreements, the International Group Agreement ('IGA') was notified to the Commission in 1981 and received a ten-year exemption which expired in February 1995. The IG requested a renewal of the exemption. However, in June 1997, as a result of a complaint by a Greek shipping organization, the Commission issued a Statement of Objections to the IG's Pooling Agreement. The IG notified amended versions of the two agreements to the Commission in 1998. Under the Pooling Agreement, claims in excess of a certain amount are shared proportionately among all the P&I Clubs. There are different layers of coverage: the first EUR 4.57 million of any claim is borne by the club whose members incurred the liability (most claims fall into this 'retention costs' category); between EUR 4.57 million and EUR 27.42 million, payment is shared by the clubs under the Pooling Agreement roughly in proportion to the number of claims each club faces, the tonnage it covers, and the total premiums it collects from shipowners; the excess of any claim over EUR 27.42 million up to EUR 1.8 billion is covered by a reinsurance contract agreed collectively by the clubs with commercial insurers; above EUR 1.8 billion up to around EUR 3.9 billion, any 'overspill' is again shared by the clubs.

The Commission considered the relevant market to be the worldwide market for P&I insurance, because its substitutability by other marine insurance products was weak from both demand and supply points of view. Because P&I insurance is 'a tailor-made product adapted to the characteristics of the insured', the Commission declined to break it down into more specific segments (for example, type of vessel insured, type and level of cover). The P&I insurance market was also considered to be separate from marine re-insurance since demand comes from different sources (professional insurers seek re-insurance, not shipowners).

On the supply side, the Commission considered that the need for technical knowledge which would take time to acquire, large networks of representatives in harbours throughout the world and very large economies of scale in order to provide high levels of P&I insurance meant that other insurers did not generally operate in the P&I field, although marine hull insurers could and did enter the P&I market for lower levels of cover.

The Commission considered the market for P&I insurance to be worldwide, as the choice of P&I Club made by shipowners was not dependent on the Club's location and the IG covered vessels registered around the world.

A number of changes were made to the Pooling Agreement in response to the Commission's Statement of Objections. The overall cap of EUR 3.9 billion was reduced from EUR 16.5 billion as the Commission considered that such a high minimum level of cover impeded clubs from competing by offering lower levels of cover, for which substantial demand existed. This concession also overcame the Commission's concern that the agreement represented an abuse of a collective dominant position, contrary to Article 82, by limiting the range of insurance cover available in the markets to the prejudice of consumers. Other changes were made to ensure that the P&I Clubs were free outside the Pooling Agreement to offer higher levels of cover than the minimum common level, and to offer lower levels individually. The IG also notified amendments to the criteria on which P&I Clubs would provide reinsurance to third insurers, either mutual or commercial, which the Commission had considered to lack objectivity and proper procedures, in infringement of Article 82. As a result of these changes, the Commission found that the Pooling Agreement did not fall within the scope of Article 81(1).

By contrast, restrictions in the notified IGA did fall within the scope of Article 81(1). It restricted the freedom of P&I Clubs to quote rates to shipowners who were looking to change clubs. Rates cover costs of claims paid by the P&I Club in question and claims shared under the Pooling Agreement, reinsurance, and administrative costs. A new club could offer lower rates only if it could demonstrate to an expert committee that the old club's rate was unreasonably high, or the holding club failed to persuade an expert committee that the new club's proposed rate was unreasonably low.

In response to the Commission's Statement of Objections, which maintained that these procedures prevented P&I Clubs from competing in relation to the rates quoted, the IG amended the IGA so that the quotation procedure would no longer apply to the club's internal administrative costs, but would be limited to costs of claims and reinsurance. This would enable a new club with lower administrative rates to charge a lower rate. The IG also inserted provisions to improve transparency about administrative costs.

The Commission also found that a provision in the IGA which reinforced the application of an annual recommendation by the IG for a minimum cost for tankers (which give rise to most claims) also represented a restriction on competition. Since this recommendation applied to retention costs, which are not shared under the Pooling Agreement, the Commission considered they were not inherent in the claim-sharing agreement. However, it recognized that it would be very complicated and unnecessarily burdensome to devise a system on the quotation rules and the minimum costs for tankers which applied only to the costs shared under the Pooling Agreement and not the retention costs. Moreover, the changes to the quotation procedure were considered to be an improvement which would enhance competition. Consequently, the Commission found the IGA was necessary to enable the benefits of the Pooling Agreement to be achieved and therefore worthy of exemption under Article 81(3).

The exemption was granted for a period of ten years from February 1999. However, the Commission considered that it should apply only as long as the Pooling Agreement was necessary for the P&I Clubs to reach the minimum scale economically required to provide the level of cover agreed at any moment within the IG. The Commission will therefore revoke the exemption 'if the members of the IG collectively hold a market share larger than twice the minimum scale'. If the detailed annual reports which the Commission requested from the IG show that the members of the IG collectively hold a market share of more than twice the minimum scale, the market will be capable of supporting two market operators and the competitive impact of the Pooling Agreement will have to be reviewed.

The Commission also found that the P&I Clubs held a collective dominant position on the worldwide market for the provision of P&I cover, but found no evidence of abuse of that position.

The Commission's treatment of competitive restrictions in the financial services sector has sometimes seemed remarkably tolerant, with insurers obtaining the blessing of arrangements restrictive of price competition which would never have been tolerated with respect to other industries. The present decision appears less tolerant than its predecessors.

(k) Dutch Banks[216] On 8 September 1999, the Commission decided, in light of the *Bagnasco* judgment,[217] that restrictions in the Dutch giro system were not caught by Article 81(1) because they did not affect trade between Member States.

The case started in 1991 when the Dutch banking association, NVB ('Nederlandse Vereniging van Banken'), notified to the Commission an amendment to its existing giro procedure (called the 'GSA' agreement).[218] The notification concerned the introduction of a multilaterally set interbank fee to be paid to the debtor bank by the creditor bank for the processing by the debtor bank of every payment involving an acceptance giro form. These forms are pre-printed credit transfer orders which a debtor remits in a standard format. They are processed on a largely automated basis. Acceptance giro forms are used for domestic business payments carried out on a regular mandatory basis without direct contact between the payor and the payee. The interbank fee is intended as partial compensation for the service provided by the debtor bank in processing the acceptance giro forms, particularly conversion of the data into electronic form. The banks took the view that the advantages of processing by the debtor bank benefited the creditor bank and the debtor bank equally, and the interbank fee was consequently set at half the debtor bank's processing costs.

The introduction of the fee increased charges for creditors, as all credit banks decided to pass on the fee to their clients. This triggered a number of complaints by major users of acceptance giro systems, who argued that the multilateral fee should be regarded as a price fixing agreement between the banks within the meaning of Article 81(1). Some complainants also alleged that the major banks had abused an individual or joint dominant position in

---

[216] [1999] OJ L271/28.

[217] Joined Cases C–215/96 and C–216/96, *Bagnasco* v. *Banca Popolare di Novara* [1999] ECR I–0135, reviewed later in this survey.

[218] The GSA agreement, which entered into force on 1 July 1991 for an indefinite period, is an amended version of the 1985 GSA agreement, which was not notified to the Commission.

breach of Article 82 by imposing unfair charges on customers using acceptance giro forms.

Initially, the Commission had three concerns about aspects of the agreement which could not be exempted: a ban on granting customers particular
advantages in connection with the holding of a particular credit account; a
ban on participants introducing their own acceptance giro procedures; and
the uniform interbank fee. Following the Commission's objections, the banks
agreed to drop the first two provisions, and they also agreed to fix the interbank fee as a maximum fee, with the possibility for individual banks to agree a
lower amount bilaterally. Nevertheless, in 1993, the Commission issued a
Statement of Objections to NVB, arguing that the interbank fee still constituted an infringement of Article 81(1) which could not benefit from an exemption. However, during the proceedings the Commission became convinced
that a multilaterally set interbank fee was more efficient than bilaterally set
interbank fees,[219] and thus indicated in its Article 19 Notice[220] that it intended
to grant an exemption to the GSA agreement. In particular, the Commission
took into account that: (i) the multilateral interbank fee was set on the basis of
the actual costs of converting payment information into electronic form, using
the most efficient method of processing; and (ii) the Dutch banks had agreed
to a periodic review of the amount of the interbank fee by an independent
expert.

The Commission held that the relevant product market was that for acceptance giros and direct debit payments. The relevant geographic market was the
Netherlands because the giro system was designed for domestic business payments there.

In its decision, the Commission found that the multilateral interbank charge
flowed from a restrictive agreement caught by Article 81(1), in so far as it
significantly limited the freedom of the banks to determine their own charging
policy. The Commission also noted that the change to a maximum fee system
had had no practical effect, since none of the banks had chosen to charge a
lower rate bilaterally. It then examined whether the interbank fee had had a
restrictive effect on the relationship between the creditor banks and their customers, since it had been established that the creditor banks systematically
passed on the fees to their customers (the payees). The Commission found
that the banks had passed on the fee to customers as a minimum charge in a
'fairly uniform fashion', but there was no evidence that they had agreed on this.

Having concluded that the agreement restricted competition within the
meaning of Article 81(1), the Commission, relying on *Bagnasco*,[221] decided
that it did not have an appreciable effect on trade between Member States and
thus did not fall under the scope of EC competition rules. The Commission
took into account the following factors in its assessment:

---

[219] Commission press release IP/99/683, 15 Sept. 1999.   [220] [1997] OJ C273/12.
[221] *Supra* n. 217.

- the agreement extended throughout the territory of the Netherlands and therefore had the effect of reinforcing compartmentalization of markets. However, this was not enough in itself to show that there was an appreciable effect on trade between Member States;
- the economic activities concerned by payment by acceptance giro were essentially domestic and thus limited to Dutch territory;
- although many branches and subsidiaries of non-Dutch banks had participated in the system (eleven out of fifty-eight from other Member States), the share of foreign banks in the Dutch acceptance giro system was very limited in terms of volume (less than 1 per cent of the acceptance giro contracts concluded);

The opportunity to offer the giro system was also found not to be a key competitive factor when foreign banks decided to enter the Dutch market (about one third of such banks did not even offer the acceptance giro product).

In light of these factors and the ruling in *Bagnasco*, the Commission concluded that the GSA agreement was not capable of appreciably affecting trade between Member States and therefore fell outside the scope of Article 81(1). The Commission indicated in the decision that if it had had jurisdiction to decide on the case, it would have taken a favourable decision. This may be interpreted as an invitation to the newly-born Dutch competition authority both to consider possible restrictions of competition in the agreement under national competition law, and to look favourably on granting an exemption. The case will doubtless be invoked frequently to discourage the Commission from intervening in matters where the effect on trade is only marginal; the leopard will have changed its spots when it declines to pursue a national restriction upon parallel trade on these grounds.

(l) CECED[222] This case concerned an agreement notified by an association of domestic appliance manufacturers, which aimed to reduce the environmental impact of washing machines in Europe. Since the parties together held around 95 per cent of the EEA market, the Commission was concerned that it might have hidden implications for competition.

The product market was found to be that for domestic washing machines, which the Commission declined to segment further according to load capacity, spinning speed, water and energy use, or sophistication of programme. The relevant geographic market was the EEA, since the major producers were found across the EEA, similar distribution channels were found in each Member State and there was potential competition in each national market from manufacturers in other Member States. The Commission considered the domestic washing machine market to be fairly stagnant, with several large manufacturers under considerable bargaining pressure from large distribution or buying groups.

[222] [2000] OJ L187/47.

Under the agreement, parties agreed to cease producing or importing less energy-efficient machines into the Community after 31 December 1997; to improve energy efficiency to 0.24 kWH/kg by 31 December 2000; to submit data on the fulfilment of objectives by class of washing machine to CECED; and to improve the availability of consumer information on environmentally friendly machines and technology. An independent consultant would aggregate the data submitted by each manufacturer, so competitors would not have access to each others' raw sales data. The joint energy efficiency target was not found to have the object or effect of restricting competition, because it was not accompanied by quotas or specific targets for each manufacturer.

However, the obstacles to production and imports that did not meet the agreed criteria were considered to restrict competition. Parties which prior to the agreement had produced or imported machines in the less energy efficient categories D to G would no longer be able to do so. The Commission considered that competition in one of the product characteristics—energy—on which competition took place, and thus consumer choice was restricted. The Commission also considered that the switch to more efficient machines would entail higher production costs and, in the short term, price increases for models which needed to be upgraded. Somewhat simplistically, the Commission found that since this would lead some manufacturers to raise their prices closer to those of competitors, the agreement would 'thereby distort price competition'. Moreover, the Commission considered that since the agreement had the effect of reducing electricity demand, electricity producers would be affected and their output restricted. This last concern is reminiscent of the Bad Old Days when every remotely conceivable economic consequence of a transaction was invoked to confirm its need for exemption.

Despite these concerns, and fortunately for the environment, the Commission found the agreement to be worthy of exemption under Article 81(3). Since washing machine energy consumption would be reduced by an estimated 15–20 per cent as a result of the agreement, pollution would thereby be reduced and economic benefits gained. The Commission also considered the agreement was likely to focus future R&D on further energy efficiency, thereby allowing for increased product differentiation among manufacturers in the long term. There was therefore a benefit for users and consumers. Individually, savings which would be made through lower electricity bills were expected to enable the cost of buying more expensive upgraded machines to be recouped within nine to forty months, and possibly reduce the prices of the most expensive (and energy efficient) machines. The Commission (on what basis we know not) estimated the 'saving in marginal damage from (avoided) carbon dioxide emissions' at EUR 41–61 per ton of carbon dioxide. Consequently, it calculated that the collective benefits to society would be over seven times greater than the increased purchase costs of more environmentally friendly machines. The presence of such calculations in a decision is rather novel: it is difficult to tell whether they are the grossest approximations or statistically defensible calculations.

It was considered that the aims of the agreement could not effectively be achieved through less restrictive means. Moreover, competition would not be eliminated, as manufacturers were free to decide how to achieve the energy efficiency required and hence compete in technologies for doing so, and in any event distributors considered price, brand name, and technical performance to be more decisive factors in purchasing decisions then energy efficiency. In addition, undertakings which were not party to the agreement could still import the less efficient categories of machines.

It was fortunate for CECED that the agreement was considered worthy of exemption, because the Commission zealously found that a concerted practice within the meaning of Article 81(1) began not in September 1997, when the agreement was signed, but back in 1996, when the parties actually began to cut down production of less efficient categories, in the spirit of the agreement they were in the process of negotiating.

(m) EPI [223] In 7 April 2000, the Commission adopted its third decision concerning the application of EC competition rules to the code of conduct of a professional body. The Institute of Professional Representatives before the European Patent Office (EPI) was set up by the European Patent Office (EPO) to organize the profession of European Patent Representative. It has adopted a code of conduct to regulate members' conduct and other activities linked to the 1973 Munich Convention on the grant of patents. The relevant market is for services associated with applications for European patents filed with the EPO, which is separate from the market in services associated with national patent applications. Following a complaint by a patent agent, the Commission issued a Statement of Objections regarding the code of conduct. The EPI subsequently submitted an amended version of the code which was the subject of the Commission's decision.

The Commission drew a distinction between certain professional rules and competitive restrictions. The decision grants negative clearance for rules in the code of conduct which are necessary to ensure professional secrecy and objectivity, or avoid conflicts of interest and misleading advertising. However, provisions prohibiting members from carrying out comparative advertising under the conditions laid down in Directive 97/55[224] and from actively offering their services to former clients of other representatives were found to be restrictions of competition in breach of Article 81(1).

The Commission held that the EPI code of conduct was a decision by an association of undertakings within the meaning of Article 81(1). Following the amendments to the notified code of conduct, most of its provisions did not restrict competition, including the rules governing members' relationship with the EPO, the avoidance of conflicts of interest and the prohibition on charging fees related to the outcome of the service provided.

---

[223] [1999] OJ L106/14.   [224] [1997] OJ L290/18.

Article 2(b)(1) and (3) of the code of conduct prohibits, in the absence of written permission, advertising which compares the professional services of one member of the EPI with those of another member, or mentions another professional entity. Article 5(c) prohibits one EPI member from soliciting the client of another EPI member who has completed a case involving the client. The Commission stated that these binding provisions might restrict the ability of more efficient EPI members to develop their services, to the detriment of less efficient patent representatives. Further, as the restrictions related to cross-border services, they were liable significantly to distort trade flows in the relevant services between Member States. These distortions might help to crystallize client relationships on national lines and create a restriction to competition.

The Commission decided that the restrictions in the code of conduct which were caught by Article 81(1) could benefit on a temporary basis from an exemption under Article 81(3), so as to give the profession time to adapt its commercial practice and permit an orderly transition which would avoid confusion and allow consumers a fair share of the resulting benefit. The expiry date of the exemption was fixed as 23 April 2000, the deadline for implementing Directive 97/55, which does not allow any exemptions for comparative advertising for the liberal professions. The Commission held that competition would not be eliminated during the period of the exemption, as representatives could compete with each other by a range of other means. An appeal against the Commission's decision is now pending.

B. ARTICLE 82

(i) Sport

(a) 1998 Football World Cup[225]   On 20 July 1999, the Commission found that the local organizing committee of the FIFA 1998 Football World Cup (the Comité Français d'Organisation de la Coupe du Monde de Football 1998, or 'CFO') had abused its dominant position by implementing discriminatory ticket sales arrangements, and therefore fined the CFO a symbolic fine of EUR 1,000. The penalty imposed, which should have been very high if the offences were as grave as asserted in the decision, was very low. To decide whether a severe penalty would have been appropriate, it is necessary to review the facts as they appeared to the public and as they were in reality under the curiously cloudy system established by the CFO.

There was much criticism of the ticketing arrangements for the 1998 World Cup, which focused on the CFO's decision to make a large proportion of tickets available only to purchasers who were able to provide a postal address in France. A total of 1,547,300 match tickets were made available for sale to the general public. Before the group draw on 4 December 1997, the CFO sold 574,200 tickets (37.1 per cent of the total) exclusively to consumers who gave a

[225] [2000] OJ L5/55.

postal address in France. Of those tickets, some 393,200 (known as the 'Pass France 98') related to all matches other than the opening match. A further 181,000 individual tickets relating to the 'high-profile matches' (the opening match, quarter and semi-finals, third and fourth place play-off and the final) were sold on the same condition. All these tickets, except those for the opening match, were sold 'blind' by the CFO, i.e. before it was known which teams would be admitted to the competition. The CFO was the only source of supply for 'blind' tickets, as national associations and tour operators were allocated tickets only following the group draw in December 1997. The CFO argued that the requirement to provide a postal address in France was intended to ensure that tickets were sold only to 'neutral' spectators, and claimed that all members of the general public with an address in France could be considered as 'neutral'.

After receiving a number of formal complaints (and doubtless also in light of the public outcry, which seemed to take the organizers completely by surprise, and which also offered the Commission the chance to be seen to do something for consumers), the Commission initiated proceedings against the CFO, in particular to establish whether the ticket distribution arrangements amounted to an infringement of Article 82.

In order to establish whether the CFO had abused a dominant position, the Commission had to determine whether it held such a position in the first place. In order to do so, it examined whether the tickets for the 1998 World Cup could be said to be substitutable to other products, relying on the SSNIP test[226] to examine the issue of 'substitutability'. Not surprisingly, the Commission established that a 10 per cent price variation would not have any significant influence on demand for the World Cup tickets. It gave four reasons for reaching this conclusion: (1) football is more popular than any other sport. In this context the Commission noted that:

While other sports command strong regional interest from the general public, only football is able to generate a broad, sustained and loyal support on a European and world-wide scale. Furthermore, sports are different, and the general public interested in one will not necessarily be followers of others. Members of the general public seeking to attend World Cup finals matches are accordingly unlikely to have considered attendance at international events involving sports other than football as adequate substitutes, whether or not the price of tickets for World Cup football matches was increased by (at least) 10% [paragraph 68].

(2) The World Cup is more important than other national and international football tournaments; (3) tickets for the European Football Championships are not substitutable for the World Cup, as the tournaments take place two years apart; (4) the great demand for World Cup tickets is a further indicator that there would be no change in consumers' behaviour in the event of a 10 per cent price increase.

[226] If a small but significant non-transitory increase in the price (10%) of certain products does not lead to a change in consumer demand to substitutable products, those products constitute a product market.

The Commission then examined whether there was any realistic substitute for the sale of the blind 'Pass France 98'. National associations and tour operators sold individual entry tickets only after the group draw, i.e. when the identities of the participating teams were known and the demand for tickets was naturally much higher. The Commission therefore concluded that the sale of the individual entry tickets by national associations and tour operators was not a product comparable with or substitutable for the 'Pass France 98' sold before the identities of the teams were known. Furthermore, even if tour operators had sold some of their allocation of tickets as 'Pass France 98', they would probably have sold them together with other services and consequently at a much higher price. The Commission took the same view as regards the sale by the CFO of blind individual tickets for the high-profile matches, partly because of the very limited supply of tickets to these matches (for both national associations and tour operators). Effectively, there was no realistic alternative source for individual blind tickets either.

Thus the Commission made a distinction between tickets sold 'blind' and other tickets sold once the identities of the participating teams were known. The CFO allocated tickets to national associations once their national teams had qualified; when selling blind tickets, it was considered to be in a dominant position. It is arguable that the commodity in question, a right to be admitted to a seat at a sports event, will change in the eyes of the consumer/spectator once the contestants' names are known; on the other hand sport, especially at the highest level, could be said to offer pleasure and excitement of high quality regardless of the participants. It is interesting that non-blind tickets were deemed to fall into a separate market. Will changes in consumer enthusiasm and the near disappearance of price elasticity of demand mean that other products may fall into a separate market? Would the rare copies of a celebrated recording constitute a market separate from good but not stellar recordings?

On the basis of this analysis, the Commission concluded that the relevant product markets were: (i) the market for the sale by the CFO before the draw to the general public of 'Pass France 98' and (ii) the market for the sale by the CFO before the draw to the general public of blind individual entry tickets to the high-profile matches.

The relevant geographic market was defined as 'at least all countries within the EEA' (paragraph 77). The CFO had argued that the geographic market was France, because only the general public living close to World Cup Stadiums would wish to purchase a blind 'Pass France 98', taking into account the need for accommodation and travel. The Commission rejected this argument, pointing to the great interest shown by consumers outside France in attending matches not involving the participation of their national team once the CFO started on 22 April 1998 to sell individual tickets to consumers providing addresses outside France. This supported the view that a significant number of consumers outside France would have wished to purchase a blind 'Pass France 98'.

The Commission therefore concluded that the CFO held a dominant position and was able to act independently and free from competitive pressure as sole supplier of tickets to the World Cup. As a 'de facto monopolist', the CFO was under a general obligation to ensure that tickets were made available to the general public throughout the EEA on non-discriminatory arrangements. Other *de facto* monopolists should worry abut their behaviour, even if they are operating on a national basis, such as the organizers of the Tour de France. Orthodox manufacturing companies are likely to be aware of their market shares; organizers of one-off events may be completely ignorant of them.

With regard to abusive behaviour the Commission held that the need to provide a postal address in France in order to purchase a ticket was an unfair trading condition which had the effect of limiting sales of the 'Pass France 98' and individual tickets to the high-profile games, to the detriment of non-French consumers and contrary to Article 82. The manner in which sales information was provided (or rather, not provided) by the CFO was also considered to be abusive. Thus, on its official World Cup website, there was no indication that entry tickets could be obtained directly from the CFO. On the contrary, it was indicated that the CFO would not sell tickets direct to the non-French public, who could obtain such tickets only through their national football associations or a tour operator. This advice had the effect of limiting demand for CFO sales of individual tickets to the high-profile matches, contrary to Article 82.

The means of reserving tickets with the CFO also discriminated against the general public outside France and constituted an additional infringement of Article 82. Consumers outside France could reserve tickets with the CFO only by applying in writing. Telephone reservations could be made only from within metropolitan France, and reservation by Minitel was available only to residents outside France via connection to the Internet, at an additional cost of 350 FF.

The CFO argued that Article 82 is not intended to give consumers' interests direct protection, so in order to constitute an infringement, abusive conduct must have at least some impact on the structure of competition.[227] The Commission rejected that argument, stating that the interests of consumers are indeed protected by Article 82. The Commission held, referring to *Continental Can*,[228] that:

Accordingly, and as has been expressly recognized by the Court of Justice, Article 82 can properly be applied, where appropriate, to situations in which a dominant undertaking's behaviour direct prejudices the interests of consumers, notwithstanding the absence of any effect on the structure of competition [paragraph 100].

Once it had established that the CFO had abused its dominant position, the next step in the Commission assessed whether there were any objective grounds for departing from the general obligation on the CFO to make tickets available on a non-discriminatory basis throughout the EEA. The Commission conceded that:

---

[227] The second part of Art. 82(1) requires the discrimination to place competitors at a disadvantage.

[228] Case 6/72, *Continental Can* v. *Commission* [1973] ECR 215.

Ensuring effective security at football matches is essential and may, in particular circumstances, justify the implementation of special ticket sales arrangements by tournament organizers [paragraph 105].

The main security concern was to ensure segregation of rival groups of supporters in the stadiums, and the CFO sought to achieve this by allocating tickets to national associations in such a way that rival supporters would be located at opposite ends of the ground. Tickets reserved for rival groups of supporters were not sold blind, but were made available only when the identities of the teams were known. The tickets sold blind by the CFO related only to seats reserved for 'neutral' spectators, and to ensure that they were in fact sold only to 'neutral' spectators, the CFO sold them exclusively to purchasers able to provide a postal address in France, who for some curious reason were considered as 'neutral' in relation to all matches. The Commission agreed that consumers buying blind tickets clearly wished to attend a football match, irrespective of the teams involved, and were not motivated by their support for any particular team. Therefore, they did not represent any specific security risk (a view which was supported by expert opinion), and consequently the obligation to provide a postal address in France was considered to be excessive. In other words, the Commission held that the CFO was wrong to regard the French public as 'neutral' and all members of the non-French public as potential security risks.

Finally, the CFO argued that because the Commission had not objected when the general arrangements for the ticketing sales had been explained in June 1997, it was contrary to the principle of legitimate expectation to initiate proceedings against the CFO at a later date. The Commission responded that at the time of the notification it had not been informed of the need to provide an address in France. Moreover, the notification made by the CFO related exclusively to the arrangements for the selection of tour operators, and the Commission was therefore free to initiate proceedings in relation to other arrangements which had not been notified.[229]

The Commission imposed a symbolic fine of EUR 1,000 on the CFO. According to the Decision, the fine was small because the CFO was unaware that the ticket sales arrangements were illegal, since they were similar to those set up for previous World Cups, and the EU competition law issues involved were of such a nature that the CFO could not rely on previous decisions or case law. As the ticket distribution system for France '98 was considered to infringe not only EU competition law but also the basic Community principle of non-discrimination, and the organizers' behaviour seems to have been ill-conceived, indeed misleading, and its notification was evidently imperfect, it is perhaps surprising, once the decision had been made to pursue the case, that the fine was only EUR 1,000.

---

[229] Interestingly, the notification by the CFO on 11 June 1997 concerning the selection of tour operators was approved by way of a comfort letter on 30 June 1997, i.e. within less than 3 weeks.

(b) *EURO 2000* In March 1999 UEFA, the continental association of European football associations, notified to the Commission the ticketing arrangements for the EURO 2000 tournament held in Belgium and the Netherlands in June 2000. The Commission took the view that these arrangements were quite unlike those for France '98. In a first period of sales, EURO 2000 offered over 400,000 blind-entry tickets (representing 34 per cent of total seating capacity) to the general public throughout the EU. Consumers could apply for tickets in writing or buy them via the Internet. A further 400,000 entry tickets were offered to the general public by UEFA member associations on a staggered basis after the group draw in December 1999. The Commission held that conditions of sale, sales information, and the ticket reservation system were transparent and non-discriminatory. In particular, all tickets sold blind by EURO 2000 (except for those taken up by sponsors and suppliers) were available to the general public throughout the EEA on a non-discriminatory basis. The Commission approved the EURO 2000 ticketing arrangements by a negative clearance comfort letter on 7 June 2000.[230]

(c) *UEFA Rules on Self Regulation and Financial Interests*[231] UEFA scored two notable successes on matters of principle. In December 1999 the Commission rejected a complaint by the owner of a stadium in Lille (Northern France) against UEFA's refusal to permit the Belgian club Excelsior Mouscron to play a UEFA cup tie in Lille. UEFA insisted that under the rules of the competition the match should take place in Mouscron's home ground. The Commission accepted that a sports organization had a legitimate right of self-regulation which could not be challenged under the competition rules. It added, as further reasons for not intervening, that no similar complaints had been received so that investigating the merits thoroughly would be disproportionately burdensome, and the national geographical organization of the sport could not be called into question by Community law.

In a separate matter,[232] the Commission indicated sympathy for a UEFA rule whereby no club in a competition could hold a financial interest in another club. The purpose of the rule is to preserve the integrity of the competition by preventing any conflict of interests between the club as minority shareholder in a rival and as sporting competitor of that rival. The matter had been decided in UEFA's favour by an award of the Court of Arbitration for Sport, located in Lausanne, in a dispute between UEFA and ENIC, a UK company with multiple investments in soccer clubs across Europe. The Commission felt the rule was not caught by Article 81(1).

The relationship between the Commission and the leadership of the world of football has been uneasy since the *Bosman*[233] case, when the European

---

[230] Commission press release IP/00/591 of 8 June 2000.
[231] Commission press release IP/99/956 of 9 June 1999.
[232] Communication under Art. 19(3) of Regulation 17: UEFA rule on 'integrity' of the UEFA club competitions: independence of club [1999] OJ L363/2.
[233] Case C–415/93, *URBSFA* v. *Bosman* [1995] ECR I–4921, (1995) 15 YEL 396.

Court of Justice imposed as legally conclusive its factual assessment of the context in which professional team sport is organized. Whereas the Commission had been reluctant to interfere with the football movement, the Court condemned as illegal two traditional pillars of the professional game. One provided for the payment of a fee by the 'buying' club to the 'selling' club on the occasion of the transfer of a talented player, in respect of the selling club's contribution to the player's training and development, a payment which offered financial incentives to grass roots clubs to seek promising young players in the expectation of selling them to wealthy teams. The other dealt with limits on the number of players of foreign nationality who could be fielded by first division clubs in national leagues.

Perhaps to compensate for its late entry to this area, the Commission has taken particularly public stances on football issues. It elected to make publicly-dramatized 'dawn raids' on national football headquarters, in search of information about the charges to makers of balls for the right to use official logos, information which was not secret and could have been obtained by a simple letter. The attempts of football authorities to propose a regime to respond to the *Bosman* ruling were chastized as inadequate: one cannot imagine the Commissioner briefing the press about the inadequacies of the board of a public company, but since sport is different, recourse to the press was doubtless deemed appropriate. It is difficult to avoid concluding that the Commission's intervention in the World Cup ticketing matter is to be viewed as part of a wish to be seen as 'tough' on football; and to play a populist role in addressing a matter which had attracted a lot of public hostility against the organizers of the event. That said, some of the practices involved in the CFO's ticketing arrangements were remarkably provocative. There may be other cases where a rare combination of exceptional public concern and the presence of a '*de facto* monopolist' lead to Commission intervention.

(ii)   Air Transport

(a)   Virgin/BA[234]   The Commission fined British Airways ('BA') EUR 6.8 million for its use of commissions and other incentives to reward the loyalty of travel agents, with the object and effect of excluding BA's competitors from the UK air transport market.

Following two complaints submitted by Virgin Atlantic Airways Ltd. in 1993 and 1998, the Commission investigated BA's discount and incentive schemes for travel agents. It found that BA was dominant on the UK markets for both travel agency services and business air travel for corporate customers, and that it abused that position through its commission arrangements with travel agents. The decision does not cover BA's arrangements with corporate customers.

The Commission considered the relevant market to be the UK market for air travel agency services, rather than air transport as a whole, following an earlier

234   [2000] OJ L30/1.

decision regarding the IATA Passenger Agency Programme.[235] It found BA to be dominant in this market: it is the dominant purchaser of air travel agency services in the UK; it offers more routes to and from the UK than any other airline; in 1992 its market share was over 46 per cent, and in 1998 it was almost 40 per cent, more than 2.2 times the combined share of its four largest rivals; it holds a substantial proportion of slots in UK airports; and a large proportion of any UK travel agent's service sales are to BA.

BA's commission schemes were considered an abuse of its dominant position. Specifically, the Commission found that they functioned as loyalty discounts and abusive discrimination between travel agents. Like all airlines participating in IATA, BA granted travel agents commission for sales of tickets on its flights. From 1976 to 1997 BA awarded 9 per cent commission on international flights and 7.5 per cent on domestic flights. In 1998, BA reduced all rates to 7 per cent and instituted a programme permitting travel agents to earn higher commission. The new commission was based on the increase in sales from the previous month. The Commission also found that since at least 1992 BA had offered travel agents special marketing agreements which awarded travel agents cash to be used for mutually agreed promotional and marketing projects, based on the agent's increased sales of BA flights over the previous year.

The Commission reviewed case law on exclusionary discounts, citing *Hoffmann-La Roche*[236] and *Michelin*,[237] and stated that BA's commission schemes were 'very close in form to that condemned by the Court in the *Michelin* case' (paragraph 101), in that they did not relate to efficiencies or other benefits secured by the supplier, but rather rewarded loyalty. It rejected BA's claim that it was cost-effective to deal with a travel agent who sold a large number of tickets, stating:

a travel agent that sells an inefficiently small number of tickets can earn the maximum commission provided its small sales represent a 25% increase over its sales in the previous year' [paragraph 102].

Because travel agents are used by airlines in about 85 per cent of UK air travel sales, the Commission found that BA's conduct had 'serious effects' on competing airlines. The Commission rejected BA's arguments that Virgin and other competitors had actually gained market share during the period involved, since 'competitors would have had *more* success in the absence of these abusive commission schemes' (paragraph 107, emphasis added).

Regarding discrimination, the Commission concluded that BA's commission schemes granted similarly situated travel agents providing the same service to BA different commission if their sales of BA tickets were different in the previous year. The Commission acknowledged that there may be cost savings when a travel agent sold a large volume of tickets, and that different travel

---

[235] [1991] OJ L258/18, (1991) 11 YEL 419, 430–1.   [236] Case 85/76, [1979] ECR 461.
[237] Case 322/81, *Michelin v. Commission* [1983] ECR 3461, (1983) 3 YEL 414.

agents might operate at different levels of efficiency and provide different levels of service to BA, but stated that this did not:

prevent the commission schemes . . . from being discriminatory. The commission schemes at issue do not respond to different volumes of sales by travel agents or different levels of service provided by travel agents to BA. Under these schemes, extra commission is related to the extent to which a travel agent meets or exceeds its previous year's sales of BA tickets.

The effect of these discriminatory commissions will be to place certain travel agents at a competitive disadvantage relative to each other. Travel agents must compete with each other to provide agency services to the public and to persuade members of the public to book air tickets through them. The resources available to the travel agents to do this by, for example, promoting their services to the public or by splitting commission with travellers, come from their commission income. By distorting the level of commission income . . . these schemes will affect the ability of travel agents to compete with each other [paragraphs 110–111].

The effect of BA's commission schemes on trade between Member States was determined from the fact that many of the competing airlines harmed by these schemes were located outside the UK, and from the exclusionary impact of these schemes for competitors desiring to enter the market for air transport originating in the UK. In reply to BA's claim that it had breached its fundamental legal obligations by not pursuing competitors for incentive schemes about which BA had formally complained, the Commission replied that while it must apply the same principles to such schemes, it did not have to 'take decisions on similar cases at the same time' (paragraph 66).

When setting the level of the fine, the Commission considered the infringement was so grave and, in particular, had lasted so long (seven years), that the fine should be increased by 70 per cent.

The decision is not perfectly clear, but it appears that the combination of a very high market share and the granting of discounts which aimed to reward not 'productivity' but merely 'loyalty' was deemed objectionable. On the other hand, it is not uncommon in many areas of commerce for those who exceed last year's figures to be rewarded. One may ask whether it is automatically objectionable to set discounts other than on a cost-justified basis.

(b)   The Airport *Cases*   In 1999 and 2000 the Commission took three decisions under Regulation 17[238] relating to the abuse of a dominant position through discriminatory landing fees and discount systems at certain Finnish, Portuguese, and Spanish airports.[239] The cases followed a Commission investigation into landing fees at European airports and a 1995 decision that the discount system at the Brussels national airport infringed EU law.[240]

---

[238]   The Commission found Regulation 17 [1968] OJ Spec. Ed. 67 rather than the procedural regulations specific to the transport sector applicable for the purposes of applying Arts. 81 and 82 EC, as it was not the air transport services provided to passengers that were in question, but rather the services associated with access to airport facilities.

[239]   *Spanish Airports* [2000] OJ L208/36; *Portuguese Airports* [1999] OJ L69/31; *Ilmailulaitos/ Luftfartsverket* [1999] OJ L69/24.

[240]   [1995] OJ L216/8, (1995) 15 YEL 340–2.

The Commission found that the system of granting discounts and setting different landing fees according to the origin of the flight discriminated in favour of national airlines, and that no objective justification for such discriminatory treatment existed. Spain and Portugal, where airports are managed by the public undertakings Aeropuertos Españoles y Navegación Aéra ('AENA') and Aeroportos e Navegaçao Aérea—Empresa Publica ('ANA'), were found to have infringed the state aid rules as well as the competition rules (Article 86(1) in conjunction with Article 82), as the charges were established by decree or laws. In Finland, where the public undertaking Ilmailulaitos/Luftfartsverket (the Finnish Civil Aviation Administration or 'CAA') itself imposed the charges, the Commission found the CAA had infringed Article 82. No fines were imposed, and the respective governments and authority were given two months in which to report to the Commission on the measures taken to end the infringements.

Regarding the question of what constitutes an undertaking under Article 82, the Commission found that according to established case law, public undertakings which administer airports are undertakings in the sense of Article 82, their core activity being to provide airlines with access services to civil airport facilities in return for a fee. The Commission referred to the case law of the ECJ in *Höfner and Elser* v. *Macrotron*[241] and *Christian Poucet*,[242] which defines an undertaking as 'every entity engaged in an economic activity, regardless of the legal status of the entity and the way it is financed'.

The Commission stated:

there is no doubt that the CAA, whose core activity is providing airlines with access services to civil airport facilities in return for a fee, is, according to the definition of the Court, an undertaking within the meaning of [Article 82] of the Treaty [*Ilmailulaitos/ Luftfartsverket*, paragraph 23].

Concerning the relevant market, the Commission used the same product market definition as in its decision concerning Brussels National Airport, i.e. the market in services linked to access to airport infrastructures for which a fee is payable. More specifically, this was said to include services linked to the operation and maintenance of runways, the use of taxiways and aprons, and approach guidance for civil aircraft. The Commission transposed the reasoning of the Court concerning the organization of port activities for third parties at a single port as a relevant market for the purposes of Article 82, to the air transport sector and access to airports.[243]

As the Court of Justice of the European Communities has held in the 'Port of Genova case', the organization of port activities for third parties at a single port may constitute a relevant market within the meaning of Article [82]. Likewise, the Court considered

---

[241] Case C–41/90, [1991] ECR I–1979, (1991) 11 YEL 482.

[242] Joined Cases C–159/91 and C–160/91, *Christian Poucet* v. *Assurances Générales de France and Caisse Mutuelle Régionale du Languedoc-Roussillon* [1993] ECR I–637, (1993) 13 YEL 471.

[243] Case C–18/93, *Corsica Ferries Italia Srl* v. *Corpo dei Piloti del Porto di Genova* [1994] ECR I–1783, (1994) 14 YEL 527.

piloting services in the Port of Genova to constitute the relevant market in its judgment in 'Corsica Ferries II'. The Court based its reasoning on the fact that, if an operator wishes to offer a transport service on a given maritime route, access to port installations situated at either end of that route is essential to the provision of the service. This reasoning can easily be transposed to the air transport sector and access to airports [*Portuguese Airports*, paragraph 14].[244]

The 41 airports administered by AENA, the seven airports administered by ANA, and the airports administered by the CAA with international traffic were each regarded as distinct geographic markets, as they were interchangeable only to a limited extent. The Commission thus found that airlines operating domestic or intra-EEA flights to and from each of the relevant airports in Finland, Spain, and Portugal had no option but to use the airports and services administered and provided by the respective authorities.

On the question of dominance, the Commission referred to the case law of the ECJ in *Corsica Ferries III*, *Höfner and Elser* v. *Macrotron* and *ERT* v. *DRP*, which held that 'an undertaking having a statutory monopoly in a substantial part of the common market may be regarded as having a dominant position within the meaning of [Article [82]'.[245] AENA, ANA, and CAA were each, by virtue of the exclusive rights granted to them, considered to hold dominant positions on the market for landing and take-off services with respect to the airports they administered, since the airports constituted the only available means of providing air transport services to a particular city, and there were high entry barriers to the market owing to the costs involved in constructing new airports.[246] AENA and ANA were held to be dominant for each of the airports they administered, and CAA was held to be dominant for its five airports with international traffic.

The Commission found that AENA's dominant position, by covering all Spain's forty-one airports and thereby the whole of Spain for landing and take-off services, affected a substantial part of the common market. Although owing to AENA's dominant position it was not thought necessary to establish the fact for the purpose of the case, the Commission stated that Spain's sixteen most important airports with high international traffic could already be considered to constitute a substantial part of the common market.[247] With regard to CAA and ANA, the Commission held that the airports which operate intra-EEA flights:

---

[244] The same reasoning was used in *Ilmailulaitos/Luftfartsverket, supra* n. 239 paras. 24–25, and AENA, *supra* n. 239, paras. 31–33.

[245] Case C–266/96, *Corsica Ferries France* v. *Gruppo Antichi Ormeggiatori del Porto di Genova* [1998] ECR I–3949, (1998) 18 YEL 587; Case C–41/90 *Höfner and Elser* v. *Macrotron* [1991] ECR I–1979, (1991) 11 YEL 482; Case C–260/89, *ERT* v. *DRP* [1991] ECR I–2925, (1991) 11 YEL 484.

[246] *Spanish Airports, supra* n. 239, para. 41.

[247] The Commission referred to Cases C–179/90 and C–266/96, *Corsica Ferries, supra* n. 245.

taken together... can... be regarded as a substantial part of the common market, if one applies the reasoning adopted by the Court in the *Crespelle* and *Almelo* judgments[248] [*Ilmailulaitos/ Luftfartsverket*, paragraph 36, and *Portuguese Airports*, paragraph 21].

The Commission went on to cite paragraph 17 of the *Crespelle* judgment:

by thus establishing, in favour of those undertakings, a contiguous series of monopolies territorially limited by together covering the entire territory of a Member State, those national provisions create a dominant position, within the meaning of [Article 82] of the Treaty, in a substantial part of the common market.[249]

The Commission concluded:

[a] fortiori, a contiguous series of monopolies controlled by the same undertaking [CAA and ANA] may represent a substantial part of the common market [*Ilmailulaitos/ Luftfartsverket*, paragraph 37, and *Portuguese Airports*, paragraph 22].

With regard to the authorities' abuse of their dominant position, the Commission was of the view that airlines were put at a competitive disadvantage by the system of landing fees and discounts, which had the effect of applying dissimilar conditions to airlines for equivalent transactions linked to landing and take-off services. AENA, ANA, and CAA were the sole administrators of the infrastructure of their airports, and provided airlines with indispensable services for which a fee had to be paid. In Portugal and Spain these fees were set by Royal Decrees and laws: they were state measures. So far CAA had set its fees independently, although if necessary they could be fixed by decree. Landing fees were calculated according to the airport, the weight of the aircraft, and the origin of the flight, and in all cases they were higher for intra-Community flights than for domestic flights. Moreover, progressive discount systems were applied; whereby lower landing fees were granted for a higher number of landings per month. To establish whether the authorities had abused their dominant positions, the Commission examined the fee differentials according to the origin of the flight separately from the discounts granted according to landing frequency.

Although rebates as such were normal business practice, according to the Commission,[250] they might constitute an abuse when they were applied by a dominant undertaking which lacked objective justification for any difference

---

[248] Case C–323/93, *Société agricole du Centre d'insémination de la Crespelle* v. *Co-opérative d'élévage et d'insémination artificielle du département de la Mayenne* [1994] ECR I–5077, (1994) 14 YEL 524, and Case C–393/92, *Commune d'Almelo et autres* v. *Energiebedrijf Ijsselmij* [1994] ECR I–1477, (1994) 14 YEL 525.

[249] *Ilmailulaitos/Luftfartsverket*, supra n. 239, para. 36, and *Portuguese Airports*, supra n. 239, para. 21.

[250] The Commission did not deal with the first question in connection with CAA, which had announced it intended to abolish its system by 1 Jan. 1999. The Spanish authorities also pointed out their intention of abolishing their system over a transitional period until 2002. However, the Commission did not accept this, as no evidence had been put forward that earlier abolition would be technically impossible or give rise to unreasonable costs; moreover, the Spanish authorities had been aware of the Commission position for a long time, and hence the delay until 2002 was unjustified.

in treatment.[251] The effect of the discount system was a difference in the treatment of airlines in terms of the price charged for landing and take-off services. However, the services provided by the authorities entailed the same work irrespective of the individual airline, and the Commission found no objective reason which would justify the difference in treatment. Although the threshold for the lowest discount[252] in the case of fifty-one to 100 landings per month was sufficient to benefit both national and foreign airlines, only the Spanish and Portuguese airlines respectively in fact benefited from the largest category of discounts,[253] given for over 200 landings per month. 'The *de facto* effect of this system, therefore, is to favour the national carriers' [*Spanish Airports*, paragraph 48, and *Portuguese Airports*, paragraph 26].[254]

Examining whether there was any objective justification for the difference in treatment, the Commission noted that airlines wishing to provide services to a particular town did not have the possibility of using an alternative airport, so there was little risk that an airline would change to another airport which charged a lower fee.[255] Possible objective justifications suggested by the Commission included economies of scale and the wish to reduce air congestion or noise. The Commission rejected the argument of economy of scale put forward by the Portuguese authorities, as it had done in its decision in the *Brussels National Airport* case (recital 16), stating that:

in the case of landing and take-off services such economies of scale do not exist. The services provided do not depend on the individual owner of the aircraft or whether they are rendered to the first or the tenth aircraft of the same airline [*Spanish Airports*, paragraph 52].

Other justifications put forward by the Portuguese authorities were competition from Madrid and Barcelona, which had similar systems, and promotion of Portugal as a tourist destination. The first of these claims was rejected by the Commission, which pointed out that it had also initiated proceedings against the Spanish authorities. The Commission also referred in this respect to the *Hedley Lomas* judgment[256] and stated that:

a Member State cannot justify an infringement of Community law on its own part by invoking the fact that another Member State has likewise failed to comply with its obligations under Community law [*Portuguese Airports*, paragraph 29].

---

[251] The Commission in *Portuguese Airports, supra* n. 239, para. 27, refers to the CFI in Case T–65/89, *BPB Industries and British Gypsum* v. *Commission* [1993] ECR II–389, para. 69, (1993) 13 YEL 462.

[252] 7.2% in Lisbon, 18.4% at other Portuguese airports, and Spanish airports 9%.

[253] 32.7% in Lisbon, 31.4% at other Portuguese airports, and Spanish airports 35%.

[254] The Spanish authorities also claimed the system of discounts was non-discriminatory, as it applied to all airlines, irrespective of whether they were Spanish or foreign. The Commission replied that although *de jure* there was no discrimination, *de facto* Spanish airlines paid lower landing charges, for which there was no economic justification.

[255] *Spanish Airports, supra* n. 239, para. 51.

[256] Case C–5/94, *The Queen* v. *Ministry of Agriculture, Fisheries and Food, ex p. Hedley Lomas (Ireland)* [1996] ECR I–2553.

The Commission also rejected the argument concerning the promotion of Portugal as a tourist destination, stating that these objectives could be achieved by non-discriminatory discounts accessible to all airlines operating services to and from the airports.[257] In reply to a similar claim from Spain regarding the Canary Islands, the Commission stated that it was not clear how the system of landing fees would help to promote tourism there, since most visitors to the Islands were Europeans from outside Spain who therefore paid higher travel costs.[258]

The Commission also found that the difference in fees for domestic and intra-Community flights was an abuse of a dominant position under Article 82(2)(c), as it had the effect of placing airlines operating EEA services at a competitive disadvantage compared to airlines providing domestic services. The Commission again transposed the reasoning by the Court of Justice and Van Gerven AG in *Corsica Ferries*[259] to the airport sector, stating that:

it becomes apparent that the system of differentiated landing fees has the effect of applying dissimilar conditions for equivalent landing and take-off services supplied to airlines. This places airlines operating EEA services at a competitive disadvantage in comparison to airlines providing domestic services. The differentiation of landing fees according to the origin of the flight therefore constitutes an abuse of a dominant position within the meaning of point (c) of the second paragraph of Article 82 [*Spanish Airports*, paragraph 56].[260]

With regard to domestic flights (excluding the Azores) the Portuguese authorities claimed that since they were so short, the landing charges would account for too high a proportion of the transport costs. The Commission rejected this argument, as the charges were based on aircraft weight rather than on distance, and:

[i]f this line of argument were accepted, flights from Portugal to Madrid, Seville, Malaga and Santiago would also have to qualify for this reduction, since these destinations are situated at a comparable distance to that involved in domestic flights [*Portuguese Airports*, paragraph 39].

The CAA claimed the system was justified on the ground that the underlying costs for internal and international flights were different because different technical and operational requirements were applicable, such as length of runways, durability of runways, operating hours, and airport availability. None of these arguments was accepted by the Commission.[261]

---

[257] *Portuguese Airports, supra* n. 239, para. 31, and *Spanish Airports, supra* n. 239, para. 67.

[258] *Spanish Airports, supra* n. 239, para. 68.

[259] Case C–18/93, *Corsica Ferries Italia* v. *Corpo dei piloti del porto di Genova* [1994] ECR I–1783.

[260] Also *Ilmailulaitos/Luftfartsverket, supra* n. 239, paras. 42–43, and *Portuguese Airports, supra* n. 239, para. 35.

[261] The latter two costs were found to be irrelevant, as they were already included in the calculation of passenger charges. The durability factor was also found to be already taken into account in the charge based on the weight of the aircraft. The argued need for runways 400 metres longer for international flights was equally rejected, as many domestic routes are of distances similar to intra-EEA flights; distance was not the sole criterion for the choice of aircraft, and most of Finland's airports had already made investments for longer runways.

The Commission referred to the recognition in *Corsica Ferries II*[262] that discriminatory practices which affect undertakings providing transport services between two Member States may affect trade between Member States.[263] Given the volume of traffic between Spain, the Community, and the EEA, the Commission found that the measures in question had an appreciable effect on cross-border trade.[264] The Spanish authorities argued that most of the discounts granted to Spanish airlines stemmed from domestic or extra-Community traffic and therefore did not affect intra-EEA traffic. The Commission, however, replied that:

this justification does not apply in respect of the main beneficiary, Iberia, which receives almost one quarter of its discounts from intra-Community flights. . . . In addition, the present system leads to lower domestic charges while imposing higher charges on intra-EEA traffic for equivalent services. Given the importance of intra-Community flights in total traffic handled at Spanish airports, there is therefore an affect on trade between Member States [*Spanish Airports*, paragraph 64].

With regard to the CAA, no statistics existed that separated intra-EEA traffic from the rest of the international traffic for each airport. The Commission nevertheless stated:

[a]s regards Helsinki airport, which handled 7,7 million passengers in 1996, the effect of the system in question on trade between Member States is beyond doubt. As regards the other Finnish airports operating intra-EEA services . . . apart from charter flights to the Mediterranean Member States and the Canary Islands, these airports operate each day to Stockholm six flights (Vaasa and Turku), five flights (Tampere), and two flights (Pori) [*Ilmailulaitos/Luftfartsverket*, paragraph 60].

Moreover, as these flights connected with flights to other EU cities, the Commission thought it legitimate to regard the system as having an effect on trade between Member States. Finally, the effect on trade between Member States was clear with regard to ANA, as the great majority of traffic volume was between Portugal and other Member States.[265]

C.   PROCEDURAL ISSUES

(i)   Supply of Incorrect Information

(a)   Anheuser-Busch and Scottish & Newcastle[266]   On 14 December 1999, the Commission fined Anheuser-Busch (AB), the world's largest brewer, and Scottish & Newcastle (S&N), the UK's largest brewer, for infringing Article

---

[262] *Supra* nn. 259 and 245.

[263] *Spanish Airports, supra* n. 239, para. 57, *Ilmailulaitos/Luftfartsverket, supra* n. 239, para. 57, and *Portuguese Airports, supra* n. 239, para. 20.

[264] In 1999 32 million passengers travelled between Spain and other Community countries, while domestic traffic volume was 25 million passengers. For the Canary Islands, intra-Community traffic is more than twice the size of domestic traffic.

[265] However, traffic for the 4 airports on the Azores archipelago was either entirely domestic or from third countries and therefore did not affect trade between Member States.

[266] [2000] OJ L49/37.

15(1)(b) of Regulation 17.[267] AB and Courage, another UK brewery, notified various agreements regarding the manufacture and sale of Budweiser beer to the Commission in 1992. Following S&N's acquisition of Courage in 1995, the Commission asked S&N to confirm the operation of the notified agreements. S&N replied that the revised arrangements had been entered into by Courage and AB in the summer of 1995 and had been legally transferred to S&N on completion of the Courage acquisition and that the Commission would be informed of the new agreements shortly.

In June 1997 the Commission formally asked AB and S&N under Article 11 for full details of any changes to the agreements since the novation, and was informed a month later that there had been no changes. However, in February 1998 AB and S&N, replying to competition concerns regarding the 1995 beer supply arrangements, sent the Commission revisions to those arrangements. The documentation included a letter dated February 1997 from AB to S&N which referred to guidelines regarding the marketing of Budweiser in the UK. A schedule to the letter detailed three main points: AB would take appropriate steps to ensure compliance with the guidelines; AB reserved the right to amend them at its sole discretion from time to time; and S&N pledged to use reasonable efforts to comply with them. S&N had signed the cover letter as 'agreed and accepted'. In April 1998 S&N, replying to a further request for information from the Commission, stated that the marketing guidelines formed an integral part of the beer supply agreement. This prompted the Commission to examine whether the parties had supplied incorrect information under the terms of Article 15(1)(b) of Regulation 17, which allows the Commission to fine undertakings for negligently supplying incorrect information.

While S&N agreed that the parties should have referred to the marketing guidelines in their July 1997 response to the Commission's request for information, AB denied having supplied incorrect information. According to AB, the guidelines were not an agreement within the meaning of Article 81(1), but simply non-contractual recommendations which S&N was free to disregard. However, the Commission held that referring to the arrangements as 'recommended guidelines' was not sufficient to prove they were not an agreement. Moreover, by signing the cover letter as 'agreed and accepted', S&N had not just acknowledged receipt of the guidelines, but acquiesced in their contents and significance.

AB also claimed that the guidelines did not change the 1995 beer supply agreement, as they were not incorporated into it. The Commission replied that whether or not they were incorporated was wholly irrelevant for determining whether they constituted a change to the agreement. In reply to AB's claim that S&N's April 1998 letter was not accurate, the Commission replied that its text clearly indicated S&N's view that the guidelines altered the overall arrangements between the parties.

---

[267] [1962] OJ L13/204.

Since both parties had co-operated with the Commission, and there was no evidence that they had intended to conceal the guidelines, the Commission considered that their failure to mention them was caused by negligence. Again S&N conceded it had erred in failing to inform the Commission of the guidelines. AB, however, claimed that it had not been negligent, as it was reasonable to consider that the guidelines were neither an agreement nor a change to the 1995 beer supply agreement. The Commission responded by observing that AB no doubt had ready access to legal advice and should have known better.

The Commission considered a fine was appropriate, as the supply of incorrect information may have a serious impact on the conduct of a case. Under Article 15, the Commission may levy fines of between EUR 100 to EUR 5,000 on undertakings which negligently supply incorrect information. As the Commission had discovered the existence of the guidelines through information provided by the parties themselves, it decided that the infringement should not be regarded as major, and accordingly fined both parties EUR 3,000. As S&N co-operated fully with the Commission, it may have reason to feel aggrieved that it received the same fine as AB. It may be recalled that in Bulloch/DCL,[268] a notification was deemed ineffective by the Commission as the notified documents did not include a list of prices which was crucial to the practices being notified.

III.   Cases before the Court of First Instance and the European Court of Justice

A.   ARTICLE 81

(i)   Obstacles to Parallel Trade

(a)   Bayer/Adalat[269]   For many commercial lawyers and the manufacturers they advise, this is one of the most important judgments the CFI has issued during the last two years. In its ruling, the CFI has given clear confirmation to suppliers of products which are sold at different prices in different Member States, and thus subject to significant parallel trade, that while they cannot prevent cross-border trade by purchasers, they do not commit an infringement if they refuse unwelcome orders. The news is particularly welcome to the pharmaceutical industry.

In 1996 the Commission condemned Bayer's marketing policy for the drug Adalat under Article 81(1) on the basis that an anti-competitive agreement existed between Bayer and its French and Spanish wholesalers, and fined Bayer heavily for the standards of the time (EUR 3 million).[270] There was an abundance of evidence to the effect that Bayer was opposed to parallel trade, that it had organized campaigns to detect and refuse orders which were likely

---

[268] Case 30/78, *DCL* v. *Commission* [1980] ECR 2229.
[269] Case T–41/96, *Bayer AG* v. *Commission*, [2000] ECR II–3383.
[270] [1996] OJ L201/1, (1996) 16 YEL 474.

to be exported, and that wholesalers knew of Bayer's reluctance to supply export orders and used a variety of tactics to get round the policy. There were many inflammatory documents from Bayer's own files and from the wholesalers which wanted supplies for export destinations. However imprudent Bayer may have been in internal record-keeping and external relations, it was clear that there were no contractual restrictions on imports. The Commission relied on the fact that the parties had 'pre-existing commercial relations' to find an agreement, and then claimed that the agreement deterred wholesalers from exporting Adalat to other Member States where prices were higher, as this would risk their supplies being cut by Bayer. The Commission decision also required Bayer to send a circular within two months to French and Spanish wholesalers stipulating that exports would be allowed within the Community and would not be penalized.

Bayer appealed the decision, and sought interim measures from the CFI so that it would not have to send the circular until the appeal had been decided. On 3 June 1996, the President of the Court of First Instance granted Bayer's request for interim measures in favour of Bayer, expressing doubts about the Commission's theory and recollecting the fundamental principle of freedom of contract. The doubts were confirmed in the CFI's final judgment on the merits. Sadly, the CFI—set up to achieve a more effective and fast system of review of Commission decisions—took over four years to issue this judgment annulling the decision. When it came, the judgment was notably robust, restating fundamental principles in a very trenchant manner.

The CFI annulled the Commission decision. Contrary to the findings of the Commission, the Court concluded that Bayer was not in breach of Article 81. In particular, the Court found that the Commission had incorrectly assessed the facts of the case, and had failed to demonstrate that there was an agreement between the parties to limit exports.

The CFI expressed itself very clearly:

The proof of an agreement between undertakings within the meaning of Article [81(1)] of the Treaty must be founded upon the direct or indirect finding of the existence of the subjective element that characterises *the very concept of an agreement, that is to say a concurrence of wills between economic operators on the implementation of a policy*, the pursuit of an objective, or the adoption of a given line of conduct on the market, irrespective of the manner in which the parties' intention to behave on the market in accordance with the terms of that agreement is expressed. . . . The Commission misjudges that concept of the concurrence of wills in holding that the continuation of commercial relations with the manufacturer when it adopts a new policy, which it implements unilaterally, amounts to acquiescence by the wholesalers in that policy, although their *de facto* conduct is clearly contrary to that policy [paragraph 173, emphasis added].

Paragraph 174 of the judgment delimits even further the scope of Article 81(1):

It follows that in the context of that article, the effects on the conduct of an undertaking on competition within the common market may be examined only if the existence of an agreement, a decision of an association of undertakings or a concerted practice within the meaning of Article [81(1)] of the Treaty has already been established. . . . *It follows that the aim of that provision is not to eliminate obstacles to intra-Community trade altogether; it is more limited, since only obstacles to competition set up as a result of a concurrence of wills between at least two parties are prohibited by that provision* [emphasis added].

In paragraph 176 the CFI spelled out the consequences for the manufacturer who has not been willing to make supplies available:

Having regard to the foregoing considerations, and contrary to what the Commission and the BAI [German wholesalers association] appear to maintain, the right of a manufacturer faced, as in this case, with an event harmful to his interests, to adopt the solution which seems to him to be the best is qualified by the Treaty provisions on competition only to the extent that he must comply with the prohibitions referred to in Articles [81 and 82]. Accordingly, *provided he does so without abusing a dominant position, and there is no concurrence of wills between him and his wholesalers, a manufacturer may adopt the supply policy which he considers necessary, even if, by the very nature of its aim, for example, to hinder parallel imports, the implementation of that policy may entail restrictions on competition and affect trade between Member States* [emphasis added].

Given the clear evidence of Bayer's policy of strongly discouraging parallel trading activity, these are strong words. This is not a new proposition, but its confirmation is valuable, especially in a case where it was quite clear from the internal documents taken by the Commission that Bayer took significant pains to achieve its goal of hindering parallel trade. However, Bayer was also extremely careful to ensure that this goal was never explicitly acknowledged to wholesalers, nor incorporated in an agreement.

The CFI in its press release stated as follows:

The Commission has not proved the existence of an agreement between Bayer and its Spanish and French wholesalers. The fine of 3 million ECU's is annulled. The continuance of commercial relations between, on the one hand, a manufacturer who unilaterally changes his distribution policy and, on the other, wholesalers who are clearly opposed to that new practice, *does not amount to an acquiescence by the wholesaler in that policy*, and is therefore not in itself sufficient to establish the existence of an agreement prohibited by Community competition law [emphasis added].

Although this statement by the CFI is not in any way binding, it is interesting to note what the CFI thinks it has in fact done. It has certainly clarified what constitutes an agreement within the meaning of Article 81(1): there must be a concurrence of wills. Only obstacles to competition established by a concurrence of wills are prohibited. Therefore, providing a manufacturer does not abuse a dominant position and there is no concurrence of wills, the manufacturer can adopt whatever unilateral policy he considers appropriate, even if its aim is to hinder parallel trade.

The judgment has been appealed by both the Commission and BAI. In the meantime, suppliers can rely on the fact that it is probably legal to supply set quantities by reference to national needs, to fix quantities to be supplied by reference to a wholesaler's past needs, or to fix thresholds in advance (instead of imposing sanctions after the event). However, the basic legal principles have not fundamentally changed. Thus, any type of written contractual provision in a distribution or dealer agreement, or on standard invoices or terms and conditions of sale, that indicates or suggests an export ban, would still constitute an infringement (even if there is no evidence that the provision was put into effect or that exports were affected). References in letters, faxes, or minutes of meetings to hindering parallel trade with the knowledge of others may show 'concurrence of wills' and thus an agreement, even if its terms are not reflected in a signed document. Conveying the message, when orders are accepted or delivered, that exports are unwelcome or that the purchaser is not free to supply any other Member State, may also be the basis of a complaint.

(b) Volkswagen AG v. Commission[271] The Commission decision[272] fining Volkswagen (VW) the extraordinary amount of EUR 102 million for preventing parallel imports of VW and Audi cars from Italy to other EU countries, particularly Austria and Germany, contrary to Article 81, was appealed to the CFI. VW sold its cars in Italy through a selective distribution system. The decision found that from 1988 to 1997 Volkswagen and its Italian subsidiary Autogerma imposed on their Italian authorized dealers the following measures contrary to Article 81: (i) a split-margin system where the dealer, instead of receiving an overall discount of 13 per cent on the amount invoiced for each vehicle ordered, was awarded a discount of only 8 per cent on invoice and a further 5 per cent to be paid later, upon registration of the vehicle in the contract territory; (ii) reduction of dealers' stocks; (iii) refusal to supply; (iv) when calculating the 3 per cent quarterly bonus, instead of taking into account all sales, those made outside the contract territory were taken into account only up to a maximum of 15 per cent of the total sales made by the dealer; and, (v) termination of dealership contracts and cancellation of the quarterly 3 per cent bonus for sales outside the contract territory. These measures were established to prevent sales not only to independent dealers and final users, but also to VW and Audi authorized dealers residing in Member States other than Italy. The Commission concluded that the Italian dealers did not participate actively in the barriers to re-export but were forced to consent to that policy.

The CFI largely upheld the decision. However, it annulled the Commission's finding that VW had adopted the split-margin system or termination to penalize dealers re-exporting VW and Audi cars from Italy to other Member States, and considered the Commission had not proved that the infringements lasted as long as claimed. The Court found that the 3 per cent bonus restricted opportunities for final users and authorized dealers to purchase cars in Italy, contrary to Article 81. It considered the Commission had not sufficiently proved the existence of a split-margin system: VW did impose supply quotas on its

---

[271] Case T–62/98, *Volkswagen AG v. Commission* [2000] ECR II–27.
[272] [1998] OJ L124/60.

Italian dealers, with the support of Autogerma, and was involved in refusals by its dealers to supply consumers, since documentary evidence referred to 'the satisfaction of solely Italian domestic demand' as the group's policy, and requests from consumers in other Member States for Italian cars were 'systematically' turned down with VW's acquiescence. Internal communications proved that VW did not make it clear that the measures were put in place only to prevent purchases by independent dealers, and therefore re-exports were also prevented *vis-à-vis* consumers and authorized dealers. VW had put in place a systematic policy of surveillance which was implemented by Autogerma; in particular, Autogerma's director had stated in a document that he thought it important to check personally each case where the 15 per cent rule had to apply. However, the Commission had not proved that VW terminated dealers because of their re-exporting activity, since VW successfully demonstrated that the only dealers terminated were those who sold vehicles to unauthorized resellers. The CFI considered that the restriction of competition caused by the measures was appreciable; in particular, the 15 per cent rule and the imposition of supply quotas reinforced compartmentalization of the markets. However, contrary to the Commission's findings, the CFI found that the duration of the restriction did not extend beyond October 1996.

The Court considered that the Commission does not need to define the relevant market when the infringement of Article 81 is an agreement which has as its object a restriction of competition. With regard to the concept of an agreement, a call by a motor vehicle manufacturer to its authorized dealers is not a unilateral act which falls outside the scope of Article 81(1), but is an agreement if it forms part of a set of continuous business relations governed by a general agreement drawn up in advance (*Ford* v. *Commission*;[273] *Bayerische Motorenwerke*[274]). A clause requiring customers not to sell a car less than six months after its purchase could be considered as an agreement between undertakings, since the group imposed as a condition of trading that the clause be signed by potential purchasers. Such a clause removed the protection of the block exemption.

Although the CFI found that VW's infringement was deliberate and serious, particularly in view of the size of the VW group and the fact that it was committed despite the warnings in settled case law on parallel imports in the motor vehicle industry, it nevertheless reduced the fine from EUR 102 million to 90 million. It is by no means clear that VW's behaviour deserved the heaviest single fine in history. It did not fix prices with its competitors. It was entitled to prohibit its distributors from reselling to unauthorized traders. It modified its incentives so as to encourage local sales rather than export sales. It knew that competition law favours cross-border trade, and went beyond what was legally permissible. Did these circumstances merit such massive punishment?

---

[273] Joined Cases C–25/84 and C–26/84 [1985] ECR 2725; (1985) 15 YEL 394.
[274] Case C–70/93, [1995] ECR I–3439; (1995) 15 YEL 353.

(c) Accinauto[275] *and* BASF[276] These judgments of May 1999 concerned a 1995 Commission decision[277] which condemned BASF and a Belgian company, Accinauto, for having concluded an agreement which effectively banned parallel imports. Accinauto was fined EUR 10,000 and BASF 2,700,000. Accinauto was the exclusive distributor in Belgium and Luxembourg for Glasurit, a motor vehicle refinishing paint manufactured by BASF. In January 1991 two UK-based distributors of vehicle refinishing paints complained to the Commission that at the instigation of BASF, Accinauto had stopped supplying them with Glasurit products, to prevent parallel imports of Glasurit into the UK. The Commission found that a 1982 agreement between BASF and Accinauto under which Accinauto was required, between 8 October 1982 and 31 December 1991, to pass on to BASF any customer enquiries coming from outside contract territory, infringed Article 81(1) because it had the object and effect of restricting competition between Accinauto and other suppliers of Glasurit paints, and in particular between Accinauto and BASF.

Both BASF and Accinauto alleged that the Commission had breached essential procedural requirements through failure to respect the rights of the defence. BASF claimed the Commission had not given it proper access to the file. The CFI agreed that the Commission has an obligation to make all documents available, except for the business secrets of other undertakings, internal Commission documents, or other confidential information. The Court also stated that the Commission must draw up a sufficiently detailed list of any documents which are not annexed to a Statement of Objections, so that the addressee can request access to specific documents likely to be useful in its rebuttal of the Commission's arguments. BASF had not made any specific request for access to additional documents, nor had it specified the origin or categories of any additional documents to which it wished to have access. Thus, the Commission could legitimately rely on its duty of confidentiality in rejecting BASF's request for full access to the file.

Both Accinauto and BASF denied that the 1982 agreement was aimed at preventing parallel imports of Glasurit products into the UK. However, since the obligation imposed on Accinauto under Article 2(2) of the 1982 agreement covered only enquiries coming from outside the contract territory, the CFI accepted the Commission's contention that the clause contained a disguised prohibition on passive export sales. The CFI rejected Accinauto's claim that it acted independently in its business dealings with BASF which exercised a close control on any sales by Accinauto outside the contract territory. As for BASF, if it had truly wished to be kept informed regarding the products concerned by the enquiries addressed to Accinauto, the passing-on obligation should have applied equally to enquiries from customers based in the contract territory.

---

[275] Case T–176/95, *Accinauto* v. *Commission* [1999] ECR II–1635.
[276] Case T–175/95, *BASF Lacke + Farben* v. *Commission* [1999] ECR II–1581.
[277] *BASF Lacke + Farben, and Accinauto* [1995] OJ L272/16, (1995) 15 YEL 321, 325–8.

A party need not be aware it was infringing the competition rules in order to commit the infringement intentionally; it was sufficient to be aware that the object of the offending conduct was to restrict competition. Accinauto must have realized the object of the offending clause in the 1982 agreement was to restrict parallel imports and thereby to obstruct competition.

The Court also upheld the Commission's decision not to take BASF's possibly difficult financial situation into account as a mitigating factor, since to have done so would have given BASF an unjustified competitive advantage over other businesses better adapted to market conditions.

Although the fine of EUR 10,000 imposed on Accinauto was not heavy, it should serve to discourage other undertakings from seeking to prevent parallel imports. BASF claimed the Commission had abused its power by imposing on it such a heavy fine, and put forward all the usual arguments why the fine should be reduced; the infringement was not serious; it had not lasted very long; it had not had a substantial effect on the internal market; it had not been committed intentionally; BASF was in financial difficulties; and so forth. The CFI refused to reduce the fines imposed.

(ii)   Market Foreclosure

(a)   Neste Markkinointi Oy v. Yötuuli Ky and Others[278]   The European Court of Justice was asked by a Finnish court for a preliminary ruling regarding the interpretation of Article 81(1) to a service-station agreement. The case raises some interesting questions in relation to exclusive purchasing agreements for motor fuels. It makes clear that a supply contract for fuels terminable at any time on one year's notice may be regarded as making only an insignificant contribution to the cumulative effect of closing off that market, and therefore does not fall under the prohibition in Article 81(1), even though the total number of such agreements concluded by a particular supplier may have an appreciable cumulative effect. It was recognized that motor fuel supply contracts are special, as any one service station sells only one brand of motor fuels. When assessing the foreclosure effect of the agreement, its duration rather than its exclusivity was decisive.

A 1986 agreement made Yötuuli a member of the Kesoil Oy (now Neste) distribution chain, which exclusively handled petrol and special products marketed by Kesoil Oy. The contract was concluded for ten years, after which Yötuuli could terminate it by giving one year's notice. In 1998 Yötuuli gave Neste one week's notice of its decision to cease buying its motor fuels. Neste sued for damage to compensate for Yötuuli's failure to respect the one-year notice requirement. Yötuuli claimed the contract was contrary to Article 81(1) because of the exclusive purchasing clause.

Yötuuli and Neste disagreed over whether the contract was concluded for an indefinite duration, and whether Regulation 1984/83[279] on the application of

---

[278] Case C–214–99, *Neste Markkinointi Oy* v. *Yötuuli Ky and Others*, judgment of 7 Dec. 2000, not yet reported.

[279] Commission Regulation 1984/83 of 22 June 1983 on the application of Art. 85(3) of the Treaty to categories of exclusive purchasing agreements, [1983] OJ L173/5, (1983) 13 YEL 420.

the Treaty competition rules was applicable. Neste claimed the contract was not concluded for an indefinite period and that Article 81(1) was not applicable. Yötuuli argued that it was concluded for an indefinite period, pointing to the fact that it was automatically renewed after ten years. The national court asked whether the prohibition in Article 81(1) was applicable to an exclusive purchasing agreement which the retailer could terminate at any time on one year's notice, if all such exclusive purchasing agreements concluded by that supplier had a significant influence on the partitioning of the market, either on their own or together with the network of exclusive purchasing agreements concluded by all suppliers, even if the agreements of a similar duration to the contract in question represented only a very small proportion of all that supplier's exclusive purchasing agreements. (The majority of Neste's agreements were concluded for a fixed term of several years.)

The ECJ referred to *Delimitis*,[280] stating that 'even if exclusive purchasing agreements do not have as their object the restriction of competition within the meaning of Article [81(1)], it is nevertheless necessary to ascertain whether they have the effect of preventing, restricting or distorting competition' [paragraph 25]. It stressed the need to assess the purchasing agreement in the economic and legal context, taken together with other agreements of the same type, in order to analyse its effects on the actual concrete opportunities of competitors to gain access to the relevant market or increase their market share. The Court repeated the conclusion in *Delimitis*[281] that:

if an examination of *all* similar contracts reveals that it is difficult to gain access to the relevant market, it is necessary to assess the extent to which the contracts entered into by the supplier concerned contribute to the cumulative effect produced by the totality of the agreements. Under the Community rules on competition, *responsibility for such an effect of closing off the market must be attributed to the suppliers who make an appreciable contribution thereto. Contracts entered into by suppliers whose contribution to the cumulative effect is insignificant do not therefore fall under the prohibition laid down in Article [81(1)].* In order to assess the extent of the contribution of the contracts concluded by a supplier to the cumulative sealing-off effect, the market position of the contracting parties must be taken into consideration. That contribution also depends on the duration of the agreements. If the duration is manifestly excessive in relation to the average duration of contracts generally concluded on the relevant market, the individual contract falls under the prohibition laid down in Article [81(1)] [paragraph 27, emphasis added].

The national court had found that the contract was part of a network of exclusive purchasing agreements closing off the major part of the market in motor fuels; the fact that only 5 per cent of Neste's service stations (representing 1.5 per cent of all the service stations in Finland) were tied to it by supply contracts terminable at any time on one year's notice and that many of the agreements entered into by Neste were exempted or had been amended for exemption under Regulation 1984/83. The European Court stressed the

---

[280] Case C–234/89, *Delimitis* v. *Henninger Bräu* [1991] ECR I–935, (1991) 11 YEL 421, 457–9.
[281] *Ibid.*, paras. 24–26.

special nature of motor fuels compared with other products such as beer or ice-cream, since any particular service station sells only one brand of motor fuels. It recognized that service-station agreements generally entail heavy investments and adaptation of sales points to the image of the brand sold. Having concluded that for technical reasons a change of supplier takes some time, the Court stated that the fundamental factor for motor fuels suppliers with contracts like the one in question was 'less the exclusivity clause itself than the duration of the supply obligation', the duration being 'the decisive factor in the market-sealing effect' (paragraph 32). It recognized that fixed-term contracts concluded for a number of years were more likely to restrict access to the market than those which could be terminated on short notice at any time, and considered that a one-year notice period would give the economic and legal interests of both parties to the contract reasonable protection, while limiting its restrictive effect on the market in motor-fuels distribution.

The Commission considered it was contrary to the *Delimitis* judgment to subdivide a supplier's network when assessing the effect of sealing off the market. The Court disagreed, stating:

the fact of *subdividing*, exceptionally, a *supplier's network is not arbitrary nor does it undermine the principle of legal certainty.* Subdividing the network in that way results from a factual assessment of the position held by the operator concerned on the relevant market, the *aim* of the assessment being, on the basis of an objective criterion of particular relevance in that it takes into account the market's distinctive feature, *to limit the number of cases in which a supplier's contracts are declared void to those which, together, contribute significantly to the cumulative effect of sealing off the market* [paragraph 37, emphasis added].

The Court, following the recommendation by Advocate General Fennelly, ruled that when contracts which may be terminated on one year's notice at any time represent only a very small proportion of all the exclusive purchasing agreements entered into by a particular supplier, they must be regarded as making no significant contribution to the cumulative effect in the sense of the judgment in *Delimitis*, and therefore as not being caught by the prohibition in Article 81(1). The judgment reflects the more liberal stand often adopted by the Court, and now influencing the Commission in its general approach to distribution.

(iii)   Cartels

The last two years have seen several important cartel judgments from the CFI and ECJ. The Commission has continued to lose some cases owing to imperfectly analysed evidence of company participation in cartel practices, and the imposition of unjustifiably high fines has not been accepted by the Court.

(a)   The Cement *Cases*[282]   The largest competition case ever dealt with by the CFI (over 40 undertakings or associations of undertakings in sixteen

---

[282] Joined Cases T–25/95, T–26/95, T–30–32/95, T–34–39/95, T–42–46/95, T–48/95, T–50–65/95, T–68/95, T–71/95, T–87–88/95, T–103/95 and T–104/95 [2000] ECR II–491.

European states) ended with a reduction of almost EUR 140 million in the fines imposed on the participants. The CFI carried out an extremely thorough analysis of all the applicants' arguments. Although its judgment was very long, it was not difficult or complicated by arcane legal reasoning.

In November 1994 the Commission decided[283] that cement producers had concluded a series of agreements and concerted practices designed to share the European markets for grey cement and white cement. According to the Commission, those agreements and concerted practices constituted a single and continuous infringement involving forty-two European undertakings and associations of undertakings. The CFI confirmed the Commission's finding that the agreement was established at the meeting of 'Head Delegates' of the industry on 14 January 1983 and confirmed at subsequent meetings of Head Delegates on 19 March and 7 November 1984 and that the agreement had an anti-competitive objective, establishing a rule of 'non-transshipment to home markets' which prohibited any export of cement within Europe that might destabilize neighbouring markets (paragraph 1085).

The Commission considered that the cement undertakings took part in the agreement either directly, or indirectly through their representation by a trade association. However, the CFI ruled that in order to prove that an undertaking had been involved in the agreement, the Commission should have demonstrated that it had clearly shown its accession to the agreement by actually participating in a measure implementing the agreement. Membership of a national association which took part in the meetings of the Head Delegates was not sufficient to prove participation in the agreement. Several applicants which did not attend the meeting on 14 January 1983 claimed that following this reasoning, the decision held they were represented at that meeting and therefore took part in the infringement from its starting date, although the Commission had not taken that approach in the Statement of Objections. The CFI agreed the Statement of Objections should have stated that the Commission had decided to adopt 14 January 1983 as the starting date of the infringement for all the addressees of the decision. It therefore ignored the Commission's test of 'representation', and itself established the date when each individual undertaking began to take part in the infringement.

The national associations of cement producers claimed that the Statement of Objections did not state the Commission's intention of fining them. The CFI agreed, and annulled the fines imposed on the associations.

The applicants complained of various infringements of their right to a fair hearing during the administrative procedure. Nearly all of them alleged that, by not giving them sufficient access to the investigation file during the administrative procedure, the Commission had deprived them of evidence which might have been useful to their defence. During the proceedings the CFI obtained the investigation file from the Commission and made it available for inspection by the parties. Much time and expenditure was devoted by

---

[283] [1994] OJ L343/1.

representatives of the applicants to photocopying reams of previously unrevealed information, and as a result two of the applicants (Cedest and Rugby) were able to exculpate themselves altogether, while others were able to offer the Court better documentation of their claims.

The CFI agreed the infringement consisted of a single agreement between cement undertakings which aimed to ensure that the rule of non-transshipment to home markets was observed. One notable feature of the story was the suggestion that a group of leading producers had organized a campaign of dissuasion and retaliation against the Greek producers who turned from the Middle Eastern markets to Western Europe. A so-called Task Force co-ordinated 'carrot and stick' actions with a view to removing 'excess tonnage' from Western Europe and reselling it in distant markets, and to punishing Greek operations in the UK, Italy, or elsewhere. It seemed difficult to believe that the Greek producers had been full participants in the 'cartel'.

The CFI ruled that the participation in the agreement of Buzzi, ENCI, Castle, Titan, Heracles, Nordcement, and Alsen Breitenburg was not sufficiently proved, and therefore annulled the fines imposed on them. The CFI found that all the other addressees of the decision had taken part in the infringement for shorter periods than those stated in the decision. Finally, since the fines were calculated according to the gravity and duration of the infringement, the CFI substantially reduced the fines imposed even on the undertakings whose participation in the agreement had been proved.

In any event, one has the impression that the Commission could better have concentrated on a small number of leading players rather than claiming that almost the entire industry was engaged in a 'single and continuous' agreement for more than a decade.

(b) PVC *Appeal*[284] Following investigations conducted in the polyvinyl-chloride (PVC) sector, the European Commission adopted a decision on 21 December 1988 penalizing fourteen PVC producers for infringement of the Community prohibition of cartels. This decision was annulled by the CFI and (on appeal) by the Court of Justice on a number of procedural grounds. Following the judgment on appeal, the Commission adopted a new decision ('the Decision') on 27 July 1994 against twelve of the producers concerned by the initial decision. The new Decision found that the twelve undertakings had infringed what is now Article 81(1) by participating in an agreement or concerted practice from August 1980 and engaging in the usual cartel activities— taking part in regular meetings in order to fix target prices and quotas, planning concerted initiatives to raise price levels and monitoring the operation of those collusive arrangements. The Decision was again appealed to the CFI by all twelve undertakings. The case raised procedural issues of particular interest, notably the question whether the Commission was entitled to adopt

---

[284] Joined Cases T–305–307/94, T–313–316/94, T–318/94, T–325/94, T–328–329/94, T–335/94 [1999] ECR II–0931.

the new Decision in 1994, after the Court had annulled the initial decision of 1988 for formal defects. On the merits, the issues relating to the calculation of fines are noteworthy.

The applicants claimed that following the annulment of the first Decision by the Court, the Commission was prevented from adopting a decision on four grounds: the principle of *res judicata;* the principle of *non bis in idem;* the passage of time; and the abuse of discretionary power.

- the applicants argued that the Court, using its powers under Article 54(1)(2) of the EC Statute of the Court of Justice,[285] had ruled on the dispute as a whole and intended its annulment of the initial decision to bring the proceedings against the PVC producers to a definitive close. Otherwise, substantive pleas would be accorded a higher status than procedural ones and procedural irregularities could be easily corrected. This plea was dismissed on the grounds that the principle of *res judicata* extends only to the matters of fact and law settled by a judicial decision. But the annulment decision was based on only one single procedural infringement, the Court having considered it not 'necessary to examine the other pleas raised by the applicants' (paragraph 78). Thus the remaining pleas were not covered by the principle of *res judicata*. Moreover, under Article 54(1)(2) of the Statute, the Court of Justice does not, when it gives final judgment in a dispute by accepting one or more pleas raised, automatically settle all the points of fact and law raised.
- the applicants alleged that by adopting the Decision the Commission had infringed the general legal principle of *non bis in idem*, which prohibits both the imposition of two penalties for the same offence and the initiation of proceedings for infringement twice in respect of the same set of facts. The Court agreed that this would indeed be the case if the Commission brought proceedings against an undertaking or imposed a fine on anti-competitive conduct on whose existence or otherwise the Community Courts had already ruled. However, this was not the case here, since the first Commission decision had been annulled and therefore did not result in a penalty. Moreover, when the CFI annulled the first decision, it had not ruled on any substantive pleas, which were therefore not foreclosed.
- the applicants alleged the Commission had infringed the requirement that it must take a decision within a reasonable time, had abused their rights, and had disregarded the principles concerning the right to a fair hearing.

The Court confirmed the general principle of Community law whereby decisions following administrative proceedings relating to competition law must be adopted within a reasonable time (paragraph 121). However,

---

[285] Art. 54 (1)(2) of the EC Statute of the Court of Justice reads: 'if the appeal is well founded, the Court of Justice shall quash the decision of the Court of First Instance. It may itself give final judgment in the matter, where the state of proceedings so permits, or refer the case back to the Court of First Instance for judgment'.

in a highly complex cartel case, the Court considered that the time taken by the Commission did not exceed what was 'reasonable'. The Court distinguished between two time periods. The first began in November 1983 with the investigation in the PVC sector and took fifty-two months, while the second started on the date when each undertaking received the Statement of Objections and lasted ten months. As a general rule, whether the time taken for a procedure is reasonable depends on the individual circumstances of the case, in particular its context, the conduct of the parties during the procedure, what is at stake for the various undertakings concerned, and its complexity. In this particular case, the Court found the length of the injury procedure reasonable in view of the bulk and complexity of the information on file. The ten-month period was not sufficiently long in itself to justify a complaint of undue delay.

- the applicants argued that the Commission was not legally obligated to adopt a new decision after an earlier decision was annulled, but had discretion to do so or not. In this case the Commission had misused its discretionary power by not observing the principle of proportionality. The objective of the new Decision was not to safeguard competition in the PVC sector, but to overrule the CFI's finding that the Commission had breached procedural rules. The Commission agreed it had discretion to refrain from acting. However, assuming that it was required to justify the adoption of the new Decision, besides its wish to ensure the competition rules were applied in the sector in compliance with the judgment concerned, the fines imposed were in themselves sufficient justification for the adoption of the Decision.

The Court found that the Commission had fulfilled its duty as guardian of the Treaty, in particular the competition rules. The Court considered the formal reference to this duty in the preamble to the Decision was sufficient reasoning to support the need for the Commission to intervene, and the proportionality of its intervention.

The applicants also argued that the CFI judgment had had the effect of annulling the initial decision in its entirety. This *erga omnes* effect precluded the adoption of a further decision, in particular because it rendered all the procedural measures invalid, and it applied to all fourteen undertakings in the case. The failure of the new Decision to condemn two undertakings condemned in the initial decision (Solvay and Norsk Hydro) therefore constituted discrimination against the twelve remaining undertakings. The Commission defined the initial decision as effectively a bundle of individual decisions, and pointed out that the individual decisions against Solvay and Norsk Hydro had become final because neither undertaking had challenged them judicially. Hence their exclusion from the new Decision did not constitute discrimination against the other undertakings.

The applicants went on to argue that the annulment of the 1988 decision necessarily nullified the procedural acts prior to that decision, since they were inextricably linked to it. Thus the Commission could not adopt a new decision without conducting a fresh administrative procedure, including further consultation of the 'Advisory Committee' and a further hearing of the parties. The Commission observed that the only ground for annulling the 1988 decision was the lack of authentication within the meaning of Article 12 of the Rules of Procedure. The prior administrative procedure was not affected and was therefore still valid. Alleged differences in wording between the 1988 decision and the new Decision were not substantial. Purely editorial changes to the text did not justify the opening of a new procedure.

The Court again upheld the Commission's view. The annulment of the decision for a procedural defect did not affect the validity of preparatory measures which were taken prior to the stage when the defect occurred, in this case the final stage of adoption. The reason for annulling the 1988 decision was its lack of authentication, so that only the manner in which it was finally adopted was defective. The entire procedure would be vitiated by illegality if important rights, for example the defence's right to have full access to a file, had been infringed. There was no need to hold a new hearing before adopting the new Decision, since the undertakings themselves agreed that it contained no new challenges to their behaviour compared with the 1988 decision.

On the merits, the Court confirmed the existence of the infringement found by the Commission and the participation by the twelve undertakings in that infringement. The Court rejected the pleas of nine of the undertakings regarding the fines in their entirety and confirmed the amounts in question. However, it accepted the arguments of the other three for a reduction. The evidence on which the Court relied to reduce the fines is noteworthy. The basis of the investigation leading to the discovery of the cartel was an unsigned, handwritten note on a sheet of paper, with the initials of companies and their market shares. In the case of Société Artésienne de Vinyle, the Court found that, contrary to the applicant's submissions, the documents produced by the Commission were sufficient to establish that the company participated in the infringement. However, the Court took into account only the participation of the company from August 1980 to June 1981 and thus reduced its fine from EUR 400,000 to EUR 135,000. (The Commission had considered that the company took part in the cartel up until April 1983.)

The Court reduced the fines imposed on Elf Atochem SA and ICI from EUR 3,200,000 to EUR 2,600,000, and from EUR 2,500,000 to EUR 1,550,000, respectively. The Court's investigation of the case showed that in fixing the amount of the fine, the Commission took account of each undertaking's market share, in order to ensure a proportionate allocation of the total fine between the undertakings concerned. In what is likely to be an important clarification for future cartel appeals, the Court stated that in general the Commission is entitled to take into account when calculating fines both the volume and value of the goods which are the subject-matter of the infringement, and the size and economic strength of the undertaking concerned, and not merely their sales in the market where the infringement took place. However, in this case the Court found that the Commission had exaggerated the market shares of the two undertakings when determining the fine.

(c)   Polypropylene *Appeal*[286]   In 1986 the Commission issued a decision[287] fining fifteen polypropylene producers almost EUR 60 million for cartel activities including price fixing and market allocation. This amount was then a record. Fourteen of the producers individually appealed to the ECJ, which three years later referred the cases to the CFI. The CFI issued its judgments between October 1991 and March 1992.[288] Nine of the fourteen producers appealed to the ECJ, which finally issued its rulings in July 1999.

During the course of its investigation into the polypropylene sector, the Commission discovered a second cartel involving the polyvinylchloride (PVC) market. The final round in the PVC cartel is reported above. Although many of the parties in the two actions were the same, the issues involved were distinct; thus the Commission handled the two cases separately. Nevertheless, the long delay between the CFI judgments and the ECJ judgments in the polypropylene cases is due in part to the link between these cases and the PVC case. Despite objections by several parties, the ECJ stayed the proceedings in the polypropylene cases shortly after they began in order to see whether there were any 'appropriate conclusions to be drawn' in relation to the appeal of the 1992 CFI judgment in the PVC case. The ECJ recommenced consideration of the polypropylene cases in September 1994, after issuing its judgment in respect to the PVC appeal.

What links the two sets of cases is a procedural discrepancy that came to light during the PVC case and posed a threat to virtually all previous Commission acts. During the oral hearing of the 1992 CFI case relating to PVC, and at a press conference following the CFI's judgment, members of the Commission's services made statements to the effect that 'all its recent decisions had been taken in the same way as in the PVC cases' (that is, in apparent breach of Article 12 of the Commission's Rules of Procedure). In the *PVC* case the Commission admitted that there had been a long-standing practice whereby the President of the Commission merely signed the minutes of the Commissioners' weekly meeting, rather than each individual decision adopted.

The ECJ rejected allegations that the CFI had committed an error of law by refusing to reopen the oral procedure and order measures of inquiry, particularly where such requests were based on '[i]ndications of a general nature con-

---

[286]   Case C–200/92, *ICI* v. *Commission* [1999] ECR I–4399; Case C–234/92, *Shell* v. *Commission* [1999] ECR I–4501; Case C–227/92, *Hoechst* v. *Commission* [1999] ECR I–4443; Case C–235/92, *Montecatini* v. *Commission* [1999] ECR I–4539; Case 51/92, *Hercules Chemicals* v. *Commission* [1999] ECR I–4235; Case C–49/92, *Commission* v. *Anic* [1999] ECR I–4125; Case C–199/92, *Huls* v. *Commission* [1999] ECR I–4287; Case C–5/93, *DSM* v. *Commission* [1999] ECR I–4695; Case C–245/92, *Chemie Linz* v. *Commission* [1999] ECR I–4643.

[287]   [1986] OJ L230/1, (1986) 6 YEL 379, 384–6.

[288]   Cases T–1/89 to T–4/89 and T–6/89 to 15/89, *Rhône Poulenc* v. *Commission et seq.* [1991] ECR II–867, (1992) 12 YEL 547, 617, 625–7, 735–6.

cerning an alleged practice of the Commission and emerging from judgment delivered in other cases [and on] statements made on the occasion of other proceedings' (*ICI*, paragraph 63). The CFI's interpretation of the circumstances capable of rendering a Commission decision null and void was correct, and the gravity of the alleged irregularities in this case was not sufficiently obvious as to merit such a finding.

The parties pleaded a variety of other claims which were dismissed by the ECJ, with the exception of Anic's case, where the Commission had appealed the CFI's judgment annulling Article 1 of the decision and reducing Anic's fine by EUR 300,000. The ECJ held that the CFI had committed an error of law in its interpretation of a concerted practice when it ruled that the undertakings' collusive practices necessarily had an effect on the conduct of the participating undertakings. The ECJ stated that the concept of concerted practice as set out in Article 81(1) includes conduct on the market pursuant to collusive conduct, as well as a relationship of cause and effect between the two. This error of law, however, had no impact on the operative part of the contested judgment, which was well founded on other legal grounds. This is thus an example of what American lawyers would call harmless error.

The Commission's appeal related to the establishment of the principle that where undertakings agree to maintain certain price levels, each undertaking is responsible for *all* the activities aimed at maintaining prices, not just those in which it participates. The ECJ held that the decision was founded on the concept of a single infringement, meaning that the decision was based on a finding that Anic was responsible for the entire infringement, not on a finding that Anic had participated in all of the activities in question. The ECJ further found that the CFI had accepted this interpretation of the decision at various points in the contested judgment. The CFI's judgment therefore contained a contradiction, since it annulled the decision in so far as it attributed to Anic responsibility for certain conduct, on the ground that the Commission had not demonstrated Anic's participation. The ECJ therefore set aside the relevant part of the CFI judgment and gave final judgment itself: although the CFI's decision to reduce the amount of the fine was based on incorrect premises as to Anic's participation in the concerted practice for a particular time period, Anic's actual participation in those activities was marginal, so the Court considered it appropriate to confirm the CFI's reduction in the fine. Thus Anic lost as to its theories, but retained its financial advantage.

The saga which began with investigations in 1983 is now finally over.

(d)   Steel Beams[289]   The CFI was presented with the question of the proper interpretation of the anti-cartel provisions of the ECSC Treaty in the steel beams appeals, in particular, whether Article 65 of the ECSC Treaty mirrored Article 81 of the EC Treaty in light of the different objectives of the two treaties,

[289] Case T–141/94, *Thyssen Stahl AG v. Commission* [1999] ECR II–347. See also Cases T–134/94 [1999] ECR II–239, T–136–138/94 [1999] ECR II–263, T–145/94 [1999] ECR II–585, T–147–148/94 [1991] ECR II–603, T–151/94 [1991] ECR II–629, T–156–157/94 [1999] ECR II–645.

and how the competition rules should be applied to a scenario where an industry is emerging from a situation of managed trade.

For much of the 1980s the steel industry was effectively in crisis. The Commission was working closely with the industry to try to resolve this. In 1988 the crisis regime formally came to an end. The Commission then took pains to make it clear that the industry had to take account of the competition rules, and in that year commenced an investigation into stainless steel price fixing. In 1990, a decision was taken in the stainless steel case.[290] Then, in 1991, the Commission carried out dawn raids at companies producing steel beams, and in 1994 the Commission fined fourteen companies around ECU 104 million in total for price fixing, market sharing and exchanging confidential information. Eleven companies appealed the Commission's decision, and were granted a partial victory by the CFI. Their fines were reduced, in some cases by as much as one-third, for a variety of reasons.

The case was delicate since it was argued that the Commission had been involved in and had encouraged or at the very least tolerated the infringements. The relationship between DG Industry (formerly DG III) responsible for working to ameliorate the situation of the steel industry under the ECSC Treaty and DG Competition (formerly DG IV) responsible for ensuring the application of the competition rules to the industry is interestingly detailed in the judgment.[291] The Commission had also got many of the facts wrong in its press release and in the way Commissioner Van Miert announced the case. This was embarrassing, even though the applicants were unsuccessful in their arguments that it constituted a breach of their procedural rights.

The Commission submitted some 11,000 documents, including internal minutes and reports, to the Court in the course of the case, and the CFI heard a number of Commission officials as witnesses, as well as expert witnesses regarding the background to the ECSC Treaty and economic issues, and even watched a video of the Press Conference with Commissioner Van Miert announcing the decision.

The Court repeated its jurisprudence that attendance by an undertaking at meetings involving anti-competitive activities suffices to establish its participation in those activities, in the absence of proof capable of establishing the contrary.[292] It confirmed that Article 65 of the ECSC should be interpreted in the same way as Article 81 of the EC Treaty (paragraphs 270, 303). It found that

---

[290] Decision 90/417/ECSC relating to a proceeding under Art. 65 of the ECSC Treaty concerning an agreement and concerted practices engaged in by European producers of cold-rolled stainless steel flat products ([1990] OJ L220/28) ('the Stainless Steel decision'), by which it imposed fines ranging from ECU 25,000 to ECU 100,000 on a number of steel undertakings.

[291] According to the Court, 'the Commission [DG Industry] was thus led to authorize, guarantee or encourage conduct apparently contrary to the normal rules governing the working of the common market, which are based on the principle of the market . . . and therefore liable to come within the prohibition of agreements under Art. 65 of the Treaty. It is also clear from a number of official documents . . . and . . . minutes that the Commission was openly in favour of certain "private arrangements", "concertations", "internal agreements" and "voluntary systems" drawn up by the undertakings' (Paragraph 494).

[292] See Case T–14/89, *Montedipe* v. *Commission* [1992] ECR II–1155, paras. 129 and 144.

the facts established by the Commission showed the existence of agreements and concerted practices to fix prices and share markets. With regard to the question of the exchange of information, the CFI upheld the Commission's view that the exchange of information substantially restricted competition between the parties, and was in fact used by the parties for collusive purposes. It confirmed the application of the case law in the *UK Agricultural Tractors case*[293] to the ECSC Treaty sector. It also agreed that the exchange of information was a separate infringement from price fixing and market sharing under Article 65(1), and the Commission was justified in imposing an element of the fine specifically in relation to that offence (paragraphs 385–411).

However, the CFI accepted that the cartel had misled the Commission about its true activities, and concealed the information which was actually in circulation from the Commission:

The Court concludes from all of the foregoing that, from 1988 on, the steel undertakings and their trade association Eurofer submitted to the Commission relatively general and imprecise information, whilst engaging, in support of their agreements in restraint of competition, in very precise and detailed discussions, individualised at the level of the undertakings, the existence and content of which they hid from both DG III and DG IV. The undertakings were fully aware of the substantive difference between those two categories of information, and they deliberately made sure that only one category, and not the other, was brought to the Commission's knowledge [paragraphs 552 and 553].

In addition, the Court found that certain elements of the price fixing had not been proved (for example, in the case of Thyssen Stahl, the CFI agreed it was not proved that there had been price fixing as regards Germany and Denmark for a certain period).

The CFI sought extremely detailed information from the Commission on the methodology employed in imposing the fines in the case. Some 100 paragraphs of the judgment are employed in setting out and assessing this methodology, and concluding that the fines were not justified. The CFI—rather contradictorily—considered the Commission had adequately set out its reasoning for the level of the fines in the decision, while accepting the 'desirability' of it providing its methodology in detail for a company (and if necessary the Court) to review:

it [is] desirable for undertakings—in order to be able to define their position in full knowledge of the facts—to be able to determine in detail, in accordance with any system which the Commission might consider appropriate, the method of calculation of the fine imposed upon them by a decision for infringement of the rules on competition, without being obliged, in order to do so, to bring court proceedings against the Commission decision.

That applies *a fortiori* where, as here, the Commission has used detailed arithmetical formulas to calculate the fines. It is desirable in such a case that the undertakings concerned and, if need be, the Court should be in a position to check that the method

---

[293] Case C–7/95 P, *John Deere* v. *Commission* [1998] ECR I–3111, paras. 88–90, and Case T–35/92, *John Deere* v. *Commission* [1994] ECR II–957, para. 51.

employed and the steps followed by the Commission are free of error and compatible with the provisions and principles applicable in regard to fines, and in particular with the principle of non-discrimination.

It must, however, be pointed out that such figures, provided at the request of one party or of the Court pursuant to Articles 64 and 65 of the Rules of Procedure, do not constitute an additional *a posteriori* statement of reasons for the Decision, but are rather the translation into figures of the criteria set out in the Decision where they are themselves capable of being quantified.

In this case, although the Decision does not contain any indications as to how the fine was calculated, the Commission provided, during the present proceedings, at the request of the Court, figures relating, in particular, to the breakdown of the fine according to the various infringements with which the undertakings were charged [paragraphs 608–611].

One reason for the reduction of the fine by the CFI was that the Commission had erred in characterizing certain companies as 'recidivists' and fining them more heavily. The Court considered that the fact that a company had been investigated by the Commission and then received a Statement of Objections in the earlier *Stainless Steel* case did not make it a recidivist, particularly in view of the fact that the infringement period in the *Steel Beams* case was prior to the *Stainless Steel* case (paragraphs 514–525). In order to be guilty of recidivism, it seems that a company must have been named in a previous decision prior to a new investigation commencing. The CFI also reduced the fine on the basis that 'the Commission had exaggerated the economic impact of the price-fixing agreements found here, as compared with the competition which would have existed had it not been for such infringements, having regard to the favourable economic climate and the latitude given to undertakings to conduct general discussions on price forecasts, between themselves and with DG III, in the context of meetings organized by DG III on a regular basis' (paragraph 645). Finally, a further reduction was made to reflect the CFI's finding that certain aspects of the price-fixing agreement found by the Commission were not proved.

(e) Cartonboard[294] In July 1994 the Commission condemned the cartel activities of nineteen cartonboard producers and imposed fines totalling EUR 131,750,000.[295] Seventeen companies and four Finnish firms which were members of the trade association Finnboard challenged that Decision before the CFI. In May 1998 the CFI reduced the fines imposed on four of those companies, bringing the total fine to EUR 120,330,000.[296] Thirteen undertakings subsequently asked the Court of Justice to annul or reduce their fines.

The original Commission investigation had resulted from complaints brought in 1990 by the British Printing Industries Federation, representing UK

---

[294] Joined Cases C–248/98 P, C–279/98 P, C–280/98 P, Cases C–282/98 P, C–283/98 P, C–286/98 P, C–291/98 P, C–294/98 P, C–297/98 P and C–298/98 P, [2000] ECR I–9641.

[295] [1994] OJ L243/1, (1994) 14 YEL 458.

[296] Cases T–295/94 and others, [1998] ECR II–813, (1998) 18 YEL 562.

printed carton producers, and the Fédération Française du Cartonnage. The Commission found that the nineteen cartonboard suppliers had infringed Article 81(1) by participating in an agreement and concerted practice from mid-1986 until at least April 1991. The cartel involved the planning and implementation of simultaneous and uniform price increases, regular meetings to discuss and agree a common plan to restrict competition, the maintenance of market shares at constant levels, the instigation from early 1990 of concerted measures to control the supply of cartonboard in the EC to ensure implementation of the price rises and the exchange of commercial information to support these measures.

The ECJ gave judgment on the appeals in November 2000. It dismissed the five appeals brought by Enso Española, Mo och Domsjö, SCA, Metsä-Serla Sales Oy (previously Finnboard), and the four Finnish companies found jointly and severally liable with Finnboard (Metsä-Serla, UPM-Kymmene, Tamrock, and Kyro). It held that none of these undertakings had succeeded in showing that the CFI had erred in its reasoning. Consequently, despite the lengthy appeal proceedings before the ECJ, none of these companies succeeded in reducing their original fines (the CFI had cut Enso Española's fine by EUR 550,000). Notably, the enormous EUR 22,750,000 fine imposed on Mo och Domsjö remains in place.

This was the first case in which the Commission had reduced fines for undertakings which had co-operated with it. It is by no means clear that the companies which volunteered the painful truth (notably Stora) felt their candour was adequately acknowledge in the levels of fines imposed.

SCA Holdings Ltd put forward an optimistic argument in its appeal to the ECJ. While some undertakings had not contested the facts found by the Commission and had had their fines reduced as a result, SCA's fine had not been reduced, although it had not expressed any view on the Commission's factual allegations. SCA claimed the CFI was incorrect to hold that its attitude did not entitle it to be treated in the same way as the other undertakings. Not surprisingly, the ECJ confirmed that:

an undertaking which . . . merely states during the administrative procedure . . . that it is not expressing any view on the Commission's factual allegations, and thus does not acknowledge the correctness of those allegations, does not in fact further the Commission's task. Where the undertaking involved does not expressly acknowledge the facts, the Commission will have to prove those facts and the undertaking is free to put forward, at the appropriate time and in particular in the procedure before the Court, any plea in its defence which it deems appropriate [paragraph 37].

The ECJ confirmed that the four Finnboard members could be held responsible for the trade association's anti-competitive behaviour because Finnboard had not determined its own behaviour on the market but had primarily carried out instructions issued by the other companies. There were also strong economic and legal ties between them. The Court also confirmed in the individual appeal brought by Metsä-Serla Sales Oy that when an association of companies is fined and the turnover of that association does not reflect its size or strength on the market, the only way to impose a sanction which is dissuasive is to take into account the turnover of its members.

Three of the remaining five appellants had their fines reduced by the ECJ. The CFI had reduced the original fine of EUR 3,000,000 on the Dutch company, NV Koninklijke KNP BT to EUR 2,700,000. The ECJ reduced the fine by a further EUR 100,000. It held that the CFI had failed to deal with KNP's argument that it had acquired the infringing company, Badische, only at the end of 1986, whereas the Commission had attributed the infringement to KNP from mid-1986.

KNP also claimed (as did other appellants) that the Commission had failed properly to explain the reasoning behind its calculation of fines and that the CFI should have annulled its Decision for this reason. The ECJ considered whether the duty to state reasons under Article 253 required the Commission to provide a more detailed explanation of its methods of calculation than simply the elements of appreciation relating to gravity and duration, and held that while it might be desirable for the Commission to give more details, its obligations under Article 253 were fulfilled if it indicated those elements. It found that the CFI had erred in law by holding that the decision must set out any basic factors which the Commission had systematically taken into account in order to fix the level of fines. However, the ECJ held that this did not mean that the CFI judgment should be annulled, as the CFI had correctly rejected the claim that the Commission had infringed its obligation to provide reasons regarding the calculation of fines.

The CFI had reduced the original fine on the German producer Moritz J. Weig GmbH from EUR 3,000,000 to EUR 2,500,000 to reflect the actual duration of its infringement (the CFI held that Weig had not participated in the first twenty-two months of the infringement). On appeal, the Court of Justice held that the CFI had discriminated against Weig by not applying the same method of calculation when adjusting its fine as it had adopted in respect of other undertakings which had likewise co-operated with the Commission. The CFI had not explicitly stated that it was using the Commission's method of calculation (relevant turnover x percentage in respect of the gravity of the infringement x percentage in respect of duration = total, less reduction for co-operation) to set the fines. However, it had not criticized this method and appeared in fact to have used it when adjusting fines for companies other than Weig. In light of this discrimination, the ECJ reduced Weig's fine to EUR 1,900,000.

The Commission had imposed on the Spanish producer Sarrió a fine of EUR 15,500,000, which the CFI had reduced to EUR 14,000,000. Sarrió raised a number of arguments on appeal. First, it argued that the CFI had failed to check whether the infringement was narrower than that found by the Commission. It claimed to have been involved only in indirect price fixing on catalogue prices, rather than direct price fixing on actual pricing. The ECJ, however, ruled that the CFI's finding was not contradictory, since it had held that Sarrío's aim in fixing catalogue prices was to increase actual customer prices. Sarrío also claimed its participation in meetings which had an anti-competitive objective did not mean that it was behaving anti-competitively; the Commission must show it had put into effect the decisions taken at those meetings. Not surprisingly, the ECJ rejected this line of argument as well. It confirmed the CFI's ruling that a company which does not implement the results of anti-competitive meetings is not absolved of responsibility unless it publicly distances itself from the content of those meetings, which Sarrió had not done. In response to another claim by Sarrió, the ECJ confirmed that the 10 per cent ceiling on fines referred to in Article 15(2) of Regulation 17[297] did indeed refer to the financial year preceding the date of the Decision, whereas it was necessary to look to the turnover at the date of the infringement (and hence the exchange rates applicable at that time) when considering the impact of a company's behaviour.

Finally, Sarrió claimed the CFI had discriminated against it by using a different method of calculation when reducing its fine from that used by the Commission. Had the CFI used the Commission's method, its fine would have been reduced by an additional EUR 250,000. The ECJ noted that the CFI had held that Sarrió's subsidiary, Prat Carton, had been involved only in collusion on price and stoppage times, and not in maintenance of market shares at constant levels, and only from June 1990 to February 1991. The CFI had not questioned the Commission's method of calculation, and if it had intended to apply a different method, it should have given its reasons for doing so. Consequently, the ECJ accepted the appellant's argument and further reduced the fine by EUR 250,000 to EUR 13,750,000. Was it worth the effort? Sarrió, having lost on its other grounds of appeal, was ordered to pay not only its own costs but also two-thirds of the Commission's costs—the total was no doubt considerably more than EUR 250,000.

The Cartonboard saga will continue to run. The ECJ referred two of the appeals back to the CFI. The Commission had imposed a fine of EUR 16,200,000 on the French producer, Cascades. The CFI had rejected most of Cascades' arguments and had not reduced its fine. However, the ECJ held that the CFI had committed an error of law in holding Cascades responsible for infringements committed by the Swedish company, Djupafors AB, and the Belgian company, Van Duffel NV, prior to their acquisition by Cascades. The ECJ held that the person or company managing the company at the time the infringement was committed must take responsibility for that infringement, even if someone else was responsible for the company by the time the decision finding infringement was taken. Djupafors and Duffel participated in the infringement independently from mid-1986 until their acquisition by Cascades in March 1989, after which they pursued their activities as subsidiaries and must therefore, in the Court's view, answer for their infringements prior to their acquisition. The ECJ therefore annulled the CFI's judgment, but since the documents before the Court did not indicate what

---

[297] *Supra* n. 1.

proportion of the overall fine was attributable to the activities of Duffel and Djupafors before their acquisition, it referred the case back to the CFI to set the new fine.

The appeal by Stora Kopparbergs Bergslags AB against the fine of EUR 11,250,000 imposed on it was also referred back to the CFI. Stora claimed the CFI had erred in law by attributing the infringement of its subsidiary Koppafors to it, without taking into consideration the Commission's inability to establish whether Stora actually exercised any influence on Koppafors' commercial policy. The ECJ reiterated that:

the fact that a subsidiary has separate legal personality is not sufficient to exclude the possibility of its conduct being imputed to the parent company, especially where the subsidiary does not independently decide its own conduct on the market, but carries out, in all material respects, the instructions given to it by the parent company [paragraph 26].

Since Stora owned the entire share capital of Koppafors and had not disputed that it was in a position to exert a decisive influence on its subsidiary's commercial policy, nor submitted any evidence to support its assertion that Koppafors behaved autonomously, the ECJ upheld the CFI's conclusion that Koppafors' behaviour could be attributed to Stora. As regards the appellant's claim that the CFI effectively placed the burden of proof on Stora by requiring it to produce evidence to support its claim that Koppafors was autonomous, the ECJ held:

As that subsidiary was wholly owned, the Court of First Instance could legitimately assume . . . that the parent company in fact exercised decisive influence over its subsidiary's conduct, particularly since it had found . . . that during the administrative procedure the appellant had presented itself as being, as regards companies in the Stora Group, the Commission's sole interlocutor concerning the infringement in question. In those circumstances it was for the appellant to reverse that presumption by adducing sufficient evidence [paragraph 29].

This is clearly a lesson for other companies not to present themselves as interlocutors for supposedly independent subsidiaries.

However, the ECJ did accept Stora's claim that the CFI had erred by arguing that it was responsible for infringements committed by its subsidiaries Feldmühle and CBC before their acquisition by Stora, because it must have been aware of their participation in the infringement. The ECJ confirmed that since Stora acquired Feldmühle and CBC only in September 1990, responsibility for their actions before that date had to be attributed to whoever managed them in the period preceding their acquisition. Since the ECJ was unable to determine from the documents before it what portion of Stora's 1990 turnover was attributable to Feldmühle and CBC, the case was referred back to the CFI to review the fine.

Another milestone in the cartel sector occurred in *Woodpulp*.[298] The ECJ overturned the CFI's ruling and confirmed that the Commission is not

---

[298] Case C–310/97 P *Assi Domän Kraft Products and Others* [1999] ECR I–5363.

required to review its original decision imposing fines as regards addressees of that decision who have chosen not to appeal it.

It seems that on the whole those who have elected to appeal the imposition on them of fines for participation in cartel matters have frequently been successful. The chances of coming away from the experience with something more than a bill for legal costs are high. In particular, arguments regarding the proven duration of the infringements, access to the file, and relevant fining criteria are likely to be taken seriously by the Courts. Furthermore, the obligation on the Commission to substantiate its fining decisions has been increased; but since the Commission does not seem to have to include this in great detail in its decision, an appeal may be necessary to elicit the information. It is not easy to see why Volkswagen had to pay EUR 90 million even after appeal to the CFI, while members of apparently long-running cartels received much lower fines.

(iv)   Tariffs for Professional Services

(a)   CNSD v. Commission[299]   In this judgment, the CFI concluded that the tariff charged by Italian customs agents for professional services constituted a restriction of competition attributable to the Consiglio Nazionale degli Spedizionieri Doganali ('CNSD') and was likely to affect intra-Community trade.

In Italy, the professional activities of independent customs agents (such as the completion of customs clearance formalities) are regulated by law. Customs agents must be authorized and entered in the national register of customs agents. The CNSD is also regulated by law. One of its tasks is to draw up the compulsory tariff for customs services. Failure to comply with the tariff may lead to penalties such as being struck off the register. In 1993, following a complaint against the tariff, the Commission adopted a decision[300] that Italian customs agents were 'undertakings' engaged in an economic activity and the CNSD was 'an association of undertakings', and that therefore the tariff for services provided by customs agents which was imposed by the CNSD constituted an infringement of Article 81(1). The CNSD lodged an application for annulment of the decision.

The CFI confirmed earlier case law[301] that the term 'undertaking' covers any entity engaged in an economic activity, regardless of its legal status or the way in which it is financed; any activity consisting in offering goods and services on a given market is an economic activity (paragraph 36). Thus, in so far as customs agents offer services for payment and assume financial risks, they are engaged in an economic activity; and therefore the CNSD is an association of undertakings, regardless of its public law status (paragraph 37).

---

[299] Case T–513/93, *Consiglio Nazionale degli Spedizionieri Doganali* v. *Commission* [2000] ECR II–1807.

[300] [1993] OJ L203/27.

[301] Case C–35/96, *Commission* v. *Italy* [1998] ECR I–3851, where the ECJ condemned Italy for fixing the tariffs charged by the CNSD and its members. Proceedings were stayed in the case under discussion pending the judgment in *Commission* v. *Italy*.

The CFI then examined whether the restrictive effects on competition were attributable solely to the operation of the national legislation or whether independent action on the part of the CNSD was at least partly responsible. The CFI confirmed the jurisprudence in *Ladbroke Racing*[302] where the ECJ held:

Articles [81 and 82] of the Treaty apply only to anti-competitive conduct engaged in by undertakings on their own initiative. . . . If anti-competitive conduct is required of undertakings by national legislation or if the latter creates a legal framework which itself eliminates any possibility of competitive activity on their part, Articles [81 and 82] do not apply. In such a situation, the restriction of competition is not, attributable, as those provisions implicitly require to the autonomous conduct of the undertakings. . . . Articles [81 and 82] may apply, however, if it is found that the national legislation does not preclude undertakings from engaging in autonomous conduct which prevents, restricts or distorts competition' [paragraphs 58 and 59].[303]

The CFI therefore concluded that the CNSD enjoyed a broad discretion in the implementation of national legislation and that the nature and the scope of competition in the sector were shaped by decisions (such as the tariff) taken by the CNSD itself; and therefore the tariff constituted a restriction of competition attributable to the CNSD (paragraph 72).

The Commission's application of Article 81(1) to a previously untouched professional activity was therefore confirmed by the CFI.

B.   ARTICLE 82

(i)   Collective Dominance and Predatory Pricing

The concept of collective dominance has been the subject of significant judicial consideration and clarification over the last two years—in 'pure' Article 82 cases *Compagnie Maritime Belge* and *Irish Sugar* and in a case considered under the Merger Regulation,[304] *Gencor*. Predatory pricing remains less than clear in EC competition law.

(ii)   Abuse of a Collective Dominant Position

(a)   Compagnie Maritime Belge II[305]   This case finally reached the ECJ in 2000. Three companies appealed the CFI judgment[306] confirming the Com-

---

[302] Joined Cases C–359/95 P and C–379/95 P, *Commission and France* v. *Ladbroke Racing* [1997] ECR I–6265; see also as regards Art. 82, Case 41/83, *Italy* v. *Commission* [1985] ECR 873; and Case C–202/88, *France* v. *Commission* [1991] ECR I–1223; and Case C–18/88, *GB-Inno-BM* [1991] ECR I–5941.

[303] See Joined Cases 209/78–215/78 and 218/78, *Van Landewyck and Others* v. *Commission* [1980] ECR 3125; Joined Cases 240/82 to 242/82, 261/82, 262/82, 268/82 and 269/82, *Stichting Sigarettenindustrie and Others* v. *Commission* [1985] ECR 3831 and Case C–219/95 P, *Ferriere Nord* v. *Commission* [1997] ECR I–4411.

[304] Regulation 4064/89, [1989] OJ L395/1.

[305] Joined Cases C–395/96 P and C–396/96 P, *Compagnie Maritime Belge Transports SA, Compagnie Maritime Belge SA and Dafra-Lines A/S* v. *Commission* [2000] ECR I–1365.

[306] Joined Cases T–24/93 to T–26/93 and T–28/93, *Compagnie Maritime Belge Transports and Others* v. *Commission* [1996] ECR II–1210.

mission Decision in the shipping case *CEWAL*.[307] The ECJ set aside the CFI ruling as regards fines, but dismissed all other arguments. The judgment was delivered some seventeen months after the Advocate General's opinion, indicating the sensitivity of the case. It raises interesting procedural and substantive issues, and sets out some important principles regarding the relationship between Articles 81 and 82, as well as abuse by a collectively dominant entity.

Associated Central West Africa Lines ('CEWAL') is a liner conference of shipping companies offering regular services between ports in Angola and Zaire (now Congo) and North Sea ports. The Commission fined CEWAL and its members for infringing Article 81(1) by entering into non-compete agreements with two other shipping conferences in order to share out the liner market between northern Europe and western Africa on a geographical basis. It also considered that the members of CEWAL had infringed Article 82 and abused their joint dominant position by implementing a co-operation agreement to match or undercut the freight rates offered by their principal independent competitor sailing on the same date, accompanied by provisions intended to establish 100 per cent loyalty with blacklists of disloyal shippers. The Commission imposed fines of between EUR 100,000 and 9.6 million. The CFI reduced the fines by approximately 10 per cent because it found no evidence that one violation had continued as long as alleged by the Commission, but dismissed the applications for annulment of the contested decision.[308]

On appeal to the ECJ, the arguments centred on the requirements necessary to prove a collective dominant position (in particular the extent to which arguments under Article 81 can be recycled as regards collective dominance under Article 82, and economic links necessary to constitute collective dominance) and question of abuse of such a position. The ECJ began by addressing the issue of whether the Commission can base a finding of abuse of a dominant position solely on circumstances or facts which would constitute an agreement under Article 81(1). It stated:

it is clear from the very wording of Articles [81](1)(a), (b), (d) and (e) and [82](a) to (d) of the Treaty that the same practice may give rise to an infringement of both provisions. Simultaneous application of Articles [81 and 82] cannot therefore be ruled out a priori [paragraph 33].

However, the ECJ, referring to *Michelin* v. *Commission*,[309] stressed that the objectives pursued by these two Articles must be distinguished. Thus, Article 81 applies to agreements regardless of the companies' market position, whereas Article 82 applies to abuse of a 'position of economic strength which enables the operator concerned to hinder the maintenance of effective competition on the relevant market by allowing it to behave to an appreciable extent independently of its competitors, its customers and, ultimately,

---

[307] Commission Decision 93/82/EEC of 23 Dec. 1992, see 12 YEL 593 (1992).
[308] Joined Cases T–24–26/93 and T–28/93 [1996] ECR II–1201; for a more detailed description see (1996) 16 YEL 553.
[309] Case 322/81, *Michelin* v. *Commission* [1983] ECR 3461, para. 30.

consumers' (paragraph 34). Further, a 'dominant position may be held by two or more economic entities legally independent of each other, provided that from an economic point of view they present themselves or act together on a particular market as a collective entity' (paragraph 36). The ECJ stressed that the three constitutive elements must be examined separately: collective position; dominant position; and abuse of that position. With regard to establishing the existence of a collective entity, it is thus necessary to ascertain whether the economic links and factors giving rise to a connection between the companies concerned enable them to act together independently of their competitors, their customers, and consumers. The ECJ said it is *not* sufficient in itself for two or more companies to be linked by an agreement within the meaning of Article 81(1)), although the agreement may mean they are linked in such a way as to act and present themselves on a particular market as a collective entity:

[t]he existence of a collective dominant position may . . . flow from the nature and terms of an agreement from the way in which it is implemented and, consequently, from the links or factors which give rise to a connection between undertakings which result from it. Nevertheless, the existence of an agreement or of other links in law is not indispensable to a finding of a collective dominant position; such a finding may be based on other connecting factors and would depend on an economic assessment and, in particular, on an assessment of the structure of the market in question [paragraph 45].

The ECJ examined the nature and objectives of liner conferences,[310] and found that they 'have a stabilising effect, assuring shippers of reliable services' and can by their nature and objectives be characterized as a collective entity. It agreed with the Commission and the CFI that CEWAL's members had abused their joint dominant position by participating in an agreement aimed at removing its only competitor from the market. The ECJ again confirmed the need for lawyers to ensure that all their arguments are included in their written pleadings by refusing to consider new procedural arguments raised at the oral hearing.

One interesting and novel issue for the Court was the question whether the practice of 'fighting ships', where CEWAL members would meet or undercut their competitors prices and share the losses incurred, constitutes an abuse of a collective dominant position. The applicants claimed that undertakings in dominant positions are entitled to react to competition from competing undertakings and may use selective price-cutting to do so, as long as it is not predatory, as defined in *Akzo*.[311] Since the CEWAL members had not set prices below costs, the applicants argued there was no abuse. Unfortunately, the Court decided to avoid any discussion of the tests laid down in *Akzo*.[312] It first

---

[310] As defined in Regulation 4056/86 laying down detailed rules for the application of Arts. 81 and 82 to maritime transport [1986] OJ L378/4.

[311] Case C–62/86, *Akzo* v. *Commission* [1991] ECR I–3359. The case establishes the definition of predatory pricing as pricing below production costs.

[312] By contrast, Fennelly AG's Opinion contains a detailed analysis of *Akzo* and its application in the Court's jurisprudence.

stated that Article 82 does not contain an exhaustive enumeration of abuses of a dominant position prohibited by the Treaty, and that in certain circumstances 'abuse may occur if an undertaking in a dominant position strengthens that position in such a way that the degree of dominance reached substantially fetters competition'[313] (paragraph 113).

It then focused on the *selective* nature of the pricing behaviour. CEWAL had over 90 per cent of the market, and only one competitor. The Court said:

where a liner conference in a dominant position selectively cuts its prices in order deliberately to match those of a competitor, it derives a dual benefit. First, it eliminates the principal, and possibly the only, means of competition open to the competing undertaking. Second, it can continue to require its users to pay higher prices for the services which are not threatened by that competition [paragraph 117].

Thus, the Court found, there was a clear abuse in this situation.

The third alleged abuse related to CEWAL's establishment of 100 per cent loyalty practices, which according to the applicants were exempted under Regulation 4056/86.[314] The ECJ predictably disagreed, noting its clear position that the grant of an exemption under Article 81(3) does not preclude the application of Article 82:

The fact that operators subject to effective competition have a practice which is authorized does not mean that adoption of that same practice by an undertaking in a dominant position can never constitute an abuse of that position [paragraph 131].

The Court pointed to settled case law that no exemption of any kind may be granted in respect of an abuse of a dominant position; and stressed that Regulation 4056/86 expressly prohibits abuse of a dominant position.

The applicants were, however, at least partly successful with regard to the fines. They claimed the CFI had erred in law by confirming that the Commission was entitled to fine companies individually, when the Statement of Objections had threatened only to impose fines on CEWAL and not on its individual members. The ECJ agreed, stressing that the Commission must specify in the Statement of Objections the persons on whom fines may be imposed:

[a] statement of objections which merely identifies as the perpetrator of an infringement a collective entity, such as Cewal, does not make the companies forming that entity sufficiently aware that fines will be imposed on them individually if the infringement is made out.

Similarly, a statement of objections in those terms is not sufficient to warn the companies concerned that the amount of the fines imposed will be fixed in accordance with an assessment of the participation of each company in the conduct constituting the alleged infringement [paragraphs 144 and 145].

---

[313] The Court referred to Case 6/72, *Europemballage and Continental Can* v. *Commission* [1973] ECR 215, para. 26.
[314] *Supra* n. 171.

The Court has, once again, made life more difficult for the Commission by insisting that it set out its position clearly and fully in the Statement of Objections, with the sanction that fundamental differences in a subsequent decision will not be accepted in a judicial review. The Commission must therefore be more rigorous in defining its case relatively early in the proceedings.

The issue of collective dominance and associated abuse came before the CFI the previous year, in the *Irish Sugar* and *Gencor* cases (considered below). The principles followed by the CFI appear to have now been confirmed by the ECJ in *Compagnie Maritime Belge*.

(b)   Irish Sugar[315]   Irish Sugar, the principal supplier of sugar in Ireland, was fined by the Commission in 1997 for infringing Article 82. The Commission found several abuses by Irish Sugar of both its own dominant position and a collective dominant position held with SDL, its Irish sugar distributor, from 1985 to 1995 on the market in granulated sugar in Ireland. It fined Irish Sugar EUR 8,800,000. Irish Sugar appealed. For the most part the CFI upheld the Commission's finding, although, perhaps interestingly, it reduced the overall fine imposed by EUR 1 million, not because it agreed with Irish Sugar that the proceedings had gone on for too long (almost seven years), or that the fine (representing 6.8 per cent of turnover) was too high for the offence in question, but because it found one element of the abusive conduct insufficiently proved.

The CFI confirmed that the Commission's view that Irish Sugar and SDL—undertakings in a vertical relationship, but not integrated to the extent of constituting one and the same undertaking—occupied a position of collective dominance in that they had the power to adopt a common market policy and act to a considerable extent independently of their competitors, their customers, and ultimately consumers.

The Court again stressed that extremely large market shares are in themselves, except for in exceptional circumstances, evidence of the existence of a dominant position. In principle, therefore, Irish Sugar's dominant position on the industrial sugar market in Ireland from 1985 to 1995 could be deduced simply from the finding that during that period it had more than 90 per cent of the sales of that market.

The Commission had accused Irish Sugar of adopting a sustained and comprehensive policy of abusive conduct, including discriminatory pricing, applying selectively low prices for potential customers, engaging in targeted discounts, and granting fidelity rebates intended to tie customers to Irish Sugar. The CFI disagreed only to the extent that the Commission could not rely on a note indicating the intention of Irish Sugar and SDL to grant selectively low prices to customers of an importer of French sugar as proof that such a policy was adopted. With regard to rebates, the CFI said:

the Commission has not committed an error of assessment in taking the view that a rebate granted by an undertaking in a dominant position by reference to an increase in

[315] Case T–228/97, *Irish Sugar* v. *Commission* [1999] ECR II–2969.

purchases made over a certain period, without that rebate being capable of being regarded as a normal quantity discount (point 153), as the applicant does not deny, constitutes an abuse of that dominant position, since such a practice can only be intended to tie the customers to which it is granted and place competitors in an unfavourable competitive position . . .

In such circumstances, the granting of target rebates by an undertaking in a dominant position, one of the immediate effects of which has been, on its own analysis, to result in a build-up of stocks and a concomitant reduction in purchases (point 80), amounts to restricting the normal development of competition (point 152 and Article 1(6)(i)) and is incompatible with the objective of undistorted competition in the common market. It is not based on any economic service justifying that advantage, but seeks to remove or restrict the purchaser's freedom of choice concerning his sources of supply and to block the access of other suppliers to the market [paragraphs 213 and 214].

The Court considered that Irish Sugar had not denied granting selective and discriminatory target rebates, and that there was no objective economic justification for this. It found that the rebates were intended to tie in certain key customers to Irish Sugar.

The message for dominant companies from *Irish Sugar*[316] and *Compagnie Maritime Belge*[317] is, again, that it may be very difficult for a company to foresee the point at which 'normal' commercial practices in pricing and rebate strategies become abusive behaviour. High market shares and an aggressive competitive stance may result in heavy penalties. The concept of predatory pricing remains opaque, and the Courts seem unwilling to delve into it. Companies which are not dominant in their own right but co-operate with others in the market may be at risk of infringing Article 82 as well as Article 81.

(iii)   Market Definition, Procedural Rights

(a)   Kish Glass & Co. Ltd. v. Commission[318]   A crucial element in the application of Article 82 is always the definition of the market. This issue was at the heart of this appeal before the CFI. Proceedings began in January 1992, when Kish Glass & Co. Ltd., an Irish glass supplier, complained to the Commission that Pilkington United Kingdom Ltd. and its German subsidiary, Flabeg GmbH, were abusing their dominant position on the Irish market for 4 mm float glass. Kish claimed that Pilkington and Flabeg applied different conditions to Kish from those proposed to other purchasers for equivalent transactions, and refused to supply Kish with 4 mm float glass beyond a certain limit, thus placing Kish at a competitive disadvantage. Pilkington denied that it held a dominant position on the float glass market, and explained that it applied a system of discounts based on customer size, time allowed for payment, and quantities purchased. Kish insisted that Pilkington supplied over 80 per cent of 4 mm float glass in Ireland, which was the relevant product and geographical market for assessing whether it held a dominant position.

---

[316] *Supra* n. 315.   [317] *Supra* n. 305.   [318] Case T–65/96 [2000] ECR I–1885.

By July 1992 the Commission had already decided provisionally that Pilkington's discount system was not discriminatory, but Kish refused to accept this conclusion. For the next four years Kish continued to provide the Commission with evidence in support of its complaint that Pilkington's customer classification system was discriminatory, because transport costs from continental Europe to Ireland were far higher than those from the UK to Ireland. Finally, on 21 February 1996 the Commission issued a decision which definitively rejected Kish's complaint and maintained its earlier conclusions: that the relevant product market was the sale of float glass of all thicknesses and the relevant geographical market the Community as a whole, or at least its northern part, and that Pilkington did not hold a dominant position on that market. Still unwilling to admit defeat, Kish asked the Court of First Instance to annul the decision. Pilkington was granted leave to intervene in support of the Commission.

Unfortunately for Kish, the CFI dismissed all its arguments. From a procedural point of view, the judgment is interesting in that it confirms the difference between the procedural rights of a complainant and the addressee of a decision. The Court agreed that the right to be heard is a fundamental principle of Community law 'in all proceedings initiated against a person which are liable to culminate in a measure adversely affecting that person'. However, the right concerns those 'in respect of whom the Commission carries out its investigation', rather than those who, like Kish, are seeking an end to an alleged infringement. Access to the file is a procedural guarantee intended to safeguard the right to be heard; but again, this right 'applies only to undertakings which may be penalised by a Commission decision finding an infringement' of the competition rules. The CFI considered that Kish had had every opportunity to give its point of view during the lengthy investigation of its complaint.

The CFI was also entirely unconvinced by Kish's argument that the Commission's final decision was vitiated by formal defects and breached the principle of legal certainty, since it was not clear that Commissioner Van Miert had seen it. The Court, referring to its decision in *Tiercé Ladbroke*,[319] considered that the decision had been taken properly, adding that Kish had 'in no way substantiated its suspicions' that the decision had been issued behind Mr Van Miert's back.

However, the crux of Kish's case lay in its pleas concerning market definitions. First, Kish claimed that the Commission had erred by defining the relevant product market as that for float glass of all thicknesses, rather than the market for 4 mm float glass only, on the basis that 'the persons active in the market, both on the supply side and the demand side, are the same for all thicknesses of glass.'

The Court prudently recalled that 'its review of complex economic appraisals made by the Commission' must necessarily be 'limited to verifying whether the relevant rules on procedure and on stating reasons have been

---

[319] Case T–504/93, *Tiercé Ladbroke* v. *Commission* [1997] ECR II–923; see (1998) 18 YEL 574.

complied with, whether the facts have been accurately stated and whether there has been any manifest error of assessment or a misuse of powers'. It considered that the Commission had satisfied this test, and rejected Kish's arguments on the proper definition of the relevant product market.

The CFI was then faced with the question of defining the geographical market, and conflicting interpretations of *United Brands*.[320] The Court noted that under *United Brands*, a geographical product market should correspond to a clearly defined geographical area where that product is marketed, and 'where the conditions of competition are sufficiently homogeneous for the effect of the economic power of the undertaking concerned to be evaluated', and referred to transport costs as a criterion for deciding whether conditions of competition are homogeneous. It considered the Commission had used a wide range of information on the costs of transporting glass in the Community to define the geographical market in this case, and had applied the criteria in *United Brands* correctly. The Court reviewed and rejected a great number of technical arguments made by Kish on transport costs and a detailed analysis of fob and cif prices of float glass.

The judgment is confirmation that perseverance does not always pay off—Kish appears to have been as active as possible as a complainant—and of the difficulty in defining the relevant market. Particularly in light of *Irish Sugar*, Kish could have been forgiven for assuming that the Commission would accept Ireland as the relevant market.

(iv) IP Rights

(a) Micro Leader Business[321]   The position of the holder of an IP right was raised again in this important judgment. The Court confirmed that a copyright holder does not exhaust its right within the EEA when it places products on a third country market, and the rightholder remains free to prevent importation of its copyrighted product into the EEA without an appropriate licence, and can maintain different pricing regimes in the EEA and elsewhere. The CFI considered, however, that if the supplier is dominant, although it can still legally impose different prices in the EEA compared to third countries for equivalent transactions, if its EEA prices are considered excessive, there is a risk that the supplier's pricing policy will be found to violate Article 82.

Micro Leader Business ('Micro'), a French parallel importer, complained to the Commission that Microsoft France prohibited software imports from Canada to France, which constituted an abuse of the dominant position held by Microsoft France and Microsoft Corporation, contrary to Article 82, and was contrary to Article 81 in that there was an agreement between Microsoft and its Canadian distributors to prevent sales to unauthorized distributors in France. The Commission rejected Micro's complaint, and Micro appealed to the CFI.

---

[320] Case 27/76, *United Brands* v. *Commission* [1978] ECR 207.
[321] Case T–198/98, *Micro Leader Business* v. *Commission* [1999] ECR II–3989.

The CFI confirmed that, in order for a violation of Article 81 to have occurred, there would have to have been an anti-competitive agreement or concerted practice between Microsoft Corporation and its Canadian distributors. The Court agreed with the Commission that the evidence did not support the assertion that there was an agreement between Microsoft Corporation and its Canadian distributors to prevent sales to unauthorized distributors in France. It also agreed that even if Microsoft Corporation did in fact restrict the ability of its Canadian distributors to sell to unauthorized dealers in France, such actions were within its legal rights as copyright holder (without prejudice to Article 82), as the placing of software products on the Canadian market did not exhaust its rights pursuant to Directive 91/250[322] in the Community.

The Court then reviewed whether the evidence adduced by Micro indicated the existence of a concerted practice between Microsoft Corporation and its authorized French distributors. The Court concluded that the Commission could justifiably view the evidence simply as instances of Microsoft informing its distributors in France that it was taking steps to prevent the importation from Canada of French-language software by parallel importers. The Court affirmed that the evidence only showed such action was being taken unilaterally by the Microsoft group as a whole.

Regarding the Article 82 allegations, the CFI observed that in response to a question by the Court, Commission representatives had confirmed that in the absence of any proof of excessive pricing, the Commission had made no attempt to establish whether Microsoft's prices on the European market were higher than those on the Canadian market or the reasons for any differences. This, the Court considered, constituted a manifest error of appreciation of the facts on the Commission's part. The Court found that the evidence supplied by Micro Leader *was* sufficient to establish that Microsoft imposed different prices for equivalent transactions in Canada and Europe. Citing *Magill*,[323] the CFI stated:

if, in principle, the exercise of a copyright by the rightholder, such as the prohibition of the importation of certain products from a third country to a Member State, does not in itself constitute a violation of Article [81] of the EC Treaty, such exercise may however, in certain exceptional circumstances, give rise to abusive conduct [paragraph 56].[324]

The Court concluded that the Commission should have fully analysed the different prices applying in Canada and France, and should do so to establish whether or not there is an abuse of Article 82. The Court therefore annulled the Commission's decision rejecting Micro's complaint.

The Commission is currently reviewing the price differences between Canada and France, so as to establish whether Microsoft's policy results in excessive pricing in France.[325] Only if this analysis shows that prices are excessive in France will the Commission be forced to investigate whether Microsoft

---

[322] Now ammended by Directive 93/98, [1993] OJ L290/2.
[323] Joined Cases C–241/91 P and C–242/91 P, *RTE and ITP* v. *Commission* [1995] ECR I–743.
[324] Unofficial translation.
[325] 'Commission examines the impact of Windows 2000 on competition', Commission Press Release IP/00/141, 10 Feb. 2000.

is in a position of dominance. Micro, one assumes, will actively push the Commission in this direction. The judgment is another step towards subjecting the enforcement of IP rights to EC competition law, albeit in unspecified 'exceptional circumstances'.

(v) Banking Terms: Effect on Trade between Member States

(a) Bagnasco[326] The applicability of the EC competition rules to standard banking conditions and the concept of appreciable 'effect on trade between Member States' in the financial services sector was the subject of an influential ruling by the ECJ in a preliminary ruling arising from two actions brought by Carlo Bagnasco and others against Banca Popolare di Novara and Cassa di Risparmio di Genova e Imperia concerning the repayment of loans Having defaulted on payment, Mr Bagnasco was required by those two banks to repay the debt balance and interest, and claims were also made on related guarantees. Bagnasco and others in the same situation argued that the claims were unenforceable, in so far as they were based on standard conditions imposed on the members of the Italian Bankers Association (IBA) which violated Articles 81 and 82 because they constituted concerted practices on the determination of interest rates.

The national court referred a number of questions to the Court concerning the compatibility of the standard banking conditions imposed by the IBA with EC competition law. In particular, it wished to know whether by allowing banks, in contracts for current account credit facilities, to change the interest rate at any time by reason of changes on the monetary market, and to do so by means of a notice displayed on their premises or whatever other way they considered most appropriate, the standard banking conditions amounted to a restriction of competition within the meaning of Article 81(1). The applicants argued that the determination of the interest rates applied by banks to their debtors in Italy involved a concerted practice. The Commission, as an intervening party, held that although it could not be ruled out that the conditions in question restricted competition, as they involved some limitation on the contractual freedom of member banks of the IBA, the right of the banks to change the interest rate did not have an appreciable effect on trade between Member States, and the conditions were therefore not incompatible with Article 81. The Court took the same view and held:

> Since, as in this case, any variation of the interest rate depends on objective factors, such as changes occurring in the money market, a concerted practice which excludes the right to adopt a fixed interest rate cannot have an appreciable restrictive effect on competition [paragraphs 35–36].

This is not an immediately obvious conclusion, since conditions restricting the freedom of a bank to conduct its own policy on interest rates appear to be a restriction on competition.

---

[326] Joined Cases C–215/96 and C–216/96, *Carlo Bagnasco and Others* v. *Banca Popolare di Novara and Cassa di Risparmio di Genova e Imperia* [1999] ECR I–135.

The national court also asked whether certain standard banking conditions relating to the provision of general guarantees to secure the opening of a current account credit facility were caught by Article 81. The conditions under scrutiny in the case had been notified to the Commission in 1993, at which time the Commission had referred the notification to the national competition authority for the banking sector (i.e. the Bank of Italy), because it considered that they did not appreciably affect trade between Member States. The theory developed by the Commission before the Court was that standard banking conditions imposed by a national banking association on all its members will only affect trade between Member States appreciably in two situations: when they apply to a financial service which is inherently of a cross-border nature, and when they may exercise a determining influence on whether or not foreign banks operate in the territory of the Member State where the conditions are applied. In dealing with this issue, the Court first repeated the standard formula on this subject which it has used in many other cases:

in order that an agreement between undertakings may affect trade between Member States, it must be possible to foresee with a sufficient degree of probability on the basis of a set of objective factors of law or fact that it may have an influence, direct or indirect, actual or potential, on the pattern of trade between Member States, such as might prejudice the realization of the aim of a single market in all the Member States. Accordingly, the effect on intra-Community trade is normally the result of a combination of several factors which, taken separately, are not necessarily decisive [paragraph 47].

The Court then observed that foreign banks with branches in Italy might as a result of the IBA agreement be pressured not to offer more favourable guarantee terms, since they might be reluctant to forego the advantages of IBA membership; by the same token, Italian customers might be deprived of the benefit of these more favourable terms. However, the Commission had already taken the position that the IBA agreements did not affect trade between Member States, and told the Court, in answer to a question, that the main customers of foreign banks were large companies and/or companies of another nationality which did not often resort to this kind of agreement. The ECJ considered that foreign banks were therefore not likely to be affected by the agreements, and therefore concluded that there was no effect on trade between Member States. An argument based on collective dominance was summarily rejected by the Court, which therefore held:

Standard bank conditions, in so far as they enable banks, in contracts for the opening of a current-account credit facility, to change the interest rate at any time by reason of changes occurring in the money market, and to do so by means of a notice displayed on their premises or in such manner as they consider most appropriate, do not have as their object or effect the restriction of competition within the meaning of Article [81(1)] of the EC Treaty; and are not, taken as a whole, liable to affect trade between Member States within the meaning of Article [81(1)] of the EC Treaty.

The Court took a relatively narrow view of the circumstances in which an agreement applied by a national banking association might have an effect on trade between Member States, endorsing (if not in precisely the same terms) the Commission's theories in this area, and backing the Commission's 'new approach' to the determination of national and EC competence. The practical results of this judgment are that (i) the Competition DG is now taking the position that most agreements on banking terms promulgated by banking associations affect trade between Member States only in certain specific circumstances, namely where the financial service concerned is cross-border in nature, or the agreement is likely to prevent or deter operations in the country in question by banks established in another country; and (ii) national courts are more likely to take a similar position in the future regarding the application of the EC competition rules to these agreements. Since all Member States now have domestic competition rules and national competition authorities to enforce them, it can be expected that in the future national competition authorities will deal with this kind of problem rather than the Commission, presumably applying the same principles as the Commission has done in its previous case law. The Court's reasoning has already been applied by the Commission in the *Dutch Banks* case.[327]

(vi) Health Funds

(a) Pavlov[328]   This case concerned the Dutch supplementary pensions system. Mr Pavlov and four other specialists at a hospital in Nijmegen objected to their compulsory membership, from 1996 onwards, of a pension fund for medical specialists. They argued that the appropriate fund for them as salaried employees of the hospital was actually the pension fund for the health sector. They therefore paid no contributions to the medical specialists' pension fund, which eventually obtained an enforcement order against them for arrears of premiums. They challenged the enforcement order before the competent national court, which asked the ECJ for a ruling on the compatibility of the medical specialists' pension fund with Community competition law.

The Court found that individual medical specialists are self-employed economic operators who provide services, collect fees, and assume financial risks, and are therefore 'undertakings' for the purposes of EC competition law. Their professional body could be regarded as an association of undertakings. Therefore, a decision by medical specialists or other members of a liberal profession to create a supplementary pension fund might restrict competition in terms of Article 81, since they would not compete against each other to obtain less costly insurance for that part of their pension (unlike the situation of agreements in the context of collective bargaining between employers and employees). However, the Court considered that such a decision would not appreciably restrict competition within the common market, contrary to Article 81, since the cost of the supplementary pension scheme, even though standardized, was not significant in relation to other costs, and would have

---

[327] [1999] OJ L271/28, *supra* n. 216.
[328] Joined Cases C–180/98 to C–184/98, *Pavel Pavlov and Others* v. *Stichting Pensioenfonds Medische Specialisten* [2000] ECR I–6451.

only a marginal and indirect influence on the final cost of the services offered by medical specialists.

The Court ruled that the medical specialists' fund was an undertaking and thus subject to EC competition law, since it determined the amount of contributions payable and benefits provided, operated on the basis of capitalization and investment performance and was supervised by the relevant insurance board. The Court also found that the fund's exclusive right to collect and manage contributions from medical specialists gave it a dominant position within the meaning of Article 82 EC, but added that it lacked sufficient information to decide whether the fund had abused its dominant position. National courts are thus entrusted with deciding whether there is a restriction of competition in this sensitive area, subject if necessary to a further reference to the ECJ for guidance.

C.   MERGERS

(i)   Extra-territoriality: Collective Dominance

(a)   Gencor Ltd. v. Commission[329]   In March 1999 the CFI rendered its long-awaited judgment in the case brought by the South African mining and metal company, Gencor Ltd. Gencor appealed the Commission decision[330] under the Merger Regulation[331] prohibiting the creation of a joint venture between Gencor and Lonrho plc in the platinum group metal ('PGM') sector. The Commission found that the concentration would lead to a reduction of market players from three PGM suppliers to two and, correspondingly, to the creation of a dominant duopoly position between the existing supplier Amplats (an associated company of Anglo American Corporation of South Africa Ltd. and a market leader) and the new joint venture in the global platinum and rhodium markets. The Commission established that a likely reduction in production following the deal would lead to higher prices. It rejected behavioural undertakings proposed by the parties, arguing that they would be difficult to police, and to enforce should they be broken. Thus, although the South African Competition Board did not oppose the concentration under South African competition law, the concentration was prohibited under EC law.

Gencor contended that the Merger Regulation concerned only mergers carried out within the Community, not to a transaction which related to economic activities conducted within the territory of a non-member country and had been approved by the authorities of that country, in this case South Africa. Gencor added that this analysis was consistent with the principle of territoriality, a general principle of public international law which the Court has accepted that the Community must observe in the exercise of its powers.[332]

---

[329]   Case T–102/96, [1999] ECR II–753.
[330]   Commission Decision 97/26/EC, [1997] OJ L11/30, see (1996) 16 YEL 456, 495–8.
[331]   Regulation 4064/89 [1989] OJ L395/1.
[332]   Joined Cases 89/85, 104/85, 114/85, 116/85 and 125/85 to 129/85, *Åhlström and Others* v. *Commission* [1988] ECR 5193 (the 'Wood Pulp' case) and Case C–286/90, *Poulsen and Diva Corp.* [1992] ECR I–6019.

The Court pointed out that the Merger Regulation applies to all concentrations with a Community dimension, as defined by certain threshold conditions based on worldwide and Community turnovers. To be regarded as a concentration having a Community dimension under the Merger Regulation, it is not necessary for the undertakings in question to be established in the Community, nor for the production activities covered by the concentration to be carried out within Community territory. The Merger Regulation ascribes greater importance to the criterion of sale within the common market than to production. Gencor and Lonrho met the Merger Regulation thresholds in terms of their sales.

The Court confirmed that concentrations which, while relating to production activities outside the Community, create or strengthen a dominant position, as a result of which effective competition in the common market is significantly impeded, fall within the scope of the Merger Regulation. The Court considered that the application of the Merger Regulation is justified under public international law when it is foreseeable that a proposed concentration will have an immediate and substantial effect in the Community, and found this requirement to be satisfied in the present case. Moreover, the Commission decision did not conflict with the jurisdiction of the South African authorities, as the courses of action required by the South African government and by the Community were not mutually exclusive.

The Court therefore concluded that the Commission's decision was not inconsistent with either the Community Merger Regulation or the rules of public international law.

On the question of collective dominance the CFI confirmed its ruling in the *Kali + Salz* cases[333] that the Community merger legislation applies to collective dominant positions where the dominant position is held by the undertaking which results from the concentration and one or more undertakings not involved in the concentration, as well as to individual dominant positions. The Court found that the Merger Regulation would lose its effectiveness if it were to cover only concentrations creating a dominant position for the parties to the concentration. Applying the ECJ's reasoning in *Kali + Salz*, the CFI confirmed that the merger would have led to a duopolistic market structure in which the parties and Amplats would have hindered effective competition, as they would have been able to act independently of their competitors and customers and adopt broadly the same strategy in the market. To establish the likelihood of collusive behaviour in the market, the Court reviewed the existing economic links between the parties. Interestingly, the CFI noted that the concept of economic links developed in the *Flat Glass*[334] and *Kali + Salz* cases should not be equated with the concept of structural links. The CFI indicated

---

[333] Joined Cases C–68/94 and C–30/95, *France and Others* v. *Commission* [1998] ECR I–1375, see (1998) 18 YEL 607.
[334] Joined Cases T–68/89, T–77/89 and T–78/89, *SIV and Others* v. *Commission* [1992] ECR II–1403 (the 'Flat Glass' case).

that the existence of structural links *was not* a precondition for the existence of a collective dominant position. It held that:

there is no reason whatsoever in legal or economic terms to exclude from the notion of economic links the relationship of interdependence existing between the parties to a tight oligopoly within which, in a market with the appropriate characteristics, in particular in terms of market concentration, transparency and product homogeneity, those parties are in a position to anticipate one another's behaviour and are therefore strongly encouraged to align their conduct in the market, in particular in such a way as to maximise their joint profits by restricting production with a view to increasing prices. In such a context, each trader is aware that highly competitive action on its part designed to increase its market share (for example a price cut) would provoke identical action by the others, so that it would derive no benefit from its initiative. All the traders would thus be affected by the reduction in price levels [paragraph 276].

A likelihood of collective dominance thus increases in markets which are already heavily concentrated and where products are homogeneous and prices transparent.

The Court then confirmed the Commission's finding that the concentration was incompatible with the common market because it would have led to the collective dominant position of the new joint venture and the existing supplier, Amplats.

The Commission's use of the Merger Regulation to challenge concentrations which reduce competition in oligopolistic markets has thus been thoroughly vindicated by the CFI in the Gencor case. Indeed, in a speech in 2000, Robert Pitofsky, Chairman of the Federal Trade Commission, argued that the EU and the USA 'have moved closer, if not to absolute convergence, because of a shared appreciation that mergers that contribute substantially to concentration can produce cartel-like effects (hence the EC has moved to expand its zone of challenge), but those effects will occur only if there is relatively high concentration, significant barriers to entry and conditions that facilitate collusion or non-collusive co-ordination (hence the U.S. has narrowed its range of targets)'. The *Gencor* judgment may be a stepping-stone in the direction of elimination of all significant differences in the approach taken by the EU and US authorities to mergers which are likely to have oligopolistic effects.

(b)   Coca-Cola[335]   In another important decision delivered under the Merger Regulation,[336] the CFI held that the Commission's finding in a decision authorizing a merger that an undertaking is in a dominant position does not in itself have binding legal effects. The background to the case involved a fairly complicated takeover arrangement between various Coca-Cola companies and Cadbury Schweppes, with the goal of reorganizing Coca-Cola's bottling system in the UK. The result was that Coca-Cola Enterprises Inc. took over the activities of a subsidiary company of Coca-Cola and Cadbury Schweppes, 'CCSB'.

---

[335] Joined Cases T–125/97 and T–127/97, T*he Coca-Cola Company and Coca-Cola Enterprises Inc* v. *Commission and Virgin Cola* [2000] ECR II–1733.
[336] *Supra* n. 331.

Virgin Cola, a rival supplier of soft drinks, was objecting both to certain discounting practices employed by Coca Cola companies and to the concentration, invoking both Article 82 and the Merger Regulation. As often happens, the
Commission's blessing was granted only after last-minute concessions by the
Coca Cola companies. The Commission decision approving the restructuring
included a statement that CCSB was in a dominant position in the British cola
market. Thus, although they had been procedurally successful, the Coca-Cola
Company and Coca-Cola Enterprises objected to the finding that CCSB was in
a dominant position, and lodged an application to have the decision annulled.

The main admissibility issue was whether a finding by the Commission of a
dominant position in a decision authorizing a merger is an act open to legal
challenge. Coca-Cola argued that in this case the finding was certainly open to
challenge, as it placed a 'special responsibility on CCSB' which would entail
significant and lasting consequences, since it meant that behaviour generally
considered lawful on the market in question might in CCSB's case be considered an abuse of a dominant position and thus have the effect of restricting
CCSB's commercial freedom The Commission could use the finding in pending and future cases, which increased the risk that Coca-Cola might be fined in
a later case; moreover, the finding might be regarded as binding by national
courts, and Coca-Cola would thus be placed in a disadvantageous position *vis-
à-vis* its competitors.

The CFI disagreed with these arguments. It conceded that while a finding
that an undertaking is in a dominant position was likely in practice to influence the policy and future commercial strategy of the undertaking concerned,
such a finding did not have binding legal effects. It was merely the outcome of
an analysis of the structure of the market and of competition prevailing at the
time when the Commission adopted a particular decision (paragraph 81). Any
future decisions by the Commission would have to be based on a fresh analysis of prevailing market structure and competition conditions (paragraph 82).
The CFI therefore concluded that the mere finding that CCSB held a dominant
position had no binding legal effects, and the applicants' challenge to its merits was inadmissible.

The CFI also examined the argument that if a company gives the Commission an undertaking to refrain from certain specified commercial practices
which, assuming the company was in a dominant position, would be illegal,
such an undertaking produced binding legal effects and should be challenge-
able. The CFI took the view that the undertaking could only be subject to
annulment if the Commission's decision was conditional upon the giving of
that undertaking. It appeared from the evidence produced that the Commission did not intend to make the 'clearance [of the transaction] conditional
upon the undertaking' (paragraph 101). The CFI therefore concluded on that
point that 'the contested undertaking has no binding legal effects in the sense
that a breach of its terms would not affect the [Commission's] decision in any
way and would not entail its revocation' (paragraph 106). The undertaking was
therefore not open to legal challenge.

The CFI did not discuss the substantive issue of whether or not CCSB was indeed in a dominant position. Therefore the effect of this judgment is that the Commission may make statements in a merger decision with clearly authoritative persuasive effects, but the views taken are not binding in subsequent Article 82 proceedings. Although they may not be binding upon the Commission in subsequent cases, they are likely to be highly persuasive for national courts before which an issue of alleged dominance arises.

(ii)   Mergers Referred to the Commission by the Member States—Effect on Trade between Member States

(a)   Kesko Oy v. Commission[337]   This case arose after the Commission decided, for only the sixth time since the Merger Regulation[338] entered into force, to block a proposed concentration between two Finnish companies, Kesko Oy and Tuko Oy. Both companies were active in Finland's wholesale and retail markets for food and non-food consumer goods. Although the deal did not meet the EU thresholds requiring notification, the merged entity would have controlled over 55 per cent of the relevant markets in Finland. The Finnish competition authority ('OFC') therefore notified the concentration to the Commission under Article 22 of Regulation 4064/89[339] as likely to create or strengthen 'a dominant position as a result of which effective competition would be significantly impeded', and requested measures 'to maintain or restore effective competition' in Finland.

Despite Kesko's offer of certain undertakings, the Commission decided[340] the takeover would give Kesko a dominant position in both the wholesale supply and retail markets and strengthen market entry barriers so as to 'make it extremely unlikely that any new competitor could establish itself' on those markets. Further, 'the change in the structure of the Finnish retail and cash-and-carry markets for daily consumer goods would have an appreciable influence, directly or indirectly, actually or potentially, on the pattern of trade between Member States'. The Commission rejected Kesko's proposed undertakings, and on 21 November informed Kesko that it 'considered it appropriate to adopt a decision . . . requiring Kesko to sell "en bloc" Tuko's daily consumer goods business'. On 7 February 1997 the Finnish entities gave an undertaking to transfer Tuko's business, provided the Commission approved the transfer or raised no objection by 30 April 1997. By this stage Kesko had already brought an action for annulment of the first decision. The Commission accepted the divestiture proposal, subject to a number of reservations and conditions set forth in a new decision. Kesko initially asked the CFI to annul this latter decision too, but subsequently withdrew the action, and the divestiture took place. However, the action for annulment of the main decision went ahead, Finland and France intervening on behalf of the Commission.

---

[337] Case T–22/97, [1999] ECR II–3775.   [338] *Supra* n. 331.
[339] Council Regulation 4064/89 of 21 Dec. 1989 on the control of concentrations between undertakings, [1989] OJ L395/1; corrected version [1990] OJ L257/13.
[340] [1997] OJ L110/53.

The CFI considered the application was admissible, despite the existence of the second decision approving the takeover, because Kesko clearly had an interest in the annulment of the decision, in order to be able to repurchase some or all of Tuko's assets at a later stage. The Court stressed that 'the fact that the contractual basis for a concentration has disappeared cannot in itself exclude judicial review of the legality of a decision of the Commission declaring that concentration incompatible with the common market'.[341] The divestiture did not constitute a 'voluntary abandonment' by Kesko of the Tuko takeover, but was a direct consequence of that decision and the subsequent 'divestiture decision', and Kesko's efforts to comply with them. However, the CFI dismissed the substance of the case in its entirety.

Kesko had argued that the Commission should have verified the competence of the OFC to request it to intervene. Fortunately for the Commission in view of all the other issues it has to verify within the tight deadlines imposed by the Merger Regulation, the CFI considered that the Commission did not need to verify the OFC's competence in terms of Finnish law, but only whether the Article 22 request to intervene was *prima facie* made by a Member State. The CFI's role was then to examine whether the Commission had discharged its duty of verification, and it found that when the decision was adopted the Commission had 'good grounds' to believe the OFC was competent.

Kesko next accused the Commission of a manifest error in assessing that the concentration would affect trade between Member States, since Kesko and Tuko achieved 99 per cent of their aggregate turnover in Finland alone. It argued that the test for effect on trade was different under the Merger Regulation from under the Treaty, and an actual effect on trade was required. The CFI referred to 'well-established and consistent case law' that in cases of alleged anti-competitive practices 'it is not necessary that the conduct in question should in fact have substantially affected trade between Member States. It is sufficient that the conduct in question is capable of having such an effect'. Such practices might include difficulties regarding market entry. The Courts had 'also held that, where the holder of a dominant position obstructs access to the market by competitors, it makes no difference whether such conduct is confined to a single Member State as long as it is capable of affecting trade and competition in the common market'.[342] The CFI further stated that it was 'apparent from the very nature of the control of concentrations established by' the Regulation that the Commission was 'required to carry out a prospective analysis of the effect of the concentration in question, and hence to consider [. . .] its effect on trade between Member States in the future'. The Court found that the Commission's analysis of the probable effects of the concentration supported the conclusion that it was likely to affect trade between Member States and therefore fell within the scope of Article 22 of the Merger Regulation.

[341] The Court cited its ruling in Case T–102/96, *Gencor* v. *Commission* [1998] ECR II–753.
[342] Case 322/81, *Michelin* v. *Commission* [1983] ECR 3461; Case T–65/89, *BPB Industries and British Gypsum* v. *Commission* [1993] ECR II–389.

(b)   Endemol Entertainment Holding BV v. Commission[343]   This concerned an appeal to the CFI of another of the rare Commission decisions declaring a concentration to be incompatible with the Merger Regulation.[344] In 1995, the Commission decided to block the proposal to form Holland Media Groep ('HMG'), a joint venture between CLT, VNU, RTL, Veronica, and Endemol, the largest Dutch and Luxembourg publisher and broadcaster, whose intended business was the 'packaging' and supply of television and radio programmes broadcast to the Netherlands and Luxembourg. Like *Kesko/Tuko*, the case was referred to the Commission by a Government (Dutch) under Article 22 of the Merger Regulation, since it did not meet the regulatory thresholds and at that time the Netherlands had no merger control legislation. The Commission decision declared the joint venture incompatible with the common market because it would have led to the creation of a dominant position in the television advertising market in the Netherlands, and strengthened Endemol's dominant position in the market for independent Dutch-language television production in the Netherlands, as a result of which effective competition in the Netherlands would be significantly impeded.

Initially all the parties to the venture lodged appeals against the decision. However, following negotiations, the Commission eventually cleared the concentration, subject to commitments which included the ending of Endemol's participation in HMG.[345] Following the Commission's clearance, CLT, VNU, RTL, and Veronica withdrew their appeals. Endemol, now the only applicant in the action, requested the CFI to annul the Commission's decision on four different grounds, all of which were rejected by the Court.

Endemol argued that the Commission was not competent to investigate the Dutch television production market, since the Dutch Government had requested an examination of the concentration only in so far as it concerned the television advertising market. The CFI confirmed that Article 22(3) of the Merger Regulation did not give Member States the power to control the Commission's conduct or define the scope of its investigation once they had referred a concentration to it. Endemol claimed the Commission had infringed its rights of defence by refusing to disclose the identity of undertakings which had not requested confidentiality; the table of contents provided with the documents to which the parties to the concentration had been given access did not indicate the nature or the content of those documents; and the Commission had relied on information obtained by telephone which was never passed on to the parties to the concentration. The CFI disagreed and considered the Commission had acted correctly in the way it had granted access to the file and passed on information. In reply to Endemol's complaint that the Commission did not draw up official minutes of one of the parties' hearings, thus preventing the advisory committee and the college of Commissioners from having full knowledge of the material facts in the case,

---

[343] Case T–221/95, [1999] ECR II–1299.   [344] [1996] OJ L134/32.
[345] [1996] OJ L294/1.

the CFI said the Commission was not required to do this by the Merger Regulation.

Endemol disputed that it held a dominant position in the market for independent Dutch-language television production in the Netherlands and that its participation in the venture strengthened its position in that market. Endemol argued that the Commission had defined the relevant market wrongly, in that it considered the market for independent production of Dutch-language television programmes as separate from the market for in-house production by the public broadcasters. Endemol also denied its preferential access to foreign and Dutch formats, the fact that it had many of the most popular Dutch television personalities under contract, and the profits made by its network outside the Netherlands were relevant factors for establishing whether it had a dominant position. As regards the strengthening of a dominant position, Endemol argued that it did not exercise joint control over HMG but was only a minority shareholder, and that it had already been the main programme supplier of RTL and Veronica for the five years prior to the merger. The Court found that independent production of Dutch-language television programmes was a separate market from the market for in-house production by public broadcasters, since the former market represented a different product subject to costs 42 per cent higher than those in the rest of the market, while in-house production by the public broadcasters was essentially intended for their own use. It considered that evidence obtained by the Commission from interested parties indicated Endemol had a dominant position in that market, and the Commission was entitled to consider Endemol's preferential access to foreign and Dutch formats, the fact that it had many of the most popular Dutch television personalities under contract and the profits made by its network outside the Netherlands were relevant factors in establishing its dominant position. The Court added that since Endemol was the main supplier of programmes to Veronica, the Commission was entitled to consider that, through the structural link created by the joint venture, Endemol would supply most of Veronica's additional programming. Finally, it noted that Endemol, Veronica, and RTL had joint control over HMG, since HMG's most important strategic decisions had to be approved by consensus of the shareholders.

This ruling is useful guidance on how the relevant market in broadcasting cases may be defined, as well as an indication of the relevant factors for finding a position of dominance in this sector; it also confirms and expands the Commission's capacity to reach intelligent conclusions based on available evidence.

(iii)   Definition of a Joint Venture under the Merger Regulation

(a)   Assicurazioni Generali SpA and Unicredito SpA v. Commission[346]   This ruling by the CFI is legally important for two reasons. First, the Court ruled that a decision finding that a joint venture does not constitute a concentration for

---

[346] Case T–87/96 [1999] ECR II–203.

the purposes of Regulation 4064/89 is a decision that brings about a distinct change in the legal position of the undertaking concerned, and is thus subject to judicial review. Secondly, the Court confirmed the demarcation of the scope of Regulation 4064/89 and Regulation 17, the two regulations being mutually exclusive.

In March 1996 the Commission found that the intention to create a joint venture known as Casse e Generali Vita SpA ('CG Vita') by Assicurazioni Generali SpA (Generali) and Unicredito SpA (Unicredito) did not constitute a concentration within the meaning of Article 3 of Regulation 4064/89,[347] and therefore did not fall within the scope of that Regulation. Consequently the operation was brought within the scope of Article 81 and the separate and distinct procedures provided for under Regulation 17. Generali and Unicredito challenged this decision before the CFI.

The Commission argued that the decision was in the nature of an interim decision which produced no immediate legal effects affecting the interests of the parent companies, and was therefore not actionable. The Court, by contrast, noted that the contested decision brought the operation within the scope of Article 81 and Regulation 17, and therefore laid down the criteria for assessing its lawfulness, as well as the procedure and, potentially, the sanctions applicable to it. Thus it affected the legal position of the parent companies and was a definitive decision which could form the subject-matter of an application for annulment.

On the substance, the parent companies argued that the Commission was incorrect in deciding that CG Vita was not autonomous. In their view CG Vita was in the nature of a concentration and was neither intended to nor had the effect of co-ordinating competitive behaviour between independent undertakings.[348]

The Court noted that a joint venture is covered by Regulation 4064/89 only if it enjoys operational autonomy and its creation does not have the object or effect of co-ordinating the competitive behaviour of the undertakings concerned. Since the Regulation gives no guidance on determining whether these two criteria are met, the CFI held that the question must be examined on the basis of the evidence available to the Commission when it adopted its decision. The Court stated that dependence on the parents for a certain period under an exclusivity clause would not necessarily deprive a joint venture of its autonomy. However, in CG Vita's case the exclusivity clause covered all ser-

---

[347] As it was worded when the decision was adopted, before being amended by Council Regulation 1310/97 [1997] OJ L180/6.

[348] Art. 3 of Regulation 4064/89 defines concentrations covered by the Regulation:

'. . . 2. An operation, including the creation of a joint venture, which has as its object or effect the co-ordination of the competitive behaviour of undertakings which remain independent shall not constitute a concentration within the meaning of para. 1(b).
The creation of a joint venture performing on a lasting basis all the functions of an autonomous economic entity, which does not give rise to co-ordination of the competitive behaviour of the parties amongst themselves or between them and the joint venture, shall constitute a concentration within the meaning of para. 1(b).'

vices, including those relating to production, management, and marketing, beyond an initial run-in period during which such assistance may be deemed justified in order to enable the joint venture to gain market access. For at least its first five years of activity, CG Vita would not be in a position to manage the services associated with the production and management of insurance policies autonomously. Moreover, documents in the Commission's possession showed that while the exclusivity clause was limited to a five-year period, action taken by the parent companies was not limited in time. Therefore the Commission was correct to declare that it was unable to conclude with a sufficient degree of probability that the joint venture actually enjoyed operational autonomy.

D.   ARTICLE 86

As in previous years, the Courts have been called to apply Article 86 (formerly Article 90) in a number of controversial areas, and the outcomes have not always been easy to predict.

(i)   Broadcasting Monopoly

(a)   VTM [349]   VTM (Vlaamse Televisie Maatschappij NV), a Belgian commercial television company broadcasting in Dutch to Belgium's Dutch-speaking regions (Flanders and Brussels Capital), sought annulment of a Commission decision[350] which condemned as an infringement of Article 86(1) and (3), read in conjunction with Article 46 of the EC Treaty, the monopoly VTM enjoyed under the Flemish legislation on TV broadcasting. (Belgium's constitution gives the Flemish Regional Government power to legislate on cultural matters in Flanders.) In 1995 a number of Flemish measures on the media were consolidated into an Order known as the 'Codex', which contained precise and narrow stipulations regarding private television broadcasting: The Court noted:

These provisions, read together, mean that only one private company having its head office in Flanders or Brussels and 51% of whose capital is held by Dutch-language publishers may be authorized to broadcast television advertising in Flanders from its territory and aimed at the Flemish community as a whole. . . . the purpose of granting a monopoly on television advertising was to protect existing Flemish newspaper and magazine publishers.

The Flemish Cultural Affairs Minister stated officially that the exclusive right conferred on VTM pursued the cultural objective of maintaining pluralism in the Flemish press, as it would 'prevent the entry of foreign operators onto the Flemish television market'. Thus the Flemish press would effectively recoup the advertising revenues which it lost to television. The only other Flemish TV company available to Belgium's Flemish community was the public company BRTN, which was not authorized to broadcast commercials, so VTM would

---

[349] Case T–266/97, *VTM* v. *Commission* [1999] ECR II–2329.   [350] [1997] OJ L244/18.

effectively enjoy a monopoly in Flanders with regard to television commercials for eight years, from 1987 to 2005.

VT4, a company established in London, complained to the Commission that VTM's privileged status led to discrimination against foreign broadcasters. VT4 held a UK non-domestic satellite broadcasting licence, and produced programmes either made or subtitled in Dutch, which were targeted at the Flemish public. The Flemish authorities told the Commission that their legislation did not prevent broadcasters established in other Member States from broadcasting advertising aimed at the Flemish public. However, in their view VT4 was really a Flemish broadcaster which had been established in the UK in order to circumvent the monopoly status granted to VTM. Belgium's federal government considered the Flemish legislation was justified on cultural grounds. The Commission, however, decided that the legislation infringed Community law and instructed Belgium to put an end to the infringement. VTM appealed to the CFI, unsuccessfully. The case gives some indication of the CFI's attitude to balancing the different goals of protecting cultural policy and achieving free competition. The Court's lack of sympathy for VTM perhaps reflects its view that an exclusive right to broadcast TV advertising was not a realistically justifiable means of protecting the Flemish culture in Belgium.

VTM claimed that by not providing it with copies of VT4's complaint or the Flemish government's observations on the objections notified to it, the Commission had breached VTM's rights of defence. However, the CFI considered the Commission was not required to give that undertaking 'an opportunity to make known its views on the observations submitted by the Member State', or provide it with a copy of the relevant complaint. The most interesting part of the case relates to the question of cultural policy objectives. VTM denied the object and effect of the contested measures were 'incontestably protectionist', claiming the Court had acknowledged[351] that 'cultural policy objectives are objectives of general interest which a Member State may lawfully pursue' when formulating the statutes of broadcasting organizations. It had been granted a temporary monopoly 'for reasons of cultural policy and, in particular, to preserve the pluralism and independence of the [Flemish] press', which was bound to lose advertising revenue following the liberalization of Flemish broadcasting.

The Court referred to its ruling in *Kraus*[352] that national measures which are likely to 'hamper or to render less attractive the exercise . . . of fundamental freedoms guaranteed by the Treaty' may be exempted because they pursue a legitimate objective or are justified by pressing reasons of public interest; but they must 'be appropriate for ensuring attainment of the objective they pursue and not . . . go beyond what is necessary for that purpose' (paragraph 32). Even a measure such as an exclusive right which pursues 'a legitimate objective compatible with the Treaty and is permanently justified by overriding

---

[351] See Cases C–23/93, *TV10* [1994] ECR I–4795 and C–368/95, *Familiapress* [1997] ECR I–3689.
[352] Case C–19/92, *Dieter Kraus v. Land Baden-Württemberg* [1993] ECR I–1663.

reasons relating to the public interest', must 'be appropriate for ensuring attainment of the objective it pursues and not to go beyond what is necessary for the purpose'. If VTM's argument that it was 'sufficient for acceptable reasons to have led to the grant of an exclusive right for it always to be justified' was accepted, it would be impossible to challenge any state measure granting an undertaking an exclusive right for 'acceptable reasons', and thus to apply the Treaty rules on fundamental freedoms. The Commission was correct in finding that VTM's monopoly infringed Article 43 by preventing competing operators from other Member States from setting up establishments in Flanders to broadcast TV advertisements to the Flemish public via Belgium's cable network; and 'since that finding alone is a sufficient indication of an impediment to freedom of establishment, it is unnecessary to examine whether these rules constitute a disguised form of discrimination whose effects are protectionist'.

Nor, in the Court's view, did the exclusive right granted to VTM actually protect press pluralism; all it in fact did was benefit publishers who existed when VTM was set up and invested in it, at the expense of those who did not. It was not a 'necessary corollary' of the public subsidies paid to BRTN for providing services of general economic interest under Article 86(2) that VTM should enjoy 'the exclusive right to broadcast advertising' throughout Flanders. VTM had offered no evidence to show that the programming requirements under the Flemish rules could not be satisfied by several competing television stations, or to explain why the Commission's suggestion that 'the cultural policy objectives and support for pluralism in the press could be attained by granting subsidies to the press' rather than by granting VTM monopoly rights was incorrect.

Finally, the CFI dismissed VTM's arguments that it should be able to rely on the Commission's earlier findings that the Flemish legislation was compatible with the Treaty, and pointed out that the Commission had applied the relevant Treaty Articles in combination as long ago as 1995.

(ii) Airports: Ground Handling

(a) Aéroports de Paris[353] In this judgment the CFI upheld a Commission decision[354] fining an airport authority, Aéroports de Paris (ADP) for abusing its dominant position as manager of the two main Paris airports, Roissy-Charles de Gaulle (CDG) and Orly, by imposing discriminatory commercial fees on suppliers or users of ground-handling or 'self-handling' services (catering, cargo handling, cleaning, and the like). Those services are normally provided to airlines by third parties rather than the airport authorities. The Commission decided that because these activities were not air transport services but airport management services, they were covered by Regulation 17[355] rather than

---

[353] Case T–128/98, *Aéroports de Paris* v. *Commission and Alpha Flight Services* [2000] ECR II–3929.
[354] [1998] OJ L230/10, (1998) 18 YEL 534–5.
[355] *Supra* n. 1.

the specific procedural rules which govern air transport services. The decision concluded that ADP imposed different levels of fees on competing suppliers of some types of ground-handling services at the same airport, and gave airlines which were licensed to self-handle an unfair advantage by charging them very low fees or no fees at all. Furthermore, since larger airlines had the highest traffic volumes at the Paris airports, they were more likely to benefit from this discrimination. The Commission did not fine ADP, but gave it two months from the date of notification of the decision in which to put an end to the infringement. ADP asked the Court to annul the decision.

ADP maintained that Regulation 17 did not apply to ground-handling services. The Court, however, upheld the Commission's view that the specific legislation governing the sector 'applies only to activities directly relating to the supply of air transport services' (paragraph 43), while groundhandling constituted 'neither transport services nor even activities directly relating to the supply of air transport services' (paragraph 46). The appropriate legislation was therefore Regulation 17.

ADP claimed the Commission had infringed its rights of defence, since, it argued, the contested decision was wholly at variance with the Commission's expressly stated position throughout the administrative procedure. The CFI succinctly replied that 'the inconsistency alleged by the applicant does not exist' (paragraph 64). Nor, contrary to ADP's claims, did the Statement of Objections or the decision require 'that the same fees be charged for self-handling and for handling for third parties'. The Commission, according to the Court, 'accepts, both in the statement of objections and in the recitals to and the operative part of the contested decision, that the fees might be different, provided that that difference is justified by objective and non-discriminatory considerations' (paragraph 69). The Court dealt in an equally short and decisive way with ADP's other complaints concerning the Commission's alleged lack of reasoning in the decision—for example, that the Commission did not indicate what ADP should or should not do in future, and that it did not explain whether the same fees should be charged at each airport. The CFI stated that the decision was 'perfectly clear' and what it required ADP to do was 'put an end to a discriminatory scheme of fees' (paragraph 89).

The Court was unsympathetic to ADP's claim that as a public body administering publicly-owned property it was not an 'undertaking' in terms of Article 82, recalling that for the purposes of competition law an undertaking is any entity that exercises an economic activity. Since the case was about ADP's allegedly discriminatory fees, it was manifest that ADP engaged in economic activities. ADP's challenge to the Commission's definition of the relevant product and geographic market as the management of airports in the Paris region was also unsuccessful. ADP was clearly in the airport management business as well as being an administrator of the public property constituted by the two airports, and CDG and Orly were not substitutable by other EU airports.

ADP argued that it did not enjoy a dominant position, that it did not abuse the dominant position which in any event it did not enjoy, and that its conduct was not discriminatory. However, the CFI held that the market to be taken into consideration was the market in management services in the Paris airports, and since ADP had a legal monopoly in that market, it clearly enjoyed a dominant position. The CFI also held that Orly and Roissy-CDG airports constitute a substantial part of the common market, regard being had to the volume of traffic and their importance within the network of European airports.

The Court noted:

in the present case, although the conduct of ADP to which the contested decision objects, namely the application of discriminatory fees, has effects on the market in groundhandling services and, indirectly, on the market in air transport, the fact remains that it takes place on the market in the management of airports, where ADP occupies a dominant position. Furthermore, where the undertaking in receipt of the service is on a separate market from that on which the person supplying the service is present, the conditions for the applicability of Article [82] are satisfied provided that, owing to the dominant position occupied by the supplier, the recipient is in a situation of economic dependence vis-à-vis the supplier, without their necessarily having to be present on the same market. It is sufficient if the service offered by the supplier is necessary to the exercise by the recipient of its own activity [paragraph 165].

The CFI then examined whether there was justification for the different fees which ADP charged groundhandlers and self-handlers. It found no legal or factual difference between them, and therefore no objective reason why they should be treated differently. ADP's suggestion that it was exempt from application of the competition rules under Article 86(2) also fell by the wayside, since the CFI replied that ADP had failed to show how either the Commission's decision or the application of the competition rules to ADP's activities would prevent it from fulfilling its public service obligations. Nor was there any reason why, as ADP claimed, the decision would have the effect of reducing the value of property belonging to the French State, i.e. the two Paris airports, since all it did was make it clear that businesses which manage state property must, like owners of private property, observe the competition rules. Finally, the CFI rejected ADP's claim that the decision was a misuse of Article 82, since its real aim was to harmonize airport charges as part of the common transport policy.

The CFI has given strong confirmation to the Commission's aim of applying the competition rules to airport services as well as airlines, and thereby increase competition and reduce overall prices. The travelling consumer can only welcome this development.

(iii)   Sectoral Pension Funds

(a)   Albany and Others[356]   In this series of judgments the ECJ ruled on the important issue of whether compulsory affiliation to a sectoral pension

---

[356] Case C–67/96, *Albany International BV* v. *Stichting Bedrijfspensioenfonds Textielindustrie* [1999] ECR I–5751; Joined Cases C–115/97, C–116/97, C–117/97, *Brentjens' Handelsonderneming BV* v. *Stichting Bedrijfspensioenfonds voor de Handel in Bouwmaterialen* [1999] ECR I–6025; and Case C–219/97, *Maatschappij Drijvende Bokken BV* v. *Stichting Bedrijfspensioenfonds voor de Vervoeren Havenbedrijven* [1999] ECR I–6025.

scheme is compatible with the EC competition rules. The question arose in the course of proceedings brought before three different Dutch courts by unrelated Dutch companies which refused to pay obligatory contributions to the sectoral pension fund for their respective sectors on, *inter alia*, the ground that the requirements violated Article 3(g), the competition rules, and other Treaty rules. The Dutch courts requested preliminary rulings.

The Court found that the Dutch pension system was based on three pillars: (i) a statutory basic pension for a limited amount calculated by reference to the statutory minimum wage, which the whole population was entitled to receive; (ii) supplementary pensions managed by collective schemes covering a particular sector of the economy; and (iii) individual pension or life insurance policies concluded on a voluntary basis.

The case concerned the second pension pillar, i.e. the sectoral pension scheme. The Dutch law on compulsory affiliation to a sectoral pension fund provides that at the request of a sectoral trade association, the relevant Minister may make affiliation to a sectoral pension fund compulsory for all or certain categories of workers in that sector. The fund's statutes and regulations must allow for exceptions to the obligation for workers to affiliate to the fund and exemptions from certain fund-related obligations, for example when they were already affiliated to another pension fund six months before the sectoral trade association asked for affiliation to be made compulsory, or could show that under another fund they would acquire rights at least equivalent to those available from the sectoral pension fund.

The applicants, a number of companies which had been refused exemption from participation in sectoral funds, challenged demands for payment of unpaid statutory contributions. They contended in particular that the system of compulsory affiliation to the funds was contrary to Articles 3(g), 43, and 49, and 81, 82, and 86 of the Treaty. The funds maintained that (i) they were not legally obliged to grant an exemption, and (ii) it was important to maintain a proper pension scheme based on the principle of solidarity for all workers and undertakings in the industries concerned. The Dutch courts pointed out that an earlier judgment[357] by the ECJ on the Dutch system had not examined the compatibility with the EC competition rules of compulsory affiliation to an occupational pension scheme.

The European Court first examined the question whether Articles 3(g), 10, and 81 prohibit a decision by the public authorities, following a request by organizations representing employers and workers in a given sector, to make affiliation to the pension fund for that sector compulsory The Court established that both the Treaty and the Agreement on Social Policy[358] recognize the importance of social policy development and provide support for contractual relations, including agreements between management and labour:

---

[357] Joined Cases C–430/93 and C–431/93, *Van Schijndel and Van Veen* [1995] ECR I–4705; see (1995) 15 YEL 95, 400–1.

[358] [1992] OJ C191/91: commonly referred to as the 'Social Protocol'.

It is beyond question that certain restrictions of competition are inherent in collective agreements between organizations representing employers and workers. However the social policy objectives pursued by such agreements would be seriously undermined if management and labour were subject to Article [81(1)] of the Treaty when seeking jointly to adopt measures to improve conditions of work and employment.

The Court doubtless had this preoccupation in mind in *Bosman*,[359] referred to above, though it did not articulate it there.

The Court held that in general, by virtue of their nature and purpose, agreements concluded in the context of collective negotiations between management and labour in pursuit of social policy objectives fall outside the scope of Article 81(1). In the specific circumstances of the *Albany* case, the Court ruled that both the nature of the agreement at issue, which was the outcome of collective negotiations between organizations representing employers and workers, and its purpose (i.e. to improve workers' remuneration) justified its exclusion from the scope of the competition rules.

The Court agreed that the Treaty imposes on Member States an obligation not to adopt laws which would render the competition rules ineffective or encourage behaviour contrary to those rules. However, since the agreements at issue did not fall within the scope of the competition rules, the Court decided that the Netherlands was free to make them binding on persons who were not bound as parties to them. Their compulsory nature formed part of a regime established under a number of national laws designed to exercise regulatory authority in the social sphere.

The Court did consider, however, that a compulsory pension fund established under a collective agreement between employers and workers in a given sector was an 'undertaking' in the meaning of Article 81(1), since it engaged in economic activities and competed with insurance companies. The fact that it was non-profit-making and certain of its characteristics were not based on an assessment of risk did not mean its activities were non-economic in nature.

The Court then examined whether, by making affiliation to a specific sectoral pension fund compulsory, and granting such funds the exclusive right to administer the contributions it collected, the Netherlands had infringed Article 82, read in conjunction with Article 86. The Court considered that the decision to make affiliation compulsory necessarily implied that the funds should be regarded as having an exclusive right within the meaning of Article 86(1). As they had a legal monopoly in a substantial part of the common market, they also occupied a dominant position. In the present cases, firms which wished to offer their employees better pension arrangements and, for reasons of efficiency, to make all their staff pension arrangements with a single insurer, were prevented from doing so by the requirement to contribute to the relevant sectoral pension fund. The resulting restriction of competition was a direct consequence of that exclusive right. The exclusive right thus resulted in an abuse of the fund's dominant position. The Court therefore considered it

---

[359] *Supra* n. 233.

necessary to examine whether the exclusive right could be justified on the basis of Article 86(2). It ruled that the pension arrangements fulfilled an essential social function in the Netherlands, where statutory pensions were low. The exclusive right was necessary, since without it the funds might be unable to fulfil their tasks of general economic interest under acceptable economic conditions, and their financial equilibrium might be endangered. In particular, 'good risks' might leave the fund, so that it held only 'bad risks' and would no longer be able to offer pensions at costs which workers could afford. This was a particular danger for the funds in question, where the solidarity factor was important. Hence the granting of exclusive rights was justified in such cases, since the pension funds would otherwise be unable to carry out the particular social task of general economic interest assigned to them. The Court thus concluded that the funds were compatible with Article 82, read with Article 86. However, that did not prevent the Commission or the national courts from monitoring, in terms of the competition rules, the way in which the Dutch sectoral pension funds exercised their exclusive rights, to avoid arbitrary or discriminatory decision making.

(b) Van der Woude[360] On the first anniversary of the *Albany* sectoral pension scheme judgments (see previous summary), the ECJ issued a preliminary ruling on a further referral by a Dutch court for interpretation of the relevance of the EC competition rules to another aspect of the Dutch system for social protection of workers. This case concerned health insurance rather than pensions, but it again raised the issue of whether a fund administering benefits for workers in a particular sector was an 'undertaking' for the purposes of the EC competition rules.

The contracts of staff at the Beatrixoord rehabilitation centre were governed by the collective labour agreement ('CLA') for the Dutch hospital sector Under Article II(G) of the CLA, 'the employer may not depart from [its] provisions or agree with the employee any conditions of employment which are not regulated by [the CLA]'. Article 32 specified that employers could only contribute towards staff health insurance premiums which were paid to the Medical Expenses Scheme of the Sickness Insurance Institute for the Hospital ('IZZ'), the compulsory sectoral health insurance fund established under the CLA. The IZZ subcontracted out these insurance activities to a mutual insurance company.

Mr van der Woude, an employee at Beatrixoord whose employment contract was governed by the CLA, wanted to use a sickness insurance scheme which offered better terms, for lower premiums, than the IZZ. He claimed that no matter which insurer he chose to use, Beatrixoord should contribute towards his health insurance premiums. Beatrixoord, however, considered itself prevented from doing so by the CLA. Mr van der Woude claimed before a Dutch court that this requirement was anti-competitive. The Dutch court had to

---

[360] Case C–222/98, *Hendrik van der Woude* v. *Stichting Beatrixoord* [2000] ECR I–7111.

decide whether the IZZ, although it did not carry on insurance business itself, constituted an 'undertaking' under Articles 81 and 82, and therefore asked the ECJ whether Articles II(G) and 32 of the CLA, read together, were contrary to Articles 81 and 82. The Court issued its rulings in the Dutch pension cases while Mr van der Woude's action was still pending. However, the Dutch court maintained its request for a further ruling by the Court on the ground that the operation of the IZZ Medical Expenses Scheme had been subcontracted to IZZ, which had in turn subcontracted it to VGZ.

The Court considered whether the nature and purpose of the CLA justified its exclusion from the scope of Article 81(1), and concluded that it was clearly a collective labour agreement under the judgments in the Dutch pension funds cases, and that the health insurance scheme which it established aimed to enable the employees concerned to pay their medical expenses and reduce the costs they would incur if it did not exist. The fact that the insurance business was contracted out did not mean that the Article 81 exception granted in the earlier judgments did not apply, since:

To accept such a limitation would constitute an unwarranted restriction on the freedom of both sides of industry who, when they enter into an agreement concerning a particular aspect of working conditions, must also be able to agree to the creation of a separate body for the purpose of implementing the agreement and this body must be able to have recourse to another insurer.

Mr van der Woude also claimed that IZZ/VGZ abused a dominant position on the Dutch private health care 'sub-market' created by the CLA, by imposing unfair prices or other unfair trading conditions. Despite the cost benefits IZZ/VGZ derived through the CLA, they offered less advantageous conditions than their competitors; moreover, they penalized those who for personal reasons did not join or left their scheme by preventing them from subsequently joining or re-joining it.

The Court found no evidence that the system established by the CLA had induced the VGZ to abuse 'any dominant position it might have', or that the services which it provided did not 'meet the needs of the employees concerned'. The alleged abuses did not 'fall within the scope of the main proceedings, which concern only the compatibility with the competition rules of rules laid own in the Collective Labour Agreement as to which sickness insurance scheme employers may contribute to'.

The Court therefore concluded that the contested provisions of the CLA were compatible with the EC competition rules, similar to the earlier *Albany* rulings.

It is clear that all elements of public activity are now open to challenge by imaginative challengers using the competition provisions of the EC Treaty, but the European Court has honourably dealt with the challenge.

(iv)   Port Services: Exclusive Right of Recognized Dockers to Perform Certain Dock Duties

(a)   Becu[361]   In this case the ECJ found that national legislation allowing only recognized dockers to perform certain dock duties does not fall under Article 86 read in conjunction with Articles 81 and 82 and Article 12 of the EC Treaty. The ruling confirms that the prohibition laid down in Article 86(1) read in conjunction with any other provision of the Treaty is applicable only to undertakings, and that Articles 81 and 82, taken separately, are concerned solely with the conduct of undertakings, and not with laws or regulations adopted by Member States. The issue was raised by a Belgian court which referred two questions for a preliminary ruling in the course of criminal proceedings against Mr Becu, Mrs Verweire, and the companies of which they were respectively director and manager, Smeg (which carried out activities relating to loading and unloading of grain boats and storage of grain for third parties) and Adia Interim (a temporary employment agency). Smeg was alleged to have breached a 1972 law requiring that all work on Belgian docks must be carried out by recognized dockers. For work carried out on quays, i.e. strict dock work, Smeg used recognized dockers who were paid a rate of 1,355 BF an hour, the minimum legal wage for dock workers. However, for related silo work, i.e. loading and unloading grain in warehouses, weighing and moving it, maintenance of facilities, operations in the silos and on the weighbridge, and the loading and unloading of trains and lorries, Smeg used hired temporary workers from Adia Interim who were not recognized dockers and were paid 667 BF an hour.

The Belgian court asked whether Article 86(1), read in conjunction with the first paragraph of Article 12 and Articles 81 and 82, gives individuals the right to challenge national legislation which requires them exclusively to employ recognized dockers for dock work, and to pay them wages fixed by law which are much higher than the wages they pay their own employees or other workers. Confirming its earlier case law, the Court stated that these directly effective provisions give individuals the right to be protected by national courts, and that public undertakings or undertakings granted special or exclusive rights by Member States are bound not to enact or maintain any measures contrary to the Treaty. The Court went on to make it clear that 'by allowing only a particular category of persons to perform certain work within well-defined areas, the national legislation at issue . . . grants to those persons special or exclusive rights within the meaning of Article [86(1)]'.

However, having established this, the Court then clarified that Article 86(1) is applicable only if the measures to which it refers concern 'undertakings'. Recognized dockers are not to be considered as undertakings, but as workers. The Court stated that:

The conditions relating to work and pay, in particular those of recognized dockers in the Ghent port area, are governed by collective labour agreements concluded on the basis of

---

[361]   Case C–22/98, *Jean Claude Becu and Others* [1999] ECR I–5665.

the 1968 Law and made mandatory by Royal Decree pursuant to that law. . . . It must therefore be concluded that the employment relationship which recognized dockers have with the undertakings for which they perform dock work is characterised by the fact that they perform the work in question for and under the direction of each of those undertakings, so that they must be regarded as 'workers' within the meaning of Article [39] of the EC Treaty, as interpreted by the case-law of the Court. . . . Since they are, for the duration of that relationship, incorporated into the undertakings concerned and thus form an economic unit with each of them, dockers do not therefore in themselves constitute 'undertakings' within the meaning of Community competition law [paragraphs 25 and 26].

The Court added that 'even taken collectively, the recognized dockers in a port area cannot be regarded as constituting an undertaking' (paragraph 27). This conclusion follows the case law that a person's status as a worker is not affected if he is linked to other workers by a relationship of association.[362] The Court found no evidence that the recognized dockers were linked by a relationship which might indicate that they operated as an entity or as workers for an entity. With regard to Article 12, the Court found no evidence that the 1972 law was discriminatory on grounds of nationality. As a result, the challenge in terms of competition law was unsuccessful.

(v) Employment Services: Exclusive Right of Public Office to Carry Out Services

(a) Giovanni Carra and Others[363]   This ruling on national monopolies for employment agencies/services concerns the legality under Articles 82 and 86 of an Italian law which reserved the right of public placement offices to act as intermediaries between demand for and supply of employment on the labour market, and prohibited other individuals or entities from doing so. The question arose in criminal proceedings against Mr Carra, Ms Colombo, and Ms Gianassi, and the Italian court referred it to the ECJ.

The Court first confirmed its established case law (including the *Becu*[364] case) that Article 82 has direct effect and confers rights on individuals, even within the framework of Article 86,[365] and that national courts have the duty to give full effect to Community law provisions when called upon to apply them. The Court then ruled on the question from the national court whether the criminal penalties laid down in Italy for acting as intermediaries in employment relationships were inapplicable under Articles 82 and 86, following the Court's ruling in *Job Centre II*.[366] The Court said they were not justified, referring to *Job Centre II*, and concluded that:

---

[362] The Court referred to Case C–179/90, *Merci Convenzionali* v. *Porto di Genova* [1991] ECR I–5889.

[363] Case C–258/98, *Giovanni Carra and others* [2000] ECR I–4217.

[364] See previous summary.

[365] See para 11. The Court refers to Case C–179/90, *Merci Convenzionali Porto di Genova* [1991] ECR I–5889; Case C–242/95, *GT-Link* [1997] ECR I–4449; and Case C–22/98, *Becu and Others* [1999] ECR I–5665.

[366] Case C–55/96, *Job Centre* [1997] ECR I–7119, where the Court held that public placement offices are subject to the prohibition contained in Art. 86 of the EC Treaty, so long as application of that provision does not obstruct the performance of the particular task assigned to them.

Public placement offices are subject to the prohibition contained in Article [82] of the Treaty, so long as the application of that provision does not obstruct the particular task conferred on them. A Member State which prohibits any activity as intermediary between supply and demand on the employment market, unless it is carried on by those offices, is in breach of Article [86(1)] of the Treaty where it creates a situation in which those offices cannot avoid infringing Article [82] of the Treaty. That is the case, in particular, in the following circumstances:

- the public placement offices are manifestly unable to satisfy demand on the market for all types of activity; and
- the actual placement of employees by private companies is rendered impossible by the maintenance in force of statutory provisions under which such activities are prohibited and non-observance of that prohibition gives rise to penal and administrative sanctions; and
- the placement activities in question could extend to the nationals or to the territory of other Member States [paragraph 13].

The Court stressed:

A national court which is called upon, within the limits of its jurisdiction, to apply provisions of Community law is under a duty to give full effect to those provisions, if necessary refusing of its own motion to apply any conflicting provision of national legislation, even if adopted subsequently, and it is not necessary for the court to request or await the prior setting aside of such provisions by legislative or other constitutional means. [paragraph 17].

(vi)   Environmental Regulations

(a)   Danish Waste/Sydhavnens[367]   An interesting referral was made to the ECJ regarding the compliance of environmental regulations with Article 86 and 82—and the ECJ came down clearly on the side of the environmentalists. Sydhavnens Sten & Grus (SS&G) organized the collection and recycling of non-hazardous building waste. On the basis of approval granted from the Municipality of Copenhagen in 1994, it established a plant for the recycling of building waste within Copenhagen's boundaries. It then concluded a contract with the Port of Copenhagen to sort and crush building waste, and applied for the necessary permit to process waste produced within Copenhagen. This approval was denied, on the basis that waste produced within the Copenhagen boundaries should be processed at another existing plant situated within the area. Under the municipal regulations, only three companies were authorized by the Municipality to receive waste produced within the Municipality, on the basis that a limit was necessary to ensure that large enough plants were established for the best quality of recycling. As a result, SS&G was able to operate its plant situated in the boundaries of Copenhagen, but only allowed to process waste coming from neighbouring municipalities.

The ECJ was asked to rule on the compatibility of the Copenhagen municipal regulations with, *inter alia*, the competition rules contained in Article 86 read with Article 82.

[367]   Case C–209/98, *Sydhavnens Sten & Grus* v. *Municipality of Copenhagen* [2000] ECR I–3743.

The ECJ established that exclusive rights had been granted to the three authorized companies by the Municipality of Copenhagen under Article 86, and looked at whether these companies were in a dominant position and were abusing that dominant position in the exercise of their rights. The ECJ provided quite firm guidance to the national court in how it should assess the relevant market:

- in determining the relevant product/service market it should decide whether the processing of environmental non-hazardous waste is a distinct market from other types of waste (paragraph 62);
- in determining the geographic market it should 'take into account' that if producers of waste in Copenhagen wish to have their waste processed in Denmark, they can only deal with one undertaking, which 'could have the effect of restricting the market to the area over which the exclusive right extends' (paragraph 62)—but in view of the importance of the municipality of Copenhagen in Denmark, might actually restrict effective competition in a wider area (paragraph 63); and
- in determining whether the area defined constitutes a substantial part of the common market, it should consider the importance of the volume of waste produced in the Copenhagen Municipality in relation to building waste processing operations in Denmark as a whole (paragraph 64).

The ECJ then emphasized the need to show that the exercise of the exclusive rights is actually leading to an abuse of a dominant position, or likely to create a situation in which an abuse occurs. It specifically noted that 'the grant of an exclusive right over part of the national territory for environmental purposes, such as establishing the capacity necessary for the recycling of building waste, does not in itself constitute an abuse of a dominant position' (paragraph 68). It then noted that the grant of exclusive rights to operate services of general economic interest might be justified under the competition rules, and said: '[t]he management of particular waste may properly be considered to be capable or forming the subject of a service of general economic interest, particularly where the service is designed to deal with an environmental problem' (paragraph 75).

The ECJ considered that the action taken by the Municipality of Copenhagen responded to a serious environmental problem: the need to provide an alternative to the burial of waste. The Municipality had considered it essential to grant exclusive rights to a limited number of recycling centres in order to guarantee a significant flow of waste to each, to ensure that the centres were viable and to ensure the quality of the recycling carried out. Even if the exclusive right led to a restriction of competition in a substantial part of the common market (in that otherwise qualified undertakings were excluded from waste processing), 'that grant was necessary for the performance of a task serving the general economic interest' (paragraph 81), and there was nothing 'to suggest that the exclusive right . . . will necessarily lead the undertakings in question to abuse their dominant position' (paragraph 82).

Therefore, the ECJ considered that the municipal regulations were compatible with Articles 86 and 82, in spite of the clear commercial disadvantage they impose on certain undertakings.

(vii)   Postal Services

(a)   Deutsche Post [368]   In this case Deutsche Post made one of its increasingly frequent visits to the European Courts, after a German court requested a preliminary ruling regarding the application of the EC competition rules to the postal sector.

Gesellschaft für Zahlungssysteme mbH (GZS), and a Citibank subsidiary, Citicorp Kartenservice GmbH (CKG) are German-based businesses which delegated the task of processing credit card statements to companies based in other EC Member States. Their letters to credit card holders resident in Germany were mailed by the Dutch and Danish postal services, which charged the normal rate for international mail and paid Deutsche Post the appropriate terminal dues (the dues which one postal administration collects from another for the delivery of its international mail). According to Article 25(1) of the Universal Postal Convention (UPC), Deutsche Post was not obliged to forward or deliver letters posted in large quantities in another Member State. Instead, under Article 25(3) of the UPC, Deutsche Post could return them to the senders or charge the senders postage on them at internal rates. Deutsche Post therefore asked CKG and GZS to pay postage at internal rates for each of their letters which it delivered in Germany, and sued them when they refused to do so. The essence of the question asked by the national court was whether, by exercising the right provided for by Article 25(3) of the UPC, Deutsche Post had breached Article 82 and 86.

The ECJ found that as Deutsche Post had been granted exclusive rights in Germany as regards the collection, carriage, and delivery of mail, it was to be regarded as an undertaking holding exclusive rights within the meaning of Article 86(1). Since these rights gave it a statutory monopoly over a substantial part of the common market, it was in a dominant position within the meaning of Article 82. There was nothing intrinsically illegal in that situation, although the ECJ recalled that Article 86(1) requires Member States not to adopt or maintain in force measures which may deprive that provision of its effectiveness. As Deutsche Post enjoyed a dominant position, there was a recognizable risk that it might misuse its right under the UPC to treat international items of mail as internal post, to the detriment of users of the postal services. However, the Court also noted that the activities of Deutsche Post, including its performance of the obligations deriving from the UPC, constituted a service of general economic interest under the terms of Article 86(2). Deutsche Post might be unable to provide such services in economically balanced conditions if it was obliged to deliver large quantities of mail which, although the senders

---

[368] Joined Cases C–147/97, *Deutsche Post AG v. Gesellschaft für Zahlungssysteme mbH (GZS)* and C–148/97, *Deutsche Post AG v. Citicorp Kartenservice GmbH* [2000] ECR I–825.

were resident in Germany, was sent using the postal services of other Member States, without receiving any compensation at all for doing so. According to the Court, a Member State's postal services cannot be expected to bear the costs entailed in the performance of the service of general economic interest of forwarding and delivering international items of mail, which is its responsibility by virtue of the UPC, while at the same time losing income because it is required to deliver bulk mailings posted in other Member States.

Therefore, the Court ruled that under the terms of Article 86(2), Deutsche Post was justified in charging internal postage on bulk cross-border mailings, so that it could continue to carry out the task of general interest entrusted to it in economically balanced conditions. However, as the forwarding and delivery costs incurred by Deutsche Post were partly offset by the terminal dues paid to it by the postal services of other Member States, it was not necessary for Deutsche Post to charge the full internal postage rates on such bulk cross-border mailings. Deutsche Post's attempt to recover the full postage rates from CKG and GZS might therefore be contrary to Article 86(1).

As a result the ECJ has not accepted the principle that companies with large mailings have a right to use the cheapest services available in the EU, without the possibility of being charged by the Post Office of origin in certain circumstances.

E.   PROCEDURAL ISSUES

(i)   *Parallel Proceedings before National Courts and the Commission*

(a)   Masterfoods[369]   In the next instalment of the long-running EC competition law 'ice cream wars', the ECJ was given an opportunity to revisit the issues covered in its *Delimitis*[370] judgment and to provide further guidance on how cases proceeding before a national court as well as before the Commission should be handled, in particular where there are conflicting decisions. Regular *YEL* readers will recall the Commission's campaign against ice cream freezer exclusivity. The issue is whether suppliers of ice cream products can provide retailers with freezer cabinets at little or no cost to display and store ice cream produced only by that manufacturer, or whether rival manufacturers' products should be given space. Since freezer cabinets are expensive and bulky objects, retailers are often happy to accept the offer of a cabinet, but then have little space in which to install other manufacturers' cabinets. If the owner of the cabinet insists on exclusivity, the retailer is then prevented from selling rival manufacturers' products.

In 1998, following a complaint by Masterfoods that it was prevented from entering the market, the Commission took a decision[371] that the exclusivity insisted upon by Van den Bergh (formerly HB Ice Cream Ltd. or 'HB') for ice cream freezer cabinets in Ireland was contrary to the EC competition rules.

---

[369] Case C–344/98, *Masterfoods Ltd. v. HB Ice Cream Ltd*, judgment of 14 Dec. 2000.
[370] Case C–234/89, *Stergios Delimitis* v. *Henninger Bräu* [1991] ECR I–935.
[371] [1998] OJ L246/1.

Masterfoods had also raised proceedings under EC competition law before the Irish High Court, and prior to the Commission decision, the High Court rejected Masterfoods' case and granted HB a permanent injunction against 'squatting' by Masterfoods' products. Masterfoods appealed against this judgment to the Irish Supreme Court. HB asked the CFI to annul the Commission decision and to suspend its effects pending the judgment on the main action, a request which—controversially—the CFI granted on 7 July 1998.[372] In these circumstances, the Irish Supreme Court decided to seek a preliminary ruling from the ECJ before ruling on Masterfoods' appeal against the High Court judgment.

The Supreme Court asked:

- whether it should stay the hearing of Masterfoods' appeal pending the resolution of HB's action against the Commission decision;
- whether, once the Commission had issued a formal decision that exclusivity provisions infringed the EC competition rules, the party condemned by that decision could continue to seek the upholding of a national court's finding that the provisions in question did not infringe the competition rules; and
- whether in the ECJ's view the exclusivity provisions were in fact contrary to the EC competition rules.

The action generated widespread interest, and France, Italy, Sweden, and the UK submitted written observations, as did the Commission.

The case presented several clearly opposed constitutional principles. HB of course relied on its judicial victory and opposed its administrative defeat, arguing that the decision was adopted in breach of the duty of 'sincere co-operation' in light of 'the principle that the decision does not bind the national court but at least gives it substantial guidance in reaching a decision' (paragraphs 30 to 32).

The Italian Government argued that the obligation of co-operation imposed by Article 10 'cannot go so far as to deprive [national courts] of their specific autonomous jurisdiction'. It added that 'if the Commission initiates proceedings regarding a particular instance of infringement of Articles [81 and 82], the national court dealing with the same matter may, but is not required to, stay proceedings before it while awaiting the outcome of the Commission's action' (paragraphs 34 and 35).

The UK Government held a quite different view, considering that the Commission decision was a valid act until declared null by the European courts, and that it followed 'from the general principle of certainty and the duty of co-operation . . . that national courts must exercise their powers so as to avoid any significant risk of conflict, not only in relation to decisions that the Commission has yet to take, but also in respect of decisions formally adopted' (paragraphs 37 and 38).

---

[372] Case T–65/98 R, *Van den Bergh Foods Ltd.* v. *Commission* [1998] ECR II–2641.

The Court of Justice started by recalling the competence of the Commission:

The Commission has exclusive competence to adopt decisions in implementation of Article [81(3)] . . . However, it shares its competence to apply Articles [81(1) and 82] with the national courts . . . the national courts thus continue to have jurisdiction to apply [those provisions] even after the Commission has initiated a procedure in application of Articles 2, 3 or 6 of Regulation No 17 [paragraph 47].

And further continued:

Despite that division of powers, and in order to fulfil the role assigned to it by the Treaty, the Commission cannot be bound by a decision given by a national court in application of [those provisions]. The Commission is therefore entitled to adopt at any time individual decisions under [those provisions] even where the agreement or practice has already been the subject of a decision by a national court and the decision contemplated by the Commission conflicts with that national court's decisions.

The Court also recalled (at paragraph 49) that the Member States have the duty to take all the appropriate measure to ensure the respect of EC law and to abstain from anything that could jeopardize the attainment of the objectives of the EC Treaty.

The Court continued :

The Court has held, in paragraph 47 of *Delimitis*, that in order not to breach the general principle of legal certainty, national courts must, when ruling on agreements or practices which may subsequently be the subject of a decision by the Commission, avoid giving decisions which would conflict with a decision contemplated by the Commission in the implementation of Articles [81(1) and 82] and Article [81(3)] of the Treaty.

It is even more important that when national courts rule on agreements or practices which are already the subject of a Commission decision they cannot take decisions running counter to that of the Commission, even if the latter's decision conflicts with a decision given by a national court of first instance [paragraphs 51 and 52].

So the national court hierarchy must look to avoid reaching decisions which conflict with Commission measures in gestation or in the public domain.

In that connection, the fact that the President of the Court of First Instance suspended the application of Decision 98/531 until the Court of First Instance has given judgment terminating the proceedings before it is irrelevant. Acts of the Community institutions are in principle presumed to be lawful until such time as they are annulled or withdrawn (Case C–137/92 P *Commission* v. *BASF and Others* [1994] ECR I–2555, paragraph 48). The decision of the judge hearing an application to order the suspension of the operation of the contested act . . . has only provisional effect. It must not prejudge the points of law or fact in issue or neutralise in advance the effects of the decision subsequently to be given in the main action (order in Case C–149/95 P(R) *Commission* v. *Atlantic Container Line and Others* [1995] ECR I–2165, paragraph 22) .

Moreover, if a national court has doubts as to the validity or interpretation of an act of a Community institution it may, or must . . . refer a question to the Court of Justice for a preliminary ruling.

If, as here in the main proceedings, the addressee of a Commission decision has . . . brought an action for annulment of that decision . . . , it is for the national court to decide whether to stay proceedings until a definitive decision has been given in the action for annulment or in order to refer a question to the Court for a preliminary ruling.

It should be borne in mind in that connection that application of the Community competition rules is based on an obligation of sincere co-operation between the national courts, on the one hand, and the Commission and the Community Courts, on the other, in the context of which each acts on the basis of the role assigned to it by the Treaty [paragraphs 53 to 56].

This means that even in such matters as timing and interlocutory procedures, the national courts must avoid conflicting with the Commission's enforcement measures. This is made even clearer by paragraph 57:

When the outcome of the dispute before the national court depends on the validity of the Commission decision, it follows from the obligation of sincere co-operation that the national court should, in order to avoid reaching a decision that runs counter to that of the Commission, stay its proceedings pending final judgment in the action for annulment by the Community Courts, unless it considers that, in the circumstances of the case, a reference to the Court of Justice for a preliminary ruling on the validity of the Commission decision is warranted.

This is powerful constitutional doctrine which offers a good template for enforcement controversies in the future. It is refreshing to see clear, firm, crisp guidance on such a sensitive topic. As we do not have a fully-integrated judicial system, and as the speed of appeals and references varies greatly, the system demands (and on this occasion obtained) guidance from the European Court which has the function of imposing uniformity. The Community is manifestly no longer driven by inter-governmental treaties. The pre-eminent role of the Commission's Directorate General for Competition is made even clearer: not just *primus inter pares* among competition enforcers, but source of guidance which national courts must both respect and defer to when hearing competition matters.

(ii)   Appeals Against Commission Rejection of Complaints

One development which has become highly noticeable over recent years is the regularity with which the Commission now faces legal challenge to its rejection of a complaint. The following cases are all examples of complainants refusing to accept the Commission's reluctance to act on their behalf. They are interesting in the first instance in that they define the standards which the Commission must meet in deciding whether or not to pursue a complaint, and also because the Court may provide helpful interpretations of the substance of the rules. The Commission's wish that EC competition law be devolved to national competition authorities and courts means that some complainants are inevitably going to be disappointed. The Court is at least attempting to ensure that where the Commission feels it is not appropriate for it to act, this is clearly set out and reasoned to the complainant concerned. The Commission has indicated that it may issue some sort of guidelines for complainants, indicating the appropriate forum for different types of complaints. This may help avoid unnecessary frustration and delay.

(a) Union Française de l'Express (Ufex) and Others v. Commission[373] This case concerned the topical issue of postal services and their liberalization, and their relationship with private courier services. The CFI in *SFEI and Others* v. *Commission*[374] rejected an application for annulment of a Commission decision refusing a complaint regarding the conduct of the French postal service, La Poste. This setback for the complainants was reversed by the ECJ on appeal by the former Syndicat Français de l'Express International ('SFEI'), now renamed Union Française de l'Express ('Ufex'), DHL International, and Service CRIE.

In 1990, several courier services lodged a complaint with the Commission that La Poste, the French Post Office, was in breach of Article 82. Their complaint concerned the logistical and commercial assistance provided by La Poste to its subsidiary Société Française de Messageries Internationales ('SFMI') which operates in the international express mail sector. Specifically, they claimed that La Poste allowed SFMI to use its infrastructure on unusually favourable terms in order to extend its dominant position on the basic postal services market to the related market in international express mail.

Four years later the Commission rejected the complaint on the ground that there was insufficient evidence to show the alleged infringements were continuing. The Commission noted that its Green Paper on postal services in the single market and Guidelines for the development of Community postal services addressed many of the problems raised in the complaint. In a recent decision under the Merger Regulation[375] regarding a joint venture (GD Net) created by TNT, La Poste, and four other postal administrations, the Commission had concluded that the joint venture did not create or strengthen a dominant position which might significantly affect competition in the common market. All these developments, according to the Commission, showed that the problems identified in the complaint regarding competition in the international express mail sector had been adequately addressed by the measures taken thus far by the Commission. The Commission noted that it considered the complaint had been made to assist the companies in an action for damages before the courts in France. This decision was unsuccessfully appealed to the CFI. A further appeal was made to the ECJ on the grounds that the CFI had erred in law by not finding that the Commission was obliged to refer to the factors set out in *Automec II*[376] when assessing whether or not there was a Community interest in pursuing a complaint.

The ECJ did not agree. Instead, it considered that the assessment of the Community interest raised by a complaint depends on the circumstances of each case, and said the criteria of assessment to which the Commission may

---

[373] Case C–119/97 P, [1999] ECR I–1341.   [374] Case T–77/95 [1997] ECR II–1.
[375] *Supra* n. 344.
[376] Case T–24/90, *Automec* v. *Commission* [1992] ECR II–2223, see (1992) 12 YEL 554, 618.

refer should not be limited, nor should it be required to have recourse only to certain criteria. On the other hand, the Court took exception to statements by the CFI to the effect that it was not part of the Commission's functions under the Treaty to establish that infringements had taken place in the past, and therefore the Commission could lawfully decide not to pursue a complaint regarding practices which had since ceased. The ECJ acknowledged that in order to perform its task of implementing competition policy effectively, the Commission was entitled to give differing degrees of priority to the complaints brought before it, but the discretion which it had for that purpose was not unlimited. First, the Commission was obliged to state reasons for declining to continue examining a complaint (not new). Secondly, the Commission, when deciding the order of priority for dealing with the complaints brought before it, could not disregard certain factors: it had to assess in each case the gravity of the alleged interference with competition and how persistent its consequences were. According to the Court, the Commission remained competent if the anti-competitive *effects* continued after the *practices* which caused them ceased. The Commission could therefore not decide that a complaint lacked Community interest merely because the practices alleged to be contrary to the Treaty had ceased, without having ascertained that the anti-competitive effects no longer continued. Rather, the Commission should consider whether the gravity of the alleged infringement or the persistence of its effects might give the complaint a Community interest. The ECJ therefore annulled the contested judgment, and remitted the case to the CFI.

When the parties returned to the CFI,[377] the applicants enthusiastically took up the point that a complaint did not necessarily lack Community interest merely because the infringement complained of had ceased. The Commission considered that appropriate measures had already been taken to put an end to anti-competitive practices in the sector.

The CFI noted that in its exercise of its discretionary power in this area the Commission must weigh the degree to which the alleged infringement was likely to disrupt the smooth functioning of the common market against the relative ease or difficulty of proving the infringement, the scope of the investigation which would be required to enable it to fulfil its role as guardian of the Treaty in the best possible conditions, and the degree of Community interest in pursuing the matter. It confirmed that the Commission could not simply decide that as the infringement had ceased there was no need to do anything. The CFI was unconvinced by the Commission's view that present and future competition problems in the sector had been adequately resolved by the conditions imposed on La Poste in the *GD Net* merger decision. It noted that the Commission's duty was not to verify whether a national court might award the complainants damages, but to defend competition by making sure that the anti-competitive effects complained of had ceased. The decision did not make it clear that this had been done, and it was not sufficient for the Commission

---

[377] *Supra* n. 374.

to explain at the oral hearing that it had taken these matters into account: a decision must be self-sufficient and not require its reasoning to be explained in subsequent oral or written arguments. The CFI therefore annulled the decision.

The judgments in this case are of considerable value to complainants. While the Courts have again confirmed the considerable latitude that lies with the Commission in deciding whether or not a case is worth pursuing, they have refused to allow the Commission to absolve itself of any responsibility for acting where an alleged infringement appears to have ceased. The judgments require the Commission to satisfy a higher test before it can confidently reject a complaint as devoid of Community interest.

(b) Florimex[378] The complex 'Florimex' affair was the subject of a lengthy summary in a previous edition of the *YEL*.[379] In brief, the Commission first condemned a set of agreements involving the VBA, a co-operative of flower and plant growers in the Netherlands, following a complaint by a large Dutch flower importer and wholesaler, Florimex. After modification and re-notification of the VBA arrangements, the Commission decided they were acceptable. Further complaints were made by Florimex and the VGB, an association of Dutch floricultural wholesalers, including Florimex, some of which were established on VBA premises. These were rejected by the Commission. The CFI[380] annulled the Commission decisions[381] rejecting the complaints, giving Florimex and the VGB another shot at challenging the VBA arrangements. The VBA appealed the CFI judgments to the Court of Justice. Interestingly, in both appeals the VBA applied to the ECJ for leave to submit written observations after the Advocate General had delivered his Opinion (relying on the case law of the European Court of Human Rights concerning the scope of Article 6(1) of the Convention for the Protection of Human Rights and Fundamental Freedoms and in particular *Vermeulen* v. *Belgium*.[382] The ECJ rejected the applications, applying its order of 4 February 2000 in *Emesa Sugar*.[383]

---

[378] Case C–265/97 P, *Coöperatieve Vereniging De Verenigde Bloemenveilingen Aalsmeer BA (VBA)* v. *Florimex BV, Vereniging van Groothandelaren in Bloemkwekerij producten (VGB) and the Commission*; Case 266/97 P, *Coöperatieve Vereniging De Verenigde Bloemenveilingen Aalsmeer BA (VBA)* v. *Vereniging van Groothandelaren in Bloemkwekerijproducten (VGB), Florimex BV and others and the Commission* [2000] ECR I–2061.

[379] 1998 18 YEL 569.

[380] Joined Cases T–70/92 and T–71/92, *Vereniging van Groothandelaren in Bloemwekerij-producten and Others* v. *Commission* [1997] ECR II–759; Case T–77/94, *VGB and Others* v. *Commission* [1997] ECR II–759, see (1998) 18 YEL 569.

[381] The original Commission decisions were IV/32.751, *Florimex/Aalsmeer II* and IV/32.990, *VGB/Aalsmeer* [1988] OJ L262/27, see (1988) I YEL 221. The first appeal to the CFI concerned a decision of 2 July 1992 rejecting complaints regarding the user fee; the second concerned the decision of 20 Dec. 1993 whereby the Commission rejected further complaints on the basis that the time limit for challenging the Commission's provisional findings had lapsed.

[382] [1996] ECHR I–224.

[383] Case C–17/98, *Emesa Sugar (Free Zone) NV* v. *Aruba* [2000] ECR I–675.

The first appeal concerned the 'user fee' charged by the VBA for the use of its premises in respect of the supply of products by suppliers who are not members of the VBA. The CFI had found that the Commission had not provided an adequate statement of reasons to justify its decision that the user fee imposed by the VBA was not contrary to EC competition law and to reject the complaint. The ECJ dismissed the appeal against this finding in its entirety. It did agree with the VBA that the CFI had erred in finding that an insufficient statement of reasons had been given by the Commission in relation to one element of the decision, concerning the equality of treatment of VBA and non-VBA members. It also agreed with the VBA that in criticizing the Commission for a manifest error of appreciation of certain facts regarding the issue of equality of treatment, the CFI did not draw the necessary distinction between the essential procedural requirement to state reasons and the plea of manifest error which goes to the substantive legality of the contested decision. However, the ECJ found that the final conclusion of the CFI was correct; there had been a manifest error of appreciation by the Commission in the finding that members and non-members were treated identically, and this vitiated the decision.

The Court reiterated the requirements that the statement of reasons required by Article 253 'must be appropriate to the act at issue and must disclose in a clear and unequivocal fashion the reasoning followed by the institution which adopted the measure in question in such a way as to enable the persons concerned to ascertain the reasons for the measure and to enable the competent Community Court to exercise its power of review. . . . It is not necessary for the reasoning to go into all the relevant facts and points of law, since the question whether the statement of reasons meets the requirements of Article [235] . . . must be assessed with regard not only to its wording but also to its context and to all the legal rules governing the matter in question' (paragraph 93).[384] The Court further noted that when a case involves balancing the interests of competition policy with those of the Common Agricultural Policy ('CAP'), a full statement of reasons is particularly important. It supported the CFI's ruling (following *Frubo* v. *Commission*[385] and *Oude Luttikhuis*)[386] that the Commission's statement of reasons for its decision failed to show that the agreements between the members of the VBA satisfied each of the objectives of the CAP set out in Article 33 and therefore qualified under that Article for a derogation from the Treaty competition rules. The fact that the CAP took precedence over the competition rules did not excuse the Commission for failing to show how these agreements contributed towards the CAP and, in particular, how the fee levied for use of the VBA's premises by non-members furthered CAP objectives.

The second appeal, which was also unsuccessful, concerned the Commission's invocation of a time limit to reject further submissions by the VGB,

[384] See Case C–367/95P, *Commission* v. *Sytraval & Brink's France* [1998] ECR I–1719, para. 63.
[385] Case 71/74, *Frubo* v. *Commission* [1975] ECR 563.
[386] Case C–399/93, *OudeLuttikhuis and Others* v. *Verenigde Coöperatieve Melkindustrie* [1995] ECR I–4515.

Florimex, and others in regard to the rejection of their complaint. It involved an equally unsuccessful cross-appeal by the VGB, Florimex, and others against the CFI's judgment in so far as it had dismissed their pleas in law and arguments concerning the Commission's refusal to uphold their complaints against the agreements relating to the 'Cultra commercial centre' concluded by the VBA with certain wholesalers. The ECJ first looked at whether the Commission could invoke a time limit which had not been respected by the applicants to close the case. The ECJ considered that in finding that 'special circumstances could preclude the Commission from closing the procedure on complaints where the complainant has not responded to a letter within the time-limit set by the Commission, the Court of First Instance correctly balanced the requirements of good administration and legal certainty on the one hand against those of ensuring the procedural safeguards provided for complainants on the other' (paragraph 71). The CFI ruled that for the Commission to assume 'silence gave consent' because the complainants failed to meet a deadline during a holiday period was not consistent with their right to a hearing. They had persisted in their complaints for over three years and had repeatedly asked the Commission for a decision; their continuing interest in the case was shown by the fact that they had instituted proceedings in a separate, related, case before the CFI;[387] furthermore their legal adviser was seriously ill at the time and a new lawyer had to be appointed.

The ECJ therefore emphasized that considerations of basic fairness must operate throughout the Commission's administrative proceedings. On the other hand, the ECJ also made it clear that its jurisdiction to hear arguments on appeal is strictly limited: in the first place, 'an appeal must indicate precisely the contested elements of the judgment which it is requested to have set aside and also the legal arguments which specifically support that request' (paragraph 78).[388] Secondly, 'in an appeal the jurisdiction of the Court of Justice is . . . confined to review of the findings of law on the pleas argued before the Court of First Instance' (paragraph 79).[389] All the other arguments made by the VBA were dismissed with the ECJ referring to its oft-repeated language that 'an appeal may be based only on grounds relating to the infringement of rules of law, to the exclusion of any appraisal of the facts' (paragraph 91).[390] Thus, the 'Court of First Instance alone has jurisdiction, first, to make a finding as to the facts, save where the substantive inaccuracy of such findings is apparent from the documents submitted to it and, second, to assess those facts . . . Furthermore, such inaccuracy must be obvious without its being necessary to undertake a fresh assessment of the facts' (paragraph 92). The Court considered that there was nothing before it to show a manifest substantive error in the findings of fact made by the CFI.

---

387 Joined Cases T–70/92 and 71/92, *supra* n. 380.
388 See the Order in Case C–317/97, *Smanor et Ségaud* v. *Commission* [1998] ECR I–4269.
389 See the Order in Case C–422/97, *Sateba* v. *Commission* [1998] ECR I–4913.
390 See Case C–8/95, *New Holland Ford* v. *Commission* [1998] ECR I–3175.

The Commission must therefore return to its analysis of the business practices of the VGB and its Alsmeer auctions for flowers and bulbs. It can be expected to outline its conclusions in an extremely detailed decision, since whatever conclusion it reaches is likely to be appealed. One issue of possible interest will be the position taken by the Commission on the effect on trade between Member States. The suggestion in its latter decisions was that, contrary to other decisions involving the Netherlands, and surprisingly in view of the pivotal position of the Dutch in the EU flower trade, the necessary effect on trade between Member States had not been shown. The Commission doubtless wishes that the new Dutch national competition authority will deal with this dispute.

(c) Stork v. Commission[391]   This case is a good example of how EC competition law may be used by parties in dispute over an agreement. It concerns an attempt by Stork, a Dutch company which produces machines for manufacturing plastic bottles by means of a 'blow moulding' technique, to escape from an agreement it concluded in 1987 with the Serac Group, a French company which produces machines for aseptically filling plastic bottles. Stork and Serac agreed to co-operate for a period of five years in marketing complete production lines for manufacturing and aseptically filling plastic bottles, by purchasing the necessary machines from each other and selling them as complete lines under their joint names. They also undertook to provide each other with the know-how required for marketing, installing, and servicing the machines. A restrictive covenant in Clause 6 of the agreement prevented either party from producing and selling equipment or parts produced by third parties without the other's prior consent, damages being payable if this requirement was breached. The non-compete requirement remained valid in certain circumstances for four years after termination of the agreement.

Some two years after its conclusion, Stork attempted to terminate the agreement, and threatened, should Serac refuse, to complain to the Commission that Clause 6 infringed Article 81. Stork did indeed make a complaint, and Serac prudently submitted the agreement to the Commission, requesting negative clearance, an exemption, or at least a comfort letter. The acting Director General for Competition replied in March 1991 that he considered Clause 6 restricted competition and was not indispensable for attaining the objectives of the agreement. He suggested that the parties amend the agreement to bring it into the spirit of the block exemption on specialization agreements (although they were not actually covered by that exemption), including deleting Clause 6.3. He said that 'given the limited economic importance of the matter at Community level, it did not seem 'appropriate, at [that] stage, to recommend to the Commission the formal opening of a procedure' (paragraph 9). In the event that the parties failed to agree to amend the clauses as suggested, they were invited to bring the matter before the proper national court

---

[391] Case T–241/97, *Stork Amsterdam BV* v. *Commission* [2000] ECR II–309.

or the competent national administrative authorities, calling attention to the Commission's letter. Finally, Stork was told that unless it reacted within four weeks, the file would be closed.

However, the dispute had not been resolved when the initial agreement expired in August 1992 without amendment. Serac again tried to obtain reassurance from the Commission, promising not to rely on Clause 6.3 except if Stork tried to use confidential know-how divulged while the agreement was in force. A senior Commission official replied in February 1993 to both parties that Serac's new arguments 'were not such as to call into question the Commission's position [that] clauses 6.2 and 6.3 of the agreement were too restrictive of competition and not indispensable to attaining the objectives of the agreement'. He added that in his view 'this matter should be considered closed'. Serac asked the CFI to annul this decision.[392] The Commission claimed that it was not 'an actionable measure' intended to produce legal effects, but only expressed a provisional view, and further 'analysis of the matter' would be pursued. On this basis, Serac withdrew its court action.

Almost a year later the Commission requested and obtained data from the parties on market shares for the types of packaging used for liquid milk, and held meetings with their legal representatives. After a further year, the Commission informed Stork that it intended to reject the complaint as 'it was not realistic to say that the agreement affords the undertakings concerned the possibility of eliminating competition in respect of a substantial part of the products in question', particularly since Serac had renounced its right under Clause 6.3. Stork disagreed and questioned whether, after twice stating in writing that the agreement restricted competition, the Commission was now entitled to conduct a fresh analysis. The Commission nevertheless adopted a decision[393] rejecting Stork's complaint and finding that although the agreement was formally caught by Article 81(1), the conditions for an exemption were met (a formal decision actually granting an exemption was not taken). Stork then brought an action for annulment, claiming that:

- since the Commission's two earlier letters already constituted 'actionable' decisions and indicated that the matter should be closed, it either lacked power to adopt the contested decision, or had abused its power by doing so and had failed to adopt a decision on the complaint within a reasonable time;
- the decision was vitiated by errors of fact and law; and
- the reasoning for the decision was inadequate or non-existent, since it did not explain why the Commission had changed its mind about the economic importance of the agreement and decided to carry out a thorough re-examination of the file.

The Court stressed that according to settled case law, any measure whose legal effects 'are binding on and capable of affecting the interests of the

---

[392] Case T–31/93, *Serac* v. *Commission*, removed from the register on 20 Dec. 1993.
[393] Decision IV/F–1/33.302 *Stork* of 20 Sept. 1989.

applicant, by bringing about a distinct change in his legal position, is an act or a decision which may be the subject of an action for annulment. . . . [t]he particular form in which acts and decisions are adopted is, in principle, immaterial' (paragraph 49).

Thus, neither preliminary observations during the first stage of the procedure for examining a complaint nor a notification that the Commission does not intend to pursue a complaint, with a request for the complainant's observations, 'can be regarded as measures open to challenge'. Comfort letters, however, are actionable, since they 'have the content and effect of a decision, inasmuch as they close the investigation, contain an assessment of the agreements in question and prevent . . . the reopening of the investigation' unless new evidence is presented.

The Court examined the Commission's two letters to Stork in light of these criteria, and concluded that they 'contained a clear appraisal of the agreement and, in particular, of its economic importance . . . made on the basis of all the information which the Commission deemed it necessary to gather. All the indications are that the decision mentioned in the letters to take no further action on the matter was meant to constitute the final step in the administrative procedure whereby the institution's position is finally determined'.[394] The fact that the letters were signed by senior officials rather than their Commissioner was irrelevant, since 'the form in which acts or decisions are cast is . . . immaterial as regards the question whether they are open to challenge by way of annulment proceedings'; what mattered was their substance.

The Court pointed out that Stork had correctly waited until the Commission had issued its final decision before disputing the validity of its decision to reopen the procedure, since 'measures of a purely preparatory character may not themselves be the subject of an application for an annulment, but any legal defects therein may be relied upon in an action directed against the definitive act'. The Commission has discretion both to decide that a complaint should not be pursued because it lacks sufficient economic importance at Community level, and subsequently to reopen the matter on the basis of new points of fact and law. But in this case the Commission gave no reason to explain its change of mind, and no new evidence regarding the economic importance or any other aspect of the agreement had come to light. Moreover, in its pleadings and its oral replies to the CFI's questions regarding its reasons for reopening the file, the Commission stated it had done so 'in response to the action brought by Serac and in order to avoid a contentious procedure', and did not mention the economic importance of the agreement at all. Stork was therefore justified in disputing the Commission's entitlement to adopt a fresh decision on a complaint relating to a matter which had already been closed because of its limited economic importance at Community level, without properly stating the reasons (in particular, the existence of fresh evidence) for

---

[394] The Court cited Case C–39/93 P, *SFEI and Others* v. *Commission* [1994] ECR I–2681, see (1994) 14 YEL 530.

reopening the administrative procedure which had led to that decision. Therefore, there was no need to examine its other arguments. The Court added that a decision on whether the agreement had infringed the competition rules could, if still required, be sought from a national court—and specifically noted that while the national court could take account of the Commission's view of the agreement, it was not bound by the comfort letters sent in this case.

The result is that Serac is in the position of having been party to an agreement which is, in the view of the Commission, formally caught by Article 81(1) and void under Article 82, although exemptable under Article 81(3). Stork presumably plans to use this in national proceedings to seek damages from Serac.

(d) Industrie des Poudres Sphériques (IPS)[395] This case involves another decision by the CFI in the context of a long-running judicial saga. It concerns a complaint made by IPS (formerly Extramet) to DG Competition that Péchiney Electrométallurgie (PEM) had abused its dominant position in the market for calcium metal by bringing an anti-dumping procedure which resulted in the imposition of an anti-dumping duty on the product,[396] thus restricting the source of supply for IPS, and also by refusing to supply IPS with the product and engaging in predatory and abusive pricing. The CFI's judgment takes thirty-nine pages to reject the appeal—a long decision, even by the standards of the CFI—possibly influenced by the lengthy and litigious, background to the case and the likelihood that its decision would be appealed to the ECJ.

IPS had already brought four cases before the Court in the context of the anti-dumping procedure which led to the imposition of duties on calcium metal from the USSR and China.[397] In *Extramet II* the Court annulled the Council Regulation imposing the anti-dumping duty, *inter alia* on the ground that the Community institutions had not actually considered whether PEM, as the only Community producer of the product, had itself, by its refusal to sell, contributed to the injury suffered. The Commission opened another investigation and a second Regulation imposing an anti-dumping duty was adopted,[398] unsuccessfully challenged before the CFI by IPS, and rejected on appeal by the ECJ.

In *Extramet II* Advocate General Jacobs specifically stated that the Community institutions had a duty to take competition policy issues into consideration in assessing cases under the anti-dumping procedure, and, in this case, to assess whether PEM had contributed to its own injury by refusing to

---

[395] Case T–5/97, *Industrie Des Poudres Sphériques (IPS)* v. *Commission*, [2000] ECR II–3755.

[396] Regulation 707/89 of 17 Mar. 1989 imposing a provisional anti-dumping duty on imports of calcium metal originating in the People's Republic of China or the Soviet Union [1989] OJ L78/10.

[397] Case C–358/89, *Extramet Industrie* v. *Council* [1991] ECR I–2501, (*Extramet I*); Case C–358/89, *Extramet Industrie* v. *Council* [1992] ECR I–3813 (*Extramet II*); Case T–2/95, *Industrie des Poudres Sphériques* v. *Council* [1998] ECR II–3939; Case C–458/98 P, *Industrie des Poudres Sphériques* v. *Council*, [2000] ECR I–8147.

[398] Council Regulation 2557/94 imposing a definitive anti-dumping duty on imports of calcium metal originating in the People's Republic of China and Russia [1994] OJ L270/27.

sell to IPS and whether this might be contrary to the EC competition rules. Meanwhile the French Competition Council, upheld on appeal, found PEM liable for abuse of a dominant position in France for the period between 1992 and 1994.

In light of this, a complaint by IPS to the Commission as regards Article 82 was clearly treated seriously. The DG Competition investigation was apparently given access to the dossier used in the anti-dumping procedure and fully reviewed it, as well as obtaining and considering further information. Nevertheless, the Commission decided to reject the complaint. Unsurprisingly, this was challenged by IPS before the CFI.

The CFI reviewed the facts of the case in some depth. It found that the Commission had not committed any manifest error of appreciation in deciding that there was no violation of Article 82 by PEM. It repeated the view in earlier jurisprudence[399] that the Commission is not obliged to take a position on every single argument invoked by a complainant, but should set out the facts and legal considerations which are of the greatest importance for its decision. In this case it considered that the Commission had provided sufficient reasoning for its conclusion that bringing an anti-dumping action is not in itself an abuse of a dominant position. Nor had the Commission infringed the complainants' procedural rights by not communicating certain documents which it had used to reach its conclusions, as it had given sufficient information on the contents of the documents in question. In particular, third parties such as complainants cannot claim a right of access to the file held by the Commission on the same basis as the undertakings under investigation,[400] and a complainant may not in any circumstances be given access to documents containing business secrets.[401]

The Court considered that even if the Commission had not had the documents which IPS had sought, the outcome of the case would not have been altered. It did send a warning to possible applicants, however—if the Commission suggests having recourse to the hearing officer regarding access to certain information, a party should do so, if only to protect its position in a subsequent appeal. The appeal was dismissed in its entirety. As a result, IPS has effectively lost the last battle in the war against PEM, fought in the different territory of competition law, subject to an appeal to the ECJ.

(iii)   Rejections of Complaints in the Car Sector

(a)   Asia Motor France and Others v. Commission[402] The CFI dealt with Episode IV of the Asia Motor France saga, featuring the heirs of the original

---

[399] For example, Case T–7/92, *Asia Motor France* v. *Commission* [1993] ECR II–669.

[400] See Case 53/85, *Akzo* v. *Commission* [1986] ECR 1965, (1986) 6 YEL 402; and Case T–17/93, *Matra Hachette* v. *Commission* [1994] ECR II–595, para. 34.

[401] See Joined Cases 142/84 and 156/84, *BAT and Reynolds* v. *Commission*, [1987] ECR 4487, para. 21.

[402] Case T–154/98 [2000] ECR II–3453.

parties,[403] in the form of their liquidators and receivers in bankruptcy.[404] Asia Motor France was an importer into France of Japanese cars which had been cleared for free circulation in other Member States of the Community. With a number of other companies in the business, it considered itself to be the victim of an unlawful cartel operated by five importers of Japanese cars into France (namely Sidat Toyota France, Mazda France Motors, Honda France, Mitsubishi Sonauto, and Richard Nissan SA) whereby they would sell no more than 3 per cent of the total number of motor vehicles registered in France in the preceding year, and would share this quota out between themselves, excluding any Japanese make of car which they did not import. The importers claimed they were not responsible for these arrangements, which were imposed on them by the French government. As noted in previous *YEL* reviews, it was plain to many observers that the real villain was the French government's unlawful unpublished ceiling on Japanese cars, which had never been challenged in the European Court. Since 1985, the Commission has been receiving complaints about the practices of this 'cartel', and refusing to act on these complaints. In its previous three decisions involving Asia Motor, the CFI ruled on the propriety of the Commission's reluctance to get involved. Episode III[405] ended when the CFI annulled a Commission decision rejecting as unfounded complaints made in November 1985 and November 1988 by Asia Motor France and its allies.

The latest episode therefore began with a supplementary investigation in which the Commission asked the importers to provide all documents for the relevant years emanating from either the French administrative authorities or the Chambre Syndicale des Importateurs d'Automobiles which dealt with 'the distribution of a quota for the import of Japanese cars', as well as evidence of 'irresistible pressure' by the French authorities, and details of why they had been unable to resist this pressure. The Commission also asked when each importer considered these restrictions had ended. This investigation culminated in a decision of 15 July 1998 duly rejecting the 1985 and 1988 complaints lodged by the applicants, on the basis that 'the replies which [the Commission] had received to its requests for information of 7 May 1997 confirm[ed] that, during the period in question, there [had] been no agreement. In any event . . . there was no Community interest sufficient to justify fresh action on its part'. The CFI was invited by the applicants to annul this decision and to take formal note that they reserved the right to claim compensation.

As a matter of admissibility, the CFI did not entertain pleas, added by the applicants at the reply stage, that the inordinate length of the proceedings had infringed the general principle of Community law according to which everyone is entitled to fair legal process. The Court considered such pleas should

---

[403] Except for Somaco, which dropped out following the CFI's ruling in Case T–387/94, *Asia Motor France III* [1996] ECR II–961, see (1996) 16 YEL 525–7.

[404] The other applicants with Asia Motor France SA were Jean-Michel Cesbrun (JMC Automobiles), Monin Automobiles SA and Europe Auto Service (EAS) SA.

[405] See (1996) 16 YEL 525–7.

have been raised at the beginning of the proceedings, and there was no duty on the Court to consider them of its own motion. The CFI then added briefly that 'the Community judicature is not required to take formal note of the fact that a party reserves the right to bring an action for compensation for damage' (paragraph 48).

On the substance of the case, the CFI noted that the essence of the action was whether or not an anti-competitive agreement between the importers existed, and pointed out, as usual,[406] that 'judicial review of Commission measures involving an appraisal of complex economic matters must be limited to verifying whether the relevant rules on procedure and on the statement of reasons have been complied with, whether the facts have been accurately stated and whether there has been any manifest error of assessment or a misuse of powers' (paragraph 53). The CFI then reviewed the Commission decisions and the reasons for their annulment. It considered that the supplementary investigation following the ruling in *Asia Motor France III* had brought to light new evidence confirming that the import restrictions on vehicles from Japan were imposed by the French authorities, and that those authorities were responsible for deciding how the 3 per cent quota thus imposed was to be shared out between the importers. The new evidence also showed that 'the French authorities ensured compliance with individual quotas and, consequently, with the overall quota by delaying or refusing certificates of conformity, which are a prerequisite to putting vehicles into circulation on French territory'. Thus, the CFI held, the new decision rejecting the complaint was based on 'objective, relevant and consistent evidence' which permitted 'a different interpretation of the evidence to which the Court of First Instance, in its judgments in *Asia Motor France II* and *Asia Motor France III*, attached strong probative force in relation to the probable existence of a concurrence of wills. . . . [I]t is clear from the documents before the Court that the importers in question had no choice but to comply with the measures taken by the French authorities' (paragraphs 87, 88). Hence the claim that the Commission had made a manifest error of assessment with regard to the facts was unfounded.

The applicants also accused the Commission of infringing Article 233 by not taking the necessary measures to comply with the judgment in *Asia Motor France III* (which, when the CFI annuls an act of an institution, requires that institution to take the measures necessary to comply with the Court's judgment), and claimed the new decision still contained errors of fact and law already identified by the CFI in that judgment. They criticized the Commission's handling of the supplementary investigation, and disputed the relevance of the evidence collected during the investigation and the Commission's analysis of it.

The CFI observed that its previous judgment criticized the Commission for having failed to check 'with the French authorities or the importers into met-

---

[406] See Joined Cases 142/94 and 156/84, *BAT and Reynolds v. Commission* [1987] ECR 4487; Case C–225/91, *Matra v. Commission* [1993] ECR I–3203; Cases T–7/92, *Asia Motor France II* [1993] ECR II–669 and Case T–387/94, *Asia Motor France III* [1996] ECR II–961.

ropolitan France' whether the authorities had put pressure on the importers to compel them to restrict imports. In the supplementary investigation the Commission had specifically asked the importers for evidence that they had been subject to 'irresistible pressure'. Thus the applicants' criticism of the supplementary investigation was unfounded.

Asia Motor may at last be drawing to a close, subject to a possible appeal to the ECJ of this judgment.

(b) SODIMA, Européenne Automobile, SGA[407]   In three judgments delivered at the end of 1999, again concerning the car distribution sector, the CFI ruled on the rejection of complaints by the Commission. The CFI confirmed the discretion of the Commission to assess which cases it wishes to pursue, and those where it considers there is no Community interest in proceeding.[408] It also ruled that the Commission is free to concentrate its efforts on pursuing one large economic enterprise where there is evidence that several enterprises have been involved in anti-competitive behaviour, and to tell companies which claim to have been damaged by these other enterprises to seek a remedy through the national courts.[409] The CFI also made it clear that failure by the Commission to respond following receipt of a complaint cannot be taken as an implied decision not to act, unless Community legislation specifically provides this.[410]

(c) Dalmasso and Others[411]   This case concerns another appeal against rejection of complaints regarding car distribution—interestingly, in view of the huge fine recently imposed by the Commission on Volkswagen, the distribution of VW cars. The CFI dismissed the application by Dalmasso and others asking it to annul three Commission decisions rejecting complaints alleging infringements of Article 81(1) and award damages for loss suffered as a result of those decisions.

After terminating their dealerships with Volkswagen between 1986 and 1991, the applicants lodged complaints with the Commission concerning refusals by Volkswagen to supply them with Audi and VW vehicles and spare parts on the sole ground that they were no longer part of Volkswagen's network in France. The Commission initiated investigation proceedings and sent Volkswagen a Statement of Objections. It considered that several provisions in the standard form agreement were anti-competitive, and that the whole

---

[407] Cases T–190/95 and T–45/96, *SODIMA* v. *Commission* [1999] ECR II–3617; Joined Cases T–9/96 and T–211/96, *Européenne Automobile* v. *Commission* [1999] ECR II–3639; Joined Cases T–189/95, T–39/96 and T–123/96, *SGA* v. *Commission* [1999] ECR II–3617.

[408] *Européenne Automobile, supra* n. 407, paras. 27–58, 61; *SGA, supra* n. 407, paras. 39–41, 61–64. The Commission is required to set out the use of its discretion with sufficient reasoning for the Court to review the decision taken.

[409] *Européenne Automobile, supra* n. 407, paras. 39, 49, 50; *SGA, supra* n. 407, para. 59, 60.

[410] *SODIMA, supra* n. 407, paras. 30–34.

[411] Joined Cases T–185/96, T–189/96 and T–190/96, *Riviera Auto Service Établissements Dalmasso SA and Others* v. *Commission* [1999] ECR II–93.

agreement therefore fell outside the scope of the car distribution block exemption regulation then in force, Regulation 123/85.[412] The Commission also found that as the standard form agreement had not been notified, it could not be covered by an individual exemption under Article 81(3).

To the surprise of the former dealers, the Commission then informed them that it had decided not to take any action against Volkswagen. The complainants submitted additional observations, but the Commission decided they contained nothing to make it alter its new point of view and dismissed the complaints definitively in September 1996. It cited the lack of sufficient Community interest in pursuing proceedings and pointed out the disproportionate work that pursuing them would entail, the fact that national courts were available to deal with the question and its intention to introduce a new Regulation in the future.

The CFI upheld the Commission's conclusions. It found that the Commission had not erred in law in finding that there was no restriction of competition in the clauses of the standard form agreements complained of. The Court also dismissed as unfounded the applicants' plea that the Commission had wrongly assessed the issue of Community interest.

The Court, in accordance with its earlier case law, specified that when dismissing a complaint on the ground that it lacked Community interest the Commission must:

weigh the significance of the alleged infringements as regards the functioning of the common market against the probability of its being able to establish the existence of the infringements and the extent of the investigative measures required in that connection. . . . It is for the Commission to gather sufficiently precise and consistent evidence to support the firm conviction that the alleged infringements constitute appreciable restrictions of competition within the meaning of Article [81(1)] of the Treaty. That requirement is not satisfied, in particular, where a plausible explanation can be given for those alleged infringements which rules out an infringement of Community rules on competition [paragraphs 46–47].

A complainant does not always have the right to obtain a decision regarding infringements of the competition rules from the Commission. In particular, there is no such right in a case such as that under examination, where the Commission does not have exclusive competence to rule that a contractual clause is incompatible with the competition rules, i.e. where a provision has direct effect and national courts share this competence (paragraph 48). Moreover, the Court agreed with the Commission in urging complainants to seek redress in the national courts in cases involving standard-form contracts for the exclusive distribution of motor vehicles, stating that it is for a national court to 'determine under its own laws, the liability which the parties to the contract may incur as a result of a refusal to sell to resellers outside the net-

---

[412] Commission Regulation 123/85 of 12 Dec. 1984 on the application of Art. [81(3)] of the EC Treaty to certain categories of motor vehicle distribution and servicing agreements [1985] OJ L15/16.

work, on the basis of a distribution agreement containing provisions which would be void' (paragraph 51).

The Court assessed the standard-form car dealership agreement in light of these principles, and came to the conclusion that the Commission had not committed a manifest error of appraisal by dismissing the complaints on the ground of insufficient Community interest. In the absence of evidence that the decision to dismiss the complaint was unlawful, and where no separate allegation of unlawfulness has been made by the applicant, the Court found that the Commission had not committed a fault of such a nature as to render the Community liable.

The applicants had some success with regard to costs, however. Although the Court found for the Commission, it ordered the parties to bear only their own costs, as the circumstances were exceptional:'it is clear from the history of the cases that the radical change in the Commission's view was likely to prompt the applicants to bring it before this Court to explain the reasons which led it to abandon its initial analysis of the provisions of the standard-form agreement' (paragraph 94).

This case therefore confirms the difficulty that applicants may have in seeking a resolution of a problem via the Commission where there may be a remedy under national law. The situation for the complainants is in fact now worse, since the CFI considered that the Commission was right in its assessment that the standard form agreements in themselves were not contrary to Article 81(1).

(iv) Failure to Act

(a) UPS v. Commission[413]   This was yet another case involving alleged abuse by Deutsche Post of its dominant position in the postal sector. The CFI upheld a complaint against the Commission for failure to act, a rare procedural development. The case was brought by UPS Europe SA ('UPS'), a member of the United Parcels Group, which distributes parcels worldwide and has offices in all the EU's Member States, including Germany. In July 1994 UPS complained to the Commission that the then Deutsche Bundespost was abusing a dominant position and receiving state aid in the form of cross-subsidization.

The Commission initially took up the complaint with enthusiasm; it met UPS early in August 1994 and very soon afterwards forwarded the complaint to Deutsche Post. However, after reading Deutsche Post's reply and discussing a non-confidential version of it with UPS, the Commission retreated a little. In March 1995 it informed UPS that it would examine only the complaint that Deutsche Post was abusing a dominant position, and that if UPS wished it could lodge a separate complaint concerning the alleged state aid, 'substantially reinforced by further evidence'. UPS filed written comments on Deutsche Post's reply. The next year brought further Commission requests for information and replies from Deutsche Post, interspersed with enquiries from UPS on the progress of its complaint under Article 82.

[413] Case T–127/98, *UPS Europe SA v. Commission,* [1999] ECR II–2633.

In November 1996—two years after the initial complaint was made—counsel for UPS sent the Commission a letter 'calling on it to act and expressly referring to Article [232] of the EC Treaty'. This, together with the lodging on 23 January 1997 of a further complaint against Deutsche Post by another operator, apparently spurred the Commission into action. On 24 January 1997 it informed Deutsche Post of its intention, 'drawing on the data available . . . to take a negative position . . . and to make a Statement of Objections with a view to proposing that the Commission consider adopting a negative decision' regarding the behaviour complained of by UPS. This ominous news was accompanied by a proposed timetable for action, starting with the sending of the Statement of Objections in April and ending with a final decision 'in the Fall of 1997'. However, the new complaint apparently disrupted the Commission's timetable, since in July 1997 it answered a further request from UPS for a progress report by explaining that owing to that complaint examination of the case would take longer. Also in July, the Commission asked outside consultants to prepare a report on data provided by Deutsche Post; but before the report was completed it told UPS that it had decided to suspend the investigation under Article 82 and instead would carry on with the investigation under Article 86.

No doubt UPS's patience had begun to wear thin, since in February 1998 it officially requested the Commission to take a position on the original complaint (now almost four years old) and reconsider its decision to suspend the procedure under Article 82. The Commission replied with a letter stating that it would open the procedure relating to Deutsche Post's alleged infringement of the state aid rules; but there were no grounds for granting UPS's application under Article 82, although the investigation might be reopened later. UPS objected to this, and asked the Commission 'to reject its complaint, if it still wished to do so, within a reasonable time'. Since a formal request to act sent four months later still produced no results, UPS turned to the CFI. UPS claimed that four years was ample time for the Commission to examine the complaint, adding at the oral hearing that the two limbs of the complaint were not mutually exclusive, and the Commission was under an obligation to conduct the investigation under Article 82 and the State aid rules at the same time.

The CFI agreed with UPS's claim, based on the case law in *Guérin Automobiles*,[414] that the Commission was obliged to adopt a definitive decision on a complaint within a 'reasonable' time 'in relation to the particular circumstances of each case and, in particular, its context, the various procedural stages to be followed by the Commission, the conduct of the parties in the course of the procedure, the complexity of the case and its importance for the various parties involved'. When UPS had formally requested the Commission to act, the procedure for examining the complaint had already reached its final stage. Thus the Commission should either have initiated proceedings against Deutsche Post or adopted a definitive decision rejecting the complaint, but

---

[414] Case C–282/95 P, *Guérin Automobiles* v. *Commission* [1997] ECR I–1503, see (1997) 17 YEL 92.

should not simply have resumed examination of the complaint. The CFI therefore rejected the Commission's defence that because it began to reconsider the complaint and to focus on the alleged Article 82 infringement only after receiving UPS's observations on its 1998 letter indicating it would proceed under the state aid rules, it had not had time to complete its analysis. The CFI also rejected all the Commission's other attempts to justify its failure to act, observing that it had done nothing more even when the oral hearing was held; moreover, during the hearing it had actually admitted that 'manifestly, there has been an infringement of Article [232]', and that it had not acted 'in an impressive manner'! UPS had asked the CFI to require the Commission to act within one month after rendering its judgment. However, citing *SDDDA*,[415] the CFI agreed with the Commission that it could only declare there had been 'an unlawful failure to act' and could not impose a deadline by which the Commission must act, since it had 'no jurisdiction to issue directions to the Community institutions'.

As we have noted in the Introduction, this case is a demonstration of how difficult the Commission finds it, without an adequate set of internal procedural rules, to dispose of a complex and hotly-contested case.

(v) Procedural Rights of Non-appellants Following a Successful Appeal

(a) AssiDomän Kraft Products and Others (Wood Pulp)[416] This judgment by the Court of Justice appears finally to have brought the fifteen-year long wood pulp proceedings to an end. The Court dealt with an appeal against a judgment by the CFI upholding the right of seven Swedish wood pulp producers which had not appealed the Commission's original decision,[417] and had paid the fines imposed under it, to have those fines repaid. The Commission challenged this initial victory,[418] and the ECJ upheld the Commission and set the CFI's decision aside.

In 1993 the Court of Justice annulled[419] the main findings of the decision finding the existence of a cartel in the woodpulp sector and imposing fines. The ECJ also annulled the fines imposed on the companies which had filed the action for annulment (twenty-six of the original forty-three addressees[420]). This judgment encouraged a number of Swedish producers which had not appealed the decision to ask for a refund of the fines they had paid. The Commission rejected these requests, arguing that the decision had fined each producer individually and the Court had merely annulled or reduced the fine

---

[415] Case T–47/96, *SDDDA* v. *Commission* [1996] ECR II–1559.

[416] Case C–310/97 P, [1999] ECR I–5363.

[417] Commission Decision 85/202/EEC of 19 Dec. 1984 in Case IV/29.725, *Wood Pulp* (the 'Wood Pulp' Decision).

[418] Reported in (1998) 18 YEL 567.

[419] Judgment of 31 Mar. 1993 in Joined Cases C–89/85, C–104/85, C–114/85, C–116/85, C–117/85 and C–125/85 to C–129/85, *Åhlström OY and Others* v. *Commission* [1993] ECR I–1307, see (1993) 13 YEL 472–5.

[420] None of the nine Swedish undertakings fined by the Commission appealed against the decision.

imposed on each undertaking which had applied for annulment of the decision. Therefore:

as the judgment does not affect the decision with regard to [the Swedish undertakings], the Commission was neither obliged nor indeed entitled to reimburse the fines paid by [those undertakings] [paragraph 11].

The CFI annulled the decision rejecting the request for repayment after examining the Commission's obligation under Article 223 to take the necessary measures to put the judgment of the CFI into effect. The CFI dismissed the companies' plea that a judgment annulling an act renders that act null and void *erga omnes* and *ex tunc*. It rejected the plea that a decision annulled on an appeal by some of its addressees was thereby also annulled with regard to addressees which had not appealed against it, but nevertheless found that a judgment annulling a measure might have consequences which went beyond the group of persons who had brought the action. Although the Swedish companies had not appealed the decision, it was addressed to them under the same administrative process, and the individual decisions concerning each Swedish company were based on the same findings of fact and the same economic and legal analysis as those annulled by the 1993 judgment.

In its appeal, the Commission argued that the 1997 judgment infringed Article 223 and disregarded Articles 230 and 249 EC Treaty. If it were upheld, it would be possible in future to disregard (i) the two-month time limit for challenging a decision; (ii) the basic legal principle that no one can sue in the name of another; and (iii) the individual nature of decisions. The Court of Justice agreed with all these arguments. It concluded by stating:

Where a number of similar individual decisions imposing fines have been adopted pursuant to a common procedure and only some addressees have taken legal action against the decisions concerning them and obtained their annulment, the principle of legal certainty . . . precludes any necessity for the institution which adopted the decisions to re-examine, at the request of other addressees, in the light of the grounds of the annulling judgment, the legality of the unchallenged decisions and to determine, on the basis of that examination, whether the fines paid must be refunded [paragraph 63].

The Court distinguished the factual situation regarding the Swedish companies' appeal from *Snupat* v. *High Authority*[421] and *Asteris and Others* v. *Commission*[422] which served as the basis for the CFI's findings. It therefore rejected the request by the Swedish companies for annulment of the decision not to refund the fines they had paid, and reversed the ruling by the CFI setting aside that decision.

As noted by Advocate General Ruiz-Jarabo Colomer, this case placed the Court before the most complex of legal dilemmas, the tension between justice and legal certainty. When Goethe considered this dilemma, he preferred 'injustice to disorder'. In its final verdict the Court refrained from expressing

---

[421] Joined Cases 42/59 and 49/59, [1961] ECR 53.
[422] Joined Cases 97/86, 99/86, 193/86, and 215/86 [1988] ECR 2181.

the issues in this way, but, following the Advocate General's opinion, found in favour of legal certainty in a situation where no superior consideration of equity in favour of the applicants existed. Doubtless (though it does not appear from the judgment), the Court was influenced by the consideration that those who do not appeal a fine tacitly acknowledge that its imposition was not intolerably unjust.

(vi)   EC Competition Law in Arbitration Proceedings

(a)   Eco Swiss China Time[423]   This judgment has important implications for companies which decide to resolve a dispute through arbitration. It also clarifies the position of competition law in the legal order. The case originated from a dispute between Benetton and two Swiss watch manufacturers, Eco Swiss and Bulova, over licensing agreements which gave the watch manufacturers the right to manufacture watches and clocks under the Benetton mark. The agreement was to continue for eight years. However, Benetton terminated it three years earlier than agreed, and the watch manufacturers therefore sought relief through arbitration. The arbitrators awarded them substantial compensation, and Benetton appealed, arguing that the original licensing agreements infringed Article 81. The case reached the Dutch Supreme Court, which made a reference to the ECJ, asking whether a failure to apply Article 81 was grounds in EC law to refuse to honour an arbitration award as being contrary to public policy.

The Court first repeated its view that arbitration tribunals are not competent to make direct references under Article 234 EC; only a national court with public status can make such a reference. The ECJ went on to find that the Treaty competition rules are fundamental objectives of the Treaty. Consequently, an infringement of Article 81 was sufficient for the annulment of an arbitration award on public policy grounds:

according to [Article 3(1)(g)] of the EC Treaty, Article 81 constitutes a fundamental provision which is essential for the accomplishment of the tasks entrusted to the Community and, in particular, the functioning of the internal market. . . .

[It] follows that where its domestic rules of procedure require a national court to grant an application for annulment of an arbitration award where such an application is founded on failure to observe national rules of public policy, it must also grant such an application where it is founded on failure to comply with the prohibition laid down in Article 81(1) EC.

The ECJ also held that an infringement of Article 81 was to be regarded as a matter of public policy within the meaning of the New York Convention on the recognition and enforcement of arbitration awards, which has been ratified by all the EU Member States and provides that the recognition and enforcement of an arbitration award may be refused only on certain specific grounds, such as public policy.

---

[423]   Case C–126/97, *Eco Swiss China Time Ltd.* v. *Benetton International NV* [1999] ECR I–3055.

The Dutch Supreme Court also asked the ECJ to consider whether Benetton could appeal on the grounds of an alleged breach of European competition rules even after the time limitation imposed by Dutch law. The ECJ found that a domestic court was not obliged to disapply its normal procedural rules when an appeal raised issues of EC law, provided that domestic time limits made it possible to exercise the rights conferred by EC law:

Community law does not require a national court to refrain from applying domestic rules of procedure according to which an interim arbitration award which is in the nature of a final award and in respect of which no application for annulment has been made within the prescribed time limit acquires the force of res judicata.

Thus parties enjoy a significant degree of freedom to determine their preferences in arbitration, including the choice of fora within the EC which entail time restrictions on challenges to arbitration awards, provided that this does not 'render excessively difficult or virtually impossible the exercise of rights conferred by Community law'.

(vii)   Procedural Deficiencies in the Adoption of Commission Decisions

(a)   Solvay (Soda-ash)[424]   On 6 April 2000 the Court of Justice confirmed rulings by the CFI annulling three Commission decisions which found that Solvay and ICI had abused their dominant positions in the soda-ash[425] market in the UK and continental Western Europe.[426] The ECJ upheld the CFI's view that the decisions should be annulled because the Commission had infringed an essential procedural requirement within the meaning of Article 230.

As regards the substance of the decisions, the Commission had imposed a fine of EUR 10 million on ICI for abusing its dominant position on the UK soda-ash market. In two separate decisions,[427] the Commission found that Solvay had engaged in market-sharing on the German market with a German producer (Chemische Fabrik Kalk) and had abused its dominant position on the Western European market for soda-ash. It imposed a fine of EUR 23 million on Solvay.

According to the decisions, Solvay and ICI had established a system of 'top slice' rebates designed to eliminate competition in their respective territories. Most glass manufacturers, the major users of soda-ash, use only one main supplier for their core requirements, but try to avoid complete dependence by also having a second supplier. To minimize the competitive impact of second suppliers, Solvay and ICI developed a two-tier pricing system where the core tonnage was sold at normal price, but the top slice, i.e. the additional quantity that the customer might otherwise have bought from another supplier, was offered at a substantial and secret discount. It was made clear to customers

---

[424] Joined Cases C–287/95 P and C–288/95, *Commission* v. *Solvay* [2000] ECR I–2391, and Case C–286/95 P, *Commission* v. *ICI* [2000] ECR I–2341.

[425] Soda-ash is a chemical product used in the manufacture of glass.

[426] Case T–31/91, *Solvay* v. *Commission* [1995] ECR II–1821; Case T–32/91, *Solvay* v. *Commission* [1995] ECR II–1825; Case T–37/91, *ICI* v. *Commission* [1995] ECR II–1901, see 15 (1995) YEL 380 ff.

[427] [1991] OJ L152/16 and [1991] OJ L152/21.

that the special price for the top slice depended on their agreeing to take most, if not all, of their requirements from ICI/Solvay. The Commission took the view that these were very serious infringements of Article 81, and the fines imposed were considered heavy at the time. Kalk did not appeal and paid a fine of EUR 1 million. Both Solvay and ICI appealed.

In 1995 the CFI found the decisions were procedurally flawed, because the texts as notified were not authenticated by the signatures of the Commission's President and Executive Secretary in accordance with the Commission's Rules of Procedure.[428] The Court held that authentication of a Commission decision must precede its notification to the addressees, as authentication was intended to guarantee legal certainty by ensuring that the text adopted by the College of Commissioners became fixed in the languages which were binding. Thus, if a dispute arose, it could be verified that the text as notified or published corresponded precisely with the adopted text and the intention of the author.[429] According to the CFI, the mere failure to observe this essential procedural requirement constituted an infringement of an essential procedural requirement under Article 230, and it was therefore irrelevant whether there were discrepancies between the texts adopted, notified, and published and, if so, whether or not those discrepancies were material and affected the addressee. The CFI therefore annulled the decisions.

On appeal to the ECJ, the Commission argued that the CFI had erred in law by failing to address the question whether the parties' interests would have been affected by the lack of authentication. The Commission referred to the judgment in *BASF*[430] and argued that lack of authentication is a procedural irregularity only when it is combined with one or more other defects affecting the notified text. The Court rejected this interpretation of the judgment:

Contrary to the Commission's submissions, it is the mere failure to authenticate an act which constitutes the infringement of an essential procedural requirement and it is not necessary also to establish that the act is vitiated by some other defect or that the lack of authentication resulted in harm to the person relying on it [*ICI*, paragraph 42; *Solvay*, paragraph 46].

The Court further held that if a Community court finds an act produced to it has not been properly authenticated, it must of its own motion raise the issue of infringement of an essential procedural requirement and as a consequence annul the act vitiated by that defect.

It should be noted that on 13 December 2000, the Commission decided to readopt the decisions against Solvay and ICI in due and proper form.[431] Their substance remains unchanged; thus, Solvay and ICI are liable to pay the same fines as those imposed by the original 1990 decisions. A procedural victory, presumably at some financial cost, but with no substantial gain for the appellants.

[428] Art. 12 of the Commission's Rules of Procedure.
[429] Case T–37/91, *ICI* v. *Commission* [1995] ECR II–1901.
[430] Case C–137/92 P, *Commission* v. *BASF and others* [1994] ECR I–2555.
[431] Commission press release IP/00/1449, 13 Dec. 2000.

(viii)   Failure to Act

(a)   TF1[432]   Although this judgment sits on the cusp between competition and state aids policy, it is reviewed here owing to its importance for the broadcasting sector. The CFI condemned the Commission for failure to act under Article 232, and confirmed that the Commission cannot extend indefinitely its preliminary examination of government measures which allegedly infringe the state aid rules (Article 87(1)).

Television broadcasting in France includes public channels (France 2 and France 3) ('France-Television') and a number of private companies, including TF1. On 10 March 1993 TF1 complained to the Commission that the methods used to finance and operate the France-Television channels infringed Articles 81, 86, and 87. In July 1993 the Commission sent TF1 a request for information, to which TF1 replied in September 1993. In July 1995, the Competition Commissioner informed TF1 that the Commission had received other similar complaints and had therefore ordered a study covering all the Member States. The results of the study were expected by summer 1995. In October 1995 TF1 formally requested the Commission to act on its complaint. In December 1995, the Commission wrote to inform TF1 that in light of the results of the study, it had sent the French authorities a request for information to help it decide what action to take with regard to TF1's complaint. In February 1996 TF1 lodged its application with the CFI. Over a year later the Commission sent TF1 a letter stating that on the basis of the information obtained, it was unable to uphold the complaint alleging infringement of Articles 81 and 82.

The Commission alleged that TF1's action was inadmissible because TF1 did not have standing. The CFI disagreed and confirmed earlier case law by stating that Article 232:

must be interpreted as entitling individuals to bring an action for failure to act not only against an institution which has failed to adopt an act which otherwise would be addressed to them but also against an institution which they claim has failed to adopt a measure which would have concerned them directly and individually [paragraph 27].

The CFI concluded that TF1 was individually and directly concerned by the Commission's decision regarding the grants made by the French authorities to the public television companies.

In order to decide whether the Commission had failed to act, the CFI examined whether, when called upon to act, it was under an obligation to do so. The CFI held that since the Commission:

has exclusive jurisdiction to assess the compatibility of a grant of State aid with the common market, it is required, in the interests of the sound administration of the fundamental rules of the Treaty relating to State aid, to conduct a diligent and impartial examination of complaints reporting the grant of aid which is incompatible with the common market [paragraph 73].

---

[432] Case T–17/96, *Télévision Française 1* v. *Commission* [1999] ECR II–1757.

Furthermore, Article 88(2) procedures must be initiated whenever the Commission has serious difficulties in determining whether an aid measure is compatible with the common market (paragraph 74).

As to whether or not the duration of the administrative procedure in the case was reasonable, the CFI confirmed that when the Commission agreed to undertake an examination of government measures which had been denounced as incompatible with Article 87(1) it could not prolong its preliminary examination indefinitely. In this case, the CFI considered that the application was well founded, because when the Commission was given formal notice to act the preliminary examination had lasted for thirty-one months, and it was unable to demonstrate that there were exceptional circumstances to explain why it had taken so long. Once again, the lack of court-like rigorous procedures, notably deadlines, and the Commission's difficulty in reaching conclusions in hotly-contested matters, led to embarrassment.

IV. Procedural and Regulatory Changes and New Legislation

A. THE NEW PROCEDURAL REGIME

1. White Paper on modernization of the rules implementing Articles 85 and 86 of the EC Treaty.[433]
2. Council Regulation 1215/1999 of 10 June 1999 amending Regulation 19/65/EEC on the application of Article 81(3) of the Treaty to certain categories of agreements and concerted practices.[434]
3. Council Regulation 1216/1999 of 10 June amending Regulation 17: first Regulation implementing Article 81 and 82 of the Treaty.[435]
4. Proposal for a Council Regulation on the implementation of the rules on competition laid down in Articles 81 and 82 of the Treaty and amending Regulations 1017/68, 2988/74, 4056/86 and 3975/87 ('Regulation implementing Articles 81 and 82 of the Treaty').[436]

B. VERTICAL RESTRAINTS

1. Commission Regulation 2790/1999 of 22 December 1999 on the application of Article 81(3) of the Treaty to categories of vertical agreements and concerted practices.[437]
2. Commission Notice—Guidelines on Vertical Restraints.[438]

C. HORIZONTAL AGREEMENTS

1. Competition rules relating to horizontal co-operation agreements— Communication pursuant to Article 5 of Council Regulation 2821/71 of 20

---

[433] COM(1999)101 final, 28 Apr. 1999 (commented on in (1998) 18 YEL 511.
[434] [1999] OJ L148/1. [435] [1999] OJ L148/5. [436] COM(2000)582 final, 27 Sept. 2000.
[437] [1999] OJ L336/21. [438] [2000] OJ C291/1.

December 1971 on the application of Article 81(3) of the Treaty to categories of agreements, decisions and concerted practices modified by
Regulation 2743/72.[439]
2. Commission Regulation 2658/2000 of 29 November 2000 on the application
   of Article 81(3) of the Treaty to specialization agreements.[440]
3. Commission Regulation 2659/2000 of 29 November 2000 on the application
   of Article 81(3) of the Treaty to categories of research and development
   agreements.[441]
4. Commission Notice—Guidelines on the applicability of Article 81 to horizontal co-operation agreements.[442]

D.   FINANCIAL SERVICES SECTOR

1. Report on the block exemption in the field of insurance.[443]

E.   TRANSPORT SECTOR

1. Commission Regulation 1083/1999 of 26 May 1999 amending Regulation
   1617/93 on the application of Article 85(3) of the Treaty to certain categories of agreements and concerted practices concerning joint planning and
   co-ordination of schedules, joint operations, consultations on passenger
   and cargo tariffs on schedules air services and slot allocation at airports.[444]
2. Commission Regulation 823/2000 of 19 April 2000 on the application of
   Article 81(3) of the Treaty to certain categories of agreements, decisions and
   concerted practices between liner shipping companies (consortia).[445]

F.   POSTAL SECTOR

1. Proposal for a European Parliament and Council Directive amending
   Directive 97/67/EC with regard to the further opening to competition of
   Community postal services.[446]

G.   TELECOMMUNICATIONS SECTOR

1. Regulation 2887/2000 of the European Parliament and of the Council of 18
   December 2000 on unbundled access to the local loop.[447]
2. Commission Directive 1999/64/EC of 23 June 1999 amending Directive
   90/388/EEC in order to ensure that telecommunications networks and
   cable TV networks owned by a single operator are separate legal entities
   (Text with EEA relevance).[448]

---

[439] [2000] OJ C118/3.   [440] [2000] OJ L304/3.   [441] [2000] OJ L304/7.
[442] [2001] OJ C3/2.   [443] COM(1999)192 final, 22 May 1999.
[444] [1999] OJ L131/27.   [445] [2000] OJ L100/24.   [446] [2000] OJ L336/4.
[447] [2000] OJ C337/220.   [448] [1999] OJ L175/39.

3. Communication from the Commission—Unbundled Access to the Local Loop.[449]
4. Commission Communication—Status of Voice on the Internet under Community law.[450]

H. PUBLIC COMPANIES

1. Commission Directive 2000/52/EC of 26 July 2000 amending Directive 80/723/EEC on the transparency of financial relations between Members States and public undertakings.[451]

I. SERVICES OF GENERAL INTEREST

1. Communication from the Commission—Services of General Interest in Europe.[452]

J. MERGER REGULATION

1. Report from the Commission to the Council on the application of the Merger Regulation thresholds.[453]
2. Commission notice on a simplified procedure for the treatment of certain concentrations under Council Regulation 4064/89.[454]
3. Commission notice on remedies acceptable under Council Regulation 4064/89 and under Council Regulation 447/98 adopted on 21 December 2000.[455]
4. Draft Commission notice regarding the treatment of ancillary restraints under the Merger Regulation.[456]

K. BILATERAL AGREEMENTS

1. Agreement between the European Communities and the Government of Canada regarding the application of their competition laws—Statement by the Commission—Exchange of Letters.[457]

---

[449] [2000] OJ C272/55.
[450] [2000] OJ C369/3.
[451] [2000] OJ L193/75.
[452] [2001] OJ C17/4.
[453] COM (2000) 399 final, 28 June 2000.
[454] [2000] OJ C217/32.
[455] [2001] OJ C68/3.
[456] Not yet published in OJ.
[457] [1999] OJ L175/49.

Common Foreign and Security Policy 1999–2000

STEVE PEERS*

I. Introduction

The European Union had a very good war. Although defence was not formally within the remit of the EU institutions at the time, EU policy strongly supported the bombing of the Federal Republic of Yugoslavia (FRY) in spring 1999 with a view to forcing a Yugoslav troop withdrawal from the Yugoslav region of Kosovo. This action was ultimately successful and, indeed, by October 2000 Slobodan Milosevic was no longer in power in Yugoslavia, raising hopes that the Western Balkans had an opportunity for peaceful development not seen for ten years. For the EU, the bombing not only saw a relatively coherent formation of policy, but also gave the final push toward the key goal of many integrationist Member States: the development of a European defence policy. With remarkable serendipity, the European Council in Cologne, meeting in June 1999, agreed to develop such a policy on the same day that Yugoslavia effectively caved in to the demands of NATO (the North Atlantic Treaty Organization) over Kosovo. Even as the European Security and Defence Policy was developed over the following eighteen months, the Union was implementing the previous reforms to the Common Foreign and Security Policy (CFSP) agreed in Amsterdam and negotiating further modest reforms as part of the Treaty of Nice.

This survey begins with an overview of the Union's CFSP measures adopted in 1999 and 2000. Then it focuses in depth on the four key issues set out above: the implementation of the Treaty of Amsterdam; the negotiation of the Treaty of Nice; the development of the EU's defence policy; and events in the former Yugoslavia. The survey indicates that although there is increasing evidence of a more effective CFSP, there are grounds on occasion to doubt its accountability, legality, and transparency.

---

* Reader in Law, Human Rights Centre, University of Essex.

II. Overview of CFSP Developments

In 1999, the Union agreed twelve Joint Actions,[1] nineteen Common Positions,[2] and twenty-four Decisions implementing, repealing, or extending Joint Actions or Common Positions.[3] In 2000, the Union agreed twelve Joint

[1] Joint Actions 1999/189 on re-establishing an Albanian police force ([1999] OJ L63/1); 1999/239 appointing a Special Envoy for Kosovo ([1999] OJ L89/1); 1999/480 on a conference to support the South-East Europe Stability Pact ([1999] OJ L188/2); 1999/522 on support for UNMIK, the civil administration of Kosovo ([1999] OJ L201/1), extended by 1999/864 ([1999] OJ L328/67); 1999/523 on appointment of the Special Representative to serve as Co-ordinator of the Stability Pact ([1999] OJ L201/2); 1999/664 extending the role of the Middle East Special Representative ([1999] OJ L264/1); 1999/523 terminating the 1998 Joint Action appointing a Special Representative for the FRY ([1999] OJ L264/2); 1999/822 amending Joint Action 1999/523 and extending it to 31 Dec. 2000 ([1999] OJ L318/40); 1999/843 amending the 1996 Joint Action on the Middle East Special Representative and extending it to 31 Dec. 2000 ([1999] OJ L326/71); 1999/844 extending the 1995 Joint Action on peace in Bosnia to 31 Dec. 2000 ([1999] OJ L326/72); and 1999/878, on non-proliferation in Russia ([1999] OJ L331/11).

[2] 1999/73 on Afghanistan ([1999] OJ L23/1), replacing a 1998 Common Position; 1999/206, establishing an arms embargo on Ethiopia and Eritrea ([1999] OJ L72/1), extended by 1999/650 ([1999] OJ L257/1); 1999/261 suspending sanctions against Libya in light of the Lockerbie trial ([1999] OJ L103/1); 1999/273 imposing a petroleum embargo on the FRY ([1999] OJ L108/1); 1999/318 imposing additional sanctions on the FRY ([1999] OJ L123/1); 1999/345 on a Stability Pact for South-Eastern Europe ([1999] OJ L133/1); 1999/346 on the biological weapons Convention ([1999] OJ L133/3), replacing a 1998 Common Position; 1999/452 on Rwanda, replacing a 1998 Common Position ([1999] OJ L178/1); 1999/479 on a referendum in East Timor ([1999] OJ L188/1); 1999/533 on the Comprehensive Nuclear Test Ban Treaty ([1999] OJ L204/1); 1999/604 exempting Montenegro and Kosovo from the EU flight ban and petrol ban to the FRY ([1999] OJ L236/1); 1999/611 removing all sanctions against Libya except the arms embargo ([1999] OJ L242/31); 1999/624 establishing an arms embargo and ban on equipment for use in repression or terrorism as regards Indonesia ([1999] OJ L245/53); 1999/670 extending a 1996 Common Position on Burma/Myanmar ([1999] OJ L267/1); 1999/691 on support for democratic forces in the FRY ([1999] OJ L273/1); 1999/722 on the democratic process in the Democratic Republic of the Congo ([1999] OJ L286/1); 1999/727 on sanctions against the Taliban ([1999] OJ L294/1); and 1999/728 on the democratic process in the Democratic Republic of the Congo ([1999] OJ L294/2), which for some reason simply copies Common Position 1999/722.

[3] Decisions 1999/54 amending the 1994 dual-use goods Joint Action ([1999] OJ L18/1); 1999/74 implementing a 1997 Joint Action on nuclear transparency ([1999] OJ L23/4); 1999/75 extending a 1998 Joint Action on a Special Representative for the Federal Republic of Yugoslavia ([1999] OJ L23/5); 1999/156 repealing a 1998 Common Position on Belarus ([1999] OJ L52/1); 1999/289 extending a 1996 Common Position on Burma/Myanmar ([1999] OJ L114/1); 1999/319, 1999/357, 1999/424, 1999/612 and 1999/812 implementing Common Position 1999/318, by establishing an entry ban against Yugoslav nationals ([1999] OJ L123/3, L140/1, L163/86, L242/32, and L314/36); 1999/320 contributing to destruction of Albanian arms, implementing a Dec. 1998 Joint Action on the issue of small arms ([1999] OJ L123/12), extended later by 1999/846 ([1999] OJ L326/74); 1999/347 repealing a 1998 Common Position on Nigeria ([1999] OJ L133/5); 1999/361 implementing a 1998 Common Position on the South-Eastern Europe Stability Pact by appointing a Special Representative ([1999] OJ L141/1); 1999/423 extending the 1996 Joint Action on the Special Representative to the African Great Lakes ([1999] OJ L163/85); 1999/434 appointing a Special Representative as Co-ordinator of the South-Eastern Europe Stability Pact ([1999] OJ L168/34); 1999/440 extending the 1997 Joint Action on assistance to the Palestinian Authority to control terrorism ([1999] OJ L171/1); 1999/481 amending a 1996 Common Position on an arms embargo to the former Yugoslavia to exempt international forces and small arms to the Bosnian police ([1999] OJ L188/3); 1999/524 repealing Joint Action 1999/239 on appointment of a special envoy for Kosovo ([1999] OJ L201/4); 1999/694 supporting the Stability Pact process ([1999] OJ L201/4); 1999/723 implementing Common Position 1999/722 on the democratic process in the Democratic Republic of the Congo ([1999] OJ L286/3); 1999/729 implementing Common Position

Actions,[4] eighteen Common Positions,[5] and twelve implementing, repealing or extending Decisions.[6]

These second pillar measures were supplemented by a number of first-pillar acts, implementing sanctions decisions in accordance with Articles 60 and/or 301 EC,[7] bringing dual-use goods (almost) fully within the scope of EC

1999/728 on the democratic process in the Democratic Republic of the Congo, which copies Decision 1999/723 for some reason ([1999] OJ L294/4); and 1999/730 and 1999/845 implementing the 1998 Joint Action on small arms as regards Cambodia and Mozambique respectively ([1999] OJ L294/5 and [1999] OJ L326/73).

4 2000/175 extending 1999/522 (*supra* n. 1) on support for UNMIK ([2000] OJ L55/78); 2000/347 extending the 1996 Joint Action on an envoy to the African Great Lakes ([2000] OJ L122/6); 2000/388 and 2000/798 extending 1999/189 (*supra* n. 1) on support for a police force in Albania ([2000] OJ L145/1 and L324/1); 2000/401 banning technical assistance related to the export of dual-use goods ([2000] OJ L159/216); 2000/402 repealing the 1994 Joint Action on dual-use goods ([2000] OJ L159/218); 2000/456 assisting the Georgian authorities to defend the observers on the Georgia/Chechnya border ([2000] OJ L183/3); 2000/717 on a meeting of Heads and State and Government in Zagreb ([2000] OJ L290/54); 2000/792 appointing the Special Representative to the African Great Lakes, replacing the original 1996 Joint Action appointing him ([2000] OJ L318/1); 2000/793 appointing the Special Representative to serve as Co-ordinator of the South-Eastern Europe Stability Pact, replacing 1999/523, *supra* n. 1 ([2000] OJ L318/3); 2000/794 appointing the Special Representative to the Middle East Peace Process, replacing the original 1996 Joint Action appointing him ([2000] OJ L318/5); and 2000/811 on the European Union Monitoring Mission ([2000] OJ L328/53).

5 2000/55 on Afghanistan, replacing 1999/73, *supra* n. 2 ([2000] OJ L21/1); 2000/56 on FRY sanctions, in particular amending and extending the entry ban in 1999/318, *supra* n. 2 ([2000] OJ L21/4); 2000/176 and 2000/454 suspending the Yugoslav flight ban ([2000] OJ L56/1 and L183/1); 2000/230 and 2000/584 extending 1999/206 (*supra* n. 2) on the arms embargo applying to Ethiopia and Eritrea ([2000] OJ L73/1 and L246/69); 2000/297 on the review conference of the Non-Proliferation Treaty ([2000] OJ L97/1); 2000/298 on EU assistance to the Palestinian Authority to prevent terrorism, replacing a 1997 Joint Action and Decision 1999/440 (*supra* n. 3) ([2000] OJ L97/4); 2000/346 placing additional sanctions on Burma/Myanmar ([2000] OJ L122/1) and 2000/601 extending this ([2000] OJ L257/1); 2000/387 repealing a 1998 Common Position on the Stability Pact ([2000] OJ L144/35); 2000/391 on Angola ([2000] OJ L146/1); 2000/420 on support for the peace process in Ethiopia and Eritrea ([2000] OJ L161/1); 2000/455 on Sierra Leone sanctions ([2000] OJ L183/2); 2000/558 on Rwanda ([2000] OJ L236/1), replacing 1999/452, *supra* n. 2; 2000/599 repealing sanctions against the FRY except those relating to Mr Milosevic and persons associated with him ([2000] OJ L255/1 and L261/1); 2000/696 applying 2000/599 in detail ([2000] OJ L287/1); and 2000/722 exempting Croatia from the arms export ban to the former Yugoslavia ([2000] OJ L292/1).

6 2000/43 amending the 1994 Joint Action on dual-use goods ([2000] OJ L82/1); 2000/82 and 2000/457, exempting further Serbian municipalities from the petrol export ban ([2000] OJ L26/1 and L183/4); 2000/177, 2000/348, 2000/370, and 2000/495 on the entry ban on Yugoslav nationals ([2000] OJ L56/2, L122/7, L134/1, and L200/1); 2000/231 supplementing a 1998 Decision on mine clearance in Croatia ([2000] OJ L73/2); 2000/724 and 2000/803 implementing the 1998 Joint Action on small arms as regards in Cambodia and South Ossetia ([2000] OJ L292/3 and L326/1); 2000/697 implementing Common Position 2000/696 by shortening the list of FRY nationals subject to the entry ban ([2000] OJ L287/2); and 2000/723 repealing 1999/320, *supra* n. 3 ([2000] OJ L292/2).

7 Regulations 214/1999 exempting Montenegro further from the ban on Yugoslav airlines flying to and from the Community ([1999] OJ L23/6); 836/1999 suspending sanctions against Libya ([1999] OJ L106/1); 900/1999 banning the sale of petrol to the FRY ([1999] OJ L114/7); 1064/1999 banning all flights between the EU and FRY ([1999] OJ L129/27), which also repealed the earlier Regulation on this subject; 1294/1999 extending the freeze on funds and ban on investment in the FRY ([1999] OJ L153/63), which also repeals two earlier Regulations on this subject; 2111/1999 exempting Montenegro and Kosovo from the petrol sanctions imposed on the FRY, and replacing Regulation 900/1999 ([1999] OJ L258/12); 2151/1999 exempting Montenegro and Kosovo from the flight ban imposed on the FRY, and replacing Regulation 1064/1999 ([1999] OJ L264/3); 2158/1999 banning exports to Indonesia of products for repression or terrorism ([1999] OJ L265/1);

law,[8] and appointing the Council Secretary-General High Representative of the CFSP.[9] The Commission also adopted a number of sanctions Regulations, pursuant to increasing powers delegated by Council Regulations.[10] In addition, the Council adopted other Decisions concerning defence issues.[11] The European Council adopted three Common Strategies, on Russia, Ukraine, and the Mediterranean.[12] Finally, the Council published documents on implementation of the 'soft-law' plan to combat arms trafficking and Code of Conduct on arms exports.[13]

It can be seen that quite apart from the amendments to the CFSP made by the Treaty of Amsterdam, there was a greater willingness to use first-pillar measures to achieve foreign policy goals during this period,[14] and an increased willingness to adopt formal second pillar measures. One particular striking feature is the gradually increasing use of the Commission to implement measures, in particular as regards sanctions and even as regards second pillar measures.[15] A closer look at the relevant measures adopted in 1999/2000 shows that the EU institutions were anxious to take advantage of the reforms introduced by that Treaty.

2421/1999 exempting certain Serbian municipalities from the petrol sanctions imposed on the FRY ([1999] OJ L294/7); 337/2000 imposing a flight ban and freeze on funds of the Taliban ([2000] OJ L43/1); 607/2000 and 1746/2000 suspending the flight ban on the FRY ([2000] OJ L73/4 and L200/24); 723/2000 and 1059/2000, amending the FRY financial sanctions ([2000] OJ L86/1 and L119/1); 1745/200 on sanctions against Sierra Leone diamonds ([2000] OJ L200/21); 1081/2000 on sanctions on Burma/Myanmar ([2000] OJ L122/29); 2227/2000 repealing Regulation 2151/1999 on the FRY flight ban ([2000] OJ L261/3 and L255/2); 2228/2000 repealing Regulation 2111/1999 on the FRY petrol export ban ([2000] OJ L261/4 and L255/3); and 2488/2000 limiting the FRY sanctions to those directed against Mr Milosevic ([2000] OJ L287/19).

[8] Regulation 1334/2000 ([2000] OJ L159/1), replacing Regulation 3381/94 ([1994] OJ L367/1), and later amended by Regulation 2889/00 ([2000] OJ L336/14). See also the index of items in the Annex to the Regulation ([2000] OJ C241/1).

[9] Decision 1999/629 ([1999] OJ L248/33).

[10] Regulations 753/1999 on Angola ([1999] OJ L98/3); 1084/1999, 1971/1999, 303/2000, and 1894/2000 on the petrol export ban to the FRY ([1999] OJ L131/29 and L244/40 and [2000] OJ L35/8 and L228/3); 1520/1999 on the FRY flight ban ([1999] OJ L177/10); and 1970/1999, 2756/1999, 826/2000, 1094/2000, 1147/2000, and 1440/2000 on the freeze on Yugoslav funds ([1999] OJ L244/39 and L331/43; [2000] OJ L101/3, L124/42, L129/15, and L161/68).

[11] Decisions 1999/190, based on Art. J.4(2) EU, requesting the WEU to implement the Joint Action concerning re-establishment of an Albanian police force ([1999] OJ L63/3); 1999/321, based on Art. 17(3) EU, on arrangements for participation of non-WEU Member States when the EU avails itself of the WEU ([1999] OJ L123/14); 1999/404 approving the arrangements on EU-WEU co-operation ([1999] OJ L153/1); 2000/143 establishing the Interim Political and Security Committee ([2000] OJ L49/1); 2000/144 establishing the Interim Military Committee ([2000] OJ L49/2); 2000/145 seconding national military experts to the Council General Secretariat for an interim period ([2000] OJ L49/3); 2000/178 on the rules governing seconded military experts ([2000] OJ L57/1); and 2000/354 establishing a committee for civilian aspects of crisis management ([2000] OJ L127/1).

[12] Respectively [1999] OJ L157/1; [1999] OJ L331/1; and [2000] OJ L183/5.

[13] See the second annual report on the former ([2000] OJ C15/1), the first two annual reports on the latter ([1999] OJ C315/1 and [2000] OJ C379/1), and agreement on the common list of military equipment covered by the latter ([2000] OJ C191/1).

[14] See also Regulation 1080/2000 on EC funding for the UN office in Kosovo and the High Representative's office in Bosnia ([2000] OJ L122/27).

[15] See the Joint Action on support for Georgia (*supra* n. 4) and the Decision on small arms in South Ossetia (*supra* n. 6).

III.   Implementation of the Treaty of Amsterdam

The new Treaty provided for a number of potentially significant reforms to the CFSP. First among these were personnel developments: the appointment of a new High Representative for the Common Foreign and Security Policy and of envoys dealing with particular issues. The next issues were institutional: the new Policy Planning and Early Warning Unit in the Council, the greatly expanded potential for the use of qualified majority voting when adopting implementing measures, and the potential use of 'constructive abstention' for Member States disagreeing with a particular policy. The next two issues relate to instruments: the new possibilities for Common Strategies to be adopted by the European Council and international agreements to implement CFSP plans. Finally, the last major development discussed here is the modest reform of the links between EU and the Western European Union (WEU) brought about by the Treaty of Amsterdam, although this development was very soon overtaken by the formal development of an EU defence policy.[16]

A.   THE HIGH REPRESENTATIVE

The Cologne European Council in June 1999 agreed on the appointment of Javier Solana as the Secretary-General of the Council, taking over as the first High Representative for the Common Foreign and Security Policy. As Mr Solana was the former Spanish Foreign Minister and the sitting Secretary-General of NATO, it was immediately evident that the EU was determined to appoint a senior political figure to serve as the High Representative, rather than an obscure bureaucrat as initially suggested by some commentators. Following the Council's formal appointment of Mr Solana,[17] there was an increasing tendency to augment his role beyond the limited powers set out in the Treaties.

The first extension of the High Representative's role in practice came with the adoption of a Joint Action in December 1999 extending the appointment of the EU special envoy in the Middle East. This measure provided expressly that the envoy would not merely be guided by and report to the Presidency but also that the Secretary-General/High Representative would assist the Presidency in this task.[18] When the mandate of the envoy to the African Great Lakes was extended, similar provision was made.[19]

More broadly, the High Representative assumed considerable powers as regards the EU Joint Action on assistance to the Palestinian Authority to fight terrorism, when that measure was revised in April 2000. He was granted two specific functions assisting the Presidency: co-ordination between the EU envoy to the Middle East and the EU special adviser on anti-terrorism actions,

---

[16]   See section V below.   [17]   Decision 1999/629, *supra* n. 9.
[18]   See Art. 3 of Joint Action 1999/843, *supra* n. 1.
[19]   Art. 3 of Joint Action 2000/347, *supra* n. 4.

and co-ordination between the EU measure, EC funding and Member States' bilateral assistance.[20] The Joint Action on support for the Georgian border and the Decision on removing small arms in South Ossetia both oblige the Commission, which is implementing these measures, to report to the Presidency assisted by the High Representative.[21]

The Council gave a particular boost to the High Representative when it adopted the Joint Action on the EU Monitoring Mission, for the first time formalizing in an official CFSP act the first *de facto* 'Joint Action' of the EU, dating back to 1991.[22] This measure requires the Mission to act in accordance with instructions from the High Representative and the Council. The High Representative has the power to define the tasks of the Mission, to receive reports from the Mission, and to ensure the effective functioning of the mission; and the Head of Mission is appointed by the Council on a proposal from the High Representative. This Joint Action appears to delegate so much power to the Secretary-General as to raise serious questions about accountability. What legal or political control can the Council exercise over his actions?

The last substantial formal increase in the High Representative's functions during this period came with the adoption of fresh Joint Actions on the EU's three Special Representatives.[23] At this time, the line of authority was altered so that Special Representatives must 'report directly' to the High Representative and shall be 'accountable' to the High Representative for administrative expenditure. On these issues, the High Representative acts alone, with no involvement of the Presidency or the Commission. Reports by the envoys are now submitted 'through' the High Representative to the Council, and are also forwarded to the Commission. Additionally, the implementation of each envoy's mandate and the constitution of each envoy's team is established in consultation with the Presidency, assisted by the High Representative and in association with the Commission.

B.   SPECIAL REPRESENTATIVES

Another new feature of the Treaty of Amsterdam was the formal power for the Council to appoint Special Representatives on certain issues, now expressly provided for in Article 18(5) EU. As previously observed,[24] despite a widespread perception that Special Representatives are among the 'reforms' of the CFSP introduced by the Treaty of Amsterdam, such posts are not really new at all. Prior to 1999 the Council had formally appointed Miguel Angel Moratino, Aldo Ajello, and Felipe Gonzalez as Special Representatives to the Middle East, the African Great Lakes, and the FRY respectively.[25] During this survey period,

[20]   See Art. 4(3) and 4(4), Joint Action 2000/298, *supra* n. 4.
[21]   Art. 2(3) of each of Joint Action 2000/496 and Decision 2000/803, *supra* nn. 4 and 6.
[22]   Joint Action 2000/811, *supra* n. 4.
[23]   For instance, see Arts. 6 and 7 of Joint Action 2000/973, *supra* n. 4.
[24]   See Peers, 'Common Foreign and Security Policy 1997' (1997) 17 *YEL* 539 at 548.
[25]   Respectively Joint Actions 96/676 ([1996] OJ L315/1); 96/250 ([1996] OJ L87/1); and 98/375 ([1998] OJ L165/2).

it also formalized the appointment of Mr Petrisch in Kosovo in March 1999. He had been informally designated as an envoy on this issue in autumn 1998, although he soon became the first EU Special Representative to cease work following the establishment of UN administration over Kosovo in July 1999.[26]

Following entry into force of the new Treaty, the new Article 18(5) was used for the first time as a 'legal base' to appoint Mr Roumeliotis as the Special Representative for the Stability Pact, up to 31 May 2000, although this appointment also expressly implemented a prior Common Position.[27] Shortly afterward, the Council adopted a Decision based on Article 18(5) appointing Bodo Hombach as the Special Representative who would serve as co-ordinator for the Stability Pact, although this decision was only temporary pending adoption of a formal Joint Action (based on both Articles 14 and 18(5) EU).[28] Mr Gonzalez' position was also ended in October 1999, this time by use of Article 14 EU as a legal base,[29] while Mr Moratinos' role was extended to encompass publicity of the Union's role amongst 'opinion leaders' in the region, without any specific legal base at all.[30]

With the expiry of Mr Roumeliotis' role in May 2000, the Union was left with three Special Representatives, and had agreed in the meantime a number of reforms relating to the logistics of the appointing procedure and administrative arrangements in March 2000. These new reforms were duly implemented when it came time to renew the mandates of Mr Moratinos, Mr Ajello, and Mr Hombach at the end of 2000.[31] In addition to placing the High Representative in charge of the Special Representatives, as discussed above, the new measures also clarified the status of Special Representatives, requiring them to agree a contract as a 'special adviser' to the Council and a contract on expenditure with the Commission and setting out rules on filling associated posts.

The outcome of formalizing the appointment of special envoys in the EU Treaty has thus been fairly modest, with fewer envoys in service at the end of 2000 than were already in service when the Treaty of Amsterdam entered into force.

C.   INSTITUTIONAL CHANGES

No Member State has yet invoked the possibility of 'constructive abstention' provided for in Article 23 EU, so in practice it seems that this clause will be used only on rare occasions. Furthermore, there is no information to indicate to what extent the Council's policy planning and early warning unit is contributing to the development and analysis of policy options. However, there has been considerable use of another institutional reform introduced by the

---

[26] See Joint Action 1999/239, *supra* n. 1 and Decision 1999/524, *supra* n. 3.
[27] Decision 1999/361, *supra* n. 3.
[28] See Decision 1999/435, *supra* n. 3, and Joint Action 1999/523, *supra* n. 1; and extension in Joint Action 1999/532, *supra* n. 1 (also based on Arts. 14 and 18(5) EU).
[29] Decision 1999/665, *supra* n. 3.   [30] Joint Action 1999/664, *supra* n. 1.
[31] Joint Actions 2000/792 to 2000/794, *supra* n. 4.

Treaty of Amsterdam: the generalization of qualified majority voting (QMV) for CFSP implementing measures.

Before 1 May 1999, there was merely a possibility for using QMV to implement Joint Actions, and this possibility was never formally invoked. Following the Treaty of Amsterdam, Article 23(2) EU requires QMV for all measures implementing Council Joint Actions or Common Positions, or all measures implementing Common Strategies adopted by the European Council. This possibility is subject to two conditions: it cannot apply to measures having military implications, and a Member State objecting to a qualified majority vote can pull the so-called 'emergency brake', blocking a vote for 'important and stated reasons of national policy', with the possibility that the Council will decide by QMV to refer the dispute to the European Council, which will settle it by unanimity.

The only way to test the usefulness of this new possibility is to examine the Council's practice closely. At first, there was considerable ambiguity about the application of the new provision. The first implementing measure adopted after entry into force of the new Treaty was a Council Decision imposing entry bans on a list of Yugoslav nationals, which expressly described itself as an 'implementing Decision' which implemented a Common Position agreed at the same time.[32] However, this initial Decision did not refer expressly to Article 23(2) EU. Nor did another implementing Decision adopted the same day, which implemented a 1998 Joint Action on control of small arms worldwide by contributing to a UN programme on collecting and destroying weapons in Albania in particular.[33] The Council also avoided referring to Article 23(2) when adopting a further three Decisions implementing the FRY entry ban and when appointing a Special Representative for the South-Eastern Europe Stability Pact, although in the latter case it was not clear whether Article 18(5) or Article 23(2) was the correct 'legal base'.[34] But in October 1999, within six months of entry into force of the new Treaty, the Council invoked Article 23(2) expressly for the first time, implementing a 1998 Joint Action on the Stability Pact for South-Eastern Europe by supporting projects related to democratization in the region.[35]

Subsequently, in November 1999, the Council expressly used Article 23(2) to adopt a measure implementing a Common Position, financing assistance to a Military Commission which would send observers to the Democratic Republic of the Congo.[36] Since then, the Council has used Article 23(2) on a number of occasions, most frequently to adopt measures implementing the 1998 Joint

[32] Decision 1999/319, *supra* n. 3.
[33] Decision 1999/320, *supra* n. 3, implementing Joint Action 1999/34 ([1999] OJ L9/1).
[34] See Decisions 1999/357, 1999/424, and 1999/612 (entry ban) and 1999/361 (Stability Pact), *supra* n. 3.
[35] Decision 1999/694, *supra* n. 3.
[36] Decisions 1999/723 and 1999/729, *supra* n. 3, implementing Common Positions 1999/722 and 1999/728, *supra* n. 2.

Action on control of small arms as regards specific projects,[37] and to update the list of Yugoslav nationals covered by the entry ban established by the Council Common Position of May 1999, starting with the fifth version of that list.[38] It follows that the implementing measures adopted on these issues shortly after the Treaty of Amsterdam *were* adopted using Article 23(2) EU, despite the Council's reluctance to refer to that provision expressly.[39] The Council has also used Article 23(2) to extend the list of Serbian municipalities exempted from sanctions on export of petrol to the FRY,[40] and to extend further funds to finance mine clearance in Croatia (implementing a 1996 land-mines Joint Action).[41] So far, the Council has only once used QMV to adopt a measure implementing a Common Strategy.[42]

Several conclusions emerge from Council practice. First, there is no doubt that Article 23(2) can be used to implement *any* Joint Actions or Common Positions, regardless of when they were adopted.[43] Secondly, the implementing Decisions on the Congo and on mine clearance in Croatia clearly indicate that the requirement for unanimity for measures having defence implications is not being interpreted broadly, even though the WEU in the latter case was actually implementing the Joint Action in question. Thirdly, while the hesitation to use Article 23(2) to implement Common Strategies has led to criticisms of the EU's approach to those measures (see below), it should nonetheless be pointed out that the use of QMV has been very extensive as regards implementation of Joint Actions and Common Positions. Also, it should be emphasized that despite no fewer than twenty-three uses of Article 23(2) from May 1999 to the end of 2000, no Member State to date has used the 'emergency brake'.[44] Of course, it is impossible to know how many times a measure under consideration has been amended or dropped because of the express or implied threat of using the emergency brake, or the extent to which the final content of implementing measures has been affected by negotiating within the 'shadow' of the emergency brake.

---

[37] Decisions 1999/730, 1999/845, and 1999/846, *supra* n. 3 (Cambodia, Mozambique, and Albania); and 2000/704, 2000/803, and 2000/723, *supra* n. 6 (Cambodia, South Ossetia, and Albania).

[38] Decision 1999/812, *supra* n. 3, and Decisions 2000/177, 2000/348, 2000/370, 2000/495, and 2000/697, *supra* n. 6.

[39] This is confirmed by Decision 1999/846, which extended the scope of Decision 1999/320 and this time referred expressly to Art. 23(2) as a legal base (both *supra* n. 3), and by Decision 2000/723, also based on Art. 23(2), which repealed Decision 1999/320 (*supra* n. 6).

[40] Decisions 2000/82 and 2000/457, *supra* n. 6.   [41] Decision 2000/231, *supra* n. 6.

[42] 1999/878, *supra* n. 1.

[43] It could have been argued that Art. 23(2) could only have been used to implement Joint Actions and Common Positions adopted after 1 May 1999, but in practice the Council has used Art. 23(2) to implement pre-Amsterdam measures, e.g. Joint Action 1999/34 on small arms.

[44] This figure includes the five uses of Article 23(2) from May to Oct. 1999 which the Council did not expressly acknowledge (*supra* nn. 32–4), but does not include the more ambiguous appointment of the Special Representative for the Stability Pact.

D.   CFSP INSTRUMENTS

Of the two new instruments introduced by the Treaty of Amsterdam, the Council did not conclude any international agreements within the CFSP Title during the survey period. However, the Joint Action on the EU Monitoring Mission expressly required it to agree one with the FRY,[45] which it did shortly after the survey period.[46]

As noted above, three Common Strategies were adopted during the survey period, with a fourth (on the Western Balkans) contemplated but eventually not adopted. These measures are all very broad in scope, encompassing objectives in all three pillars of the European Union. Frankly, the validity of such an approach is surely highly doubtful, particularly if Common Strategies are considered binding. True, there are statements following each Common Strategy noting that implementation of each of them must occur in accordance with the relevant institutional provisions. But such implementation will doubtless take account of the Common Strategy agreed by the European Council, which was agreed by means of a procedure different from the requirements of the first and third pillars. The wording of Articles 3 and 13 EU clearly requires that Common Strategies limit themselves to matters within the scope of the second pillar; if Common Strategies had been intended to function as cross-pillar measures, it would have been easy for the drafters of the Treaty of Amsterdam to refer to them in Article 3 EU along with the other amendments made to that Article.

A critical appraisal of the three Common Strategies can be found in a report of the High Representative in late 2000, declassified after discussion in the Council.[47] In his view, those 'Common Strategies adopted so far have not contributed to a stronger and more effective EU in international affairs'. In particular, this was because the initial areas chosen for Common Strategies were areas in which there was already a considerable EU and EC *acquis*, raising questions of the relationships between the new Common Strategies and the older instruments. Moreover, the third parties involved tried to influence the adoption of the Common Strategies and even, in Russia's case, adopted their own 'Common Strategies' towards the EU. The Common Strategies have not really helped the EU adopt policies towards important areas, and have led to little use of QMV for implementation; they have been negotiated from the 'bottom up', leading to very broad, slickly produced, and encyclopaedic policy statements that are difficult to apply to changing situations in practice. Presidency work plans on implementation of the Common Strategies have been treated as routine bureaucratic exercises.

The High Representative suggests solving these problems by treating Common Strategies as purely internal documents, possibly keeping part of them confidential in future. They should also be limited to a fairly specific

---

[45]   See Art. 6 of Joint Action 2000/811, *supra* n. 4.
[46]   See Decision 2001/352 ([2001] OJ L125/1.   [47]   Council doc. 14871/00, 21 Dec. 2000.

topic, rather than addressing a country, region, or theme; and they should have added value, particularly by way of clearly delineating prospects for implementation by QMV. To avoid the 'bottom-up' negotiating approach, the Common Strategies should be preceded by clear directions from the European Council, and suggestions for Common Strategies could be made by the High Representative. Work plans should be better co-ordinated and include review of implementation. Their implementation in the other pillars could be co-ordinated by means of inviting the Commission to act in the first pillar and allocating responsibility to the relevant senior Council committees to ensure implementation.

Ministers reacted to these proposals early in 2001, and their view will therefore be examined in the next edition of this survey. But while the High Representative makes a number of well-considered suggestions which would improve drafting and implementation of Common Strategies, some of his suggestions are problematic. First of all, it may be impractical to keep part of Common Strategies confidential, given their adoption by the European Council following a proposal by the Council. So many people will have seen them that a leak is surely likely, and with the massive publicity that always surrounds European Councils, any attempt to adopt a partly secret document during them will inevitably lead to frenzied activity by journalists and great suspicion of the Union's intentions by the general public and the third parties concerned. In any event, the High Representative's arguments for secrecy are not convincing on the merits. The CFSP involves regular mild or even stinging criticisms of various third countries by means not only of formal CFSP instruments but also of the release of Declarations and Conclusions. It seems pointless for the Union to avoid publishing controversial policy positions in Common Strategies in order to avoid offending the third states in question, when the mere decision not to publish such positions is equally, if not more, likely to enrage those third states. As for giving the High Representative the power to make proposals for Common Strategies, it is not clear whether this role would be exhaustive and whether it would apply only to the initial suggestion for a Common Strategy or to the detailed suggestion for a measure to be adopted; the latter power is arguably vested solely in the Council by the terms of the EU Treaty, and it seems overly restrictive to give any one CFSP actor a monopoly over the former, particularly given the subsidiary role of the High Representative in the TEU. Next, the suggestion that Common Strategies focus on areas of great interest where there is little *acquis* is contradictory; after seven years of the CFSP, there is inevitably a substantial *acquis* in any area of great interest, to say nothing of the EC's external relations, which include a treaty between the Community and nearly every country in the world. Finally, the Secretary-General does not consider the possibility that the problems with adopting Common Strategies are inherent in their nature: since they can be adopted only at lengthy intervals they cannot easily be adapted to changing events and the process of adopting them is very cumbersome in any event. If a foreign policy issue is particularly pressing or imminent, surely the Council should focus on adopting measures to address it as soon as possible, rather than delay matters by negotiating a Common Strategy and recommending it to the European Council some months later, then waiting to implement it? After all, the prospect of adopting implementing measures by QMV is not unique to Common Strategies; as discussed above, the Council has made extensive use of the power to implement Joint Actions and Common Positions by QMV already.

So if the chief consideration is efficiency, the CFSP should let Common Strategies wither on the vine and focus on adopting Joint Actions, Common Positions, and measures implementing them instead. If the chief criterion is legitimacy, it might be argued that acts adopted by the European Council are more legitimate; however, attempting to adopt secret Common Strategies would surely be one of the quickest ways to lose legitimacy for both the European Council and the Common Strategies themselves.

E.   DEFENCE

The EU and the WEU were very quick to act on the new prospects for co-operation posed by the Treaty of Amsterdam. An agreement between the two was concluded very shortly after entry into force of the new Treaty, although this agreement was not expressly a measure pursuant to Article 24 EU.[48] Additionally, the Council soon formalized the arrangements it had already agreed concerning non-WEU members' participation in Petersberg tasks pursuant to Article 17 EU.[49] However, there were no new examples of EU/WEU co-operation in practice following entry into force of the new Treaty; the two Unions simply continued with the co-operation on Croatian mine clearance agreed in 1998 and the co-operation on an Albanian police force, agreed early in 1999.[50]

IV.   Negotiation of the Treaty of Nice

A.   INTRODUCTION

At first sight there is no reason why the Treaty of Nice, agreed in December 2000 and signed in February 2001,[51] should have addressed *any* CFSP issues. According to the Protocol attached to the EU and EC Treaties by the Treaty of Amsterdam concerning the EU institutions and future Intergovernmental Conferences (IGCs), the Union was committed to a short IGC on the sole issues of the number of Commissioners and the weighting of Council votes (issues which the Treaty of Amsterdam negotiators had failed to agree upon), with a later IGC on the broader reform of the institutions. However, following

---

[48] Decision 1999/404, *supra* n. 11.   [49] Decision 1999/321, *supra* n. 11.
[50] See respectively Decisions 2000/231, *supra* n. 6, and 1999/190, *supra* n. 11.
[51] [2001] OJ C80/1.

signature of the Treaty of Amsterdam, enlargement negotiations with no fewer than twelve applicant countries got under way. As a result, some Member States pressed for a broader agenda than the 'mini-IGC' foreseen in the Protocol on the institutions. The Cologne European Council in June 1999 therefore called for the forthcoming Finnish Presidency to prepare a full report on the issues which the planned IGC should tackle, including not only on the two mandated issues but also the 'possible extension of qualified majority voting [QMV] in the Council' and 'necessary amendments to the Treaties arising as regards the European institutions in connection with the above issues and in implementing the Treaty of Amsterdam'.[52]

After consulting the EP, the Commission, and the Member States, the Finnish Presidency duly reported to the Helsinki European Council in December 1999.[53] The Presidency found that there was wide interest in considering the issue of QMV in the planned Treaty negotiations, although the Presidency's discussion of the possible extension of QMV did not mention any CFSP issues.[54] It also noted that the parallel talks then under way on the EU's nascent defence policy[55] might require separate amendments to the EU Treaty,[56] but that this issue could not be addressed until discussions on development of the defence policy had proceeded further. However, the Presidency reported that there was limited interest among Member States in pursuing the issue of 'flexibility' (allowing some Member States to integrate faster than the others) in the planned negotiations,[57] or in restructuring the Treaties.[58]

IGC negotiations then opened as planned during the Portuguese Presidency in February 2000 and concluded as planned in December during the French Presidency, although not without considerable rancour among Member States on many issues. Ultimately during the early months of 2000 it proved that there was indeed considerable interest in developing the principle of 'flexibility', and the Santa Maria de Feira European Council in June 2000 therefore formally agreed to place this issue on the IGC agenda. However, there was no interest in expressly addressing the issue of the EU's legal personality.

For the CFSP, the Treaty negotiations raised four separate but interconnected issues. The first was the issue of QMV, concerning the extent to which simplified voting should be extended into CFSP matters. The second issue was the matter of international agreements concluded within the scope of the CFSP. The third, and most complex, was the issue of whether 'flexibility' should be allowed for the CFSP in the same way that it has potentially existed for the

---

[52] The issue of extended QMV had in fact been raised by a Declaration to the Treaty of Amsterdam by several Member States, which had insisted that further Treaty amendments must entail extensions of QMV to ensure that the Union still functioned effectively following enlargement.

[53] 'Efficient Institutions After Enlargement: Options for the Intergovernmental Conference', Council doc. 13636/99, 7 Dec. 1999.

[54] Part One, s. 3 of *ibid.*   [55] See Sect. V below.

[56] Part Two, s. 5(I) of the report, *supra* n. 53.

[57] Part Two, s. 6(I) of the report, *supra* n. 53; this disinterest applied equally to the issue of *second* pillar flexibility.

[58] Part Two, s. 6(II) of the report, *supra* n. 53.

first and third pillars since the entry into force of the Treaty of Amsterdam. If it is allowed, what substantive conditions should govern it? Fourthly, should the Treaty amendments reflect the decision to launch an EU defence policy and, if so, how? This last issue is addressed separately in the context of the detailed analysis of the development of EU defence policy as a whole.[59]

B.   QUALIFIED MAJORITY VOTING

The first issue proved the easiest to agree. At present, following the Treaty of Amsterdam, voting on CFSP matters is governed by Article 23 of the EU Treaty,[60] providing for unanimous voting as the norm and QMV as an exception for implementing measures, subject to an 'emergency brake' and an exception for defence.

There was no prospect of changing the voting practice of the European Council when it adopted Common Strategies, but what about the Council? It could be argued either that the 'emergency brake' procedure should be weakened, or that *all* Council decisions on CFSP should be subject to QMV, given the protection extended to Member States by Article 23. However, from the outset, the Treaty negotiators considered more limited reforms. The first list of specific Treaty clauses that should shift to QMV, as unveiled by the Portuguese Presidency, suggested instead QMV for appointment of CFSP envoys pursuant to Article 18(5) EU and for agreement on CFSP treaties pursuant to Article 24 EU, wherever the Council acts by QMV to adopt an internal measure. This parallelism between the voting rules for internal and external treaties is also found in the first pillar.[61] In parallel, the Presidency suggested extending QMV to two first pillar matters highly relevant to QMV: the appointment of the Council Secretary-General, who performs the task of High Representative for the CFSP,[62] and the decisions amending the list of arms which are not subject to the rules of the EC Treaty.[63]

Ultimately three of these four proposed extensions of QMV became part of the final Treaty of Nice. The only proposal which failed was the proposed amendment of Article 296 EC regarding arms. As for the other three extensions of QMV, the amendment to allow appointment of the Council Secretary-General was accomplished by a simple amendment to Article 207(2), providing simply that the Council votes by a different procedure. It should be emphasized that there is still no democratic participation in this appointment, unlike the extensive EP powers over appointment and censure of the Commission, despite the enhancement of the Council Secretary-General's

---

[59] Sect. V below.

[60] On negotiation of this clause, see Peers, 'CFSP 1997', *supra* n. 24 at 552–3. There are also separate decision-making rules on decisions to instigate an EU defence policy or to absorb the WEU into the EU (European Council decision ratified by the Member States: see Art. 17 EU) or as regards derogations from the rules concerning CFSP expenditure and the EU budget (unanimity in the Council: see Art. 28(4) EU).

[61] See Art. 300(2) EC.   [62] See Arts. 207(2) EC and 18(3) EU.   [63] Art. 296 EC.

status by the Treaty of Amsterdam. It should also be emphasized that, as an EC Treaty appointment, the Secretary-General's appointment could in principle be challenged in the EC courts and is *not* subject to any form of 'emergency brake' procedure or military and defence condition.[64]

The amendment to appoint special envoys by QMV was adopted as an amendment to Article 23(2) EU, adding a third derogation to the general rule that the Council adopts CFSP measures by a unanimous vote. Here it should be emphasized that this new derogation is still subject to the two conditions (the 'emergency brake' and the military/defence limitation) that apply to the other two derogations. It seems unusual that the Council Secretary-General is now appointed by the Community version of QMV, without those two limitations, even though his or her position is obviously more important than the appointment of an envoy and even though the appointment of the Secretary-General has military or defence implications. This is already true given the EU's existing impact on defence policy and will obviously be more true in the future following development of an EU defence policy. Also, it should be emphasized that in some cases the appointment of an envoy could have fallen under one of the existing two exceptions.[65]

Finally, the amendment to Article 24 EU did not take the form of an amendment to Article 23 EU, but of an amendment to Article 24 itself. However, qualified majority voting pursuant to the new Article 24(3) EU will still be the CFSP version of QMV, because the new paragraph refers back to the voting conditions (with the two limits on QMV) set out in Article 23(2).[66] Moreover, the initial text of the proposed amendment was altered during the negotiations in order to narrow its effect significantly. Originally the amendment would have allowed QMV in *all* cases where the Council would have voted by QMV internally,[67] but ultimately the new Article 24(3) allows for QMV only where the Council is *implementing a Joint Action or Common Position*.[68] This leaves out the other two cases covered by the derogation for QMV in Article 23(2) EU: the appointment of envoys and the implementation of Common Strategies. The former appears irrelevant to the conclusion of international agreements but the latter could be very relevant indeed, given the broad scope of the Common Strategies agreed to date. It is surprising that the Member States insisted upon this limitation upon QMV for international agreements, given the parallel possibility for internal QMV and the guarantees offered by the limitations on QMV in Article 23(2) EU.

---

[64] Presumably the so-called 'Luxembourg Compromise' could be applied, but that is a political rule which is not legally binding; in any event, Member States would likely be vastly more reticent to threaten to use the Luxembourg Compromise in the first pillar context than they would be to invoke the second pillar 'emergency brake'.

[65] For instance, see Decision 1999/361, *supra* n. 3.

[66] Art. 24(4) also extends QMV to implementation of some third pillar treaties.

[67] See Council doc. 4770/00, 14 Sept. 2000; from Council doc. 4776/00, 28 Sept. 2000, the drafts suggested that QMV would apply for implementation of Joint Actions, Common Positions and Common Strategies.

[68] The change to the proposed text was first made in the version proposed on 30 Nov. 2000 (4815/00) and was maintained in subsequent versions.

C. CFSP INTERNATIONAL AGREEMENTS

In addition to the important change to the voting requirements of Article 24, Member States took the opportunity to redraft other aspects of this Article. This was an unusual and unexpected move, since there had been no interest in formally placing the issue of the EU's legal personality on the agenda of the IGC. None of the IGC documents concerning the redrafting of Article 24 suggested why the changes to the text were being proposed.

Since the text of Article 24 EU was agreed during negotiations of the Treaty of Amsterdam, it has been at the heart of the dispute whether the European Union has legal personality. The Article does not expressly grant legal personality to the Union, but provides for a mechanism for the Council to agree treaties with third countries or organizations in order to implement the CFSP Title.[69] In its current form, Article 24 provides that the treaties in question shall be negotiated by the Presidency (possibly assisted by the Commission), after authorization by the Council acting unanimously. The treaties shall then be concluded by a unanimous vote on a recommendation from the Presidency. As a result of the Treaty of Nice, these provisions are now Article 24(1) to (3) and provide for QMV in certain circumstances, as discussed above.[70]

The crucial issue is whether the Council is acting on behalf of the Member States collectively, or rather on behalf of the Union as a distinct entity. On this point, the present Article 24 states that agreements shall not be binding on a Member State which states that it must first comply with its constitutional procedure, but that the other Member States may agree that the agreement applies provisionally to them. A Declaration to the Treaty of Amsterdam asserted that any agreements concluded pursuant to the present Article 24 did not transfer competence to the Union. Arguably these provisions make it clear that such agreements are concluded on behalf of the Member States, but equally it could be argued that they do not necessarily have this effect.[71]

The amendments agreed as part of the Treaty of Nice make no reference to the previous Declaration, but amend one of the two principles already set out in the present Article 24 and add another principle. Following the amendments, the future Article 24(5) will still provide that some Member States can delay the binding effect, while the other Member States may nonetheless agree that the agreement shall apply provisionally;[72] but this clause will no longer specify *who* is bound provisionally.[73] Moreover, the future Article 24(6) will

---

[69] A parallel clause exists for the negotiation of treaties relating to police and criminal law co-operation (Art. 38 EU).

[70] Sect. IV/B.   [71] See the discussion in Peers, 'CFSP 1997', *supra* n. 24 at 561–4.

[72] The conference rejected the prospect, in early drafts (see Council doc. 4770/00, 14 Sept. 2000), that Member States' ability to delay effect upon them would apply only when the Council voted *unanimously* (dropped beginning with Council doc. 4790/00, 3 Nov. 2000).

[73] The negotiators dithered on this point during negotiations, with texts first explicitly keeping the reference to provisional effect on Member States (Council doc. 4770/00, 14 Sept. 2000), then referring to provisional effect on the 'Union' (starting with Council doc. 4776/00, 28 Sept. 2000); the final wording appeared late in the negotiations (starting with Council doc. 4815/00, 30 Nov. 2000).

provide that the agreements concluded pursuant to Article 24 are binding on the *institutions of the Union*.[74]

What is the effect of the new amendments? At the outset, the argument that there is no legal personality for lack of an express reference to it should be dismissed, for the International Court of Justice has long established that international personality need not be express. Under one scenario, the Union is a legal person already as a result of Article 24, and the revised Article 24 will merely confirm the existing situation.[75] Under another scenario, Article 24 as revised will create legal personality, in particular by providing expressly that treaties concluded pursuant to it will bind the institutions of the Union. With this amendment, it can be argued that the references to Member States in Article 24 EU merely mean that Member States are bound to implement Article 24 treaties as an internal obligation to the Union, rather than as an external obligation to third states, and that the references to Member States in Article 24 do not preclude the existence of legal personality for the Union. This follows from a comparison with the parallel provisions in Article 300 EC. In any event, the argument may be of limited importance in future, since the first use of Article 24 (falling outside this survey period) has been concluded in the name of the European Union and appears to treat the Union as a distinct entity from its Member States.[76]

D. CFSP 'FLEXIBILITY'

Imagine a speech by the High Representative, a Commissioner, or a representative of the Council Presidency at a conference or at a negotiating table. The speaker persuasively argues with great conviction on behalf of the 'Union's' policy on such important issues such as arms control, support for human rights, or conflict prevention. But at the end of the speech, she has to point out that at least one EU Member State does not actually agree with what she just said. In fact, she was speaking on behalf of only *some* Union members.

Such a scenario would obviously seriously weaken the policy which the 'Union' was trying to implement. Third parties might well discover which parts of the policy certain Member States disagreed with and draw attention to the split (and away from themselves). Union policy could be ignored or even ridiculed as a result.

While the EC Treaty has provided for 'flexibility' in one sense (a potentially *indefinite* distinction between Member States as regards their participation in certain EU policies, while still using EU institutions and forms of co-operation)

---

[74] Initially the texts provided expressly that the treaties would be binding on the Union institutions *and Member States*, subject to the possible delay which a Member State could insist upon (Council doc. 4770/00, 14 Sept. 2000; the final wording was used starting with Council doc. 4810/00, 23 Nov. 2000).

[75] See the Opinion of the Council legal service on this issue (Council docs. 5332/1/00, 24 Nov. 2000 and SN 1628/00, 16 Feb. 2000).

[76] See Decision 2001/352, *supra* n. 46.

since entry into force of the Treaty of European Union in 1993,[77] the prospect of broader flexibility clauses applying to all aspects of EU policy was raised only with the negotiation of the Treaty of Amsterdam in 1996–7. As a result of the Treaty of Amsterdam, the TEU contains a Title VII setting out general rules relating to flexibility in all areas of EU co-operation,[78] while the first and third pillars supplement this Title with further specific rules concerning flexibility in each of those areas,[79] although these provisions have not yet been used at time of writing. In contrast, the second pillar contains no specific provisions on flexibility supplementing Title VII of the EU Treaty; instead it provides for 'constructive abstention' in the event of some Member States disagreeing with the majority and for specific rules on defence. Until the very late stages of the Treaty of Amsterdam negotiations, the negotiators had been considering specific provisions on CFSP flexibility, but the idea was dropped at some point during the final ten days of negotiations.[80]

As noted above, flexibility was initially kept off the agenda of the Treaty of Nice negotiations, but was formally added in June 2000. The French Presidency then launched discussions on the issue formally with a discussion paper on the issue. Ultimately the negotiators agreed not only to insert specific provisions on flexibility for the second pillar,[81] but also to amend the general rules governing flexibility and the specific rules governing first and third pillar flexibility, all previously agreed in the Treaty of Amsterdam.[82] Under the current rules, objecting Member States have an 'emergency brake' similar to Article 23(2) EU, which means that they can block a proposed authorization of flexibility in the Council by asserting that they have 'important and stated reasons of national policy' to block it; the Council can then decide by QMV to refer the issue to the Council at head of state and government level (in the first pillar) or the European Council (in the third pillar) to resolve the dispute with a unanimous vote.[83] The amendments to the existing provisions concerning the first and third pillars alter the decision-making procedure governing the decision to start flexibility in each pillar, allowing flexibility to go ahead merely on a qualified majority vote in the Council.[84] Following the new amendments, objecting Member States will merely be able to force a *discussion* at the level of

[77] As is well known, flexibility as formally provided for in the Treaties initially applied only to economic and monetary union (since applied in practice since 1999) and social policy (terminated with the entry into force of the Treaty of Amsterdam in May 1999).

[78] Arts. 43–45 EU; the formal term for this flexibility will be changed from 'closer co-operation' to 'enhanced co-operation' by the Treaty of Nice.

[79] Arts. 11 EC and 40 EU. In addition, the EC Treaty since the Treaty of Amsterdam contains detailed rules on flexibility within the specific fields of immigration, asylum, and civil co-operation law.

[80] See discussion of the second pillar flexibility negotiations and the results in Peers, 'CFSP 1997', *supra* n. 24, at 553–5.

[81] These will become Arts. 27a–27e EU.

[82] Arts. 43–45 EU (general rules) will be entirely replaced with six Arts. (Arts. 43, 43a, 43b, 44, 44a, and 45 EU); Art. 11 EC will be replaced by Arts. 11 and 11a EC; and Art. 40 EU will be replaced by Arts. 40, 40a, and 40b EU.

[83] See respectively the present Arts. 11(2) EC (first pillar) and 40(2) EU (third pillar).

[84] See future Arts. 11(2) EC and 40a(2) EU.

the European Council, but following this discussion the Council can then act by QMV. The position of the Commission and the EP as regards the initial decision to authorize flexibility has also been altered.

There are also amendments to the substantive conditions for launching flexibility, which apply to flexibility in all three pillars.[85] There are ten such conditions, which include the condition that eight Member States (instead of a 'majority' of Member States, as at present) must be participants in order for the action to go ahead. The conditions also comprise rules aiming to protect the central principles of first pillar law.[86] Furthermore, the general rules have been revised to provide that flexibility measures are not part of the '*acquis*' which acceding Member States must apply,[87] although this does not preclude new Member States from joining if they choose to.

In parallel to agreeing these amendments, Member States discussed the development of the specific flexibility rules which will apply to the second pillar. The three key issues throughout these negotiations were: the specific conditions that would apply to second pillar flexibility; the scope of that flexibility; and the decision-making rules that would apply. There were two further, less contentious, issues: the role of the High Representative and the rules for 'party-crashing' Member States.

Negotiations began with a French Presidency discussion paper in July 2000, which raised questions about whether CFSP flexibility provisions were needed.[88] Shortly afterward, a further Presidency note elaborated upon the issues,[89] followed in the autumn first by a detailed policy paper and then by a summary of possible guidelines for negotiations.[90] In the meantime the Belgians had released a policy paper, the Spanish had proposed a text for CFSP flexibility clauses, and the German and Italian delegations had jointly proposed flexibility provisions, including CFSP provisions.[91] The Presidency then proposed a text of all flexibility provisions in mid-October,[92] which was revised in a number of further drafts over the following seven weeks until agreement on the final text in Nice.[93]

(i) Conditions for Flexibility

The initial draft second pillar flexibility clauses discussed during the Treaty of Amsterdam negotiations set out three conditions before CFSP flexibility could be authorized.[94] Second pillar flexibility had to respect EC powers as well as

---

[85] Future Art. 43 EU.
[86] See particularly future Art. 43(c), (e) and (f).
[87] Future Art. 44(1) EU.
[88] Confer 4758/00, 11 July 2000.
[89] Confer 4761/00, 18 July 2000.
[90] Confer 4766/00, 30 Aug. 2000 and Confer 4780/00, 5 Oct. 2000.
[91] Respectively Confer 4760/00, 14 July 2000; Confer 4765/00, 28 Aug. 2000; and Confer 4783/00, 4 Oct. 2000.
[92] Confer 4786/00, 18 Oct. 2000.
[93] Confer 4790/00, 3 Nov. 2000 (summary of all IGC texts); Confer 4798/00, 9 Nov. 2000 (new flexibility draft); Confer 4803/00, 17 Nov. 2000 (new flexibility draft); Confer 4810/00, 23 Nov. 2000 (revised summary of texts); Confer 4815/00, 30 Nov. 2000 (revised summary of texts); and Confer 4816/00, 6 Dec. 2000 (draft Treaty of Nice).
[94] Council doc. 3813/97, 11 Feb. 1997.

the objectives of the CFSP and any guidelines developed by the European Council; it had to aim to promote the identity of the Union as a cohesive force in international relations; and it would have to involve at least two-thirds of the Member States. Later versions reduced the threshold for participation in all types of flexibility to a majority of Member States, added the proviso that CFSP flexibility would also have to respect strategies agreed by the European Council, and would have instead required CFSP flexibility to *refrain from impairing* the cohesiveness of the Union as a cohesive force.[95] The drafters had obviously noticed the utter absurdity of suggesting that Union measures involving not all Member States could in any way promote cohesiveness of the Union, rather than the reverse.

These issues were inevitably raised again during negotiations on the Treaty of Nice. Ultimately the future Article 27a EU sets out a slightly more elaborate version of the conditions discussed during the Amsterdam negotiations, leaving the condition concerning the number of participants to Article 40 EU.[96] CFSP flexibility 'shall be aimed at safeguarding the values and serving the interests of the Union as a whole'; following the initial Amsterdam proposals, it must entail 'asserting [the Union's] identity as a coherent force on the international scene'. There are three specific rules that it must respect: the 'principles, objectives, general guidelines and consistency' of the CFSP, along with existing CFSP decisions; the powers of the EC; and 'consistency between all the Union's policies and its external activities'. It can be seen that the agreed conditions have built upon the initial proposals, in particular by inserting language concerning the CFSP from other provisions of the EU Treaty, obviously with the intent of ensuring close links between CFSP flexibility and the CFSP 'mainstream'. The obligation to safeguard EU values comes from Article 11(1) EU; the obligation to assert identity comes from Article 2 EU; the objectives of the CFSP are set out in Article 11 EU; CFSP general guidelines and principles are defined pursuant to Article 12 EU; the Council is obliged to ensure the internal consistency of the CFSP pursuant to Article 13(3) EU; and consistency between various EU policies is addressed by Article 3 EU. Where the flexibility provisions expand upon the general CFSP provisions is in the references to acting as a *coherent* force as serving the interests of the Union *as a whole*. Both these provisions are clearly designed to ensure that CFSP flexibility will not detract from the principle of *unity* of CFSP actions toward the outside world.

However, respect for this principle is also dependent upon the scope of CFSP flexibility, the most difficult CFSP issue discussed during the IGC negotiations.

(ii)   Scope of Flexibility

It is surely evident that, in principle, CFSP flexibility runs a strong risk of shattering the unity of the Union's foreign policy. The central flaw in the provisions

---

[95] See Peers, *supra* n. 24.

[96] This condition is discussed in the next subsection, since it is closely related to the issue of the scope of CFSP flexibility.

discussed at Amsterdam was that allowing some Member States to go ahead without others would have fragmented the Union's relations with the outside world, announcing formally that the Union was split and conflicting by its very nature with the central principle of a 'common' policy with third states.

The only possible way to square coherence with flexibility in the CFSP context was to limit it to measures *implementing existing policy*, not setting *new* policy, a prospect not discussed during the Amsterdam negotiations. At first, the French Presidency suggested that CFSP flexibility could also be used to develop new policies,[97] but from an early point, the Treaty negotiators accepted that CFSP flexibility could only be used for implementation, except possibly for defence and armaments issues.[98] The important question then was the scope of that implementation. For a long period, the negotiators considered allowing CFSP flexibility as regards implementation of a common strategy, joint action, or common position; but ultimately the future Article 27b EU limits CFSP flexibility to 'implementation of a joint action or a common position'.[99] So if the EU wants to use flexibility to implement a common strategy, it will have to adopt a Joint Action or Common Position first.

Until the last session of negotiations at the level of EU leaders, the French Presidency also hoped that the Treaty would authorize flexibility as regards defence matters. Its initial discussion paper considered the use of flexibility on such matters especially important,[100] and proposals from Spain and Belgium echoed this view.[101] There was no specific reference to defence matters in the draft texts until some time into the negotiations on flexibility; at that point the proposal expressly stated that defence and security initiatives within the sphere of crisis management could form one of the objects of enhanced co-operation. This proviso remained until the final version of the Treaty, which (due to the opposition of the UK in particular) states instead in Article 27b EU that enhanced co-operation 'shall not relate to matters having military or defence implications'.

Next, the issue of the number of participants was closely linked to the issue of the scope of flexibility. The Member States broadly agreed at the outset of discussions on flexibility that the 'quorum' for the number of participants for all types of flexibility should be altered from a majority to eight;[102] this change makes of course no difference at present but is intended to facilitate flexibility after enlargement. However, it was argued that an exception should be made for CFSP flexibility. Initially, the Presidency proposed that as few as three or four Member States could be entrusted with CFSP flexibility,[103] but ultimately

---

[97] See Council doc. 4766/00, 30 Aug. 2000.

[98] See Art. J(2) of the first proposed Presidency text, 4786/00, 18 Oct. 2000; the only proposed text to suggest the application of CFSP flexibility to developing initial policies was Council doc. 4790/00, 3 Nov. 2000 (see Art. J(3)).

[99] This limitation was first accepted in Council doc. 4803/00, 17 Nov. 2000 (see Art. J).

[100] Council doc. 4766/00, 30 Aug. 2000.

[101] Council docs. 4760/00, 14 July 2000 and 4765/00, 28 Aug. 2000.

[102] Future Art. 43(g) EU.   [103] Council doc. 4786/00, 18 Oct. 2000 (Art. J(2)).

the Treaty negotiators rejected this prospect,[104] imposing the threshold of eight Member States equally as regards CFSP matters.

The Nice version of CFSP flexibility is vastly preferable to the version under consideration at Amsterdam. By limiting flexibility to measures implementing existing policy, there is only a limited danger of fragmentation of policy. Indeed, by comparison with constructive abstention, the new version of flexibility will lead to less fragmentation, because there is no oppositional stance in merely opting out of implementation after agreeing to the policy. It should also be noted that the threshold for constructive abstention is different from the threshold for flexibility, since constructive abstention will block a proposal if Member States constituting only a third of Council voting weight invoke the clause.[105]

The new provisions can also be compared with the provision on appointing some Member States as 'agents', which was considered at length during the Amsterdam negotiations, but ultimately rejected.[106] That draft provision would have allowed appointment of 'one or more' Member States as agents, and would have applied only to implementing a Joint Action. Here the provisions will apply to Common Positions as well and require much greater participation.

Finally, because the CFSP provisions relate only to implementation, they should influence the interpretation of the 'last resort' clause governing all types of flexibility,[107] as regards CFSP flexibility. This clause appears to govern the situation where some Member States are unwilling for political reasons to agree to an initiative; but in the CFSP context it should arguably also apply to a situation where a small Member State is willing to agree in principle to an implementation measure but lacks sufficient staff to contribute effectively. Arguably, the clause should also be interpreted to allow small Member States to concentrate their commitments to a limited number of EU operations in the interests of efficiency, even where it may be technically possible for them to spread their personnel more thinly.

(iii)   Decision-making

During the Amsterdam discussions, it had always been accepted that any launch of CFSP flexibility would require a unanimous vote. However, during the Nice discussions, this issue was revisited, likely because of the parallel discussions on simplifying the voting rule applying to third and first pillar flexibility. At various times, it was suggested that 'ordinary' QMV in Council, unanimity, and Article 23(2) EU should apply to various parts of CFSP flexibility, depending variously on the number of Member States participating, the subject-matter (defence, implementation measures, or setting fresh policy),

---

[104] The idea was dropped starting with the draft of 30 Nov. 2000 (Council doc. 4815/00).

[105] However, logically any Member State which invokes the constructive abstention clause will not be participating in implementation of a policy.

[106] See the text of the draft Amsterdam provision in Peers, *supra* n. 24, 549 at n. 50.

[107] Future Art. 43a EU.

and whether the Commission objected.[108] However, in the final Treaty, with the agreement to limit CFSP flexibility to implementation of prior policy, the voting rule in all cases is simply Article 23(2) EU.[109] This is eminently logical, since of course Article 23 governs implementation of Joint Actions and Common Positions in any case. The Commission shall give an opinion particularly on whether the proposal 'is consistent with Union policies', a wider remit than examining consistency with Community policies (as considered in some drafts), and the EP must be forwarded the request for information.

(iv)   High Representative

Initially the High Representative was to be 'associated' with second pillar flexibility actions,[110] but his or her responsibility was altered throughout the negotiations. The final future Article 27d EU instead provides that the High Representative 'shall in particular' ensure that all Council members and the EP are informed of second pillar flexibility measures. This is without prejudice to the powers of the Presidency and the Commission. The Treaty of Nice will therefore create a new task for the High Representative, in addition to his or her current roles assisting the Presidency to represent and implement the CFSP and assisting the Council generally, 'in particular' in formulating and implementing policy decisions and conducting political dialogue on the Council's behalf.[111] On this issue, it is striking that the second pillar flexibility texts considered during the Treaty of Amsterdam never foresaw a role for the High Representative, so he or she at least has an enhanced role compared to the previously contemplated Treaty texts. But while the High Representative's new role as a messenger may appear relatively demeaning, it should be noted that this is the first task for which the High Representative is not expressly under the control of the Presidency or the Council, and that the High Representative's other functions in respect of the CFSP will still apply equally to second pillar flexibility.[112]

(v)   Late-coming Member States

The second pillar flexibility text under discussion during the Treaty of Amsterdam negotiations had foreseen rules on late-coming Member States identical to the rules ultimately agreed for third pillar flexibility (which will still apply following the Treaty of Nice).[113] Right from the initial second pillar flexibility proposal during the Nice negotiations, this proposal was revived and ultimately agreed.[114] During the negotiations, there was a prospect that the Commission would not be invited to give its view where flexibility concerned

---

[108] For example, see Art. K of Council doc. 4810/00, 23 Nov. 2000, with three different voting rules.

[109] Future Art. 27c EU.   [110] See Art. K in Council doc. 4786/00, 18 Oct. 2000.

[111] Arts. 18(3) and 26 EU.   [112] This follows clearly from the future Art. 27a(2) EU.

[113] See 30 May 1997 Amsterdam draft, discussed in Peers, *supra* n. 24; on the third pillar rules, see current Art. 40(3) EU and future Art. 40b EU.

[114] Art. 27e EU.

defence matters,[115] but that potential distinction was set aside when the negotiators agreed that second pillar flexibility would not apply to defence matters. The sole distinction between the future second and third pillar 'party-crashing' rules will be that the opinion to be issued by the Commission in the second pillar need not expressly make recommendations on the modalities of how the late-comer will join in with the others. Otherwise the same rules apply: the Commission will give an opinion within three months and the Council will decide within four months, with deemed acceptance of the application unless there is a QMV against, in which case the Council must give reasons and set a deadline for re-examining the application. However, it is striking that this clause is the first CFSP provision ever to allow for a 'normal' qualified majority vote, rather than the CFSP version of QMV.

V.   EU Defence Policy

A.   OVERVIEW

The limited agreement to extend EU defence policy in the Treaty of Amsterdam was soon superseded by events, with the UK government concerned to find an area of EU policy which it could play a large role developing and the crisis in Kosovo convincing other Member States dubious about an EU defence role that the Union should develop capabilities to act. The Cologne European Council in June 1999, meeting on the same day as the conclusion of the NATO bombing of Kosovo, therefore agreed to develop a European Security and Defence Policy (ESDP), with a formal decision launching the policy to be agreed by the end of 2000. Matters developed over the following three Presidencies, with aspects of the policy developing through reports agreed at the Helsinki, Feira, and Nice European Councils.

In Cologne, the European Council decided that the EU defence policy would focus on implementation of the 'Petersberg tasks' defined in Article 17(2) EU (humanitarian and rescue tasks, peacekeeping tasks, and tasks of combat forces in crisis management, including peacemaking). These tasks fall short of creating a full military alliance, and there was no interest in pursuing such an alliance at EU level, given the neutrality of several Member States and the existence of NATO and the WEU, which entail collective defence obligations for their members. As a result, despite the creation of an EU defence policy, the WEU will still exist as an organization, albeit only as a shell concerned solely with the issue of collective defence, as regards which it adds nothing to NATO. WEU functions as regards all other matters are simply going to be addressed by the EU institutions instead, although there will be no formal transfer from the WEU to the EU. As such an EU defence policy is being developed without

---

[115] This was first suggested in the 9 Nov. draft (Council doc. 4798/00), and remained in every subsequent draft until the final Treaty was agreed.

the integration of the WEU into the EU, as envisaged in the current Article 17(1) EU.

The Cologne European Council also decided upon the basic aspects of the decision-making system for EU defence policy, although these were subsequently augmented substantially in later discussions, and agreed upon a number of issues that would have to be addressed for the development of the EU defence policy. The Helsinki European Council then agreed the 'headline goal' of deploying 50,000–60,000 troops by 2003 within sixty days for one year, backed up by military assets and logistics and intelligence capabilities. This would have to be supported by agreement with NATO to use NATO assets and modalities for third states to participate in actions, particularly the six non-EU European members of NATO and other countries which were candidates for EU membership (totalling fifteen countries). It decided to establish an interim Political and Security Committee and Military Committee and to second military personnel to the Council, with a view to preparing for a future Military Staff organization within the Council.[116]

By now, non-military crisis management was also on the agenda, with a short report launching the process of discussion of this issue. In spring 2000, following the urging of the Lisbon European Council, an interim committee on civilian crisis management had also been established within the Council.[117] The Feira European Council took this issue forward by endorsing the headline goal of deploying 5,000 police by 2003 for crisis management operations, 1,000 of them within thirty days. The same European Council also agreed guidelines on relations with NATO and with third states in the context of EU defence policy. In November 2000, the Council arranged a 'Commitments Conference' at which the Member States pledged forces that could contribute to the headline goals of force deployment for 2003. Finally, in a report by the Presidency endorsed by the Nice European Council, all aspects of the development of the EU's defence policy were further developed. Ultimately it did not prove possible at Nice to agree a Decision of the European Council formally establishing the ESDP, so the deadline was moved to the end of 2001 at the planned Laeken European Council, with the Swedish Presidency to issue a report on progress at the Gothenburg European Council in June of that year.

The development of the new policy is surveyed below from the perspective in turn of institutional development, operational commitments, relations with NATO, relations with third states, and amendment of the EU Treaty.

B.   DEFENCE INSTITUTIONS

The lynchpin of the ESDP is the Political and Security Committee (PSC), which is to be a standing committee made up of senior officials of Member States.[118] This Committee, which is to replace the long-standing Political Committee

---

[116] *Supra* n. 11.   [117] *Supra* n. 11.
[118] See Annex III to the Presidency Report to the Nice European Council.

referred to in the present Article 25 EU, is to keep track of situations and monitor developments. It may be chaired by the High Representative, after consulting the Presidency, in particular during a crisis. Its roles include giving guidelines to other committees, including the Military Committee, and to lead political dialogue with third parties as regards the ESDP. In a crisis, it will propose political objectives and recommend options, including an opinion recommending a Joint Action. It also has the role of supervising implementation and assessing effects of decisions. A Situation Centre under the direction of the High Representative will support the Committee and provide it with intelligence. During an operation, a Joint Action will determine the High Representative's role in implementation, and the High Representative will act only with the Committee's assent. The Council will be informed of events through Committee reports submitted by the High Representative as chair of the Committee.

The next Committee is the Military Committee,[119] consisting of EU Member States' chiefs of defence or their representatives. It is the senior military body in the EU framework, and gives military advice to the PSC and military direction to the EU Military Staff. Its mission is to give military direction of military activities. It does that by offering military advice and recommendations, developing an overall concept of crisis management, assessing risks, and conducting military relations with third states and organizations. In a crisis situation, it controls the EU Military Staff and gives recommendations, while during an operation, it monitors the military aspects of that operation. It will have a standing chair, appointed for a three-year term, who will be a four-star flag officer, ideally a former Chief of Defence in a Member State. The Chair is to represent the Military Committee before the PSC and, when a military issue is being discussed, the Council, and also serves as the chief military adviser to the High Representative. He (or, improbably, she) is to chair the Military Committee impartially with a view to reaching consensus, give instructions to the Director-General of the Military Staff, liaise with the Presidency, and be a point of contact with an Operations Commander during an operation. He is supported by his personal staff, assisted by the Military Staff, and also supported by a Military Committee working group.

Next is the Military Staff, taking the form of a Directorate-General of the Council, composed of military staff seconded by the Member States in an international capacity, and headed by a Director-General, a three-star flag officer of a Member State.[120] Its mission is to provide early warning, strategic assessment, and strategic planning of Petersberg tasks, and to implement policies and decisions as directed by the EU Military Committee. Its roles are to link the EU Military Committee with military resources, provide military expertise, contribute to elaboration, assessment, and review of capability goals, and monitor, assess, and make recommendations regarding forces as

---

[119] See Presidency Report to the Nice European Council, Annex IV.
[120] See *ibid.*, Annex V.

regards training, exercises, and interoperability. It may set up a 'Crisis Action Team' during a crisis.

C. COMMITMENTS

As noted above, the headline commitment for the EU is to be able to deploy 50,000–60,000 troops quickly by 2003, along with associated military equipment.[121] On paper, Member States have promised to provide the personnel and equipment by the deadline, but it remains to be seen whether they have the funds and the political will to ensure that the forces are available at that date.

As regards civilian crisis management,[122] the Feira European Council originally set goals in four areas: policing, the rule of law, civil administration, and civil protection. Initial work has focused on policing, with the headline goal of 5,000 officers mentioned above. These officers are to be ready for the full range of assignments, should have a clear remit and an appropriate mandate, and integrate with the other three elements. Less work has been done on them, but by the end of 2000 the Council had established a database compiling information on Member States' capacities in this area.

D. EU–NATO RELATIONS

Relations between the EU and NATO should, in the EU's view, be based on the autonomy of the EU's decision-making, with the two organizations on an equal footing and non-discrimination between EU Member States.[123] Before a crisis, there are to be stepped-up contacts between the two organizations at the level of Secretary-General and military and foreign policy officials. During a crisis, contacts must be increased further and, if the EU uses NATO assets, there are detailed rules concerning how NATO assets must be handed over at the EU's request and the subsequent supervision of the EU's use of them. An Annex sets out the EU's expectations as regards 'guaranteed permanent access' to NATO's planning capabilities and the 'presumption of availability' of previously identified NATO assets and capabilities.

While the EU's goals for its relations with NATO are understandable goals from its point of view, there are obvious problems in expecting NATO to endorse them without qualification. If the EU wants guaranteed access to NATO assets because it lacks significant assets of its own, it is not really on an equal footing in practical terms, and it could be seen as contradictory to demand access to NATO assets but deny other NATO members influence on EU decisions whether and how to use those assets. Moreover, it may seem odd to other NATO members that EU Member States which have not joined NATO expect equal treatment from NATO as compared to those EU Member States that have joined the organization. These are precisely the problems that led

---

[121] See *ibid.*, Annex II.   [122] See *ibid.*, Annex II.   [123] See *ibid.*, Annex VII.

Turkey to reject a deal on the EU's terms as regards NATO assets and its own potential participation (see below) throughout 2000.

E.   THIRD STATES

As noted above, the two most important groups of third states for the ESDP are the six non-EU European NATO states and the other nine candidates for EU accession,[124] hereinafter called the 'ESDP associates'. Although Canada, Russia, and Ukraine have also expressed a strong interest in potentially participating in EU operations, the focus to date has been on these associates. The arrangements which the Union has worked out for these try to balance competing objectives: the autonomy of Union action, as against the need to have access to NATO assets and the additional capabilities of states associated with the ESDP, and the concomitant expectations by third states that they are entitled to an equal say in the conduct of operations.[125]

The Union has agreed on permanent consultation of these states outside crises, with two meetings per Presidency with all fifteen states generally and with the six NATO countries in particular. These third states are welcome to appoint representatives to the PSC and officers accredited to the EU Military Staff. If a crisis breaks out, there is to be stepped-up contact before an operation; the six NATO states must be contacted in particular if the EU is examining the option of using NATO assets for an operation. Once the EU has decided to begin an operation, the planning work will be presented to the associated countries and they may decide whether to participate. There is a distinction here between the NATO associates, who have the right to participate where NATO assets are involved and will be invited to participate where NATO assets are not involved; and the other associates, who *may* be invited to participate at the discretion of the Council. If NATO assets are used, entailing planning within NATO bodies, the NATO associates will be involved in planning in accordance with NATO rules; if not, then planning will be undertaken by the EU Military Staff and all the associates may send liaison officers.

The day-to-day management of operations will be conducted by a 'Committee of Contributors'. This Committee will be a forum for discussing operations following a PSC decision, and will contribute to PSC discussions. The PSC will 'take account' of this Committee's views. All associates contributing significant forces will have the same rights and obligations over day-to-day operations. The Committee will be chaired by a representative of the Presidency or the High Representative, assisted by the Chair of the Military Committee; the Operation Commander, and the Director-General of the Military Staff may attend.

---

[124] Respectively Norway, Iceland, Turkey, Poland, the Czech Republic, and Hungary; and Estonia, Latvia, Lithuania, the Slovak Republic, Slovenia, Romania, Bulgaria, Cyprus, and Malta.

[125] See Annex VI to the Presidency Report to the Nice European Council, Council doc. 14056/3/00, 13 Dec. 2000.

Article 17 EU was amended by the Treaty of Amsterdam following a complex compromise between Member States with dramatically different views of the development of an EU defence policy.[126] First, Article 17(1) states that the CFSP includes the 'progressive framing of a common defence policy', which 'might lead to a common defence' if the European Council so decided. In that case, it would be up to Member States to ratify that decision. The same paragraph provides that the WEU is 'an integral part of the development of the Union', giving access to an operational capability. The Union is to develop closer relations with the WEU, with a possibility of merger if the European Council so decided, again subject to ratification by Member States. EU defence policy must not prejudice the neutrality or NATO commitments of Member States and could be supported by co-operation in the field of armaments.

Article 17(2) then limits the ambit of Article 17 to the so-called 'Petersberg tasks'. In turn, Article 17(3) specifies the role of the WEU in implementing EU policy with defence implications more precisely. Article 17(4) specifies that EU defence policy cannot prejudice co-operation between Member States bilaterally or in the WEU or NATO framework, while Article 17(5) calls for a review of Article 17 in future IGCs.

In light of the power of the European Council to decide on an EU defence policy, did the EU Treaty need to be revised? A report by the Council Legal Service to the Feira European Council was ambiguous. In the Legal Service's view, the decisions at Cologne and Helsinki did not necessarily require a Treaty amendment. However, Treaty amendment would be needed if the Council's decision-making powers were to be transferred to a body made up of officials, or to amend the provisions regarding the WEU. In any event, besides the legal question, it was up to Member States to decide on the political and operational desirability of any amendments.

Some Member States, while supporting the development of an EU policy, would have preferred to have no Treaty amendment in relation to the ESDP, in particular because they feared that it would complicate domestic ratification of the Treaty of Nice. Others were more enthusiastic, and Italy and the Benelux submitted drafting amendments to Articles 17 and 25 towards the close of negotiations.[127] In their view, for political and operational reasons, Article 17 should be amended to delete all reference to the WEU as a body assisting the EU, and Article 25, which sets out the role of the Political Committee, should be amended to alter that Committee's powers as planned as part of the EU defence policy. This would consist of renaming the Committee when it met as a crisis management body and adding three new paragraphs to that Article, which would consist in turn of giving the

---

[126] For a detailed discussion of the Amsterdam negotiations on defence see Peers, *supra* n. 24 at 555–61.
[127] Council doc. 4788/00, 23 Oct. 2000.

Committee formal power over the 'political control and strategic direction' of operations, governing the relationship between the Council and the Committee, and formalizing the existence of the Military Committee and the Committee for civilian crisis management.

The French Presidency kept the issue off the IGC agenda until the final weekend of negotiation between leaders. At that point, amendments to Articles 17 and 25 were agreed, along with a Declaration on the issue. The amendments were close to those suggested by Italy and Benelux. First, Article 17(1) has been amended by dropping the second sub-paragraph, which referred to EU–WEU relations and the possibility of an EU–WEU merger. The cross-reference to that sub-paragraph in the first sub-paragraph had to be deleted also. Secondly, almost all of Article 17(3) on the specific role of the WEU has been deleted; the only survivor is the fourth sub-paragraph, which will provide in future that EU defence policy, rather than (at present) the EU–WEU link, is without prejudice to neutrality and NATO activity. Article 17 as redrafted thus still refers to the progressive framing of a defence policy, the possible decision on a common defence, the Petersberg tasks, review at future IGCs, and NATO and WEU membership, although the WEU is now referred to only in its role as a military alliance.

As for Article 25, the Treaty ultimately renamed the Committee and added two paragraphs. First, the Committee will exercise 'political control and strategic direction' of operations, but only within the scope of the CFSP Title of the EU Treaty. Secondly, a new paragraph allows the Council to authorize the committee to take decisions regarding the operation, 'without prejudice to Article 47', which provides that EU Treaty activity may not encroach upon EC Treaty activity. There is no reference to the other new committees and the Committee has been renamed for *all* purposes; it will not, as suggested by Italy and Benelux, have a different name depending on what capacity it is acting in. Finally, a Declaration states that the objective is for the EU to become operational quickly, with a decision to be taken as soon as possible in 2001 based on the existing Treaty provisions. Therefore, ratification of the Treaty of Nice is not a precondition for applying the ESDP.

At first sight, the Treaty negotiators took due care to implement the legal analysis of the Council legal service, which concluded convincingly that amendments as regards the WEU and delegation of Council powers were necessary. On the other hand, the Declaration attached to the new Treaty seems to reach the opposite conclusion. True, the European Council can decide upon an EU defence policy without amending the Treaty, but it cannot decide on a policy which entails amendments to the role of the WEU or upon delegation of Council powers without Treaty amendments. Since the EU policy will involve those elements, it seems instead that ratification of the new Treaty *is* a precondition for a defence policy in this form to get under way. Since the ESDP will in any event be dependent upon national ratification and the 'headline goals' underpinning it are not due to be implemented until 2003, it is difficult to see the reason for the rush in any event.

It is striking that the amendments to Article 25 limit its scope not merely to the EU Treaty but to the CFSP Title, preserving the decision-making machinery not only of the Community but also of the third pillar. This is unmistakably a legally binding constraint upon the Committee, limiting its tasks to CFSP activities. Any activity beyond those limits would encroach on first or third pillar prerogatives and could be attacked by virtue of Article 47 EU.[128] Although the Committee is not listed as a potential defendant in either the EC or EU Treaty, any encroachment by it could be attacked either by means of attacking the validity of a Council CFSP measure which purported to give it the power to encroach upon the first or third pillar,[129] or by arguing that the Court should extend to this Committee the principle that any body taking legally binding decisions is subject to judicial review, regardless of the wording of the Treaties.[130]

In drafting terms, the new clauses are relatively clear, and in fact they perform a service in removing certain convoluted provisions from Article 17 that were poorly drafted by EU leaders at the very end of the Amsterdam negotiations. It is odd, however, that the EU Treaty will still refer to EU defence policy merely as a possible development after that policy has already entered into force. There is a good possibility therefore that the next Treaty amendment, set for 2004, will officially make reference to the defence policy in the Treaties.

VI. The Former Yugoslavia

By the beginning of 1999, EU relations with the former Yugoslavia looked rather different from the way they did in the early 1990s. In place of a floundering attempt to stop an ongoing war, the Union was co-ordinating a complex and comprehensive policy designed to win the peace. The main focus of policy since 1995 had been securing application of the Dayton agreement, with a hierarchy regarding EU trade and aid policy set up for the Western Balkans states (including Albania but excluding Slovenia) based on the extent to which they met EU political and economic criteria.[131] At the close of 1998, the EU had fairly good relations with the Former Yugoslav Republic of Macedonia (FYROM), civil relations with Albania and Bosnia-Herzegovina, troubled relations with President Tudjman's Croatia, and very poor relations with the FRY. Two years later, the outlook for the region was dramatically improved, and the EU's relations with Croatia and the FRY in particular were transformed beyond recognition. In addition to the improved relations with

---

[128] See Case C–170/96, *Commission* v. *Council* [1998] ECR I–2763.

[129] If action by the Committee came so long after the Council conferred on it powers that the two-month deadline to attack the measure in Art. 230 EC or Art. 35 EU had expired, it would still be possible to use Art. 241 EC to attack the basic decision as regards the first pillar, although the EU Treaty does not expressly refer to the existence of a similar principle in the third pillar.

[130] Case 294/83, *Les Verts* v. *EP* [1986] ECR 1339.

[131] See Peers, 'Common Foreign and Security Policy 1998', (1998) 18 *YEL* 659 at 679–81 for more detail.

individual countries, the Union held a conference to endorse its 'Stability Pact' for the region, and backed up this process with second pillar measures.[132]

Negotiations between the EC and FYROM on a new form of association agreement, a Stabilization and Association Agreement, were completed in November 2000.[133] Following the death of President Tudjman, negotiations began on a parallel agreement with that state. But the most complex and important relationship was with the FRY.

The Union's concern about the situation in Kosovo had been expressed in escalating sanctions which had been imposed during 1998.[134] First, the EU imposed a ban on entry of persons who it believed were primarily responsible for oppression in Kosovo,[135] along with a ban on export to the FRY of equipment that could be used to further terrorism and a ban on publicly-financed export credit;[136] secondly, it froze bank accounts of the Serbian and FRY governments;[137] thirdly, it banned new investment in the FRY;[138] and fourthly, it banned flights from Yugoslav carriers to and from the Union, excepting one charter flight to and from Montenegro.[139] In a separate move, the Union had also imposed a ban on entry for persons who it believed were responsible for suppressing the independent media,[140] and it had appointed both a formal envoy to the FRY (Felipe Gonzalez) and an informal envoy to Kosovo (Wolfgang Petrisch).[141]

In early 1999, attention was focused on encouraging the Milosevic government to agree peacefully to a solution to the crisis. If it failed to agree, it faced the threat of NATO bombing attacks. During this period, the EU sanctions were maintained, albeit relaxed for flights to and from the pro-Western region of Montenegro,[142] and Wolfgang Petrisch was confirmed officially as a Special Envoy.[143] Ultimately NATO forces were indeed used to bomb the FRY, beginning in March 1999, and the EU duly escalated the sanctions. First, it imposed a ban on petroleum sales to the FRY,[144] and then it imposed a package of further sanctions: extending the entry ban; freezing more funds (now including all funds of persons associated with President Milosevic and companies controlled by or acting for the FRY and Serbian governments); banning private sector export finance; banning all private or commercial flights to and from the FRY (not just Yugoslav airline flights); and banning the sale of goods, service, technology, or equipment used to repair damage caused by NATO air

---

[132] Joint Actions 1999/489 and 1999/523, *supra* n. 1; Common Position 1999/345, *supra* n. 2; Decisions 1999/361, 1999/434, and 1999/694, *supra* n. 3; Joint Action 2000/793, *supra* n. 4; and Common Position 2000/387, *supra* n. 5.

[133] COM (2001)90, 19 Feb. 2001.   [134] See Peers, 'CFSP 1998', *supra* n. 131, 665–9.

[135] Common Position 98/240 [1998] OJ L95/1.

[136] *Ibid.*, and Regulation 926/98 [1998] OJ L130/1.

[137] Common Position 98/326 [1998] OJ L143/1 and Regulation 1295/98 [1998] OJ L178/33.

[138] Common Position 98/374 [1998] OJ L165/1 and Regulation 1607/98 [1998] OJ L209/16.

[139] Common Position 98/426 [1998] OJ L190/3 and Regulation 1901/98 [1998] OJ L248/1.

[140] Common Position 98/725 [1998] OJ L345/1.

[141] See sect. III/B above.   [142] Regulation 214/1999, *supra* n. 7.

[143] Joint Action 1999/239, *supra* n. 1.

[144] Common Position 1999/273, *supra* n. 2 and Regulation 900/1999, *supra* n. 7.

strikes.[145] The entry ban was applied by an implementing second pillar Decision,[146] frequently updated,[147] while the other measures were applied by Community legislation adopted pursuant to Articles 60 and 301 EC,[148] although a proposed regulation banning exports of goods and services to repair damage caused by the air strikes was proposed but not adopted in light of the end to the bombing.[149]

Following the FRY's decision to pull its forces out of Kosovo, the Union began a two-track policy. One track consisted of assisting the UN to establish a civil administration in Kosovo.[150] The second track consisted of pressure against the FRY to change its government, implemented by retaining the sanctions put into place prior to and during the conflict in Kosovo. However, the Union again decided to distinguish carefully between Serbia on the one hand, and Montenegro (now joined with Kosovo) on the other. The latter were exempted from the petrol ban and flight ban by autumn 1999.[151] By this time, the Union also decided to encourage 'democratic forces' within Serbia itself, establishing a Common Position which was 'geared in particular' to developing dialogue with democratic leaders, establishing a process for shared discussion, providing Serbian municipalities with energy, and intensifying support for democratic media.[152] This was implemented in part by exempting certain Serbian municipalities controlled by opposition forces from the petrol export ban applying to Serbia.[153]

In early 2000, the Union again modulated its policy, suspending the flight ban for a limited period in response to requests from the Serbian opposition,[154] but coupling this liberalization with an extension in the list of persons covered by the entry ban.[155] The Regulation establishing a freeze on funds and a ban on new investment was also amended, in particular to ensure that investment could flow to Kosovo and Montenegro.[156] Finally, following the mass uprising in October 2000 which ensured recognition of the election of an opposition candidate as President of the FRY, the Union swiftly rescinded the

---

[145] Common Position 1999/318, *supra* n. 2. [146] Decision 1999/319, *supra* n. 3.
[147] See *supra* nn. 3 and 6.
[148] See Regulation 1064/1999, *supra* n. 7, strengthening the flight ban and repealing Regulation 1901/98 on that issue, and Regulation 1294/1999, *supra* n. 7, extending the freeze on funds and ban on new investments and repealing Regulations 1295/98 and 1607/98 on that issue.
[149] COM(1999)266, 31 May 1999.
[150] See Joint Action 1999/522, *supra* n. 1, ultimately replaced by Regulation 1080/2000, *supra* n. 14.
[151] See Common Position 1999/604, *supra* n. 2 and Regulations 2111/1999 and 2151/1999, *supra* n. 7. For the sake of 'transparency and simplicity', the latter Regulations replaced Regulations 900/1999 and 1064/1999 respectively.
[152] Common Position 1999/621, *supra* n. 2.
[153] Regulation 2421/1999, *supra* n. 7, and Commission Regulations 303/2000 and 1894/2000, *supra* n. 10.
[154] Common Positions 2000/176 and 2000/454, *supra* n. 5, implemented by Regulations 607/2000 and 1746/2000, *supra* n. 7.
[155] Common Position 2000/56, *supra* n. 5, implemented by Decision 2000/177 and later Decisions, *supra* n. 6.
[156] Regulation 723/2000, *supra* n. 7; part of the new Regulation had a later entry into force by virtue of Regulation 1059/2000, also *supra* n. 7.

ban on sales of petrol and the ban on flights,[157] and revised the remaining
sanctions so that they apply only to persons related to Mr Milosevic.[158]

These sanctions, like the previous round of sanctions against the former
Yugoslavia, were tested in the EC Courts. In *Invest Import und Export and
Invest Commerce* v. *Commission*, two Yugoslav companies challenged their
inclusion on the list of companies affected by the freezing of funds, when
those sanctions were clarified by the Council and implemented by the
Commission in spring 2000.[159] In two orders, the two Courts both dismissed
the claim by the plaintiffs, which claimed that they had wrongly been included
within the scope of the ban since they had no dealings with Mr Milosevic or the
Serbian or Yugoslav state. Before the Court of First Instance, they pleaded the
principle of proportionality, but before the Court of Justice, they pleaded that
their fundamental rights to property and to exercise of an economic activity
had been breached. The Court of Justice ruled, following the earlier case of
Bosphorus,[160] that any economic sanctions imposed by the Community
entailed an effect on economic operators, and that such damage had to be
weighed up against the human rights which the Community was willing to
protect. Moreover, the plaintiffs had not shown concrete evidence of how the
rights in question were affected. With great respect, the sanctions in this case
were very clearly aimed only at certain FRY organizations, and so it would not
have been inappropriate for the Court to examine whether the plaintiff organizations (which claimed to be operated by a workers' collective) actually fell
within the class of companies closely related to Mr Milosevic and his associates, which the Regulations were designed to cover. As regards the effect on the
plaintiffs' rights, surely even in the rarefied world of Luxembourg judicial reasoning should be sufficiently connected to the real world to conclude that
freezing bank accounts must necessarily affect the account-owners' property
and right to carry on a business.[161]

In the second case, *Royal Olympic Cruises and others* v. *Council and
Commission*,[162] the plaintiffs argued that the NATO bombing of Yugoslavia
was illegal and had caused them considerable damage as operators of cruises
in the south-east Mediterranean. In their view, the Union and the Community
constitute a single legal and political entity, so any illegal activity within the
framework of the Union engages the non-contractual liability of the
Community institutions. Since the Community institutions had participated
in the illegal activity by means of adopting sanctions measures, they too were

[157] Common Position 2000/599 and Regulations 2227/2000 and 2228/2000, *supra* nn. 5 and 7.
[158] Common Position 2000/696 and Regulation 2488/2000, *supra* nn. 5 and 7; the latter
repealed Regulations 1294/1999 and 607/2000 establishing a freeze on funds, a ban on new investment, and a flight ban, along with Art. 2 of Regulation 926/98, banning export credits. The ban on
sale of goods for use for repression, established by Art. 1 of Regulation 926/98, was maintained in
force.
[159] Case T–189/00 R [2000] ECR II–2293; appeal in Case C–317/00 P (R) [2000] ECR I–9541.
[160] Case C–84/95 *Bosphorus Hava Yollari Turizm* v. *Minister for Transport, Energy and
Communications, Ireland and the Attorney-General* [1996] ECR I–3953.
[161] See comments by Peers in (2001) *Nott. HR Law Review* 145 at 166–7.
[162] Case T–201/99 [2000] ECR II–4005; appeal pending as Case C–49/01 P.

liable. The Court of First Instance took the view that since the plaintiffs had claimed to suffer damage only as a result of the armed intervention, not the economic sanctions, and had admitted that the Court had no jurisdiction over acts within the framework of the EU,[163] they had not shown that the behaviour of the EC institutions within the first pillar was linked with the armed intervention or the damage which they suffered.

Is the Court's analysis correct? Politically speaking, the Community sanctions measures were of course linked with the armed intervention. Legally, however, the Community measures did not refer expressly to the armed intervention, although one Regulation contained exemptions from its scope in order to facilitate that intervention.[164] Moreover, there was no funding from the EU budget as regards that intervention, even by means of a second pillar measure. The proposed (but not adopted) Regulation banning exports of goods and services to repair certain damaged installations carefully refrains (even in the explanatory memorandum) from noting how those installations had become damaged. Of course, in the absence of an EU defence policy, the bombings were carried out by NATO, rather than within the second pillar framework. However, a link with the armed intervention can still be found in the key second pillar Common Position stepping up sanctions during the air strikes: the preamble argues that 'the most extreme measures, including military action' were 'both necessary and warranted', and both the preamble and an Article refer to preventing repair to damage 'caused by air strikes to assets, infrastructure or equipment'.[165] It is submitted that any measures linked to this Common Position by virtue of Articles 60 and 301 EC are therefore measures linked to the air strikes,[166] and it would have been harder still to deny a link between the air strikes and the Community institutions if the proposed Regulation banning repair to damage had been adopted. It can be argued that even where the institutions did not themselves conduct a given military action as such, their behaviour might be so closely connected with it as to justify imputing non-contractual liability as regards any Community measures. So, with great respect, it is submitted that the Court was wrong to find that there was an insufficient link between the air strikes and the acts of the Community institutions.

However, this is not the end of the analysis. It is logically necessary to examine separately the two issues that the Court dealt with together, and determine whether in this case, despite the links between the *EC legislation* and the air strikes, there was a sufficient link between the *damage suffered* and the air strikes, which there must be for a damages case to succeed. The answer to this question is easy, since the plaintiffs themselves admitted that they suffered

---

[163] If the plaintiffs indeed 'admitted' this, they were not legally correct to do so and the Court should have corrected them, as the EC Courts have some jurisdiction over *third* pillar matters.

[164] See Art. 3 of Regulation 900/1999, *supra* n. 7.

[165] Common Position 1999/319, *supra* n. 2, preamble and Art. 5.

[166] The earlier Common Position 1999/273 imposing the petrol export ban, which refers to 'extreme measures' but does not expressly refer to air strikes, is more ambiguous.

purely because of the air strikes, not because of the economic sanctions linked
to them. Whether or not the Community is separate from the Union, the
bombing in this case was not even an act of the Union, and as long as the
source of the damages which the plaintiffs suffered is severable from the acts
of the Community, there is simply no Community nexus in this case. If the limitation on the Court's jurisdiction in Article 46 EU is to mean anything, that
should put paid to any legal action against the Community institutions.
However, while this finding is enough to dispose of this case, it is important to
emphasize that if the plaintiffs had rather suffered because of the *Community
acts*, the Community institutions would potentially be liable as there would be
a sufficient nexus with Community law, and the legality of the bombing and
Community measures would have to be examined together, because the Court
was wrong to conclude that there was no link between the two at all. Since the
liability of the Community can arise from participation in illegal activity at the
international level,[167] it should follow that in such a case the EC courts would
have to examine whether the underlying military activity was legal.

Finally, the legality of the Union second pillar measures imposing entry bans
was challenged by two Yugoslav nationals who argued that those measures
should have been adopted under the first pillar, following the Treaty of
Amsterdam.[168] This would have proved a golden opportunity to delimit the
scope of the first and second pillars following the Treaty of Amsterdam, but
this prospect disappeared when the cases were withdrawn following the
removal of many names (including the plaintiffs' names) from the entry ban in
late 2000.

The second saga of EU sanctions against the former Yugoslavia led to legislation of quite fiendish complexity. One would hope that the institutions have
learned the lesson for the future that if many forms of sanctions are to be
applied against a third state, the legislative regime must be clearer and simpler
to apply. A number of traders may well have been uncertain about the extent
of trade which was actually permitted with the FRY, and with which parts of the
FRY. Additionally, as before, it has led to litigation against the Community, with
rather dubious judgments apparently more concerned with ensuring the
unfettered discretion of the Community institutions than with imposing effective judicial scrutiny of whether the application of sanctions has been over-
zealous.

VII. Conclusion

The Treaty of Amsterdam amendments on the CFSP have had a more
significant impact than perhaps some observers anticipated. The regular use
of qualified majority voting and the expanding activities of a high-profile High
Representative have clearly added to the efficiency and visibility of EU policy.

---

[167] See Case C–572/93, *Odigitria* [1995] ECR II–2025.
[168] Cases T–349/99 and T–350/99, *Miskovic and Karic* v. *Council* [2000] OJ C79/35 and 36.

Although the EU had failed to prevent the dispute over Kosovo breaking out into armed conflict, it maintained a unified policy on the issue throughout and developed a highly-nuanced policy in the form of various sanctions and benefits imposed or withdrawn to parts or all of the FRY during the final years of the Milosevic era. It seems, following on from questions posed in previous surveys, that there is considerable evidence both that the EU has reformed the CFSP institutions effectively and that there is growing political will to use them.

Yet any increase in effectiveness of the CFSP brings with it new problems. Just as the increased efficiency of first-pillar decision-making, beginning in the mid-1980s, led to considerable doubts about the legitimacy and transparency of Community decision-making, a more effective CFSP may come to raise the same concerns. There are considerable grounds over the last two years to indicate that this may be the case. A symptomatic incident was the High Representative's decision, nominally wearing his Council Secretary-General's hat, to push through major amendments to the Council's transparency rules which would automatically exclude access to many documents related to foreign and defence policy.[169] Since this proposed measure was suggested to Member States' representatives in Council working bodies shortly before the summer break, with no prior warning and no chance for national parliaments to discuss it, it raised disturbing questions about the apparently high-handed political approach by Mr Solana in this case, to say nothing of the grave legal doubts about the validity of the new Decision, which has been attacked by the European Parliament and several Member States in the Court of Justice.

Similar doubts about the legality of Union activity may be raised about the rush to decide on the new defence policy before certain elements of that policy have been ratified by national parliaments by means of the amendments found in the Treaty of Nice. Certainly, the defence policy of the Union is an important objective that will have a significant impact on the effectiveness of the CFSP. But that is not an excuse for major attacks on the principle of transparency and the obligation for the Union to act legally, particularly since the CFSP still falls fully outside the purview of the EU Courts. Even where it falls within the purview of the Courts, by means of a first pillar link, those Courts have been reaching unconvincing judgments about the legality of Community acts and the Community institutions' liability for them. With very limited transparency, marginal parliamentary control, excluded or supine courts, and potentially strained political accountability, a more 'effective' CFSP is surely not merely a cause for congratulation but also for concern.

---

[169] Decision 2000/527 [2000] OJ L212/9.

REVIEWS OF BOOKS

The Administrative Supervision & Enforcement of EC Law: Powers, Procedures and Limits by Alberto Gil Ibañez, Hart Publishing, Oxford, 1999, xlv + 324 pp. ISBN 1–84113–056–7.

While the academic literature has extensively discussed the ongoing development of EC substantive law, it has paid distinctly less attention to its supervision and enforcement, a legal area that raises questions that are as important as they are intricate. The book by Alberto Gil Ibañez addresses this thorny issue and provides a study of the roles played by the two enforcers of EC law: the Commission and the national administrations. As the author acknowledges in the introduction, the process of application of the law is a complex one in any legal system, but it becomes more so in EC law due to a concurrence of factors. These include the unique position of national authorities as both enforcers and subjects of the law, the tenuous division of competences between the Community and national administrations, the distinctive character of the Community legal order and the practicalities of rationally organizing a system involving fifteen different national administrations. Enforcing the law in the face of such an involved reality seems, by any standards, a daunting task.

The book, a revised version of the author's Ph.D dissertation, is divided into three Parts. The First Part (Chapters 1 and 2), attempts to clarify the meaning of terms commonly used in this area, such as supervision, enforcement, and administration, and also considers the problem of the division of powers between the Community and the Member States. The Second Part of the book examines the procedures for the supervision and enforcement of EC law and the limits to their use. Chapter 3 explores the process whereby the Commission obtains information and studies the tensions between the Commission's power to carry out inspections and the duty of the Member States to submit to them. The author observes, *inter alia*, that the Commission is bereft of independent powers of investigation in areas where they are crucial, such as environment (at 72), and that in areas where these powers have been granted, the means of inspection vary from one policy to another. The general infringement procedure in Article 226 EC, the specialized procedures provided in Articles 86(3), 88, and 104 EC and those set out by secondary legislation in the areas of public procurement, air transport policy, clearance of accounts in the context of the EAGGF, and heath and safety are examined in Chapter 4. The author highlights the unsystematic process of creation of new enforcement mechanisms by secondary legislation and questions whether there are adequate legal bases in the Treaty to warrant their existence. Finally, Chapter 5 illustrates how difficult it is to set limits to the use of those procedures, given the absence of clear criteria on when the Commission or the national authorities should be responsible for pursuing a breach.

The Third Part of the book is devoted to the study of selected topics in the administrative supervision and enforcement of EC law. The time constraints under which the enforcers of EC law operate are considered in Chapter 6. The author focuses his attention on the lack of a regulatory framework for the application of deadlines and makes some thoughtful suggestions on how the system could be improved. In Chapter 7, the discretion bestowed on the Commission and on the national authorities in the enforcement of EC law is examined. One of the most interesting sections in that Chapter is the analysis of the limits imposed on the Commission's discretion, although a more detailed study of the impact of the principles of legitimate expectations and of proportionality would have been welcomed. Chapter 8 deals with the difficult issue of the co-ordination between the Commission and the Member States. The author reasons that although the Commission is, theoretically, in a position of authority with regard to the Member States, it effectively lacks the resources and the power to carry out that role. In practice, therefore, the relationship between the two enforcers of EC law seems to be one of co-operation rather than one of hierarchy. The fostering of mutual trust between the Commission and the national authorities, the encouragement of a further degree of decentralization, and the clarification of the criteria that apply to the enforcement of EC law, are persuasively argued by the author in his concluding Chapter as constituting the essential tools for the reform of the present system.

The book by Gil Ibañez is a judicious combination of methodical exposition and critique. It provides a detailed picture of the current mechanisms of enforcement, but it also draws the attention of the reader to their weaknesses and, in particular, to the striking lack of consistent rules, which emerges as a recurrent theme in the book. Only the failure to adopt the new numbering of Treaty provisions, introduced by the Treaty of Amsterdam, is a disappointing feature in a well-researched and valuable book. The author should be congratulated for tackling a topic of such inherent complexity, for articulating it, and for offering a set of stimulating suggestions on improvement. He also manages to convey a message of enthusiasm for a reform that is long overdue. The last sentence of the book appropriately emphasizes that 'both the Commission and the national authorities must continue their struggle with complexity if they want the Community system to survive'. Gil Ibañez's work certainly does much to illuminate that complexity and, what is more, to show the way forward.

ALBERTINA ALBORS-LLORENS

*L' évolution de la responsabilité de l'Etat sous l'influence du droit Communau-
taire*, by Petra Senkovic, Bruylant, Brussels, 2000, 490 pp.

The judgment of the European Court of Justice in the *Francovich* case creating
a Community remedy in damages for breach of Community law, and the
jurisprudence that follows it, have been the object of much close attention in
legal literature. This, in itself, augurs well for the future of this new remedy.
Indeed, as some national experiences illustrate, the consolidation of this
judge-made principle will depend largely on the contribution of legal scholarship to the conceptualization of its theoretical foundation. This work by Petra
Senkovic on the influence of Community law in the evolution of state liability
for damage caused by the legislator is a further valuable contribution to this
debate. Moreover, the author's insight on the reaction of national legal systems
to the European Court's case law is an important addition to the ongoing discussion concerning the development of a new *jus commune*.

The book under review, based on a Ph.D thesis submitted at the University
of Paris I Panthéon-Sorbonne, is divided into two parts: the first focuses on the
principle of state liability for breaches of Community law attributable to the
legislator; the second examines the impact of this principle on the national
legal systems. It also includes a comprehensive bibliography and an index of
the relevant case law, providing a valuable reference point for those with an
interest in the area.

The analysis of the principle of state liability for breach of Community law
commences with an interesting excursus into the arguments made to support
parliamentary immunity from actions for damages and the doctrinal developments that led, in national and international law, to the acceptance of compensation for legislative harm. Only then does the author proceed to consider
the problem of state liability from the perspective of Community law. Senkovic
contends that state liability for breach of Community law cannot be compared
to state liability for legislative wrong under national and international law. At
the heart of her reasoning is the claim that the national legislator, when intervening within the ambit of Community law, plays a merely executive role (4,
54). This finding derives from the premiss that the legislator is bound by
Community law and its margin of discretion is therefore considerably
reduced. I do not dispute these findings, but I am not convinced that they supply an adequate basis for the argument that the interventions of the legislator
in the field of Community law have an executive character. Such assertion
needs to be grounded in deeper considerations. Moreover, I believe that
Senkovic's assertion may be difficult to defend in light of the subsidiarity principle and the express reference of the authors of the Treaty to the role of
national parliaments in the European Union.

This introductory Chapter is followed by a sound and detailed analysis of
the Court's rulings concerning state liability for breach of Community law.
Chapter 2 focuses on the theoretical foundation of the principle of state liability, offering the reader a thorough but somewhat uncritical account of the

arguments developed by the Court. Chapter 3 deals with the conditions under which liability is deemed to arise. This Chapter is divided into four sections. The first deals with the question of the Court's legitimacy to define the conditions of liability; the second with the problem of reconciling the regime of liability for breaches of Community law by Community institutions with the regime of liability applicable to Member States. The final sections deal with both the substantive and procedural conditions of liability and the extent of compensation. The result is a clear and informative account of the legal debate surrounding the Court's jurisprudence.

One would have welcomed, however, a more detailed discussion concerning the convergence of the two Community liability systems. Surprisingly the author does not explore whether, and the extent to which, the specificity of the Community decision-making process and the lack of a formal definition of legislative act in Community law may affect the harmonization of these tort systems.

In addition, the jurisprudence concerning the relationship of the action for damages with other remedies would merit a closer scrutiny. In my view, the author's attempt to define the place and role of the damages remedy in the system of legal protection of rights derived from Community law is weakened by her narrowly focused research. Cases such as *Sutton* (C–66/95 [1997] ECR I–2163) and *Comateb* (C–192 to 218/95 [1997] ECR I–165) are overlooked, despite their importance for ascertaining the Court's position regarding the relation of actions for damages for breach of Community law with other national remedies. Furthermore, the controversial response of the Court to the problem raised by the relationship between the action for damages against the European Community, under Article 288(2) of the EC Treaty, and the action for damages against national authorities, in the case of concurrent liability of the European Community and a Member State, is also ignored.

However, the most disappointing feature of this part is the failure to explore the impact of the subsidiarity principle on the interpretative role of the European Court of Justice. One would expect that, when addressing questions like the legitimacy of the Court's rulings, or the level of harmonization required by Community law, the author would feel tempted to participate in the emerging but already vibrant debate on judicial subsidiarity.

The second part of the book is devoted to examining the compliance of national legal orders with the principle of state liability for breach of Community law. The inquiry is limited to three legal systems—the English, French, and German, a selection that presents the additional interest of comparing the reaction of common law and civil law systems to this judge-made principle.

Senkovic's work contains a careful and detailed analysis of these three legal systems, bringing to light disparities such as to the normative justification and the scope of the right to obtain compensation for legislative harm. The author gives a thorough account of the application of the damages remedy in case of legislative wrong by national courts, before and after the *Francovich* judgment. She also takes the reader through a stimulating inquiry on the possibility of interpreting national tort law in accordance with the requirements of Community law. This inquiry leads the author to the conclusion that national legal systems do not allow an effective application of the principle of state liability for breaches of Community law attributable to the legislator. Based on this conclusion, Senkovic calls for further action on the part of the European Court in determining and harmonizing the conditions of state liability, in order to satisfy the requirement of uniform application of Community law in the Member States.

The book concludes by raising a number of very interesting questions which offer the reader some of the most thought-provoking pages of the work. Senkovic alerts us to the consequences of harmonization in the coherence of national legal systems and asks whether the increase in the role of national judges will not provoke a shift in the balance of powers between the legislator and the judiciary. These final considerations illustrate that the impact of the *Francovich* jurisprudence may exceed the realm of public liability and they indicate areas of future research.

Luísa Verdelho Alves

Thoughts from a Bridge: A Retrospective of Writings on New Europe and American Federalism, by E. Stein, The University of Michigan Press, Ann Arbor, Mich., 2000, xv + 497 pp., and *Democracy & Constitutionalism*, by G.F. Mancini, Hart, Oxford, 2000, xxvii + 268 pp.

Few scholars are blessed with the ability of being able to discern the extent to which, if at all, their research may be said to constitute a benefit and not a burden to the academic community, or indeed, as in some cases, society as a whole. Goethe, for instance, believed that the most important and perhaps the only legacy he would leave behind was his writings on the natural sciences, a view he based on the fact that they were a product of experiences which were salient, formative, and were central to his intellectual development—perhaps a good illustration of how difficult it can be to stand back from one's own experience! Even those who possess this blessing (or curse!) are all too often dismissed as suffering from 'objectivity deficit disorder'.

In academia, the ascertainment of *Leitmotivs* of one's own intellectual achievements is usually delegated to others by way of the *Festschrift*. The attempts made during periods of self-reflection over the contributions to science are usually haphazard, cursory, and yield insights which may explain symptoms but not their causes, so to speak. How many scholars get to write their own *Festschrift*, one wonders? The sources of the process of 'self-reflection' are usually discernible from things ranging from the list of acknowledgements in the opus of one's choice or the 'old faithful' selection of the anecdotes to be told during faculty dinners or indeed at any available opportunity, as those sources close to academics, the 'nearests and dearests' would no doubt testify. Putting together a collection of articles written during one's career is perhaps the closest one comes to writing one's own *Festschrift* which, if done wisely, escapes the label of self-indulgence and is, instead, a source of enlightenment and inspiration not only to oneself but for others also. It is safe to say that it is the latter and not the former which applies to the case at hand. Both books provide the reader with an invaluable selection of articles which are highly informative and thought-provoking. Moreover, she is invited to draw her own conclusions concerning the nature of the contribution to research on European integration especially because both authors are, in their own way, honest about the link between their experience and their research.

Stein is candid about the events which, in his view, informed his own biography including his rites of passage as a lawyer beginning with his work as a soldier-lawyer with the Allied Commission for Italy during the Second World War, the years spent working for the US Department of State in charge of constitutional developments and the United Nations and teaching at Michigan Law School, which was the first American law school to include a course on European Community law (as it was then). He concludes that the consequences of these experiences were mainly twofold. First, they explain his need for a myth and something to believe in after the Second World War which, as he states, explain his interest in a new international legal order and a new art of governance. Secondly, it accounts for Stein's ability to reconcile the variety of roles which lawyers are called upon to exercise, namely as government advisers, negotiators, diplomats, and corporate counsel and attorney in international legal practice as well as his concern to employ the most appropriate analytical framework for legal research, a phenomenon which Stein refers to as the 'living law'. One is reminded of the 'law in context' approach to law. Stein, however, succeeds where law in context failed. First, its disciples defended it with such vigour—perhaps understandable in view of the opposition which they faced, namely the legacy of legal positivism—that much of the scholarship which was conducted under its aegis tended to be too self-referential. There is a time to defend a movement as a good in itself. There is also, however, a time to practise what one preaches, which brings us to the second flaw. Scant attention was paid to the detail concerning method which was, to some extent, the project's undoing. Nothing speaks more eloquently than scholarship which is completed with erudition, precision, and sophistication. It is, after all, better not to do something at all than to do it badly, which as regards law in context is a warning which its disciples would have done well to heed.

All academics interested in European Union studies sooner or later come across the famous lines, '[t]ucked away in the fairyland Duchy of Luxembourg and blessed, until recently, with benign neglect of the powers that be and the mass media, the Court of Justice of the European Communities has fashioned a constitutional framework for a federal-type structure in Europe'. This passage appears in an article which Stein wrote in 1981 and represents, as Weiler points out in the 'Foreward', the roots of the constitutional paradigm for a field of law which was an unknown quantity for lawyers from the moment the European Court of Justice upheld the right of an individual to rely directly on a treaty before a domestic tribunal in *Van Gend en Loos*. What many lawyers failed to grasp was that from this moment onwards, not only was EC law *sui generis* but also the legal reasoning upon which it was based was, to some extent, *sui generis*. Lawyers would have to transcend, qualify, and, in some cases, even abandon the tools with which their legal training had furnished them, in order to come to grips with the different legal systems of the Member States of the EC as well as respond to the conceptual challenge which EC (not to mention EU) law represents to law and legal reasoning. It is not easy, as Stein points out, for any lawyer born and bred in a national system to abandon 'hallowed national constitutional practices'. Moreover, one cannot expect a national lawyer to be an enthusiast of a legal system which erodes not only national power but also her own career interests (see 37).

Lawyers and judges have consistently been the principal actors in the European integration process. Indeed, the historical development of EC law is what Egon Ehrlich referred to, albeit in another context, as *Juristenrecht*. *Juristenrecht*, however, raises problems of democratic legitimacy if one accepts that judges and lawyers alike are supposed to be beneath the law and not, as the *praxis* of EC law testifies, above it. According to a judicial model, the citizen is never the originator of the norms. In political terms, however, the citizen is able informally to determine the content through the weakly democratic mechanism of the European Parliament and by way of Non-Governmental Organizations (NGOs) and lobbyists. The normative order which constitutes EC law is not only the product of legal pluralism; it is also entrenched in multilevel governance given that it is based on an increasingly interconnected international order. This may seem like stating the obvious. The collection of Stein's writings, however, testifies to the fact that he was aware of these issues long before this became obvious to the community of academics interested in the European integration project. However, not only was he aware of these issues but he consistently attempted to devise models of legal reasoning which could take this into account.

The *Leitmotiv* which spans Stein's career is the art of governance and the management of power in a complex divided-power system which he has addressed in a variety of contexts throughout his distinguished career. It is his meticulous attention to the detail of devising a suitable conceptual legal framework within which the European integration project is best understood which enabled him to develop a 'universal grammar' which could be used across the board, that is to say, not exclusively within the constitutional paradigm. Furthermore, the quality of his analysis is such that his arguments are as appropriate now as they were when the articles were published. Consider this extract taken from page 75 of his book: 'where abstract legal argument is eschewed, bargaining is the order of the day, and solutions at times are reached in the privacy of the chairman's office', which appears in an article on the harmonization of European company laws. Substantively speaking, European company law has moved on a great deal from 1971. However, it is precisely because Stein takes the law's social and political context seriously, not to mention the benefits of a systematic comparative study that his ideas cut across a compartmentalized approach to EC law (i.e. private law, public law). Indeed, Stein's ideas are as relevant to the study of the European integration project now as they were in 1971, which is the measure of a true scholar. Moreover, his writings bear testimony to the value which is added to scholarship by integrity.

The overall impression one gains from this collection is of a scholar who is able to achieve a balance between rigorous scientific study (see 'Uses, Misuses—and Nonuses of Comparative Law' at 89–111, and the comparisons between the American Federal experience and the European Union in 'Courts and Free Markets—Perspectives from the United States and Europe' at 112–60), concern for accountability and the role of the judiciary in a modern administrative state ('Citizen Access to Judicial Review of Administrative Action in a Transnational and Federal Context' at 161–90), and the complex division of powers between the EU Member States and the Community institutions ('Towards a European Foreign Policy? The European Foreign Affairs System from the Perspective of the United States Constitution with Excerpts from *External Relations of the European Community: Structure and Process*'). An annotation appears at the beginning of each article in this collection in which Stein outlines not only the context of the research but also comments on the articles with the benefit of hindsight, a device which is truly fascinating for the reader, particularly when Stein openly acknowledges the link between his experiences and his intellectual endeavours.

The admission of this link by no means detracts from the quality of the articles; in fact it is the opposite which is true, for Stein's attempt to make sense of his experiences shines through the scholarship which is underpinned with honesty, particularly as regards the conclusions he draws from his analyses. Consider an article which arose as a consequence of the return to the country of his birth, the former Czechoslovakia, where he followed the post-Communist Czech–Slovak constitutional negotiations at first hand (see 'Excerpts from *Czecho/Slovakia*: Ethnic Conflict, Constitutional Fissure, Negotiated Breakup' at 417–75) with, he concedes, mixed emotions, something which enabled him to view the negotiation with a degree of realism which was all too often absent during those heady days after 1989.

In another article written during research leave in Berlin in 1984, Stein assesses the German law on free speech ('History against Free Speech: German Law in European and American Perspective' at 347–409) and draws attention to cases in America which have arisen under the constitutional right to free expression, such as the *Skokie* case (*Village of Skokie* v. *Nationalist Socialist Party of America*, 69 Ill. 2d 605, 375 NE 2d 21 (1978)), in which ordinances of the village of a Chicago suburb prohibiting a neo-Nazi party to march through a village where 40,000 of the 70,000 inhabitants were Jewish was struck down as unconstitutional by the Illinois state and lower federal courts. Part of his conclusion is that the resolution of such a case would be quite different in the Federal Republic of Germany. It would indeed be interesting to see whether Professor Stein would still maintain this position today in the light of the exponential increase in racist incidents since unification and the marches by neo-Nazis in cities throughout the Federal Republic which have become all too commonplace, the latter being repeatedly upheld on the basis of the constitutional right of freedom of expression and the freedom of assembly.

Be that as it may, the quality of Stein's craftsmanship is such that his objectivity is unquestionable, particularly given that he is aware of the dangers of observers seeing only what they want to see (see 9) Applied to the context of European integration, he articulates this approach, arguing for balance in an academic debate which is all too often susceptible to the competing ideologies of *Euroeuphoria* and *Europessimism*, both of which, as Stein argues, are inappropriate (see 474).

Judge G. F. Mancini, who sadly died in 1999, navigated the perilous straits of competing ideologies with finesse. This is particularly impressive given that, as a former judge of the European Court of Justice, the likelihood of presenting the case for European integration selectively is high. Here again, we are faced with a scholar whose aim in publishing his collected writings is to benefit readers and is not merely an act of self-indulgence.

Mancini's vision of Europe is a European political entity organized along the lines of a state without a nation but which respects the identity of the peoples of which it is composed and which is provided with two chambers, an executive chamber and a chamber of guaranteeing organs whose objective is democracy. His main concern is a method whereby this may be achieved which he articulates by advocating a model of federalism which is based on fair, accountable, transparent decision-making. This process is one conducted by actors which are bound by the 'checks and balances' inherent in a constitutional framework which the ECJ has gone some way towards creating as part of its innovative jurisprudence (see Chapter 1, 'The Making of a Constitution of Europe'). Indeed, whilst acknowledging the constraints of the political stalemates of the 1960s and 1970s, which allowed the Court sufficient room for manœuvre to catalyse the integration process (one may be forgiven for thinking that the Court achieved this almost single-handedly, on reading Mancini's review of the Court's decisions), he acknowledges the limits of judicial activism (see 14) and the importance of a balance created by other institutions. Thus, in Chapter 2 ('The Constitutional Challenge Facing the European Court of Justice'), he underlines the necessity for a system of checks and balances based on the principle of democracy which the Court has consistently recognized, particularly in the cases concerning the standing of the European Parliament to bring proceedings against acts of the Council and the Commission (see, for example, the *Chernobyl* case: Case C–70/88, *European Parliament* v. *Council* [1990] ECR I–2041). Generally speaking, Mancini manages to achieve a balance by presenting arguments which are highly informed without getting sidetracked by detail, and his writing retains an awareness of the relevance of political and socio-economic considerations without being superficial, an ability which is not always common amongst lawyers, particularly those interested in the context in which law operates.

In Chapter 5, 'The Euro: A Currency in Search of a State' he succeeds in providing an overview of monetary union which is full of insights such as the need for a political counterpart of the European Central Bank (see 75–6) in order to maintain an institutional balance. Credit must be given where it is due and, to this extent, Mancini must be applauded for being honest in his arguments and for showing that he has the interests of the individual at heart and not the vested interests which a scholar in his position, i.e. as a former Judge of the ECJ, might be forgiven for having. Indeed, he does not mince his words when he states that the *status quo* as regards monetary union exacerbates the democratic deficit. The individual is never far from Mancini's thoughts. It is here where he might be forgiven for presenting the case selectively, a siren call which he is, however, able to withstand. For example, even though he applauds the Court's authorship of human rights protection he is openly critical about the fact that the ECJ has let the individual down as regards *locus standi* of natural and legal persons under the second paragraph of Article 177 EC Treaty (now Article 234 EC), and the onus on the individual to show that a regulation singles him out and affects him in a genuinely distinctive way in order to be able to mount a direct challenge, as well as being critical of the ECJ's excessive caution and indulgence towards Community institutions (see 46 ff.). Notwithstanding this, he acknowledges that the ECJ has consistently reached decisions which extend beyond a rationale which is exclusively economic (see for example the discussion of Case C–13/94 *P.* v. *S. and Cornwall County Council* [1996] ECR I–2143 in Chapter 9 at 156) ensuring that Europe is not just for 'traders' (see 100).

Indeed, Mancini is at his best when he discusses the jurisprudence of the ECJ. Jean Monnet's words, which Mancini refers to at 100, '*d'abord on décide, puis on explique*' (see 49), could equally be applied to Mancini in the sense that his writings are reminiscent of the tradition of the glossators. This is particularly welcome especially given the complexity of the issues on which the ECJ has been asked to adjudicate and the fact that its rationales are not always easy to deduce from its decisions. After all, one man's method may be another's madness.

In Chapter 14, Mancini draws from the opinion of the ECJ on the establishment of the Agreement establishing the World Trade Organization (WTO). His analysis is consistent with his ideas concerning the need for effective representation of European interests by unanimity. Thus, he advocates legal measures which enable the Community's external economic policy to be both consistent (see 235 ff.) and based on unanimity. However, one cannot help but wonder, given that unanimity often brings with it the corollary of the lowest common denominator, whether legal measures should be denied which not only take the diversity of the EU's members into account but also draw strength from it and perceive it as a quality to be protected. This is the stone upon which the federalist approach to law is built. For example, could one conceive of legal measures which endorse a federalist framework for foreign policy which reformulates the saying 'united we stand, divided we fall', to 'divided we stand' whilst, at the same time, preventing the latter's corollary, namely, united we fall. This is but one query amongst the plethora of questions which this collection of Judge Mancini's writings provokes.

Both books are to be commended and recommended for fostering the pursuit of further enquiry in a field over which a veritable 'lake' of ink, to borrow terminology more commonly associated with the Common Agricultural Policy, has been spilled, which has not always been a credit to the juridical study of European integration. Indeed, given the deluge of literature on the subject, it is interesting to speculate on what will remain timeless, particularly in the 'publish or perish' climate in which a 'less is more' backlash remains the wishful thinking of many a scholar. At page xvii of the introduction of his book, Judge Mancini writes, 'History alone can judge the stones which we contributed to the construction of the cathedral which our predecessors commenced'. This quotation may be reformulated *ad personam*: if the academic study of the European integration project may be regarded as the cathedral, then the collected writings of Stein and Mancini may be regarded as indispensable additions to the pillars of that hallowed artifice, not least because the discipline is, from a historical point of view, still in its formative years according to some, in arrested development according to others, and in the throes of a 'mid-life crisis' according to others still. The law of the European Union can do many things but can neither navel gaze nor can it write its own *Festschrift*, even if systems theorists would have us believe otherwise. This is a task which, as Eric Stein and the former Judge Mancini show, has to be delegated to others.

Miriam Aziz

General Principles of EC Law by John A. Usher, Longman, London, 1998, 168 pp.

The General Principles of EC Law by Takis Tridimas, Oxford University Press, Oxford, 1999, 356 pp.

General Principles of European Community Law by Ulf Bernitz and Joakim Nergelius (eds.), Kluwer, The Hague, 2000, 244 pp.

In the last three years, three books have been published under the same title, *General Principles of EC Law*. Nevertheless each of the books is different in approach, content, and aim, and none of them exhausts the rich topic with which they deal.

I begin with an overview of the book by Usher. This is a handy book, brief (in particular if compared to the Tridimas volume) and with a short format. It is addressed mainly to students, although it is also a valuable book for academics and practitioners. This book provides a sound overview of the function of some of the general principles of EC law emerging from the case law of the European Court of Justice and Court of First Instance.

General principles of EC law are introduced to the reader with reference to the functions these principles have in EC law, to their sources, to the different names that the principles have in the different legal orders, and to the innovative approach of the Court of Justice to former Article 215(2) EC. The status and functions of general principles (as interpretative devices, as grounds for annulment, as a basis for the award of damages, or as constraints on Member States' activities) are examined in Chapter 8.

In Chapters 2 to 7 the author examines the following general principles of EC law: Community preference, non-discrimination, proportionality, legitimate expectations, legal certainty, procedural rights (the right to be heard, the prohibition of self-incrimination, the privilege of legal profession, the principle of effective judicial protection), the right to privacy, the principle of protection of property rights, and the principles of good administration (administrative good faith, consistency, diligence, and communication).

This book provides a clear overview of the function of general principles deriving from the case law of the Community Courts. The case law is certainly not exhaustively covered, but the approach of the European Courts to each topic is well explained. In order to show the judicial practice clearly, the author selects for each issue relevant areas where case law evidences the approach of European Courts. Staff cases and the field of competition are predominant areas, in this sense. The chapters are well structured, and this helps to provide a clearer understanding of the way in which the European Courts apply general principles of law.

Throughout the book the author pays accurate attention to the influence that national legal systems have had on the development of general principles of EC law. I found particularly interesting the attention paid by Usher to the national origin of some EC general principles. Thus, it is shown that despite the national origin of a principle, when the Court of Justice adopts it in EC law, it does not necessarily adopt the meaning the principle has in the national legal order of origin. The 'Community' character of general principles of EC law, whatever their national origin, is easily perceived from the reading of the book. It is similarly recalled that at times a given principle is named differently depending on the national legal order to which it belongs. This feature of the book is important since it highlights the mutual influence of national legal orders and EC law.

In this same line of the mutual influence of legal orders, the book includes a final chapter devoted to the influence of general principles of Community law in the United Kingdom legal systems. This Chapter is very interesting since it does not deal merely with situations in which UK authorities administer EC law, but also explores the influence of general principles of Community law in situations where there is not a direct connection with EC law.

Finally, it is worth noting that the book was published before the entry into force of the Amsterdam Treaty, and consequently it follows the former numbering of provisions although the text of the Amsterdam Treaty was taken into account.

The Tridimas volume is, by contrast with that of Usher, a dense book. It is certainly a suitable volume for practitioners and academics and for those who seek an accurate account of the development and current state of case law of the Community Courts in relation to the application of general principles of EC law.

This book deals more specifically with the 'general principles of law recognized in the Community legal order', as the author notes himself. General principles of law are the clearest example of judicial law-making, and the book aims to give an account of the state of case law. Thus, to some extent this is more a book about outcomes, about the concrete practice that the application of general principles by the European Court has generated. Consequently the book entails a great effort of systematization of the rich practice of the European Court of Justice and the Court of First Instance. At the same time, in the examination of case law the author reflects also on the general approach of the European Courts to each of the principles under review.

In the first chapter the author introduces the reader to the main issues and questions to which the application of general principles of law by Community Courts gives rise. These include: the origin of the principles, the mandate of the Court of Justice, the sources of inspiration, the three main functions that general principles fulfil, the scope of application, and the position of general principles in the hierarchy of Community norms. He addresses the interesting and unsettled point of the application of general principles against individuals.

The general principles of law which the author analyses are equality, proportionality, legal certainty, legitimate expectations, fundamental rights, rights of defence, effective remedies in national courts, and the principles governing liability in damages.

The following Chapters (2 to 9) are devoted to each of the general principles referred to above. The internal distribution of chapters is more or less similar in each chapter. Thus, the examination of each topic is introduced by some general considerations and subsequently the functioning of the principle is explained through its application in selected areas. Agriculture, competition, and staff cases are recurrent areas. Although the brief introduction to each principle varies from one principle to another, the source of inspiration of the Court of Justice is generally recalled (whether adopted from a specific legal tradition or deduced from the EC legal order itself), followed by the content of the principle, or the schema of reasoning of the Court of Justice.

With regard to each principle, the author describes the evolution of the Courts' practice and the current state of case law. In addition to this, he emphasizes specific and challenging questions generated by judicial practice together with unsettled topics or trends under evolution. It is worth noticing that throughout the book the author gives an account of the relationship between the European Courts and national courts. Thus, this book also calls attention to the process of mutual influence and relationship between EC law and national legal orders.

However, issue can be taken with some aspects of Tridimas' volume. Particularly I do not agree with the way in which he distributes the headings and sub-headings within each chapter. The author does not appear to follow a coherent approach, which creates more confusion than clarity in the understanding of the case law. Further, the author is not fully consistent with some of the terms employed, for example, with regard to the 'functions' of general principles. This divergence in the use of the term may cause confusion.

Finally, let us turn to the recent book edited by Bernitz and Nergelius. This book brings together sixteen essays, by different eminent legal scholars, concerning diverse aspects of the general principles of Community law. The essays are the result of a conference held in Malmö (Sweden) in August 1999, organized by the Swedish Network of European Legal Studies in co-operation with the Faculty of Law at the University of Lund.

Although any book about general principles of law necessarily concerns case law, this book is more about principles than about case law, albeit that the latter is also included. Thus, with the support of the practice of the European Court of Justice and Court of First Instance, the authors show the role and application of general principles in Community law, emphasizing the sources of inspiration of Community Courts, the underlying values of the principles, and the objectives each principle aims at securing.

The conference was intended to emphasize the ongoing process of cross-fertilization, nevertheless, what predominates in the book is the analysis of the application of the selected general principles by the European Courts.

The essays are in four groups. The first group contains three introductory articles about general aspects of principles. The second deals with the protection of Human Rights. The third is devoted to the analysis of institutional principles. The fourth part of the book is devoted to the general principles and the legal system. The volume concludes with a block in which conclusions are drawn.

This book provides the reader with an excellent analysis of the main issues that the application of principles of Community law generate. Throughout the book the different authors present the current practice of the European Courts, criticize inconsistencies, pose challenging questions, and try to devise the possible ways of future trends.

Clearly this book is broader in scope than the other two books reviewed above, in the sense that it covers not only 'classical' general principles of EC law. By comparison, it is the third block of this volume which contains topics not dealt with in the previous books. This block brings together four interesting essays about 'institutional' principles. The issues discussed in the essays are the principle of proportionality and subsidiarity, Article 10 EC, the question of the role of constitutional principles in EC law and the issue of general principles of institutional law as a category of general principles that regulate institutional relations, and are used by the Court in the construction of the EU legal order. Block four of the book contains as well a brief overview of the general principles in Swedish law.

The fact that the issues are dealt with by different authors at times produces repetition of some points; thus, the origin of the principles, the sources of inspiration of the European Courts are highlighted in different essays. Nevertheless, this fact is balanced by the richness arising from the fact that each author provides her or his own view of the issue under examination.

As was said above, none of the books exhausts the topic of general principles of EC law. It is apparent from this review that, although there are principles examined by all three, others are dealt with only in one, for example, subsidiarity or the principle of Community preference. Yet, in the examination of certain principles, like the principle of legal certainty, authors select different outcomes to focus on, as is clearly seen in the Usher and Tridimas books. I agree that this basic principle is so vast that it may deserve a whole study of its own.

All three books mainly concern the practice of the European Courts, and similarly all three contain comparative references to the national legal orders, above all when the principles applied by the European Courts clearly have a national origin. It results from the reading of these books that there is a topic still to be developed: the reception in national legal orders of the general principles of Community law, some of which are, as mentioned, of national origin and others are specific to EC law.

All three books are very rich and challenging, each with the specificities mentioned in this review.

ANGELES MAZUELOS

Regulating Social Europe: Reality and Myth of Collective Bargaining in the EC Legal Order by Antonio Lo Faro, Hart Publishing, Oxford, 2000, 288 pp.

Antonio Lo Faro's impressive monograph explores the function of European collective bargaining in the context of the Community legal order. As befits an analysis of European labour law, the author's approach is rich, drawing not only on legal, but also institutional, political and industrial relations sources. His central thesis is that European collective bargaining is best understood not, as one might first imagine, with reference to national collective bargaining systems, as a manifestation of collective autonomy at European level, but rather as an imperfect response to the crisis in the Community regulatory system. The thesis is compelling. It deserves to be heeded by both the Commission and Council which have done no more than to provide 'lame' normative support for collective bargaining at European Community level (at

159), and by the social partners themselves, in particular UNICE, CEEP, and the ETUC, whose readiness to be manipulated as pawns in the regulatory and legitimacy game strangely escapes the author's censure.

The '*pars destruens*' tells us what Community collective bargaining is not. Chapters 3 and 4 demonstrate that European collective bargaining is not analogous to national collective bargaining. The argument is well made. Indeed, it seems rather odd that Lo Faro chooses to use the term 'collective bargaining' with reference to the activities of the social partners at the Community level. The Community term 'social dialogue', though inelegant, is more apposite in relation to the 'enfeebled' (at 153) version of collective bargaining which is outlined in Chapter 5. The '*pars construens*' tells us what Community collective bargaining is. It is part of the, as yet inadequate, response of the Community institutions to the regulatory and legitimacy crisis.

The contours of the Community's crisis are helpfully sketched in Chapters 1 and 2 with reference to the writings of, among others, Teubner, Habermas, and Ladeur. Lo Faro's account focuses on the possibilities for 'non-legislative regulation' (at 28) at the Community level. He describes the inadequacy of the Community's traditional institutional arrangements. Moreover, he argues that 'none of the alternatives to legislative harmonisation which have so far made an appearance on the scene of Community law seems appropriate to the particular nature of the system of regulation and set of principles which traditionally characterise the sources of labour law' (at 50). Thus, collective bargaining was 'conceived' by the Community institutions 'as a feasible alternative to the traditional method of legislative harmonisation' (at 134). As a 'regulatory resource' (at 132–8) collective bargaining has been moderately successful, as the Directives on parental leave, part-time work, and fixed-term work testify.

Lo Faro, however, demands more from Community collective bargaining. He explores the constitutional framework which would be required in order to allow European collective bargaining to play a full part as a 'legitimacy resource' for the European Community (at 138–54). He argues, largely with reference to national experience (he is acutely aware of the methodological problems here), that changes to the current structure are required. Collective bargaining cannot contribute to the Community's legitimacy in the continuing absence of Community recognition of freedom of association and the right to strike. There is a contradiction between assigning a regulatory function to collective bargaining and 'forgetting' to provide the conditions that would enable it to become independent (at 158). The author warns that the current Treaty provisions will not be such 'as to trigger the launch of bargaining processes which are constitutionally significant, normatively relevant and socially widespread' (at 145). There is, accordingly, a strong plea for 'new constitutional provisions' on Community collective bargaining, to give rise to 'a reinvigorated conception of the social dialogue as the principle for informing a consensus-based administration of social and labour policies' (at 153).

It is inevitable that, in a book of only 160 pages which deals specifically with collective bargaining in the EC legal order, various other aspects of the regulatory and legitimacy crisis do not receive adequate consideration. Lo Faro is concerned with the decision-making process. He is rather less concerned with outcomes. But the legitimacy of Community regulation depends not only on the identity of the regulators, but also on the form and content of the ensuing regulation. The objectives of Community labour law are not clearly defined in the Treaties. Contrary to what many seem to assume, uniformity is not, and never has been, the ultimate objective. The challenge involves the formulation of more flexible forms of regulation which allow various national systems to evolve together in a way which is compatible with the establishment and functioning of the market in Europe. Co-ordination strategies, such as those in the Employment Title (Articles 125–130 EC), and in the Social Provisions (see Article 137(2)(a) EC as amended at Nice) have a role to play. So too does minimum standard setting, if only so as to set the baseline rules of economic ordering within the European market. To date, the efforts of the regulators, in particular as regards the absence of a convincingly articulated rationale for intervention, have been disappointing. If the legitimacy of the Community is to be enhanced, these lessons must be learned by the Commission and Council, and, to bring us back to Lo Faro, by the social partners themselves, whatever the constitutional framework in which they are permitted to operate.

Regulating Social Europe seems to be directed primarily towards an academic audience. It is not an easy read, though the author's 'succinct and schematic' retracing of his 'multi-faceted and necessarily heterogeneous logic path' (at 155–61) is indeed useful. At times Lo Faro is perhaps a little over-indulgent; to pick one example, the historical account of the divisions within the pluralist tradition (at 83–9) adds little to the argument which the author is seeking to advance. However, those who find themselves deterred should persevere. The book offers many insights into the operation of the social dialogue and provides the opportunity for profound reflection on the future of the making of labour law within the European legal order.

PHIL SYRPIS

Competition Law and Regulation in European Telecommunications by P. Larouche, Hart Publishing, Oxford and Portland Oregon, 2000, 466 pp.

As we all know the telecommunications industry has undergone in Europe a major transformation during the last decade. That transformation is probably not the last one as the Commission and other European institutions have announced their desire again to adapt the European regulatory framework. A new version of that framework should indeed be adopted in the course of this year. It should constitute a general platform the aim of which would be to organize all electronic communications throughout the European Union—as well as those affecting the European territory even if they emanate from a third State or are directed towards such a state.

In this context, studies on telecommunications are welcome. It is important to analyse where we are coming from (what has been done in the past, in terms of regulation and market development) and to propose guidelines on what the future may bring. Several authors have answered that demand, by bringing a contribution to the debate. A variety of books and articles have thus been published, among which it is not always easy to make a selection. The book written by Pierre Larouche will certainly help in that regard. It is very well documented and mentions all studies which have dealt with the subject matter, with comments in the body of the book. Larouche's book probably constitutes one of the basic reference works just about everyone with an interest in European communications should have in his library.

The book primarily deals with competition law as well as sector-specific regulation. These are the two bodies of law which have been used by European authorities to organize the telecom markets in Europe. Telecommunications are also affected by other sorts of rules—for instance those regarding the protection of privacy. The author has however made a clear choice of the perspective he wants to pursue in the book: the objective is to analyse the relations among undertakings in the telecom markets—hence this choice in favour of competition as well as sector-specific economic rules.

The book is based on a central assumption. According to the author, EC telecommunications law is driven by specific policy objectives. Hence, it must be considered a distinct Community law area that goes above and beyond the mere application of general goals or provisions expressed in the EC Treaty. The book aims at analysing how these specific EU telecom policy objectives have so far been defined and implemented, given the distribution of power and competence among different Community institutions.

Chapter 1 provides an overview of the regulatory models that were successively adopted by these institutions. As we may recall, major initiatives were adopted to that effect in the 1980s. They encompass the enactment of several directives by the European Commission with the goal of liberalizing the sector. The initiatives by the Commission were subsequently complemented by a general regulatory framework adopted by the Council, with the intervention of the Parliament. The goals pursued by the latter institutions were, principally, to promote the existence of Open Networks and to ensure the free circulation of equipment and services throughout the Community.

Chapter 2 investigates the use which has been made of the rules of competition to give an impulse to the liberalization process. Particular attention is devoted by the author to Article 86 EC (formerly Article 90 EC). As we know, that provision deals, among other things, with special and exclusive rights. It was used in order to bring to an end the monopolies national operators enjoyed for decades as well as—in connection with other EC law provisions—to force dominant operators to open their networks to newcomers on reasonable terms. Article 86 EC was also instrumental in allowing the Community institutions to determine in what conditions exceptions to free competition should be recognized. It thus played an essential role in the definition of obligations which may be imposed on certain undertakings as a result of the universal service which has to be made available to all citizens *on* reasonable terms and conditions.

Chapter 3 discusses the link between competition law and sector-specific regulation. It examines whether the former may be used to structure the sector, thus to what extent the rules of competition provide instruments likely to make possible the definition and implementation of the public policy objectives underlying EC telecom policy. So far, it has generally been considered that sector-specific regulation should be used in order to ensure a transition between what were in essence monopolistic markets to an era where transactions would be dominated by competition. A transition would thus take place, which should be as short as possible and should organize the relations among undertakings so as to make it possible for markets spontaneously to produce by themselves the welfare that is necessary for society. After the transitional period, the European authorities would only need to apply the rules of competition to ensure a smooth functioning of the markets. The telecom policy objectives would then be realized by a combination of spontaneous behaviour by economic actors, as directed or oriented by an adequate application of competition rules.

That vision is challenged by Larouche in Chapter 4. For the author, the rules of competition are meant to ensure a proper functioning of the markets. They should not be used as regulatory tools, to organize markets, and determine questions such as who is going to be allowed on the markets, what kind of goods and services will the operators have to provide, as well as under what conditions should these goods and services be made available. To take an example, the markets for telecommunications differ widely among the Member States. Some are organized in a more competitive manner than others. A regulatory policy will take into account these differences, in order to ensure smooth progress towards a common goal—an efficient market throughout the European Union. Yet, European competition law has by nature to be applied uniformly throughout the EU. As such, it cannot easily allow for differences between Member States.

Competition law, furthermore, lacks flexibility. The implementation of the policy objectives pursued by the European authorities makes it necessary to determine, in view of the circumstances, whether or not intervention is mandated. For the author, such flexibility does not exist within the ambit of competition law. In applying such rules, authorities have to concentrate on one goal—making sure markets produce the most efficient outcome. They may not suspend that objective, in situations where they may feel other objectives should have priority.

In fact, competition law may probably be used to open and liberalize the sector. However, these two goals are not the only objectives pursued in the framework of EC telecom law and policy. These numerous and sometimes complicated objectives may be implemented only by resorting to sector-specific economic regulation. Telecommunications are indeed essential for all economic and social activity. Thus, it is not sufficient to promote efficiency exclusively. Other values are to be implemented, including those which underlie the concept of universal service and which cannot be realized through an application of competition rules. Furthermore, telecommunications are based on networks. Yet network effects may prevent competition from producing full benefits. For these reasons, it is important to 'keep an eye' on the sector. Such task should be entrusted to a regulator that will ensure that nothing prevents the sector from fully contributing to overall welfare.

The author is in an excellent position to make a significant contribution to the debate. He was educated in several legal systems, which certainly gave him the background necessary to place the European developments in perspective. Larouche obtained a law degree in Canada (McGill), graduated as a Master in Germany (Bonn), and subsequently joined the University of Maastricht (The Netherlands), where the book was originally presented as his doctoral dissertation and where he worked in association with colleagues from other European universities, particularly the Katholieke Universiteit Leuven (Belgium).

Larouche was furthermore engaged in private practice in the 1990s as an attorney in Brussels, where the important decisions are taken regarding EC competition rules as well as the EC telecom policy. According to information provided in the preface (at 11), he was closely associated with important telecom alliances including the joint venture entered into by Deutsche Telecom, France Telecom, and US Sprint at the beginning of the 1990s, which collapsed after the offer made for Sprint by Worldcom-MCI, as well as the decision by Deutsche Telecom to enter the battle to conquer Telecom Italia. There is little doubt that the combination of high-level private practice and strong academic background helped the author to analyse European telecom reform in a systematic, far-reaching manner without losing sight of the concrete implications for the organization of the sector.

Finally, Larouche's research interests are wide. Besides his engagement in research concerning telecommunications, he actively investigates other sectors where rules are sometimes used as tools for regulation. For instance, he is contributing to a vast project on the emergence of a common law of torts throughout the European Union. This multidisciplinary perspective within the legal system obviously creates an extraordinary position, allowing the author to evaluate in a critical fashion the use that is currently made of the legal system by the authorities.

One can agree—or not—with the position advocated in the book, that competition law does not make it possible to define and implement the objectives which are pursued in EC telecommunications policy. A possible disagreement does not, however, affect the quality which is inherent in the publication. Obviously, we have here a very serious, well grounded, solid, and systematic analysis which will prove essential in all legal systems where telecommunications are liberalized, together with other utility industries. The structure is logical. The reasoning is crystal clear. The organization is perfect: besides the text, the readers will find a table of frequently cited materials, a table of abbreviations, a table of cases, a table of legislation, a bibliography, and an index. The book was updated before publication, in order to include the views of the European Commission concerning the 1999 Telecommunications Review.

PAUL NIHOUL

Judicial Review and the Rights of Private Parties in EC Law by Angela Ward, Oxford University Press, Oxford, 2000, lxviii + 368 pp. including a bibliography.

The Future of Remedies in Europe edited by Claire Kilpatrick, Tonia Novitz, and Paul Skidmore, Hart Publishing, Oxford, 2000, xlii + 303 pp.

Angela Ward has produced a detailed account of the legal rules governing actions in which private parties seek either to enforce or to challenge laws emanating from the European Community legal order. The central focus of the work is an in-depth comparison between the effectiveness of the remedies available to individuals who seek to enforce Community measures before the national courts, and the avenues of redress available to those private parties who attempt to challenge the legality of Community legislative measures. Ward's careful analysis provides clear evidence of the 'double standard' that has emerged in the judicial review case law. While the European Court of Justice has adopted an active and expansive approach towards the enforcement of Community norms within national legal systems, attempts by private parties to challenge the legality of Community measures have generally met with a cool response from the Community judicature.

Ward charts how the Court of Justice attempted to justify a steady erosion of Member State autonomy in the field of national procedural rules and remedies by drawing on the concepts of 'effective judicial protection' and 'individual rights' (Chapters 2, 3, and 4). Chapter 5 illustrates how the two concepts have also substantially underpinned developments in the case law on the enforcement of directives in national law. These concepts, however, have not been actively deployed by the Court in the context of judicial review of Community measures. Chapters 6, 7, and 8 vividly illustrate 'the formidable difficulties' that confront individuals who seek judicial review of Community measures pursuant to Articles 230, 234 (validity review), and 288(2) respectively. The result, it is argued, 'has been the evolution of a system that tends to insulate Community institutions from judicial accountability for their activities' (at 323).

The work does not ignore the broader constitutional context in which the Community judicature operates. The absence of an express, Treaty-based mandate undoubtedly raises concerns over the legitimacy of the Court's endeavours to craft a federal legal architecture. Against this background, the justifications offered by the Court in support of its intensification of the reach of Community law into national legal systems are closely scrutinized. Ward suggests that the Court is likely to come under increasing pressure to improve standards of judicial review of Community measures. In particular, the ever-growing influence of Directives in the affairs of private sector actors serves further to underline the importance of an effective system of judicial review whereby individuals may challenge directives that are detrimental to their interests.

Throughout the work, Ward delivers detailed analysis of the Court's judicial review case law. However, the discussion of the decision in *Kraaijeveld* (Case C–72/95, *Aannemersbedrijf PK Kraaijeveld BV* v. *Gedeputeerde Staten van Zuid-Holland* [1996] ECR I–5403) is surprisingly brief (at 182). In *Kraaijeveld* the Court ruled that even though Member States enjoy a discretion under Articles 2(1) and 4(2) of the Environmental Impact Assessment Directive (Directive 85/337/EEC), this did not 'preclude judicial review of the question whether the national authorities exceeded their discretion' (at paragraph 59). The Court reasoned that the Directive imposed an obligation on the Member States to pursue a particular course of conduct and that the effectiveness of the Directive would be weakened 'if individuals were prevented from relying on it before their national courts' (at paragraph 56). The Court instructed the national court to take account of the provisions of the Directive in the course of national judicial review proceedings without expressly ruling on whether the relevant provisions of the Directive had direct effect. The Court has confirmed this approach in its recent rulings in *Bozen* and *Linster*. (Case C–435/97, *World Wildlife Fund* (*WWF*) v. *Autonome Provinz Bozen* [1999] ECR I–5613 and Case C–287/98, *Luxembourg* v. *Linster*, ruling of 19 September 2000, not yet reported). An examination of the potential scope of the *Kraaijeveld* doctrine and how (if at all) it fits with classical direct effect doctrine would have enhanced the analysis presented under the heading 'The Right to an Effective Remedy as a General Principle of Law?' (at 179–83).

At a more general level, the account of current issues in the jurisprudence governing national procedural rules and remedies is particularly thorough (Chapter 3). Readers who are already familiar with this case law will appreciate the self-contained 'Policy Discussion and Conclusions' provided in Chapter 4. It is also worth noting that a number of the individual chapters are complemented by brief summaries that greatly assist the reader in forming a clear overview of the main trends (and inconsistencies) in the ever-expanding judicial review jurisprudence. The inclusion of a brief analysis of the legal rules governing access to documents, and the acknowledgement of the potential of the right of access to documents in terms of enhancing the effectiveness of the right to judicial review (at 245–9), is also useful. 'General Conclusions' are presented in Chapter 9. This chapter also incorporates (albeit very briefly) a number of tentative proposals (including Treaty amendments) designed 'to enhance justice' (at 342–4). In terms of access to justice, a discussion of the potential role of the Ombudsman (at both European and national level) in filling perceived gaps in the system of judicial protection would have enhanced the conclusion.

The reviewer was disappointed to find that the work did not consider, even briefly, the *actual* effectiveness of the judicial protection offered by national courts where individuals seek to argue that national law is not in conformity with Community law. In the final analysis, the effectiveness of Community law at local level depends on the willingness of the national courts to apply it faithfully. Practical considerations, such as the absence of an equitable and efficient scheme of civil legal aid, may result in individuals being locked out of the national courts. Where individuals do gain access to the national courts and present arguments based on Community law, the national judge(s) may fail correctly to interpret and/or apply Community law. Furthermore, it is not uncommon for national courts to fail to make a reference to the Court of Justice where a clear question regarding the correct interpretation of a Community norm is at issue. It is submitted that practical issues, such as those listed above, constitute an important, but often neglected, dimension of the concept of effective judicial protection.

In conclusion, to echo the remarks of Judge Forwood (at page viii), the provocative analysis presented in this book provides much cause for reflection on the part of both Community and national judges. Overall, Ward's detailed and insightful study is an important contribution to the growing literature on remedies in Community law.

The Future of Remedies in Europe presents a very different approach to the subject of European remedies. The essays presented in this collection aim to go beyond simply recounting and analysing Court of Justice jurisprudence on remedies. Rather, it is argued that greater attention should be paid to the national dimension. Furthermore, it is claimed that a sectoral analysis of procedures and remedies for enforcing Community law rights may well provide 'a new and challenging research agenda for reassessing the past and considering the future of remedies in the Luxembourg Court's jurisprudence' (at 14). These twin themes run through the collection of essays which is organized into four parts: Chapters 1–3 focus on the ongoing dialogue between the Court of Justice and the national courts; Chapters 4–6 take a sectoral approach to EC remedies; Chapters 7–10 consider the coexistence and interaction of Community law with other European legal orders (namely private international law and the Council of Europe system); Chapters 11–13 are concerned with the broader issue of access to courts and other forms of remedial control. It is impossible to do justice to the breadth and depth of the contributions in the limited space available here. The following appraisal aims to provide an impression of the main arguments canvassed by the various contributors.

Kilpatrick's introductory essay provides a very useful overview of the development of remedies in Europe. Her clear *précis* helps the reader to locate the subsequent contributions within their broader constitutional and institutional context. The potential usefulness of a sectoral analysis of European remedies as a key to unlocking the intricacies of the (often conflicting) jurisprudence is a dominant theme here (at 14–16). Part I opens with an analysis of the now very familiar principles of equivalence and effectiveness by Tridimas. The interrelationship between the two principles is examined in light of the decision in *Levez* (Case C–326/96, *Levez* v. *T. H. Jennings (Harlow Pools) Ltd.* [1998] ECR I–7835). The two principles, it is argued, 'are not to be treated as terms of art but rather as facilitating the judicial enquiry' (at 49). According to Tridimas, the Court of Justice has successfully drawn the balance between the need to ensure the effective application of Community law and respect for the autonomy of national legal systems. Next, Flynn presents a detailed and provocative account of the 'extensive judicial rewriting' of the decision in *Emmott* (Case C–208/90, *Emmott* v. *Minister for Social Welfare and Attorney-General* [1991] ECR I–4629). He concludes that notwithstanding steady judicial retrenchment, *Emmott*'s underlying logic (a broad application of the principle of effectiveness of remedies) 'remains viable and potentially applicable' (at 65) (see, for example, *Levez*). One of the many thought-provoking arguments canvassed by Harlow in Chapter 3 is that developments in the remedies jurisprudence of the Court of Justice and the European Court of Human Rights create additional pressure for '*judicial* resolution of every problem and denies its rightful place to the extralegal tradition' (at 74). Harlow challenges the feasibility of approximation of European remedies by means of Court of Justice initiatives founded on the Article 234 preliminary reference procedure. The critical importance of the national dimension is emphasized. The way forward, it is argued, 'is to trust national courts, *best fitted to understand the national context*, to decide routine points of EC law for themselves . . .' (at 82, emphasis added).

The following three chapters (together comprising Part II) present sectoral approaches to EC remedies. In a wide-ranging study, Weatherill exposes the imbalance in the effective application of Community law—contrasting the vigour with which commercial actors exploit the law with the limited scope for redress in the context of diffuse interests (for example, environmental damage). It is suggested, (convincingly) that '[t]he way in which the EC legal system has chosen to channel access to the courts falls well short of allowing a general right to secure the observance of EC Law' (at 102). Potential solutions to this 'implementation imbalance' are briefly canvassed. These include the argument that the Court should revise its traditionally negative attitude to horizontal direct effect. Poiares Maduro (Chapter 5) forcefully demonstrates that the provision of European remedies does not always have to be centred in the Court of Justice. Different institutional alternatives are capable of delivering effective remedies. In particular, greater empowerment of the national courts is advocated (at 139–40). Ryan continues the sectoral analysis of European remedies by reference to labour law, demonstrating *inter alia* the weaknesses in the rules governing the private enforcement of EC labour law.

Part III begins with an enlightening (and specialist) contribution from Beaumont that persuasively demonstrates the significance of private international law in the future development of European remedies. This detailed exposition is followed by an analysis of the potential consequences of incorporation of the European Convention on Human Rights (*via* the Human Rights Act 1998) for the remedial landscape in the United Kingdom. Here, White anticipates that obligations arising under the Convention may well lead to the gradual erosion of national procedural autonomy. In the following chapter, Schermers argues that with the expansion of the jurisdiction of the Court of Justice in the field of fundamental rights, overlaps between its jurisdiction and that of the European Court of Human Rights are more likely. He suggests that one means of resolving this undesirable practical problem would be to reconsider the introduction of the same system of preliminary rulings for both courts. Next, Ward laments the fragmentation of legal remedies brought about by the Amsterdam Treaty. The obvious shortcomings inherent in the scheme of judicial review that applies to challenges to measures concerning visa, asylum, and immigration policy (Title IV EC) and Police and Judicial Co-operation in Criminal Matters (Title VI TEU) are the subject of detailed scrutiny. The negative impact of this recent fragmentation of remedies on the uniform application of Community law is emphasized. The potential of European human rights law to cure the deficiencies in the system of judicial review crafted under Amsterdam are considered briefly (at 225–6). The strong emphasis on the importance of the uniform application of Community law in Ward's contribution raises, yet again, a familiar thorny issue—how much uniformity is required in order to secure the effective enforcement of Community law rights? It is important to recall that the principle of uniform application is not unlimited. Member States obviously retain a degree of autonomy over their procedural rules and remedies for sound practical reasons. The importance of the *national* legal context of remedial protection is stressed by a number of contributors (especially Harlow) who acknowledge the obvious limits of the principle of uniformity. For reasons of local effectiveness, the provision of remedies cannot be neatly detached from the relevant national legal culture. Ward's perspective may be somewhat at odds with this view.

In Part IV (where the broad underlying theme is access to the courts and other forms of remedial control), Novitz examines the control systems applicable to the European Convention on Human Rights and the European Social Charter. Both instruments create distinct supervisory machinery. The focus of Novitz's piece is the critical role the relevant supervisory machinery plays in determining the privileged status enjoyed by Convention rights (which enjoy Court supervision) and the more contested and ambivalent status of the social rights set out in the Charter (where supervision is limited to mere recommendations and reports). Syrpis examines *inter alia* the role of the Community judicature in ensuring the legitimacy of the social dialogue mechanism (Article 138 EC). The decision of the Court of First Instance in *UEAPME* (Case T–135/96, *UEAPME* v. *Council* [1998] ECR II–2335), in the context of access to judicial review, is the subject of critical scrutiny here. The challenge facing the Court, it is argued, is to provide 'a public law underpinning to the social dia-logue mechanism' (at 266). Syrpis urges the Court to take a bold approach to judicial review and thereby facilitate the development of social democracy in the Community legal order. A forward-looking contribution by Rawlings is very suitably placed at the end of the collection. Here, the underlying dynam-ics of the public enforcement process are scrutinized and deficiencies in the Article 226 infringement procedure (from the complainant's perspective) care-fully teased out. The potential of the European Ombudsman to fill gaps left in the wake of judicial failure effectively to police the Article 226 process is under-scored. To date, it is argued, this potential has been frustrated by the unneces-sarily legalistic approach to the concept of 'maladministration' adopted by the Ombudsman. However, Rawlings is optimistic about the future. A number of practical suggestions are canvassed as to how the Article 226 process could be reinvigorated. The objective, it is argued, is to put in place 'a form of regulatory proceeding that more accurately reflects the demands for more responsive and participatory forms of decision-making, which are associated with ideas of a Community "public sphere" and active citizenship' (at 268). An underlying theme of this insightful contribution is the complementary roles played by the public and private mechanisms of Community law enforcement. The way for-ward, it is suggested, is to promote a 'coupling of public advocacy with private initiative, which points in turn to a greater recognition of the role of the citizen in the shaping of the process' (at 295).

One of the many strengths of this collection (notwithstanding some minor overlaps) is that the varied contributions challenge the reader really to think about the potential future development of remedies in Europe from a number of different perspectives. The reviewer was very pleased to note the emphasis given to the national dimension (including the ongoing 'conversations' between the national courts and the Court of Justice) in a number of the con-tributions. Apart from the earlier innovative work of Slaughter *et al.* (eds.), *The European Courts and National Courts—Doctrine and Jurisprudence: Legal Change in Its Social Context* (Hart Publishing, Oxford, 1998), the national dimension (including the attitudes and behaviour of national courts) is rarely the focus of detailed, contextual analysis. In order to deepen our understand-ing of European legal integration, more comparative, systematic studies are required. To take just one obvious example, there remains a striking absence of empirical country-studies of legal integration in specific policy sectors. Overall, and in conclusion, *The Future of Remedies in Europe* succeeds admirably in raising important agendas for future research.

ÁINE RYALL

Implementing Amsterdam: Immigration and Asylum Rights in EC law edited by
   Elspeth Guild and Carol Harlow, Hart Publishing, Oxford and Portland, 2001,
   320 pp.

In *Implementing Amsterdam*, the editors, Guild and Harlow, have managed to
bring together some of the most outstanding scholars and practitioners in the
field of European asylum and migration law. Each of these authors gives his or
her view on the development of this field of law after the coming into force of
the Treaty of Amsterdam (ToA) in May 1999. Some of the contributions are
highly theoretical, whereas others adopt a practitioner's point of view and look
at the individual rights of asylum seekers and of applicants for immigration. A
very wide range of topics is covered in in-depth discussions, in a way that does
justice to the complexity and the versatility of this area of law.

   An alternative title for the book, reflecting the feeling that might come over
the reader, is 'Between Hope and Fear'. The contributions indeed have this element in common: the idea that the Treaty of Amsterdam constitutes a landmark in the development of European asylum and immigration law, which
until then had been characterized by intergovernmental co-operation and has
now been lifted to the First Pillar, the supranational level of the EU.

   Some authors seem to consider the period before the ToA as the 'middle
ages' of European migration law. The new Treaty, and especially its Title IV
on 'visas, asylum, immigration and other policies related to the free movement of persons' contain the promise of enlightenment. They see it as a
new start for the development of a real European approach towards immigration. The contributions suggesting this positive input do not neglect,
however, the dangers the ToA contains, which are emphasized by other contributors. The ToA does give new powers to the EC, but at the same time
limits the competences of the different institutions: at least during the first
five years, the role of the Commission, the European Parliament, and the
Court are limited. But even after this initial period, it remains to be seen
what Member States are willing to leave to the EC, giving up a part of their
national sovereignty. Some authors express the fear that the applicants for
asylum and immigration may be the dupes of the ongoing battle between
national and Community authorities.

   Gortazar, writing about individual rights and the abolition of internal borders, questions the importance of the changes made by the ToA. The limited
role of the Community institutions is not necessarily of a temporary nature.
Majority voting in the Council prevails and the access to the Court, which she
sees as the most important way to implement the 'new area of freedom, security and justice', will be limited. What is the actual transformation with regard
to the situation pre-Amsterdam, she asks?

   Boeles provides a theoretical background to the discussion by comparing
the 'normal', everyday meaning of the words 'area of freedom, security and
justice' with their particular meaning in EU and Community law. According
to this author, once an immigrant has been allowed entrance to the labour

market, etc., there is ever less justification for treatment which is different from that accorded to nationals.

Crowly takes the same concept of 'an area of freedom, security and justice' as a starting point, but looks at it from a sociological point of view. He comes to the conclusion that this area 'in which the free movement of persons is assured' is not only not compatible with, but actually premised upon, the existence of internal borders. As for the 'Fortress Europe', he claims that this edifice is fundamentally unstable, because it tries to combine freedom for some and restrictions for others.

From a more legal viewpoint, Guild describes the same paradox. On the one hand, at least during the last ten years, the Member States have sought to improve labour mobility because it is believed to improve the economic welfare of all parties involved. On the other hand, they maintain at the same time a discourse against primary economic migration from outside the Union. Guild investigates the dichotomy between that discourse and the actual actions of the Member States as regards the admission of persons for employment, or indeed the Union's own actions as revealed in its championing of a new international framework for the movement of workers. In the ToA, this dichotomy comes down to the fact that, at least for the time being, the competence to rule on the free movement of EU citizens is almost entirely in the hands of the EC, whereas for third-country nationals, they largely depend on Member States. In her conclusion on the 'great myths' of primary immigration, Guild concludes that 'the reality and the discourse on labour migration have become detached: the reality is a highly active and expanding legal framework for labour migration; the discourse is a focus of insecurity on economic migrants. . . . A firmer commitment by Europe's policy makers to providing leadership in explaining the reality is urgently needed.'

Several authors, Blake, Goodwin-Gill, and Van der Klaauw, take the individual rights of asylum seekers as a starting point for their discussion of the changes (to be) brought about by the ToA. Blake concentrates on the Dublin Convention, from the perspective of an individual asylum seeker, based essentially on the UK experience. The basic problem with the Dublin Convention, according to Blake, is 'that it does not really work'. Happily the author does not present this affirmation as a conclusion, but as a point of departure to describe the particular problems to which the Convention gives rise, and the way in which the EU may be able to solve the different problems.

The authors writing on asylum seekers have one element in common: they emphasize the importance for the EU to respect and implement international agreements, conventions, etc. Blake pleads in favour of a comprehensive system of asylum law, including substantive criteria, effective procedures, reasoned decision-making, access to the courts, proper support during the process, etc. Van der Klaauw, on the other hand, highlights the importance of a common instrument on *procedural* asylum law. The first priority is to achieve consensus on minimum standards. He expresses the fear that Member States will turn out not to be willing to adopt standards higher than

those representing the lowest common denominator. 'If Member States continue on the old road of intergovernmental co-operation and consultation,
preserving the particularities of their own asylum systems, these minimum
standards are at risk of developing into maximum standards, particularly if the
rule of unanimous voting is to be maintained during the next five-year transition period in which the various asylum instruments need to be adopted.'

This affirmation is undoubtedly valid not only in the field of asylum law, but
equally with regard to legal migration. Two aspects of this part of migration law
are described by Groenendijk and Brinkmann. Where Brinkmann focuses on
the conditions for entry and residence for family members of EU citizens and
third-country nationals, Groenendijk discusses the legal position of settled
third-country nationals, equally called 'long-term residents'. They both plead
in favour of equal treatment with EU citizens as a final goal, in order to stimulate integration and to combat racial discrimination.

Groenendijk discerns five different models of existing legislative practices
that could be used by the Commission when drawing up a proposed directive
concerning long-term residents. He considers the possibility of extension of
existing rights of EU citizens to established third-country nationals the most
appropriate, where free movement rights are concerned. On the other hand,
the issue of their legal status could better be determined with reference to the
existing rights of Turkish workers and their families under the Association
rules. The European Council in the Tampere conclusions does not, however,
seem to have followed Groenendijk's proposal.

Another very interesting proposal for classification of migrants, and thus the
way in which legal instruments should or could deal with them, is put forward
by Peers. With a view to adopting new legislation after the entry into force of
the ToA, the EU has the choice between several possible models. It can base its
immigration law rules on: the 'alien' model as in the restrictive pre-Amsterdam
soft law instruments; the 'worker' model as in the rules in agreements with
third states (particularly Turkey); or on the 'citizen' model of the rules applying
to EU citizens. Finally, the EU could improve the rules applying to European
Union citizens and develop a 'human' model of migration law. Unlike most
authors in this book, Peers includes illegal entry and illegal residence in his
study.

Finally, the contributions of Curtin and of Guild and Peers jointly should be
mentioned. These two contributions suggest how the principles of legal certainty and the rule of law, both of eminent importance in the field of migration
law, can be better ensured. Curtin argues for the right to information on decision-making in the fields of asylum and immigration. Her main concern is the
question how and if transparency has been established or will be established
in the field of migration issues by the ToA. She therefore first studies the
shaded inclusion of the Schengen *acquis* in the EU legal order in the ToA itself.
She then analyses the position with regard to citizen access to information on
immigration and asylum policy areas from the date of entry into force of the
ToA. She has a particular interest in the case law on the subject.

It is this latter element, the case law of the Court of Justice, that most interests Guild and Peers, who make a study of the activism of the ECJ in the field of immigration and asylum law and the way in which the Court is conditioned by the ministries of the interior. According to the authors, 'the Court's relationship with national interior ministries as regards movement of natural persons, particularly where they are third-country nationals, became increasingly tense through the 1980s and reached a decisive stand-off in 1991 with the Maastricht Treaty. The policies of the interior ministries towards the Court have been perhaps more restrictive in the field of third-country nationals than in almost any other.' Guild and Peers examine the evolving role of the court in the field and its implications for individual immigrants and asylum seekers in the Union. They come to the conclusion that not only has the Court been assigned less jurisdiction, its jurisprudence has equally become ever more restrictive. Indeed, in a report issued by the Court in 1999, the restrictions on the Court's jurisdiction in Article 68 EC have been backed by the Court itself! It appears at present that an alliance has developed between national interior ministries anxious to preserve maximum discretion over entry and movement of third-country nationals, and Community judges with protracted concerns over their workload. The objective justifications adduced are tried by Guild and Peers, and found wanting.

Unfortunately, this chapter was finalized before the European Council meeting in Nice in December 2000, which brought about some potentially important changes for the workload of the Community's judicial body. Thus, the new Treaty allows the Court of First Instance to be given jurisdiction to hear and determine most classes of direct action, as well as certain questions referred for a preliminary ruling. The creation of judicial panels attached to the Court of First Instance is intended to relieve the burden on that Court. With a view to enlargement of the Union, the new Treaty establishes an express link for the first time between the number of Member States and of Judges. As a result of these and other changes, it is hoped that the Court's overload will be relieved and that at least one of the sources of the alliance between the ECJ and the interior ministers will be removed.

The coming years will further demonstrate whether the hopes and fears expressed by the different authors in this book are justified. In any case, it gives a very good overview of the *current* law and jurisprudence, and the possible consequences of recent legislative developments. Only time will tell if these academic hypotheses are proven, and if the warnings and recommendations are properly heeded by policy makers.

SANDRINE VAN DER VELDE

Legitimate Expectations in Administrative Law by Søren Schønberg, Oxford
University Press, Oxford, 2000, 338 pp.

This book comprehensively analyses how the protection of legitimate expectations created by administrative decisions and representations is conceived
and applied in English, French, and EC law. It is thus a comparative study that
aims to answer three main questions. First, why should expectations be
protected? Secondly, how are legitimate expectations currently protected in
the three referred legal orders? Thirdly, whether the current English system of
protection of legitimate expectations is satisfactory.

The study is predominantly based on and supported by case law, since there
are few constitutional or statutory provisions dealing with the issues in question. However, constitutional, statutory, and administrative sources are duly
taken into account where relevant.

The principle of protection of legitimate expectations has been developed in
administrative law. It is assumed that expectations arise when public authorities adopt formal decisions or when their statements and behaviour give rise
to informal representations. Expectations deserve (or may deserve) protection
when they are disappointed, either because decisions are revoked or because
authorities depart from representations. The author articulates his analysis
around four situations on the ground that the justification for protection of
expectations varies in each of them: revocation of administrative decisions
(situation 1), departure from individualized assurances (situation 2), departure from policy in individual instances (situation 3), and departure from policy in the light of a general shift in policy (situation 4). The author uses a rather
large definition of 'representations' that covers 'explicit or implicit administrative pronouncements of fact and law or intent which cannot be categorised as
final decisions or determinations'.

The book has a coherent and clear structure. The first chapter explores the
ultimate foundations for the protection of legitimate expectations. It is submitted that fairness justifies the protection of legitimate expectations. First,
because according to the reliance theory preventable harm should be avoided.
Secondly, because expectations are one aspect of the principle of legal certainty, which is ultimately concerned with the individual's autonomy (rule of
law theory). Besides, it is also notable that the protection of legitimate expectations concerns not only fairness and control of administration, but also
administrative efficacy and, at times, economic efficiency.

Chapters 2 to 6 explore in full the different ways by which legitimate expectations are protected. Chapter 2 deals with the procedural protection of
expectations. The author focuses on three procedural guarantees: notice,
hearing, and the giving of reasons. Chapters 3 and 4 explore the substantive
protection of legitimate expectations, that is, to what extent public authorities are bound by their decisions and representations. Finally, Chapters 5 and
6 engage in an analysis of compensatory protection of legitimate expectations, that is, the extent to which individuals can seek and get compensation

for the loss caused by reliance upon administrative decisions and representations.

In so far as the book addresses these three ways of protection (procedural,
substantial, and compensatory protection), it provides a complete picture of
the question under review. Further, it is pointed out that the protection of
legitimate expectations entails a combination of all three ways, consequently
the analysis would be somewhat incomplete if it merely focused on one of
them.

The comparative analysis is approached in a functional way, in the sense
that the author compares rules that have the function of protecting the expectations of individuals in all three legal orders. Thus, it is of no importance that
the French system does not have an explicit concept of legitimate expectations, for the author focuses on the rules that *de facto* amount to the protection of legitimate expectations in French law.

There are some points that may deserve further explanation. For instance,
whereas it is submitted that the book is concerned with 'individualized decision-making' (at 2), it is not clear to what extent the fourth situation singled
out by the author fulfils this criterion. Actually, situation 4 basically concerns
the adoption of general rules (the expression of a certain administrative policy) and the consequences that their change entail for individuals in terms of
expectations. Secondly, at times the distinction between situations 2 and 3
does not hold. Thus, amongst the measures through which administrative
authorities assume individualized assurances the author refers to circulars,
reports, communications, or codes of conduct (at 120). It could be argued that
such measures are of general character and would fit more in situation 4.

Thirdly, with regard to EC law, more detailed explanation would be welcome
of the concept of 'administrative' situations in EC law, since this is not a settled
question. Actually, it may be argued that situation 4 amounts in EC law to what
the Court of Justice calls 'normative' or 'legislative' situations.

In any case, the book perfectly reflects the existing tensions between, on the
one hand, the freedom of the administration in the adoption and application
of policy choices and, on the other hand, the protection of individuals' reliance
on administrative decisions and representations. It is wisely noticed at different points of the book that individuals are these days faced with the complexity of administrative law and do not have the necessary tools for discovering
the lawfulness or unlawfulness of administrative decisions and conduct.

The fact that the book consists of comparative research is welcome in many
other respects. In the first place, reading of the book highlights that, despite
the conceptual differences that exist between the three legal orders, the
material outcomes do not significantly differ in each of them. Secondly, a
number of improvements are suggested with regard to the English system,
many of which are inspired by the French and Community practice. The
author also suggests how the French and EC systems could be improved, for
example, with regard to procedural protection of expectations, where the
English system is more developed. The comparative analysis allows the reader

himself to evaluate the merits and deficiencies of each of the three legal orders and to draw conclusions about cross-fertilization among them.

This is a sound book that provides the reader with a comprehensive analysis of the principle of protection of legitimate expectations in administrative law in English, French, and EC law.

ANGELES MAZUELOS

Restitution and European Community Law by Alison Jones, Mansfield Press, London, 2000, xxxxii + 206 pp.

In this book, Jones examines in detail which rules of Community law are capable of affecting restitutionary claims commenced in English courts, and to what extent these rules could influence the development of such claims. The book is part of a series of books dealing with spheres within which the English law of restitution relates to other areas of law.

Restitution, related to the principle against unjust enrichment, is nowadays a frequently used legal instrument in English law, as well as in Community law. It is only since the last third of the twentieth century however, that it has received serious recognition. The House of Lords in 1991 in *Lipkin Gorman* v. *Karpnale Ltd.* acknowledged the principle against unjust enrichment underlying various existing restitutionary claims. Although the European Court of Justice has acknowledged such a principle in Community law also, it has long been reluctant to require specific remedies for breaching Community law, preferring to respect the principle of national procedural (and remedial) autonomy. However, on various occasions the Court has made clear that money paid in breach of Community law must in principle be repaid. Since restitution must, in the absence of Community rules, be carried out in conformity with the applicable rules of national (procedural) law, it is therefore important to examine which rules of national law could be applicable and how these rules comply with the conditions of equivalence and effectiveness.

The structure of Jones' book is based on three situations in which restitutionary claims in English law may be affected by Community law requirements. The first situation is when charges have been levied by a public authority in breach of Community law (Chapters 2, 3, and 4). The second situation is when sums have been paid by a public authority in breach of EC law (Chapter 5). The third is when benefits have been conferred on a private party under a contract or contractual term infringing the EC Treaty competition rules (Chapter 6). The discussion of these three situations is prefaced by an introduction about European law in general and about how national rules could be influenced by requirements of Community law. Each of these three situations is discussed in a very well structured way: first an overview of the applicable rules of English law, secondly the requirements of Community law, and thirdly a thorough analysis of the impact of Community law on the English rules in every particular situation. Within this structure Jones deals consistently with three major topics, namely the grounds for a restitutionary claim, interest, and possible defences against such a claim.

The way in which the discussion of every situation is structured has an advantage as well as a disadvantage. The advantage is that not only is the impact of Community law on national rules described, but also a thorough overview is given of English as well as of Community law as far as restitutionary issues are concerned. In that respect the author gives a clear overview of the national and European case law in this field of law. The disadvantage is that many things said in the analysis section have already been dealt with in the two previous parts, which sometimes results in duplication. Although every situation is discussed in the same structured way, that does not mean, however, that the same weight has been given to the discussion of each different situation. The major part of the book consists of a discussion of the first situation in which charges have been levied in breach of Community law. Jones spends three chapters on these types of restitutionary claim, whereas the other two situations merit only two separate chapters.

As far as the substance of the book is concerned, Jones draws three important conclusions. In the first place she argues that it would be better to consider the case law of the Court of Justice dealing with restitution in the light of the principle of effectiveness together with the principle against unjust enrichment, instead of taking only the former into account. Traditionally, only the principle of effectiveness has been used to explain the rather strict case law of the Court with regard to restitution. The principle of effectiveness requires the effective enforcement of Community law in the Member States, as well as the effective protection of Community rights for private parties. But, as Jones demonstrates, the principle against unjust enrichment is very much intertwined with the principle of effectiveness, at least as far as restitutionary claims by and against public authorities are concerned. For that reason, Jones argues that a remedy intended to remove an unjust enrichment within Community law is essential to guarantee the effectiveness of that law.

The strength of Jones' reasoning is not only that the reason restitutionary claims should be enforced becomes clearer, it also serves a better understanding of why interest should be awarded. When, for example, state aid has been granted in breach of Community law, competitors will have the possibility to ask for recovery before national courts on the basis of Article 88(3) [ex Article 93(3)] EC, which is directly effective. Recovery in that case is meant to remove the unjust enrichment of the recipient. The enrichment, however, often consists not only of the pure benefit conferred on the recipient, but also of indirect advantages as a result of the main benefit. The effectiveness of the EC state aid rules would be undermined if such additional benefits could be obtained. By arguing that they form a kind of unjust enrichment, a valid ground has been given to impose on the recipient an obligation to pay interest as well.

Jones' reasoning is also useful in relation to possible defences against restitutionary claims. A major part of the book consists of a thorough analysis of such defences available in English law (statutory law as well as common law). Often these defences concern procedural rules of national law (for example, limitation periods) which could bar a claim for restitution. But also defences such as 'passing on' and 'unjust enrichment of the claimant' could be invoked. As soon as the enforcement of restitutionary claims based on Community law is at stake, such defences will be capable of being invoked only if they comply with the principles of equivalence and effectiveness. It cannot be denied that the principle of effectiveness in particular is rather a vague concept. For that reason it will very much depend on the circumstances of a given situation whether or not a rule of national law as a defence against a restitutionary claim will be applicable. That could make it rather difficult sometimes to understand the rationale of the case law of the Court of Justice. Jones, however, argues that the principle against unjust enrichment should also be taken into account in relation to the case law concerning defences based on national (procedural) law. That would make it easier to understand why some defences are declared compatible with Community law standards of effectiveness, whereas others are declared incompatible. In particular with regard to the strict interpretation of defences in state aid cases, Jones' reasoning is rather useful.

The second and third conclusions drawn in the book concern the concrete impact of Community law on the English rules dealing with restitutionary claims. Since until now a general ground for recovery in English law has been denied, Jones wonders whether sufficient judicial protection could be given in all cases in which restitutionary claims could be raised. It will be the task of national judges to guarantee this protection. For that reason national judges may have to change or to expand their current interpretation of English law as far as restitutionary claims based on Community law are concerned. Jones is particularly critical with regard to claims based on void contracts which have been concluded in breach of EC competition rules. It has to be seen in future whether her expectations will be met, since no national case law on this subject yet exists. This book could certainly serve then as a guide for national judges to resolve problems concerning new restitutionary claims.

Many books have already been written about the enforcement of EC law by national courts and remedies to be granted in case of breach of EC law, but none has dealt with restitution and European Community law in such a careful and interesting way as Jones has done in her book. It is not always an easy book to read, but that is not the fault of the author. Taking into account the complex and difficult nature of the subject, Jones has produced a very clear analysis based on case law which is often unclear, and she does so being rather critical of this case law. But that is not the only strength of the book. It is also a particularly 'just enrichment' of the fundamental debate concerning enforcement and remedies in European Community law.

PAUL ADRIAANSE

Competition Law—Alignment and Reform by Imelda Maher, Round Hall Sweet
& Maxwell, Dublin, 1999. ISBN 1–889738–52–5; lxvii + 514 pp.

Although it may not be clear from the title, this book focuses on competition
law in Ireland. The title captures two facets of the Irish experience of competition law over the last decade: greater alignment of substantive rules on EC law
and (more slowly) reform of competition procedures. The alignment was a relatively straightforward matter: the Competition Act 1991 adopted the same
rules as Articles 81 and 82 (as they now are) of the EC Treaty. As regards procedure, the picture is more complex. The 1991 Act created a Competition
Authority with powers to rule on notifications (the notification procedure was
based on the current EC system) but limited enforcement powers. Breaches of
the 1991 Act could be brought before the civil courts by the Competition
Authority or unhappy victims, but there was no criminal penalty. There was
widespread criticism that this was insufficient, and the Act was modified in
1996 to make breaches of competition law a criminal offence (which can lead
to fines and imprisonment). At the same time, the government commissioned
a major review of the legislation and the ensuing report of the Competition
and Mergers Review Group (June 1998) suggested a number of reforms. At the
time of writing the government is considering proposals to modify the legislation again, although the precise details have not yet been announced.

As far as this reviewer is aware, this book is the most recent work on Irish
competition law to be published. The author describes the situation up to
early 1999, so it covers the Commission's initial proposals for 'modernization'
of the procedures at EC level and the report of the Competition and Mergers
Review Group mentioned above.

The first half of the book deals with the fundamentals of Irish and EC competition law. After an introduction to competition theory, the book sets out the
background and procedural framework to the 1991 Act. The author then outlines the EC competition rules (emphasizing ECJ cases or Commission decisions with an Irish dimension). There is also a survey of how the EC rules have
been applied in the Irish courts. Some of these cases are relatively unimpor-
tant and many never proceeded beyond preliminary stages. However, the
author gives the Irish background to some cases which have led to important
decisions at EC level: *Magill* is one, and the 'ice cream wars' being fought in the
Irish courts may turn out to be another (already, these have led to a judgment
of the European Court of Justice of 14 December 2000 in Case C–344/98
Masterfoods, which casts light on the procedural issues involved).

After this, there is a further chapter illustrating how the Irish courts and
Competition Authority have applied the Competition Act. The Irish Act did not
explicitly state whether the new competition rules were to be interpreted in
the light of EC precedents, or whether the Irish courts and the Competition
Authority were to start afresh as if it were a free-standing piece of legislation to
be interpreted without reference to decisions elsewhere. The author notes
that, after some hesitation, the Irish courts have largely applied EC judgments

by analogy, although the Supreme Court caused some surprise when its first decision on the Competition Act held that the notion of an 'undertaking' in the Act was different from the term as it is used in EC law.

The treatment of mergers is similar: after a long chapter on EC merger control, a shorter chapter on Irish mergers analyses the few published decisions in this field. The author plunges into the *Woodchester* controversy (named after a decision of the Competition Authority which caused even more surprise by applying the Competition Act to aspects of a merger cleared under another statute). Different views have been expressed for and against this approach, but here the author concludes that the Competition Acts should be redefined so as to exclude mergers.

Until this point in the book, the author has presented the general Irish and EC rules in separate chapters. In the next section, she focuses on a series of specific topics (vertical restraints, pricing, and intellectual property) and compares the Irish and EC law side-by-side. This makes for a clearer exposition, and perhaps a future edition may apply this approach more widely. On vertical restraints, the rules in Ireland and the EC have both changed recently—the author gives the new rules a cautious welcome.

On the controversial issues of the day, the author's position on the *Woodchester* issue has been noted above. She seems to support the 'essential facilities' doctrine, though she argues that it can reduce incentives to invest. In the chapter on economic theory, the author describes as 'extreme' the view of some Chicago economists that predatory pricing brings few gains. On pricing, she explodes the myth that price controls have vanished in Ireland and calls the survival of the Groceries Order an 'anachronism'. This is a rule predating the Competition Act which provides special rules for the groceries sector—in particular it prevents supermarkets and the like from selling grocery goods for less than the net invoice price at which they were purchased. The author's view is that the rules in the Groceries Act are no longer needed now that the Competition Act is in place.

As regards the question whether the common law rules on restraint of trade may have survived the passage of the 1991 Act, the author considers that they have. She explores the effect of this on contracts for the sale of land or contracts of employment (in passing, she seems to suggest that the Competition Acts should not apply to real property). If the common law rules still allow challenges to agreements, beyond the grounds contained in the Competition Acts, it would have been interesting to explore what effects this has on a certificate or licence issued by the Competition Authority (these are the Irish equivalents of a negative clearance and exemption, respectively, under the present EC system).

Overall, the book is a welcome addition to the small number of works on Irish competition law. It would be most valuable to students or practitioners in Ireland who want a single-volume guide to both Irish and EC competition law (much like Richard Whish and Brenda Suffrin's work in the United Kingdom). For readers who are familiar with EC law and but wish to know how a particular transaction may be viewed in Irish law, the volume will also be very helpful.

BARRY DOHERTY

The European Union and its Court of Justice by Anthony Arnull, Oxford University Press, Oxford, 1999, 593 pp.

Arnull's *The European Union and its Court of Justice* is a legal book on the contribution of the European Court of Justice to the development of European law. It undertakes a twofold task. First of all, it examines various fields of law and the evolution that these have undergone by taking account of the Court's complex case law. Indeed, European Union law is the law as it has been or will be interpreted by the main judicial institution of the European Union. While examining the Court's case law, Arnull undertakes a second task, namely defending the Court from accusations of activism in having taken a leading role in the process of European integration.

It is uncontested that the Court has used (and uses) its adjudicative powers in a creative way: in shaping the legal framework in which it operates, the Court has expanded the scope of the Treaty and its own jurisdiction. In this respect, however, Arnull makes two important claims. The first one is of a normative nature. The creative role of the Court in the elaboration of the constitutional basis of European law and its evolution of European law itself can be explained by the inner logic of the law, and in particular by the principle of the Rule of Law. This is particularly true when Arnull analyses the contribution of the Court in the 'constitutionalizing process' of European law. Supremacy, direct effect, and the generation of rights which individuals can vindicate before national courts in his view are, among other things, necessary legal tools in establishing the foundations of democracy. Arnull does not see a tension between law and politics, but rather a relationship of dependency. Legitimate political decision-making exists only if due process, legal principles such as legal certainty and effectiveness, fundamental rights, and the protection of individual rights against the executive and legislature are established and protected by the law. Arnull is correct in recollecting the role played by the Rule of Law in democratic polities, and in analysing the role of the Court from that perspective, that is, from the perspective of the contribution of the Rule of Law to the European legal system.

The second claim is a methodological one: 'if we are to play the game of activism-spotting, some cases might be presented as examples of both activism and restraint' (at 564). The very same case can be seen through the activism lens or the restraint lens depending on the viewer's normative understanding of the Court's role. Moreover, this normative understanding is normally presupposed and not spelled out, which increases the analytically misleading effect that the activism/restraint oversimplification has.

The analysis of the Court's case law which Arnull develops in his book is well exemplified in the introductory chapter on 'Europe's Judges'. Arnull's knowledge of the Court's case law is outstanding. A great number of cases are provided to explain numerous detailed aspects of European law. From this point of view, the book is extremely useful for practitioners and academics with a sound knowledge of European law. It is also noteworthy that the analysis of the case law is undertaken by someone who has spent quite some time working in the Court. His experience and 'inside knowledge' benefit the study, pointing out features of cases and practices that might otherwise pass unnoticed by academics, including everyday problems the Court has to face, such as the workload and the plurality of official languages.

The book is divided into three main themes. First, *legal foundations*, where Arnull analyses the role played by the Court in shaping and reinforcing the Rule of Law; this part of the book deals most with constitutional themes. Secondly, *substantive law,* in which Arnull analyses the contribution of the Court's cases in shaping several fields of European law. Finally, in the *Court's general approach,* Arnull juxtaposes very different and unrelated chapters on legal argumentation, on sources of law, and on political theory.

In the first part, Arnull undertakes three main areas of research: the jurisdiction of the Court, the relationship between European law and national law, and, finally, the judicial protection of individual rights. All three areas share the same theme: the great contribution of the Court in elaborating the Rule of Law. In the chapter devoted to the jurisdiction of the Court, Arnull analyses the case law on judicial standing. Access to the Court via actions for compliance (Article 226), actions concerning the legality of Community rules (Article 230), and preliminary questions (Article 234) have been interpreted by the Court in such a way that the effectiveness of Community law (Case C–479/83, *Francovich* [1995] ECR I–3849) and the existence of judicial remedies to control European institutions (Case 190/84, *Les Verts* [1986] ECR 1217) were formally guaranteed. There is also space for criticism from the point of view of the Rule of Law, since the Court's case law on judicial standing of private legal and natural parties prevents the executive and legislature from being subject to effective judicial review. Again the connection to democracy is spelt out: '[n]ot only does a more relaxed approach [to judicial standing] protect the public interest in observance of the law by the administration, it may also be said to promote the proper functioning of the democratic process by facilitating public participation in decision making. . . . From this perspective, standing might be seen as an aspect of citizenship' (at 47).

In the chapters devoted to the relationship between European law and national law, Arnull sees a tension between legal systems rather than a conflict between European institutions and Member States. This explains the attention he pays to the reception by national courts of the direct effect and primacy doctrines, and he reaches a conclusion on the importance of the judicial co-operation model. This is described as the tacit compromise the Court and national courts have reached: the Court has to respond to the concerns of national courts because the values embedded in the legal systems of Member States may contribute to the healthy development of Community law, whereas the national courts 'need to recognize the importance of the Court's role as the ultimate arbiter of the meaning and effect of Community law' (at 105).

The tension between the Court and national courts is latent in the chapter on European rights and national remedies (Chapter 5). The problem is posed in pure legal terms: on the one hand national courts are bound to protect European rights; on the other hand, the principle of autonomy of national procedures should be upheld. Can both legal principles be reconciled? Arnull extensively analyses the Court's case law by differentiating three judicial stages (restraint, activism, and retrenchment), and concludes with a 'legal' criticism relating to the increase of legal uncertainty due to the lack of consistency and the fine distinctions drawn between cases which apparently are similar (at 143).

In Chapter 6 Arnull analyses the connection between the general principles of law and fundamental rights: the Court (Case 29/69, *Stauder* v. *Ulm* [1969] ECR 419) protects fundamental rights as a general principle of law (at 204). The contribution to the Rule of Law made by the Court could not be greater in this sense, for the Court, Arnull explains, 'equipped the Community with a uniform standard of fundamental rights distinct from yet inspired by the constitutional traditions of the member states and international treaties to which the Community was not itself a party' (at 219). This was the 'ingenious' way the Court had to solve the dilemma of protecting fundamental rights which were not mentioned in the Treaty. According to a strict reading of the principle of legal certainty, the Treaty did not refer to the judicial protection of fundamental rights. However, the legitimacy of the Court would be called into question if violations of fundamental rights remained unprotected by a constitutional-like court.

The second part of Arnull's book is devoted to the contribution of the Court in the development of main fields of European law: the four European freedoms, the law of competition, and equal treatment for men and women. Arnull offers a rich analysis of the Court's very extensive case law, which makes the book especially appropriate for practitioners.

The chapters belonging to this part share the same perspective: the Court has greatly contributed to the systematicity and coherence of the legal system. For example, when evaluating the contribution of the Court in the free movement of goods case law, Arnull does not analyse decisions such as Case 8/74, *Dassonville* [1974] ECR 837 and Case C–267/91, *Keck* [1993] ECR I–6097 from the normative perspective of the function of the judiciary and the role of the Court. He rather reads the case law as the struggle to find an equilibrium between legal certainty (*Keck*) and effectiveness of European law (*Dassonville*). The Court reaches, Arnull argues, neither of these principles. The reasons for this failure are internal to the law: (i) the Court is unwilling to abandon *Dassonville*; (ii) the Court did not explicitly overrule prior judgments; and (iii) the Court did not offer a definition of the notion of selling arrangements (at

296). All these reasons concern the principle of legal certainty, and as a consequence the principle of effectiveness of Community law.

Similarly, in the chapter devoted to the freedom to provide services (Chapter
9) Arnull explains that the Court's case law on Articles 43 and 49 of the Treaty
and the adoption of the rule of reason in this area of law should not be interpreted as a sign of the Court's will to expand the force of the Treaty and its own
jurisdiction. The rule of reason is a device to find a compromise between the
principle of freedom of movement for persons and services and the need to
ensure the legitimate interest of the Member States (at 353).

Likewise, in the remaining chapters on substantive law Arnull refers to a
large number of cases and provides a rich and detailed analysis of them. In so
doing, Arnull is keen on highlighting that, rather than the exercise of judicial
activism, the reasons for the creative interpretation of the Treaty are to be
found in the Treaty itself and in the legal principles which give coherence to
the Community legal system. This lends a hybrid quality to all the chapters on
substantive law, for not only does Arnull aim to describe the law as it is, and in
this sense the chapters are addressed to European law academics and practitioners; he also wants to legitimate the contribution of the Court and defend
this institution from the accusation of activism. The Rule of Law, rather than
the activism/restraint perspective, favours the consistency and coherence of
the legal system, and allows the best perspective to criticize constructively the
Court's contribution.

The final part of Arnull's book entitled *The Court's general approach* contains reflections on two particular issues, namely the justification of teleological argumentation and the use of precedent (Chapters 14 and 15), and a
general reflection on the contribution of the Court to date.

The title of Chapter 14, 'Methods of interpretation', is rather misleading,
since it is devoted mainly to the use of teleological argument, or rather its
justification in European law. The reasons which justify the use of the teleological method of interpretation are, the author argues, to be found in the
characteristics of the legal system: teleological argumentation is 'especially
well suited to the problems of interpretation to which the Community law
sometimes gives rise' (at 515). He refers to Case 283/81, *CILFIT* v. *Ministry of
Health* [1982] ECR 3415, where the Court established the main features of
Community law: it is drafted in several languages, so that the purpose and
context of the Treaty provisions are necessary points of reference to ensure
uniform interpretation; moreover, every proviso must be placed in its context
and interpreted in the light of the purposes of the Treaty, so that the judiciary
can clarify the ambiguity of the text and fill gaps (at 517).

The chapter 'Precedent' contains a reflection on the use of this source of law
by the Court. Although it is a source of law, even more so in Community law,
the Court, Arnull argues, 'is not bound by its previous decisions but in practice
it does not often depart from them' (at 529). That is, although there is no theory of binding precedent in Community law—national courts can address preliminary questions even if the issue has previously been dealt with—there is a

practice of following them. Arnull reconstructs this practice by focusing not only on judgments where the Court follows its decisions, but also on when the Court distinguishes and overrules previous cases. This practice of consciously taking account of precedents (both in following and abandoning) is welcomed by Arnull for the same reasons that justifies much of the activity of the Court: due to the volume of previous case law, good practice on the use of precedents increases legal certainty and the consistency of the legal system.

The final chapter is indeed a general reflection on the role of the Court. Although Arnull has judged Europe's judges within the previous chapters, in his final chapter he does so by differentiating between several stages over time and by taking account of the institutional context in which the Court under-takes its functions. The first phase lasted until the breakdown of the Luxembourg Compromise, when the Court's main task was to elaborate the pillars of a constitutional legal order. Direct effect and primacy were elabo-rated as essential legal tools to guarantee the uniform application of Community law and, therefore, the proper functioning of the internal market. The protection of individual rights by the Court was another of the Court's major preoccupations (at 542). The Court's activism in this area reinforced the constitutional role that the Court aims to play, and at the same time guaran-teed the effectiveness of Community law. Finally, during this stage, the much criticized active role of the Court in areas of substantive law is explained by Arnull as the necessary corollary to the legislative deadlock caused by the Luxembourg Compromise.

This situation was to change when the Luxembourg Compromise broke down and voting in accordance with the Treaty became the normal practice (at 544). The SEA reinforced this trend. However, the change in voting practice did not reduce the role of the Court. On the contrary, during this second phase, the Court reinforced its constitutional role as protector of individual rights (Case C–46/93, *Factortame* [1996] ECR I–1029, Case C–6/90 *Francovich* [1991] ECR I–5357, and Case C–208/90, *Emmott* [1994] ECR I–4269), and as observer of the institutional balance, especially since co-operation law-making processes were established.

The third phase started with the Maastricht Treaty. The TEU excluded from the Court's jurisdiction all the new provisions on foreign and security policy and practically all those on justice and home affairs. This, Arnull argues, does not mean that Member States wanted to neglect the important role of the Court. On the contrary, the TEU endorsed the Court's case law on fundamen-tal rights and the standing of the Parliament in annulment proceedings. It also granted to the Court important powers such as the power to impose sanctions on Member States which failed to comply with rulings against them under Article 226. The so-called judicial restraint exercised by the Court during this stage was due to the new emphasis on defining more precisely the scope of the Community's powers in order to protect the prerogatives of the Member States (at 554). Probably this way was the most appropriate to deal with the Court's workload, which eventually was taken seriously.

Is Arnull's analysis too benign a reading of the Court's role? Many of the Court's judgments have been criticized in terms of lack of consistency and legal certainty; however, what Arnull has tried to do in his book is to stress the Court's concern for consistency and the rational basis of the vast majority of its decisions. Is this too legalistic a view of the Court's role? This has to be answered in the negative. Arnull's book is clearly a book on law. However, he has rightly stressed the importance of the Rule of Law as necessary to the development of democratic policies, and the social legitimacy of the Court gained by its crucial role in strengthening the Rule of Law: '[a] court which is taken seriously by lawyers deserves to be taken seriously by the public in the absence of clear evidence that something is amiss' (at 563).

LEONOR MORAL SORIANO

The European Court of Justice. The Politics of Judicial Integration by R. Dehousse, Macmillan, London, 1998, 213 pp.

Dehousse's *The European Court of Justice*, in contrast to that of Anthony Arnull which is also reviewed in this volume, is a book on the role of the law rather than a legal book, as the author himself explains. It aims at providing answers to crucial 'why' questions concerning the role of the main judicial European institution which have puzzled many: Why did the Court undertake an active role (Chapter 4)? Why did the Court's active role remain uncontested? Why did the Member States and the majority of institutions affected by the creative approach to interpretation not counter 'with fierce resistance' the innovative decisions of the Court (Chapter 5)? Why did the Court start to exercise judicial self-restraint in the late 1980s (Chapter 6)? Why did the change from judicial activism to judicial self-restraint take place?

To provide convincing answers, Dehousse elaborates the pillars of his analysis: the multifaceted role of the Court as constitutional court, as law-maker, and as policy-maker (Chapters 1–3); the overlap and interaction between law and politics as exemplified by the juridification of the policy process (Chapter 4); the political and strategic role played by the Court (Chapter 3); the rejection of mono-causal explanations; and the importance equally attributed to the behaviour of the Court and its environment to explain the function of this judicial institution.

Part of the analysis of the Court's case law is devoted to explaining the contribution of the Court in the constitutionalizing process of European law (Chapters 1 and 2) and in the process of European integration (Chapter 3). However, the book's main theme is the analysis of the Court's case law from the point of view of the relationship between law and politics. Dehousse identifies two consecutive judicial models with which the Court has been engaged and which explain the role of the law in its environment: the activism and the self-restraint models (Chapters 4–6). What these models are and why they took place are the main queries Dehousse tries to answer.

When using the judicial activism and judicial self-restraint categories, Dehousse is very cautious not to confuse the reader. He uses them to refer to different ways of depicting the web of relations between the Court and the other (institutional) players—mainly the Member States—and the interaction between the Court and its (political) environment. Therefore, judicial activism and judicial self-restraint are working categories that Dehousse uses neither as a reproach nor as a eulogy. The author rightly does so because he does not attach any normative claim to either category: rather than focusing on what the judiciary should do, he focuses on the reception given to judicial activities. Since normative considerations are left aside, Dehousse's reader should certainly not be looking for the definition of 'the function' of the judiciary or 'the function' of the Court. The book poses apparently less normative questions, namely how does the Court understand its own function, and how do the main features of the Court's environment (institutional and political) affect the function of the Court?

Both judicial and self-restraint models are examined by paying great attention to the interaction between the Court and its environment. Obviously any account of the Court's environment has to describe the complex web of relations of the Court and other European institutions, the Member States, and the national courts. However, Dehousse also takes account of the policy-making process, that is, the political environment in which institutional relations take place. Here is where Dehousse's major contribution lies: a particular set of institutional relations can be characterized as activist or self-restricted; however, the reason why either model developed and why it is tolerated or rejected depends on the dominant model of policy-making embraced by the institutions. In this sense, the author's main thesis is that the exercise of judicial activism or judicial self-restraint depends very much on the Court's environment, namely on the level of toleration of the environment towards judicial inventiveness, and the capacity of the Court to adapt to new environments.

First, Dehousse deals with the activist model which dominated the judicial function of the Court until the late 1980s—to Dehousse, the turning point is the institutional reform introduced by the SEA first, and the Maastricht Treaty later, which also encouraged a different policy-making model. Generally, the following are considered signs of judicial activism: a generous interpretation of fundamental principles contained in the Treaties; the understanding of principles such as obligation on Member States and source of rights for individuals; the opportunity to enforce these rights before the courts and tribunals (at 75); the integration process boosted by law (at 78 ff); the influence of the Court in the policy-making process—either by suggesting new policy avenues as in the *Cassis de Dijon* case, or by legitimizing choices made by other political players, or by catalysing EC legislation in deadlock situations (at 85 ff). Without doubt, the Court's creative interpretation of the Treaties has achieved two aims: first, it has strengthened the effectiveness of Community law and, therefore, the institutional interest of the Court; and, secondly, it has defined the limits of competence of European institutions, and in particular it has called into question the level of discretion of Member States under Community law.

Why? Or better, as Dehousse puts it, why was there no sign of resistance by the majority of institutions affected? Here is where the political environment comes into play. Chapter 4 is devoted to the analysis of the policy-making process model dominant until the Maastricht Treaty. To Dehousse, this model is characterized by the political void: Community institutions with a democratic deficit hold Community political power; the legislative deadlock caused by the renunciation of majority voting had to be remedied by the Court's atypical role; and the Community decision-making process is less politicized (at 128–9) and more juridicized (at 97 ff). The judicial policy-making is the result of the strategic use of litigation by both European institutions—exemplified by the European Parliament gaining access to the courtroom—and private parties, since the Court interprets principles as obligations on Member States, and as sources of rights for individuals which can be enforced by the judiciary.

This model of the policy-making process brings uncertainty and lacks democratic legitimacy, but these drawbacks are overcome by the 'non-partisan' character of judicial decision-making: 'by replacing "conflicts of interests" with "matters of principle", they clearly contribute to the depoliticization of the political process. Partisan conflict is transformed into allegedly non-partisan questions about the proper interpretation of the treaty' (at 115). The Court, says Dehousse, 'has always been careful to present its analyses— even the most audacious—as the outcome of interpretation of a rule of law' (at 125). By so doing, the Court has favoured a teleological interpretation of the Treaty. Again, this statement is uttered without stamping on it any normative claim concerning the very nature of legal interpretation. And rightly so, because Dehousse's work does not aim at elaborating a normative model of legal interpretation or legal reasoning, but rather at exploring the area of convergence between law and politics.

To the activism model, Dehousse opposes the Court's exercise in self-restraint since the late 1980s. The Court:

is more sensitive to the need to preserve member states' capacity to conduct their own public policies, even when this may entail (limited) costs in terms of market unity; it seems reluctant to expand the scope of Community competence against the wishes of national governments; and it has indicated on several occasions that it cannot substitute its own views for those of Community institutions when the latter enjoy discretionary power [at 148].

As in the analysis of the web of relations taking place in the activism model, in Chapter 6, Dehousse analyses both the institutional and the political environments of the Court. As for the institutional environment, this has been profoundly modified by the SEA. Majority voting and the larger role given to the Parliament in the law-making process have intensified the legislative activity, and increased the number of institutional frictions. In this new institutional environment, the Court has intensified its role in solving institutional disputes, that is, it has intensified its constitutional role. In contrast, its role in policy-making has shrunk, for majority voting remedied the deadlock situation which dominated the pre-SEA era.

As for the political environment, this has become less juridified and more politicized: European institutions and Member States try to retain some policy areas away from the Court's hands. The Maastricht Treaty excludes the 'third pillar' from the scrutiny of the Court. Member States perceived this area as belonging to the hard core of national sovereignty, and did not want this area to be developed by the case law of the Court (at 164). In the same re-politicization line, Member States, Dehousse points out, start politically to overrule Court's decisions. This is the interpretation of the *Barber* case (Case C–262/88 [1994] ECR I–4583) on private pensions and Protocol No. 2 which overrule the interpretation of Article 119; the *SPUC* v. *Grogan* case (Case C–159/90 [1991] ECR I–4685) on the compatibility with the Treaty of Irish legislation prohibiting the advertising of possibilities of abortion abroad and the special protocol introduced by the Irish government; and the *Commission* v. *Greece* case (Case C–305/87 [1989]) on the acquisition of second homes by foreigners, and Protocol No. 1 which authorized Denmark to retain legislative competence in this field. To Dehousse, the message that the Member States wanted to send to the Court was to stay out of sensitive policy areas because policy-making is a matter of policies rather than a matter of principles.

The reinvigorated political environment explains the role of the Court, which exercises greater deference towards Member States' policy choices, and at the same time enhances the effectiveness of Community law (at 168) via 'constitutional' case law. Hence, as far as the content of the Court's decisions is concerned, this judicial European institution is neither activist nor self-restraining, and yet is both.

The move from the judicial activism model to the judicial self-restraint one, Dehousse argues, cannot be described as a U-turn (at 186), because in both models the Court follows the same pattern: it is sensitive to political constraints. 'Its frequent attempts to identify a middle path when it has had to rule on a thorny political case clearly suggest its awareness that its authority can be challenged in the event of open conflicts with political actors' (at 179). In this sense, Dehousse's main conclusion holds that the Court must be seen as a strategic actor, because in order to ensure compliance it has to be more responsive to factual situations, and reach decisions in the form of compromises.

The Court seen as a strategic actor is the corollary of Dehousse's analysis of the role of the Court (Chapter 7). If there is an area of convergence between law and politics, if law influences politics as much as politics influence law, and if the Court is sensitive to its institutional and political environments, then the Court is a strategic actor pursuing a 'values agenda' which it considers to be enshrined in the Treaty, and interacting with its environment to obtain compliance. Indeed, the Court consolidates its institutional position and the effectiveness of European law, but does not become involved in political disputes (at 185) as a consequence of the interaction with its environments.

It is at this point of Dehousse's analysis, at the end of the book, that normativity comes into play. Dehousse has tried to explain the role of the Court by looking at the relation between law and politics, and rejecting normative claims when describing either the activism or the self-restraint model. He has answered many 'why' questions, and to those answers, eventually, the normative question has to be posed: 'which should be the role of the judiciary?'

Explaining the evolution from an intrusive to a deferential attitude towards Member States' policy choices, Dehousse argues that:

Although this evolution might alarm traditional supporters of court-driven integration, it can also be seen as a sign of institutional maturity for the EU as a whole—a sign that in the European political system, as in 'normal' ones, political decisions tend to be left to the political process, with judges ensuring the fairness and the correct functioning of this process [at 186].

This statement is based on a strict division between the normative notion of democracy and the Rule of Law. The political domain is the arena for democracy, whereas the judiciary ensures the Rule of Law. But if something is to be learned from the first decades of 'court-driven integration' it is that, in order to have a mature democracy, those principles upon which the constitutional design of Europe is built have to be elaborated by the interaction of law and politics, that is, by the interaction of the Rule of Law and democracy.

In conclusion, Dehousse's *The European Court of Justice* is a marvellous attempt at explaining the role of the Court by taking into account its institutional and political environment. The web of relations in a juridified policy-making process is characterized as the activism model. By contrast, the politicized policy-making process taking place after the Maastricht Treaty leads to a self-restraint model. Although the description of the activism and restraint models is free from normative claims, Dehousse's final pages show how difficult it is to provide answers to the role of the Court without addressing the normative dimension of the role of the judiciary. Ensuring the fairness and the correct functioning of this process is the responsibility of the judiciary according to the Rule of Law. But it is also to guarantee the protection of individual rights against executive and legislative actions; to identify the general principles of the legal system; and to interpret the law in a way that promotes the consistency and coherence of the legal system.

LEONOR MORAL SORIANO

Tables of Cases

Court of First Instance

(Alphabetical order)

European Court of Justice

(Numerical order)

Court of First Instance (Numerical order)

Opinions

TABLE OF COMMISSION COMPETITION DECISIONS

TABLE OF CASES BEFORE THE EUROPEAN COURT OF HUMAN RIGHTS

TABLE OF CASES BEFORE THE INTERNATIONAL COURT OF JUSTICE

TABLE OF NATIONAL CASES

United States of America

Tables of Legislation

EUROPEAN COMMUNITY LEGISLATION, TREATIES, AND
RULES OF PROCEDURE

REGULATIONS

COUNCIL DECISIONS

TREATIES

TABLE OF NATIONAL LEGISLATION

Table of International Conventions and Agreements

Index